BARRON'S

THE TRUSTED NAME IN TEST PREP

AP®

African American Studies

PREMIUM

Rashad K. Brown, M.Ed.

AP® is a registered trademark of the College Board, which is not affiliated with Barron's and was not involved in the production of, and does not endorse, this product.

© Copyright 2026 by Kaplan North America, LLC d/b/a Barron's Educational Series

AP® is a registered trademark of the College Board, which is not affiliated with Barron's and was not involved in the production of, and does not endorse, this product.

All rights reserved.
No part of this book may be reproduced in any form or by any means without the written permission of the copyright owner.

Published by Kaplan North America, LLC d/b/a Barron's Educational Series
1515 West Cypress Creek Road
Fort Lauderdale, Florida 33309
www.barronseduc.com

ISBN: 978-1-5062-9834-4

10 9 8 7 6 5 4 3 2 1

Kaplan North America, LLC d/b/a Barron's Educational Series print books are available at special quantity discounts to use for sales promotions, employee premiums, or educational purposes. For more information or to purchase books, please call the Simon & Schuster special sales department at 866-506-1949.

About the Author

Greetings, ambitious scholars of AP African American Studies! I am **Rashad K. Brown, M.Ed.**, a graduate from the highest of seven hills, Florida Agricultural & Mechanical University, hailing from the capital city of Tallahassee, Florida. As you embark on the journey to conquer the AP African American Studies exam, I stand ready to be your guiding light. My advocacy for students' rights and educational reform has been a cornerstone of my work, most notably in Georgia, where I built a historic coalition to ensure that students gained access to the AP African American Studies course. This passion has been spotlighted in my features on *Fox 5 News*, on CNN with Victor Blackwell, and in *USA Today*. I have shared insights and challenges through an op-ed in the *Atlanta Journal-Constitution* and delivered a historic, impassioned speech at the Georgia State Capitol, championing the importance of AP African American Studies in education to ensure official adoption in the state of Georgia and state funding for the course.

As the 2023–2024 Equity Champion for Atlanta Public Schools, I proudly stood at the forefront of initiatives to ensure that every student has equitable access to transformative learning opportunities. My dedication to excellence in teaching earned me the prestigious Outstanding Social Studies Teacher Award, underscoring my commitment to engaging, meaningful education and advocacy for social justice and equity for all students.

Our journey is interdisciplinary, sharpening your skills in historical analysis, literary interpretation, visual comprehension, and data evaluation. As I shared on the *Rickey Smiley Morning Show*, AP African American Studies stands as a testament to our collective advocacy and commitment to education's power to uplift and empower.

Let's prepare to make history together!

Acknowledgments

This work reflects the many individuals whose love, guidance, and inspiration have shaped my journey. To my late mother, **Jacquelyn W. Brown**, thank you for instilling in me a love of reading at an early age and providing the framework for passion and perseverance. Your influence is the foundation of everything I do. To my father, **William E. Brown Jr.**, I thank you for inspiring me to attend Florida A&M University to receive the higher education necessary to become a productive citizen in America.

To my late grandmother, **Willie Ruth Williams**, affectionately known as "*Gensie*," your unwavering commitment to educational advocacy, equity, and social justice taught me the importance of standing up for students and ensuring fairness for all. To my late grandfather, **John A. Williams Sr.**, your life of strong determination and hard work showed me the transformative power of resilience and dedication.

To my loving wife, **Paris S. Brown**, your unwavering support has been my anchor. Thank you for walking this journey with me, hand in hand, and for being the loving mother and guiding force for our four kings: **Rashad M. Brown, Adonis M. Brown, Makhai M. Brown, and Zavion M. Brown**. Together, we build legacies.

Atlanta Public Schools & Atlanta Board of Education

I would like to extend my sincere gratitude to Atlanta Public Schools & Atlanta Board of Education for their unwavering advocacy in protecting students' right to take AP African American Studies and for championing inclusive, high-quality education. I am especially thankful for the visionary leadership of the Superintendent and my principal, **Dr. Adam Danser**, for volunteering Maynard Jackson High School to serve as one of only 60 schools nationwide selected to pilot this historic course—allowing me to serve as one of just 60 teachers in the country to lead it.

The College Board

I would like to extend my deepest gratitude to the College Board for the visionary leadership and educational courage it took to create and design the AP African American Studies course. This groundbreaking initiative affirms the importance of centering Black history, culture, and intellectual traditions within advanced academic study, and it stands as a testament to the transformative power of education to uplift, inspire, and empower future generations.

I am especially grateful to my professional mentors from the College Board, including **Dr. Brandi Waters**, Senior Director and Program Manager for AP African American Studies and Strategic Partnerships & Engagement, whose leadership and vision have guided my journey. I also extend deep appreciation to **Dr. Teresa Reed**, Dean of the University of Louisville School of Music, a distinguished member of the committee that developed the AP African American Studies course and current Chief Reader for the AP African American Studies exam, whose scholarship and stewardship have elevated the field. Finally, I am thankful for **Antoinette Dempsey-Waters, M.Ed.**, Co-Chair of the Development Committee and Lead Consultant for AP African American Studies, whose expertise and dedication have helped shape this groundbreaking course and its national expansion.

Each has provided invaluable mentorship and opportunities that have shaped my growth as an educator and deepened my commitment to educational equity. Their guidance has led me to serve as a national consultant for AP African American Studies and a state policy advocate, roles that advance the mission of expanding access to this historic course for all students.

Florida A&M University

Finally, I extend special gratitude to two mentors whose influence at Florida A&M University helped shape my academic and artistic journey. **Dr. David H. Jackson Jr.**—now Professor of History at North Carolina Central University, where he formerly served as Provost and Vice Chancellor for Academic Affairs—was Associate Provost and Dean of the School of Graduate Studies and Research, and Professor of History at Florida A&M University. As a sophomore in his History of Africa course at Florida A&M, I developed a deep and lasting appreciation for the depth, complexity, and global impact of African history. That course profoundly shaped my worldview and ignited my commitment to truth-telling through education. Dr. Jackson's scholarship, mentorship, and passion continue to inspire my work and my purpose.

Dr. Julian E. White, Distinguished Professor of Music and retired Director of Bands and Chair of the Department of Music at Florida A&M University, nurtured my artistic and musical voice from middle school through college. Under his leadership of the world-renowned "Marching 100," I developed a deep appreciation for the African diaspora's influence on music, dance, and cultural expression. He taught me that rhythm and movement are not merely performance—they are acts of pride, resistance, and storytelling. His mentorship empowered me to carry that legacy onto global stages, including the Grammy Awards and the Super Bowl, where I proudly represented the excellence of our cultural heritage.

This book stands as a testament to the wisdom and support of these incredible individuals. Thank you for your love, lessons, and legacy. With unwavering support and determination,

Rashad K. Brown, M.Ed.

Founder, African American Studies Guru LLC

Table of Contents

PART 3: UNIT 2—FREEDOM, ENSLAVEMENT, AND RESISTANCE

PART 4: UNIT 3—THE PRACTICE OF FREEDOM

PART 6: PRACTICE TESTS

How to Use This Book

Review and Practice

This book's review topics are aligned with the curriculum for the AP African American Studies course as outlined in the College Board's 2024 *AP African American Studies Course and Exam Description* (CED). You may find it helpful to read the CED along with your classroom assignments when you are first learning the material and studying for classroom tests. Alternatively, you may choose to read the topics of this book together with the CED as a review after you have completed most of your AP African American Studies course. By answering the practice questions that follow each chapter, you will be able to test your learning as you progress through the book.

Practice Tests

The final section of this book challenges you to put your knowledge and skills to the test with two full-length practice exams that mirror the rigor and format of the actual AP African American Studies exam. These exams feature all question types you'll encounter, allowing you to build familiarity with the test structure.

To maximize your preparation, it is recommended that you time yourself as you complete each exam. This practice will help you develop the pacing needed to excel under exam conditions. After completing the tests, consult the detailed answer explanations for the multiple-choice questions and review examples of high-scoring responses for the written sections. These insights are designed to clarify any material or concepts you find challenging and help you sharpen your approach.

Online Practice

Beyond the two practice tests in this book, you'll also gain access to one additional full-length practice exam online. This test can be taken in either timed or untimed practice mode, giving you flexibility to refine your skills. Each question is accompanied by clear and thorough explanations, ensuring that you understand not only the correct answers but also the reasoning behind them.

BARRON'S ESSENTIAL 5

As you prepare for the AP African American Studies exam and work toward earing a **5**, you **MUST** learn five core areas. These essential concepts aren't just about memorizing facts, they're about thinking critically, analyzing sources, and crafting compelling arguments.

1 **Think like a historian: understanding course skills.** To truly excel in AP African American Studies, you need to think like a historian. This means approaching the material with a critical eye—analyzing historical events, trends, and social processes. You'll be tasked with making connections between key events and understanding their broader significance. By developing this historian mindset, you'll be able to see how African American experiences have shaped, and been shaped by, history. This skill is foundational and will help you understand how the past influences the present.

2 **Skill 1: Applying Disciplinary Knowledge**. One of the most important aspects of the AP exam is your ability to explain and analyze course concepts. You'll need to demonstrate your understanding of developments and processes—whether cultural, historical, political, or social. This involves recognizing connections between different periods in history, explaining how they relate to each other, and understanding patterns of change or continuity. You'll also need to tie these concepts back to the field of African American Studies, showing how everything you learn in this course is connected to a larger narrative. This skill will be assessed through multiple-choice questions, free-response questions, and the document-based question.

3 **Skill 2: Conducting Source Analysis**. Much of your analysis in this course will involve interpreting and evaluating sources, whether they're historical documents, works of art or music, or even modern-day data like charts and surveys. The key is not just understanding what a source says but also evaluating how and why it says it. You'll need to identify the claim a source is making, the evidence it uses, and the reasoning behind it. Beyond that, you'll assess the source's perspective, purpose, and intended audience. Understanding the context and significance of each source will allow you to draw deeper connections and draw conclusions that reflect a thorough understanding of African American history.

Skill 3: Mastering Argumentation. A crucial part of the exam is your ability to develop and support an argument. In short-answer responses and the document-based question, you'll be asked to formulate a clear claim and back it up with specific, relevant evidence. This means not only stating your argument but also using the evidence you've learned to defend it. Your argument should be logical, well-supported, and grounded in course content. This skill will be assessed across multiple question types, so it's essential to practice structuring your responses with a solid line of reasoning.

5

Identifying and explaining course concepts, developments, and patterns. Finally, it's important to have a clear grasp of key concepts, developments, and historical patterns in African American history. You'll need to recognize how different historical events are connected, what causes and effects are at play, and how these connections shape the African American experience. Whether you're analyzing continuities, changes, or comparisons, your ability to explain these patterns will help you build a comprehensive understanding of the course material. Recognizing how these concepts fit into a broader historical and cultural context will set you up for success on the exam and beyond.

PART 1
Introduction

Preparing for the AP African American Studies Exam

Congratulations on taking the Advanced Placement (AP) course in African American Studies. The AP African American Studies exam is not just a test—it's an opportunity to explore and engage with the rich, complex history and culture of the African American experience. As you prepare for this groundbreaking exam, this test prep book will serve as your guide to mastering the skills and knowledge required to succeed. Through carefully designed exercises, practice tests, and strategic insights, this book aims to deepen your understanding and sharpen your analytical skills, providing the tools necessary to excel on the AP exam.

Understanding the AP African American Studies Exam Structure

The first step in preparing for the AP African American Studies exam is to understand its structure. The College Board's *AP African American Studies Course and Exam Description* is available online. It breaks down the components of the exam, including the distribution of multiple-choice questions (MCQs), free-response questions (FRQs), and document-based questions (DBQs), as well as the suggested timing for each section. This information is crucial. It will help you familiarize yourself with the format of the test and manage your time effectively during the exam.

The exam itself is a comprehensive assessment designed to evaluate your understanding of the four thematic units outlined in the AP African American Studies course. Each of these units presents a distinct area of study, spanning from the historical roots of the African diaspora to the modern-day movements shaping contemporary society. This test prep book mirrors this structure, with a focus on building the knowledge and skills you'll need to answer questions thoughtfully and effectively.

A Comprehensive Approach to Exam Preparation

This book is organized to enhance both your understanding of the material and your ability to apply that knowledge in a test setting. The learning journey is divided into units that reflect the course's four thematic sections. Each unit is carefully crafted to build on the previous one, creating a fluid, interconnected learning experience.

Within each chapter, you'll encounter practice questions designed to stimulate your analytical thinking and challenge you to consider the material from multiple perspectives. These questions are specifically crafted to help you develop a deeper, more nuanced understanding of African American history, culture, and experiences. They push you not just to memorize facts but to think critically and make connections among different time periods, events, and cultural shifts.

In addition to practicing the types of questions you'll encounter on the exam, this book provides answer keys and detailed explanations. These explanations are designed to clarify why certain answers are correct, helping you understand the reasoning behind each concept, while also reinforcing your test-taking strategies. This ensures you're not just prepared to answer questions but also equipped to approach each one with the right mindset.

Finally, this test prep book provides you with two full-length practice exams that mirror the rigor and format of the actual test. These practice exams include all the question types you'll encounter on the exam, giving you the opportunity to build familiarity with the test structure and pacing. Remember to time yourself during these practice exams to simulate the real test experience. If any material or questions feel unclear, be sure to consult the explanations and descriptions provided to clarify your understanding. Good luck as you prepare for the AP exam and stay focused as you work toward mastering these important concepts. You've got this!

1

Mastering the Skills and Themes of AP African American Studies

Learning Objectives

In this chapter, you will learn:

- ➔ Understanding course skills
- ➔ Themes in African American Studies

The College Board's AP African American Studies course is carefully designed to reflect what experts in the field agree students must master to earn college credit or placement. Success on the AP African American Studies exam—and the opportunity to receive college credit—requires students to develop and demonstrate three essential skills.

1. **APPLYING DISCIPLINARY KNOWLEDGE.** Students must be able to explain course concepts, identify patterns, and analyze processes integral to African American Studies. This skill will be critical in answering multiple-choice questions and crafting responses to free-response prompts.
2. **ANALYZING AND EVALUATING PRIMARY SOURCES.** The exam challenges students to interpret a wide variety of materials, such as historical documents, data, and visual sources. Developing the ability to assess claims, evidence, and context is crucial to navigating source-based questions.
3. **CRAFTING EVIDENCE-BASED ARGUMENTS.** Students are required to write clear, persuasive, and well-supported arguments. This skill is the foundation for the free-response and document-based questions, where success hinges on constructing coherent arguments grounded in credible evidence.

Understanding Course Skills

Mastering these skills is not just beneficial—it's essential to passing the AP African American Studies exam and achieving the college credit you've worked so hard to earn. Throughout this book, you'll find resources, exercises, and practice questions designed to sharpen your abilities in these key areas. By engaging with these materials and practicing consistently, you'll gain the confidence and proficiency needed to excel.

Skill 1: Applying Disciplinary Knowledge

Mastering the skill of applying disciplinary knowledge is a cornerstone of success in AP African American Studies. This skill goes beyond memorizing facts—it challenges you to engage critically with the material, making connections and analyzing concepts to uncover deeper meanings. Each component of this skill builds your ability to think like a scholar, providing the foundation for understanding African American history and its broader implications. Let's explore each aspect in detail.

Identify and Explain Course Concepts, Developments, and Processes

At its core, this skill asks you to recognize and articulate the key ideas, historical developments, and processes that define African American Studies. For example, you might examine the cultural significance of the Harlem Renaissance or the political impact of Reconstruction. To succeed, focus on clearly identifying these concepts and explaining their importance within historical or contemporary contexts.

- **What This Looks Like on the Exam:** You might encounter multiple-choice or free-response questions asking you to define a specific concept, such as pan-Africanism, and explain its historical impact.
- **How to Practice:** Regularly review key terms and events, ensuring you can both identify and explain their significance. Engage with course readings and lectures to deepen your understanding of these foundational ideas.

Identify and Explain the Context of a Specific Event, Development, or Process

Context is everything when it comes to understanding history. This aspect of the skill asks you to situate a specific event, development, or process within its broader historical, cultural, or social framework. For example, explaining the context of the Montgomery Bus Boycott involves understanding the systemic racism of the Jim Crow era and the rise of grassroots activism.

- **What This Looks Like on the Exam:** You might be asked to analyze the Civil Rights Act of 1964, explaining the social and political conditions that led to its passage.
- **How to Practice:** Practice identifying the bigger picture surrounding significant events. Ask yourself: What conditions led to this event? What were its immediate and long-term impacts? Use timelines and historical narratives to place events within their proper context.

Identify and Explain Patterns, Connections, or Other Relationships

This can also be called "causation, changes, continuities, and comparison." History is not a collection of isolated moments. Instead, it's a tapestry of interconnected events and ideas. This component challenges you to identify patterns, draw connections, and analyze relationships such as causation, change over time, and continuity. For instance, you might compare the abolitionist movements in the United States to global antislavery efforts, highlighting similarities and differences.

- **What This Looks Like on the Exam:** You might encounter a question asking you to explain how the Great Migration influenced cultural developments such as the Harlem Renaissance.
- **How to Practice:** Develop skills in comparative analysis by examining case studies and connecting them across time periods and themes. Consider cause-and-effect relationships, and analyze what changed versus what remained constant over time.

Explain How Course Concepts, Developments, and Processes Relate to African American Studies

African American Studies is an interdisciplinary field, weaving together history, sociology, art, politics, and more. This component requires you to situate course concepts, developments, and processes within the broader framework of African American Studies. For example, you might explore how the Black Arts Movement contributed to both cultural expression and political activism.

- **What This Looks Like on the Exam:** You may be asked to connect a specific historical development, such as the rise of Black feminist thought, to its broader impact on African American Studies as a discipline.
- **How to Practice:** Familiarize yourself with the interdisciplinary nature of African American Studies. Reflect on how events, movements, and cultural developments intersect with the field's key themes, such as identity, resistance, and empowerment.

Applying disciplinary knowledge equips you with the tools to engage deeply with the material, making meaningful connections and analyzing the past with a critical lens. By mastering these subskills, you'll not only be prepared to excel on the AP exam but also gain a richer understanding of African American history and its role in shaping our world today. This is your opportunity to think critically, analyze deeply, and bring a scholar's perspective to your studies.

Skill 2: Analyzing and Evaluating Primary Sources

Source analysis is a vital skill in AP African American Studies, empowering you to evaluate diverse written and visual materials critically. These sources range from historical documents and literary texts to music lyrics, works of art, and data representations like maps, charts, and graphs. Mastering this skill requires more than comprehension—it calls for a nuanced understanding of how sources convey information, their underlying purpose, and their broader significance. Let's break down each component of this skill.

Identify and Explain a Source's Claim(s), Evidence, and Reasoning

The ability to dissect a source starts with identifying its main claim. What argument or perspective is the author presenting? Equally important is evaluating the evidence the author provides to support the claim and understanding the reasoning that connects the evidence to the argument. For example, analyzing a speech by Frederick Douglass requires identifying his stance on abolition, the specific examples he uses to support his points, and how he crafts his argument to appeal to his audience.

- **What This Looks Like on the Exam:** You might encounter a source-based multiple-choice question asking you to pinpoint the claim made in a historical document or a free-response prompt requiring you to explain how evidence supports a particular claim.
- **How to Practice:** Practice breaking down sources into their components: What is being argued? What evidence is provided? How does the evidence support the argument? Annotate texts and visuals to identify these elements.

Describe a Source's Perspective, Purpose, Context, and Audience

Every source is created with a specific perspective, purpose, and audience in mind. Understanding these elements provides insight into why the source was created and how it should be interpreted. For instance, examining a political cartoon from the Jim Crow era involves recognizing the creator's perspective, the intended message (purpose), the historical conditions of its creation (context), and the audience it targeted.

- **What This Looks Like on the Exam:** You might be asked to describe the purpose of a propaganda poster or explain how a literary text reflects its historical context.
- **How to Practice:** When engaging with a source, ask yourself: Who created this? Why did they create it? What was happening historically at the time? Who was the intended audience? Develop a habit of annotating sources with these questions in mind.

Explain the Significance of a Source's Perspective, Purpose, Context, and Audience

Understanding the elements of a source is just the beginning. This component requires you to analyze why those elements matter. How does the source's perspective reveal bias or unique insight? How does the purpose shape the way information is presented? What does the context tell us about the historical moment? Why does the intended audience matter? For example, the significance of W. E. B. Du Bois's *The Souls of Black Folk* lies not only in its literary quality but also in its purpose to illuminate the double consciousness experienced by African Americans during the early twentieth century.

- **What This Looks Like on the Exam:** You may be asked to evaluate the significance of a speech's purpose in shaping its impact or explain how an audience's reception of a source influences its historical importance.
- **How to Practice:** Go beyond surface-level analysis by asking "so what" questions: Why does this perspective matter? What does the purpose reveal about its creator? How does the audience influence its tone or content?

Describe and Draw Conclusions from Patterns, Trends, and Limitations in Data

Data analysis is a key aspect of source evaluation. This component requires you to interpret information from graphs, tables, charts, and maps, identifying patterns or trends and acknowledging limitations. When describing and drawing conclusions, you must make connections to relevant course content. For example, analyzing migration data during the Great Migration reveals patterns of African Americans relocating to urban centers in the North, but it's equally important to consider what the data may omit, such as personal experiences or cultural impacts.

- **What This Looks Like on the Exam:** You might analyze a graph showing voter turnout trends among African Americans after the Voting Rights Act, identifying patterns and connecting them to the broader Civil Rights Movement.
- **How to Practice:** Engage with diverse data sets by asking: What do the numbers or visuals show? Are there any gaps or limitations in the data? How does this information connect to the historical or cultural context I've studied?

Source analysis is at the heart of African American Studies, allowing you to engage critically with the voices and artifacts of the past. By mastering these skills, you'll not only excel on the AP exam but also deepen your ability to interpret and evaluate the rich tapestry of African American history and culture. This skill transforms you from a passive reader into an active, critical thinker—equipped to draw meaningful conclusions and understand the world through a scholarly lens.

Skill 3: Crafting Evidence-Based Arguments

Argumentation is a cornerstone of success in AP African American Studies, allowing you to construct well-reasoned and evidence-based arguments that reflect your understanding of course concepts and themes. Developing this skill goes beyond forming opinions. It involves crafting defensible claims, supporting them with credible evidence, and organizing your ideas into logical, persuasive arguments. Let's delve into the components of this skill and explore how to master each one.

Formulate a Defensible Claim

The foundation of any strong argument is a clear, defensible claim. A defensible claim is one that can be supported with evidence and reasoning, even if others might disagree. For example, you might argue that the Harlem Renaissance was one of the most significant cultural movements in American history. A defensible claim takes a position that can be examined, analyzed, and supported with facts.

- **What This Looks Like on the Exam:** You might be asked to write a short-answer response that begins with a clear thesis or claim about the significance of a historical event, such as the impact of the Civil Rights Act of 1964.
- **How to Practice:** Practice crafting thesis statements that are specific, arguable, and supported by evidence. Avoid vague or overly broad claims, and ensure your position directly addresses the question or prompt.

Support a Claim or Argument Using Specific and Relevant Evidence

A strong claim is only as good as the evidence that supports it. This component requires you to draw on specific, relevant examples from course materials to back up your argument. For example, if your claim is that enslaved people actively resisted their oppression, you might support this with evidence of rebellions, the Underground Railroad, or cultural expressions of resistance.

- **What This Looks Like on the Exam:** You may need to write an essay that integrates examples from primary sources, historical events, or cultural artifacts to substantiate your argument.
- **How to Practice:** Regularly review course content and practice identifying evidence that directly supports various claims. Make sure your evidence is precise and clearly linked to your argument.

Strategically Select Sources to Support a Claim Effectively

Not all evidence is created equal. This component emphasizes the importance of evaluating the reliability, credibility, and relevance of your sources. For example, when using a nineteenth-century editorial to support an argument, you should consider the perspective of the author, the purpose of the writing, and the context in which it was created. This critical evaluation helps ensure that your argument is built on strong, credible foundations.

- **What This Looks Like on the Exam:** You might be presented with multiple sources and be asked to determine which is the most credible or relevant source to support a specific claim.
- **How to Practice:** Develop the habit of questioning your sources. Ask yourself: Who created this? What was their purpose? How reliable is the evidence provided? Practice selecting and defending your choice of sources in response to prompts.

Select and Consistently Apply an Appropriate Citation Style

Proper citation is essential for academic integrity and clarity. This skill requires you to choose an appropriate citation style (such as MLA, APA, or Chicago) and apply it consistently when referencing sources in your work. Although the AP African American Studies exam does not mandate a specific style, using citations correctly shows your ability to present evidence in a professional and scholarly manner.

- **What This Looks Like on the Exam:** You might be required to cite a source in a document-based question or free-response essay.
- **How to Practice:** Familiarize yourself with the basics of different citation styles. Practice integrating source citations into your writing seamlessly, ensuring that your work maintains a professional tone.

Use a Line of Reasoning to Develop a Well-Supported Argument

A well-supported argument is not just about having evidence; it's about organizing that evidence in a logical, coherent manner. This component challenges you to connect your claims and evidence using a clear line of reasoning. For instance, when arguing about the impact of the Great Migration, you might outline how economic opportunities in the North attracted African Americans, which in turn led to cultural movements like the Harlem Renaissance.

- **What This Looks Like on the Exam:** You'll be expected to construct essays with clear introductions, organized paragraphs, and strong conclusions, all tied together with a logical flow of ideas.
- **How to Practice:** Outline your arguments before writing. Identify your claim, evidence, and reasoning for each paragraph. Practice linking your ideas clearly so your reader can follow the progression of your argument.

The ability to construct compelling arguments is a hallmark of scholarly success. In AP African American Studies, argumentation allows you to engage deeply with the material, making meaningful connections and presenting your insights with clarity and conviction. By mastering these subskills, you'll not only excel on the AP exam but also gain a critical thinking framework that will serve you well in college and beyond. This is your opportunity to showcase your intellectual rigor and academic mastery—embrace it!

Themes in AP African American Studies

The themes of AP African American Studies act as the connective tissue of the course, weaving together the units into a cohesive and meaningful exploration of African American history and culture. These themes are not isolated ideas. Instead, they are the threads that run throughout the course, encouraging students to create meaningful connections across historical periods, disciplines, and cultural contexts.

Revisiting these themes across different units allows students to see the interplay of historical events, cultural movements, and intellectual debates, deepening their conceptual understanding. By applying these themes in various contexts, students gain a more profound appreciation of the complexities and contributions of African American experiences throughout history.

This thematic approach encourages critical thinking, interdisciplinary analysis, and a holistic understanding of African American Studies. The information that follows explores the major themes of the course and how they provide the foundation for understanding the rich tapestry of African American life. There are four themes:

- Migration and the African diaspora
- Intersections of identity
- Creativity, expression, and the arts
- Resistance and resilience

Migration and the African Diaspora

Migration is a cornerstone theme in African American Studies, encapsulating the movement of African peoples across time and space, both by force and by choice. This theme serves as a lens through which students can explore the formation and evolution of African diaspora communities worldwide and African American communities within the United States.

The concept of **diaspora** refers to the dispersal of a group of people from their place of origin to new locations, often reshaping identities and cultural practices in profound ways. For the African diaspora, this dispersal begins with Africa as the ancestral homeland—a shared point of origin that binds the histories, experiences, and legacies of African-descended peoples across continents, including the Americas, Europe, and Asia.

Forced migration: Central to this theme is the transatlantic slave trade, a devastating chapter in global history that forcibly removed millions of Africans from their homeland. This forced migration was the foundation of the African diaspora in the Americas, where enslaved people endured unimaginable hardships while also planting the seeds of resilience, cultural preservation, and resistance.

Voluntary migration: Over time, voluntary migrations—such as the Great Migration of the twentieth century—transformed African American communities in the United States. Millions of African Americans moved from the rural South to urban centers in the North and West, seeking opportunities and escaping the oppressive conditions of Jim Crow segregation. This migration not only reshaped the demographics of the nation but also fueled cultural renaissances, political movements, and economic advancements that left an indelible mark on American society.

Africa itself remains a powerful symbol within the diaspora, influencing cultural practices, artistic expression, and political ideologies in diverse ways. From the pan-Africanist movements of the early twentieth century to the contemporary embrace of African heritage in music, art, and fashion, the connection to Africa serves as a unifying thread across the global African diaspora. This symbolic relationship continues to evolve, reflecting the dynamic interplay between shared ancestry and the unique experiences of African-descended communities worldwide.

By examining migration and the African diaspora, students gain a deeper understanding of how movement shapes identity, culture, and community. This theme encourages critical reflection on the ways African Americans and other members of the diaspora have navigated displacement, sought opportunity, and maintained a connection to their ancestral homeland, all while contributing immeasurably to the societies they inhabit.

Intersections of Identity

The theme of **intersections of identity** lies at the heart of African American Studies, offering a framework to explore the complexity and diversity within African American and Black communities across the African diaspora. This theme challenges the notion of a monolithic Black experience, emphasizing how distinct categories of identity—such as race, ethnicity, class, nationality, gender, region, religion, and ability—interact to shape individual experiences and perspectives in unique ways.

Identity as multidimensional: African Americans and members of the African diaspora exist at the intersection of multiple identities, each contributing to how they experience the world and how the world perceives them. For example, the experiences of a Black woman in twentieth-century America are shaped not just by her race but also by her gender, her socioeconomic status, and her geographic location. This intersectionality is essential for understanding the nuanced realities of individuals and communities.

Historical and social contexts: The course examines how intersecting identities have influenced historical processes, cultural expressions, and social movements. From the overlapping struggles of race and class during the Civil Rights Movement to the role of gender in the fight for voting rights, intersections of identity reveal how systemic oppression often operates along multiple axes. At the same time, they highlight the resilience and agency of individuals navigating these challenges.

Intersections in African diaspora communities: Across the global African diaspora, categories of identity intersect in ways that reflect unique cultural, political, and social contexts. For instance, the experiences of Afro-Caribbean communities in the United Kingdom differ from those of African Americans in the United States, yet both reflect the interplay of race, nationality, and migration. Recognizing these intersections helps illuminate the diversity within the broader Black experience while fostering a sense of connection across different communities.

Developing critical skills: In line with the discipline of African American Studies, this theme encourages students to develop the skill of analyzing how intersections of identity impact the sources, debates, and historical processes they study. Whether examining the writings of bell hooks on race and feminism or analyzing data on regional economic disparities, students learn to approach each topic with a nuanced understanding of identity's layered complexities.

By exploring the intersections of identity, students gain a deeper appreciation for the rich diversity within African American and Black communities and the interconnected nature of social categories. This theme invites critical reflection on how these intersections have shaped individual lives, collective histories, and the ongoing pursuit of equity and justice. Through this lens, students are equipped to engage thoughtfully with the complexities of identity, both in the past and the present.

Creativity, Expression, and the Arts

Creativity, expression, and the arts is central to understanding the experiences, struggles, and triumphs of African American communities throughout history. In AP African American Studies, this theme serves as a powerful lens for examining how African Americans have used artistic forms to define their identities, challenge oppression, celebrate culture, and influence society on a global scale. Through direct encounters with Black art, literature, music, and performance, students gain a deeper appreciation of the role creativity has played in shaping African American life from its earliest origins to the contemporary moment.

African Influences on Creativity and Expression

The foundation of African American artistic traditions can be traced back to early African societies, where creativity was deeply intertwined with spiritual, social, and political life. From the rhythmic storytelling of griots to the intricate symbolism of African textiles, these early forms of expression laid the groundwork for the cultural innovations that would emerge across the diaspora. Students explore how these influences persisted and evolved, becoming central to religious expression, language, and artistic forms in African American communities.

Art as Advocacy and Justice

Throughout history, African American creativity has been a powerful tool for advocacy and resistance. Photography, poetry, music, and biography have been used to confront injustices, highlight systemic inequalities, and inspire action. For example, the poetry of Langston Hughes gave voice to the struggles and dreams of African Americans during the Harlem Renaissance, while the photography of Gordon Parks captured the raw realities of segregation and poverty during the Civil Rights Movement. Students analyze how these forms of expression communicated powerful messages and mobilized communities to fight for justice.

Debates on the Role of Black Artists

The course also engages students in critical debates about the responsibilities and roles of Black writers, artists, and performers in society. Should art reflect the harsh realities of oppression or focus on celebrating joy and resilience? How do artists balance creative freedom with the expectations of their communities? These questions have been at the center of conversations about African American expression for centuries, from the literary debates between Booker T. Washington and W. E. B. Du Bois to modern discussions on the portrayal of Black characters in film and television.

Celebration of Black Beauty and Identity

Creativity and expression are also deeply tied to affirmations of Black identity and beauty. Students examine how Afrocentric hairstyles, fashion, and other forms of self-presentation have celebrated African heritage while challenging Eurocentric beauty standards. Whether through the natural hair movement or the bold styles of contemporary designers, these expressions of identity have empowered African Americans to reclaim their narratives and define beauty on their own terms.

Global Influence and Evolution

African American creativity has resonated far beyond the borders of the United States, influencing cultures and movements across the world. From jazz and hip-hop shaping global music scenes to African American literature inspiring anti-colonial movements in Africa and the Caribbean, the global impact of African American expression cannot be overstated. Students are encouraged to examine how these forms of creativity have evolved over time and how they continue to shape global conversations on race, identity, and justice.

By exploring the theme of creativity, expression, and the arts, students develop an appreciation for the transformative power of artistic expression in African American communities. This theme celebrates the resilience, innovation, and brilliance of Black creativity while encouraging students to analyze its context, purpose, and lasting impact on the world critically.

Resistance and Resilience

The twin themes of **resistance and resilience** are woven deeply into the fabric of the AP African American Studies course, serving as a lens through which students explore the enduring strength and creativity of African American communities. These themes illuminate the diverse methods African Americans have used to confront oppression, assert their agency, and maintain authenticity across political, economic, cultural, and artistic domains. By engaging with these themes, students uncover the profound ways African Americans have not only survived but have thrived in the face of systemic adversity.

Resistance as a Catalyst for Change

Resistance has been central to African American experiences, from the earliest moments of the transatlantic slave trade to contemporary struggles for justice. Students explore how enslaved Africans resisted their captivity through revolts, sabotage, escape, and the preservation of cultural practices. These acts of defiance laid the groundwork for larger movements, such as abolitionism and the Civil Rights Movement, which sought to dismantle systemic oppression and demand equality. Resistance also manifests in subtler forms, such as the creation of counternarratives in literature, music, and art that challenge stereotypes and reclaim African American identities.

Resilience as a Foundation for Survival and Growth

Resilience complements resistance, highlighting the ways African Americans have adapted, persevered, and built thriving communities despite persistent challenges. Students examine how resilience has taken shape in various forms, from the establishment of mutual aid societies and historically Black colleges and universities (HBCUs) to the celebration of cultural traditions that affirm African heritage and identity. Resilience is not just about surviving adversity—it is about finding joy, building communities, and creating spaces where Black life can flourish.

Political and Economic Agency

The course emphasizes how African Americans have asserted political and economic agency as acts of resistance and resilience. From the formation of Black-owned businesses during the Reconstruction era to contemporary movements advocating for wealth equity and political representation, these efforts have sought to empower African American communities. Students study examples such as the role of women's clubs in advocating for economic and social rights and the significance of grassroots political organizations in shaping policy and public opinion.

Cultural and Artistic Expressions of Resistance

African American cultural and artistic practices have long been vehicles for resistance and resilience. Students analyze how music, literature, and visual arts have provided platforms to resist oppression, challenge societal norms, and celebrate Black identity. For instance, spirituals and protest songs have been used to inspire movements for justice, while visual arts and literature have offered profound critiques of systemic racism and inequity. These expressions not only reflect the struggles of African Americans but also serve as enduring symbols of strength, hope, and defiance.

Connections to the Broader African Diaspora

The themes of resistance and resilience are not confined to the United States. They are shared across the African diaspora, where African-descended communities have drawn upon their collective heritage to challenge colonialism, oppression, and inequality. From the anti-apartheid movement in South Africa to the cultural renaissance in the Caribbean, students explore how these themes connect African American experiences to global struggles for justice and liberation.

Evolving Forms of Resistance and Resilience

Throughout the course, students are encouraged to identify how resistance and resilience evolve in response to changing historical and social contexts. Whether examining the formation of abolitionist societies in the nineteenth century, the strategies of the Civil Rights Movement, or the rise of Black Lives Matter, students gain a deeper understanding of how these themes adapt to meet new challenges while drawing strength from a rich history of advocacy and empowerment.

By examining the themes of resistance and resilience, students uncover the ingenuity, strength, and creativity that have defined African American communities throughout history. These themes celebrate the enduring spirit of African Americans while inspiring students to reflect on how acts of resistance and resilience continue to shape the present and future.

2

Navigating the AP African American Studies Exam

Learning Objectives

In this chapter, you will learn:

- ➔ How to answer multiple-choice questions
- ➔ How to answer free-response questions
- ➔ How to answer document-based questions
- ➔ How to prepare for the Individual Student Project: Exam Day Validation Question

The AP African American Studies exam is the culmination of your journey through this transformative course. It is designed to assess your mastery of the skills and learning objectives outlined in the framework. This exam is not just about testing your knowledge; it evaluates your ability to think critically, analyze sources, and articulate your understanding of African American history, culture, and contributions. To earn college credit or placement, you'll need to demonstrate proficiency both in the classroom and on the exam.

In addition to the end-of-course exam, you will complete an individual student project by May 31. This project is a unique opportunity to delve deeply into a topic of your choice within the field of African American Studies, showcasing your research and analytical skills. As part of the project, you'll present your findings in class and participate in an **oral defense**, where you will respond to questions about your work. This process mirrors the rigor of collegiate academic standards and prepares you for higher-level research and presentation skills.

Exam Structure

The end-of-course exam is 2 hours and 40 minutes long and is divided into multiple components to comprehensively assess your skills and knowledge.

- **Multiple-Choice Questions:** The exam includes 60 multiple-choice questions (MCQs) designed to evaluate your understanding of course concepts and your ability to apply skills such as source analysis, argumentation, and identifying patterns and connections.
- **Free-Response Questions:** You'll also tackle three free-response questions (FRQs) that challenge you to construct well-supported arguments, analyze sources, and engage deeply with the material. These questions are your opportunity to showcase your ability to think critically and express your ideas clearly and persuasively. Of the three short-answer questions, two will be source-based—one connected to a text and another to a visual—while the third will require students to respond without a source, relying on their knowledge and critical understanding of course content.
- **Document-Based Question:** Students will encounter one document-based question that presents students with five documents offering various perspectives on a historical development or process. The topic of the document-based question will be within the scope of the required content in the Course Framework.
- **Project Validation Question:** On exam day, you will encounter one question specifically tied to your individual student project. This written response question will mirror the types of oral defense questions you addressed during your project presentation, allowing you to reflect on and articulate your findings in writing.

Units of Review	Exam Weight
Unit 1: Origins of the African Diaspora This book reviews the genesis of the African diaspora, delving into Africa's sociopolitical, economic, and aesthetic tapestry prior to the transatlantic slave trade, spanning the era from 3000 B.C.E. to 1580 C.E. Sample multiple-choice questions and free-response questions from this unit offer a foundational understanding of the origins that shaped this profound historical journey.	**20–25%**
Unit 2: Freedom, Enslavement, and Resistance This book reviews the intricate web of enslavement and the pursuit of freedom in the Americas. It unravels the complexities of Black resistance against the chains of enslavement while also examining the emergence of the global abolitionist movement. Sample multiple-choice questions and free-response questions will help readers analyze a critical period that shaped the narratives of struggle and resilience within the African American experience.	**30–35%**
Unit 3: The Practice of Freedom This book reviews the dynamic landscape of post-abolition Black communities as they navigated the arduous path to securing and safeguarding their rights as citizens. Sample multiple-choice questions and free-response questions help readers explore the birth of educational, artistic, and communal organizations that blossomed amid African American migrations across the United States from 1865 to 1925.	**20–25%**
Unit 4: Movements and Debates This book reviews the vibrant tapestry of social movements and political aspirations that continue to enrich the intellectual legacy of African American Studies. Review chapters, sample multiple-choice questions, and free-response questions help readers traverse the extensive terrain of the long Civil Rights Movement, the dynamic Black Power movement, the impactful Black feminism, and the contemporary Movement for Black Lives from the 1930s to 2000s.	**20–25%**

The AP score you earn—ranging from 1 to 5—is a combination of your project score and your performance on the end-of-course exam. Your teacher will evaluate your project presentation and oral defense using the rubric provided by the College Board, which ensures consistency and fairness. Together, these scores reflect your comprehensive understanding of the course material and your readiness for college-level African American Studies.

Understanding Section I: Multiple-Choice Questions

- Number of questions: 60
- Exam weight: 60%
- Suggested completion time: 70 minutes

The multiple-choice section is the cornerstone of the AP African American Studies exam, accounting for the largest portion of your overall score. This section evaluates your ability to analyze course concepts, explore thematic connections, and interpret primary and secondary sources with precision and critical thinking. Designed to assess your comprehension of African American history, culture, and contributions, this section also tests your mastery of applying disciplinary knowledge to real-world and historical contexts.

Structure and Question Types

The 60 multiple-choice questions (MCQs) are organized into sets, each containing three to four questions linked to one or two stimulus materials. These stimulus materials serve as the foundation for the questions, challenging you to draw on both the provided sources and your broader understanding of the course content.

Source Materials in the MCQ Section

The stimulus materials for the multiple-choice section include a mix of text-based, visual, and quantitative sources. Here's what you can expect.

- **Text: Historical Primary Sources**—Speeches, letters, and documents from key historical figures.
- **Text: Literary Sources**—Excerpts from poems, novels, or essays reflecting African American experiences.
- **Text: Secondary Sources**—Scholarly analyses or interpretations of historical events and cultural phenomena.
- **Data: Maps, Charts, Tables, or Graphs**—Visual representations of demographic, economic, or social trends.
- **Images: Art or Architecture**—Visual media showcasing cultural expression or historical context.
- **Images: Historical Photos or Maps**—Snapshots of pivotal moments or locations tied to African American history.

Key Features

The exam uses a variety of sources:

- Most questions (about 13–14) will include a single source as a stimulus, which may be text, data, or imagery.
- A smaller number of questions (about 4–5) feature paired sources, offering two stimuli for comparison or analysis. These pairings may consist of the same source type (e.g., two texts) or a combination of different types (e.g., one text and one image).

Both required and related sources are used:

- Up to half of the stimulus materials will be drawn from the required sources outlined in the course framework, ensuring a direct connection to what you've studied.
- The remaining sources will be related to the required content but may introduce new material to assess your ability to make broader connections and apply your knowledge to unfamiliar contexts.

The focus of the questions varies:

- Some questions focus explicitly on analyzing the source material provided, requiring you to evaluate claims, evidence, and context.
- Other questions challenge you to move beyond the stimulus, drawing connections to related concepts and events from the course content.

How to Excel in the Multiple-Choice Section

Mastering multiple-choice questions requires a combination of content knowledge and strategic thinking. Use these tips to improve your performance and maximize your score:

- **Read the Question Carefully:** Before looking at the answer choices, read the question carefully to understand what it's asking. Pay attention to keywords like *not, except,* and *best* to determine the type of answer required.
- **Predict the Answer:** Before you look at the answer choices, try to predict the answer based on your knowledge of the topic. This can help you eliminate obviously wrong choices and narrow down your options.
- **Eliminate Wrong Answers:** If you're unsure of the correct answer, start by eliminating choices that you know are incorrect. This increases your chances of selecting the right answer even if you're not entirely sure.
- **Consider Context:** Consider the historical context in which the question is framed. Think about the time period, location, and events surrounding the topic. This can provide valuable clues for selecting the correct answer.

- **Be Mindful of Chronology:** If the question involves a historical timeline, pay attention to chronology. Sometimes the timing of events can help you eliminate choices that don't fit the timeline.
- **Avoid Second-guessing:** Once you've selected an answer, unless you're certain it's incorrect, avoid changing your choice. Your first instinct is often correct.
- **Pace Yourself:** Don't spend too much time on a single question. If you're stuck, move on to the next one and come back later if you have time. It's important to manage your time effectively to answer as many questions as possible.
- **Use the Process of Elimination:** If you're unsure about an answer, use the process of elimination. Cross out answers you're certain are wrong, which increases the likelihood of choosing the correct answer.
- **Watch for Key Phrases:** Pay attention to key phrases, such as "which of the following," as these can indicate that there may be multiple correct answers. Remember that you need to choose the best answer.
- **Don't Leave Questions Blank:** In most AP exams, there is no penalty for guessing. If you're running out of time and have unanswered questions, take a guess. You have a chance of getting them right, while unanswered questions are guaranteed to be wrong.

Test-Taking Strategies

Analyze the stimulus materials thoroughly:

- Carefully review the source material provided with each question.
- Focus on identifying main claims, evidence, and historical context.

Practice efficiency:

- Develop the skill to analyze sources quickly while maintaining accuracy.
- Efficient time management is critical to completing all 60 questions in 70 minutes.

Build connections:

- Relate new material to essential course knowledge and themes.
- This skill is vital for questions that extend beyond the immediate stimulus.

Engage with diverse sources:

- Familiarize yourself with historical documents, literature, art, and data like maps or graphs.
- Practice interpreting these sources to connect them to broader course concepts.

KEEP IN MIND

Tips for Multiple-Choice Questions

Success on multiple-choice questions comes from preparation, strategic thinking, and familiarity with the format. Practice with the sample questions in this book to hone your skills and approach each question with focus and confidence.

Understanding Section II: Free-Response Questions, Exam Day Validation Question, and Document-Based Questions

The second section of the AP African American Studies exam challenges students to demonstrate their analytical skills, critical thinking, and ability to construct well-supported arguments. This section consists of three short-answer questions, one document-based question (DBQ), and one project exam day validation question. Each component is designed to assess your mastery of key course concepts and skills.

Source-Based Short-Answer Questions

- Number of questions: 3
- Exam weight: 18%
- Suggested completion time: 40 minutes

This section includes three short-answer questions that require you to analyze and interpret a source or set of sources. Each question consists of three to four parts and assesses multiple learning objectives and essential knowledge statements.

Key Features

- One question will use a required source from the course framework.
- The other question will use a related source that is not part of the required course content.
- Each question will include:
  - At least one part directly assessing the source and its associated content.
  - At least one part moving beyond the source to evaluate related course content.
  - At least one part assessing your ability to make thematic, chronological, or multidisciplinary connections across the course framework.

Source Types

- **Text-Based Sources:** Speeches, letters, literary excerpts, or historical documents.
- **Visual Sources:** Photographs, works of art, charts, or maps.

Short-Answer Question (No Source)

This question presents a broad thematic concept that recurs across multiple course units. It tests your ability to synthesize course material and provide specific examples.

Key Features

- Provide specific examples related to the thematic concept.
- Address at least one of the following:
  - **Causality:** Explain causes or effects.
  - **Contextualization:** Situate the concept within its historical or cultural framework.
  - **Comparison:** Highlight similarities or differences.
  - **Continuities and Changes over Time:** Analyze patterns of stability or transformation.
  - **Significance:** Explain the importance of the thematic concept.

Tips for Free-Response Questions

- **Read the Prompt Carefully:** Begin by carefully reading the FRQ prompt. Understand what it's asking you to do, whether analyzing, explaining, evaluating, or providing evidence. Pay attention to the specific historical context or time period mentioned.
- **Organize Your Thoughts:** Restate the question in your answer to help focus your response. Before you start writing, take a moment to outline your response. Jot down key points or arguments you want to include. This will help you stay focused and ensure your response is well structured.
- **Answer All Parts of the Question:** FRQs often have multiple parts. Make sure you address each part of the question in your response. Failure to do so can result in lost points.
- **Use Specific Historical Evidence:** Back up your arguments with specific historical evidence. Mention names, dates, events, and details from your knowledge of history to support your points. This demonstrates your depth of understanding.

- **Be Clear and Concise:** Write clearly and concisely. Avoid vague or overly complex language. Your points should be easy for the reader to understand.
- **Stay Relevant:** Stick to the topic and avoid going off on tangents. Every sentence in your response should directly contribute to answering the prompt.
- **Provide Context:** When discussing historical events or concepts, provide some context. Explain why they are significant in the broader historical narrative.
- **Analyze and Interpret:** Don't just provide facts; analyze and interpret them. Explain the significance of the evidence you present. What does it reveal about the historical period or issue?
- **Proofread:** Take a few minutes at the end to proofread your essay. Check for spelling and grammar errors. A well-edited essay is more likely to earn higher marks.
- **Manage Your Time:** Keep an eye on the time, especially if there are multiple FRQs to answer. Allocate your time wisely to ensure you have enough for each response.
- **Practice, Practice, Practice:** The more you practice writing responses to FRQs, the better you'll become at it. Use this test prep book to practice writing FRQs and compare correct sample answer choices.

Document-Based Question (DBQ)

- Number of questions: 1
- Exam weight: 12%
- Suggested completion time: 45 minutes

The document-based question (DBQ) requires students to analyze a set of five documents offering diverse perspectives on a historical development or process. The DBQ is a critical component of the AP African American Studies exam, offering you the opportunity to showcase your analytical abilities, evidence-based reasoning, and understanding of historical context. To excel, you must construct a well-supported argument that integrates evidence from the provided sources while demonstrating broader historical and disciplinary connections. Below is a detailed explanation of the scoring criteria, guiding you through each element of the DBQ.

Thesis or Claim (0–1 Point)

Criteria: To earn the point for your thesis, your response must:

- Present a clear, defensible claim that directly addresses the prompt.
- Establish a line of reasoning that guides your argument.
- Be located in one place, in either the introduction or the conclusion.

Your thesis is the foundation of your argument. It should not merely restate the prompt but, instead, should take a position that you will defend using evidence and analysis. For example, if the prompt asks you to evaluate the impact of the Harlem Renaissance, your thesis should make a specific claim about how this cultural movement shaped African American identity and contributions.

> **TIPS FOR SUCCESS**
>
> - Write a concise and focused thesis that outlines your argument clearly.
> - Ensure your thesis is specific enough to guide your essay but broad enough to address the scope of the prompt.

Example

The impact of the Harlem Renaissance is (insert evidence and analysis).

Context (0–1 Point)

Criteria: To earn the context point, your response must:

- Describe broader historical, cultural, or disciplinary developments that are relevant to the topic of the prompt.
- Provide more than a passing reference; context should add depth to your argument.

Context situates your argument within the larger historical or disciplinary framework.

TIPS FOR SUCCESS

- Think of context as the bigger picture surrounding your argument.
- Use context to enhance the reader's understanding of why your argument matters in its historical or cultural setting.

Example

When discussing the Civil Rights Movement, you might provide context by describing the broader social and political landscape of post–World War II America, including the persistence of segregation and the rise of grassroots activism.

Evidence (0–3 Points)

Criteria: To earn the evidence points, your response must:

- Accurately describe the content of at least two sources in relation to the prompt. (1 point)
- Accurately describe the content of at least three sources and use them to support your argument. (2 points)

To receive the third point, your response must go beyond quoting the sources. Instead, interpret and connect their content to the argument you are making.

TIPS FOR SUCCESS

- **Show, Don't Just Quote**: Go beyond repeating what the sources say—explain why the evidence matters. Connect each source to your argument by highlighting themes, historical context, or significance.
- **Weave Sources Together**: Use at least three sources and show how they relate to one another. Linking ideas across sources strengthens your argument and demonstrates deeper analysis.

Example

When analyzing a speech by Frederick Douglass, explain how its themes of freedom and equality bolster your thesis.

Evidence Beyond the Sources (0–1 Point)

Criteria: To earn this point, your response must use at least one additional piece of evidence not provided in the sources that is relevant to your argument.

Bring in outside knowledge to strengthen your essay. For example, if the DBQ focuses on Reconstruction, you might reference specific legislation, such as the Civil Rights Act of 1866, to enhance your argument.

TIPS FOR SUCCESS

- Be selective with your evidence—focus on quality and relevance rather than quantity.
- Use your own knowledge strategically to reinforce the argument and demonstrate mastery of the course content.

Source Use (0–1 Point)

Criteria: To earn this point, your response must explain how or why the perspective, purpose, context, or audience of at least two sources is relevant to your argument.

Show that you understand the intent behind the sources and how their creation influences their content and relevance.

TIPS FOR SUCCESS

- Use phrases like "The purpose of this document is . . ." or "This source's perspective highlights . . ." to clarify your analysis.
- Avoid simply identifying these elements—explain their significance to your argument.

Example

When analyzing a political cartoon, discuss how its intended audience and historical context shape its message.

Reasoning (0–1 Point)

Criteria: To earn this point, you must use reasoning to structure your argument, employing strategies like causation, comparison, or continuity and change over time.

Reasoning connects your thesis, evidence, and analysis into a cohesive argument.

TIPS FOR SUCCESS

- Structure your essay logically, ensuring that each paragraph builds on the previous one.
- Explicitly link your evidence back to your thesis using reasoning to strengthen your argument.

Example

If discussing the Great Migration, you might use causation to explain how economic opportunities in the North and oppressive conditions in the South drove African Americans to relocate.

Key Takeaways for Success

A strong DBQ is well organized, clearly written, and deeply analytical. Focus on crafting a defensible thesis, integrating multiple sources, and connecting your argument to broader historical contexts. Practice using reasoning to link your evidence to your thesis, ensuring your essay is both logical and persuasive. By mastering the DBQ, you demonstrate your ability to think critically, analyze sources, and construct evidence-based arguments. These are key skills that reflect the rigor of AP African American Studies and prepare you for college-level scholarship.

Individual Student Project

In AP African American Studies, students will undertake a dynamic individual research project designed to connect scholarship with critical analysis. Each student will select a topic of personal and historical significance, explore four interrelated sources, and craft an argument that reflects both depth of understanding and mastery of disciplinary skills. This project is more than an academic exercise—it is an opportunity for students to uncover untold narratives, amplify diverse voices, and present their findings with intellectual rigor.

Teachers will guide students through every stage of the process, offering structured support as they refine their research, develop their presentations, and defend their analysis. Educators also have the flexibility to incorporate additional components, such as written reflections or annotated bibliographies, that can be factored into the student's overall course grade.

Project Scoring

Teachers will evaluate each student's project using the official scoring rubric provided in this manual. The project consists of three key components, scored as follows:

- **Selected Sources Template (2 points)**
- **8-Minute Presentation and Oral Defense (10 points)**
  - *5-minute presentation*
  - *3-minute oral defense*

This structure ensures that students are not only evaluated on research and content but also on their ability to clearly articulate and defend their ideas—skills essential to success in AP African American Studies and beyond.

A Call to Scholars

This project is your chance to think like a historian, storyteller, and cultural critic all at once. Choose a topic that matters—not just to history, but to you. Whether you're uncovering the brilliance of Black women leaders, the cultural influence of hip-hop, or the hidden narratives of resistance and resilience, let your research reflect both intellectual curiosity and cultural pride. Approach this work boldly, as if your voice is the one shaping the next chapter of history—because it is!

Project Exam Day Validation Question

- Number of questions: 1
- Exam weight: 1.5%
- Suggested completion time: 10 minutes

The project exam day validation question is an essential part of the AP African American Studies exam's free-response section. It offers students a unique opportunity to showcase their analytical and reflective skills. This component connects directly to the individual project you completed during the course and assesses your ability to articulate your research findings in writing. The question is worth 2 points and will be evaluated alongside the rest of your exam by official AP readers.

Connection to the Project

This question mirrors the types of oral defense questions you addressed during your project presentation. However, instead of responding verbally, you will craft a written response that demonstrates your ability to analyze, compare, and evaluate the sources you selected for your project.

Focus of the Question

The validation question will require you to reflect on one or more aspects of your research. These aspects include the strategic selection of sources, the reliability and depth of your evidence, or the connections between your project and the course content.

Purpose

This section evaluates your ability to think critically about your research process, justify your choices, and draw meaningful insights from your work. It emphasizes the importance of deep engagement with sources and the ability to connect them to broader course themes.

Possible Areas of Focus for the Validation Question

A strategic selection of sources question requires you to analyze how and why you chose specific sources for your project. It assesses your ability to think critically about the quality and relevance of the materials you used. Examples include:

- Why did you choose a specific source for your project? Explain the source's relevance and how it contributed to your research.
- Which source most deepened your understanding of the topic and why? Reflect on how the source provided unique insights or added depth to your analysis.
- How would excluding one of your sources have weakened your argument? Analyze the role of a key source and how it bolstered the strength of your project.
- How did you determine the reliability of one of your sources? Discuss the criteria you used to evaluate the source's credibility and accuracy.

A comparison of sources question challenges you to assess how your sources interact with one another, whether through differing perspectives, similarities, or varying degrees of reliability. Examples include:

- How do two of your sources provide different perspectives on an aspect of your topic? Highlight contrasting viewpoints and discuss their significance to your argument.
- How do two of your sources provide similar perspectives on an aspect of your topic? Identify commonalities and explain how they reinforced your understanding.
- Why is one of your sources more convincing than another? Evaluate the strength of evidence, clarity of argument, or depth of insight in one source compared with another.
- Why is one of your sources more reliable than another? Analyze factors like the author's credentials, publication context, or use of evidence.

An additional insights and connections question encourages you to reflect on what you learned during the research process and how your findings connect to course content in new or unexpected ways. Examples include:

- What is one piece of information you learned from a source that was not covered in your classroom instruction? Discuss how this new information expanded your understanding of the topic.
- What is one piece of information you learned that builds on what you studied in class? Explain how the source added depth or nuance to what you already knew.
- How did your research connect to a course topic in unexpected ways? Reflect on any surprises or discoveries you encountered while completing your project.
- How did your research raise additional questions or insights about your topic? Analyze how the project opened new avenues for inquiry or revealed complexities in your topic.

TIPS FOR SUCCESS

- **Be Reflective:** Go beyond summarizing your project. Analyze and evaluate your choices, demonstrating a deep understanding of your research process.
- **Use Evidence:** Support your response with specific examples from your project, showing how your sources contributed to your argument and insights.
- **Connect to Course Content:** Highlight how your project relates to broader themes and learning objectives in AP African American Studies, emphasizing its relevance and significance.
- **Practice Articulating Your Process:** Prepare for this section by reviewing your project, reflecting on your sources, and practicing responses to potential validation questions.

The project exam day validation question is your chance to showcase your ability to think critically, reflect deeply, and connect your research to the rich field of African American Studies. By approaching this section with confidence and preparation, you'll not only reinforce the significance of your work but also demonstrate the scholarly rigor expected in college-level studies.

Task Verbs for Free-Response Questions and the Research Project

Understanding the meaning behind task verbs is essential for writing high-scoring responses on the AP African American Studies exam and completing your project. These task verbs tell you exactly what the question is asking you to do.

Cite: Provide information about a source, such as the title, author, type, and/or date.

Compare: Describe or explain similarities and/or differences between two or more things (events, ideas, perspectives, etc.).

> **TIPS FOR SUCCESS**
>
> For DBQs, simply referencing the source by its letter (e.g., Source A) is sufficient.

Define a Research Question: Clearly identify your topic of interest, develop guiding questions, and reference relevant sources that will deepen your analysis.

Describe: Give the key characteristics or details of a specific topic without needing to explain causes or effects.

Develop an Argument: Make a claim and support it with evidence and reasoning.

Draw a Conclusion: Use evidence to form an accurate statement or interpretation that shows your understanding of the issue or topic.

Evaluate: Make a judgment about the significance, accuracy, or quality of an idea, argument, or source based on evidence.

Explain: Provide information on how or why something happens, supported by evidence.

Explain How: Provide information on how or why something happens, supported by evidence. Focus on processes, relationships, or developments.

Explain Why: Provide information on how or why something happens, supported by evidence. Focus on causes, motivations, or reasons.

Identify: Name or point out a fact, feature, or idea related to the topic. (Note: No explanation is required.)

Support an Argument: Use specific examples and explain how they reinforce your claim.

Synthesize: Bring together ideas, perspectives, or evidence from multiple sources to create or support a unified, well-developed position.

Each of the task verbs listed point to a specific skill. Paying close attention to what a question is really asking will help you plan your response, choose the right evidence, and stay focused.

PART 2

Unit 1—Origins of the African Diaspora

3

The Strength and Complexity of Early African Societies

Key Themes

- Africa as the cradle of humanity—Africa was home to the earliest humans and civilizations.
- Technological and cultural innovation—Early African societies demonstrated complex governance, ironworking, and artistic excellence.
- Powerful empires and economic systems—Ghana, Mali, and Songhai controlled trans-Saharan trade routes and became centers of learning.
- Linguistic and ethnic diversity—Africa's rich ethnolinguistic makeup shaped its societal development.
- Foundation of African American Studies—Exploring Africa's deep past anchors the discipline and instills historical pride.

TIMELINE

Date/Period	Event/Development	Related Topics
c. 300,000 B.C.E.	**Origins of *Homo sapiens* in East Africa** (e.g., Omo Valley, Ethiopia)	Topic 1.2—African Continent
c. 10,000 B.C.E.	Agricultural communities begin forming in the Nile Valley and West Africa	Topic 1.4—Ancient Societies
c. 3,100 B.C.E.	**Unification of ancient Egypt** under Narmer/Menes	Topic 1.4—Africa's Ancient Societies
c. 2500 B.C.E.–500 C.E.	**Nok culture** develops in present-day Nigeria; known for advanced ironworking and terracotta art	Topic 1.4—Ancient Societies
c. 800 B.C.E.–400 C.E.	**Kingdom of Kush** (Nubia) thrives in Nubian region; rules Egypt at its peak	Topic 1.4—Ancient Societies
c. 300 C.E.–1100 C.E.	**Kingdom of Ghana** rises; controls trans-Saharan gold and salt trade routes	Topic 1.5—Sudanic Empires
c. 1235 C.E.–1400s C.E.	**Empire of Mali** flourishes under Sundiata and Mansa Musa; becomes a center of Islamic learning in Timbuktu	Topic 1.5—Sudanic Empires
c. 1460s C.E.–1591 C.E.	**Songhai Empire** becomes dominant under Sunni Ali and Askia Muhammad	Topic 1.5—Sudanic Empires

Date/Period	Event/Development	Related Topics
Pre-1600s C.E.	Expansion of diverse **ethnolinguistic groups** (e.g., Bantu migrations, Afroasiatic and Niger-Congo families)	Topic 1.3—Population and Language
Ongoing/ contemporary	Study of early Africa continues through African American Studies as a discipline	Topic 1.1—What Is African American Studies?

Early African societies represent some of the most vibrant and influential civilizations in human history. These societies laid the groundwork for global trade, cultural exchange, and intellectual innovation. Through their diverse kingdoms, city-states, and cultural practices, early African communities shaped the social, political, and economic landscapes of their time while creating enduring legacies that continue to inspire. Understanding the strength and complexity of these societies not only provides insight into Africa's rich history but also deepens our appreciation for its foundational role in shaping the African diaspora.

Topic 1.1 What Is African American Studies?

Key Terms

- African American Studies
- Interdisciplinary approach
- Black Campus Movement
- Black Student Union Strike (1968)
- National Council for Black Studies
- Hunter College Black and Puerto Rican Studies
- Diaspora
- Rigorous scholarly inquiry
- Freedom struggles
- Misconceptions about Africa
- Documented African history

African American Studies is an interdisciplinary field dedicated to the comprehensive exploration of the history, culture, experiences, and contributions of people of African descent. Rooted in the struggles for justice and equity, the discipline examines the intersections of race, identity, politics, art, and social movements, both within the United States and across the African diaspora. African American Studies draws from multiple academic disciplines, including history, sociology, literature, political science, and anthropology, to provide a holistic understanding of the African American experience. By critically analyzing systems of oppression and highlighting the resilience, creativity, and agency of African-descended communities, the field challenges traditional narratives and amplifies historically marginalized voices. More than a study of the past, African American Studies is a dynamic and evolving discipline that connects historical contexts to contemporary issues, fostering critical thinking and empowering scholars to engage with the world in meaningful ways.

After engaging with this topic, scholars will be able to:

- Identify the defining characteristics of African American Studies as a discipline.
- Examine the historical movements that drove the creation of African American Studies programs in U.S. colleges and universities during the 1960s and 1970s.
- Evaluate how African American Studies deepens our understanding of early African societies and their relationships with African diasporic communities globally.

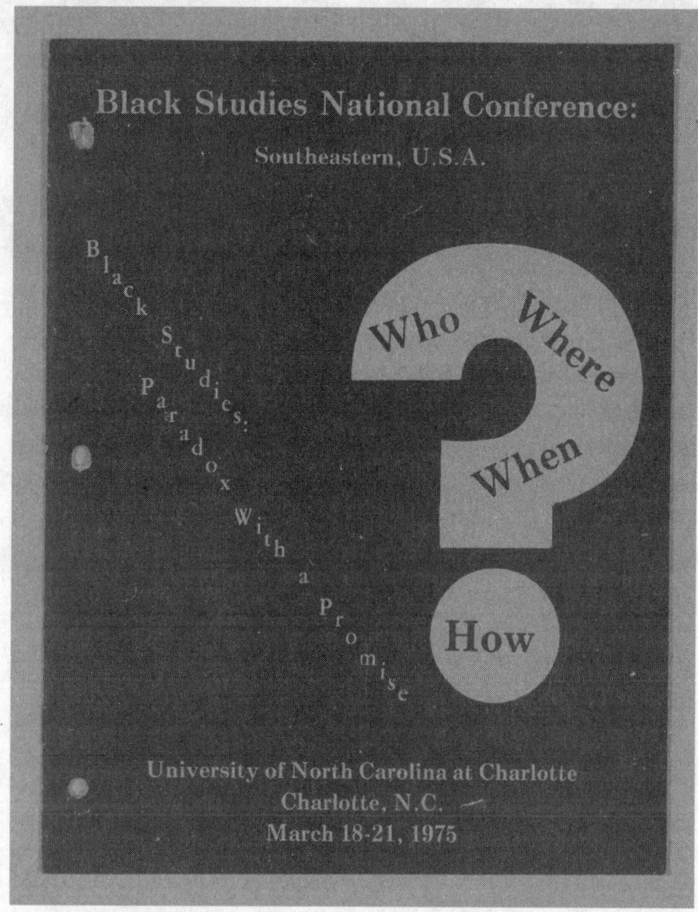

The program for the first National Council for Black Studies annual conference, *Black Studies: Paradox with a Promise*, held at the University of North Carolina at Charlotte, March 18–21, 1975. (Source: Collection of the Smithsonian National Museum of African American History and Culture)

How did a movement for academic justice spark one of the most transformative disciplines in modern history? African American Studies is an interdisciplinary field born out of the struggles for equity and representation during the Civil Rights and Black Power Movements of the 1960s and 1970s. It seeks to illuminate the histories, cultures, contributions, and struggles of people of African descent while challenging the systemic exclusion of Black voices from traditional academic narratives.

During the Black Campus Movement (1965–1972), hundreds of thousands of Black students, supported by Latino, Asian, and white allies, organized protests across more than 1,000 colleges nationwide. Their demands for greater inclusion led to the establishment of African American Studies programs, marking a pivotal moment in academia. These programs not only centered the histories and contributions of Black people but also pushed for institutional support for Black students, faculty, and administrators.

A Black student union leader in front of a crowd of demonstrators at San Francisco State College in December 1968

At its core, African American Studies acknowledges Africa as the cradle of humanity and the ancestral home of African Americans. The field delves into the cultural, political, artistic, and technological advancements of early African societies—monumental architecture, dynamic political systems, and artistic brilliance—that continue to shape identities and inspire communities worldwide. Through this lens, students explore how the legacies of Africa are deeply connected to the experiences of the African diaspora.

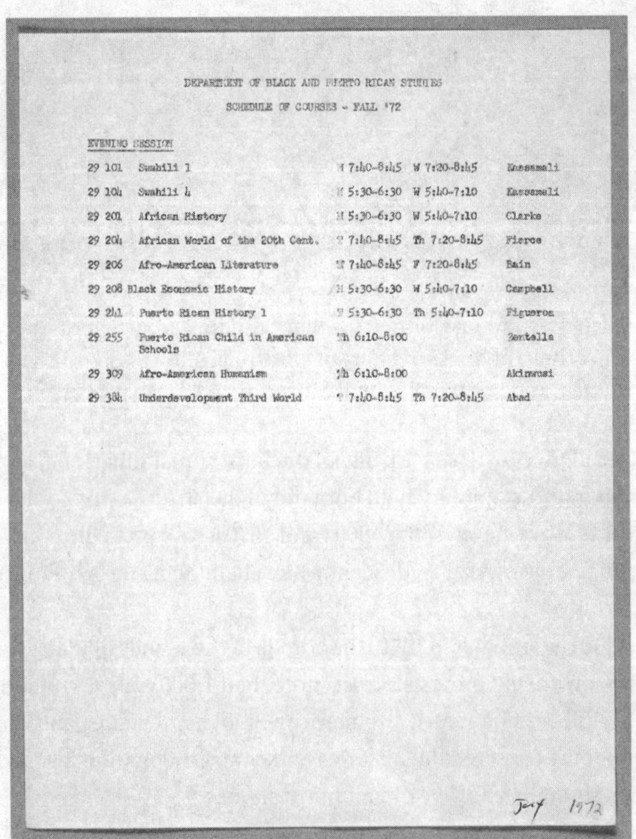

DEPARTMENT OF BLACK AND PUERTO RICAN STUDIES

SCHEDULE OF COURSES - FALL '72

EVENING SESSION

29 101	Swahili 1	M 7:40-8:45	W 7:20-8:45	Kassameli
29 104	Swahili 4	M 5:30-6:30	W 5:40-7:10	Kassameli
29 201	African History	M 5:30-6:30	W 5:40-7:10	Clarke
29 204	African World of the 20th Cent.	T 7:40-8:45	Th 7:20-8:45	Pierce
29 206	Afro-American Literature	M 7:40-8:45	F 7:20-8:45	Bain
29 208	Black Economic History	M 5:30-6:30	W 5:40-7:10	Campbell
29 241	Puerto Rican History 1	T 5:30-6:30	Th 5:40-7:10	Figueroa
29 255	Puerto Rican Child in American Schools	Th 6:10-8:00		Zentella
29 309	Afro-American Humanism	Th 6:10-8:00		Akinwusi
29 384	Underdevelopment Third World	T 7:40-8:45	Th 7:20-8:45	Abad

July 1972

Schedule of courses for Black and Puerto Rican Studies at Hunter College in New York City, July 1972

By using interdisciplinary research, African American Studies dismantles misconceptions that early Africa lacked history or global significance. Instead, it reveals a continent rich in complexity and innovation, whose societies were globally connected long before the transatlantic slave trade. This deeper understanding of Africa's legacy not only enriches the study of African American experiences but also challenges dominant narratives, inspiring a reimagining of history itself.

African American Studies is more than a discipline; it is a call to action. It empowers scholars to analyze the intersections of race, culture, power, and resistance critically, equipping these scholars to address contemporary issues and advocate for justice. It bridges the past with the present, offering a transformative lens through which to view the world and envision a more equitable future. African American Studies is a dynamic and evolving field, and you are now part of its legacy. Let's explore its depth and impact together!

Why African American History Starts in Africa

The story of African American history begins with deep roots—not in slavery but in Africa's civilizations, cultures, and ideas. Understanding these early societies helps reclaim a legacy that was too often erased.

You're Practicing: Recognizing why certain histories are told and why others were left out.

Connect This To: Origins and diasporic identity.

Theme: Identity and Culture

Practice: Contextualize

African American Studies emerged as an academic response to both scholarly omission and demands for racial justice.

(A) Describe the historical context in which African American Studies developed as a distinct academic discipline.

(B) Explain how African American Studies challenged dominant narratives in traditional academic fields.

(C) Analyze the significance of the interdisciplinary nature of African American Studies in shaping a fuller understanding of Black life and history.

SAMPLE RESPONSES

(A) African American Studies developed as a distinct discipline during the Black Campus Movement, when hundreds of thousands of Black students organized protests across more than 1,000 colleges and universities nationwide. They demanded the creation of academic programs that centered on Black history, culture, and contributions, which led to the establishment of African American Studies departments across the country.

A key context for the emergence of African American Studies was the San Francisco State College student strike of December 1968, where the Black Student Union and the Third World Liberation Front led the longest student strike in U.S. history. Their activism resulted in the creation of the nation's first Department of Black Studies and served as a model for similar programs nationwide.

(B) African American Studies challenged stereotypical academic narratives by centering the histories and contributions of African-descended peoples. For example, Hunter College's Black and Puerto Rican Studies Program reframed Africa as a site of cultural, political, and technological innovation, dismantling the false narrative that early African societies lacked global significance.

African American Studies challenged Eurocentric frameworks by connecting African American history to the African diaspora. It revealed how precolonial African societies built complex political systems, artistic traditions, and global trade networks long before European contact, providing a fuller understanding of Africa's enduring global influence.

(C) The interdisciplinary nature of African American Studies is significant because it draws from history, sociology, literature, political science, and art to provide a holistic understanding of Black life and culture. By integrating these disciplines, scholars uncover the interconnected forces shaping the African American experience—from systemic oppression to cultural resilience—creating a more accurate and nuanced historical narrative.

African American Studies is significant because it links African American experiences to global diasporic struggles, fostering a broader understanding of identity and resistance. By examining Africa's legacy alongside African-descended communities worldwide, the field highlights patterns of migration, innovation, and solidarity, reshaping historical perspectives across borders.

Skills Assessed: Contextualize historical developments; use sources and evidence; analyze relationships among developments.

Topic 1.2 The African Continent: A Varied Landscape

Key Terms

- Climate zones (desert, semiarid/Sahel, savannah, rainforest, Mediterranean)
- Major rivers (Niger, Congo, Zambezi, Orange, Nile)
- Trade routes
- Geographic diversity
- Fertile land/agriculture
- Nomadic herders and salt trade
- Kola trees, yams, gold

How has the African continent's diverse geography shaped the development of civilizations, cultures, and trade? Africa, which is often referred to as the cradle of humanity, is a land of extraordinary geographic diversity. From vast deserts and lush rainforests to expansive savannahs and towering mountain ranges, Africa's varied landscape has profoundly influenced the settlement patterns, cultural interactions, and economic systems of its peoples. This chapter invites scholars to explore the richness of Africa's physical environment and its pivotal role in shaping human history.

After engaging with this topic, scholars will be able to:

- Describe the geographic features that define the African continent.
- Explain how Africa's diverse landscape influenced patterns of settlement and facilitated trade between distinct cultural regions.

Africa's geography is not just a backdrop to its history; it is a dynamic force that has driven innovation, fostered connections, and presented challenges that civilizations have creatively addressed. By studying the relationship between Africa's environment and its peoples, scholars will uncover the ways in which geography has been a catalyst for cultural exchange and economic growth.

As the second-largest continent in the world, Africa boasts extraordinary geographic diversity that has profoundly influenced its history and global significance. The continent is characterized by five primary climate zones: vast deserts such as the Sahara, semiarid regions like the Sahel, expansive savannah grasslands, lush tropical rainforests, and the temperate Mediterranean zone. This variety of landscapes has shaped settlement patterns, agricultural practices, and trade networks. This variety has also fostered cultural and economic development over millennia.

Natural Boundaries and Global Connections

Africa's borders are defined by seas and oceans—the Red Sea, Mediterranean Sea, Atlantic Ocean, and Indian Ocean—that facilitated the emergence of early societies and fostered global interactions. The continent's five major rivers—the Nile, Niger, Congo, Zambezi, and Orange—served as lifelines, connecting regions within Africa's vast interior. The proximity of waterways like the Red Sea and Mediterranean Sea played a pivotal role in creating early trade networks and establishing Africa's place in the interconnected ancient world.

Population Centers and Key Geographic Features

Population centers in Africa, particularly in the Sahel and savannah grasslands, emerged due to three critical factors:

1. **TRADE AND TRANSPORTATION.** Major water routes, such as the Niger and Nile Rivers, facilitated the movement of people, goods, and ideas. These major water routes also enabled the growth of vibrant trade networks.
2. **AGRICULTURAL INNOVATION.** Fertile land in regions like the savannah grasslands supported the expansion of agriculture and the domestication of animals. This fertile land also laid the foundation for stable and prosperous communities.
3. **TRADE LINKAGES ACROSS REGIONS.** The Sahel and savannah grasslands served as vital bridges, connecting communities in the Sahara to the north with those in the tropical regions to the south. This connectivity encouraged cultural exchanges and economic interdependence.

Climate Variations and Trade Opportunities

Africa's diverse climates created opportunities for specialized trade, reflecting the adaptability and ingenuity of its people:

- **Deserts and Semiarid Regions:** Nomadic herders traversed these areas in search of food and water, trading valuable resources like salt.
- **The Sahel:** In this transitional zone, livestock became a key commodity of trade.
- **Savannah Grasslands:** These fertile lands were ideal for cultivating grain crops, which became staples in regional and interregional trade.
- **Tropical Rainforests:** In the lush rainforest regions, people cultivated kola trees and yams while engaging in the trade of gold, a resource that would become central to Africa's global economic influence.

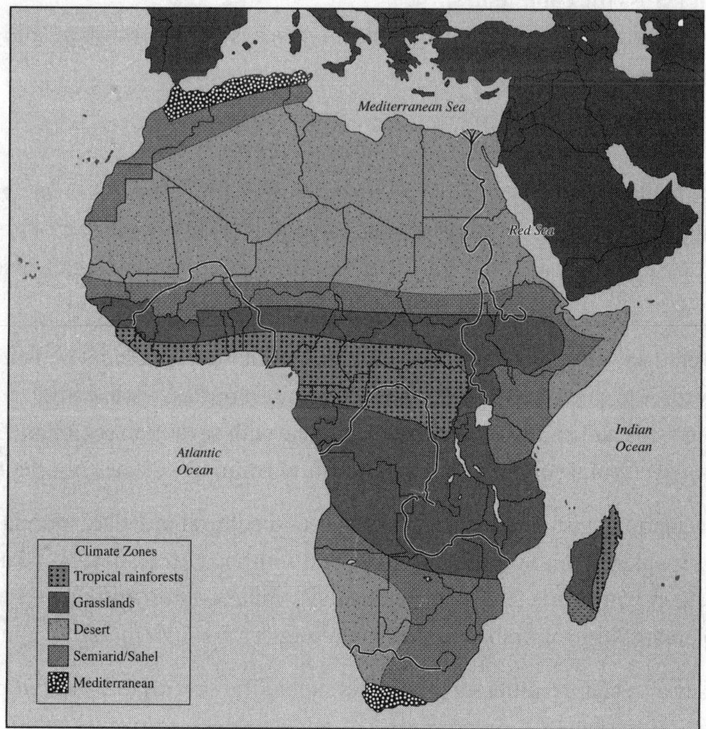

Major climate regions of Africa

A Dynamic Continent

The geographic diversity of Africa not only shaped the livelihoods of its peoples but also positioned the continent as a critical hub of trade and cultural exchange. Its landscapes, rich with natural resources and opportunities, supported the development of complex societies that contributed to the interconnectedness of the ancient world.

Africa's varied geography and resourcefulness of its people provide a lens through which scholars can better understand the continent's enduring influence. The fertile soils of the savannah, the nomadic resilience of desert herders, and the global trade networks originating from Africa remind us of the continent's foundational role in human history.

Geography Shapes Civilizations

Africa's rivers, deserts, and valleys didn't just shape the land—they shaped empires. Natural features like the Nile and the Sahara created trade routes, supported farming, and connected societies. Studying geography helps us see how the environment and innovation shaped the rise of powerful African civilizations.

You're Practicing: Making connections between the land and historical developments.

Connect This To: Environment, trade, and empire building.

Theme: Origins and Encounters

Practice: Explain the Significance or Importance

The African continent is often misrepresented as geographically and culturally uniform, yet its environmental and social diversity is vast.

(A) Explain how the physical geography of Africa (e.g., deserts, rainforests, savannahs, and river systems) has shaped patterns of human settlement, trade, and cultural development.

(B) Describe how regional diversity has contributed to the emergence of distinct societies, languages, and political systems across the continent.

(C) Analyze why understanding the varied geography of Africa is important when studying African and African American histories.

SAMPLE RESPONSES

(A) The Niger and Nile rivers shaped settlement patterns by providing fertile soil for agriculture and reliable transportation routes. These waterways facilitated the rise of population centers like Timbuktu and Jenne, enabling the exchange of grain, gold, and kola nuts while connecting diverse societies across West, North, and East Africa.

Africa's diverse climates created specialized economies that fueled regional and global trade. For example, nomadic herders in the Sahara traded salt across desert routes, while communities in tropical rainforests cultivated yams, kola nuts, and gold for exchange with savannah societies. These interdependent networks promoted cultural contact and economic innovation across the continent.

(B) Africa's varied geography fostered distinct languages and cultural practices among different regions. For instance, Bantu-speaking communities in central and southern Africa developed agricultural innovations and migrated widely, spreading their language family, while Swahili-speaking societies along the East African coast blended African, Arab, and Persian influences through Indian Ocean trade.

Regional diversity also shaped different political systems. The savannah-based empires of Mali, Ghana, and Songhai centralized power through control of gold and salt trade routes, while smaller rainforest communities relied on decentralized governance rooted in kinship networks. These contrasting systems highlight how societies adapted to their environmental and economic contexts.

(C) Understanding Africa's varied geography is important because it challenges stereotypes that depict the continent as culturally and environmentally uniform. Recognizing the diversity of deserts, savannahs, rainforests, and fertile river valleys highlights Africa's role as a center of innovation, migration, and cultural exchange long before European colonization.

Studying Africa's landscapes is also significant because it reveals how environmental diversity shaped cultural traditions carried into the African diaspora. Foods like yams and rice, spiritual practices tied to river systems, and gold-based trade legacies influenced the development of African American communities in the Americas, demonstrating the deep continuities between African and diasporic identities.

Skills Assessed: Explain the significance of geographic context; use sources and evidence; analyze relationships among developments.

Topic 1.3 Population Growth and Ethnolinguistic Diversity

Key Terms

- Bantu expansion
- Agricultural innovations
- Iron tools
- Ethnolinguistic groups
- Linguistic diversity (e.g., Swahili, Zulu, Xhosa)
- Migration patterns
- Genetic ancestry of African Americans

How did a single migration shape the linguistic, cultural, and genetic landscape of an entire continent? The Bantu expansion, one of the most significant population movements in human history, serves as a powerful example of how migration can transform societies. Beginning around 3000 B.C.E. and spanning thousands of years, this migration spread Bantu-speaking peoples across much of sub-Saharan Africa, leaving an indelible mark on the continent's cultural and genetic heritage.

After engaging with this topic, scholars will be able to:

- Describe the factors that spurred the Bantu expansion across the African continent.
- Explain how the Bantu expansion influenced the linguistic diversity of West and Central Africa and contributed to the genetic heritage of African Americans.

The Bantu Expansion: A Catalyst for Population Growth and Ethnolinguistic Diversity

Africa's rich linguistic and genetic diversity owes much to one of the most remarkable population movements in history: the Bantu expansion. Spanning over two millennia (1500 B.C.E.–500 C.E.), this migration of Bantu-speaking peoples from West and Central Africa transformed the cultural, linguistic, and demographic landscape of the continent.

Technological and Agricultural Innovations as Catalysts

The Bantu expansion was fueled by advancements in both technology and agriculture that supported population growth in West and Central Africa. Technological innovations, such as the development of tools and particularly of ironworking techniques, enabled communities to cultivate land more effectively, expand agricultural output, and establish stable settlements. Agricultural innovations, such as the cultivation of bananas, yams, and grains, provided reliable food sources. They also supported larger populations and the need to migrate to new, fertile lands. These innovations created a ripple effect, triggering migrations that carried Bantu-speaking peoples across sub-Saharan Africa in search of arable land and resources.

The Linguistic Legacy of the Bantu Expansion

As Bantu-speaking peoples migrated, they brought with them not only their agricultural practices and technologies but also their languages.

- **Diversity of Bantu Languages:** Today, the Bantu linguistic family encompasses hundreds of languages spoken throughout West, Central, and Southern Africa, including widely known languages such as Swahili, Zulu, Kikongo, and Xhosa.
- **A Unifying Thread:** Although distinct, these languages share common roots, reflecting the deep historical connections among Bantu-speaking communities. The spread of these languages underscores the cultural cohesion that accompanied the physical movement of people.

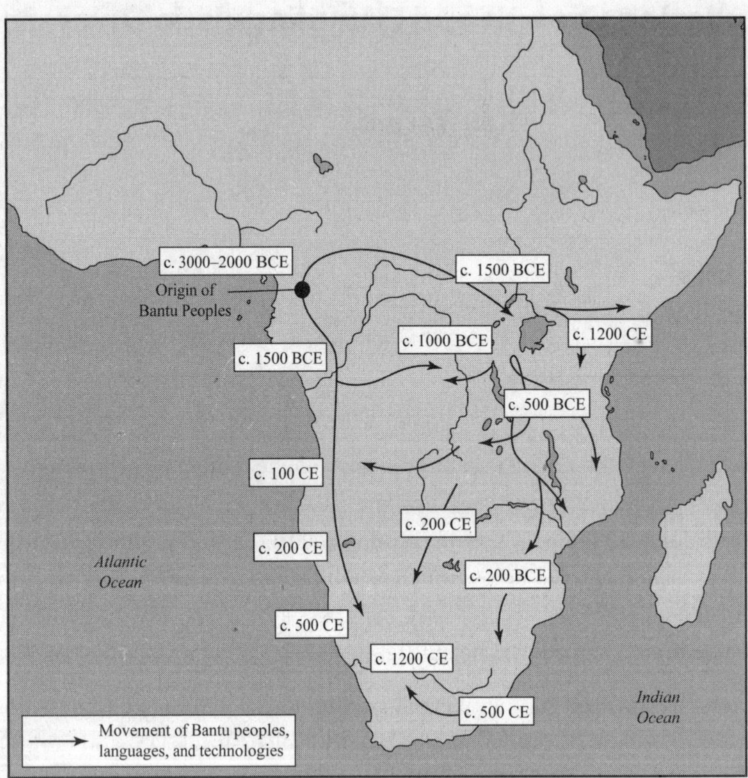

The movement of Bantu peoples, languages, and technologies

The Power of Language and Movement

What do Bantu, Swahili, and Yoruba have in common? They're all part of Africa's rich linguistic heritage. As people moved, they spread more than language—they spread farming techniques, ironworking, and ideas. These movements shaped the African societies from which many enslaved people came.

You're Practicing: Understanding how migration spreads culture.

Connect This To: Identity, memory, and connection across time.

Theme: Migration and Diaspora

Ethnolinguistic Diversity and the African Diaspora

Africa is home to thousands of ethnic groups and languages, making it one of the most linguistically and culturally diverse continents in the world. The Bantu expansion played a significant role in shaping this diversity. There is a deep connection to African Americans. A substantial portion of the genetic ancestry of African Americans traces back to communities in West and Central Africa, many of which spoke languages belonging to the Bantu linguistic family. The cultural and genetic legacy of the Bantu expansion is thus deeply woven into the heritage of African-descended peoples across the diaspora.

The Bantu expansion highlights the dynamic interplay of innovation, migration, and cultural exchange in Africa's history. It is a story of resilience and adaptability, illustrating how human ingenuity fosters growth and connection across vast regions. By understanding the enduring influence of the Bantu expansion, scholars gain a richer appreciation for the foundations of Africa's ethnolinguistic diversity and its profound impact on the African diaspora.

Practice: Explain the Significance or Importance

Africa is home to a rapidly growing population and the greatest ethnolinguistic diversity in the world.

(A) Explain how population growth has influenced economic, social, and political developments in different African regions.

(B) Describe the significance of Africa's ethnolinguistic diversity in shaping cultural expression, identity, and historical continuity.

(C) Analyze the importance of recognizing Africa's ethnolinguistic diversity when studying diasporic African identities and the development of African American culture.

SAMPLE RESPONSES

(A) Population growth during the Bantu expansion transformed African societies by fueling migrations into fertile regions, where agricultural innovations like banana and yam cultivation sustained larger populations. These migrations spread ironworking, farming practices, and trade networks across sub-Saharan Africa, integrating distant regions into shared economic and cultural systems.

In West Africa, population growth supported the rise of powerful states like Ghana and Mali, where abundant labor enabled control of gold and salt trade routes. These kingdoms used their growing populations to strengthen military capacity, expand political authority, and create centralized governments that dominated regional commerce.

(B) The Bantu expansion produced hundreds of related languages, including Swahili, Kikongo, and Zulu, which continue to connect millions across the continent. This shared linguistic foundation reflects historical continuity while enabling distinct regional identities to flourish within the broader Bantu cultural heritage.

Africa's ethnolinguistic diversity also shaped unique artistic, religious, and political traditions. Distinct storytelling styles, musical forms, and kinship-based governance systems developed in different regions, reflecting adaptation to local environments while preserving ancestral knowledge and reinforcing collective identities across generations.

(C) Recognizing Africa's ethnolinguistic diversity clarifies the multiple cultural origins of African Americans, many of whom trace ancestry to West and Central African societies. Traditions such as drumming, call-and-response singing, and spiritual practices carried by Bantu-speaking peoples shaped African American music, faith, and community life in the Americas.

Acknowledging this diversity also reveals how enslaved Africans from different cultural and linguistic backgrounds blended traditions under oppression. New diasporic identities emerged, combining African, Indigenous, and European influences while preserving connections to ancestral heritage, shaping African American culture as a dynamic expression of resilience and adaptation.

Skills Assessed: Explain the significance of historical and cultural diversity; use sources and evidence; analyze relationships among developments.

Topic 1.4 Africa's Ancient Societies

Key Terms

- Egypt and Nubia (Kush)
- Black pharaohs (Twenty-Fifth Dynasty)
- Aksumite Empire (Eritrea/Ethiopia)
- Ge'ez script
- Nok culture (Nigeria)
- Ironworking and terracotta sculptures
- Christianity in Africa (King Ezana)
- Early African influence on African American identity
- Sacred/secular texts in early Black literature

What made the ancient societies of Africa centers of innovation, trade, and cultural brilliance? Africa's ancient civilizations, from the bustling trade hubs of West Africa to the architectural marvels of East Africa, were among the most advanced and influential societies of their time. Their contributions continue to resonate, providing a rich foundation for the cultural identity and historical significance cherished by Black communities worldwide.

This chapter invites you to explore the richness of Africa's ancient civilizations, uncovering their achievements in trade, governance, and culture. By understanding the significance of these societies, scholars gain insight into the foundational role Africa played in shaping the heritage and identity of the African diaspora.

After engaging with this topic, scholars will be able to:

- Describe the defining features of ancient East and West African societies, including the goods these societies produced and their economic contributions.
- Explain the cultural and historical significance of Africa's ancient societies to Black communities and their enduring legacy in shaping global history.

Africa's ancient societies stand as testaments to the ingenuity, cultural richness, and resilience of the continent. These civilizations—spanning from the fertile banks of the Nile to the ironworking communities of West Africa—were among the earliest complex societies in human history. Their achievements in trade, governance, technology, and religion not only shaped the ancient world but continue to inform and inspire global history and the identity of African-descended peoples today.

The Kingdoms of Egypt and Nubia

Among the first large-scale societies to emerge in Africa were Egypt and Nubia (also known as Kush or Cush), which developed along the Nile River around 3000 B.C.E. Nubia was rich in gold and luxury goods. It became a vital trading partner—and occasional adversary—of Egypt. Their interactions, shaped by both cooperation and conflict, culminated in a remarkable reversal of power around 750 B.C.E. when Nubia conquered Egypt and established the Twenty-Fifth Dynasty. For a century, the Black pharaohs of Nubia ruled Egypt, leaving an indelible mark on Egypt's cultural and political history.

The Aksumite Empire

Located in present-day Eritrea and Ethiopia, the Aksumite Empire emerged around 100 B.C.E. as a key player in global trade. Strategically situated along the Red Sea, Aksum connected Africa to the Mediterranean, the Roman Empire, and India. Its thriving economy was supported by maritime trade and bolstered by the creation of its own currency. Aksum's script, Ge'ez, became a cornerstone of its cultural legacy, with enduring significance as the liturgical language of the Ethiopian Orthodox Church.

Ancient Africa Was Global and Advanced

Think pyramids, stone churches, gold trade, and advanced medicine: African civilizations like Egypt, Kush, and Aksum were deeply connected to the ancient world. They traded with Asia and Europe and built cities with temples, libraries, and marketplaces. This history shows how African societies were far from isolated. Instead, they were global, intellectual, and powerful.

You're Practicing: Analyzing how cultural and political systems reflect power.

Connect This To: Religion, trade, and innovation.

Theme: Resistance and Autonomy

AXUM, Ezanas, circa 330–360 C.E.

Aksum exemplifies Africa's agency in adopting Christianity on its own terms. Under King Ezana's leadership, Aksum became the first African society to embrace Christianity, free from the influence of colonialism or the transatlantic slave trade. This independent adoption of a global religion highlights the complexity and autonomy of African civilizations during this period.

The Nok Civilization

The Nok society, which emerged around 500 B.C.E. in present-day Nigeria, represents one of the earliest ironworking cultures in West Africa. Known for their intricate terracotta sculptures depicting humans and animals, the Nok created artifacts that reveal a deep appreciation for artistry, adornment, and symbolism. These sculptures, along with stone tools, are the oldest evidence of a settled, complex society in sub-Saharan Africa, underscoring the technological and cultural advancements of the region.

A terracotta Nok sculpture of a seated man by an unknown artist, created between 500 B.C.E. and 500 C.E. in modern-day Nigeria

The Significance of Ancient Africa to Black Communities

The historical and cultural significance of Africa's ancient societies has long been a source of pride and empowerment for Black communities.

- **Countering Racist Stereotypes:** From the late eighteenth century onward, African American writers highlighted the complexity of ancient African societies to challenge stereotypes portraying Africa as lacking culture or governance. By reclaiming the achievements of civilizations like Egypt, Nubia, and Aksum, these writers contributed to the early foundations of African American Studies.
- **Inspiring Political Movements:** In the mid-twentieth century, research into Africa's ancient societies provided crucial support for anti-colonial movements. Demonstrating the sophistication of these societies reinforced African leaders' demands for self-rule and independence from European colonial powers.

Africa's ancient societies are far more than remnants of the past; they are vibrant examples of the continent's enduring influence on world history. By exploring these civilizations, scholars uncover the origins of technological innovation, cultural exchange, and political autonomy. These legacies challenge historical misconceptions and serve as a profound source of pride and connection for African-descended peoples worldwide.

Practice: Explain the Significance or Importance

Long before European colonization, Africa was home to complex and sophisticated societies with rich political, cultural, and economic systems.

(A) Describe the political, technological, and cultural achievements of one or more ancient African societies, such as Egypt, Kush, Axum, Mali, or Great Zimbabwe.

(B) Explain how these societies interacted through trade, migration, and religion and how they contributed to a broader African and global history.

(C) Analyze why the study of Africa's ancient civilizations is important for challenging Eurocentric historical narratives and shaping African American identity and pride.

SAMPLE RESPONSES

(A) The Kingdom of Kush demonstrated political and cultural sophistication by conquering Egypt around 750 B.C.E. and establishing the Twenty-Fifth Dynasty. The Black pharaohs unified the Nile Valley under

Nubian leadership, blending Egyptian and Kushite traditions in governance, religion, and art, leaving an enduring legacy in architecture and cultural identity.

The Aksumite Empire (100 B.C.E.–700 C.E.) achieved technological and cultural innovation through its development of the Ge'ez script and a thriving maritime economy. Under King Ezana, Aksum became one of the earliest African societies to adopt Christianity independently, demonstrating both political autonomy and Africa's integration into global religious and intellectual networks.

(B) The Aksumite Empire linked Africa to the Mediterranean, India, and the Roman world via Red Sea trade routes, exchanging gold, ivory, and spices for luxury goods and knowledge. This connectivity fostered technological diffusion and made Aksum a key player in early global commerce, shaping transcontinental cultural exchange.

The Mali Empire (c. 1235–1600) became a hub of cultural and economic interaction through control of trans-Saharan trade networks. Under Mansa Musa, Mali's wealth and influence expanded, and his famous pilgrimage to Mecca in 1324 strengthened Islamic scholarship and forged global connections, positioning West Africa as a center of education, religion, and diplomacy.

(C) Studying Africa's ancient civilizations challenges Eurocentric stereotypes that portray Africa as lacking history or cultural achievement. Recognizing the political sophistication of Egypt, Kush, and Aksum highlights Africa's role as a center of innovation and cultural influence, restoring agency and complexity to African history.

For African Americans, exploring Africa's ancient achievements fosters cultural pride and identity. Civilizations like Mali and Great Zimbabwe demonstrate Africa's longstanding contributions to science, governance, and education, offering a counter-narrative to colonial histories and deepening connections to ancestral legacies across the African diaspora.

Skills Assessed: Explain the significance of historical developments; use sources and evidence; analyze relationships among developments.

Topic 1.5 The Sudanic Empires: Ghana, Mali, and Songhai

Key Terms

- Ghana Empire (seventh to thirteenth centuries)
- Mali Empire (thirteenth to seventeenth centuries)
- Songhai Empire (fifteenth to sixteenth centuries)
- Mansa Musa
- Trans-Saharan trade
- Gold trade
- Islamic influence
- Hajj (pilgrimage to Mecca)
- *Catalan Atlas*
- Mali equestrian figure
- West African origins of African Americans

How did the wealth of gold and the power of trade transform ancient West African empires into global influencers? The Sudanic empires of Ghana, Mali, and Songhai were some of the most advanced and prosperous civilizations of their time. Their wealth and influence extended far beyond Africa's borders. Through gold, trade, and cultural exchange, these empires shaped political, economic, and religious developments that connected Africa to the broader Mediterranean world and left an enduring legacy for African-descended peoples.

This topic uncovers the remarkable achievements of Ghana, Mali, and Songhai. These empires stood as beacons of wealth, scholarship, and cultural ingenuity. By studying their legacies, scholars will see how the stories of these ancient civilizations are interwoven with the histories of the African diaspora.

After engaging with this topic, scholars will be able to:

- Analyze how the influence of gold and trade shaped the political, economic, and religious development of Ghana, Mali, and Songhai.
- Explain how Mali's extraordinary wealth and power enabled the empire to extend its influence across Africa and the Mediterranean.
- Understand the historical connections between the Sudanic empires and the experiences of early generations of African Americans.

The Sudanic empires of Ghana, Mali, and Songhai are often called the Sahelian empires. They represent some of the most influential and dynamic civilizations in African history. Between the seventh and sixteenth centuries, these empires rose and fell in succession, each building upon the legacy of its predecessor. Renowned for their vast wealth, cultural innovations, and strategic importance in global trade, these empires shaped not only West Africa but also the broader Mediterranean world, leaving an enduring impact on the African diaspora.

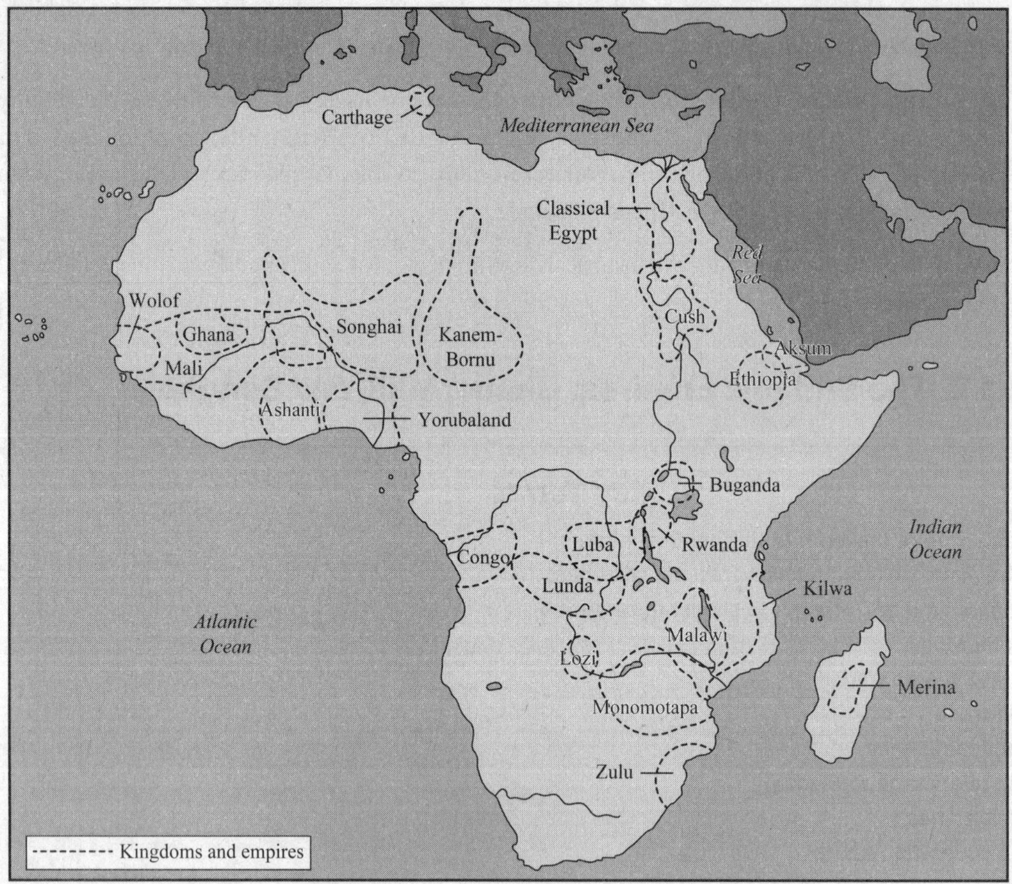

Africa's kingdoms and empires, circa 600–1600 C.E.

A Legacy of Successive Empires

The three empires flourished sequentially, with each reaching their peak during different periods. Ghana, the earliest of the Sudanic empires, thrived between the seventh and thirteenth centuries, primarily due to its abundant gold mines and its strategic location at the crossroads of trans-Saharan trade routes. This wealth enabled Ghana to establish itself as a dominant political and economic power in the region.

Following Ghana's decline, Mali rose to prominence in the thirteenth century and continued its dominance into the seventeenth century. Under leaders such as Mansa Musa, Mali became an unparalleled center of trade, culture, and scholarship. Mali extended its influence across Africa and into the Mediterranean.

Songhai, the last and largest of the Sudanic empires, emerged in the fifteenth century, building on the foundations laid by Mali. Spanning a vast territory, Songhai exemplified the height of West African political and military organization before its eventual decline due to shifting trade routes and external pressures.

The Influence of Gold and Trade

Gold was the lifeblood of the Sudanic empires, serving as the cornerstone of their wealth and global influence. Positioned at the nexus of trans-Saharan trade routes, these empires facilitated the exchange of gold, salt, textiles, and other valuable goods between sub-Saharan Africa and North Africa, Europe, and the Mediterranean world. This trade network not only enriched the empires but also established the Sudanic empires as key players in global commerce.

Trans-Saharan commerce brought more than goods to the region—it introduced new ideas and cultural influences. North African traders, scholars, and administrators brought Islam to West Africa, fostering its growth and embedding it into the political and intellectual fabric of the Sudanic empires. The spread of Islam further strengthened ties between West Africa and the broader Islamic world, enriching local traditions with new religious, architectural, and scholarly influences.

The Mali Empire and the Legacy of Mansa Musa

The Mali Empire reached its zenith under the reign of Mansa Musa, who ruled in the fourteenth century. Known for his immense wealth and devotion to Islam, Mansa Musa positioned Mali as a beacon of prosperity, trade, and cultural sophistication. His legendary hajj (pilgrimage) to Mecca in 1324 showcased Mali's wealth to the world. While carrying vast amounts of gold and accompanied by a grand entourage, Mansa Musa's pilgrimage attracted the attention of merchants, scholars, and cartographers from the Mediterranean to Europe. His pilgrimage can be seen on the *Catalan Atlas*, which was created in 1375 by Abraham Cresques. This solidified Mali's global reputation.

Catalan Atlas by Abraham Cresques, 1375
(Source: Copia de 1959 del original de 1375, CC BY 3.0 via Wikimedia Commons)

Mali's wealth also underpinned its military and territorial expansion. Access to trans-Saharan trade routes enabled the empire to acquire advanced weaponry and powerful horses, which strengthened its ability to exert influence over neighboring regions. This combination of military might and economic power allowed Mali to maintain its dominance for centuries.

Image of Mali equestrian figure, thirteenth to fifteenth centuries

Mansa Musa Changed the World's View of Africa

Mansa Musa's fourteenth-century pilgrimage to Mecca put West Africa in the spotlight. He handed out so much gold that it affected the economies of entire cities. His empire, Mali, became known for wealth, learning, and architecture—especially the libraries and mosques in Timbuktu.

You're Practicing: Using visual and historical evidence to understand cultural influence.

Connect This To: Global trade, Islamic scholarship, and political leadership.

Theme: Power and Politics

Songhai's Rise and Decline

The Songhai Empire, emerging in the fifteenth century, became the largest of the Sudanic empires, extending its reach across vast swathes of West Africa. Songhai built upon the trade networks and administrative systems established by its predecessors, creating a powerful and centralized state. However, the emergence of Atlantic trade routes in the fifteenth century, driven by Portuguese exploration along Africa's western coast, marked a turning point. The shift from trans-Saharan trade to Atlantic commerce diminished Songhai's wealth and influence, contributing to its eventual decline.

Connections to the African Diaspora

The Sudanic empires' influence extended far beyond their historical period, leaving a legacy that shaped the African diaspora. The geographic reach of these empires, spanning regions from Senegambia to Côte d'Ivoire and parts of Nigeria, encompassed many of the communities from which enslaved Africans were forcibly taken. The cultural, linguistic, and historical connections between the Sudanic empires and African-descended peoples in the Americas highlight the enduring impact of these civilizations.

Many African Americans trace their ancestry to societies in West and West Central Africa, regions that were integral to the Sudanic empires. The intellectual achievements, governance systems, and cultural traditions of Ghana, Mali, and Songhai remain a source of pride and identity for African-descended peoples worldwide. These empires serve as a reminder of Africa's central role in global history and its enduring contributions to humanity.

A Legacy of Resilience and Ingenuity

The Sudanic empires exemplify the resilience, ingenuity, and cultural richness of African civilizations. By understanding their histories, we gain a deeper appreciation of the interconnectedness of the ancient world and the foundational role of Africa in shaping global culture and commerce. The legacies of Ghana, Mali, and Songhai continue to inspire, providing a vital link between the past and the present.

Practice: Explain the Effects of Historical Development

The Sudanic empires of Ghana, Mali, and Songhai flourished through control of trans-Saharan trade and played a major role in shaping West African history.

(A) Describe the political structures and economic systems of the Sudanic empires.

(B) Explain the effects of trans-Saharan trade on the development and influence of these empires, especially regarding wealth, Islam, and urbanization.

(C) Analyze how the legacy of these empires contributes to African and African American historical consciousness today.

SAMPLE RESPONSES

(A) The Mali Empire established a highly centralized government under rulers like Mansa Musa, who used wealth from gold and salt trade to expand military power and control vast territories. Mali's strong bureaucracy managed taxation, trade routes, and Islamic scholarship, making the empire a major political and cultural center.

The Songhai Empire developed an advanced administrative system by dividing its large territory into provinces governed by appointed officials. Positioned at the crossroads of trans-Saharan trade, Songhai controlled gold, salt, and agricultural production, generating immense wealth that funded military expansion and urban growth.

(B) Mansa Musa's hajj in 1324 demonstrates how trade fueled Mali's wealth and spread its influence globally. Control over gold routes allowed Mali to finance massive caravans, and the pilgrimage strengthened diplomatic and religious ties with the broader Islamic world, promoting Islamic scholarship and cultural exchange.

In Songhai, trade-driven prosperity fostered the rise of Timbuktu and Gao as urban centers of learning and commerce. Merchants, scholars, and architects from North Africa introduced Islamic practices, mosques, and schools, integrating Songhai into wider religious and intellectual networks that connected Africa to the Mediterranean and Middle East.

(C) The achievements of the Sudanic empires affirm Africa's role as a center of wealth, scholarship, and innovation long before European colonization. For African Americans, learning about civilizations like Mali and Ghana provides a counter-narrative to Eurocentric histories, fostering cultural pride and reinforcing ancestral connections.

These empires also connect directly to the African diaspora, as many enslaved Africans brought to the Americas descended from regions once ruled by Ghana, Mali, and Songhai. Their traditions, languages, and religious practices survived across generations, influencing African American culture and strengthening ties to Africa's rich historical legacy.

Skills Assessed: Explain the effects of historical developments; use sources and evidence; analyze relationships among developments.

KEY TAKEAWAYS

1. **Africa as the Cradle of Humanity**
   - Modern humans *(Homo sapiens)* originated in East Africa around 300,000 B.C.E., highlighting the continent's foundational role in global human history.
   - African American Studies emphasizes this origin to underscore Africa's centrality, not marginality, in world development.
2. **Geography Shapes History**
   - Africa's five climate zones—desert, Sahel, savannah, rainforest, and Mediterranean—greatly influenced human settlement, agriculture, and trade.
   - Major rivers like the Nile, Niger, and Congo facilitated transportation, trade, and the growth of civilizations.
   - Natural features encouraged cultural interconnectivity across the continent long before European colonization.
3. **Bantu Expansion and Ethnolinguistic Diversity**
   - The Bantu migrations (c. 1500 B.C.E.–500 C.E.) were pivotal in spreading languages, agriculture, and iron technology across sub-Saharan Africa.
   - This expansion shaped much of Africa's linguistic and genetic diversity, with enduring connections to African American heritage.
4. **Advanced Ancient Civilizations**
   - Societies such as Egypt, Nubia (Kush), Aksum, and Nok developed systems of writing, ironworking, religion, and international trade.
   - These civilizations counter myths of African primitivism and illustrate Africa's historical depth and sophistication.
5. **Sudanic Empires and Global Trade Networks**
   - The Ghana, Mali, and Songhai empires controlled vast trade routes linking West Africa with North Africa, the Middle East, and Europe.
   - Gold and salt were key economic drivers, while Islam deeply influenced political and cultural life.
   - Mansa Musa's hajj in 1324 showcased Mali's global wealth and prestige, placing Africa on the world map in medieval cartography.

6. **Continuity and Legacy in African American Studies**
   - The academic discipline of African American Studies arose in the 1960s–1970s, inspired by student activism and the Civil Rights and Black Power Movements.
   - The field uses an interdisciplinary lens to reclaim African history and connect it with diasporic identity, resistance, and empowerment.
   - Understanding Africa's early achievements fosters pride and deeper insight into the global African diaspora's roots.

Practice Multiple-Choice Questions

DIRECTIONS: Pick the letter that best answers the following questions.

Questions 1 through 3 refer to the following.

Program for the First National Council for Black Studies Annual Conference, 1975

1. What is the primary emphasis of African American Studies?
   (A) Exploring the history, culture, and significant contributions of individuals of African heritage
   (B) Investigating the historical aspects of Africa
   (C) Scrutinizing the diaspora experiences of African Americans
   (D) Examining the profound repercussions of slavery in the United States

2. How does African American Studies differ from other disciplines?
   (A) It combines an interdisciplinary approach with scholarly inquiry.
   (B) It focuses solely on the history of African Americans.
   (C) It emphasizes the contributions of African Americans to the arts.
   (D) It is primarily concerned with political movements in the United States.

3. What does the term *African diaspora* refer to in the context of African American Studies?
   (A) The migration of African Americans from Africa to the United States
   (B) The dispersion of people of African descent around the world
   (C) The cultural exchange between Africa and other continents
   (D) The formation of African American communities in the United States

Questions 4 and 5 refer to the following.

The Mediterranean Sea as shown in the *Catalan Atlas* by Abraham Cresques

4. The Muslim merchant's journey to Mali was most likely motivated by which of the following?
   (A) A desire to crossbreed powerful North African camels with Central Asian camels
   (B) An interest to conduct commerce at the crossroads of the Arab, Persian, Indian, and Chinese empires
   (C) The appeal of lucrative trade with a wealthy and powerful West African empire
   (D) The invitation from Mali's rulers to expand the number of converts to Islam

5. What does the *Catalan Atlas* reveal about Mali?
   (A) Its military conquests and cultural diversity
   (B) The wealth and influence of the ruler Mansa Musa and the Mali
   (C) Its agricultural practices and territories
   (D) Its technological and architectural advancements

Answer Explanations

1. **(A)** African American Studies primarily centers on the culture and significant contributions of individuals of African ancestry. Choice (B) is incorrect because African American Studies centers on the experiences and contributions of people of African heritage in the United States and in the diaspora, not on the African continent's history. Choice (C) is incorrect because it is less precise than Choice (A) and doesn't explicitly encompass the comprehensive exploration of history, culture, and contributions of individuals of African heritage. Choice (D) is incorrect because African American Studies extends beyond the impact of slavery to encompass a broader exploration of African American history, culture, and contributions.

2. **(A)** An interdisciplinary approach is something unique to African American Studies, compared with traditional history courses, as it incorporates history, culture, art, and literature. Choice (B) is incorrect because African American Studies goes beyond solely focusing on history. Although history is a significant component, African American Studies also encompasses the study of culture, literature, art, sociology, politics, and various other disciplines. Choice (C) is incorrect because African American Studies is not limited to just the arts. It certainly acknowledges and emphasizes contributions in the arts. However, African American Studies extends to all areas of life, including history, politics, sociology, literature, and more. Choice (D) is incorrect because, although political movements are an essential aspect of African American Studies, it is not limited to politics alone. African American Studies covers a wide range of topics, including history, culture, art, literature, social issues, and more.

3. **(B)** The concept of diaspora refers to the dispersal of a group of people from their place of origin to new locations, often reshaping identities and cultural practices in profound ways. Choice (A) is incorrect because it oversimplifies the African diaspora, which extends beyond African Americans' migration to the United States. Choice (C) is incorrect because it focuses on cultural exchange, whereas the diaspora encompasses more than just cultural aspects. Choice (D) is incorrect because it narrows down the definition to African American communities in the United States, excluding the broader global context of the African diaspora.

4. **(C)** The Mali Empire, particularly during the reign of Mansa Musa, was known for its immense wealth, especially in gold. The appeal of lucrative trade with such a wealthy and powerful West African empire would have been a significant motivator for Muslim merchants to undertake the journey. Choice (A) is not a historically supported reason for the journey of Muslim merchants to Mali. Although camels were important for trade routes, this particular motivation is unlikely. Choice (B) may have been a motive for trade along the trans-Saharan routes, but it doesn't specifically address the Mali Empire or its wealth. Choice (D) does not align with historical accounts of why Muslim merchants traveled to the Mali Empire. The primary motivation was economic and trade related rather than religious conversion.

5. **(B)** The *Catalan Atlas* depicts Mansa Musa holding a golden nugget that symbolizes his vast wealth, and it demonstrates the Mali Empire's significant position in the context of medieval West Africa. Choice (A) is not a primary focus of the *Catalan Atlas*, which is more known for depicting the wealth and influence of Mali. Choice (C) is not a central theme of the *Catalan Atlas*, which primarily emphasizes the empire's wealth and power. The technological and architectural advancements described in Choice (D) are not prominently featured in the *Catalan Atlas*.

Foundations of Power: Early African Kingdoms, Trade, and Global Influence

Key Themes

- Intellectual traditions sustained through oral and ritual practices
- Spiritual pluralism and resilience in the face of colonial imposition
- Cultural hybridization through intercontinental trade and contact
- Governance systems rooted in community and kinship
- Diasporic agency beyond slavery narratives

TIMELINE

Date/Period	Event/Development	Related Topics
Prehistoric–Present	**Oral tradition** emerges as a central method of preserving history, values, and knowledge across African societies	Topic 1.6—Learning Traditions
Ancient–Modern	**Griots** (oral historians) and **praise poets** become custodians of cultural memory in West Africa	Topic 1.6—Learning Traditions
Pre-1500s	Development of **Indigenous belief systems**, including ancestor veneration, nature spirits, and divination	Topic 1.7—Indigenous Cosmologies
Post-7th century C.E.	Spread of **Islam** and **Christianity** leads to **religious syncretism** in African societies	Topic 1.7—Religious Syncretism
1st–15th centuries C.E.	Growth of **Swahili Coast city-states** (e.g., Kilwa, Mombasa); blend of African, Arab, and Persian cultures	Topic 1.8—Culture and Trade in East Africa
8th–15th centuries C.E.	Flourishing of **Great Zimbabwe** and Mapungubwe; key trading centers for gold and ivory	Topic 1.8—Southern African Trade
c. 1390–1914 C.E.	Rise of the **Kingdom of Kongo** in West Central Africa; complex centralized governance and Christian conversion	Topic 1.9—Kingdom of Kongo
c. 1500s C.E.	**Manikongo Nzinga a Nkuwu** (Afonso I) converts to Christianity and corresponds with the Portuguese Crown	Topic 1.9—Kingdom of Kongo
Ancient–Modern	Kinship structures guide **inheritance, governance, and social roles** across matrilineal and patrilineal societies	Topic 1.10—Kinship and Leadership

Date/Period	Event/Development	Related Topics
Across eras	Role of **chiefs, elders, and councils** in Indigenous political systems	Topic 1.10—Kinship and Leadership
Pre-1500s–Present	African diasporas form through **trade, migration, exploration, and forced displacement**	Topic 1.11—Global Africans
Early modern era	Africans travel to Europe, the Americas, and the Islamic world as traders, soldiers, and scholars	Topic 1.11—Global Africans
1490s–1600s C.E.	Individuals such as **Estevanico**, **Juan Garrido**, and **Yasuke** participate in global exploration and empires	Topic 1.11—Global Africans

Topic 1.6 Learning Traditions

Key Terms

- Timbuktu—center of trade and Islamic scholarship
- Griot—oral historian, storyteller, and musician
- *Epic of Sundiata (Sunjata)*—foundational Mande epic
- Oral tradition—transmission of history and culture through the spoken word
- Gender and griots—both women and men held this role
- Learning communities—intellectual hubs in cities like Timbuktu
- Book trade and manuscripts—especially in Mali
- Astronomy, mathematics, architecture, jurisprudence—subjects studied

How did early West African societies foster knowledge and pass down wisdom to future generations? Education in early West African societies was deeply rooted in community values, cultural practices, and institutional frameworks. These societies recognized the importance of knowledge in sustaining their political power, economic prosperity, and cultural identity. Through oral traditions, apprenticeships, and formal learning centers, they developed robust systems to educate their members and preserve their legacies.

Education in early West Africa was not limited to formal settings; it was embedded in the fabric of daily life. Communities took collective responsibility for the transmission of knowledge, emphasizing values, skills, and traditions essential for social cohesion and survival. Formal institutions, such as Qur'anic schools and centers of higher learning in cities like Timbuktu, played a crucial role in advancing scholarship in theology, astronomy, medicine, and the arts. By exploring these educational models, scholars will gain a deeper appreciation for how early African societies cultivated learning and innovation, laying the intellectual foundations for their global influence.

After engaging with this topic, scholars will be able to:

- Describe the institutional- and community-based models of education that flourished in early West African societies.

Learning Traditions in Early West African Societies

The West African empires of Mali, Ghana, and Songhai were not only centers of trade and wealth but also hubs of intellectual and cultural flourishing. Education in these societies took many forms, from formal learning centers to oral traditions that preserved and transmitted cultural knowledge. These systems of education reflected the values, creativity, and interconnectedness of West African societies, leaving a legacy of innovation and scholarship.

Centers of Learning in West African Empires

The trading cities of West African empires were home to thriving intellectual communities. In Mali, the city of Timbuktu stood as a beacon of learning, attracting scholars from across the Islamic world. Timbuktu's renowned book trade and university culture established the city as a hub for disciplines such as astronomy, mathematics, architecture, and law. Manuscripts from this period, some of which survive today, testify to the depth and diversity of knowledge produced and preserved in West Africa. These centers of learning were not isolated. They were deeply interconnected with global intellectual networks, linking Africa to the Mediterranean, the Middle East, and beyond.

The Role of Griots in Preserving Knowledge

Education in West Africa extended beyond formal institutions to community-based systems, where griots played a central role. Griots were esteemed historians, storytellers, and musicians who served as the living repositories of a community's history, traditions, and cultural practices. They preserved knowledge of key events, genealogies, and societal values through oral traditions, passing this information from generation to generation. You can see the image *Griot Basimana with Guitar*, from Mali, on page 54 of the CED.

The griot tradition was not static. Instead, it was dynamic and adaptive, ensuring that the histories the griots preserved remained relevant to the communities they served. This role required immense skill. Griots not only memorized extensive histories but also interpreted them, weaving them into narratives that inspired and guided their audiences.

Gender and the Griot Tradition

The griot tradition was inclusive, with both men and women serving as custodians of cultural memory. African Women who served as griots played an essential role in preserving knowledge related to births, deaths, marriages, and other pivotal events in the life of the community. Their contributions ensured that the griot tradition reflected the full spectrum of human experience and underscored the importance of gender balance in the preservation of cultural heritage.

A Legacy of Knowledge and Innovation

West African learning traditions, whether housed in formal institutions like Timbuktu or embodied in the oral artistry of griots, represent a profound commitment to knowledge and cultural preservation. These traditions highlight the intellectual richness of African societies and their ability to balance innovation with the preservation of history and identity.

By understanding these educational practices, scholars gain insight into the values and achievements that defined West African societies and shaped their enduring influence on the global stage. The learning traditions of West Africa remind us that education is not solely about the transmission of information but is about the cultivation of wisdom, creativity, and community.

Words That Keep History Alive

In West Africa, people didn't need books to learn history. Stories, poems, and songs that passed through generations carried all the knowledge they needed. Griots, or oral historians, knew thousands of years of family and community memory.

You're Practicing: Understanding how people preserve knowledge outside of written texts.

Connect This To: Cultural memory, oral tradition, and identity

Theme: Identity and Culture

Practice: Explain the Significance or Importance

Education in African societies took diverse forms prior to European colonization, including oral traditions, Islamic scholarship, and community-based instruction.

(A) Describe the different methods of knowledge transmission in African societies before the transatlantic slave trade.

(B) Explain the importance of oral traditions, including griots and communal storytelling, in preserving historical and cultural knowledge.

(C) Evaluate the historical significance of centers of learning like Timbuktu and their legacy in the global history of education.

SAMPLE RESPONSES

(A) In West Africa, knowledge was transmitted through formal centers of learning like Timbuktu, where scholars studied astronomy, mathematics, architecture, and law. Qur'anic schools and universities preserved thousands of manuscripts, creating a vibrant intellectual hub connected to North Africa and the Middle East.

Community-based apprenticeships and oral instruction played an equally important role. Skills such as farming, ironworking, and medicine were taught collectively, ensuring that practical knowledge and cultural traditions were passed from one generation to the next to maintain social cohesion.

(B) Griots served as historians, musicians, and storytellers who preserved genealogies, cultural values, and collective memory. Through works like the *Epic of Sundiata*, griots ensured that political histories and community identities were transmitted across generations, reinforcing cultural continuity.

Communal storytelling allowed African societies to preserve historical events, religious beliefs, and social norms. These narratives were dynamic and adapted to contemporary contexts, enabling communities to retain their heritage while interpreting lessons relevant to changing times.

(C) Timbuktu became one of the world's foremost intellectual centers during the Mali and Songhai Empires, housing universities and manuscript libraries that attracted scholars from across the Islamic world. Its integration into global networks positioned West Africa as a vital contributor to the advancement of knowledge before European colonization.

The legacy of Timbuktu extends beyond Africa, shaping modern understandings of education and cultural preservation. Its surviving manuscripts reveal West Africa's contributions to science, literature, and theology, challenging Eurocentric narratives and affirming Africa's role in global intellectual history.

Skills Assessed: Explain the significance or importance; use sources and evidence; analyze relationships among developments.

Topic 1.7 Indigenous Cosmologies and Religious Syncretism

Key Terms

- Syncretism—blending of traditional African beliefs with Christianity or Islam
- Orishas—deities in Yoruba cosmology (e.g., Shango, Oya, Ogun)
- Ancestor veneration—spiritual reverence for forebears
- Divination—seeking knowledge through spiritual means
- Collective ceremonies—music, dance, and healing rituals
- Louisiana voodoo—example of diasporic religion
- Afro-Cuban religions—like Santería and Regla de Ocha
- Islam and Christianity in Africa—often blended with Indigenous practices
- Ceremonial artifacts—like the *Oshe Shango* wand

How do spiritual traditions evolve while preserving their essence across continents and centuries? Indigenous cosmologies and religious practices in early West and West Central African societies were deeply rooted in their cultural landscapes, shaping how communities understood the world, their place within it, and their connections to the divine. These traditions were not static. They adapted and blended with other belief systems to create syncretic practices that survived the transatlantic slave trade and flourished in African-descended communities in the Americas.

This chapter explores the dynamic interplay between Indigenous African cosmologies and external influences, highlighting the resilience of African spiritual traditions. From the blending of African and Christian elements in Afro-Caribbean religions to the preservation of African cosmologies in rituals and community practices, scholars will uncover how faith became a source of strength, identity, and resistance.

After engaging in this topic, scholars will be able to:

- Explain how syncretic religious practices developed in early West and West Central African societies.
- Analyze how these practices were carried forward and adapted in African-descended communities in the Americas.

The spiritual traditions of early West and West Central African societies were deeply rooted in their understanding of the cosmos, the community, and the divine. These traditions were dynamic, evolving as African societies encountered and adapted external influences such as Islam and Christianity. The blending of Indigenous African cosmologies with introduced faiths created syncretic practices that not only enriched cultural and spiritual life in Africa but also crossed the Atlantic, becoming central to the identity and resilience of African-descended communities in the Americas.

The Emergence of Syncretic Faiths in Africa

The adoption of Islam and Christianity by African leaders often marked a blending rather than a replacement of spiritual practices. In empires like Mali and Songhai, where Islam became prominent, and in the Kingdom of Kongo, where Christianity took root, subjects retained elements of their Indigenous cosmologies while incorporating teachings from these introduced religions.

This blending manifested in practices such as using traditional rituals alongside Islamic or Christian prayers or integrating local symbols and ceremonies into worship. These syncretic traditions were not simply adaptations. Instead, they were affirmations of African cultural agency, preserving Indigenous beliefs while embracing aspects of new faiths to create unique, hybrid spiritual identities.

Syncretic Practices in the African Diaspora

When Africans were forcibly transported to the Americas during the transatlantic slave trade, they carried with them the rich spiritual traditions of their homelands. Approximately one-quarter of enslaved Africans came from Christian societies in Africa, while another quarter came from Muslim societies. These individuals brought a wealth of syncretic religious practices that blended Indigenous African beliefs with elements of Christianity and Islam, reshaping spiritual landscapes in the Americas.

Key elements of African spiritual traditions—such as ancestor veneration, divination, healing practices, and communal singing and dancing—endured in the diaspora. These practices became foundational to African diasporic religions such as Louisiana voodoo, Candomblé in Brazil, and Santería in Cuba. Through these faiths, enslaved Africans and their descendants maintained a connection to their heritage, creating spaces for spiritual resilience and cultural preservation even under the brutal conditions of slavery.

Symbolism and Syncretism in African and Afro-Diasporic Spiritual Practices

Among the Yoruba people of Nigeria, the ***Oshe Shango*** ceremonial wand is a powerful emblem of devotion and connection to **Shango**, the orisha of thunder, fire, and lightning. Shango, revered as both a deity and a deified ancestor, was a legendary monarch of the Oyo kingdom. The *Oshe Shango* is central to dances and rituals honoring this orisha, embodying his power and presence through its intricate symbolism.

Belief Systems That Blend and Evolve

African spirituality wasn't pushed aside by new religions—it adapted and thrived. Many African societies combined their beliefs with elements of Islam and Christianity, creating unique religious identities. This blending is part of a long tradition of resilience and cultural innovation.

You're Practicing: Noticing how people adapt to change without losing who they are.

Connect This To: Religion, resistance, and community belief systems.

Theme: Cultural Expression and Resistance

Dance wand *(Oshe Shango)*.
(Source: Frank L. Babbott Fund and Designated Purchase Fund. "Dance Wand *(Oshe Shango)*" *Brooklyn Museum*, 2024, www.brooklynmuseum.org/objects/105029)

This ceremonial wand consists of three key elements:

- A handle, representing the human connection to the divine.
- Two stone axes, symbolic of Shango's lightning bolts, signifying his control over natural and cosmic forces.
- A female figure, often depicted carrying the axes on her head and representing balance, strength, and the integral role of women in Yoruba spiritual practices.

The *Oshe Shango* is not merely an object but a living symbol, reflecting the interplay of history, mythology, and spirituality in Yoruba cosmology.

Syncretism in Afro-Cuban Religious Performance

The influence of African spiritual traditions extends far beyond the continent, evolving and blending with other cultural elements across the African diaspora. Groups like **Osain del Monte**, an Afro-Cuban performance ensemble, vividly illustrate this syncretism through their artistic expressions. Their performances merge the spiritual practices of Afro-Cuban religions with elements of music, dance, and storytelling to create a dynamic representation of faith and cultural heritage.

Visual Syncretism in Art: *Oya's Betrayal*

The painting ***Oya's Betrayal*** offers a striking example of how African spiritual traditions have been visually reimagined through the lens of other artistic styles. This work portrays a conflict among the orishas Oya, Ogun, and Shango, blending the oral traditions of the Yoruba with Renaissance artistic techniques. The juxtaposition of African cosmology with European art forms creates a powerful visual narrative that bridges cultural boundaries and highlights the adaptability of African spiritual traditions. See page 56 of the CED for a visual reference.

Spirituality as a Tool of Resistance

Syncretic faiths were not only a means of preserving culture but also a source of empowerment and resistance. Enslaved Africans often performed spiritual ceremonies before revolts, drawing strength and solidarity from their shared traditions. These ceremonies reaffirmed communal bonds, instilled hope, and provided a spiritual framework for resistance against oppression.

A Legacy of Adaptation and Survival

The blending of Indigenous African cosmologies with introduced religions demonstrates the resilience and adaptability of African spiritual traditions. From the royal courts of Mali and Kongo to the plantations of the Americas, these syncretic practices affirmed the humanity and creativity of African peoples in the face of profound challenges.

Today, the influence of these traditions is evident in the vibrant religious and cultural practices of African-descended communities around the world. They are living testaments to the enduring strength of African cosmologies and the ability of these cosmologies to adapt, evolve, and inspire. By exploring these traditions, scholars gain a deeper understanding of the cultural richness and resilience that define the African diaspora.

Practice: Visual Analysis and Cultural Interpretation

Examine the *Oshe Shango* ceremonial wand and *Oya's Betrayal* by Harmonia Rosales.

(A) Identify and explain how each piece of art reflects core principles of Yoruba cosmology and spiritual symbolism.

(B) Analyze how these works illustrate religious syncretism or cultural adaptation in diasporic contexts.

(C) Evaluate the broader cultural significance of art in sustaining religious identity and affirming community resilience across time and space.

SAMPLE RESPONSES

(A) The Oshe Shango ceremonial wand reflects Yoruba cosmology through its depiction of Shango, the orisha of thunder and lightning. The double-headed axe symbolizes divine power and control over natural forces, while the female figure balancing the axe represents harmony, resilience, and the central role of women in Yoruba spirituality.

Harmonia Rosales' *Oya's Betrayal* visually reimagines Yoruba mythology, portraying the orishas Oya, Ogun, and Shango in conflict. By integrating traditional narratives with Renaissance-style techniques, Rosales captures Yoruba beliefs about divine agency, human struggle, and cosmic balance, demonstrating how spiritual myths remain alive through artistic interpretation.

(B) The Oshe Shango wand embodies religious syncretism by showing how Yoruba cosmology survived transatlantic slavery and evolved within Afro-Caribbean religions such as Santería and Candomblé. Ceremonial objects like the wand were adapted into new ritual contexts, blending Indigenous practices with Catholic iconography while preserving Shango's spiritual essence.

Oya's Betrayal illustrates cultural adaptation by merging African spiritual traditions with Western artistic techniques. By portraying Yoruba orishas using European visual styles, the painting reflects how diasporic communities preserved sacred narratives while embedding them within broader global art forms, making Yoruba cosmology legible to wider audiences.

(C) The Oshe Shango wand demonstrates how ceremonial art functions as a living symbol of faith, sustaining Yoruba identity across centuries. In the Americas, similar objects became central to community rituals, affirming continuity with ancestral traditions despite forced migration and cultural suppression.

Oya's Betrayal highlights the transformative power of art in preserving and revitalizing African cosmologies for contemporary audiences. By reframing Yoruba spiritual narratives through modern visual language, Rosales affirms the enduring relevance of these traditions and celebrates diasporic resilience across time and place.

Skills Assessed: Connect course content to African American experiences; analyze artistic and visual sources; evaluate the significance of historical and cultural perspectives.

Topic 1.8 Culture and Trade in Southern and East Africa

Key Terms

- Great Zimbabwe—stone city and center of trade
- Shona people—builders of Great Zimbabwe
- Granary tower—architectural symbol of surplus and power
- Swahili Coast—East African trade network
- Indian Ocean trade routes—connected Africa to Asia and the Middle East
- Swahili language—Bantu-Arabic fusion
- Islam in East Africa—shared religion across city-states
- Portuguese colonization—disrupted trade in the 1500s
- Cultural fusion—Arab, Persian, African influences in art and trade

How did monumental architecture and thriving trade networks shape the history of Southern and East Africa? The region's rich history of innovation and interconnectedness is exemplified by the awe-inspiring stone structures of Great Zimbabwe and the vibrant city-states of the Swahili Coast. These societies, defined by their cultural sophistication and economic influence, highlight the dynamic interplay of geography, culture, and politics in shaping the rise and fall of powerful African civilizations.

This topic explores the enduring legacies of Southern and East African societies, emphasizing their contributions to global trade, cultural exchange, and architectural innovation. By examining the rise and fall of Great Zimbabwe and the Swahili city-states, scholars gain a deeper understanding of how these civilizations navigated and thrived within the complex networks of the ancient world.

After engaging with this topic, scholars will be able to:

- Describe the function and significance of Great Zimbabwe's monumental stone architecture.
- Analyze how geographic, cultural, and political factors influenced the development and decline of city-states along the Swahili Coast.

Culture and Trade in Southern and East Africa

The Kingdom of Zimbabwe and the city-states of the **Swahili Coast** represent two of the most remarkable examples of Southern and East African innovation, trade, and cultural sophistication. These societies flourished as hubs of wealth, power, and influence. They shaped the region's history through their resourcefulness and connections to global trade networks. Their legacies, embodied in monumental stone architecture and thriving mercantile cities, continue to inspire awe and underscore Africa's role in the ancient world.

The Kingdom of Zimbabwe and Great Zimbabwe

From the twelfth to the fifteenth century, the Kingdom of Zimbabwe flourished in Southern Africa, with its capital city, Great Zimbabwe, serving as a symbol of power and prosperity. Inhabited by the Shona people, the kingdom grew wealthy from its abundant gold, ivory, and cattle resources, which positioned it as a critical link in trade networks extending to the Swahili Coast and beyond.

Great Zimbabwe is best known for its monumental stone architecture, which demonstrates the ingenuity and engineering prowess of its builders. The Great Enclosure, with its towering walls and intricate designs, was likely a site for religious and administrative activities, reflecting the city's role as a spiritual and political center.

Great Zimbabwe ruins
(Source: Janice Bell, CC BY-SA 4.0, via Wikimedia Commons)

The conical tower, a striking feature within the enclosure, is believed to have served as a granary. It probably symbolized the wealth and agricultural abundance of the kingdom.

Conical tower—great enclosure
(Source: Andrew Moore from Johannesburg, South Africa, CC BY-SA 2.0 via Wikimedia Commons)

These stone ruins remain a testament to the prominence, autonomy, and agricultural advancements of the Shona kings. They challenge outdated narratives that underestimated the capabilities of early African societies and stand as enduring symbols of African ingenuity and resilience.

Stone ruins

The Swahili Coast: A Nexus of Global Trade

Stretching from Somalia to Mozambique, the Swahili Coast emerged as a vibrant trading network that connected Africa's interior with Arab, Persian, Indian, and Chinese trading communities. Between the eleventh and fifteenth centuries, the city-states of the Swahili Coast thrived. Their prosperity was underpinned by their strategic coastal locations and access to rich trade goods such as gold, ivory, and spices.

The city-states were united by a shared language and a shared religion. The language—Swahili—is a Bantu lingua franca enriched by Arabic influences. The religion—Islam—provided a unifying cultural framework and facilitated connections with Muslim trading partners. These cultural commonalities fostered a sense of identity and cooperation among the diverse trading communities along the coast.

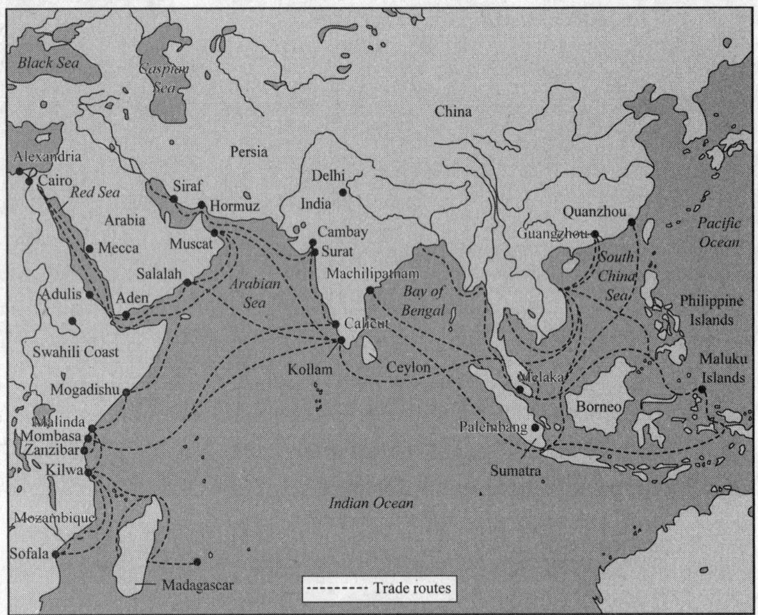

Map showing Indian Ocean trade routes from the Swahili Coast

The prominence of the Swahili Coast drew the attention of European powers, particularly the Portuguese. In the sixteenth century, Portuguese forces invaded major city-states and established settlements, seeking to control the lucrative Indian Ocean trade. Although this marked a turning point in the region's history, the resilience of the Swahili culture ensured that its legacy endured.

A Legacy of Innovation and Connection

The Kingdom of Zimbabwe and the Swahili Coast city-states exemplify the dynamism of early African societies. Great Zimbabwe's stone architecture stands as a symbol of African autonomy and innovation, while the Swahili Coast demonstrates the continent's role as a vital participant in global trade networks. These societies were not isolated. Instead, they were deeply connected to the world, influencing and being influenced by cultures and economies far beyond their borders.

By examining the achievements of these civilizations, scholars gain a deeper appreciation for the strength, adaptability, and cultural richness of Southern and East Africa. Their legacies continue to inspire and remind us of Africa's enduring contributions to global history.

Trade That Built Cities

Did you know that huge stone cities like Great Zimbabwe were built from profits made through trading gold and ivory? African merchants weren't just participating in the global economy—they were shaping it. These trade networks helped grow powerful and artistically rich societies.

You're Practicing: Understanding how trade connects to cultural and political power.

Connect This To: Global connections and economic development.

Theme: Origins and Encounters

Practice: Map and Monument Analysis

Base your answers on the image of Great Zimbabwe's conical tower and the map of Indian ocean trade routes.

(A) Identify what each source reveals about African participation in regional and global trade networks.
(B) Explain the role of geographic location in shaping political and economic power in Southern and East Africa.
(C) Analyze how these sources challenge common misconceptions about early African societies.

SAMPLE RESPONSES

(A) The conical tower of Great Zimbabwe demonstrates the Shona people's control over wealth generated from gold, ivory, and cattle trade. Its monumental architecture symbolizes agricultural surplus and political authority, showing that Great Zimbabwe was a central hub linking Southern Africa's resources to Swahili Coast city-states and Indian Ocean markets.

The Indian Ocean trade routes map reveals that the Swahili Coast connected Africa to Arab, Persian, Indian, and Chinese trading networks. African merchants exchanged gold, ivory, and spices for textiles, ceramics, and luxury goods, demonstrating Africa's integral role in premodern global commerce long before European dominance.

(B) Great Zimbabwe's inland location near gold and ivory reserves, combined with its access to trade routes leading to the Swahili Coast, allowed Shona rulers to control both resource extraction and regional commerce. Its strategic placement enabled the kingdom to accumulate wealth and consolidate political power over surrounding territories.

The Swahili Coast's proximity to the Indian Ocean facilitated the rise of cosmopolitan port cities like Kilwa and Mombasa. These city-states thrived because their coastal locations provided direct access to maritime trade, fostering economic prosperity and cultural exchange while strengthening their influence across East Africa and beyond.

(C) The conical tower of Great Zimbabwe challenges stereotypes that early African societies lacked architectural sophistication or political organization. Its intricate stone construction, without mortar, reflects advanced engineering, centralized authority, and an economy capable of sustaining monumental projects.

The Indian Ocean trade map refutes outdated narratives portraying Africa as isolated from global exchange. The Swahili Coast city-states were active participants in international trade centuries before European colonization, shaping economic and cultural networks that spanned Asia, the Middle East, and Africa.

Skills Assessed: Describe and interpret sources; explain continuity and change; use reasoning to explain connections.

Topic 1.9 West Central Africa—the Kingdom of Kongo

Key Terms

- Nzinga Mbemba (Afonso I)—Kongo king, converted to Catholicism
- Roman Catholicism—adopted voluntarily by Kongolese royalty
- Christian syncretism—Africanized Catholicism
- Portuguese-Kongo relations—trade and military alliances
- Transatlantic slave trade—Kongo was major source region
- Ivory, copper, textiles, salt—key exports
- Christian names—passed through African traditions (e.g., João, Juan)
- African Catholic iconography—*Triple Crucifix*

How did the Kingdom of Kongo navigate the intersection of religion, politics, and global trade during a transformative era in African and Atlantic history? The Kingdom of Kongo, one of West Central Africa's most powerful states, offers a compelling example of how African societies adopted Christianity, engaged in political alliances, and became entangled in the transatlantic slave trade. These dynamics shaped the kingdom's cultural identity and left a profound legacy on early generations of African Americans.

The Kingdom of Kongo represents both the resilience and complexity of African societies as they adapted to external influences and navigated the challenges of global interconnectedness. By exploring the religious, economic, and political transformations of this kingdom, scholars will uncover its pivotal role in shaping African and Atlantic histories. Let us delve into the story of the Kingdom of Kongo and its lasting impact on the African diaspora.

After engaging with this topic, scholars will be able to:

- Explain how the adoption of Christianity influenced the economic and religious aspects of the Kingdom of Kongo.
- Analyze how the kingdom's political relationship with Portugal affected its participation in the transatlantic slave trade.
- Describe how Kongo's Christian culture shaped the experiences and identities of early African Americans.

The Kingdom of Kongo: Christianity, Trade, and the Transatlantic Slave Trade

The **Kingdom of Kongo**, a formidable state in West Central Africa, stands as a testament to the complex interplay of religion, trade, and politics during the early modern era. Its voluntary adoption of Roman Catholicism in 1491 under **King Nzinga** a **Nkuwu (João I)** and his son **Nzinga Mbemba (Afonso I)** not only transformed the spiritual life of the kingdom but also established pivotal economic and political ties with Portugal. These developments placed Kongo at the center of transatlantic exchanges, leaving a profound legacy on the African diaspora, including early African Americans.

The Adoption of Christianity and Its Transformations

The voluntary conversion of the Kingdom of Kongo's ruling elite to Christianity was a significant turning point in the kingdom's history. This religious shift strengthened diplomatic and trade relationships with Portugal, bringing increased wealth to Kongo through the exchange of ivory, salt, copper, and textiles. Unlike in many other regions, the introduction of Christianity in Kongo was not accompanied by colonial occupation. This allowed for the development of a distinctly African form of Catholicism.

This syncretic faith blended Christian theology with Indigenous aesthetic and cultural traditions, creating a unique spiritual identity that resonated across the kingdom. Practices such as naming children after saints or according to the day of the week on which they were born, a preexisting tradition in the Kongo, became integrated into this Christian framework. These naming conventions, carried across the Atlantic by enslaved individuals, influenced early African American kinship and cultural practices, with names like Juan, João, and John reflecting this enduring connection.

Political Ties and the Transatlantic Slave Trade

The Kingdom of Kongo's alliance with Portugal came at a steep cost. In exchange for military assistance, the Portuguese demanded access to the trade of enslaved people. Although Kongo's rulers initially sought to regulate the number of captives sold to European powers, their efforts proved ineffective against the growing demands of the transatlantic slave trade.

As the trade expanded, Kongo and the greater West Central African region became the largest source of enslaved Africans transported to the Americas. Approximately a quarter of those forcibly brought to what became the United States originated from West Central Africa, and many of them were already Christians before their arrival. This religious foundation provided a framework for cultural resilience and adaptation in the Americas, influencing the practices of faith, kinship, and identity in African-descended communities.

In 1526, King Nzinga Mbemba, who had adopted the Christian name Afonso I, initiated a remarkable correspondence with King João III of Portugal, writing a series of 24 letters that stand as powerful appeals for justice. These letters urged an end to the growing reliance on the slave trade, which had come to dominate the once mutually beneficial relationship between Kongo and Portugal.

Although the two kingdoms had established a trading partnership as early as the 1480s, Afonso grew increasingly alarmed by how this relationship had deteriorated. What began as an exchange of goods and ideas had devolved into a dynamic centered on the capture and sale of his people. His letters, which were both eloquent and impassioned, reflect his deep concern for the moral and societal consequences of the slave trade as well as his struggle to balance the political realities of his kingdom with his Christian faith. These documents remain a poignant testament to Kongo's agency and resistance during a tumultuous era.

Excerpt of letter from Nzinga Mbemba to Portuguese King João III

> And we cannot reckon how great the damage is, since the mentioned merchants are taking every day our natives, sons of the land and the sons of our noblemen and vassals and our relatives, because the thieves and men of bad conscience grab them wishing to have the things and wares of this Kingdom which they are ambitious of, they grab them and get them to be sold; and so great, Sir, is the corruption and licentiousness that our country is being completely depopulated, and Your Highness should not agree with this nor accept it as in your service. And to avoid it we need from those Kingdoms no more than some priests and a few people to reach in schools, and no other goods except wine and flour for the holy sacrament. That is why we beg of Your Highness to help and assist us in this matter, commanding your factors that they should not send here either merchants or wares, because it is our will that in these Kingdoms there should not be any trade of slaves nor outlet for them.

Source: "Excerpt of letter from Nzinga Mbemba to Portuguese King João III," in World History Commons, https://worldhistorycommons.org/excerpt-letter-nzinga-mbemba-portuguese-king-joao-iii [accessed May 24, 2025].

The Enduring Legacy of Kongo's Christian Culture

The Kingdom of Kongo's integration of Christianity into its cultural and political fabric illustrates the adaptability and agency of African societies in the face of external influences. The voluntary nature of the conversion allowed Christianity to be molded to fit local traditions, ensuring its acceptance and longevity. This cultural syncretism carried across the Atlantic, where West Central Africans brought their faith, traditions, and naming practices into the New World.

The legacy of Kongo's Christian culture can be seen in the survival of religious practices, linguistic traditions, and kinship systems among early African American communities. These cultural threads highlight the enduring influence of Kongo on the African diaspora and underscore the deep connections between African societies and the Americas.

The ***Triple Crucifix*** is a remarkable composite artifact, likely representing an interpretation of the Christian Trinity, that was crafted between the sixteenth and nineteenth centuries. This unique crucifix features three individually cast Christ figures, each affixed to a wooden cross using nails and copper loops. Notably, the central figure is more finely rendered, suggesting it may have been created earlier than the others.

Triple Crucifix, sixteenth to nineteenth centuries
(Source: LaGamma, Alisa. *Kongo: Power and Majesty*. New York: The Metropolitan Museum of Art, 2015, p. 110, fig. 64)

The Kingdom of Kongo's history reveals a complex narrative of cultural innovation, economic ambition, and political entanglement. Its legacy as a center of African Catholicism and a key player in the transatlantic slave trade illustrates the profound ways African societies shaped and were shaped by global dynamics.

Faith, Diplomacy, and the Kingdom of Kongo

The Kingdom of Kongo chose to convert to Christianity—but on its own terms. Its leaders used religion as both a spiritual and political tool, connecting with European powers while maintaining local traditions. This is a powerful example of how Africans shaped their relationships with the world.

You're Practicing: Thinking critically about how power and belief are connected.

Connect This To: Political negotiation and cultural change.

Theme: Power and Resistance

Practice: Causation and Perspective Analysis

Read the excerpt from King Nzinga Mbemba's letter to King João III. Then answer the following.

(A) Identify the central concern of King Nzinga Mbemba and the audience he addresses.
(B) What specific evidence does he use to support his position?
(C) How does this letter reflect the tensions between religious alliance and political sovereignty?

SAMPLE RESPONSES

(A) King Nzinga Mbemba, also known as Afonso I, expresses deep concern over the illegal capture and sale of Kongo's people, including nobles and relatives, by Portuguese merchants. His audience is King João III of Portugal, whom he appeals to directly for intervention and protection, emphasizing their shared Christian alliance.

Afonso warns that the slave trade is destabilizing Kongo's society, leading to depopulation and social breakdown. Addressing King João III, he frames his appeal as a plea between Christian rulers, underscoring his expectation that their spiritual and political partnership obligates Portugal to curb these abuses.

(B) Nzinga Mbemba highlights that Portuguese merchants are "taking every day our natives, sons of the land and the sons of our noblemen and vassals and our relatives" to demonstrate the widespread harm caused by the slave trade. By naming nobles and kin, he shows that the trade is dismantling Kongo's social hierarchy and governance.

Afonso requests that Portugal "send here neither merchants nor wares" and instead provide only priests and teachers, demonstrating his desire to limit commercial exploitation while maintaining Kongo's Christian development. This contrasts the kingdom's spiritual goals with the material ambitions driving Portuguese interference.

(C) The letter reveals Afonso's dual reliance on and resistance to Portugal. While Kongo voluntarily adopted Catholicism to strengthen diplomatic and trade ties, Afonso resists Portuguese domination over his people and resources. His plea shows that religious solidarity did not guarantee political autonomy in the face of growing European economic interests.

Afonso's appeal demonstrates the contradictions of Christian partnership: he assumes that shared faith should ensure Portugal's protection of Kongo, yet João III's merchants exploit this relationship through the slave trade. The letter exposes the fragile balance between spiritual unity and Kongo's sovereignty as the kingdom faced pressures from expanding global trade networks.

Skills Assessed: Explain causation and the effects of historical developments; analyze historical perspectives; evaluate the significance of a source in its historical context.

Topic 1.10 Kinship and Political Leadership

Key Terms

- Kinship networks—basis for governance and social organization
- Women's leadership—in politics, religion, economy, and military
- Queen Idia (Benin)—first *iyoba* (queen mother), advisor and warrior
- Queen Njinga (Ndongo and Matamba)—warrior queen who resisted Portuguese
- FESTAC mask—symbol of Queen Idia's legacy
- Spiritual authority and diplomacy—attributes of female rulers
- Guerilla warfare—Njinga's military strategy
- Slave trade participation—complex political choices for African leaders

How did kinship structures and the leadership of remarkable women shape the societies of early West and Central Africa? In many African societies, kinship served as the foundation for political, social, and economic organization. It was through these networks that individuals defined their roles, formed alliances, and maintained communal cohesion. Within this framework, women often played critical roles, not only within families but also as political and military leaders. Figures such as **Queen Idia of Benin** and **Queen Njinga of Ndongo-Matamba** exemplify the strength and resilience of African leadership, leaving legacies that continue to inspire.

This topic explores how kinship systems structured early African societies and highlights the transformative leadership of two iconic queens. By examining their achievements and the cultural contexts that shaped their reigns, scholars will gain a deeper understanding of how leadership, resilience, and kinship were central to African civilizations. Let us celebrate the legacies of Queen Idia and Queen Njinga and their indelible impact on history.

After studying this topic, scholars will be able to:

- Describe the central function of kinship and the diverse roles women played in early West and Central African societies.
- Compare the political and military leadership of Queen Idia of Benin and Queen Njinga of Ndongo-Matamba.
- Analyze the enduring legacy of their leadership and contributions to African and global history.

Kinship and Political Leadership in West and Central Africa

In the intricate social and political landscapes of early West and Central African societies, kinship ties served as the bedrock of community organization. These extended familial connections fostered alliances that shaped governance, trade, and cultural continuity. Within these systems, women held dynamic and influential roles, shaping their societies as spiritual leaders, political advisors, economic strategists, educators, and agricultural innovators. Among the most notable figures were Queen Idia of Benin and Queen Njinga of Ndongo-Matamba, whose leadership and resilience continue to resonate across the African diaspora.

Kinship as the Foundation of African Societies

Kinship networks were essential to the structure of many early African societies, providing a framework for political alliances, economic collaboration, and social cohesion. These networks allowed families to pool resources, protect their communities, and maintain cultural traditions across generations. Through kinship, leaders consolidated power, secured loyalty, and fostered unity within their kingdoms, creating a foundation for both governance and resistance.

Women's Multifaceted Roles in African Societies

Women in West and Central Africa played diverse and integral roles within their communities. As spiritual leaders, they guided rituals and ensured the spiritual well-being of their societies. As political advisors, they counseled kings and influenced governance. Many women also served as market traders, controlling local and regional economies, while others worked as educators and agriculturalists, passing down knowledge and sustaining their communities. These roles underscore the significance of women's contributions to both daily life and the broader political landscapes of their societies.

Queen Idia: The *Iyoba* of Benin

In the late fifteenth century, **Queen Idia** became the first ***iyoba* (queen mother)** of the **Kingdom of Benin**, which was located in present-day Nigeria. She served as a trusted political advisor to her son, **Oba Esigie**, and played a critical role in the military and spiritual success of his reign.

Queen Idia was not only a strategist but also a warrior. She led armies into battle, relying on her deep knowledge of spiritual power and medicinal practices to secure victories for Benin. Her influence extended beyond the battlefield, solidifying her status as a powerful and enduring figure in African history. Her legacy as a symbol of Black women's leadership was further cemented in 1977 when an ivory mask of her likeness was chosen as the emblem for FESTAC (the Second World Black Festival of Arts and Culture).

Leadership in Many Forms

Not all leaders were kings. Some African societies were led by councils or lineage-based systems. Many African societies recognized the authority of queens and female elders. Power in early Africa looked different in different places—and that variety is part of what made it so strong.

You're Practicing: Comparing leadership styles and understanding how they reflect culture.

Connect This To: Gender roles, authority, and tradition.

Theme: Governance and Autonomy

Queen Njinga: The Resilient Leader of Ndongo-Matamba

In the early seventeenth century, as Portuguese incursions into Central Africa intensified, Queen Njinga rose to power as the ruler of Ndongo and later Matamba, in present-day Angola. Her reign began during a period of upheaval; people from her kingdom were among the first large groups of enslaved Africans forcibly transported to the Americas.

Queen Njinga's leadership was defined by her fierce resistance to Portuguese colonization. For over 30 years, she waged guerrilla warfare to protect her kingdom's sovereignty, employing strategic alliances, diplomatic skills, and military ingenuity. While participating in the transatlantic slave trade to consolidate her political influence, she also expanded Matamba's military by offering sanctuary to those who escaped enslavement, integrating them into her forces. Her reign not only preserved her kingdom's autonomy but also paved the way for nearly a century of women rulers in Matamba, a testament to the enduring power of her leadership.

Queen Nzinga with military entourage,
Kingdom of Matamba, Angola, seventeenth century
(Source: Photo by Fine Art Images/Heritage Images/Getty Images)

Queen Njinga's reign stands as a testament to the ability of African leaders to resist colonization and maintain sovereignty in the face of overwhelming challenges. Her strategic brilliance and diplomatic skill earned her a lasting place in history as one of Africa's most formidable leaders, inspiring generations of women across the diaspora.

Legacies Across the African Diaspora

The legacies of Queen Idia and Queen Njinga extend far beyond their lifetimes, resonating across the African diaspora as symbols of resilience, strength, and leadership.

Queen Idia's image, immortalized through the FESTAC ivory mask, has become a global emblem of the power and influence of Black women in leadership roles. Her contributions to Benin's military and her spiritual successes highlight the vital role women played in shaping African societies. The sixteenth-century ivory mask of Queen Idia, crafted as a pendant to inspire Benin's warriors, symbolizes her extraordinary leadership. Faces atop the mask represent her diplomatic and trade relations with the Portuguese. Iron scarifications on her forehead mark her as a warrior, while beads above her face depict Afro-textured hair, celebrating her natural beauty and cultural pride.

Queen Mother Pendant Mask: *Iyoba*, sixteenth century
(Source: The Met, "Queen Mother Pendant Mask: *Iyoba*." *Metmuseum.org*, 2020)

Practice: Comparative Evaluation

Compare the leadership of Queen Idia and Queen Njinga.

(A) How did kinship structures support their rise to power?
(B) What leadership qualities did they share? In what ways were their strategies or legacies different?
(C) How might these leaders be used to challenge stereotypes in modern discussions of African history?

SAMPLE RESPONSES

(A) Queen Idia's rise to influence as the first iyoba (queen mother) of Benin was rooted in the kingdom's kinship system, which positioned mothers of kings as spiritual and political advisors. Her role as the mother of Oba Esigie granted her the authority to counsel on governance, lead armies, and perform spiritual rituals, illustrating how kinship ties elevated women to powerful positions in Benin's political hierarchy.

Queen Njinga's ascent to the throne of Ndongo and later Matamba in seventeenth-century Angola was similarly tied to kinship networks. As a royal daughter and sister, she leveraged familial connections to claim authority during a period of crisis caused by Portuguese incursions. Her status within the royal lineage allowed her to consolidate alliances and secure loyalty, enabling her to lead both diplomatically and militarily.

(B) Both queens demonstrated military acumen, political strategy, and cultural influence. Queen Idia led armies and combined spiritual power with medicinal knowledge to secure victories for Benin, while Queen Njinga commanded forces using guerrilla warfare and forged alliances with escaped captives to resist Portuguese colonization. However, their strategies diverged, as Idia's leadership strengthened Benin's centralized monarchy and cultural heritage, while Njinga's prolonged armed resistance preserved Matamba's independence and extended female rule for nearly a century.

The legacies of these leaders differed in global recognition. Queen Idia's influence is immortalized through the FESTAC ivory mask, symbolizing cultural pride and spiritual authority, while Queen Njinga's legacy endures as a model of anti-colonial resistance and military innovation. Both leaders challenge assumptions of passive female roles, but Njinga's sustained defiance against European domination distinguishes her in African and diasporic histories.

(C) Queen Idia's accomplishments dismantle stereotypes that portray African women as excluded from political power. Her dual role as a spiritual leader and military strategist underscores the complexity of women's authority in precolonial Africa. Highlighting her achievements challenges Eurocentric narratives that undervalue Africa's governance systems and intellectual traditions.

Queen Njinga challenges stereotypes of African societies as passive victims of European colonization. Her thirty-year resistance against Portuguese forces, mastery of diplomacy, and integration of freed captives into her army reveal a narrative of agency, resilience, and strategic adaptation. Presenting her story elevates Africa's role in shaping global history and counters depictions of Africans as historically powerless.

Skills Assessed: Describe the historical context; compare historical developments; explain the significance of evidence and reasoning.

Topic 1.11 Global Africans

Key Terms

- *Chafariz d'El-Rey*—sixteenth-century Lisbon painting showing Africans in European life
- Pre-slave trade relations—diplomatic, religious, and trade travel
- African elites in Europe—ambassadors, scholars, children of royalty
- Iberian Peninsula—cities like Lisbon and Seville hosted free and enslaved Africans
- Roles of Africans in Europe—guards, knights, vendors, entertainers
- Portuguese-African gold and slave trade—predated transatlantic routes
- Bypassing Saharan routes—direct Atlantic trade initiated

How did early interactions between Africans and Europeans shape global relationships before the transatlantic slave trade? Long before the forced migration of millions during the transatlantic slave trade, Africans and Europeans engaged in dynamic exchanges of ideas, culture, and commerce. These interactions, driven by exploration, trade, and early forms of labor systems, laid the groundwork for the slave-based economies that would later dominate the Americas.

This topic explores the interconnected histories of Africans and Europeans in the pre-slavery era. It highlights the agency of African individuals in global networks and examines the Portuguese role in establishing systems of enslaved labor. By tracing these early interactions, scholars will gain a deeper understanding of how these relationships evolved and set the stage for the profound transformations brought about by the transatlantic slave trade. Let us delve into the lives of these global Africans and their pivotal role in shaping the world.

After engaging with this topic, scholars will be able to:

- Explain the motivations behind African migration to Europe and European travel to Africa prior to the transatlantic slave trade.
- Analyze how early forms of enslaved labor introduced by the Portuguese influenced the development of slave-based economies in the Americas.

Global Africans: Early Interactions and the Foundations of Enslaved Labor

In the late fifteenth century, the expanding trade networks between West African kingdoms and Portugal reshaped global relationships, bypassing traditional trans-Saharan routes. This trade, centered on gold, goods, and enslaved people, increased the wealth and influence of African kingdoms, where slavery was already a common feature of hierarchical societies. These exchanges not only transformed the economies of both regions but also deepened cultural and demographic connections between Africa and Europe.

Trade and Migration Between Africa and Europe

The growth of trade between Portugal and West African kingdoms brought an increasing European presence to West Africa and a notable population of sub-Saharan Africans to Mediterranean port cities like Lisbon and Seville. Africans arrived in these cities for various reasons. Among them were elites, such as ambassadors and the children of rulers, who traveled for diplomatic missions, education, and religious instruction. In these cosmopolitan hubs, free and enslaved Africans held diverse roles, including domestic workers, boatmen, guards, entertainers, vendors, and even knights. This highlights the broad scope of African contributions to European urban life.

Chafariz d'El-Rey (The King's Fountain), 1570–1580
(Source: Berardo Collection Museum, public domain, via Wikimedia Commons)

The ***Chafariz d'El-Rey***, a sixteenth-century painting that is also called *The King's Fountain*, vividly captures the significant African presence and the diverse roles Africans played in Iberian port cities like Lisbon, where they constituted 20 percent of the population. This artwork highlights the interconnectedness of African and European societies long before the peak of the transatlantic slave trade.

Prominently featured is **João de Sá Panasco**, an African-Portuguese knight of the Order of Saint James, riding a horse with dignity and authority. In the lower right corner, two African noblemen, dressed in European attire and bearing swords, underscore the integration of African elites into European society. The upper left of the painting depicts an African court guard and Muslim African traders, illustrating the varied contributions of Africans to urban life and commerce.

This remarkable scene exemplifies the cultural and social exchanges between African and European societies during this era. It challenges the narrow narratives of Africa's historical role and highlights the breadth of African influence in premodern Europe.

The Portuguese Colonization of Atlantic Islands

The Portuguese colonization of the Atlantic islands of **Cabo Verde** and **São Tomé** in the mid-fifteenth century marked a critical turning point. These islands became key sites for agricultural production, with plantations cultivating cotton, indigo, and sugar. To meet the labor demands of these enterprises, the Portuguese relied heavily on enslaved Africans, forcibly removing tens of thousands from the continent by 1500. This system of plantation labor not only exploited African people but also established a model for the slave-based economies that would later dominate the Americas.

The Foundations of Slave-Based Economies

By the turn of the sixteenth century, approximately 50,000 enslaved Africans had been transported to Portuguese-controlled Atlantic islands and Europe. These early plantations demonstrated how enslaved labor could generate immense profits, laying the groundwork for the transatlantic slave trade. The systems of exploitation refined on Cabo Verde and São Tomé would later be exported to the Americas, shaping the social, economic, and political dynamics of the New World.

A Precursor to the African Diaspora

These early interactions illustrate the agency of African kingdoms in global trade and the forced migration of African people that preceded the transatlantic slave trade. The presence of Africans in European cities, as both free individuals and enslaved laborers, reflects the complex realities of these early exchanges. At the same time, the plantation systems of the Atlantic islands foreshadowed the devastating impact of slavery in the Americas, underscoring the foundational role of African labor in the development of modern global economies.

Africans on the World Stage—Before Slavery

Long before the transatlantic slave trade, Africans were sailors, traders, and even knights in Europe and Asia. Art like *Chafariz d'El-Rey* shows Black people participating fully in global life. Their presence reminds us that African history is also world history.

You're Practicing: Challenging common assumptions about when and how Africans entered global stories.

Connect This To: Representation, early global connections, and movement.

Theme: Migration and Diaspora

Practice: Visual Interpretation and Argumentation

Analyze the *Chafariz d'El-Rey* painting. Then answer the following questions.

(A) What roles do Africans appear to play in sixteenth-century Lisbon?
(B) How does this image complicate simplistic narratives of African-European relationships?
(C) What does this source suggest about African agency prior to the height of the slave trade?

SAMPLE RESPONSES

(A) The Chafariz d'El-Rey painting shows that Africans played roles of political and social prominence in sixteenth-century Lisbon. João de Sá Panasco, an African-Portuguese knight of the Order of Saint James, is depicted riding a horse with dignity, symbolizing African integration into elite military and chivalric orders. This challenges stereotypes by highlighting African contributions to European political and military life.

The painting also depicts Africans working as vendors, guards, court attendants, and traders, showing their participation in Lisbon's economic and social networks. These roles illustrate that Africans were essential to urban labor systems in Iberian port cities and demonstrate the cosmopolitan diversity of Lisbon's population, where Africans comprised roughly 20 percent of residents.

(B) The Chafariz d'El-Rey painting complicates simplistic narratives by showing that Africans were not solely enslaved laborers but also integrated elites. The presence of African noblemen wearing European clothing and bearing swords reflects their social influence and demonstrates that African ambassadors, scholars, and military leaders participated actively in European society prior to the height of the transatlantic slave trade.

The image also reveals that African-European relationships involved diplomatic, economic, and cultural exchange, not just domination. Muslim African merchants depicted in the painting represent Lisbon's thriving trade networks, where African kingdoms exchanged gold, textiles, and goods with Portugal. This challenges Eurocentric narratives by emphasizing African agency in shaping early global commerce.

(C) The painting suggests that Africans exercised significant agency in shaping their roles in Europe before the height of the transatlantic slave trade. Figures like João de Sá Panasco demonstrate that African individuals could gain prominence, wealth, and status within European institutions, participating in military orders and courts while maintaining transnational influence.

The Chafariz d'El-Rey also suggests that Africans were key actors in early global trade and diplomacy. The depiction of African traders and Muslim intermediaries highlights their roles in negotiating exchanges between African kingdoms and Portuguese merchants, shaping the flow of goods, wealth, and knowledge long before widespread plantation slavery. Africans were not passive participants; they were foundational architects of early Atlantic networks.

Skills Assessed: Analyze visual evidence; make a defensible claim; explain your reasoning.

KEY TAKEAWAYS

1. **Black Political Power and Economic Advancement**
   - African Americans made significant political and economic gains throughout the late twentieth and early twenty-first centuries, achieving increased representation in government and breaking barriers in business and entrepreneurship.
   - Black mayors, congresspeople, and other elected officials transformed local and national politics, while organizations and initiatives focused on closing the racial wealth gap.
2. **Religious and Cultural Diversity in Black Communities**
   - Contemporary Black communities reflect wide-ranging religious and cultural identities, including Christianity, Islam, African diasporic religions, and nonreligious worldviews.
   - This pluralism enhances intracommunity solidarity and is a legacy of African and diasporic spiritual resilience and adaptation.
3. **Evolution and Global Influence of African American Music**
   - From spirituals and blues to hip-hop and Afrofuturism, Black music has served as a vehicle for self-expression, resistance, and cultural pride.
   - Genres such as jazz, gospel, R&B, and rap have shaped global soundscapes and continue to reflect the social realities and political aspirations of Black communities.
4. **Black Excellence in the Visual and Performing Arts**
   - African American achievements in theater, television, and film have reshaped cultural narratives and challenged stereotypes.
   - Artists like Ava DuVernay and movements such as #OscarsSoWhite have highlighted the need for inclusive representation and storytelling.
5. **Athletics as a Platform for Activism**
   - Black athletes have used their prominence to spotlight racial injustice, from Muhammad Ali and Tommie Smith to Colin Kaepernick and Naomi Osaka.
   - Sports have been both a space of opportunity and a microcosm of broader racial dynamics in society.

6. **Contributions to Science, Technology, and Health**
   - Black inventors, scientists, medical professionals, and engineers have long contributed to advancements in both U.S. society and the global society.
   - Contemporary figures in tech and health equity continue this tradition, innovating while addressing disparities in access and outcomes.
7. **Afrofuturism and Visions of Black Futures**
   - Afrofuturism fuses science fiction, technology, and African diasporic culture to imagine liberated Black futures.
   - Works like *Black Panther* and the music of Janelle Monáe use speculative storytelling to challenge historical erasure and envision new possibilities.
8. **The Legacy and Future of African American Studies**
   - Black Studies remains a vital field that centers African diasporic knowledge, resistance, and liberation.
   - As a discipline, it equips scholars to examine systems of oppression and articulate pathways toward equity and justice.

Practice Multiple-Choice Questions

DIRECTIONS: Pick the letter that best answers the following questions.

Questions 1 through 3 refer to the following image.

Queen Nzinga with Military Entourage,
Kingdom of Matamba, Angola

1. Which of the following strategies did Queen Njinga use to resist Portuguese colonization during her reign over Ndongo and Matamba?

   (A) She aligned exclusively with neighboring African kingdoms to form a coalition against the Portuguese.
   (B) She waged guerrilla warfare and used diplomacy to maintain sovereignty.
   (C) She relied solely on spiritual rituals to inspire resistance among her people.
   (D) She ceded key territories to the Portuguese in exchange for trade agreements.

2. What was one of Queen Njinga's key contributions to her kingdom during her reign?

   (A) Establishing Matamba as a sanctuary for those escaping enslavement
   (B) Signing an exclusive trade agreement with the Portuguese
   (C) Introducing Christianity as the state religion
   (D) Abandoning all diplomatic relations with European powers

3. Queen Njinga's leadership paved the way for nearly 100 years of women rulers in Matamba. Which aspect of her reign contributed most to this legacy?

   (A) Her victory over the Portuguese in all major battles
   (B) Her political and military strategies, which preserved Matamba's autonomy
   (C) Her religious reforms that centralized power under a divine monarchy
   (D) Her emphasis on trade, which made Matamba a leading economic power in Africa

Questions 4 and 5 refer to the following excerpt.

Excerpt of letter from Nzinga Mbemba to Portuguese King João III

"And we cannot reckon how great the damage is, since the mentioned merchants are taking every day our natives, sons of the land and the sons of our noblemen and vassals and our relatives, because the thieves and men of bad conscience grab them wishing to have the things and wares of this Kingdom which they are ambitious of, they grab them and get them to be sold; and so great, Sir, is the corruption and licentiousness that our country is being completely depopulated, and Your Highness should not agree with this nor accept it as in your service. And to avoid it we need from those Kingdoms no more than some priests and a few people to reach in schools, and no other goods except wine and flour for the holy sacrament. That is why we beg of Your Highness to help and assist us in this matter, commanding your factors that they should not send here either merchants or wares, because it is our will that in these Kingdoms there should not be any trade of slaves nor outlet for them."

Source: "Excerpt of letter from Nzinga Mbemba to Portuguese King João III," in World History Commons, https://worldhistorycommons.org/excerpt-letter-nzinga-mbemba-portuguese-king-joao-iii [accessed May 24, 2025].

4. What primary concern does Nzinga Mbemba (Afonso I) express in his letter to King João III regarding the transatlantic slave trade?

   (A) The lack of Portuguese military support for the Kingdom of Kongo
   (B) The role of Portuguese merchants in depopulating the kingdom through the slave trade
   (C) The need for more European goods, such as wine and flour, for the kingdom's prosperity
   (D) The inability of the kingdom to access priests and schools for religious instruction

5. What solution does Nzinga Mbemba propose to address the negative impact of the slave trade in the Kingdom of Kongo?

   (A) Halting all trade with Portuguese merchants except for priests and goods needed for religious sacraments
   (B) Expelling all Portuguese merchants from the kingdom and banning Christian missionaries
   (C) Strengthening the military to prevent Portuguese influence and protect the population
   (D) Allowing trade with Portuguese merchants only if they restrict the slave trade to criminals and prisoners of war

Answer Explanations

1. **(B)** Queen Njinga effectively combined guerrilla warfare with diplomatic strategies to resist Portuguese colonization for over 30 years. Her use of military tactics, such as ambushes and mobile warfare, and her diplomatic efforts, including forming alliances with the Dutch, showcased her adaptability and strategic brilliance. Choice (A) is incorrect because, although Njinga formed alliances, her resistance strategies extended far beyond this, incorporating warfare and negotiations. Choice (C) is incorrect because, although spiritual rituals were significant in rallying the people, they were not Queen Njinga's primary means of resistance. Choice (D) is incorrect because Queen Njinga actively resisted territorial concessions to the Portuguese and fought to maintain her kingdom's sovereignty.

2. **(A)** Queen Njinga provided refuge for people who escaped Portuguese enslavement, incorporating them into her military forces and strengthening Matamba's defenses. This act showcased her commitment to protecting her people and resisting external domination. Choice (B) is incorrect because, although Queen Njinga engaged in trade, she did not sign exclusive agreements that prioritized Portuguese interests over her kingdom's sovereignty. Choice (C) is incorrect because, although she adopted Christian practices for diplomatic purposes, Christianity was not established as the state religion in her kingdom. Choice (D) is incorrect because Queen Njinga skillfully used diplomacy, including negotiating with the Portuguese and making alliances with the Dutch, to advance her goals.

3. **(B)** Queen Njinga's combination of military innovation and political acumen allowed Matamba to maintain its independence despite intense Portuguese pressure. Her leadership demonstrated the capability of women rulers and set a precedent for female leadership in the kingdom for nearly a century. Choice (A) is incorrect because, although she resisted the Portuguese effectively, Queen Njinga did not win all battles outright. Choice (C) is incorrect because Queen Njinga's leadership was not characterized by a centralized divine monarchy through religious reforms. Choice (D) is incorrect because, although trade was a significant aspect of her reign, Queen Njinga's legacy as a leader was rooted more in her resistance strategies and statecraft than solely in her economic achievements.

4. **(B)** Nzinga Mbemba's letter focuses on the harmful effects of the transatlantic slave trade. It emphasizes how Portuguese merchants, motivated by greed, were depopulating the Kingdom of Kongo by abducting its citizens, including nobles and vassals. Choice (A) is incorrect because the letter does not address a lack of military support. Choice (C) is incorrect because, although wine and flour are mentioned, they are requested only for religious purposes, not as primary concerns. Choice (D) is incorrect because, although Mbemba mentions a need for priests and schools, his main concern is stopping the slave trade.

5. **(A)** Nzinga Mbemba explicitly requests that no merchants or wares, except for priests and goods such as wine and flour needed for religious sacraments, be sent to the kingdom in order to eliminate the slave trade entirely. Choice (B) is incorrect because Mbemba welcomes priests for education and religious instruction and does not place to expel them. Choice (C) is incorrect because the letter does not propose military strengthening as a solution. Choice (D) is incorrect because Mbemba's letter advocates for the complete cessation of the slave trade, not its regulation.

PART 3

Unit 2—Freedom, Enslavement, and Resistance

5

Unbreakable: Roots of Resistance, Rise of Liberation

Key Themes

- African exploration and intellectual presence long before enslavement
- Violent commodification of Black bodies in labor, trade, and law
- Global systems of power that enforced race as a social construct
- Resistance at every stage—from ships to courtrooms to cultural survival
- Intersection of law, economy, and ideology in institutionalizing slavery

TIMELINE

Date/Period	Event/Development	Related Topics
Early 1500s	**Juan Garrido** and **Estevanico**, African explorers, take part in Spanish expeditions in Mexico and the Southwest	Topic 2.1—African Explorers in the Americas
1500s–1800s	Establishment and growth of **departure zones** along West African coasts: Senegambia, Gold Coast, Bight of Benin, Kongo	Topic 2.2—Departure Zones and the Slave Trade
17th–18th centuries	Political instability and expansion of warfare in West Africa due to slave trade demand	Topic 2.3—Capture and the Impact of Slave Trade
Middle Passage era	**Shipboard resistance** by enslaved Africans; examples include revolts, hunger strikes, and suicide	Topic 2.4—Resistance on Slave Ships
Mid-1700s–Early 1800s	Growth of **abolitionist thought**, Quaker opposition, and petitions in Britain and the United States	Topic 2.4—Antislavery Movement
1600s–1800s	**Slave auctions** become institutionalized in U.S. port cities; families are separated for profit	Topic 2.5—Slave Auctions and Domestic Trade
1808	The United States outlaws the **transatlantic slave trade**, increasing reliance on the domestic slave economy	Topic 2.5—Domestic Slave Trade
Colonial-Antebellum era	Enslaved Africans and their descendants shape plantation **labor systems, spiritual life**, and **folk cultures**	Topic 2.6—Labor, Culture, and Economy
Slave labor	Fueled U.S. agricultural and economic growth—especially cotton, tobacco, and rice industries	Topic 2.6—Labor, Culture, and Economy

Date/Period	Event/Development	Related Topics
Colonial 1600s–1800s	**Slave codes** passed to restrict movement, literacy, and autonomy; laws differ by colony but share harsh enforcement	Topic 2.7—Slave Codes and Law
Landmark cases	***Somerset v. Stewart*** **(1772);** ***Dred Scott v. Sandford*** **(1857)**—affirmed Black noncitizenship under U.S. law	Topic 2.7—Landmark Cases
17th century onward	Development of **racial caste systems**—white racial identity becomes legal and social status marker	Topic 2.8—Social Construction of Race
Hereditary slavery	Enslavement becomes **matrilineal and perpetual**, legally reproducing status through birth	Topic 2.8—Reproduction of Status

Topic 2.1 African Explorers in the Americas

Key Terms

- Esteban/Estevanico—Moroccan-born enslaved explorer with Cabeza de Vaca
- Pre-Columbian African presence theories—including references to Mali sailors
- Juan Garrido—African conquistador, fought in Mexico
- Zamoranos—people of African descent in Spanish America
- Colonial Spanish expeditions—with African participants
- Conquistadors of African descent

Did you know that there were Africans in the Americas before the slave trade? Before the transatlantic slave trade reached its height, Africans were already present in the Americas—not as enslaved laborers but as explorers, translators, settlers, and cultural intermediaries. Their presence reveals a critical and often overlooked dimension of early American history: Africans were not merely passive subjects of European conquest but active participants in the unfolding colonial world. Among these figures, the ladinos—Africans who had lived in Iberia and adopted Spanish or Portuguese language and culture—played especially significant roles as some of the first Africans to arrive in territories that would later become the United States.

After engaging with this topic, scholars will be able to:

- Explain the significance of the roles ladinos played as the first Africans to arrive in the territory that became the United States.
- Describe the diverse roles Africans played during the colonization of the Americas in the sixteenth century.

African Explorers in the Americas

Long before the rise of plantation slavery and racialized bondage, Africans were already present in the Americas—not as mere subjects of colonial systems but as explorers, intermediaries, and agents of cross-cultural navigation. These individuals, many of whom were known as ladinos, played a crucial role in the earliest European ventures into the New World, including in territories that would become the modern-day United States.

Ladinos and Atlantic Creoles: Agents of Early Contact

In the early sixteenth century, both free and enslaved Africans familiar with the Iberian language and culture journeyed across the Atlantic alongside Spanish and Portuguese explorers. Known as ladinos, these Africans had been acculturated in Iberia, often speaking Spanish or Portuguese and practicing Christianity. They were part of a broader group known as **Atlantic creoles**—Africans whose lives reflected the early stages of the Atlantic world and who served as cultural intermediaries during a formative historical moment.

Atlantic creoles were not defined solely by enslavement. Many were multilingual and versed in the commercial and diplomatic protocols of both European and African societies. This fluency in multiple worlds gave them rare—and at times significant—social mobility. As interpreters, navigators, craftsmen, and envoys, they became essential figures in early contact zones, negotiating across the fault lines of empire, commerce, and colonization.

Claiming La Florida: Africans and Early Colonization

The role of ladinos extended directly into the colonial aspirations of Spain in North America. As Spain sought to lay claim to vast territories it named *La Florida*—an area encompassing present-day Florida, Georgia, and South Carolina—Africans were present in these expeditions from the outset. Their inclusion reflected not only Spain's leading role in the early transatlantic slave trade but also the pragmatic need for skilled, adaptable, and acculturated African labor.

Whether free or enslaved, ladinos in Spanish exploration parties were far more than laborers; they were often cultural and political figures. Their presence in the earliest phases of colonization challenges reductive narratives that equate African arrival in the Americas solely with bondage. These individuals laid tracks not only through geography but through history itself—shaping early American societies in ways that are too often ignored in conventional accounts.

Africans in the Early Colonization of the Americas

In the fifteenth and sixteenth centuries, Africans played critical and multifaceted roles in the shaping of the Americas. Their experiences challenge narrow narratives that place Africans solely within the confines of bondage. Instead, they illuminate a far richer story of African presence, influence, and resistance in the early Americas.

Three Major Roles: Conquistadores, Laborers, and Artisans

Africans in the early Americas occupied three major social and economic roles:

- As conquistadores, some Africans joined Spanish military expeditions in hopes of earning freedom and material gain. These men were often motivated by the promise of social mobility, land, or legal recognition in exchange for their participation in the brutal campaigns of conquest against Indigenous nations.
- As free skilled workers and artisans, Africans contributed their craftsmanship, agricultural knowledge, and commercial expertise to the development of colonial settlements. Their labor, though often overlooked in historical narratives, was essential to the functioning of these fragile and growing societies.
- As enslaved laborers, countless Africans were forced to perform grueling work in the mines, fields, and construction projects that funded European imperial expansion. In the Caribbean and Latin America, African labor became the backbone of colonial economies, especially in silver mining and early sugar cultivation.

Juan Garrido: African Conquistador and Trailblazer

One of the most remarkable early African figures in North America was **Juan Garrido**, a free African conquistador born in the Kingdom of Kongo. After moving to Lisbon, Garrido joined Spanish military expeditions to the New World. In 1513, he became the first known African to set foot in what is now the United States, arriving in Florida as part of a Spanish force.

Garrido maintained his freedom by serving as a soldier and actively participating in Spain's campaigns to conquer Indigenous peoples. He later settled in Mexico, where he contributed to urban development and even claimed to be the first person to grow wheat in the Americas. His life reflects the complexity of African involvement in empire building—not only as victims but also as agents operating within imperial structures for survival, opportunity, and advancement.

Conquistador Negro Duran
(Source: Diego Durán, public domain, via Wikimedia Commons)

Juan Garrido's Petition, 1538

In 1538, Juan Garrido submitted a formal petition to the Spanish Crown, seeking recognition and compensation for his years of military service and contributions to Spanish colonial expansion in the Americas. As a free African conquistador who had participated in key expeditions—including the conquest of present-day Florida and Mexico—Garrido used this petition to assert his identity, defend his legacy, and claim rights typically reserved for Spanish-born settlers.

The petition is significant not only because it documents Garrido's personal achievements but because it challenges assumptions about race, status, and power in the early colonial world. In his own words, Garrido situates himself as a loyal subject of the Crown, a Christian, and a contributor to the Spanish imperial project. His appeal reveals the limited yet strategic avenues available for Africans to claim agency and recognition in colonial legal systems.

> **The opening of Juan Garrido's probanza (petitionary proof of merit) of September 27, 1538**
>
> I, Juan Garrido, black in color, resident of this city [Mexico], appear before Your Mercy and state that I am in need of providing evidence to the perpetuity of the king [a perpetuidad rey], a report on how I served Your Majesty in the conquest and pacification of this New Spain, from the time when the Marqués del Valle [Cortés] entered it; and in his company I was present at all the invasions and conquests and pacifications which were carried out, always with the said Marqués, all of which I did at my own expense without being given either salary or allotment of natives [repartimiento de indios] or anything else. As I am married and a resident of this city, where I have always lived; and also as I went with the Marqués del Valle to discover the islands which are in that part of the southern sea [the Pacific] where there was much hunger and privation; and also as I went to discover and pacify the islands of San Juan de Buriquén de Puerto Rico; and also as I went on the pacification and conquest of the island of Cuba with the adelantado Diego Velázquez; in all these ways for thirty years have I served and continue to serve Your Majesty—for these reasons stated

above do I petition Your Mercy. And also because I was the first to have the inspiration to sow wheat here in New Spain and to see if it took; I did this and experimented at my own expense.

Source: Juan Garrido, Petition to Charles V, Holy Roman Emperor and King of Spain, 1538

Estevanico: Enslaved Explorer, Translator, and Healer

Another foundational figure in the story of Africans in early America is **Estevanico**—also known as Esteban the Moor. Born in Morocco and enslaved by Spanish colonizers, Estevanico was forced into service as part of a failed expedition to colonize parts of the Gulf Coast. By 1528, he was traversing what is now Texas and the American Southwest.

As one of the few survivors of the expedition, Estevanico used his linguistic and cultural knowledge to act as a translator, guide, and even healer among Indigenous communities. Despite his contributions, his position remained precarious. He was ultimately killed by Indigenous people who resisted Spanish colonial encroachment. His death is a reminder of the brutal contradictions embedded in conquest, servitude, and empire.

These stories underscore the early and enduring presence of Africans in the Americas—not only as enslaved laborers but as navigators, mediators, builders, and survivors. They operated in a colonial world shaped by violence, ambition, and survival. Their stories speak to the resilience, adaptability, and complexity of African experiences in the early Atlantic world.

Before Columbus: Africans in the Americas

What if Africans were in the Americas before Columbus? Some historians and cultural traditions say they were. These stories challenge the timeline most textbooks follow—and remind us that history isn't just about what's proven but also about what's remembered.

You're Practicing: Evaluating different types of historical evidence.

Connect This To: Oral tradition, origin stories, and global migration.

Theme: Migration and Diaspora

Practice: Contextualization

Use the narrative description of West African societies and the start of the slave trade from this section to respond to the following.

(A) Identify one way in which West African societies were affected by the emergence of the transatlantic slave trade.

(B) Explain one way the transatlantic slave trade shaped global commerce or labor systems in the Americas.

(C) Using your knowledge beyond the text, explain how this trade impacted cultural retention or transformation among enslaved Africans.

SAMPLE RESPONSES

(A) West African societies were affected by the emergence of the transatlantic slave trade because it destabilized kingdoms such as Kongo, Dahomey, and Oyo by fueling conflicts over access to trade routes and captives. As European demand for enslaved labor grew, African leaders were drawn into complex political rivalries, resulting in the fragmentation of traditional governance systems.

The transatlantic slave trade also transformed West African economies by shifting production away from local markets toward goods demanded by European traders, such as weapons, textiles, and alcohol. This dependency on European trade destabilized long-standing economic networks within Africa and reshaped regional power structures, creating lasting inequalities.

(B) The transatlantic slave trade shaped global commerce by fueling the growth of plantation economies in the Americas, particularly in sugar, tobacco, and rice production. Enslaved Africans became the backbone of these labor systems, generating massive profits for European empires and integrating Africa, Europe, and the Americas into a triangular trade network.

The trade also shaped global commerce by providing the labor needed to extract silver from mines in places like Potosí in modern-day Bolivia. The silver enriched European powers and was funneled into global trade routes, linking the Americas to Europe, Africa, and Asia. Enslaved African labor thus became central to the emergence of a truly interconnected global economy.

(C) Despite forced migration and enslavement, Africans preserved elements of their cultural heritage in the Americas through religion, language, music, and foodways. Practices such as ring shouts, call-and-response traditions, and drumming survived in regions like the Caribbean and the Gullah-Geechee communities of the U.S. South, maintaining connections to ancestral identities.

The trade also resulted in the transformation of African cultures, leading to the creation of new diasporic identities. Through the blending of African, Indigenous, and European traditions, enslaved Africans developed Creole languages, syncretic religions such as Santería and Vodun, and hybrid music and dance traditions, forging cultural expressions that remain vital across the African diaspora today.

Skills Assessed: Explain the historical context; support a claim with evidence; connect the content to African American life and culture.

Topic 2.2 Departure Zones in Africa and the Slave Trade to the United States

Key Terms

- Transatlantic slave trade
- Departure zones—Senegambia, Windward Coast, Bight of Benin, Bight of Biafra, Angola
- Slave forts and castles—Elmina Castle, Goree Island
- Barracoons—temporary slave-holding pens
- Middle Passage
- Ouidah (Whydah)—major slaving port
- Abolition of U.S. slave trade (1808)—led to internal trade boom
- Cultural retention—African ethnic identities in the U.S. South

The transatlantic slave trade was one of the largest and most devastating forced migrations in human history. Over the course of more than three centuries, millions of Africans were violently uprooted from their homelands and transported across the Atlantic to fuel the economic ambitions of European empires. This trade system connected four continents—Africa, Europe, South America, and North America—and transformed the cultural, political, and demographic landscapes of the modern world.

Understanding the transatlantic slave trade is essential not only to African American history but to the very foundation of the Americas. It is a story of global capitalism, imperial expansion, racial ideology, and profound resistance.

After engaging with this topic, scholars will be able to:

- Describe the scale and geographic scope of the transatlantic slave trade.
- Identify the primary slave-trading zones in Africa from which Africans were forcibly taken.
- Explain how the distribution of distinct African ethnic groups during the era of slavery shaped the development of African American communities in the United States.

The Scope and Structure of a Global System

The transatlantic slave trade was not a spontaneous or isolated event. It was a carefully coordinated system that connected Africa to the Americas and Europe through commerce, colonization, and violence. Portugal, Great Britain, France, Spain, and the Netherlands emerged as the top five enslaving nations, each profiting from the trade in African lives through state sponsorship, private shipping networks, and imperial expansion. Though over 12.5 million Africans were transported across the Atlantic, of those who survived the journey, *only about 5 percent—roughly 388,000 individuals—came directly to what is now the United States.*

The majority were taken to Brazil, the Caribbean, and Spanish America. Yet despite their smaller numbers, Africans in North America built powerful and enduring communities that preserved and adapted African cultural traditions in profound ways.

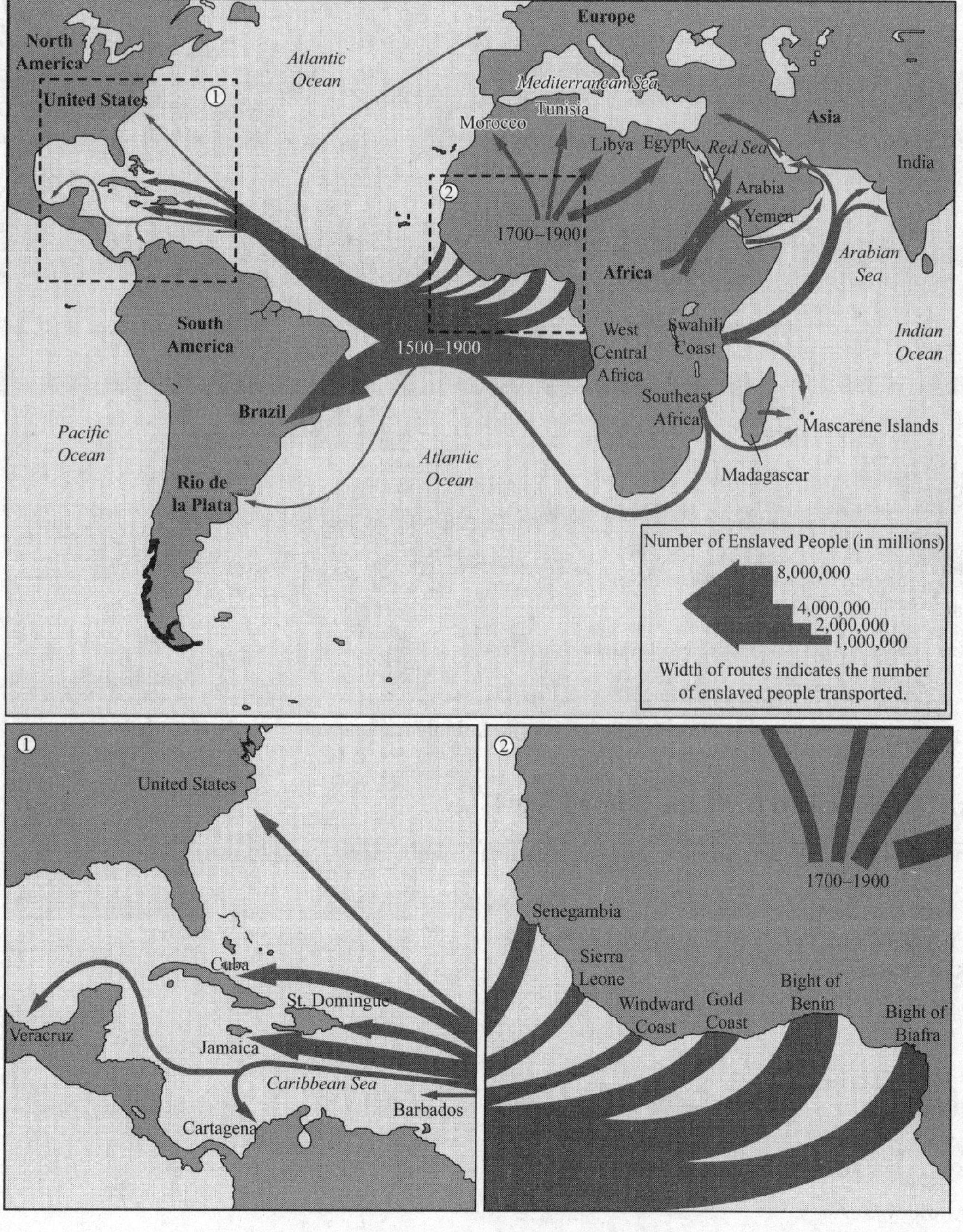

Overview of the slave trade out of Africa

Charleston, South Carolina: A Major Port of Entry

Of the Africans who were brought directly to the United States, *48 percent disembarked in Charleston, South Carolina,* making it the most significant slave-trading port in North American history. Charleston was the epicenter of the domestic slave economy. Its role as a gateway city means it also became a site of concentrated African cultural retention.

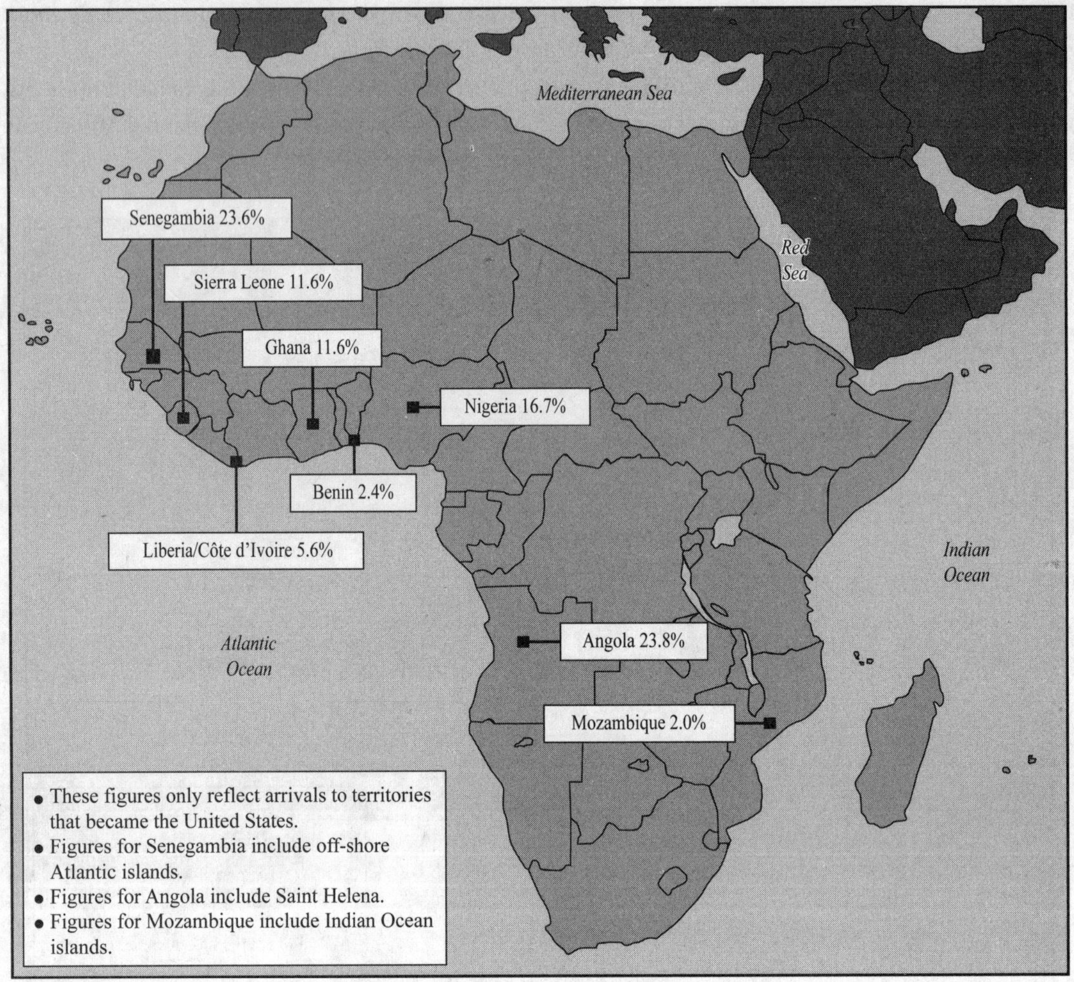

Regional origins of enslaved people forcibly transported to North America

Where Did Enslaved Africans Come From?

Africans who were brought to North America came primarily from nine geographic regions that align with modern-day countries:

- Senegambia
- Sierra Leone
- Liberia
- Côte d'Ivoire
- Ghana
- Benin
- Nigeria
- Angola
- Mozambique

Africa's Role in the Slave Trade

The transatlantic slave trade didn't start in North America. Instead, it began on African coasts where kingdoms, traders, and colonizers clashed over power and profit. Understanding where and how people were taken helps us see the human cost behind the numbers.

You're Practicing: Tracing causes and consequences across continents.

Connect This To: Global trade networks and African resistance.

Theme: Origins and Encounters

Among these, captives from **Senegambia** and **Angola** made up nearly half of those transported directly to the U.S. mainland. These regions were deeply connected to African social, spiritual, and political systems. The people who were taken from them brought those systems with them, preserving elements of their languages, beliefs, and practices in their new, enslaved communities.

African Ethnic Diversity and the Making of African American Culture

Enslaved Africans in the United States did not arrive as a monolith. Instead, they came from distinct ethnic, linguistic, and religious backgrounds, including Wolof, Akan, Igbo, and Yoruba societies. These groups each had their own governance systems, artistic traditions, culinary practices, and spiritual worldviews. Nearly half of those brought to the United States came from regions where **Islam** or **Christianity** had taken root, adding layers of complexity to how religion, literacy, and identity unfolded in African American life.

> **TIP**
>
> **Use the Process of Elimination**
>
> When answering multiple-choice questions (MCQs), first eliminate obviously wrong answers to increase your chances of choosing the correct answer from the remaining options.

Once in the Americas, these diverse Africans were often forced into shared spaces on plantations, in towns, and in emerging Black communities. Their interactions produced new cultural syntheses: blending languages, merging spiritual practices, and cocreating the foundations of African American identity. This process did not erase African origins; it reimagined them in a new world shaped by survival, resistance, and cultural continuity.

Understanding the scale and ethnic complexity of the transatlantic slave trade deepens our appreciation for the cultural genius, resilience, and influence of early African Americans. Their journey across the Atlantic was a forced one, but what they carried with them transformed the world.

Short-Answer Practice Question

Use your knowledge of the transatlantic slave trade to answer all parts of the question below in complete sentences.

(A) Describe the geographic scope of the transatlantic slave trade.

(B) Explain one piece of evidence that illustrates the scale of the transatlantic slave trade before the nineteenth century.

(C) Identify and explain the significance of Charleston, South Carolina, within the history of the transatlantic slave trade.

SAMPLE RESPONSES

(A) The transatlantic slave trade connected Africa, the Americas, and Europe, with enslaved Africans transported primarily to the Caribbean, South America, and North America.

(B) Over 12.5 million Africans were forcibly transported to the Americas during the 350-year span of the slave trade, with more Africans arriving than people from any other region in the world before the 1800s.

(C) Charleston, South Carolina, was the main entry point for enslaved Africans in the United States, with 48 percent of Africans brought directly to the U.S. landing there, making it the center of the American slave trade.

Skills Assessed: Contextualization; connect to broader African American experiences; line of reasoning.

Topic 2.3 Capture and the Impact of the Slave Trade on West African Societies

Key Terms

- Capture raids—interethnic warfare and kidnapping
- Dahomey, Asante, Oyo Empires—involved in slave raiding
- Disruption of societies—depopulation, political destabilization
- Guns-for-slaves trade
- Loss of artisans and scholars
- Portuguese and British traders—key actors in West Africa
- Elmina Castle dungeons—symbolic of African trauma

What did it mean to be captured, shackled, and torn from one's homeland—only to endure a journey of unimaginable horror and arrive in a world defined by bondage? The transatlantic slave trade was not a single event but a three-part ordeal that began long before Africans reached the shores of the Americas. From inland raids and forced marches to coastal imprisonment, oceanic terror, and eventual arrival in the Americas, the journey itself was a site of violence, trauma, and transformation.

The trade's impact was not limited to individuals, though. It reshaped entire African societies. As European demand for human labor intensified, the slave trade destabilized West African kingdoms, inflamed regional warfare, and disrupted centuries-old systems of governance, culture, and kinship. At the same time, African survivors—once they were in the Americas—reclaimed their voices through personal narratives that now serve as irreplaceable historical testimony.

After engaging with this topic, scholars will be able to:

- Describe the conditions of the three-part journey enslaved Africans endured during the transatlantic slave trade.
- Explain how the transatlantic slave trade destabilized West African societies.
- Describe the key features and purposes of narratives written by formerly enslaved Africans.

Capture and the Impact of the Slave Trade on West African Societies

The transatlantic slave trade was more than a mass relocation of human beings—it was a process of violent dislocation that unfolded in three devastating stages. From the moment of capture in West Africa to the crushing brutality of the Middle Passage and the disorienting reality of arriving in the Americas, the journey that enslaved Africans endured was both a physical and a spiritual trauma. Yet, even in the face of that brutality, survivors reclaimed their voices through slave narratives—literary and political acts of truth telling that reshaped the moral conscience of the modern world.

The Three-Part Journey of the Enslaved

The path from freedom to bondage unfolded in three interconnected stages, each marked by profound suffering and separation.

- **The First Passage** began with capture. Many enslaved Africans were seized in the interior of West Africa—often as prisoners of war, victims of raids, or individuals kidnapped from their communities. From there, they were forced to march for weeks or even months toward coastal trading forts. This brutal overland journey was characterized by exhaustion, starvation, and violence. Once they reached the Atlantic coast, many captives were confined to overcrowded, disease-ridden dungeons, where they waited—often in darkness—for ships to arrive.
- **The Middle Passage**, the second and most infamous stage, was the transatlantic crossing. A voyage that could last up to three months, the Middle Passage was defined by unimaginable horror. Packed tightly into slave ships, Africans endured malnourishment, untreated wounds, beatings, sexual violence, and rampant disease. Deprived of dignity and fresh air, many lost their lives. Historians estimate that *15 percent* of all enslaved Africans died during this voyage—a staggering human toll. For most, this passage marked a permanent rupture from homeland, family, and ancestry.
- **The Final Passage** began upon arrival in the Americas. Survivors were often quarantined, forcibly inspected, and then resold—many at multiple ports. Their journey did not end at the dock. After being sold, they were transported again—by foot, cart, or ship—to plantations or settlements hundreds of miles away. This relocation could take just as long as the Middle Passage itself, fracturing bonds between those who had survived the earlier stages together.

The Destabilization of West African Societies

While the trade uprooted individuals, it also devastated the social and political fabric of entire African societies. European demand for human labor reshaped local economies, governance, and warfare across West Africa.

- The promise of profit from slave trading gave rise to new cycles of violence and militarization. Coastal kingdoms grew wealthy by raiding interior communities, and war captives were frequently sold to European traders. The arrival of **firearms** intensified these conflicts, transforming local disputes into large-scale warfare fueled by foreign incentives.
- Although some coastal states amassed wealth and political power, many interior regions suffered chronic instability. Communities lived under the constant threat of being raided or betrayed. In many cases, African leaders—seeking to preserve their own dominance—sold captured soldiers or rival ethnic groups into slavery, feeding the cycle of violence.
- The long-term consequences were profound. West African societies experienced a deep loss of human capital—particularly of young men and women who would have become leaders, farmers, artisans, and elders. This disruption to generational continuity robbed communities of cultural transmission, kinship networks, and future prosperity.

Slave Narratives: Memory, Resistance, and Testimony

From this history of trauma emerged a tradition of powerful storytelling. Formerly enslaved Africans began documenting their experiences through poems and slave narratives, a literary genre that served not only as historical record but as a moral indictment of slavery itself.

Slave narratives became foundational texts in early American literature—memoirs, testimonies, and political declarations. These works sought to end slavery and dismantle the ideological structures that justified it. Writers like Phillis Wheatley, Olaudah Equiano, Frederick Douglass, and Harriet Jacobs illuminated the humanity, intellect, and resilience of Black people in a society that tried to deny them all three.

These narratives had a triple purpose:

- **Historical:** preserving firsthand accounts of enslavement and resistance.

- **Literary:** using powerful storytelling to connect with readers across boundaries.
- **Political:** advocating for abolition, civil rights, and the inclusion of African-descended people in the promises of American democracy.

Phillis Wheatley and the Politics of Voice

In 1773, Phillis Wheatley—an enslaved African girl taken from West Africa and raised in colonial Boston—published *Poems on Various Subjects, Religious and Moral,* becoming the first African American woman to publish a book. Through verse, Wheatley asserted Black intellect, spiritual depth, and moral reason during an era that denied all three to people of African descent.

Her most famous and most debated poem, "On Being Brought from Africa to America," offers a deeply complex reflection on race, religion, and belonging. At first glance, Wheatley appears to accept her enslavement as a form of divine mercy—suggesting she found salvation in Christianity. Closer reading, though, reveals a piercing critique of white hypocrisy.

"On Being Brought from Africa to America"

'Twas mercy brought me from my Pagan land,
Taught my benighted soul to understand
That there's a God, that there's a Saviour too:
Once I redemption neither sought nor knew.
Some view our sable race with scornful eye,
"Their colour is a diabolic die."
Remember, Christians, Negros, black as Cain,
May be refined and join the angelic train.
"On Being Brought from Africa to America,"

—Phillis Wheatley

Source: "On Being Brought from Africa to America." *Learning for Justice*, 7 July 2014, www.learningforjustice.org/classroom-resources/texts/on-being-brought-from-africa-to-america (public domain).

The following excerpt, from Chapter 2 of *The Interesting Narrative of the Life of Olaudah Equiano*, offers a firsthand account of the horrors of enslavement and the Middle Passage. Written by Olaudah Equiano in 1789, the narrative stands as a foundational text in both African American literature and the global abolitionist movement.

> The closeness of the place, and the heat of the climate, added to the number in the ship, which was so crowded that each had scarcely room to turn himself, almost suffocating us. This produced copious perspirations, so that the air soon became unfit for respiration, from a variety of loathsome smells, and brought on a sickness among the slaves, of which many died, thus falling victims to the improvident avarice, as I may call it, of their purchasers. This wretched situation was again aggravated by the galling of the chains, now become insupportable; and the filth of the necessary tubs [large buckets for human waste], into which the children often fell, and were almost suffocated. The shrieks of the women, and the groans of the dying, rendered the whole a scene of horror almost inconceivable.

Source: Olaudah Equiano, *The Interesting Narrative of the Life of Olaudah Equiano, Or Gustavus Vassa, The African*. Written by Himself (London, 1789), Project Gutenberg, https://www.gutenberg.org/ebooks/15399.

The journey into slavery began with capture, but it never fully silenced African voices. The writings of those who survived—alongside the cultural memory of those who did not—form a vital archive of truth, grief, endurance, and transformation. By studying these accounts and the systems that produced them, scholars gain not only historical knowledge but moral clarity.

When Communities Collapse

The transatlantic slave trade didn't just tear families apart—it devastated entire regions of West Africa. Raids, wars, and kidnappings became more common, and some communities never recovered. The loss of so many people affected everything: politics, economies, and culture.

You're Practicing: Understanding how outside forces reshape communities.

Connect This To: Long-term impact, regional instability, and legacy.

Theme: Resistance and Autonomy

Practice: Causation

Using the text in this section, respond to the following prompt.

Explain how the economic development of European nations and the United States was directly tied to the institution of slavery. In your response, be sure to do the following.

(A) Identify at least two sectors or industries (e.g., agriculture, finance, shipping) that benefited from slavery.
(B) Use evidence from the reading to support your explanation.
(C) Explain how this economic system contributed to ideas of racial hierarchy or racial capitalism.

SAMPLE RESPONSES

(A) The cotton and textile industries in the United States and Britain depended heavily on enslaved labor for raw materials. The shipping and finance sectors in cities like Liverpool and New York profited from the transatlantic slave trade and the insurance of enslaved people as property.

(B) The profitability of the U.S. cotton industry relied on the labor of millions of enslaved Africans, who produced the majority of the world's cotton by the mid-19th century. This cotton fueled textile factories in Britain and the northern United States, linking enslaved labor directly to industrial growth and global trade networks.

(C) The economic success of slavery was often justified through racist ideologies that claimed African-descended people were suited for enslavement, which institutionalized a racial hierarchy. This racial capitalism intertwined economic profit with racial oppression, as enslaved people were treated as commodities whose labor and reproduction were monetized for the benefit of white elites.

Skills Assessed: Explain historical context and developments; support claims with evidence; use reasoning to show cause-and-effect relationships.

Topic 2.4 African Resistance on Slave Ships and the Antislavery Movement

Key Terms

- Slave ship uprisings—*La Amistad*, Creole revolts
- Resistance during Middle Passage—suicide, hunger strikes, rebellion
- Olaudah Equiano—memoir as abolitionist tool
- Maritime maroons
- Quakers and abolitionism
- Transatlantic abolitionist networks
- Shipboard mortality—impact of rebellion and disease

What does it mean to resist when your very body has been reduced to cargo? During the transatlantic slave trade, enslaved Africans were not passive victims—they were *fighters, defenders of dignity*, and *architects of rebellion*, even in the face of unthinkable violence. From hunger strikes and sabotage to full-scale revolts aboard slave ships, African captives challenged their commodification at every stage of the Middle Passage.

At the same time, artists, abolitionists, and formerly enslaved people documented and exposed the inhumanity of the trade. One of the most enduring tools of protest was the **slave ship diagram**—a visual weapon that transformed statistics into a moral reckoning. These diagrams became powerful antislavery propaganda, inspiring activism, outrage, and ultimately, a movement.

After engaging with this topic, scholars will be able to:

- Describe the methods by which Africans resisted their commodification and enslavement individually and collectively during the Middle Passage.
- Describe the features of slave ship diagrams created during the era of the slave trade.
- Explain how Africans' resistance on slave ships and slave ship diagrams inspired abolitionists and Black artists during the era of slavery and after.

African Resistance on Slave Ships and the Antislavery Movement

The Middle Passage was designed to strip Africans of their names, languages, identities, and dignity. While even in chains—below deck and suffocating in darkness—resistance surged. Across thousands of voyages, Africans refused to surrender to the machinery of slavery. They fought back—through defiance, through uprising, and through memory.

These acts of resistance sparked fear among enslavers, reshaped slave ship architecture, and inspired a growing antislavery movement. Artists and abolitionists transformed that resistance into political power, using slave ship diagrams as tools of moral reckoning. Long after the ships stopped sailing, Black artists have continued to resurrect these images—not to relive the trauma but to reckon with it, reclaim it, and honor the defiant spirit of those who resisted.

Rebellion in the Belly of the Ship

Aboard slave ships, African captives resisted their dehumanization through both individual and collective acts. Some refused to eat, asserting control over the only thing left—their bodies. Others attempted to jump overboard, choosing death over bondage. In some cases, captives overcame linguistic and cultural barriers to organize revolts, seizing weapons, overpowering crews, and attempting to redirect or escape the ship's course.

These uprisings were not rare. They were a persistent reminder that Africans could not—and would not—be reduced to cargo. Their resistance exposed the moral failure of the trade and made it logistically riskier and more expensive for enslavers. To suppress revolts, slavers modified the ships themselves. New designs included barricades, nets to catch jumpers, iron instruments to force-feed those on hunger strike, and guns to quell any spark of rebellion. The structure of the ship became a weapon—but so too did the resistance of those it tried to contain.

The Revolt on *La Amistad*

One of the most famous examples of shipboard resistance occurred in 1839, long after the transatlantic slave trade was declared illegal. A young Mende man named Sengbe Pieh, also known as Joseph Cinqué, led a rebellion aboard the Spanish schooner *La Amistad*. The enslaved Africans overpowered the crew and attempted to sail back to Africa.

Though eventually captured and put on trial in the United States, their story gripped the nation. After two years of legal battles, the U.S. Supreme Court ruled in favor of the Mende captives, granting their freedom. The *Amistad* case galvanized the abolitionist movement, revealing not only the brutality of slavery but the intelligence, courage, and legal agency of Africans themselves. Here is the **Plea to the Jurisdiction of Cinque and Others, 1839** and sketches of some of the survivors from *La Amistad*.

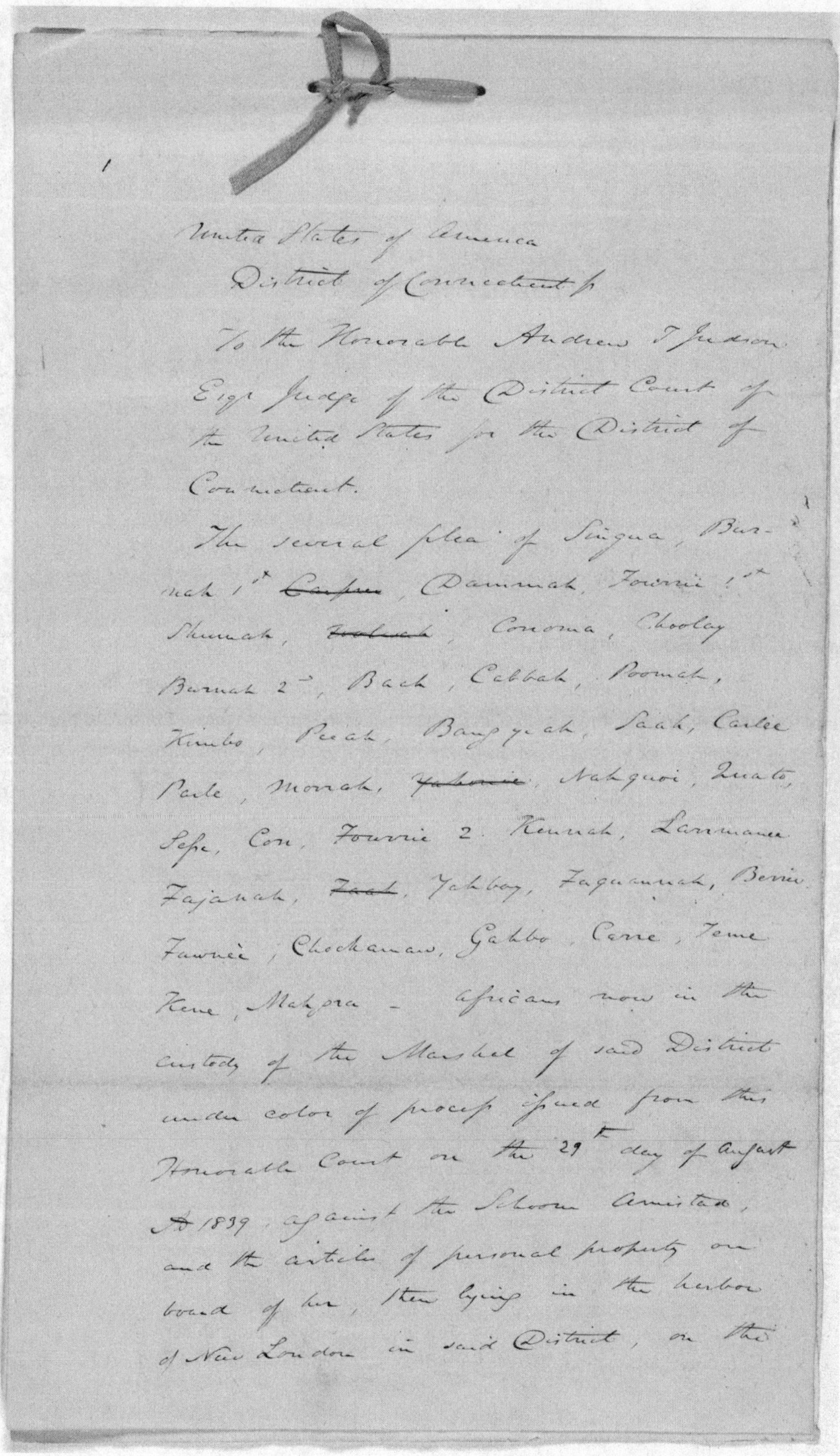

1

United States of America
District of Connecticut ss

To the Honorable Andrew T Judson Esqr Judge of the District Court of the United States for the District of Connecticut.

The several plea of Singua, Burnah 1st, Dammah, Fowrie 1st Shumah, Conoma, Chooley Burnah 2d, Bach, Cebbah, Poomah, Kimbo, Peeah, Baugyeah, Saah, Carlee Pale, Morrah, Nahquoi, Quato, Sepe, Con, Fowrie 2. Kenuah, Lammanee Fajanah, Yahboy, Faguannah, Berrie Fawrie, Chockamaw, Gabbo, Carre, Teme Kene, Mahgra - Africans now in the custody of the Marshal of said District under color of process issued from this Honorable Court on the 29th day of August AD 1839, against the Schooner Amistad, and the articles of personal property on board of her, then lying in the harbor of New London in said District, on the

Plea to the Jurisdiction of Cinque and Others, 1839

Sketches of the captive survivors from the *Amistad* trial, 1839
(Source: Sketches of the *Amistad* captives by William H. Townsend, Beinecke Rare Book and Manuscript Library at Yale University)

The Power of Slave Ship Diagrams

In the eighteenth and nineteenth centuries, abolitionists used a new kind of visual rhetoric: the slave ship diagram. The most famous image—depicting the British ship *Brookes*—showed Africans packed tightly in rows, lying shoulder to shoulder in the belly of the vessel. These diagrams standardized horror, presenting slavery not as abstract injustice but as measurable, visible, and systemic violence.

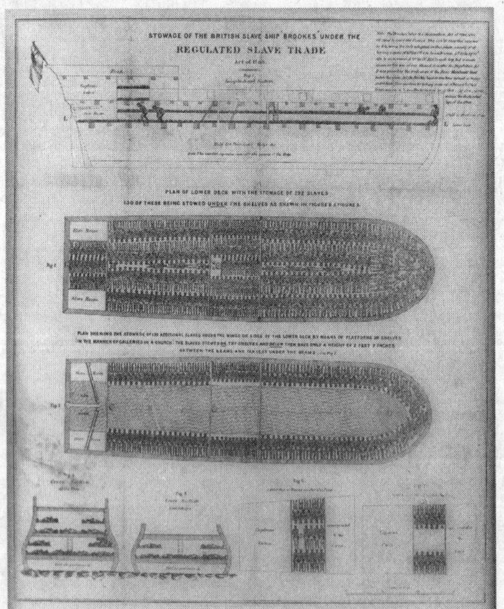

Stowage of the British slave ship *Brookes*, early nineteenth century
(Source: Library of Congress Rare Book and Special Collections Division)

- These diagrams typically displayed only half the number of enslaved people a ship actually carried, meaning the reality was even more inhumane than what the images depicted.
- They revealed cramped, unsanitary conditions that bred disease, disability, and death during voyages lasting up to 90 days.
- Most excluded the instruments of control: the guns, nets, iron force-feeding devices, and physical restraints used to maintain order and suppress resistance.

By circulating these images, abolitionists—Black and white alike—used visual evidence to make the Middle Passage undeniable. The diagram became one of the most effective pieces of antislavery propaganda in world history.

Legacy: Art as Resistance, Memory as Power

The diagram of the slave ship did not vanish with abolition. It has since been reclaimed and reimagined by Black artists, poets, and performers who use it to confront historical trauma and pay tribute to ancestral resilience. Whether through performance art, sculpture, digital media, or installation, contemporary creators revisit the visual language of enslavement—not to relive it but to insist on its recognition. In doing so, they ensure that the memory of the more than *12.5 million Africans forced onto over 36,000 voyages* is not lost to silence but is etched permanently into the moral consciousness of our time.

> **TIP**
>
> **Read Source Titles and Captions Carefully**
>
> For primary source images or documents, the titles and captions often reveal helpful context. Use them to frame your interpretation to assist in answering multiple-choice questions.

Fighting Back at Sea

Enslaved Africans didn't wait for freedom—they fought for it. Some revolted on ships. Others jumped into the ocean, refusing to be stolen. Their resistance inspired abolitionists and shaped how slavery was challenged even before arriving on land.

You're Practicing: Recognizing resistance in unexpected places.

Connect This To: Rebellion, survival, and resistance movements.

Theme: Resistance and Autonomy

Practice: Comparison

(A) Describe one method Africans used to resist enslavement aboard slave ships during the Middle Passage.

(B) Describe one feature of slave ship diagrams that highlights the dehumanizing conditions of the Middle Passage.

(C) Compare how Africans' resistance on slave ships and slave ship diagrams each contributed to the antislavery movement.

SAMPLE RESPONSES

(A) Africans staged hunger strikes to refuse food, attempted to jump overboard rather than live enslaved, and sometimes organized collective revolts despite linguistic barriers.

(B) Slave ship diagrams often showed tightly packed rows of captives arranged to maximize profit, illustrating the cramped, unsanitary, and inhumane conditions that led to high rates of disease and death during voyages lasting up to 90 days.

(C) Africans' direct resistance, such as revolts and refusals to submit, made the slave trade riskier and more costly, forcing changes in ship design and generating stories of bravery like the *Amistad* revolt, which inspired abolitionist activism.

In contrast, slave ship diagrams served as powerful visual propaganda, helping abolitionists in the 18th and 19th centuries expose the brutality of the Middle Passage to the public and rally support for ending the trade.

Together, both forms of resistance—physical defiance and visual documentation—brought global attention to the inhumanity of the slave trade.

Skills Assessed: Historical comparison; relevance to African American life; constructing defensible claims.

Topic 2.5 Slave Auctions and the Domestic Slave Trade

Key Terms

- Auction blocks
- Plantation economy
- New Orleans, Charleston, Richmond—key auction hubs
- Second Middle Passage—forced migration within the United States
- Separation of families
- Fancy trade—sexual exploitation
- Slave pens and holding facilities
- Economics of slavery

After the transatlantic slave trade was officially abolished, the business of human trafficking did not end—it simply moved inland. The rise of the domestic slave trade in the United States became one of the most brutal and expansive forced migration systems in American history. Enslaved people were sold, auctioned, and transported across state lines to fuel the growth of plantation economies in the Deep South.

At the center of this system were slave auctions, which were public spectacles where Black men, women, and children were inspected, dehumanized, and sold to the highest bidder. These markets fractured families, commodified bodies, and made clear that slavery was not just a labor system; it was a system of racial capitalism that turned people into property.

Yet even within this system, enslaved people resisted—through coded communication, escape, and the unbreakable will to reunite with loved ones. To understand slavery in America, one must understand the trauma of the auction block and the scale of the domestic slave trade that reshaped the nation's geography, economy, and soul.

After engaging with this topic, scholars will be able to:

- Describe the logistics and dehumanizing practices of slave auctions in the United States.
- Explain the scale and economic motivations behind the domestic slave trade.
- Analyze the emotional and cultural impact of forced migration on enslaved communities and families.

Slave Auctions and the Domestic Slave Trade

The abolition of the transatlantic slave trade in 1808 did not bring an end to slavery in the United States. Instead, it gave rise to a new, insidious system: the **domestic slave trade**. This was a vast network of forced migration, auctions, and sales that shattered African American families and restructured the geography of slavery across the American South. This internal trade, driven by the cotton boom and protected by both law and racial ideology, displaced over a million African Americans in what historians now call the **Second Middle Passage**—a forced migration greater in scale than the original transatlantic trade.

The Auction Block: Violence, Spectacle, and Dehumanization

Slave auctions were more than commercial transactions. They were performances of power. Enslaved men, women, and children were examined like livestock. They were probed for strength, endurance, and reproductive potential. The auction block reduced human beings to property, transforming the trauma of separation into a public spectacle.

Enslavers used both legal authority and white supremacist doctrine to justify these atrocities. Resistance was often met with severe punishment. Those who dared to speak out, run, or weep in defiance of their sale were whipped—sometimes publicly and often in front of their own families. The goal was to break not just the body but the spirit and to communicate ownership through pain.

When you analyze the advertisement for slave auctions, you can see how everything from a person's age, gender, name, and perceived occupation was listed to entice buyers to purchase humans as property.

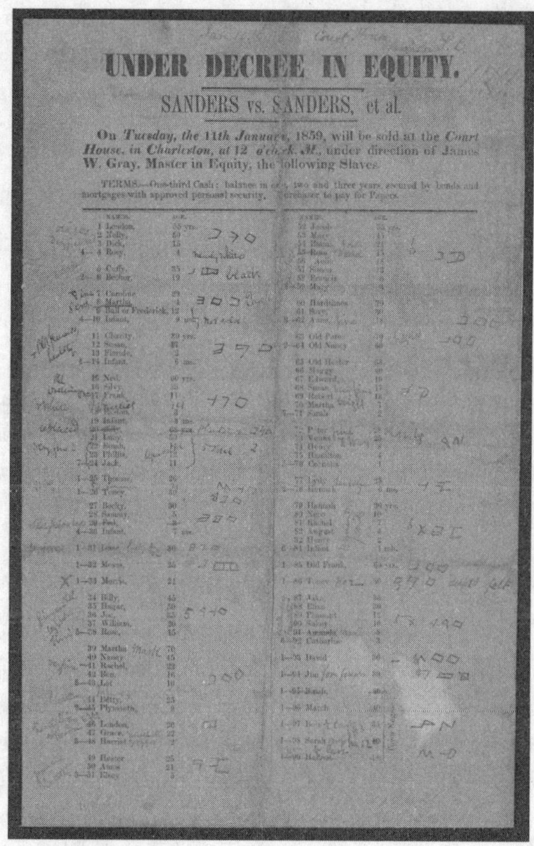

UNDER DECREE IN EQUITY.

SANDERS vs. SANDERS, et al.

On *Tuesday, the 11th January*, 1859, will be sold at the *Court House, in Charleston, at 12 o'clock M.*, under direction of James W. Gray, Master in Equity, the following Slaves.

Broadside for an auction of enslaved persons at the Charleston Courthouse, 1859
(Source: Collection of the Smithsonian National Museum of African American History and Culture, 1859)

The Rise of the Domestic Slave Trade

With the transatlantic trade closed, slavery in the United States became a self-sustaining system. The enslaved population grew primarily through childbirth, and enslaved children became commodities the moment they were born. In the lower South—states like South Carolina, Georgia, Alabama, Mississippi, Louisiana, and Texas—the cotton economy exploded and so did the demand for enslaved labor.

Families for Sale

At slave auctions, human beings were bought and sold like livestock. Children were torn from parents, and spouses were separated forever. The pain of those separations shaped African American life for generations, and the echoes of that trauma still resonate today.

You're Practicing: Recognizing the human cost behind economic systems.

Connect This To: Family, loss, and survival.

Theme: Identity and Culture

To meet that demand, enslaved people were forcibly relocated from the upper South—places like Virginia, Tennessee, and Kentucky. Families were torn apart and marched in coffles—chained groups forced to walk hundreds of miles to new markets in the Deep South. This massive, organized migration, known as the Second Middle Passage, resulted in the forced relocation of over 1 million African Americans. It was the largest internal forced migration in American history.

Literature as Resistance: Black Voices on the Auction Block

African American writers responded to the trauma of the auction block with truth telling. In their narratives, poems, and essays, formerly enslaved people described the emotional terror of being sold into unknown territory, often separated from spouses, children, and siblings. These texts gave voice to the pain that the ledgers and auction records erased.

More than just personal reflections, these works refuted the lie that slavery was a "civilizing" or "benevolent" institution. Authors like **Harriet Jacobs**, **Frederick Douglass**, and **Solomon Northup** exposed the cruelty of the domestic slave trade and made it clear that no part of slavery, especially the sale of human beings, was anything less than an act of terror.

> **"It Was a Mournful Scene Indeed": Solomon Northup Remembers the New Orleans Slave Market, recounting his personal experience**
>
> The slave auction was one of the most barbaric practices of the harsh system of slavery. The slave trade within the United States destroyed families and tore apart communities, especially after 1840 when slavery was extended into the newer lands of the lower South and Southwest. Planters in the older settled areas of the upper South could realize substantial profits selling enslaved people, and New Orleans became the center of the trade. The resulting forced migration involved hundreds of thousands of African Americans. Some moved with their masters, but the migration also tore apart slave families residing on different plantations. Others were sold on the block.
>
> Source: Solomon Northup, *Twelve Years a Slave: Narrative of Solomon Northup, a Citizen of New-York, Kidnapped in Washington City in 1841, and Rescued in 1853, from a Cotton Plantation near the Red River, in Louisiana* (Auburn, NY: Derby and Miller, 1853), 78–82.

The Scale of Displacement

The Second Middle Passage marked an unprecedented demographic shift. Over two and a half times more people were displaced during the domestic slave trade than had arrived from Africa during the entire transatlantic trade to what would become the United States.

This relocation reshaped the Black experience in America—geographically, culturally, and emotionally. It concentrated African American populations in the Deep South, changed family structures, and left a legacy of trauma, resilience, and resistance that still echoes across generations.

To understand American slavery, one must understand that the auction block was not just a moment. It was a system: a mechanism of profit, control, and dismemberment. Even in the face of sale, separation, and surveillance, Black people remembered, resisted, and wrote. Their stories endure, so the truth cannot be auctioned off.

Practice: Causation

Drawing on the descriptions in this section about forced migration, family separation, and auction practices, complete the following.

(A) Identify one way slave auctions or the domestic slave trade affected enslaved individuals or families.

(B) Explain how the domestic slave trade reinforced the system of racial capitalism.

(C) Using your broader knowledge, explain how enslaved people responded to or resisted the trauma of separation.

SAMPLE RESPONSES

(A) Slave auctions often led to the permanent separation of families, as spouses, children, and parents were sold to different owners, severing kinship ties.

The domestic slave trade subjected enslaved individuals to constant dehumanization, as they were inspected like commodities and stripped of personal identity.

(B) The domestic slave trade turned human beings into property, treating their bodies and labor as financial assets that could be bought, sold, or mortgaged to generate profit.

The trade fueled the expansion of plantation economies—particularly the cotton industry—by ensuring a steady supply of labor, thus intertwining white wealth accumulation with the exploitation of Black lives and the maintenance of a rigid racial hierarchy.

(C) Enslaved individuals preserved family bonds by creating fictive kinship networks, calling other enslaved adults “aunt,” “uncle,” or “brother” to maintain a sense of community and belonging.

Spirituals and oral traditions, such as storytelling and African-derived folktales, offered ways to process grief and preserve cultural identity.

Some enslaved people engaged in flight or rebellion, using resistance as a direct challenge to the system that commodified and tore apart their families.

Skills Assessed: Describe historical context and development; connect content to African American experiences; support claims with specific textual evidence; explain the significance and reasoning.

Topic 2.6 Labor, Culture, and Economy

Key Terms

- Enslaved labor systems—task vs. gang system
- Rice, cotton, tobacco, sugar plantations
- Skilled labor—blacksmiths, carpenters, boat builders
- Cultural retention—foodways, music, language
- Gullah Geechee culture—coastal South Carolina/Georgia
- Enslaved economic activity—night gardens, hiring out
- Creolization—fusion of African and European cultures

The story of enslaved African Americans is not only one of forced labor—it is also a story of specialized skill, cultural survival, and economic power. Enslaved people were more than agricultural workers. They were blacksmiths, seamstresses, cooks, midwives, carpenters, musicians, and linguists. Each contributed not only to the wealth of the plantation economy but also to the cultural identity of African American communities.

Across fields, cities, and households, the labor of enslaved people shaped the foundation of the American economy. At the same time, enslaved Africans brought with them vibrant musical traditions, linguistic patterns, and communal practices that formed the roots of what we now recognize as African American culture. This topic explores the dual legacy of forced labor and creative resilience—how work, though weaponized by the slave system, also became a site of cultural expression, survival, and resistance.

After engaging with this topic, scholars will be able to:

- Describe the range and variety of specialized roles performed by enslaved people.
- Explain how slave labor systems affected the formation of African American musical and linguistic practices.
- Evaluate the economic effects of enslaved people's commodification and labor, both within and beyond African American communities.

Labor, Culture, and Economy

To understand the full weight of American slavery, we must move beyond the image of the cotton field. Enslaved African Americans labored not only in agriculture but also in cities, homes, institutions, and skilled trades. Their work was foundational to the economic rise of the United States. Yet the wealth they created was stolen, their genius exploited, and their legacies buried beneath the myth of the plantation.

At the same time, through the very systems designed to oppress them, enslaved people cultivated powerful traditions of cultural survival—through music, language, and community. Whether in the rhythms of a field song or the quiet preservation of African linguistic structures, enslaved African Americans made meaning in the margins of forced labor.

The Diversity of Enslaved Labor

Enslaved people performed an astonishing range of work. Across rural plantations and growing cities, in domestic service and industrial settings, African Americans of all ages and genders were forced into specialized roles that supported every facet of American life.

- On plantations, enslaved people were tasked with growing and harvesting crops like cotton, tobacco, rice, and indigo. In homes, they labored as cooks, wet nurses, laundresses, and caretakers—their skills taken for granted and their presence often unacknowledged.
- Enslaved people were also skilled laborers: blacksmiths, carpenters, painters, seamstresses, and musicians whose talents brought prestige and profit to their enslavers. Many of these skills were brought from Africa and became the basis for cultural continuity and communal pride.
- In some cases, enslaved individuals were bound not to private owners but to churches, factories, and even universities. This institutional slavery reveals how deeply embedded forced labor was in every corner of American society.

Even within these exploitative systems, African Americans used their skills to build communities, sustain families, and express identity. Labor was not just oppression; it was also a site of cultural resistance and spiritual survival.

Sugarcane harvest, Antigua, West Indies, 1823
(Source: William Clark, CC0, via Wikimedia Commons)

Labor Systems and Cultural Expression

Two major systems governed enslaved agricultural labor in the United States: the gang system and the task system.

- In the **gang system**, enslaved people worked in large groups from sunup to sundown under the constant surveillance of overseers. This system, used primarily on cotton, sugar, and tobacco plantations, was relentless in pace and punishment. Yet even here, enslaved people resisted erasure through the creation of **work songs**—songs sung in English but infused with African rhythmic structures, syncopation, and spiritual meaning. These songs helped keep time, lift morale, and pass down stories.
- In the **task system**, which was more common in rice-growing regions like the South Carolina and Georgia low country, individuals were assigned daily quotas. Once tasks were completed, some enslaved people used the remaining time to grow food, tend to family, or preserve language and religious practices. It was under this system that **Gullah**, a creole language rooted in West African linguistic traditions, developed. This shows how cultural memory persisted, even under constraint.

Commodification, Capital, and Inequality

The economic footprint of slavery reached far beyond the plantation. Even cities and regions that did not participate directly in the African slave trade benefited from the industries slavery sustained—including banking, textile production, shipping, and insurance. Northern cities profited from the labor of Southern plantations, creating an economy of interdependence masked by distance.

Enslaved people were not just laborers, they were commodities, appraised for their productivity, skills, and reproductive potential. Their bodies were wealth, yet they and their descendants were excluded from the wealth they generated. They received no wages. They had no legal claim to property or inheritance. They built the infrastructure of America yet were legally barred from participating in its prosperity.

VALUABLE

SLAVES

AT AUCTION,

AT THE CITY HOTEL COMMON ST.

BY C. E. GIRARDEY & CO.,

Office No. 6, Banks' Arcade.

WILL BE SOLD AT AUCTION ON

THURSDAY, Feb. 3, 1859,

AT 12 O'CLOCK, AT THE CITY HOTEL,

THE FOLLOWING DESCRIBED SLAVES TO WIT:

1. ISAM, black, aged about 40 years, a superior engineer and blacksmith: has worked over 20 years with the late Wm. Chapman; is well known for character and qualification throughout the Parish of St. James.
2. JOHN, griffe, aged 24 years, a No. 1 carpenter and ship caulker.
3. TOM, black, aged 24 years, a No. 1 blacksmith and machinist.
4. ALEXANDER, mulatto, aged 28 years, a No. 1 stone cutter.
5. STEPHEN, black, aged 24 years, field hand.
6. EDWARD, black, aged 14 years, field hand,
7. JACK, black, aged 21 years, field hand,
8. HIRAM, black, aged 13 years, field hand.
9. GEORGE, mulatto, aged 30 years, house and confidential servant.
10. JAROTT, black, aged 24 years, field hand.
11. MADORA, black, aged 18 years, extra likely.
12. MATILDA, black, aged 17 years, good cook, washer and ironer.
13. PAULINE, black, aged 13 years, speaks French and English, good house gir' and child's nurse.
14. BETSY, black, aged 12 years, house girl.
15. PHŒBY, black, aged 20 years, extra likely.
16. MARY, black, aged 25 years, superior washer and ironer.
17. CLARISSY, black, aged 40 years, field hand.
18. MARY, black, aged 30 years, cook, washer and ironer.
19. MARY JANE, black, aged 30 years, field hand.
20. PHILUS, black, aged 30 years, good cook, washer and ironer, and her child aged 2 years.

—ALSO—

Several other Plantation Hands.

TERMS---CASH.

☞ The Slaves may be seen at the office of the Auctioneers. ☜

A broadside advertising "Valuable Slaves at Auction" by C. E. Girardy & Co. in New Orleans, February 3, 1859 (Source: Collection of the Smithsonian National Museum of African American History and Culture)

Over centuries, this economic system entrenched **racial wealth disparities** that continue to shape American life. The legacy of this alienation is visible today in generational poverty, lack of access to capital, and the ongoing fight for reparative justice. The labor of enslaved African Americans was never just work. It was the foundation of an economy, the fuel for a culture, and the canvas for resistance. Their stories are not just about suffering, they are about endurance, creativity, and the making of a nation.

A rice fanner basket, circa 1863
(Source: Collection of the Smithsonian National Museum of African American History and Culture)

The **rice fanner basket**, circa 1863, is a powerful artifact of enslaved African Americans' agricultural expertise, particularly in low country South Carolina and Georgia. Woven with West African techniques, it reflects the cultural retention and specialized knowledge enslaved people used in rice cultivation—an industry that enriched the South and depended entirely on the labor of enslaved African Americans.

Building More than Wealth

Enslaved Africans didn't just provide labor—they shaped the entire economy of the Americas. From rice-growing skills to ironwork and music, their knowledge and culture became part of daily life. Even under brutal conditions, they created new traditions that still influence food, music, and language today.

You're Practicing: Seeing how cultural influence can grow under oppression.

Connect This To: Labor, creativity, and survival.

Theme: Cultural Expression and Resistance

Practice: Visual Interpretation and Causation

Examine the painting entitled Sugarcane harvest, Antigua, West Indies, 1823, presented in this section that depicts enslaved people working on a sugar plantation. Then respond to the following.

(A) Describe what this painting conveys about the conditions and structure of enslaved labor in plantation economies.

(B) Explain how this image helps illustrate the connection between forced labor and the development of global capitalism.

(C) Using your knowledge beyond the image, discuss how visual representations like this can influence historical memory and public understanding of slavery.

SAMPLE RESPONSES

(A) The painting shows enslaved people engaged in intensive, backbreaking labor, emphasizing the hierarchical organization of plantation life, where overseers supervised large groups of workers.

It conveys the dehumanizing and grueling nature of sugar production, illustrating how enslaved Africans were forced to labor in fields under harsh conditions, often from sunrise to sunset, with little autonomy or rest.

(B) The painting reflects how sugar plantations in the Caribbean were key drivers of global trade networks, supplying sugar to European markets and generating vast wealth for European colonizers and investors.

By depicting the scale and organization of enslaved labor, the image highlights how the exploitation of enslaved Africans fueled the triangular trade, linking African enslavement, New World plantation economies, and European industrial and financial growth.

(C) Visual sources such as this painting can both reveal and obscure aspects of slavery: while they document the existence of forced labor, they may also sanitize or romanticize the brutality of the institution.

Modern scholars and artists reinterpret such images to confront the realities of violence, resistance, and exploitation that shaped slavery, ensuring these histories are not forgotten.

Skills Assessed: Analyze visual sources; explain the historical context; support interpretation with evidence; explain the significance and use reasoning.

Topic 2.7 Slavery and American Law—Slave Codes and Landmark Cases

Key Terms

- Slave codes—legal restrictions on enslaved people
- Chattel slavery—permanent, inherited status
- *Partus sequitur ventrem*—child inherits status of the mother
- Fugitive Slave Acts (1793, 1850)
- *Dred Scott v. Sandford* (1857)—denied Black citizenship
- *Somerset v. Stewart* (1772, UK)—ruled slavery unsupported in England
- Legalized racial hierarchy

Law was not neutral in the history of American slavery—it was a weapon. From the seventeenth to the nineteenth centuries, legal systems across the American colonies and later the United States were constructed to protect the institution of slavery and deny citizenship, freedom, and basic human rights to African Americans. Through **slave**

codes, court decisions, and constitutional exclusions, the law codified Black subjugation and criminalized Black resistance.

Yet it was precisely because African Americans resisted—through escape, rebellion, education, and self-liberation—that these laws became increasingly severe. At the same time, landmark legal cases exposed the contradictions at the heart of American ideals and forced the nation to reckon with the legal and moral crises slavery created.

After engaging with this topic, scholars will be able to:

- Explain how American law affected the lives and citizenship rights of enslaved and free African Americans between the seventeenth and nineteenth centuries.
- Explain how slave codes developed in direct response to African Americans' resistance to slavery.

Slavery and American Law: Slave Codes and Landmark Cases

From the founding of the colonies to the eve of emancipation, American law did more than accommodate slavery; it actively built and sustained slavery. Through a complex web of constitutions, statutes, and court decisions, lawmakers codified Black subjugation while avoiding the plain language of slavery. Enslaved and free African Americans alike were denied legal personhood, targeted through race-based restrictions, and criminalized simply for resisting oppression or pursuing freedom.

Law was used as a tool of white supremacy. But the very need for slave codes, constitutional clauses, and landmark decisions reflected something deeper: African Americans refused to accept the status assigned to them. Resistance in body, spirit, and intellect forced American lawmakers to tighten control. In this way, American legal history is also a record of Black resistance and white retaliation, of freedom pursued and freedom denied.

The Constitution and the Legal Silencing of Slavery

When the U.S. Constitution was ratified in 1787, it made key references to slavery—without ever using the words *slave* or *slavery*. The framers deliberately chose euphemisms.

Article I, Section 2 counted enslaved individuals as "three fifths of all other Persons" for purposes of representation and taxation.

> Article I
>
> Section 2
>
> The House of Representatives shall be composed of Members chosen every second Year by the People of the several States, and the Electors in each State shall have the Qualifications requisite for Electors of the most numerous Branch of the State Legislature.
>
> No Person shall be a Representative who shall not have attained to the Age of twenty five Years, and been seven Years a Citizen of the United States, and who shall not, when elected, be an Inhabitant of that State in which he shall be chosen.
>
> Representatives and direct Taxes shall be apportioned among the several States which may be included within this Union, according to their respective Numbers, which shall be determined by adding to the whole Number of free Persons, including those bound to Service for a Term of Years, and excluding Indians not taxed, <u>three fifths of all other Persons</u>. The actual Enumeration shall be made within three Years after the first Meeting of the Congress of the United States, and within every subsequent Term of ten Years, in such Manner as they shall by Law direct. The Number of Representatives shall not exceed one for every thirty Thousand, but each State shall have at Least one Representative; and until such enumeration shall be made, the State of New Hampshire shall be entitled to chuse three, Massachusetts eight, Rhode Island and Providence Plantations one, Connecticut five, New-York six, New Jersey four, Pennsylvania eight, Delaware one, Maryland six, Virginia ten, North Carolina five, South Carolina five, and Georgia three.

> When vacancies happen in the Representation from any State, the Executive Authority thereof shall issue Writs of Election to fill such Vacancies.
>
> The House of Representatives shall chuse their Speaker and other Officers; and shall have the sole Power of Impeachment.

Article IV, Section 2 required the return of fugitives "held to Service or Labour" who escaped to free states.

> Article IV
>
> Section 2
>
> The Citizens of each State shall be entitled to all Privileges and Immunities of Citizens in the several States. A Person charged in any State with Treason, Felony, or other Crime, who shall flee from Justice, and be found in another State, shall on Demand of the executive Authority of the State from which he fled, be delivered up, to be removed to the State having Jurisdiction of the Crime.
>
> No Person held to Service or Labour in one State, under the Laws thereof, escaping into another, shall, in Consequence of any Law or Regulation therein, be discharged from such Service or Labour, but shall be delivered up on Claim of the Party to whom such Service or Labour may be due.
>
> Source: United States Constitution, 1787. See the full transcription on the National Archives website. (National Archives)

This legal avoidance of the word *slave* reflected the contradictions at the heart of the American project—a republic that proclaimed liberty while protecting human bondage. It was not until the **Thirteenth Amendment** in 1865 that the Constitution explicitly used the word *slavery*—and abolished it.

Slave Codes and the Construction of Racial Hierarchy

Slave codes formed the legal backbone of slavery across the Americas. These laws defined enslavement as a lifelong, inheritable, race-based condition, passed from mother to child and immune to merit or humanity.

- These codes criminalized basic acts of autonomy: movement without permission, gathering in groups, practicing African cultural rituals such as drumming, and learning to read or write.
- In colonies like South Carolina, Louisiana, and Virginia, codes included bans on wearing certain fabrics or carrying weapons. These laws were about control but also about status, making clear that Blackness itself was associated with unfreedom.

The **Code Noir** in French colonies and the **Código Negro** in Spanish colonies served as foundational legal frameworks for maintaining slavery across the Atlantic world. Both sets of laws restricted the lives of enslaved Africans, dictated the rights and duties of slaveholders, and codified the forms of violence and control deemed legally permissible within these societies.

In **French Louisiana**, a version of the Code Noir was formally introduced in **1724**, modeled closely after the 1685 code established for the French Caribbean colonies. This legal code, known in English as the **Black Code**, remained in effect until the United States acquired Louisiana in 1803. Comprising 54 articles, it regulated nearly every aspect of enslaved life, defined the status of free Black people, and outlined the legal relationship between enslavers and the enslaved.

The following selection includes Articles 1–10 of the 1724 Louisiana Code Noir, offering direct insight into how law was used to uphold white dominance, control Black life, and structure the racial hierarchy of colonial Louisiana.

BLACK CODE OF LOUISIANA

I. Decrees the expulsion of Jews from the colony.

II. Makes it imperative on masters to impart religious instruction to their slaves.

III. Permits the exercise of the Roman Catholic creed only. Every other mode of worship is prohibited.

IV. Negroes placed under the direction or supervision of any other person than a Catholic, are liable to confiscation.

V. Sundays and holidays are to be strictly observed. All negroes found at work on these days are to be confiscated.

VI. We forbid our white subjects, of both sexes, to marry with the blacks,under the penalty of being fined and subjected to some other arbitrary punishment. We forbid all curates, priests, or missionaries of our secular or regular clergy, and even our chaplains in our navy to sanction such marriages. We also forbid all our white subjects, and even the manumitted or free-born blacks, to live in a state of concubinage with blacks. Should there be any issue from this kind of intercourse, it is our will that the person so offending, and the master of the slave, should pay each a fine of three hundred livres. Should said issue be the result of the concubinage of the master with his slave, said master shall not only pay the fine, but be deprived of the slave and of the children, who shall be adjudged to the hospital of the locality, and said slaves shall be forever incapable of being set free. But should this illicit intercourse have existed between a free black and his slave, when said free black had no legitimate wife, and should said black marry said slave according to the forms prescribed by the church, said slave shall be thereby set free, and the children shall also become free and legitimate; and in such a case, there shall be no application of the penalties mentioned in the present article.

VII. The ceremonies and forms prescribed by the ordinance of Blois, and by the edict of 1639, for marriages, shall be observed both with regard to free persons and to slaves. But the consent of the father and mother of the slave is not necessary; that of the master shall be the only one required.

VIII. We forbid all curates to proceed to effect marriages between slaves without proof of the consent of their masters; and we also forbid all masters to force their slaves into any marriage against their will.

IX. Children, issued from the marriage of slaves, shall follow the condition of their parents, and shall belong to the master of the wife and not of the husband, if the husband and wife have different masters.

X. If the husband be a slave, and the wife a free woman, it is our will that their children, of whatever sex they may be, shall share the condition of their mother, and be as free as she, notwithstanding the servitude of their father; and if the father be free and the mother a slave, the children shall all be slaves.

Source: "Translation and Summary of the Black Code of Louisiana," in Benjamin Franklin French, Historical Collections of Louisiana: Embracing Translations of Many Rare and Valuable Documents Relating to the Natural, Civil, and Political History of That State, Part III (New York: D. Appleton, 1851), 89–95.

TIP

Answer FRQs Using the Claim, Evidence, and Reasoning Method

When answering free-response questions, restate the question as a claim, provide specific evidence, and explain your reasoning for how the evidence supports your claim.

The Stono Rebellion and Legal Retaliation

In 1739, enslaved Africans in South Carolina launched the **Stono Rebellion**, the largest uprising of enslaved people in colonial British North America. In response, white lawmakers passed the **1740 South Carolina Slave Code**, a brutal legal overhaul designed to choke off any future resistance.

- The law classified all Black people and Indigenous individuals who did not submit to colonial rule as presumed slaves and "non-subjects" under British law.
- It banned enslaved people from gathering, traveling, rebelling, reading, drumming, or leaving the colony—even for self-emancipation.
- If an enslaved person defended themselves against violence from a white person, the law condemned the enslaved person to death.

This code was not just about punishing rebellion—it was about erasing any trace of Black autonomy.

Law and Citizenship: Free States, Free in Name Only

Even in free states, laws worked to suppress Black freedom. Northern states passed **Black Codes** that restricted the rights of free African Americans:

- Some states banned the entry of free Black people altogether.
- In New York, free Black men could not vote unless they met high property requirements.
- In Ohio, they could not testify against white citizens in court.
- Before the **Fifteenth Amendment** was ratified in 1870, only Iowa and Wisconsin had granted Black men the right to vote.

These laws made it clear that freedom did not mean equality and that Black exclusion was a national, not just a Southern, reality.

Dred Scott and the Legal War on Black Citizenship

One of the most devastating legal assaults on Black citizenship in American history came in 1857, when the United States Supreme Court issued its ruling in ***Dred Scott v. Sandford***. Dred Scott, an enslaved man, had sued for his freedom after living for several years in free territory. His argument was grounded in the widely held belief that residence in a free state conferred emancipation.

In a sweeping and inflammatory decision, **Chief Justice Roger B. Taney**, writing for the majority, declared that Scott could not bring suit in federal court because, as a Black man, he was "not included, and was not intended to be included, under the word 'citizens' in the Constitution." Taney went further, stating that African Americans "had no rights which the white man was bound to respect."

The Court also struck down the **Missouri Compromise of 1820**, arguing that it violated white citizens' constitutional protection of property rights. By this logic, enslaved people were legally indistinguishable from other forms of property, and Congress had no authority to prohibit slavery in federal territories. Taney's decision opened the door for the expansion of slavery nationwide; nullifying decades of legislative compromise.

The following excerpts from Chief Justice Roger B. Taney's majority opinion in *Dred Scott v. Sandford (1857)* reveal the stark legal arguments that shaped one of the most infamous decisions in Supreme Court history. Together, they illustrate how the highest court in the nation codified racial exclusion and denied citizenship to all African Americans, free or enslaved.

> The question is simply this: Can a negro, whose ancestors were imported into this country, and sold as slaves, become a member of the political community formed and brought into existence by the Constitution of the United States, and as such become entitled to all the rights, and privileges, and immunities, guaranteed by that instrument to the citizen? One of which rights is the privilege of suing in a court of the United States in the cases specified in the Constitution. . . .

We think [people of African ancestry] are not, and that they are not included, and were not intended to be included, under the word "citizens" in the Constitution, and can therefore claim none of the rights and privileges which that instrument provides for and secures to citizens of the United States. . . .

They had for more than a century before been regarded as beings of an inferior order, and altogether unfit to associate with the white race, either in social or political relations; and so far inferior, that they had no rights which the white man was bound to respect; and that the negro might justly and lawfully be reduced to slavery. . . . He was bought and sold, and treated as an ordinary article of merchandise and traffic, whenever a profit could be made by it. This opinion was at that time fixed and universal in the civilized portion of the white race.

. . . For if they were so received, and entitled to the privileges and immunities of citizens, it would exempt them from the operation of the special laws and from the police regulations which they considered to be necessary for their own safety. It would give to persons of the negro race, who were recognized as citizens in any one State of the Union, the right to enter every other State whenever they pleased, singly or in companies, without pass or passport, and without obstruction, to sojourn there as long as they pleased, to go where they pleased at every hour of the day or night without molestation, unless they committed some violation of law for which a white man would be punished; and it would give them the full liberty of speech in public and in private upon all subjects upon which its own citizens might speak; to hold public meetings upon political affairs, and to keep and carry arms wherever they went. And all of this would be done in the face of the subject race of the same color, both free and slaves, and inevitably producing discontent and insubordination among them, and endangering the peace and safety of the State.

The act of Congress, upon which the plaintiff relies, declares that slavery and involuntary servitude, except as a punishment for crime, shall be forever prohibited in all that part of the territory ceded by France, under the name of Louisiana, which lies north and not included within the limits of Missouri. And the difficulty which meets us at the threshold of this part of the inquiry is, whether Congress was authorized to pass this law under any of the powers granted to it by the Constitution; for if the authority is not given by that instrument, it is the duty of this court to declare it void and inoperative, and incapable of conferring freedom upon any one who is held as a slave under the laws of any one of the States.

. . . The power to expand the territory of the United States by the admission of new states is plainly given. But the power of Congress over the person or property of a citizen [is] regulated and plainly defined by the Constitution itself. And when the Territory becomes a part of the United States, the Federal Government enters upon it with its powers over the citizen strictly defined, and limited by the Constitution. It has no power of any kind beyond it; and it cannot, when it enters a Territory of the United States, put off its character, and assume discretionary or despotic powers which the Constitution has denied to it.

. . . [T]he rights of private property have been guarded with . . . care. Thus the rights of property are united with the rights of person, and placed on the same ground by the fifth amendment to the Constitution, which provides that no person shall be deprived of life, liberty, and property, without due process of law. And an act of Congress which deprives a citizen of the United States of his liberty or property, merely because he came himself or brought his property into a particular Territory of the United States, and who had committed no offence against the laws, could hardly be dignified with the name of due process of law.

Upon these considerations, it is the opinion of the court that the act of Congress which prohibited a citizen from holding and owning property of this kind in the territory of the United States north of the line therein mentioned, is not warranted by the Constitution, and is therefore void; and that neither Dred Scott himself, nor any of his family, were made free by being carried into this territory; even if they had been carried there by the owner, with the intention of becoming a permanent resident.

Source: "Scott v. Sandford." *LII/Legal Information Institute*, 2019, www.law.cornell.edu/supremecourt/text/60/393 (public domain).

More than Chains: Enslavement and the Law

Slave codes weren't just rules, they were tools of control. Laws defined Black people as property, restricted their movements, and punished freedom. But over time, these same legal systems were also used to fight back—through lawsuits, petitions, and landmark cases.

You're Practicing: Analyzing how laws reflect power structures.

Connect This To: Legal battles, civil rights, and oppression.

Theme: Power and Politics

Widely condemned by legal scholars, the Dred Scott decision is often regarded as the worst ruling in the history of the Supreme Court.

The court's ruling was devastating:

- African Americans, enslaved or free, were not—and could never become—citizens of the United States.
- Because Scott was not a citizen, the court ruled he had no standing to sue.
- The ruling also declared the Missouri Compromise unconstitutional, effectively expanding slavery into western territories.

Its legacy was reversed only through the adoption of the **Thirteenth Amendment (1865)**, which abolished slavery, and the **Fourteenth Amendment (1868)**, which established birthright citizenship and equal protection under the law.

Practice: Contextualization and Causation

Use the discussion in the text about the *Dred Scott v. Sandford* decision to answer the following.

(A) Identify one key claim made in Chief Justice Taney's opinion in *Dred Scott v. Sandford.*

(B) Explain how this decision reinforced the legal foundations of racial slavery and white supremacy in the United States.

(C) Using your knowledge beyond the text, explain how the Dred Scott case shaped African American political or legal activism in the years before the Civil War.

SAMPLE RESPONSES

(A) Chief Justice Taney claimed that African Americans, whether free or enslaved, were not citizens of the United States and therefore had no legal standing to sue in federal court.

(B) The ruling declared that African Americans had "no rights which the white man was bound to respect," affirming the belief that Black people were property rather than citizens.

By denying the federal government the authority to prohibit slavery in the territories (striking down the Missouri Compromise), the decision expanded the power of enslavers and entrenched white supremacy as a legal doctrine.

(C) The decision fueled abolitionist movements and African American activism, as leaders like Frederick Douglass condemned the ruling and argued it revealed the moral bankruptcy of the U.S. legal system.

It galvanized Black communities to intensify efforts for freedom petitions, legal challenges, and grassroots organizing, while also energizing antislavery political parties such as the Republican Party.

The ruling's blatant defense of slavery heightened sectional tensions and motivated African Americans to demand constitutional change, laying the groundwork for the 14th Amendment's guarantee of citizenship.

Skills Assessed: Describe claims made in a legal source; analyze the purpose, audience, and historical impact of the case; support claims with evidence from the ruling; connect to broader African American historical experiences.

Topic 2.8 The Social Construction of Race and the Reproduction of Status

Key Terms

- Scientific racism—pseudoscience to justify slavery
- Polygenism—theory that races were created separately
- Racial caste system
- One-drop rule—legal/social determination of Black identity
- Sexual violence—enforcement of racial hierarchy
- Miscegenation laws—banned interracial relationships
- Motherhood and reproductive control—enslaved women as property
- Breeding practices—for profit and control

Race was not merely a biological reality in America, it was a social invention, forged through law, power, and economic interests. In colonial and early American society, race became a mechanism to define identity, justify slavery, and assign status across generations. At the heart of this system was the legal doctrine of ***partus sequitur ventrem***—the idea that a child's status followed that of the mother. This rule ensured that the children of enslaved women, regardless of the father's identity, even if he was white, were also enslaved.

As this legal principle took root, it gave rise to racial taxonomies, which were categories used to organize, control, and rank human beings based on ancestry and appearance. These taxonomies reinforced a racial hierarchy that privileged whiteness while institutionalizing the generational subjugation of Black people. This topic examines how race was constructed not simply as a category of identity but as a tool of inheritance, exclusion, and domination.

After engaging with this topic, scholars will be able to:

- Explain how *partus sequitur ventrem* affected African American families and informed the emergence of racial taxonomies in the United States.
- Explain how racial concepts and classifications emerged alongside legal and social definitions of status.

The Social Construction of Race and the Reproduction of Status

Race in the United States was never simply about skin tone—it was about power, property, and control. During the seventeenth century, colonial lawmakers began crafting a legal system that would make slavery not just a condition of labor but a condition of birth. Central to this system was the legal doctrine of *partus sequitur ventrem*, a Latin phrase meaning "that which is born follows the womb." This law made enslaved status **hereditary**: if a mother was enslaved, so too would be her child—regardless of the father's status, race, or identity.

This reversal of English common law (which traditionally followed the father's status) allowed white enslavers to avoid legal responsibility for the children they fathered through sexual coercion and assault while simultaneously expanding their property holdings. Over time, laws like *partus sequitur ventrem* worked in tandem with emerging racial classifications to create a rigid social hierarchy in which race, status, and rights were inseparable.

The 1849 image "Am I Not a Woman and a Sister?" published in *The Liberator* served as a powerful symbol of abolitionist and feminist solidarity. It appealed to both conscience and citizenship by foregrounding the humanity, suffering, and moral agency of enslaved Black women.

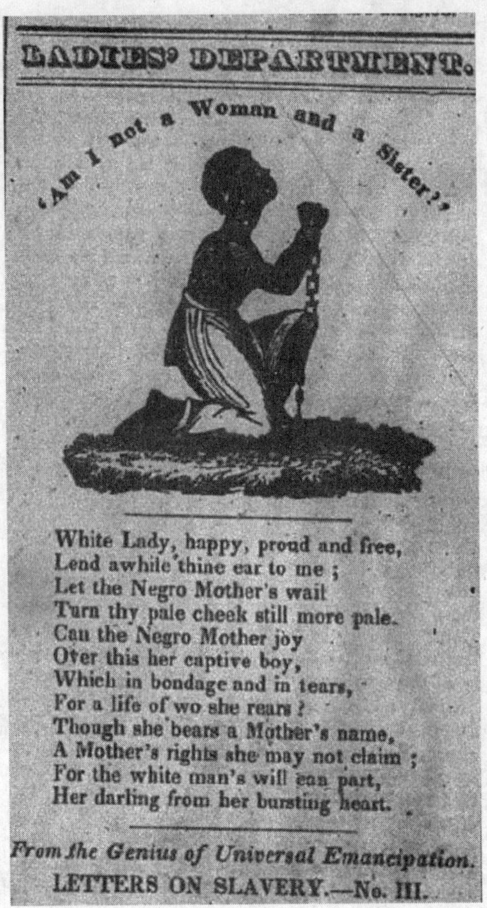

LADIES' DEPARTMENT.

"Am I not a Woman and a Sister?"

White Lady, happy, proud and free,
Lend awhile thine ear to me;
Let the Negro Mother's wail
Turn thy pale cheek still more pale.
Can the Negro Mother joy
Over this her captive boy,
Which in bondage and in tears,
For a life of wo she rears?
Though she bears a Mother's name,
A Mother's rights she may not claim;
For the white man's will can part,
Her darling from her bursting heart.

From the Genius of Universal Emancipation.

LETTERS ON SLAVERY.—No. III.

"Am I not a woman and a sister?" from *The Liberator*, 1849
(Source: *The Liberator*, vol. 2, no. 5 (February 4, 1832), accessed July 1, 2025, https://fair-use.org/the-liberator/1832/02/04/the-liberator-02-05.pdf)

In the 1662 Virginia law titled Negro Women's Children to Serve According to the Condition of the Mother, the colonial legislature codified a significant departure from English common law by declaring that a child's legal status would follow that of the mother, not the father. This statute served to *legally entrench hereditary racial slavery*, enabling enslavers to reproduce and expand their labor force through the children of enslaved women—regardless of the father's identity or status.

> WHEREAS some doubts have arisen whether children got by any Englishman upon a negro woman should be slave or free, Be it therefore enacted and declared by this present grand assembly, that all children born in this country shall be held bond or free only according to the condition of the mother, And that if any Christian shall commit fornication with a negro man or woman, he or she so offending shall pay double the fines imposed by the former act.
>
> Source: "Negro Women's Children to Serve According to the Condition of the Mother," 1662, in William Waller Hening, ed., *The Statutes at Large; Being a Collection of All the Laws of Virginia from the First Session of the Legislature, in the Year 1619*, vol. 2 (New York: R. & W. & G. Bartow, 1823), 170.

Partus Sequitur Ventrem and the Legal Inheritance of Slavery

The legal doctrine of *partus sequitur ventrem* contradicted English common law, which assigned status through the father. It was explicitly designed to preserve slavery for mixed-race children born to white men and enslaved Black women. It permitted white enslavers to sexually exploit Black women without accountability and to profit from the children born of such violence. Enslaved women were thus not only laborers—they were also forced reproducers of future generations of the enslaved.

Partus sequitur ventrem exemplifies how slavery in the United States was systemically racialized and biologically reproduced through legal code.

Hypodescent and the Rise of the One-Drop Rule

In the United States, the logic of **hypodescent**—the idea that a child inherits the racial status of the more socially "subordinate" parent—was used to reinforce the racial order. Although different states had varying thresholds for what percentage of African ancestry constituted Blackness, by the late nineteenth and early twentieth centuries, the **one-drop rule** became dominant: any degree of African ancestry rendered a person legally Black.

- This racial classification excluded African Americans from claiming multiracial or multiethnic identities, even when they had European or Indigenous ancestry.
- It also ensured that those with African lineage could be easily identified and denied access to land, education, legal standing, and citizenship.

Through hypodescent, racial identity became fixed, legal, and unescapable. Racial status was now a status not just imposed but inherited.

The Invention of Race

Race isn't just about skin color—it's a social idea created to justify slavery and inequality. Colonists built systems where whiteness meant freedom and Blackness meant bondage. Learning how race was invented helps us understand how it still shapes society today.

You're Practicing: Connecting past ideas to present realities.

Connect This To: Status, identity, and inequality.

Theme: Identity and Culture

Practice: Continuity and Change over Time

Based on the content of this section, respond to the following.

(A) Identify one example from the text that shows how race was socially or legally constructed in the United States during slavery.
(B) Explain how that example contributed to the reproduction of racial hierarchy or social status.
(C) Using your broader knowledge, explain how these ideas about race continued to shape laws, policies, or cultural norms after slavery ended.

SAMPLE RESPONSES

(A) Slave codes were created to legally define African-descended people as property and to restrict their rights, such as forbidding them from learning to read or marrying freely.

Laws like the "one-drop rule" classified individuals with any African ancestry as Black, reinforcing rigid racial boundaries.

(B) By legally codifying racial categories and limiting the rights of enslaved Africans, slave codes institutionalized white supremacy and created a system in which Blackness was equated with permanent enslavement and social inferiority.

The "one-drop rule" ensured that mixed-race individuals, regardless of appearance, were classified as Black, preventing them from escaping systemic oppression and maintaining white social dominance.

(C) After emancipation, Jim Crow laws in the South reinforced racial segregation, using the same logic of white superiority and Black inferiority that had existed during slavery.

Plessy v. Ferguson (1896) upheld the doctrine of "separate but equal," legally entrenching racial hierarchy in public life.

Culturally, stereotypes and discriminatory practices—such as housing redlining and employment discrimination—emerged from these racial constructs and persisted well into the 20th century.

Skills Assessed: Explain historical context and systems; develop a defensible claim; support the claim with evidence; use reasoning to explain the long-term significance; connect content to broader African American experiences.

KEY TAKEAWAYS

1. **African Presence and Exploration in the Americas**
   - Africans were present in the Americas before and alongside European colonizers, with figures like Juan Garrido and Estevanico participating in Spanish expeditions.
   - These narratives challenge the idea that Africans arrived only as enslaved people and highlight early contributions to American history.
2. **Departure Zones and the Impact of the Slave Trade**
   - West and West Central Africa served as major departure zones for enslaved Africans, who were forcibly transported to the Americas.
   - The transatlantic slave trade had devastating effects on African societies, including demographic shifts, political destabilization, and cultural disruption.
3. **Capture, Resistance, and Survival**
   - Africans resisted enslavement at every stage—from capture and the Middle Passage to plantation life—through revolts, escape, and cultural preservation.
   - Shipboard rebellions and suicide were forms of defiance against dehumanization and captivity.
4. **Slave Auctions and the Domestic Slave Trade**
   - Enslaved Africans were commodified and sold through brutal public auctions, contributing to the expansion of slavery in the United States, especially after the 1808 ban on the transatlantic trade.
   - The domestic slave trade uprooted families and reinforced slavery's integration into the American economy.
5. **Labor, Culture, and Economic Foundations**
   - Enslaved Africans provided vital labor in agriculture, skilled trades, and domestic work, forming the economic backbone of American prosperity.
   - Despite harsh conditions, they developed rich cultural traditions—music, cuisine, and language—that laid the foundation of African American identity.

6. **Law and the Construction of Race**
   - Slave codes and landmark legal cases institutionalized racial slavery and codified Black inferiority under the law.
   - The legal system played a central role in the reproduction of status, linking racial identity to inherited enslavement.
7. **Race as a Social and Economic Tool**
   - The concept of race was constructed to justify and perpetuate slavery, defining Blackness in opposition to whiteness and freedom.
   - This social construct became a mechanism for sustaining systems of exploitation, disenfranchisement, and inequality.

Practice Multiple-Choice Questions

DIRECTIONS: Pick the letter that best answers the following questions.

Questions 1 through 3 refer to the following.

The opening of Juan Garrido's probanza [petition] to the King of Spain, September 27, 1538

"I, Juan Garrido, black in color, resident of this city [Mexico], appear before Your Mercy and state that I am in need of providing evidence to the perpetuity of the king, a report on how I served Your Majesty in the conquest and pacification of this New Spain, from the time when the Marqués del Valle [Cortés] entered it; and in his company I was present at all the invasions and conquests and pacifications which were carried out, always with the said Marqués, all of which I did at my own expense without being given either salary or allotment of natives [repartimiento de indios] or anything else. As I am married and a resident of this city, where I have always lived; and also as I went with the Marqués del Valle to discover the islands which are in that part of the southern sea [the Pacific] where there was much hunger and privation; and also as I went to discover and pacify the islands of San Juan de Buriquén de Puerto Rico; and also as I went on the pacification and conquest of the island of Cuba with the adelantado Diego Velázquez; in all these ways for thirty years have I served and continue to serve Your Majesty—for these reasons stated above do I petition Your Mercy. And also because I was the first to have the inspiration to sow wheat here in New Spain and to see if it took; I did this and experimented at my own expense."

Source: Juan Garrido, probanza (petitionary proof of merit), September 27, 1538, *Archivo General de Indias* (Seville), México 204, f.1; transcription in Ricardo Alegría, *Juan Garrido, el conquistador negro en las Antillas, Florida, México y California, 1503–1540* (San Juan, PR: Centro de Estudios Avanzados de Puerto Rico y el Caribe, 1990); English translation by Matthew Restall in "Black Conquistadors: Armed Africans in Early Spanish America," *The Americas* 57, no. 2 (October 2000): 171.

1. Which of the following best explains Juan Garrido's main purpose in writing this petition?

   (A) To protest the mistreatment of enslaved Africans in the Caribbean
   (B) To request financial compensation and official recognition from the Spanish Crown
   (C) To argue against the practice of religious conversion in New Spain
   (D) To advocate for the rights of Indigenous peoples in Spanish colonies

2. What does Garrido's mention of sowing wheat in New Spain suggest about his role in colonial society?

   (A) He was primarily an enslaved agricultural laborer.
   (B) He served as a missionary promoting Christian farming practices.
   (C) He contributed to the introduction of European agricultural practices in the Americas.
   (D) He resisted European settlement by encouraging Indigenous agricultural systems.

3. Which of the following best characterizes the status of Juan Garrido in colonial Spanish society based on this document?

   (A) A subordinate laborer with no military experience
   (B) A free Black man asserting his loyalty and service to the empire
   (C) A rebellious figure challenging Spanish conquest
   (D) An Indigenous advocate seeking reforms to the encomienda system

Questions 4 and 5 refer to the following.

Negro Women's Children to Serve According to the Condition of the Mother

"WHEREAS some doubts have arisen whether children got by any Englishman upon a negro woman should be slave or free, Be it therefore enacted and declared by this present grand assembly, that all children borne in this country shall be held bond or free only according to the condition of the mother, And that if any Christian shall commit fornication with a negro man or woman, he or she so offending shall pay double the fines imposed by the former act."

Source: "Negro Womens Children to Serve According to the Condition of the Mother," 1662, in William Waller Hening, ed., *The Statutes at Large; Being a Collection of All the Laws of Virginia from the First Session of the Legislature, in the Year 1619*, vol. 2 (New York: R. & W. & G. Bartow, 1823), 170.

4. What was the most significant long-term consequence of the law codified in this 1662 statute?

   (A) It prevented mixed-race children from inheriting land from their fathers.
   (B) It established that slavery in the colonies would be passed down through the maternal line.
   (C) It encouraged English men to marry enslaved African women to free their children.
   (D) It abolished the legal use of the term *slave* in colonial Virginia.

5. According to the law, why did the General Assembly specify increased penalties for Christians who committed fornication with African individuals?

   (A) To encourage the formal conversion of enslaved Africans to Christianity
   (B) To criminalize interracial relationships and reinforce racial boundaries
   (C) To regulate marriage within enslaved communities
   (D) To ensure that children of enslaved fathers remained in bondage

Answer Explanations

1. **(B)** Garrido petitions the Spanish Crown to recognize his thirty years of service and contributions—including military expeditions and agricultural innovation—without compensation. His request for recognition and reward reflects a desire for financial support and acknowledgment. Choice (A) is incorrect because the petition does not reference enslaved Africans. Choice (C) is incorrect because religion is not a topic in this document. Although Garrido mentions conquests, his focus is not on Indigenous rights, making Choice (D) incorrect.

2. **(C)** Garrido explicitly states that he was the first to attempt wheat cultivation in New Spain, indicating his role in transferring European agricultural knowledge to the Americas. Choice (A) is incorrect because he identifies as a free man and petitioner, not an enslaved laborer. No religious mission is mentioned, making Choice (C) incorrect. Choice (D) is incorrect because Garrido represents European colonial interests, not resistance to them.

3. **(B)** Garrido identifies himself as "black in color," a free man and long-serving military participant in Spanish conquests. He petitions the Crown based on loyal service, asserting his value to the empire. Choice (A) is incorrect because Garrido lists his extensive military expeditions. Choice (C) is incorrect because he reinforces imperial objectives, not rebellion. Garrido makes no mention of Indigenous rights or of challenging the encomienda, making Choice (D) incorrect.

4. **(B)** The statute formalized *partus sequitur ventrem*, meaning a child's legal status—enslaved or free—followed that of the mother. This law entrenched hereditary racial slavery, ensuring the perpetual reproduction of a captive labor force. Although inheritance was impacted, the law does not mention landownership, making Choice (A) incorrect. Choice (C) is incorrect because the law discouraged interracial unions through increased fines. (D) is incorrect because the statute uses language that supports slavery and defines it through maternal status.

5. **(B)** The statute explicitly imposes double fines on Christians who engage in sexual relationships with Africans. This was intended to deter interracial intimacy and reinforce racial separation within colonial society. Choice (A) is incorrect because conversion is not addressed in this law. Choice (C) is incorrect because the law targets relationships across racial lines, not within enslaved communities. The law ties status to the mother, not the father, thereby making Choice (D) incorrect.

6

The Spark of Knowing: Enlightenment and the Rise of Resistance

Key Themes

- Cultural resilience and innovation as forms of survival
- Armed and intellectual resistance fueled by global Black consciousness
- Pan-African and diasporic awareness predating modern nationalism
- The Enlightenment's contradictory role—ideals of liberty met with slavery's expansion
- Black leadership and collective organizing emerge as transformative forces

TIMELINE

Date/Period	Event/Development	Related Topics
1700s–1800s	Enslaved Africans in North America begin forming **distinct African American cultures**—language, religion, music	Topic 2.9—Creating African American Culture
Early 1700s	Emergence of **Black naming practices** and early expressions of **racial identity and pride**	Topic 2.10—Identity and Naming
1739	**Stono Rebellion** in South Carolina; one of the largest slave revolts in colonial America	Topic 2.11—Stono Rebellion
1738–1740s	**Fort Mose** established in Spanish Florida as a refuge for escaped enslaved people	Topic 2.11—Fort Mose
1791–1804	**Haitian Revolution**—led by **Toussaint Louverture**, inspires enslaved and free Black people globally	Topic 2.12—Legacies of the Haitian Revolution
Early 1800s	Fears of revolution prompt stricter laws in U.S. slave states	Topic 2.12—Reaction to the Haitian Revolution
1800–1830s	Series of revolts in the United States—**Gabriel's Rebellion (1800), German Coast (1811), Nat Turner's Rebellion (1831)**	Topic 2.13—Resistance and Revolts
1820s–1850s	**Black organizing in the North:** freedom schools, antislavery societies, women's rights groups	Topic 2.14—Organizing in the North
1830s–1860s	Figures like **Maria Stewart**, **Sojourner Truth**, **Frederick Douglass**, and **Harriet Jacobs** rise in activism	Topic 2.14—Freedom and Education

Date/Period	Event/Development	Related Topics
1700s–1800s	**Maroon communities**—autonomous societies formed by self-liberated people (e.g., in Jamaica, Brazil, Florida)	Topic 2.15—Maroon Societies
19th century	Ongoing maroon resistance in **Palmares (Brazil)** and **Quilombos** reflects diaspora-wide struggle	Topic 2.15—Autonomous Black Communities
1820s–1888	Brazil becomes last country in Western Hemisphere to abolish slavery (1888); strong Afro-Brazilian cultural ties	Topic 2.16—Diasporic Connections (Brazil)
Across 18th–19th centuries	Rise of **diasporic identity and shared resistance ideologies** among Black communities in the Americas and Caribbean	Topic 2.16—Diasporic Resistance

Topic 2.9 Creating African American Culture

Key Terms

- Cultural retention and transformation
- Creolization
- Ring shout—spiritual dance with African roots
- Call and response—African musical tradition
- Gullah Geechee—language and culture along the U.S. Southeast coast
- African spiritual practices—blended with Christianity
- African naming traditions
- Folk medicine
- Storytelling and oral tradition

Against the backdrop of bondage, surveillance, and displacement, African Americans created something extraordinary: a vibrant, enduring culture rooted in African traditions and transformed through the realities of life in the Americas. Through art, music, language, and spiritual expression, enslaved people carved out spaces for joy, resistance, memory, and identity.

The development of African American culture was not passive adaptation. It was intentional preservation and innovation. Enslaved Africans retained rhythmic structures, tonal patterns, and communal rituals passed down for generations, blending them with local influences to create distinctly African American forms of expression that would forever shape American music, language, and visual culture.

After engaging with this topic, scholars will be able to:

- Describe African American forms of self-expression in art, music, and language that combine influences from diverse African cultures with local sources.
- Describe ways enslaved African Americans adapted African musical elements from their ancestors and influenced the development of American musical genres.
- Explain the multiple functions and cultural significance of spirituals in enslaved communities.

Creating African American Culture

Culture is not merely inherited. It is forged, preserved, and adapted across time and circumstances. In the face of slavery's brutality, African Americans created a rich cultural legacy that drew upon African traditions, responded to the conditions of enslavement, and transformed the cultural landscape of the Americas.

From spirituals that encoded resistance to the rhythmic foundations of blues and gospel, from creole languages born out of necessity to pottery and quilts that preserved memory and identity, enslaved people cultivated forms of expression that were not only resilient but revolutionary. These creative forms nurtured dignity, affirmed community, and became a vital means of survival.

Cultural Fusion Through Art, Language, and Instrumentation

African American culture developed through a continuous process of blending African traditions with European and Indigenous influences, forming unique styles of art, language, and music in the Americas.

- African Americans retained aesthetic traditions from West and Central Africa in pottery, basket weaving, and quilt making. They used these practices not only for utility but also as vehicles for storytelling and cultural memory. Quilts, for example, often symbolized generational knowledge, encoded stories of escape, or marked significant family events.

A cream and red appliqued quilt, circa 1850
(Source: Collection of the Smithsonian National Museum of African American History and Culture)

- Enslaved artisans created musical instruments inspired by their heritage. These Included rattles made from gourds, African-style drums, and the banjo, whose roots trace directly to West African stringed instruments. These instruments became central to ritual, community celebration, and musical innovation.
- Enslaved Africans brought with them linguistic diversity and fluency in multiple languages from their involvement in long-distance trade. In the Americas, this linguistic adaptability resulted in the development of creole languages, such as Gullah in the Carolina low country. Gullah blended West African grammar and vocabulary with European linguistic structures, allowing enslaved communities to maintain cultural continuity even under forced separation.

This excerpt from Chapter 6 of *My Bondage and My Freedom* (1855) by Frederick Douglass offers a powerful reflection on how literacy became both a personal awakening and a profound act of resistance against the institution of slavery.

DEAR FRIEND: I have long entertained, as you very well know, a somewhat positive repugnance to writing or speaking anything for the public, which could, with any degree of plausibilty, make me liable to the imputation of seeking personal notoriety, for its own sake. Entertaining that feeling very sincerely, and permitting its control, perhaps, quite unreasonably, I have often refused to narrate my personal experience in public anti-slavery meetings, and in sympathizing circles, when urged to do so by friends, with whose views and wishes, ordinarily, it were a pleasure to comply. In my letters and speeches, I have generally aimed to discuss the question of Slavery in the light of fundamental principles, and upon facts, notorious and open to all; making, I trust, no more of the fact of my own former enslavement, than circumstances seemed absolutely to require. I have never placed my opposition to slavery on a basis so narrow as my own enslavement, but rather upon the indestructible and unchangeable laws of human nature, every one of which is perpetually and flagrantly violated by the slave system. I have also felt that it was best for those having histories worth the writing—or supposed to be so—to commit such work to hands other than their own. To write of one's self, in such a manner as not to incur the imputation of weakness, vanity, and egotism, is a work within the ability of but few; and I have little reason to believe that I belong to that fortunate few.

These considerations caused me to hesitate, when first you kindly urged me to prepare for publication a full account of my life as a slave, and my life as a freeman.

Nevertheless, I see, with you, many reasons for regarding my autobiography as exceptional in its character, and as being, in some sense, naturally beyond the reach of those reproaches which honorable and sensitive minds dislike to incur. It is not to illustrate any heroic achievements of a man, but to vindicate a just and beneficent principle, in its application to the whole human family, by letting in the light of truth upon a system, esteemed by some as a blessing, and by others as a curse and a crime. I agree with you, that this system is now at the bar of public opinion—not only of this country, but of the whole civilized world—for judgment. Its friends have made for it the usual plea—"not guilty;" the case must, therefore, proceed. Any facts, either from slaves, slaveholders, or by-standers, calculated to enlighten the public mind, by revealing the true nature, character, and tendency of the slave system, are in order, and can scarcely be innocently withheld.

I see, too, that there are special reasons why I should write my own biography, in preference to employing another to do it. Not only is slavery on trial, but unfortunately, the enslaved people are also on trial. It is alleged, that they are, naturally, inferior; that they are so low in the scale of humanity, and so utterly stupid, that they are unconscious of their wrongs, and do not apprehend their rights. Looking, then, at your request, from this stand-point, and wishing everything of which you think me capable to go to the benefit of my afflicted people, I part with my doubts and hesitation, and proceed to furnish you the desired manuscript; hoping that you may be able to make such arrangements for its publication as shall be best adapted to accomplish that good which you so enthusiastically anticipate.

FREDERICK DOUGLASS

Source: Frederick Douglass, *My Bondage and My Freedom* (New York and Auburn: Miller, Orton & Mulligan, 1855), 90–106.

The *Storage Jar* by David Drake, created in 1858, stands as a rare and extraordinary example of artistic expression by an enslaved African American potter in the antebellum South. Drake, also known as Dave the Potter, inscribed his name and original poetry onto his ceramic vessels—an audacious act of literacy, identity, and resistance in a time when enslaved people were legally forbidden to read or write. His work embodies the enduring power of craftsmanship as a form of cultural memory, defiance, and self-assertion.

Storage Jar by David Drake, 1858 (Source: Purchase, Ronald S. Kane Bequest, in memory of Berry B. Tracy, 2020)

Music was one of the most powerful ways African Americans retained ancestral identity while creating something entirely new. Enslaved people adapted Christian hymns taught by missionaries but infused them with distinctly African musical elements: call and response, rhythmic clapping, improvisation, and syncopation.

- These spiritual songs became acts of survival, embedding hope, protest, and communal strength into every note.
- The musical innovations of enslaved people laid the foundation for future American genres, including gospel, blues, jazz, and hip-hop.
- The influence of Senegambian and West Central African musical systems, particularly in regions like Louisiana, can be heard in the development of the blues, which echoes the *fodet* tradition of West Africa in both scale and structure.

The Function and Power of Spirituals

Spirituals—also called sorrow songs or jubilee songs—were more than devotional music. They were multidimensional expressions of faith, pain, and strategy.

- Through spirituals, enslaved African Americans found ways to articulate suffering, express hope, and sustain their humanity in the face of dehumanization.
- Many spirituals functioned as coded resistance, providing enslaved communities with ways to communicate escape routes, issue warnings, or affirm their belief in freedom and divine justice.

Spirituals were profound cultural expressions that carried far more than melody. They embodied the soul of a people, combining theology, resistance, and encoded communication in a way that only the enslaved could fully decipher.

The lyrics of many spirituals held double meanings. On the surface, they expressed Christian faith and longing for redemption, drawing on biblical stories such as Moses and the Exodus, Daniel in the lions' den, or Jesus as deliverer.

Beneath the surface, however, they functioned as covert messages, alerting enslaved communities to escape routes, safe houses, and opportunities to flee via the Underground Railroad.

- Songs like "Swing Low, Sweet Chariot" or "Go Down, Moses" were not only calls to divine liberation—they were maps for survival.
- Spirituals employed African oral traditions, emphasizing call and response, improvisation, and communal performance. These elements were not simply aesthetic—they were vital tools for preserving memory, building unity, and defying silence.

Songs like "Steal Away to Jesus" conveyed both theology and tactics, using metaphor and biblical allusion as shields for liberation plans. In every refrain, African Americans declared their presence, their intelligence, and their refusal to be erased.

Steal Away to Jesus

Steal away, steal away,
steal away to Jesus!
Steal away, steal away home,
I ain't got long to stay here.

My Lord, He calls me,
He calls me by the thunder;
The trumpet sounds within my soul;
I ain't got long to stay here. [Refrain]

Green trees are bending,
Poor sinners stand a trembling;
The trumpet sounds within my soul;
I ain't got long to stay here. [Refrain]

My Lord, He calls me,
He calls me by the lightning;
The trumpet sounds within my soul;
I ain't got long to stay here.

Source: "Steal Away to Jesus," in *Jubilee Songs: Complete. As Sung by the Jubilee Singers of Fisk University, Under the Auspices of the American Missionary Association* (New York: Bigelow & Main, 1872), University of Wisconsin–Madison Libraries.

In this way, spirituals represent a fusion of African heritage and American experience. They preserved the rhythmic patterns and performance styles of West Africa while expressing the realities of bondage and the aspirations for freedom in America. As cultural artifacts, spirituals are more than songs. They are historical testimony, spiritual lifelines, and strategic instruments of resistance.

TIP

Look for Signal Words in MCQs

Phrases like *most likely, best explains,* or *primary cause* indicate what the question is asking. Make sure you understand what is being asked to ensure you choose the right answer choice

Culture That Can't Be Taken

Even while enslaved, African Americans made something new, blending African traditions with new realities. Music, language, religion, and community were reimagined in ways that gave people strength and identity. Culture wasn't just a comfort—it was a form of resistance.

You're Practicing: Understanding how communities survive by creating.

Connect This To: Resilience, memory, and creativity.

Theme: Cultural Expression and Resistance

Practice: Cultural Source Analysis and Thematic Reasoning

In this topic, the text discusses how African Americans formed a distinct culture through food, religion, language, family, music, and storytelling, often drawing on African traditions adapted under enslavement.

(A) Identify one specific example from the text of how African Americans created a new cultural tradition from African and American influences.

(B) Explain how that tradition helped maintain community and identity under conditions of enslavement.

(C) Using your broader knowledge, discuss how this cultural formation contributed to later African American resistance, identity, or artistic expression.

SAMPLE RESPONSES

(A) African Americans blended African rhythms and call-and-response patterns with Christian hymns to create spirituals, which became a distinct musical tradition.

Enslaved Africans also developed ring shout dances, combining African spiritual movements with Christian religious practices.

(B) Spirituals and ring shouts provided a means of spiritual resistance and emotional survival, fostering a shared sense of hope and solidarity among enslaved people.

These traditions allowed enslaved Africans to retain cultural connections to their African heritage while creating a collective identity rooted in faith and resilience.

(C) The spirituals laid the foundation for later African American musical forms such as gospel, blues, jazz, and hip-hop, which became both cultural expressions and vehicles for political resistance.

During the Civil Rights Movement, songs derived from spirituals (e.g., "We Shall Overcome") served as rallying cries for freedom and equality.

These traditions also shaped Harlem Renaissance artists, who celebrated African heritage and used music, poetry, and visual arts to challenge racial stereotypes and assert Black pride.

Skills Assessed: Connect historical content to African American experiences; support a claim using textual and cultural evidence; explain how cultural developments reflect broader historical significance.

Topic 2.10 Black Pride, Identity, and the Question of Naming

Key Terms

- Self-identification—African, Negro, Black, African American
- Cultural nationalism
- Naming as resistance
- James Forten, Frederick Douglass—thinkers on Black identity
- Naming conventions—renaming after freedom
- African cultural memory
- Pan-African consciousness
- Ethnic vs. racial identity

The power to name oneself is the power to define one's place in the world. Throughout American history, African Americans have used language not only to resist externally imposed labels but to assert their dignity, humanity, and evolving cultural identity. As the demographics of the Black population changed and communities expanded across geography and generation, so too did the terms used to express identity. Each of these terms carried deep political, social, and emotional meaning.

From *African* to *Negro*, from *Colored* to *Black* and *African American*, these naming practices were never static. They reflected ongoing debates about ancestry, belonging, nationalism, and pride. They continue to shape how people of African descent see themselves and are seen by others.

After engaging with this topic, scholars will be able to:

- Explain how changing demographics and popular debates about African Americans' identity influenced the terms they used to identify themselves in the nineteenth century and beyond.

Names, Identity, and the Assertion of Black Pride

The words a people use to name themselves are never just labels—they are declarations of identity, belonging, and pride. For African Americans, the question of naming has always carried deep historical weight, shaped by forced displacement, survival, and the pursuit of freedom. As the African American population shifted across generations, so too did the language used to define who they were and where they stood within American society.

In the early nineteenth century, changes in migration, memory, and movement reshaped how Black people described themselves. With the United States' official ban on the transatlantic slave trade in 1808, the number of African-born individuals in the enslaved population declined significantly even as illegal smuggling persisted. This demographic shift gave rise to a growing population of African Americans born on U.S. soil, many of whom began to reconsider what it meant to be "African" in an American context.

Rejecting the Term *African* and Asserting American Identity

During this same period, the emergence of the **American Colonization Society (ACS)** reflected a broader racial tension within the country. White leaders who founded the ACS in 1816 proposed a plan to deport free Black Americans to Africa, viewing them as outsiders in the nation they helped build. In response, many Black leaders and communities rejected the term *African*, distancing themselves from the narrative that they were not truly American.

By the late 1820s, the term *African* began to decline in favor as a primary racial identifier, especially among free Black populations. For many, embracing an American identity—even as second-class citizens—was an assertion of both birthright and belonging. It was a rejection of exile and an affirmation of their stake in the nation's future.

The Politics and Power of Self-Naming

As the struggle for freedom and citizenship continued throughout the nineteenth and twentieth centuries, African Americans adopted a **range of ethnonyms** to reflect evolving political identities, cultural pride, and social movements. These included terms such as:

- **Negro**—once widely used but later critiqued for its associations with slavery and subservience
- **Afro-American**—a term that reclaimed African heritage and stressed diasporic unity
- **Black**—boldly redefined during the Black Power movement as a symbol of pride, solidarity, and resistance
- **African American**—popularized in the late twentieth century to center both ancestry and national identity

Each of these terms has reflected different moments in the African American journey—moments of cultural resistance, political awakening, and strategic redefinition.

Powerful letters were originally published between 1831 and 1841 in prominent Black and abolitionist newspapers like *Freedom's Journal*, *The Liberator*, and *The Colored American*. These letters reflect the voices of African Americans who boldly challenged racism, inequality, and calls for emigration. Collected in *Call and Response*, the excerpts from these letters that are reproduced below capture the urgency, intellect, and resilience of Black writers who demanded justice and full belonging in American society. Their words offer a firsthand glimpse into the political and moral debates shaping early Black activism.

A QUESTION.

Sir—I write at the request of a friend, to ask this question:—Why do our friends, as well as our enemies, call us "negroes?" We feel it to be a term of reproach, and could wish our friends would call us by some other name. If you, Sir, or one of your correspondents, would condescend to answer this question, we would esteem it a favor.

I was much pleased with your remarks on the absurd practice of placing the people of color behind all others, in our houses of worship. I, Sir, would have gladly sat among the humblest of my despised race; but have been obliged, for conscience' sake, to sit with white Christians; and often as I have met the look of scorn, and heard the whispered remark of "This bench is for the black people,"—"This bench is for the people of color," has the tear gathered in my eye, and the prayer ascended from my heart to God, that he would in his own time take away our reproach; and oh! most firmly do I believe he will. This belief alone is sufficient to keep me in the path of duty.

Allow me, Sir, to return you my thanks and the thanks of my friends, for your unwearied and noble efforts in our cause. May Heaven's best blessings rest on you, and on all connected with you, for your sake. Words are too poor to express my emotions of gratitude towards the authoress of the lines, entitled "The Black at Church," for expressing in such beautiful language, the sentiments of my heart.—May the Almighty bless her—

And in her last, extremest need,
When soul and body sever,
For this one act may all her sins
Be blotted out forever.

ELLA.

Philadelphia, May 25, 1831.

Source: Ella, "A Question," *The Liberator*, June 4, 1831, p. 2, Boston Public Library Rare Books Department/Digital Commonwealth.

CHANGE OF APPELLATION.

To the Editor of the Liberator.

Dear Sir—I observe in one of your late papers, the complaint of a correspondent, that the term "negro" should be applied to the colored citizens by those who are friendly to them; not aware that from the use that has been made of that term, it is understood among those, to whom it is applied, as an insulting and offensive appellation. The term "colored" is not a good one. There are several objections to it. The most important is, that whenever used, it recals to mind the offensive distinction of color, a distinction which the philanthropist is endeavoring to do away, and should not therefore remind the two parties of, (both white and black,) whenever he has occasion to name the latter. The name of "African" is more objectionable yet, and is no more correct than that of Englishman would be to a native born citizen of the United States. The colored citizen of America is an American of African descent. Cannot a name be found that will express these two facts? I suggest one; and I beg you and your readers to reflect on it, before you reject it as unsuitable or of little importance; and if you approve of it, to do your best to introduce it to general adoption. It is "Afric-American," or, written in one word, "Africamerican." I think much may be said in favor of this term. One of its recommendations is, that it asserts that most important truth, that the colored citizen is as truly a citizen of the United States of America as the white. I suggest to the editor of the proposed new philanthropic newspaper in Philadelphia, to exchange the intended title of his sheet from American to Africamerican. A SUBSCRIBER.

Source: A Subscriber, "Change of Appellation," *The Liberator*, July 16, 1831, pp. 2–3, Boston Public Library Rare Books Department/Digital Commonwealth (public domain).

The suggestion of "A Subscriber" is worthy of some consideration, For our own part, we are pleased with it; but, ere we adopt it, we should like to hear from our readers—especially our colored readers, (for we must use this term at present,) on the subject. It is to be regretted that necessity demands a distinctive appellation, by which to designate a portion of our fellow-countrymen; but as this is the case, we think the least objectionable one would be, "Afric-Americans," or "Africo-Americans," written as a compound and not as one word. The terms "negroes," "blacks," and "people of color," ought, if possible, to be repudiated.

Source: Untitled response to "A Subscriber," *The Liberator*, July 16, 1831, p. 3, Boston Public Library Rare Books Department/Digital Commonwealth.

AFRIC-AMERICAN.

Mr Editor—Your correspondent, "A Subscriber," has suggested the appropriateness of the term Afric-American, in lieu of the many common names which are made use of, to distinguish us from other American born citizens. It appears to me, that the suggestion is as absurd as the sound of the name is inharmonious. It is true, that we should have, and the time demands, a distinct appellation for us—we being the only class of people in America, who feel all the accumulated injury which pride and prejudice can suggest; but, sir, since we have been so long distinguished by the title, men of color, why make this change, so uncouth and jargon-like? A change we do want, and a change we will have; and when it comes, we shall be called, in common with others, citizens of the United States and Americans. I think we should no sooner subscribe to the term Afric-American, than the descendants of any part of the world, (natives of the United States,) would suffer the name of the country of their forefathers to be linked to the title of their native country.

With much respect,

A Subscriber and Citizen of the United States.

Philadelphia, Sept. 1, 1831.

Source: A Subscriber and Citizen of the United States, "Afric-American," *The Liberator*, September 24, 1831, p. 1, Boston Public Library Rare Books Department/Digital Commonwealth.

A Resolution Rejecting the Use of the Terms *Colored* and *Africans* at the Fifth Annual Convention for the Improvement of the Free People of Colour (1835) offers a vivid account of how free African Americans in the antebellum North actively shaped their political and cultural identities. Held in Philadelphia, the 1835 convention reflects growing resistance to externally imposed labels and a call for unity, dignity, and self-definition. By rejecting terms like *Colored* and *Africans*, delegates demonstrated a sophisticated awareness of language as a tool of both empowerment and marginalization—laying early groundwork for the enduring struggle over naming, belonging, and Black political identity in America.

> On motion of W. Whipper, seconded by R. Purvis,
>
> Resolved, That we recommend as far as possible, to our people to abandon the use of the word "colored," when either speaking or writing concerning themselves; and especially to remove the title of African from their institutions, the marbles of churches &c.
>
> Which motion was under consideration when the Convention adjourned. . . .
>
> William Whipper's resolution in relation to us, using the words "colored" and "Africans," was called up, and after an animated and interesting discussion, it was unanimously adopted.
>
> Source: Minutes of the Fifth Annual Convention for the Improvement of the Free People of Colour in the United States (William P. Gibbons: Philadelphia, 1835), pp. 14–15 (public domain).

What's in a Name? Everything.

Names can be a form of power or a tool of erasure. Enslavers often renamed people to control them. However, African Americans resisted by choosing new names or nicknames or by reclaiming their African heritage. Naming is about more than identity—it's about freedom.

You're Practicing: Recognizing the deeper meaning in everyday choices.

Connect This To: Naming, pride, and language as resistance.

Theme: Identity and Culture

Practice: Significance and Cultural Analysis

Using examples from the reading, develop an argument for how naming practices and self-presentation were acts of resistance and identity formation for African Americans during slavery. In your response, do the following.

(A) Reference at least two examples from the text (e.g., naming children, adopting honorifics, dress).

(B) Explain the relationship between identity formation and cultural pride.

(C) Connect your analysis to broader patterns in African American history where naming or image were used to assert autonomy.

SAMPLE RESPONSES

(A) Enslaved African Americans often named their children after African ancestors or leaders to preserve cultural memory and assert a connection to their heritage despite the attempts of enslavers to erase their identity.

Clothing and self-styling on Sundays or special occasions were also subtle acts of defiance, allowing enslaved people to present themselves with dignity and challenge stereotypes of inferiority.

(B) By preserving African-derived names and customs, enslaved people constructed a collective identity rooted in cultural pride, rejecting the imposed narrative that they were merely property.

Identity formation through naming, music, and dress affirmed a sense of humanity, resilience, and belonging, reinforcing solidarity within the enslaved community and maintaining spiritual resistance against the institution of slavery.

(C) After emancipation, African Americans often changed their surnames to break ties with former enslavers and assert independence, mirroring the cultural defiance seen during slavery.

During the Harlem Renaissance, artists and writers embraced African-inspired aesthetics and celebrated Black identity through self-presentation and creative works.

In the Black Power era, slogans like "Black is Beautiful" and the adoption of Afrocentric names and styles (e.g., "Kwame," "Malik," or natural hair) reflected a continuing tradition of using names and images to challenge systemic racism and affirm cultural pride.

Skills Assessed: Develop a defensible claim; use historical and cultural evidence; connect course content to African American experience and continuity; explain the historical and cultural significance.

Topic 2.11 The Stono Rebellion and Fort Mose

Key Terms

- Stono Rebellion (1739)—South Carolina slave revolt
- Fort Mose—first free Black settlement in what is now the United States
- Spanish Florida—offered asylum for escaped enslaved people
- Catholic conversion and military service
- Rebellion suppression and slave codes
- Gracia Real de Santa Teresa de Mose—full name of Fort Mose
- Francisco Menendez—leader of Fort Mose militia

Throughout the seventeenth and eighteenth centuries, the fight for freedom in the Americas was not just waged on battlefields or in courtrooms. Instead, it unfolded through uprisings, alliances, and escapes that redefined the political geography of slavery. For many enslaved Africans in British North America, **Spanish Florida** represented hope, resistance, and the possibility of sanctuary.

This topic explores how the Spanish Crown's offer of asylum to fugitive slaves in exchange for conversion to Catholicism challenged British colonial authority and sparked one of the most significant slave uprisings in early American history: the **Stono Rebellion of 1739**. In its wake, the establishment of **Fort Mose**, the first free Black settlement legally sanctioned in what is now the United States, offered both refuge and resistance.

After engaging with this topic, scholars will be able to:

- Explain key effects of the asylum offered by Spanish Florida in the seventeenth and eighteenth centuries.

Revolt and Refuge: The Stono Rebellion and Fort Mose

In the colonial Americas, geography shaped the contours of resistance. While British colonies sought to expand slavery through brutal codes and legal restrictions, Spanish Florida emerged as a beacon of hope—a rare refuge where enslaved Africans could gain their freedom in exchange for religious conversion. This political and religious offer not only disrupted colonial hierarchies but also catalyzed one of the most consequential acts of collective resistance in early American history: the Stono Rebellion of 1739.

At the heart of this topic is the story of how flight, faith, and freedom converged in the formation of Fort Mose, the first legally sanctioned free Black town in what is now the United States. The settlement was more than a safe haven—it was a symbol of autonomy, defiance, and Black leadership under siege.

Asylum in Spanish Florida and the Birth of Fort Mose

Founded in **1565**, the city of **St. Augustine** stands as the oldest continuously occupied settlement of European and African origin in the United States. Beginning in the seventeenth century, enslaved Africans who escaped plantations in the Carolinas and Georgia fled southward to Spanish Florida, where the Spanish Crown offered a unique form of emancipation: freedom in exchange for conversion to Catholicism.

This policy led to the creation of **Fort Mose (Gracia Real de Santa Teresa de Mose)** in **1738** under the leadership of **Francisco Menéndez**, an enslaved Senegambian who had previously fought against the British during the Yamasee War. Fort Mose became a military outpost and community of free Black men and women—many of whom had risked everything to escape bondage. As such, Fort Mose stands as the first free Black town formally recognized by a European colonial power in North America.

This excerpt from *An Account of the Stono Rebellion* (1739) offers a firsthand colonial perspective on one of the largest and most organized slave uprisings in British North America. It captures the fear and urgency felt by white settlers in South Carolina as nearly 100 enslaved Africans, many from the Kingdom of Kongo, rose up in pursuit of freedom and marched toward Spanish Florida.

> Sometime since there was a Proclamation published at Augustine, in which the King of Spain (then at Peace with Great Britain) promised Protection and Freedom to all Negroes Slaves that would resort thither. Certain Negroes belonging to Captain Davis escaped to Augustine, and were received there. They were demanded by General Oglethorpe who sent Lieutenant Demere to Augustine, and the Governour assured the General of his sincere Friendship, but at the same time showed his Orders from the Court of Spain, by which he was to receive all Run away Negroes. Of this other Negroes having notice, as it is believed, from the Spanish Emissaries, four or five who were Cattel-Hunters, and knew the Woods, some of whom belonged to Captain Macpherson, ran away with His Horses, wounded his Son and killed another Man. These marched f [sic] for Georgia, and were pursued, but the Rangers being then newly reduced [sic] the Countrey people could not overtake them, though they were discovered by the Saltzburghers, as they passed by Ebenezer. They reached Augustine, one only being killed and another wounded by the Indians in their flight. They were received there with great honours, one of them had a Commission given to him, and a Coat faced with Velvet. Amongst the Negroe Slaves there are a people brought from the Kingdom of Angola in Africa, many of these speak Portugueze [which Language is as near Spanish as Scotch is to English,] by reason that the Portugueze have considerable Settlement, and the Jesuits have a Mission and School in that Kingdom and many Thousands of the Negroes there profess the Roman Catholic Religion. Several Spaniards upon diverse Pretences have for some time past been strolling about Carolina, two of them, who will give no account of themselves have been taken up and committed to Jayl in Georgia. The good reception of the Negroes at Augustine was spread about, Several attempted to escape to the Spaniards, & were taken, one of them was hanged at Charles Town. In the latter end of July last Don Pedro, Colonel of the Spanish Horse, went in a Launch to Charles Town under pretence of a message to General Oglethorpe and the Lieutenant Governour". On the 9th day of September last being Sunday which is the day the Planters allow them to work for themselves. Some Angola Negroes assembled, to the number of Twenty; and one who was called Jemmy was their Captain, they surprised a Warehouse belonging to Mr. Hutchenson at a place called Stonehow [Stono]; they there killed Mr. Robert Bathurst, and Mr. Gibbs, plundered the House and took a pretty many small Arms and Powder, which were there for Sale. Next they plundered and burnt Mr. Godfrey's house, and killed him, his Daughter and Son. They then turned back and marched Southward along Pons Pons, which is the Road through Georgia to Augustine, they passed Mr. Wallace's Tavern towards day break, and said they would not hurt him, for he was a good Man and kind to his Slaves, but they broke open and plundered Mr. Lemy's House, and killed him, his Wife and Child. They marched on towards Mr. Rose's resolving to kill him, but he was saved by a Negroe, who having hid him went out and pacified the others. Several Negroes joyned them, they calling out Liberty, marched on with Colours

displayed, and two Drums beating, pursuing all the white people they met with, and killing Man Woman and Child when they could come up to them. Colonel Bull Lieutenant Governour of South Carolina, who was then riding along the Road, discovered them, was pursued, and with much difficulty escaped & raised the Country. They burnt Colonel Hext's house and killed his Overseer and his Wife, They then burnt Mr. Sprye's house, then Mr. Sacheverell's, and then Mr. Nash's house, all lying upon the Pons Pons Road, and killed all the white People they found in them. Mr. Bullock got off, but they burnt his House, by this time many of them were drunk with the Rum they had taken in the Houses. They increased every minute by new Negroes coming to them, so that they were above Sixty, some say a hundred, on which they halted in a field, and set to dancing, Singing and beating Drums, to draw more Negroes to them, thinking they were now victorious over the whole Province, having marched ten miles & burnt all before them without Opposition, but the Militia being raised, the Planters with great briskness pursued them and when they came up, dismounting, charged them on foot. The Negroes were soon routed, though they behaved boldly, several being killed on the Spot, many ran back to their Plantations thinking they had not been missed, but they were there taken and Shot, Such as were taken in the field also, were taken in the field also, were after being examined, shot on the Spot, and this is to be said to the honour of the Carolina Planters, that not withstanding the Provocation they had received from so many Murders, they did not torture one Negroe, but only put them to an easy death. All that proved to be forced & were not concerned in the Murders & Burnings were pardoned. And this sudden Courage in the field, & the Humanity afterwards hath had so good an Effect that there hath been no farther Attempt, and the very Spirit of Revolt seems over. About 30 escaped from the fight, of which ten marched about 30 miles Southward, and being overtaken by the Planters on horseback, fought stoutly for some time and were all killed on the Spot, The rest are yet untaken, In the whole action about 40 Negroes and 20 whites were killed. The Lieutenant Governour sent an account of this to General Oglethorpe, who met the advices on his return from the Indian Nation. He immediately ordered a Troop of Rangers to be ranged, to patrole through Georgia, placed some Men in the Garrison at Palichocolas, which was before abandoned, and near which the Negroes formerly passed, being the only place where Horses can come to swim over the River Savannah for near 100 miles, ordered out the Indians in pursuit, and a Detachment of the Garrison at Port Royal to assist the Planters on any Occasion, and published a Proclamation ordering all the Constables &c. of Georgia to pursue and seize all Negroes, with a Reward for any that should be taken. It is hoped these measures will prevent any Negroes from getting down to the Spaniards.

Source: James Oglethorpe, "An Account of the Negroe Insurrection in South Carolina," TNA, CO 5/640, fols. 392–96, National Archives, Kew, UK.

This October 1739 letter from Governor William Bull provides a firsthand colonial account of the Stono Rebellion, one of the largest uprisings of enslaved Africans in British North America. Governor Bull details the rebels' march toward Spanish Florida, the violent encounters that followed, and the colony's swift retaliation. The letter also reflects British anxieties about future resistance and outlines efforts to enlist native nations to prevent further escapes.

My Lords,

I beg leave to lay before your Lordships an account of our Affairs, first in regard to the Desertion of our Negroes.... On the 9th of September last at Night a great Number of Negroes Arose in Rebellion, broke open a Store where they got arms, killed twenty one White Persons, and were marching the next morning in a Daring manner out of the Province, killing all they met and burning several Houses as they passed along the Road. I was returning from Granville County with four Gentlemen and met these Rebels at eleven o'clock in the forenoon and fortunately deserned the approaching danger time enough to avoid it, and to give notice to the Militia who on the Occasion behaved with so much expedition and bravery, as by four a'Clock the same day to come up with them and killed and took so many as put a stop to any further mischief at that time, forty four of them have been killed and Executed; some few yet remain concealed in the Woods expecting the same fate, seem desperate....

It was the Opinion of His Majesty's Council with several other Gentlemen that one of the most effectual means that could be used at present to prevent such desertion of our Negroes is to encourage some Indians by a suitable reward to pursue and if possible to bring back the Deserters, and while the Indians are thus employed they would be in the way ready to intercept others that might attempt to follow and I have sent for the Chiefs of the Chickasaws living at New Windsor and the Catawbaw Indians for that purpose....

My Lords,

Your Lordships Most Obedient and Most Humble Servant

Wm Bull

Source: Don Manuel de Montiano, Official Letters from Don Manuel de Montiano, Governor of East Florida, to Don Juan Francisco de Guemes y Horcasitas, Captain-General of the Island of Cuba, 1737 Sept. 30 to 1741 Jan. 2, trans. 1846 from the original in the City Archives of St. Augustine, Florida, p. 28, Digital Library of Georgia.

Colonial Backlash and the Destruction of Fort Mose

In response to the Stono Rebellion, South Carolina's colonial government passed the **1740 Slave Code**. This sweeping set of legal restrictions prohibited enslaved Africans from gathering, reading, drumming, and traveling without permission. The code criminalized self-defense by enslaved people and sharply curtailed any remaining avenues to freedom.

That same year, British colonial forces invaded Spanish Florida and destroyed Fort Mose, seeing it as a direct threat to British colonial order. Although the settlement was later rebuilt, its destruction symbolized the ongoing tension between Black freedom and colonial expansion. Fort Mose's brief existence nevertheless left a powerful legacy as a site of refuge, Black autonomy, and resistance to slavery long before emancipation.

The First Sparks of Rebellion

In 1739, enslaved Africans in South Carolina rebelled and marched toward freedom in Spanish Florida. This wasn't just an isolated event, it was part of a broader pattern of resistance. Rebellions like Stono helped shape policies and fears across colonial America.

You're Practicing: Connecting small events to big systems.

Connect This To: Armed resistance and early freedom movements.

Theme: Resistance and Autonomy

Practice: Causation and Contextualization

This topic explores the Stono Rebellion and Fort Mose as early examples of African resistance and community formation in colonial America. Respond to the following.

(A) Identify one factor that motivated the Stono rebels to seek freedom in Spanish Florida.

(B) Explain how geographic or political conditions in Florida (e.g., Spanish sanctuary policy) helped shape Fort Mose as a site of Black autonomy.

(C) Using your broader knowledge, discuss how these events challenge typical narratives of colonial America that focus solely on British rule and enslaved passivity.

SAMPLE RESPONSES

(A) The Spanish Crown's sanctuary policy, which promised freedom to enslaved Africans who escaped British colonies and converted to Catholicism, motivated the Stono rebels to flee South Carolina.

News of earlier fugitives finding refuge and freedom at Fort Mose, the first free Black settlement in Spanish Florida, inspired enslaved Africans to resist British enslavement.

(B) Florida's position as a Spanish-controlled territory allowed the Crown to offer legal freedom and land grants to formerly enslaved Africans, creating a community where Black residents could govern themselves under Spanish protection.

The fort's strategic military role—defending Spanish Florida from British incursions—meant that Black men at Fort Mose were not only free but also recognized as soldiers and defenders of their community.

(C) The Stono Rebellion and the existence of Fort Mose highlight that enslaved Africans were active agents of resistance rather than passive victims, using both armed rebellion and strategic alliances to pursue freedom.

These events broaden the narrative of colonial America by showcasing Spanish colonies as alternative sites of freedom, where Black communities could secure autonomy and resist British dominance.

Skills Assessed: Describe the historical context (colonial laws, Spanish vs. British rule); use reasoning to explain cause and consequence; connect developments to African American traditions of resistance and autonomy; analyze how the audience and purpose shaped Spanish and British policy toward enslaved people.

Topic 2.12 Legacies of the Haitian Revolution

Key Terms

- Haitian Revolution (1791–1804)
- Toussaint Louverture—revolutionary leader
- Jean-Jacques Dessalines
- Saint-Domingue—former French colony
- Only successful enslaved-led revolution
- Influence on Black Americans—inspiration and fear
- Haitian immigration to United States
- Impact on U.S. slavery laws
- Louisiana Purchase—geopolitical result of Haitian independence

The Haitian Revolution (1791–1804) was nothing short of world-shaking. Led by enslaved Africans and maroons who rose against French colonial rule, it became the first successful revolt to establish an independent Black republic and abolish slavery. Its impact reverberated far beyond the shores of Saint-Domingue, inspiring freedom movements, striking fear into slaveholding societies, and reshaping Black political consciousness throughout the African diaspora.

This topic explores the revolution's global significance, the central role played by maroon communities, and the way its example fueled both resistance and radical thought in African American communities and across the Atlantic world.

After engaging with this topic, scholars will be able to:

- Explain the global impacts of the Haitian Revolution.
- Describe the role of maroons in the Haitian Revolution.
- Explain the impacts of the Haitian Revolution on African diasporic communities and Black political thought.

Legacies of the Haitian Revolution

The Haitian Revolution was a defining moment in global history. From 1791 to 1804, enslaved Africans and maroons on the island of **Saint-Domingue** overturned the most profitable slave-based colonial economy in the world and established **Haiti**, the first independent Black republic and the second free nation in the Western Hemisphere. This uprising not only dismantled the institution of slavery in one of France's wealthiest colonies but also sent shockwaves across the Atlantic world, altering the course of politics, trade, and Black liberation.

The Global Impact of a Black Republic

The Haitian Revolution was the only successful slave revolt in world history to result in the permanent abolition of slavery and colonial rule. This victory deeply disrupted European imperialism and challenged global systems of racial hierarchy and forced labor.

- France, reeling from the loss, was forced to sell the **Louisiana Territory** to the United States in 1803. While this nearly doubled U.S. territory, it also expanded the geographic reach of slavery as the new land was rapidly developed into a slave-based economy.
- The revolution triggered France's temporary abolition of slavery across its empire from 1794 to 1802, affecting colonies such as Guadeloupe and Martinique.
- With the destruction of Saint-Domingue's plantation economy, the global sugar market shifted. Cuba, Brazil, and the United States filled the economic vacuum, leading to an increase in enslaved labor elsewhere.
- Haiti's independence created **a migration wave**—both white planters and formerly enslaved Haitians fled to U.S. cities like Baltimore, New York, and Philadelphia, heightening white anxiety about potential revolts and helping spur the passage of restrictive policies like the **Alien and Sedition Acts (1798)**.
- Despite its revolutionary success, Haiti's future was shaped by economic coercion. In order to gain diplomatic recognition from France, Haiti was forced to pay reparations for lost "property"—including formerly enslaved people—for over a century, which crippled the new nation's development.

The Role of Maroons in Haitian Liberation

At the heart of the Haitian Revolution were **maroons**—Afro-descendants who had escaped slavery and formed independent communities in the mountainous interior of the island. These communities were not only self-sustaining; they were strategic strongholds of resistance.

- Maroons played a pivotal role in the revolution by sharing intelligence, forging alliances across plantations, and launching coordinated attacks against French forces.
- Many of the revolution's most effective fighters were former soldiers from the Kingdom of Kongo, enslaved during internal African conflicts and transported to Haiti. Their military training, combined with their knowledge of terrain and tactics, helped shape the revolution's effectiveness and endurance.

The Preliminary Declaration from the Constitution of Haiti (1805) boldly asserts Haiti's sovereignty, racial equality, and independence from colonial rule in the wake of the Haitian Revolution. Drafted under Emperor Jean-Jacques Dessalines, the declaration redefined Black citizenship, rejecting slavery in all forms and proclaiming freedom as a permanent, irrevocable condition for all Haitians. It stands as a radical vision of liberty, dignity, and Black nationhood in the early nineteenth century.

> Preliminary Declaration.
>
> Art. 1. The people inhabiting the island formerly called St. Domingo, hereby agree to form themselves into a free state sovereign and independent of any other power in the universe, under the name of empire of Hayti.

2. Slavery is forever abolished.

3. The Citizens of Hayti are brothers at home; equality in the eyes of the law is incontestably acknowledged, and there cannot exist any titles, advantages, or privileges, other than those necessarily resulting from the consideration and reward of services rendered to liberty and independence.

4. The law is the same to all, whether it punishes, or whether it protects.

5. The law has no retroactive effect.

6. Property is sacred, its violation shall be severely prosecuted.

7. The quality of citizen of Hayti is lost by emigration and naturalization in foreign countries and condemnation to corporal or disgrace punishments. The fist case carries with it the punishment of death and confiscation of property.

8. The quality of Citizen is suspended in consequence of bankruptcies and failures.

9. No person is worth of being a Haitian who is not a good father, good son, a good husband, and especially a good soldier.

10. Fathers and mothers are not permitted to disinherit their children.

11. Every Citizen must possess a mechanic art.

12. No whiteman of whatever nation he may be, shall put his foot on this territory with the title of master or proprietor, neither shall he in future acquire any property therein.

13. The preceding article cannot in the smallest degree affect white woman who have been naturalized Haytians by Government, nor does it extend to children already born, or that may be born of the said women. The Germans and Polanders naturalized by government are also comprized [sic] in the dispositions of the present article.

14. All acception (sic) of colour among the children of one and the same family, of whom the chief magistrate is the father, being necessarily to cease, the Haytians shall hence forward be known only by the generic appellation of Blacks.

Source: Haitian Constitution of 1805, as translated in *New-York Evening Post*, July 15, 1805, NYS Historic Newspapers.

In his 1893 lecture at the Chicago World's Fair, Frederick Douglass delivered a powerful tribute to Haiti's revolutionary legacy, challenging the racist erasure of the first Black republic from global narratives of freedom. Speaking as the former United States Minister to the Republic of Haiti, Douglass honored the Haitian people's courage in overthrowing slavery and colonialism while also condemning the hypocrisy of nations that denied Haiti diplomatic respect. His words reasserted Haiti's rightful place at the center of Black political history and global liberty.

In beginning his address, Mr. Douglass said:

> No man should presume to come before an intelligent American audience without a commanding object and an earnest purpose. In whatever else I may be deficient, I hope I am qualified, both in object and purpose, to speak to you this evening.
>
> My subject is Haiti, the Black Republic; the only self-made Black Republic in the world. I am to speak to you of her character, her history, her importance and her struggle from slavery to freedom and to statehood. I am to speak to you of her progress in the line of civilization; of her relation with the United States; of her past and present; of her probable destiny; and of the bearing of her example as a free and independent Republic, upon what may be the destiny of the African race in our own country and elsewhere.

If, by a true statement of facts and a fair deduction from them, I shall in any degree promote a better understanding of what Haiti is, and create a higher appreciation of her merits and services to the world; and especially, if I can promote a more friendly feeling for her in this country and at the same time give to Haiti herself a friendly hint as to what is hopefully and justly expected of her by her friends, and by the civilized world, my object and purpose will have been accomplished.

There are many reasons why a good understanding should exist between Haiti and the United States. Her proximity; her similar government and her large and increasing commerce with us, should alone make us deeply interested in her welfare, her history, her progress and her possible destiny.

Haiti is a rich country. She has many things which we need and we have many things which she needs. Intercourse between us is easy. Measuring distance by time and improved steam navigation, Haiti will one day be only three days from New York and thirty-six hours from Florida; in fact our next door neighbor. On this account, as well as others equally important, friendly and helpful relations should subsist between the two countries. Though we have a thousand years of civilization behind us, and Haiti only a century behind her; though we are large and Haiti is small; though we are strong and Haiti is weak; though we are a continent and Haiti is bounded on all sides by the sea, there may come a time when even in the weakness of Haiti there may be strength to the United States.

Now, notwithstanding this plain possibility, it is a remarkable and lamentable fact, that while Haiti is so near us and so capable of being so serviceable to us; while, like us, she is trying to be a sister republic and anxious to have a government of the people, by the people and for the people; while she is one of our very best customers, selling her coffee and her other valuable products to Europe for gold, and sending us her gold to buy our flour, our fish, our oil, our beef and our pork; while she is thus enriching our merchants and our farmers and our country generally, she is the one country to which we turn the cold shoulder.

We charge her with being more friendly to France and to other European countries than to ourselves. This charge, if true, has a natural explanation, and the fault is more with us than with Haiti. No man can point to any act of ours to win the respect and friendship of this black republic. If, as is alleged, Haiti is more cordial to France than to the United States, it is partly because Haiti is herself French. Her language is French; her literature is French, her manners and fashions are French; her ambitions and aspirations are French; her laws and methods of government are French; her priesthood and her education are French; her children are sent to school in France and their minds are filled with French ideas and French glory.

But a deeper reason for coolness between the countries is this: Haiti is black, and we have not yet forgiven Haiti for being black [applause] or forgiven the Almighty for making her black. [Applause.] In this enlightened act of repentance and forgiveness, our boasted civilization is far behind all other nations. [Applause.] In every other country on the globe a citizen of Haiti is sure of civil treatment. [Applause.] In every other nation his manhood is recognized and respected. [Applause.] Wherever any man can go, he can go. [Applause.] He is not repulsed, excluded or insulted because of his color. [Applause.] All places of amusement and instruction are open to him. [Applause.] Vastly different is the case with him when he ventures within the border of the United States. [Applause.] Besides, after Haiti had shaken off the fetters of bondage, and long after her freedom and independence had been recognized by all other civilized nations, we continued to refuse to acknowledge the fact and treated her as outside the sisterhood of nations.

Frederick Douglass's Lecture on Haiti at the Chicago World's Fair, 1893

Source: An excerpt from Frederick Douglass's Lecture on Haiti: The Haitian Pavilion Dedication Ceremonies Delivered at the World's Fair, in Jackson Park, Chicago, Jan. 2d, 1893. Chicago: Violet Agents Supply Co., 1893. pp. 35–36.

Jacob Lawrence's series *The Life of Toussaint L'Ouverture* powerfully illustrates the revolutionary legacy of the Haitian leader through bold forms, vivid color, and visual storytelling. In *L'Ouverture* (1986), Lawrence portrays

Toussaint as a resolute and dignified figure, capturing the intensity of his leadership. *To Preserve Their Freedom* (1988) reflects the collective will of the Haitian people to defend the liberty they fought to achieve, while *Strategy* (1994) emphasizes the intellectual force and tactical brilliance that guided the revolution.

For more in-depth analysis, scholars can view the images and explore their historical significance online for free at The Gilder Lehrman Institute of American History: https://www.gilderlehrman.org/ap-african-american-studies/unit-2/resistance-revolt.

Reverberations Across the African Diaspora

The Haitian Revolution inspired more than fear in slaveholding societies—it ignited hope and transformed Black political thought.

- For African Americans, Haiti symbolized the realization of ideals left unfulfilled by the American Revolution—freedom, equality, and Black sovereignty.
- It inspired direct action: the **Louisiana Slave Revolt of 1811**, led by Charles Deslondes, and the Malê Muslim uprising in Brazil in 1835 were both rooted in Haitian influence and its example of successful rebellion.
- Haiti became a touchstone in Black political discourse, shaping abolitionist rhetoric and becoming a symbol of liberation referenced by leaders across the Americas for generations.

The Revolution That Shook the World

Haiti's revolution wasn't just a win for Haitians—it was a shockwave. The idea that enslaved people could rise up and win their freedom terrified slaveholders and inspired the enslaved across the Americas. Even today, Haiti's story is a symbol of defiance and possibility.

You're Practicing: Understanding how one struggle sparks others.

Connect This To: Freedom movements and revolutionary influence.

Theme: Power and Politics

Practice: Explain the Effects of Historical Developments and Connect Transnational Influences

The Haitian Revolution (1791–1804) had far-reaching effects across the Atlantic world, influencing African American communities and shaping political responses in the United States. Respond to the following.

(A) Identify one way the Haitian Revolution influenced free or enslaved African Americans in the early nineteenth century.

(B) Explain how U.S. laws or public reactions reflected fear of the revolution's impact on slavery or racial hierarchy.

(C) Analyze whether the Haitian Revolution had a greater effect on Black political consciousness or white responses rooted in repression. Use specific historical examples to support your explanation.

SAMPLE RESPONSES

(A) The Haitian Revolution inspired enslaved African Americans to resist bondage by proving that an enslaved population could overthrow a powerful colonial regime.

Free Black leaders like Richard Allen and Prince Hall celebrated Haiti as a symbol of Black independence, using its success to advocate for abolition and equal rights in the United States.

(B) In response to fears that the Haitian Revolution would inspire similar uprisings, the U.S. government passed laws restricting Black immigration from Haiti, including a ban on "importation" of "any negro, mulatto, or other person of colour" (1803) (effective 1808).

Southern states tightened slave codes, increasing surveillance and punishment of enslaved people, while white mobs targeted free Black communities, fearing the spread of revolutionary ideas.

The Gabriel Prosser rebellion (1800) and later slave conspiracies were directly linked to heightened anxieties over Haiti's influence on African American resistance.

(C) The Haitian Revolution arguably had a greater effect on Black political consciousness, as it served as a powerful example of successful resistance and self-governance. African American activists and writers, such as David Walker in his "Appeal to the Colored Citizens of the World" (1829), referenced Haiti as proof that freedom could be won through collective struggle.

However, white responses rooted in repression were also significant, as illustrated by the Louisiana Territory's Black Codes and the intensification of pro-slavery rhetoric, which sought to prevent the spread of "Haitian-style revolts."

Overall, the revolution's dual legacy—inspiring African Americans while hardening white fears—shaped the polarized racial and political climate leading up to the Civil War.

Skills Assessed: Explain the effects of historical developments; connect global Black resistance to African American identity formation; support claims with historical evidence; evaluate the significance of transnational developments.

Topic 2.13 Resistance and Revolts in the United States

Key Terms

- Nat Turner Rebellion (1831)
- Gabriel's Rebellion (1800)
- Denmark Vesey Plot (1822)
- Day-to-day resistance—work slowdowns, sabotage, escape
- Slave patrols and harsh retaliation
- Black agency and collective resistance
- Enslaved women's resistance—reproductive and household roles
- Religious messaging in revolts

Across the landscapes of bondage, African Americans—both enslaved and free—refused to accept their oppression in silence. Resistance was not limited to open rebellion; it was woven into everyday acts of defiance, survival, and solidarity. From quiet forms of cultural preservation and work slowdowns to bold revolts and abolitionist organizing, Black people throughout the United States and the wider Americas resisted slavery in every form it took. This topic explores the strategies, motivations, and lasting significance of these efforts, from the daily resistance of those in bondage to the revolutionary visions that guided rebellions and movements for abolition. It highlights how Black resistance shaped American history, challenged colonial power structures, and laid the moral foundation for freedom struggles across generations.

After engaging with this topic, scholars will be able to:

- Describe the daily forms of resistance demonstrated by enslaved and free African Americans.
- Describe the inspirations, goals, and struggles of different revolts and abolitionist organizing led by enslaved and free African descendants throughout the Americas.

Revolts, Resistance, and the Struggle for Freedom

The history of African American resistance is a history of courage, defiance, and the unrelenting pursuit of freedom. Whether through everyday acts of quiet rebellion or bold collective uprisings, both enslaved and free African Americans challenged the brutal systems that sought to deny their humanity. This resistance—spiritual, cultural, physical, and political—was not merely reactive. It was strategic, inspired, and central to the broader abolitionist struggle that reshaped the course of American and global history.

Everyday Resistance and the Power of Persistence

Although some revolts captured headlines and prompted legal backlash, the most consistent form of resistance occurred in the daily lives of enslaved people. From slowing work, breaking tools, and stealing food to feigning illness or escaping bondage, these everyday acts of defiance chipped away at the authority of the enslaver and reaffirmed one's agency under a dehumanizing system.

- These methods were not isolated. They helped preserve cultural knowledge, sustain hope, and forge solidarity, laying the moral and spiritual groundwork for the broader movement toward emancipation.
- Churches and religious gatherings, especially in the North, became key sites of resistance. Black congregations not only provided space for spiritual uplift but also for political organizing, mourning communal losses, planning escapes, and circulating abolitionist ideas.

Revolt, Rebellion, and Revolutionary Imagination

The transatlantic slave trade often brought to the Americas individuals who had military experience in Africa. These skills were sometimes crucial to organizing large-scale revolts, especially in regions where enslaved populations were concentrated.

- As early as 1526, Africans brought to assist with Spanish exploration along the Carolina-Georgia coastline launched the first known slave revolt in what is now the United States, escaping into nearby Indigenous communities in resistance.
- The **Haitian Revolution** served as a model of Black sovereignty and armed resistance. In 1811, Charles Deslondes, influenced by Haiti's success, led the **German Coast Uprising**—the largest slave revolt on U.S. soil. Nearly 500 enslaved people and maroons marched toward New Orleans in a bold attempt to claim freedom, but the rebellion was ultimately suppressed with brutal violence.
- In **1841**, an enslaved cook aboard the slave ship *Creole* named **Madison Washington** led a mutiny that redirected the vessel to the British-controlled Bahamas, where slavery had been abolished in 1833. Nearly 130 enslaved people gained their freedom—making the *Creole* revolt one of the most successful slave uprisings in U.S. maritime history.

Spiritual Resistance and the Call to Liberation

Religion also became a catalyst for revolution. Leaders such as **Nat Turner** and **Denmark Vesey** believed their missions were divinely inspired and used biblical language to rally others against slavery. Their resistance drew directly from Christian theology while also channeling African spiritual traditions and communal forms of justice.

Likewise, Black abolitionists such as **Maria W. Stewart** and **Henry Highland Garnet** merged faith with activism, delivering fiery sermons and speeches that linked spiritual salvation to political emancipation. They called on African Americans to rise against slavery and injustice.

The following 1802 letter from Thomas Jefferson to Rufus King reveals the deep anxieties held by American leaders regarding the Haitian Revolution and its implications for slavery in the United States. Jefferson, then president, reflects on the challenges of maintaining diplomatic relations with Haiti while suppressing fears of Black rebellion spreading to American soil. The letter offers insight into how revolutionary Black freedom in Haiti unsettled the foundations of racial hierarchy in the early American republic.

To Rufus King

Washington July 13. 1802.

Dear Sir

The course of things in the neighboring islands of the West Indies appears to have given a considerable impulse to the minds of the slaves in different parts of the US. a great disposition to insurgency has manifested itself among them, which, in one instance, in the state of Virginia broke out into actual insurrection. this was easily suppressed: but many of those concerned, fell victims to the law. so extensive an execution could not but excite sensibility in the public mind, and beget a regret that the laws had not provided, for such cases, some alternative, combining more mildness with equal efficacy. the legislature of the state, at a subsequent meeting, took the subject into consideration, and have communicated to me through the Governor of the state, their wish that some place could be provided, out of the limits of the US. to which slaves guilty of insurgency might be transported; and they have particularly looked to Africa as offering the most desirable receptacle. we might, for this purpose, enter into negociations with the natives, on some part of the coast, to obtain a settlement, and, by establishing an African company, combine with it commercial operations, which might not only reimburse expences but procure profit also. but there being already such an establishment on that coast by the English Sierra Leone company, made for the express purpose of colonising civilized blacks to that country, it would seem better, by incorporating our emigrants with theirs, to make one strong, rather than two weak colonies. this would be the more desireable, because the blacks settled at Sierra Leone, having chiefly gone from these states, would often recieve, among those we should send, their acquaintances and relations. the object of this letter therefore is to ask the favor of you to enter into conference with such persons private & public as would be necessary to give us permission to send thither the persons under contemplation. it is material to observe that they are not felons, or common malefactors, but persons guilty of what the safety of society, under actual circumstances, obliges us to treat as a crime, but which their feelings may represent in a far different shape. they are such as will be a valuable acquisition to the settlement already existing there, and well calculated to cooperate in the plan of civilisation.

As the expence of so distant a transportation would be very heavy, & might weigh unfavorably in deciding between the modes of punishment, it is very desirable that it should be lessened as much as is practicable. if the regulations of the place would permit these emigrants to dispose of themselves, as the Germans & others do who come to this country poor, by giving their labour for a certain term to some one who will pay their passage; and if the master of the vessel could be permitted to carry articles of commerce from this country & take back others from that which might yield him a mercantile profit sufficient to cover the expences of the voyage, a serious difficulty would be removed. I will ask your attention therefore to arrangements necessary for this purpose.

The consequences of permitting emancipations to become extensive, unless a condition of emigration be annexed to them, furnish also matter of solicitude to the legislature of Virginia, as you will percieve by their resolution inclosed to you. Altho provision for the settlement of emancipated negroes might perhaps be obtainable nearer home than Africa, yet it is desirable that we should be free to expatriate this description of people also to the colony of Sierra Leone, if considerations respecting either themselves or us should render it more expedient. I will pray you therefore to get the same permission extended to the reception of these as well as those first mentioned. nor will these be a selection of bad subjects; the emancipations for the most part being either of the whole slaves of the master, or of such individuals as have particularly deserved well. the latter is most frequent.

The request of the legislature of Virginia having produced to me this occasion of addressing you, I avail myself of it to assure you of my perfect satisfaction with the manner in which you have conducted the several matters confided to you by us; and to express my hope that through your agency we may be able to remove every thing inauspicious to a cordial friendship between this country & the one in which you are stationed: a friendship dictated by too many considerations not to be felt by the wise & the dispassionate of both nations. it is therefore with the sincerest pleasure I have observed on the part of the British government various manifestations of just and friendly disposition towards us. we wish to cultivate peace & friendship with all nations, believing that course most conducive to the welfare of our own. it is natural that these friendships should bear some proportion to the common interests of the parties. the interesting relations between Great Britain and the US. are certainly of the first order; & as such are estimated, & will be faithfully cultivated by us. these sentiments have been communicated to you from time to time in the official correspondence of the Secretary of state: but I have thought it might not be unacceptable to be assured that they perfectly concur with my own personal convictions, both in relation to yourself and the country in which you are. I pray you to accept assurances of my high consideration & respect. Th: Jefferson

Source: A letter from President Thomas Jefferson to US Minister to Great Britain Rufus King, July 13, 1802, conveying Virginia's request to send insurrectionists to Sierra Leone (Founders Online, National Archives. [Original source: The Papers of Thomas Jefferson, vol. 38, 1 July–12 November 1802, ed. Barbara B. Oberg. Princeton: Princeton University Press, 2011, pp. 54–57.]).

Revolts That Made the United States Nervous

Enslaved people didn't accept their fate. From Nat Turner's rebellion to countless smaller acts of defiance, resistance was constant. Each revolt brought fear to slaveholders and led to tighter laws and harsher punishments. However, they also kept the fight for freedom alive.

You're Practicing: Exploring cause and effect between rebellion and law.

Connect This To: Legal backlash and fear of liberation.

Theme: Resistance and Autonomy

Practice: Historical Comparison

The enslaved rebellions described in this topic differed in execution, motivation, and impact but shared a common thread of resistance and pursuit of freedom. Respond to the following.

(A) Identify one specific revolt or conspiracy described in the text and summarize its central goal.
(B) Explain one way this event influenced laws or public opinion in the United States.
(C) Compare the motivations or strategies of two revolts described in the text (e.g., Gabriel's vs. Nat Turner's) and explain how these reflect broader political or religious ideas in African American history.

SAMPLE RESPONSES

(A) Nat Turner's Rebellion (1831) sought to overthrow the system of slavery by leading a coordinated uprising of enslaved people in Virginia, with the ultimate goal of creating freedom for African Americans through armed resistance.

Alternatively, Gabriel Prosser's planned revolt (1800) aimed to capture Richmond, Virginia, and negotiate an end to slavery, reflecting both revolutionary ideals and the influence of Haitian independence movements.

(B) Nat Turner's Rebellion led to harsher slave codes in Virginia and other Southern states, including laws that prohibited the education of enslaved people and limited the ability of free Blacks to gather or travel.

Public opinion in the South hardened in favor of slavery as a means of maintaining racial control, while Northern abolitionists pointed to the rebellion as evidence of slavery's moral corruption and the inevitability of resistance.

(C) Gabriel Prosser's conspiracy was inspired by the ideals of the Haitian Revolution and the American Revolution, focusing on political liberation and strategic planning to seize weapons and negotiate freedom. Nat Turner's uprising, on the other hand, was heavily influenced by religious visions and prophetic leadership, with Turner believing he was divinely chosen to lead his people to freedom.

Together, these revolts reflect a broader tradition of African American resistance rooted in both political radicalism and spiritual conviction, demonstrating how faith and revolutionary ideals often intertwined in the struggle against slavery.

Skills Assessed: Compare developments across time/events; use text-based evidence to support claims; use reasoning to explain significance; connect political rebellion to broader African American intellectual traditions.

Topic 2.14 Black Organizing in the North: Freedom, Women's Rights, and Education

Key Terms

- Abolitionist societies
- Free African Schools
- Mutual aid societies—Free African Society and others
- Black women's organizing—Maria W. Stewart, Sojourner Truth
- National Negro Convention Movement
- African Methodist Episcopal (AME) Church—Richard Allen
- Education as liberation
- Intersection of race and gender in reform

In the decades before the Civil War, free Black communities in the North—facing legal discrimination, economic inequality, and racial violence—built networks of mutual aid, political resistance, and cultural pride. At the forefront of this organizing were Black women, whose advocacy for education, abolition, and women's rights laid the foundation for later civil rights and feminist movements. Through churches, schools, conventions, and the press, they reimagined what freedom meant, not only for African Americans but for the nation as a whole.

After engaging with this topic, scholars will be able to:

- Explain how free Black people in the North and South organized to support their communities.
- Describe the techniques used by Black women activists to advocate for social justice and reform.
- Explain why Black women's activism is historically and culturally significant.

Northern Black Activism: Freedom, Women's Rights, and Education

In the face of deep systemic oppression, free Black communities across the United States—especially in the North—developed powerful infrastructures of resistance, resilience, and renewal. From building schools and churches to advancing abolitionist and feminist thought, free African Americans shaped a political and cultural blueprint for community empowerment. At the center of this transformation stood Black women. Their voices, writings, and organizing strategies formed one of the earliest intersections of racial and gender justice in American history.

Community Building and Mutual Aid

By 1860, free Black people made up 12 percent of the total Black population in the United States. Although more free Black people lived in the South in absolute numbers, the proportion was far greater in the North, where they used their relative mobility to organize, educate, and resist.

- In cities like Philadelphia, New York, and New Orleans, free African Americans established mutual aid societies that served as financial, educational, and cultural lifelines for their communities.
- These societies funded the growth of Black schools, independent businesses, and self-governed churches. They also supported the work of early Black writers, lecturers, and newspaper editors, ensuring that African American perspectives reached a wider audience.

This self-determined infrastructure helped lay the groundwork for collective advancement, even as Black communities continued to face racial violence, economic exclusion, and legal inequality in both the North and the South.

Black Women Lead the Way

Black women were not only present in these movements—they were visionaries, architects, and truth tellers.

- In the 1830s, **Maria W. Stewart** became the first Black woman in American history to publish a political manifesto and one of the first women of any race to speak publicly on political issues. In boldly addressing both Black audiences and white critics, Stewart helped launch what would become the first wave of American feminism.
- Throughout the nineteenth century, Black women continued to use oratory, essays, and religious platforms to spotlight their unique position at the intersection of race and gender. They called on abolitionist movements to center the voices of Black women, challenging both racism and sexism in their communities and beyond.

Maria W. Stewart (1803–1879) was a pioneering African American intellectual, educator, journalist, and activist whose life defied the constraints placed on Black women in the early nineteenth century. A former domestic servant, Stewart became the first African American woman to deliver a public lecture. She was also the first American woman of any race to speak before a mixed-gender audience on political and social issues. On September 21, 1832, she delivered her groundbreaking speech Why Sit Here and Die?, presented at Franklin Hall in Boston. She addressed the New England Anti-Slavery Society, founded by abolitionist William Lloyd Garrison, editor of *The Liberator*. Stewart's bold voice helped shape both the abolitionist and early women's rights movements.

Here is an excerpt of her speech:

> Why sit ye here and die? If we say we will go to a foreign land, the famine and the pestilence are there, and there we shall die. If we sit here, we shall die. Come let us plead our cause before the whites: if they save us alive, we shall live—and if they kill us, we shall but die. Methinks I heard a spiritual interrogation—"Who shall go forward, and take off the reproach that is cast upon the people of color? Shall it be a woman?" And my heart made this reply—"If it is thy will, be it even so, Lord Jesus!" I have heard much respecting the horrors of slavery; but may Heaven forbid that the generality of my color throughout these United States should experience any more of its horrors than to be a servant of servants, or hewers of wood and drawers of water! Tell us no more of southern slavery; for with few exceptions, although I may be very erroneous in my opinion, yet I consider our condition but little better than that. Yet, after all, methinks there are no chains so galling as the chains of ignorance—no fetters so binding as those that bind the soul, and exclude it from the vast field of useful and scientific knowledge. O, had I received the advantages of early education, my ideas would, ere now, have expanded far and wide; but, alas! I possess nothing but moral capability—no teachings but the teachings of the Holy Spirit. I have asked several individuals of my sex, who transact business for themselves, if providing our girls were to give them the most satisfactory references, they would not be willing to grant them an equal opportunity with others? Their reply has been—for their own part, they had no objection; but as it was not the custom, were they to take them into their employ, they would be in danger of losing the public patronage. And such is the powerful force of prejudice. Let our girls possess what amiable qualities of soul they may; let their characters be fair and

spotless as innocence itself; let their natural taste and ingenuity be what they may; it is impossible for scarce an individual of them to rise above the condition of servants. Ah! why is this cruel and unfeeling distinction? Is it merely because God has made our complexion to vary? If it be, O shame to soft, relenting humanity! "Tell it not in Gath! publish it not in the streets of Askelon!" Yet, after all, methinks were the American free people of color to turn their attention more assiduously to moral worth and intellectual improvement, this would be the result: prejudice would gradually diminish, and the whites would be compelled to say, unloose those fetters! Though black their skins as shades of night, their hearts are pure, their souls are white. Few white persons of either sex, who are calculated for any thing else, are willing to spend their lives and bury their talents in performing mean, servile labor. And such is the horrible idea that I entertain respecting a life of servitude, that if I conceived of there being no possibility of my rising above the condition of a servant, I would gladly hail death as a welcome messenger. O, horrible idea, indeed! to possess noble souls aspiring after high and honorable acquirements, yet confined by the chains of ignorance and poverty to lives of continual drudgery and toil. Neither do I know of any who have enriched themselves by spending their lives as house-domestics, washing windows, shaking carpets, brushing boots, or tending upon gentlemen's tables. I can but die for expressing my sentiments; and I am as willing to die by the sword as the pestilence; for I and a true born American; your blood flows in my veins, and your spirit fires my breast.

TIP

Practice "Quick Reads" for Sources

Read the question first to understand what is being asked. You don't need to read every word of a long source. Skim for thesis statements, evidence, and context related to the question.

Source: Maria W. Stewart, "Lecture Delivered at the Franklin Hall, Boston, September 21, 1832," in *Meditations from the Pen of Mrs. Maria W. Stewart*, Washington: W. Lloyd Garrison & Knap, 1879.

A Legacy of Intersectional Activism

Black women's activism during this era did not merely participate in dominant conversations about race or gender—it reshaped those conversations entirely.

- These activists demonstrated how racism, sexism, and class exploitation were linked and demanded to be addressed together. Their analysis and organizing anticipated the political theories that would later define intersectionality.
- Their work fueled both the abolitionist movement and the early women's suffrage movement, even as they were often excluded from the leadership ranks of both.

From local churches to national lecture halls, from the printed page to grassroots protests, Black women expanded the meaning of freedom—insisting that it must be inclusive, holistic, and unapologetically just. The fight for racial and gender justice in the United States was not simply inherited. It was built. The builders were Black communities, led in large part by Black women, whose voices still echo in the movements of today.

Learning as Liberation

Northern Black communities didn't just hope for freedom—they organized for it. Schools, churches, women's groups, and abolitionist societies laid the groundwork for future civil rights movements. Education was a tool for survival and a weapon for change.

You're Practicing: Seeing how communities build power together.

Connect This To: Collective action, education, and advocacy.

Theme: Community and Power

Practice: Explain the Significance of Historical Developments and Evaluate Their Impact

This section explores how Black Northerners in the nineteenth century advocated for civil rights, education, and gender equality through speeches, publications, and organizing efforts. Respond to the following.

(A) Identify one strategy used by Black activists to advocate for legal equality, education, or women's rights.

(B) Explain one way Black women challenged racial or gendered exclusions in reform movements of the time.

(C) Using your broader historical knowledge, argue whether the most lasting impact of this period was in formal politics, cultural identity, or institution building. Support your answer with evidence.

SAMPLE RESPONSES

(A) Black activists such as Frederick Douglass and Maria W. Stewart used public speeches and abolitionist publications to challenge racial inequality and argue for equal education and suffrage rights.

Black communities also established mutual aid societies and independent schools to provide education and foster civic participation outside of exclusionary white institutions.

(B) Sojourner Truth's "Ain't I a Woman?" speech (1851) directly confronted the exclusion of Black women from both abolitionist and women's rights circles, demanding recognition of their equal humanity.

(C) The most lasting impact was institution building, as Black Northerners established schools, newspapers, churches, and civic organizations that laid the foundation for later civil rights activism.

For example, independent Black churches like the AME Church not only provided spiritual refuge but also served as hubs for political organizing and education.

These institutions sustained African American cultural identity, leadership, and resistance well into the twentieth century, influencing movements from Reconstruction to the Civil Rights era.

Skills Assessed: Make a defensible historical argument; use textual evidence to support claims; connect content to African American civic development; evaluate tensions within reform movements (race, gender, class).

Topic 2.15 Maroon Societies and Autonomous Black Communities

Key Terms

- Maroon communities—formed by escaped enslaved people
- Quilombos (Brazil), Palmares, Suriname maroons
- Seminole alliances—in Florida
- Self-governance and military defense
- African traditions in isolation
- Treaties with colonial powers
- Autonomy and landholding
- Black republics—as forms of resistance

Throughout the African diaspora, many enslaved Africans refused to remain in bondage. They escaped into forests, mountains, and remote territories. There they built independent communities known as **maroon societies,** bold expressions of resistance, survival, and self-governance. These communities were formed by self-emancipated

Africans and their descendants. They stood as enduring symbols of Black autonomy, often challenging colonial rule through armed defense and political negotiation.

After engaging with this topic, scholars will be able to:

- Describe the characteristics of maroon communities and the regions where they emerged.
- Describe the purposes and outcomes of maroon wars throughout the African diaspora.

Freedom Beyond Slavery: Maroon and Independent Black Communities

Across the Americas, wherever slavery was imposed, African-descended people fought to create spaces of freedom. Maroon societies—formed by self-emancipated Africans and their descendants—were bold declarations of autonomy and resistance. These communities did more than escape slavery; they built new worlds rooted in African cultural survival, collective defense, and self-determination.

Defiant Settlements of Freedom

Maroon communities emerged in remote environments that offered natural protection from colonial surveillance: dense forests, mountainous terrain, swamps, and hidden valleys. Though some lasted only a few years, others endured for decades or even centuries, forming sophisticated and resilient societies outside the reach of colonial power.

- These communities often included formerly enslaved individuals as well as people born free, who passed down traditions of resilience and independence.
- Within maroon settlements, African-based languages, belief systems, and cultural practices blended with local influences, creating unique diasporic identities. Despite facing hardships—such as disease, food scarcity, and the looming threat of capture—maroons cultivated thriving networks of survival, kinship, and political structure.

In the United States, maroon communities were found in the Great Dismal Swamp, located between Virginia and North Carolina. They were also found within **Indigenous nations**, where African Americans sometimes found refuge and solidarity. Beyond the United States, maroon societies took other forms:

- In Spanish America, they were known as ***palenques.***
- In Brazil, the largest and most famous maroon society was the **Quilombo dos Palmares**, which lasted for nearly 100 years and stood as a beacon of organized Black resistance in the Western Hemisphere.

An engraving of *Leonard Parkinson, a Captain of the Maroons, taken from the Life* by Abraham Raimbach, 1796 (Source: Abraham Raimbach, public domain, via Wikimedia Commons)

Maroon Wars and Political Sovereignty

Maroon societies were not passive settlements. They were active military and political forces that confronted European empires. These were not isolated rebellions; they were organized wars for territorial control and sovereignty.

- In sixteenth-century Panama, **Bayano** led a series of sustained wars against Spanish forces, resisting colonization through guerrilla tactics and fortification of maroon settlements.
- In eighteenth-century Jamaica, **Queen Nanny**, a spiritual and military leader of the Windward Maroons, orchestrated effective campaigns against the British. Her leadership earned her legendary status and contributed to the negotiation of treaties that temporarily secured maroon autonomy.

Some maroon communities negotiated formal agreements with colonial powers—agreements that recognized the independence of maroon communities in exchange for assisting in suppressing future slave revolts. These arrangements, while pragmatic, highlight the complexity of maroon politics as they sought to balance survival with their commitment to freedom.

This 1796 drawing by Abraham Raimbach depicts **Leonard Parkinson**, a prominent maroon leader and Captain of the maroons in Jamaica. As a commander during the Second Maroon War, Parkinson led guerrilla resistance against British colonial forces, defending the autonomy of the maroon communities. His image stands as a powerful representation of Black military leadership and the long tradition of African-descended resistance in the Americas.

This 1801 image *The Maroons in Ambush on the Dromilly Estate in the Parish of Trelawney, Jamaica*, by J. Bourgoin and J. Merigot, captures a dramatic moment during the Second Maroon War. It illustrates the strategic guerrilla warfare used by Jamaican maroons to defend their autonomy against British colonial forces. The image highlights the intensity of resistance and the determination of maroon fighters to preserve freedom on their own terms.

The Maroons in Ambush on the Dromilly Estate in the Parish of Trelawney, Jamaica
by J. Bourgoin and J. Merigot, 1801

Painted in 1862, *The Hunted Slaves* by Richard Ansdell is a striking portrayal of two fugitive enslaved people seeking refuge while being pursued through hostile terrain. Created during the height of the American Civil War, the image evokes both the terror of enslavement and the unyielding courage of those who resisted it. The painting stands as a powerful visual narrative of survival, dignity, and the human cost of slavery.

The Hunted Slaves by Richard Ansdell, 1862
(Source: Richard Ansdell, public domain, via Wikimedia Commons)

Maroon societies remind us that resistance to slavery was not only individual but communal. They also remind us that Black freedom making was often accompanied by governance, military strategy, and cultural preservation. These societies created models of Black autonomy long before emancipation was won through law. Their legacies endure as testaments to the global dimensions of African-descended peoples' resistance and resolve.

Freedom in the Wild

Some enslaved people didn't wait for laws to change. They ran. In remote swamps, mountains, and forests, they built Maroon communities: independent villages where freedom was real. These communities weren't just survival stories—they were political statements that proved a different way of life was possible.

You're Practicing: Recognizing resistance beyond protest or rebellion.

Connect This To: Autonomy, hidden histories, and community power.

Theme: Resistance and Autonomy

Practice: Resistance, Autonomy, and Comparative Analysis

The maroon communities discussed in this section demonstrate how formerly enslaved Africans created independent, often militarized societies in resistance to enslavement. Respond to the following.

(A) Identify one maroon or autonomous Black community discussed in the text and describe how it maintained independence.

(B) Compare the strategy or structure of that community to one other from the text (e.g., Palmares vs. Jamaican maroons or Black Seminoles).

(C) Explain how these societies challenged traditional narratives about Black agency during slavery and influence modern African diasporic identity.

SAMPLE RESPONSES

(A) The Jamaican Maroons maintained independence by forming fortified settlements, conducting guerrilla warfare against colonial forces, and negotiating treaties in the 18th century that recognized their freedom in exchange for peace.

Similarly, Palmares in Brazil survived for nearly a century by establishing a self-sufficient economy, cultivating crops, and defending against repeated Portuguese military campaigns.

(B) Unlike the Jamaican Maroons, who signed treaties with colonial authorities to secure autonomy, Palmares rejected diplomatic agreements and relied on continuous military resistance to maintain sovereignty.

The Black Seminoles combined African and Native American cultural practices, aligning with the Seminole tribe in Florida, which gave them greater mobility and access to trade networks, contrasting with the more isolated structure of the Jamaican Maroons.

(C) Maroon communities defied the narrative of enslaved passivity by demonstrating that African-descended people actively resisted slavery, formed independent societies, and preserved African cultural traditions.

Their success stories inspired later resistance movements and remain symbols of Black autonomy, influencing modern pan-African and diasporic identities that celebrate self-determination and cultural resilience.

Contemporary cultural expressions, such as music and literature, often draw from the legacy of maroons to highlight the longstanding tradition of African resistance and community building in the Americas.

Skills Practiced: Compare historical developments across regions; use reasoning to explain historical significance; connect historical autonomy to cultural continuity in the African diaspora; support analysis with evidence from case studies in the chapter.

Topic 2.16 Diasporic Connections: Slavery and Freedom in Brazil

Key Terms

- Atlantic slave trade to Brazil—largest recipient
- Quilombo dos Palmares—largest maroon settlement
- Candomblé—Afro-Brazilian religious practice
- Manumission—buying freedom
- Racial mixing and fluidity in Brazil
- Brazilian abolition (1888)—last in Western Hemisphere
- Zumbi dos Palmares—freedom fighter
- Afro-Brazilian cultural heritage—music, food, religion
- Comparative slavery systems—United States vs. Brazil

When studying the African diaspora, it is essential to move beyond U.S. borders to understand the full scope of transatlantic slavery. Brazil—the largest destination for enslaved Africans in the Americas—was home to both the deepest horrors of enslavement and some of the most enduring legacies of African cultural survival and resistance. By examining slavery in Brazil, students gain critical insight into the global dimensions of the African American story and the broader fight for Black freedom.

After engaging with this topic, scholars will be able to:

- Describe features of the enslavement of Africans in Brazil.
- Explain shifts in the numbers of enslaved Africans in Brazil and the United States during the nineteenth century.

Slavery and the Struggle for Freedom in Brazil

To understand the African diaspora fully, students must engage with Brazil—the largest importer of enslaved Africans in the transatlantic slave trade. Although the United States often dominates conversations about slavery, Brazil received nearly half of all Africans who survived the Middle Passage. The legacy of this history is visible today in Brazil's language, music, religion, foodways, and ongoing struggle for racial justice. This topic invites scholars to explore Brazil's unique role in the global system of slavery and the enduring cultural impact of African-descended communities across the Americas.

Brazil as the Heart of the Diaspora

More enslaved Africans arrived in Brazil than in any other part of the Americas. Of the estimated 10 million Africans who survived the transatlantic crossing, *approximately 5 million were taken to Brazil.*

- Enslaved Africans were forced to labor in multiple industries that shaped Brazil's economy for centuries, including sugar plantations, gold and diamond mining, coffee production, cattle ranching, and local food and textile production.
- Despite the violence of enslavement, African communities in Brazil managed to preserve and transform their cultural traditions, forming the foundation for uniquely Afro-Brazilian expressions.

Practices such as **capoeira**, a martial art disguised as dance, and the **congada**, a festival honoring both African royalty and Catholic figures, reflect the depth and resilience of Black cultural life under slavery.

Freedom and Legal Culture in Brazil vs. the United States

Although both Brazil and the United States depended heavily on enslaved labor, the paths to freedom and the demographic makeup of the enslaved population varied greatly between the two nations during the nineteenth century.

- In Brazil, **manumission**—the legal release from slavery—became increasingly common due to influences from Iberian Catholicism and legal traditions that allowed for more flexibility in granting freedom.
- By the time slavery was abolished in Brazil in 1888 (the last country in the Americas to do so), nearly *4 million Afro-Brazilians were already free* and abolition liberated approximately *1.5 million people still in bondage.*

In contrast, the United States—despite banning the transatlantic slave trade in 1808—saw its enslaved population grow dramatically due to natural increase, i.e., people being born into slavery. By the time of the **Emancipation Proclamation** in 1863, the United States held about 4 million enslaved African Americans, nearly half of all enslaved people in the Americas at that time. These individuals were born into a system of hereditary chattel slavery that denied them the possibility of manumission or legal personhood.

The *Festival of Our Lady of the Rosary*, painted by Carlos Julião in the 1770s, captures the vibrant public celebration of Black Catholic devotion in Rio de Janeiro, highlighting how Afro-Brazilian communities blended African spiritual traditions with Catholicism under slavery.

A print by artist Carlos Julião, *Festival of Our Lady of the Rosary, Rio de Janeiro, Brazil*, circa 1770s (Source: https://slaveryimages.org/database/image-result.php?objectid=276)

Photographed nearly a century later, *Escravo Mina* and *Escrava Mina* by José Christiano de Freitas Henriques Junior (1864) offer rare portraits of enslaved West African–descended individuals in Brazil. These photographs preserved the dignity, identity, and humanity of two individuals at a time when slavery still shaped Brazilian society. Together, these works serve as powerful visual records of Black cultural resilience and religious life in the African diaspora.

Photographs *Escravo* ("Enslaved Man") *Mina* and *Escrava* ("Enslaved Woman") *Mina*, taken by José Christiano de Freitas Henriques Jr. (also known as Christiano Junior), Brazil, 1864 (Source: https://slaveryimages.org)

This image of capoeira players and musicians on the beach in Salvador da Bahia captures the dynamic blend of martial arts, music, and dance that defines capoeira—an Afro-Brazilian tradition rooted in resistance. Developed by enslaved Africans in Brazil, capoeira was both a form of self-defense and a cultural expression disguised as play. Today, it stands as a living symbol of Afro-diasporic resilience and identity.

Brazilian capoeira group performs for a crowd in the Barra neighborhood
(Source: Shutterstock)

Different Places, Shared Struggles

Brazil received more enslaved Africans than any other country—and its story is deeply connected to the African American experience. From capoeira to candomblé, enslaved people found creative ways to preserve their culture and resist. Looking across the African diaspora helps us see patterns of both oppression and brilliance.

You're Practicing: Making global connections in the Black experience.

Connect This To: Shared resistance, cultural roots, and freedom movements.

Theme: Migration and Diaspora

Practice: Transnational Comparison and Cultural Reasoning

This topic presents Brazil as a key site of both massive enslavement and powerful resistance. Quilombos like Palmares and cultural practices like Candomblé and capoeira demonstrate how Afro-Brazilians preserved their identity and fought for freedom. Respond to the following.

(A) Identify one way Afro-Brazilians resisted or survived slavery in culturally significant ways.

(B) Compare that example to a resistance or survival strategy used by African Americans in the United States.

(C) Using your broader knowledge, explain how such comparisons can expand our understanding of Black freedom struggles across the diaspora. You might compare quilombos to maroon communities or Candomblé to African American religious traditions such as the ring shout or praise houses.

SAMPLE RESPONSES

(A) Afro-Brazilians formed quilombos like Palmares, independent communities of escaped enslaved people that preserved African languages, religious traditions, and martial arts like capoeira while resisting recapture.

Through spiritual practices like Candomblé, Afro-Brazilians maintained African religious traditions by blending them with Catholic rituals to protect their cultural identity and resist forced conversion.

(B) Similar to Palmares, maroon communities in the U.S., such as those in the Great Dismal Swamp, provided refuge for runaway enslaved people, practiced communal living, and used the environment for defense against slave catchers.

Like Candomblé, African Americans preserved cultural identity through ring shouts and spirituals, which blended African rhythms and call-and-response traditions with Christian worship to create spaces of cultural resistance.

(C) These comparisons reveal that enslaved Africans across the Americas engaged in parallel strategies of cultural survival and resistance, whether through maroon communities or spiritual traditions, highlighting a shared diasporic resilience.

Understanding the similarities between quilombos and U.S. maroons, or Candomblé and ring shouts, shows how Black freedom struggles were interconnected and global, adapting African traditions to challenge enslavement in unique but related ways.

Skills Assessed: Compare diasporic developments across regions (Brazil and United States); connect experiences across the African diaspora; make a claim about Black resistance across contexts; use evidence from both the text and historical knowledge; explain the historical and cultural significance.

KEY TAKEAWAYS

1. **Cultural Creation Amid Captivity**
   - Enslaved Africans in the Americas cultivated new cultural forms by blending African, European, and Indigenous influences.
   - Religion, music, language, and kinship networks became powerful tools of identity and endurance, shaping early African American culture.
2. **Black Pride and the Politics of Naming**
   - African-descended communities asserted pride through naming practices that reflected their cultural heritage and spiritual beliefs.
   - The act of renaming—whether by enslavers or as an act of resistance—was central in the fight over autonomy and self-definition.
3. **Rebellion and Strategic Resistance**
   - Armed uprisings like the Stono Rebellion (1739) and the creation of Fort Mose (Florida) illustrate organized resistance and Black military strategies.
   - These acts exposed the vulnerabilities of the slave system and led to harsher laws by colonial authorities.
4. **The Haitian Revolution's Revolutionary Ripple Effect**
   - The 1791–1804 Haitian Revolution inspired fear among slaveholders and hope among the enslaved.
   - It shifted global politics and influenced Black movements in the United States and throughout the Americas.
5. **Resistance and Rebellion in the United States**
   - Enslaved and free Black individuals resisted through escape, sabotage, and insurrection.
   - Events like Gabriel's Rebellion and Nat Turner's Rebellion heightened the tension between slavery and growing abolitionist sentiment.
6. **Black Organizing in the North**
   - Free Black communities in the North founded schools, mutual aid societies, and abolitionist organizations.
   - Black women were central to these movements, fighting for both racial and gender equity and expanding the meaning of citizenship.
7. **Maroons and Diasporic Autonomy**
   - Maroon societies—formed by escaped slaves in remote regions—created self-governing communities rooted in African traditions.
   - These societies symbolized the enduring struggle for sovereignty and the continuity of African culture in the diaspora.
8. **Diasporic Ties Across the Americas**
   - African-descended peoples in Brazil, Haiti, the United States, and other parts of the Americas developed shared identities and resistance practices.
   - Black resistance and cultural expression were both local and interconnected across the Atlantic world.

Practice Multiple-Choice Questions

DIRECTIONS: Pick the letter that best answers the following questions.

Questions 1 through 3 refer to the following.

Leonard Parkinson, a Captain of the Maroons
by Abraham Raimbach, 1796

1. What does the image of Leonard Parkinson most directly represent?

   (A) The militarization of enslaved Africans in British colonies
   (B) The leadership and resistance efforts of Jamaican maroon communities
   (C) The forced conscription of Africans into British colonial armies
   (D) A romanticized depiction of African royalty in the Caribbean

2. What do the posture and weaponry shown in the engraving most clearly signify?

   (A) A passive stance while awaiting orders from British forces
   (B) A ceremonial tradition among enslaved African communities
   (C) Preparedness for guerrilla resistance against colonial authority
   (D) British propaganda emphasizing African docility

3. What broader historical development does this image help illustrate?

   (A) The assimilation of maroons into British military regiments
   (B) The establishment of plantation economies in Jamaica
   (C) The long-standing resistance of Afro-descended communities in the Americas
   (D) The failure of African cultural practices to survive in the Caribbean

Questions 4 and 5 refer to the following.

1739 Letter from Governor William Bull.

"My Lords,

I beg leave to lay before your Lordships an account of our Affairs, first in regard to the Desertion of our Negroes.... On the 9th of September last at Night a great Number of Negroes Arose in Rebellion, broke open a Store where they got arms, killed twenty one White Persons, and were marching the next morning in a Daring manner out of the Province, killing all they met and burning several Houses as they passed along the Road. I was returning from Granville County with four Gentlemen and met these Rebels at eleven o'clock in the forenoon and fortunately deserned the approaching danger time enough to avoid it, and to give notice to the Militia who on the Occasion behaved with so much expedition and bravery, as by four a'Clock the same day to come up with them and killed and took so many as put a stop to any further mischief at that time, forty four of them have been killed and Executed; some few yet remain concealed in the Woods expecting the same fate, seem desperate....

It was the Opinion of His Majesty's Council with several other Gentlemen that one of the most effectual means that could be used at present to prevent such desertion of our Negroes is to encourage some Indians by a suitable reward to pursue and if possible to bring back the Deserters, and while the Indians are thus employed they would be in the way ready to intercept others that might attempt to follow and I have sent for the Chiefs of the Chickasaws living at New Windsor and the Catawbaw Indians for that purpose....

My Lords,

Your Lordships Most Obedient and Most Humble Servant

Wm Bull"

Source: Official letters from Don Manuel de Montiano, Governor of East Florida, to Don Juan Francisco de Guemes y Horcasitas, Captain-General of the Island of Cuba, 1737 Sept. 30 to 1741 Jan. 2, p. 28. Translation from 1846 from the original in the City Archives of St. Augustine, Florida, held in the Digital Library of Georgia.

4. What primary concern does Governor William Bull express in his 1739 letter regarding the Stono Rebellion?
   (A) The loss of property caused by the destruction of crops
   (B) The influence of Spanish Florida in inciting rebellion
   (C) The dangers posed by armed, organized Black resistance
   (D) The reluctance of local militias to respond to threats

5. According to Bull's letter, what tactic was proposed to prevent future rebellions like the Stono Rebellion?
   (A) Increasing the number of white settlers in the interior
   (B) Deploying British troops along the Carolina border
   (C) Using allied Indigenous nations to capture escapees
   (D) Offering freedom to enslaved people who report conspiracies

Answer Explanations

1. **(B)** Leonard Parkinson was a prominent leader during the Second Maroon War in Jamaica. This engraving highlights his role as a captain of the maroons—Africans who escaped slavery and formed autonomous, militarized communities in Jamaica. Choice (B) is correct because the image reflects the organized resistance of the maroons. Choice (A) is incorrect because it refers to colonial militarization of enslaved Africans, not autonomous resistance. Choice (C) is incorrect because Parkinson was not conscripted; he led guerrilla warfare against British forces. Choice (D) is incorrect becausee the image depicts resistance, not royalty.

2. **(C)** Parkinson is shown in an alert, active pose with a rifle, which indicates readiness for battle. This visual language underscores the military organization and resistance tactics of the maroons. Choice (A) is incorrect becausee the stance is dynamic and assertive, not passive. Choice (B) is unrelated; there is no indication of ceremony or tradition here. Choice (D) is incorrect because the image reflects strength, not docility.

3. **(C)** This engraving is a powerful representation of the autonomy and military resistance of Jamaican maroons—descendants of Africans who refused enslavement and established independent communities. Choice (A) is incorrect because maroons resisted British control, not assimilated into it. Choice (B) is too narrow and does not reflect the theme of resistance. Choice (D) is false; maroon communities preserved African cultural practices.

4. **(C)** Governor Bull describes the "great Number of Negroes" who took up arms, killed colonists, and marched with "Daring" intent. His alarm centers on the scale, organization, and violence of the rebellion. Choice (A) is incorrect because, although destruction occurred, the letter emphasizes human casualties and the military nature of the resistance. Choice (B) is not explicitly mentioned in this letter, though Spanish Florida is contextually relevant to the rebellion. Choice (D) is incorrect; Bull praises the militia's "expedition and bravery," not reluctance.

5. **(C)** Bull specifically mentions enlisting Chickasaw and Catawba chiefs to track and intercept runaways. This reflects colonial reliance on strategic alliances with Indigenous nations to suppress Black resistance. Choices (A) and (B) are not proposed in the letter. Choice (D) is a tactic sometimes used but not mentioned by Bull in this correspondence.

7

Mapping Freedom: Land, Liberation, and the Long Struggle to Belong

Key Themes

- Freedom as contested and mobile—across native lands, international borders, and underground networks
- Intellectual and political debates within Black communities about where and how to belong
- Radical self-definition through writing, art, and armed resistance
- Memory and ritual (e.g., Freedom Days) as tools of resilience and cultural continuity

TIMELINE

Date/Period	Event/Development	Related Topics
1700s–1800s	**African-descended people live among and alongside native nations**—intermarriage, alliance, and shared resistance	Topic 2.17—African Americans in Indigenous Territory
1830	**Indian Removal Act** accelerates conflict and displacement of both native and Black communities	Topic 2.17—Indigenous Territory
1816–1860s	Rise of **emigration and colonization debates**—e.g., American Colonization Society (ACS) and Liberia	Topic 2.18—Emigration and Belonging
1829	**David Walker's *Appeal*** demands Black self-determination and revolution	Topic 2.19—Radical Resistance
1830s–1850s	Growth of **Black abolitionist voices—Frederick Douglass, Henry Highland Garnet, Maria Stewart**	Topic 2.19—Radical Resistance
1830s–1860s	Expansion of **Underground Railroad** networks; **Harriet Tubman** leads dozens to freedom	Topic 2.20 - Abolitionism and the Underground Railroad
1850	**Fugitive Slave Act** increases danger for escaped and free Black people	Topic 2.20—Underground Railroad
1800s–present	**Art and photography** document and interpret Black freedom struggles—e.g., daguerreotypes, portraits, murals	Topic 2.21—Resistance in Art and Photography
1830s–1860s	Enslaved women write **narratives of resistance**—e.g., **Harriet Jacobs, Sojourner Truth**	Topic 2.22—Gender and Slave Narratives

Date/Period	Event/Development	Related Topics
1861–1865	**Civil War**; African Americans fight for Union, freedom, and family reunification	Topic 2.23—The Civil War and Black Communities
1863	**Emancipation Proclamation** redefines purpose of war and sparks mass Black enlistment	Topic 2.23—Civil War and Black Communities
June 19, 1865	**Juneteenth**—enslaved people in Texas learn of emancipation, celebrated as **Freedom Day**	Topic 2.24—Freedom Days
Post-1865 to present	Annual celebrations of **emancipation anniversaries** (e.g., Emancipation Day, Juneteenth) commemorate struggle	Topic 2.24—Ongoing Struggle for Freedom

Topic 2.17 African Americans in Indigenous Territory

Key Terms

- Black-Indigenous alliances
- Five Large Indigenous Nations—Cherokee, Choctaw, Chickasaw, Creek, Seminole
- Enslavement by native nations—especially among the Cherokee
- Black Seminoles—Afro-Indigenous maroon communities
- Trail of Tears—displacement of both Native Americans and Black people
- Freedmen treaties
- Citizenship debates—especially after Reconstruction
- Intermarriage and shared culture

In the eighteenth and nineteenth centuries, as the institution of slavery spread across the U.S. South and into newly acquired territories, African Americans and Indigenous peoples found themselves navigating shared landscapes shaped by displacement, resistance, and survival. While some African Americans sought refuge in Indigenous nations, others were enslaved within them—highlighting the diverse and often contradictory relationships between Black and native communities. In places like Indian Territory and the southeastern woodlands, these interactions produced new kinship ties, cultural exchanges, and political alliances while also raising tensions over land, labor, and sovereignty. The expansion of slavery transformed Indigenous spaces into contested zones where race, power, and survival intersected.

After engaging with this topic, scholars will be able to:

- Explain how the expansion of slavery in the United States South affected relations between Black and Indigenous people.

Black-Seminole Solidarity and Resistance

In the early nineteenth century, some African American maroons—freedom seekers who escaped slavery—found refuge among the Seminole people in Florida. More than welcomed, they were embraced as kin. Their alliance was not only cultural but military. During the Second Seminole War (1835–1842), Black and Indigenous fighters stood united in resisting forced relocation and U.S. expansion. This historic partnership challenged the racial hierarchies of the time and reflected the possibilities of coalition building in the face of empire.

Abraham, a prominent Black Seminole leader, was a strategist, interpreter, and political liaison who played a critical role during the Second Seminole War. Born into slavery and later emancipated, he became an advisor to Seminole chiefs and a key negotiator with U.S. officials. His leadership exemplifies the enduring alliance between African American maroons and the Seminole Nation in their shared struggle for sovereignty and survival.

Gopher John, also known as John Horse, was a Black Seminole leader, military scout, and interpreter whose influence spanned both the Second Seminole War and the U.S. Civil War. A fierce advocate for Black freedom and Seminole sovereignty, he used his multilingual skills and political acumen to navigate among Indigenous, African American, and U.S. military interests. His legacy reflects the enduring resistance and resilience of Black Seminole communities in the face of displacement and oppression.

Abraham, a black Seminole leader, 1863 (Source: Schomburg Center for Research in Black Culture, Manuscripts, Archives and Rare Books Division, The New York Public Library)

Gopher John, a black Seminole leader and interpreter, 1863 (Source: Schomburg Center for Research in Black Culture, Manuscripts, Archives and Rare Books Division, The New York Public Library)

Slavery Along the Trail of Tears

While some Indigenous nations sheltered the formerly enslaved, others practiced chattel slavery themselves. The Cherokee, Chickasaw, Choctaw, Creek (Muscogee), and Seminole nations—often referred to as the five large Indigenous nations—held enslaved African Americans within their communities. When the federal government executed forced removals through the Trail of Tears, these enslaved individuals were uprooted once more and transported westward alongside their enslavers, making them victims of both racial slavery and settler colonialism.

An 1836 diary entry recounting General Thomas Sidney Jesup's military campaign offers a chilling window into the violent displacement of Black Seminoles during the Second Seminole War. As the U.S. Army escalated efforts to suppress resistance in Florida, Jesup's troops targeted maroon settlements with calculated precision. This excerpt captures the moment when 41 Black Seminoles were seized, their village burned in a predawn raid:

> Tracks and Indian tracks supposed to be from one to two weeks old. Moved forward to Palalikaha on the Volusia road—found the way strewed with dead horses. Passed a large encampment of the Tennesseans & friendly Indians—here numerous beaver had been killed. Passed through two hammocks, and after dark encamped a short distance from the latter near a pond. Went forward, crossed the Ocklawaha at the lower end of a lake on a temporary bridge constructed by General Eustis—Soon after captured an Indian from whom information was obtained of the situation of a negro village at the head of the lake. Detached Lt. Col. Caulfield with two companies of his battalion, accompanied by Capt. Crossman and Lieut. Chambers, also by an interpreter and the Indian prisoner—Genl. J. moved forward with the remainder of the command about five miles encamped on a beautiful lake—Lieut. Col. Caulfield returned about 9 p.m. with forty one negro prisoners, having surprised the village, captured the greater part of its inhabitants, and burnt the houses and property which they could not bring in.
>
> Source: Entries from the diary of General Thomas Sidney Jesup while commanding his first campaign of the Second Seminole War, October 1, 1836, to May 30, 1837, pp. 32–35 (State Archives of Florida, Collection M86-12).

Slave Codes and Surveillance in Native Nations

In an effort to codify their social order and align with American power structures, some Indigenous nations developed slave codes and enforcement systems that mirrored those found in the American South. They established slave patrols, restricted the mobility of enslaved people, and participated in the recapture of those who fled. These measures reflected a broader pattern of internalized racial hierarchies shaped by U.S. expansion and white supremacist influence.

The *Arkansas Petition for Freedmen's Rights* (1869) was a powerful document submitted by newly emancipated African Americans demanding equal protection, landownership, and full civil rights during the Reconstruction era. Signed by freedmen determined to claim their place in American democracy, the petition reflected both the urgency and hope of Black political activism in the post–Civil War South. It stands as a testament to the struggle for justice amid ongoing racial violence and resistance to Black citizenship.

> To the Honorable Senators and Representatives in the Congress of the United States Representing the State of Arkansas.—
>
> Gentlemen,
>
> We the undersigned Petitioners; Members of the General Assembly of the State of Arkansas, do most respectfully represent that information has been received that there are <u>three thousand</u> persons of African descent living and residing in the Choctaw and Chickasaw Nations, who were formerly held in servitude by Said Nations, and who are desirous of remaining in said Nations and enjoying all the rights and privileges of Citizens thereof. Therefore. We request that you use your influence for the passage of an Enabling Act by

the Congress of the United States, to allow the Choctaw and Chickasaw Nations to amend or rescind Article III of a Treaty entered into by and between the Government of the United States and the said Choctaw and Chickasaw Nations dated April 26th 1866, so that all persons of African descent may remain in said Nations; select and hold forty (40) acres of Land each—and be entitled to all the rights and privileges of any other class of Citizens in said Nations, including the right of Suffrage.—

Arkansas Petition for Freedmen's Rights (1869)

Source: General Assembly of the State of Arkansas, Petition for Freedmen's Rights to the US Congress, 1869 (National Archives, Records of the U.S Senate).

Racial Boundaries and Erased Kinship

As native nations absorbed the logic of racial slavery, they began to harden social boundaries that once allowed for Black-Indigenous kinship. Laws and cultural shifts redefined people of mixed African and Indigenous ancestry as outsiders, stripping them of tribal affiliation and disrupting generations of family and cultural connection. This legacy of exclusion reverberates in modern debates around tribal citizenship, sovereignty, and reparative justice.

Two Histories, One Land

African Americans and Indigenous peoples often shared land—and sometimes struggles. From intermarriage to military alliances, their stories are deeply linked. These shared spaces offer a rich picture of resistance, survival, and identity in early America.

You're Practicing: Connecting overlapping historical narratives.

Connect This To: Cultural exchange, territory, and resistance.

Theme: Migration and Diaspora

Practice: Explain the Effects of Historical Developments and Evaluate Their Significance

Using your knowledge of the interactions between African Americans and Native American communities in the eighteenth and nineteenth centuries, complete the following.

(A) Describe one example of cooperation or alliance between African-descended people and Indigenous nations.

(B) Explain one way in which U.S. expansion and Indian removal policies affected African Americans in Indigenous territories.

(C) Evaluate the extent to which these interactions supported African American freedom and belonging.

SAMPLE RESPONSES

(A) The Black Seminoles in Florida formed alliances with the Seminole Nation, where African-descended people lived in autonomous villages, intermarried, and fought alongside Seminoles during the Seminole Wars against U.S. forces.

Many Indigenous nations, such as the Creek and Cherokee, provided refuge to runaway enslaved Africans, allowing them to integrate into tribal communities, sometimes as free farmers or warriors.

(B) The Indian Removal Act of 1830 and the Trail of Tears led to the forced migration of Indigenous nations that had previously harbored free and fugitive Black people, resulting in their re-enslavement or displacement by white settlers.

As U.S. expansion seized tribal lands, African-descended people who had gained relative autonomy in Native communities—such as the Black Seminoles—were targeted by slave catchers and military campaigns seeking to destroy these alliances.

(C) These alliances provided significant opportunities for freedom, as seen with the Black Seminoles, who secured land, protection, and a shared resistance against U.S. encroachment.

However, the support was limited and fragile, since U.S. government policies and pressure on Native nations often forced them to adopt slaveholding practices or sign treaties that undermined Black autonomy.

Skills Assessed: Describe and explain historical developments and processes; evaluate Evidence for historical argumentation; argumentation with complex understanding.

Topic 2.18 Debates About Emigration, Colonization, and Belonging in America

Key Terms

- American Colonization Society (ACS)
- Liberia—African nation founded by freed Black Americans
- Paul Cuffe—early emigration advocate
- Henry Highland Garnet—supporter of African emigration
- Martin Delany—father of Black nationalism
- Debates over loyalty vs. liberation
- Citizenship and belonging
- Black nationalism vs. integrationism

In the nineteenth century, African Americans engaged in passionate debates about whether true freedom and equality could ever be realized in the United States. Some leaders, disillusioned by the deep-rooted racism and violence that followed emancipation, advocated for emigration as a pathway to Black sovereignty and self-determination—especially to Africa, Canada, Haiti, or Central America. Others rejected emigration, insisting that the struggle for justice must remain rooted in the American landscape. They argued that African Americans had earned their place through labor, sacrifice, and citizenship.

After engaging with this topic, scholars will be able to:

- Explain how nineteenth-century emigrationists aimed to achieve the goal of Black freedom and self-determination.
- Explain how transatlantic abolitionism influenced anti-emigrationists' political views about the potential for African Americans' belonging in American society.

A Future Beyond the United States

By the mid-nineteenth century, many African American leaders had grown disillusioned with the failure of the United States to uphold promises of liberty and equality. In the wake of the 1857 *Dred Scott v. Sandford* decision—which denied African Americans any claim to citizenship—emigrationists proposed leaving the United States altogether. They viewed the creation of autonomous Black communities abroad as a viable path toward freedom, safety, and self-governance beyond the reach of American racism.

Shared Histories, Shared Destinies

African American emigrationists considered West Africa, the Caribbean, and Latin America to be ideal destinations because of their sizable Afro-descendant populations and cultural, historical, and linguistic ties to the African diaspora. These regions also offered warm climates and fertile land, which were seen as practical for agricultural development, self-sufficiency, and the building of Black-majority societies grounded in a shared struggle and ancestral connection.

Black Nationalism and Self-Determination

Figures such as Paul Cuffee and Martin R. Delany advanced Black nationalism as both a political philosophy and survival strategy. They argued that unity, racial pride, and control over their own political destinies were essential to resisting systemic oppression. These leaders envisioned emigration not as retreat but as a radical act of sovereignty—a rejection of white supremacy and an affirmation of global Black solidarity.

Paul Cuffee's Vision in Action

Paul Cuffee, a wealthy African American Quaker and sea captain, acted on his beliefs by organizing and financing the first African American–led emigration voyage to Africa. In 1815, he transported 39 African Americans to Freetown, Sierra Leone—a settlement originally founded by the British for formerly enslaved Africans. His journey marked the beginning of an enduring emigrationist tradition rooted in Black agency and global connection.

Birthright Citizenship and the Fight Within

In contrast, many Black abolitionists rejected emigration, arguing that African Americans were entitled to the rights and liberties promised by the U.S. Constitution. They believed in fighting to claim their rightful place as full citizens and saw themselves as having an undeniable claim to "birthright citizenship." For these anti-emigrationists, the struggle for justice was a fight for inclusion within the American body politic—not abandonment of it.

In a 1832 publication entitled "Emigration to Mexico" in *The Liberator*, a woman identified only as A Colored Female of Philadelphia boldly critiques the limits placed on African American life in the United States. Arguing in favor of Black emigration to Mexico, she challenges the nation's failure to uphold liberty and envisions a freer, more dignified future beyond its borders.

> **"Emigration to Mexico" by A Colored Female of Philadelphia in *The Liberator*, January 28, 1832:**
>
> Mr. Editor,—I am happy to learn that the sentiments of some of my Trenton brethren are in accordance with my own, in regard to our locating in Mexico and Upper Canada; for, in my humble opinion, one thing is needful for us as a people, even emigration; but not to Africa; nor to place ourselves as a distinct people any where; but to attach ourselves to a nation already established. The government of these United States is not the only one in this hemisphere that offers equal rights to men; but there are others, under whose protection we may safely reside, where it is no disgrace to wear a sable complexion, and where our rights will not be continually trampled upon, on that account. We profess to be republicans, and such I hope we are; but wherein do we show our republican spirit, by sitting still and sighing for that liberty our white brethren tell us we shall never obtain; or in hoping that in some fifty or a hundred years hence, our children's children will be made free? I think we do not evince republicanism by this conduct, but verily believe that the time has arrived, when we too ought to manifest that spirit of independence which shines so conspicuously in the character of Europeans, by leaving the land of oppression, and emigrating where we may be received and treated as brothers; where our worth will be felt and acknowledged; and where we may acquire education, wealth and respectability, together with a knowledge of the arts and sciences; all of which may be in our power—of the enjoyment of which the government of the separate states in the union is adopting means to deprive us.

The author of this article is aware, that the subject is not popular, and perhaps will not be kindly received; but it is one that I hope will be deeply pondered in the mind of every colored citizen of this country, before he passes sentence against it.

Some of your readers may inquire, where is that country to which we may remove, and thus become free and equal? I believe that country to be Mexico. There is an independent nation, where indeed "all men are born free and equal," possessing those inalienable rights which our constitution guarantees. The climate is healthy and warm, and of course adapted to our nature; the soil is rich and fertile, which will contribute to our wealth; and there we may become a people of worth and respectability; whereas in this country we are kept poor, and of course, cannot aspire to any thing more than what we always have been. I have been waiting to hear of some way being pointed out, that will tend to better the present generation; but, as yet, have heard of nothing that appears to be permanent. I would not wish to be thought pleading the cause of colonization, for no one detests it more than I do. I would not be taken to Africa, were the Society to make me queen of the country; and were I to move to Canada, I would not settle in the colony, but take up my abode in some of the cities where a distinction is not known; for I do not approve of our drawing off into a separate body any where. But, I confess, I can see no just reason why we should not cultivate the spirit of enterprise as well as the whites. They are found in every quarter of the globe, in search of situations to better their condition; and why we may not "go and do likewise?"

I am informed that the population of Mexico is eight millions of colored, and one million of whites; and by the rapid growth of amalgamation amongst them, there is every probability that it will ere long become one entire colored nation. I am of opinion that Mexico would afford us a large field for speculation, were we to remove thither; and who can say, that the day will not soon arrive, when the flag of our colored American merchants' ships from the Mexican ports shall be seen, proudly waving in the breeze of the American harbors? And shall not our sons feel proud to enlist under the Mexican banner, and support her government? Surely they will.

There is one objection, however, that may arise in the minds of some; that is, the religion of that nation being Papist; but we can take with us the Holy Bible, which is able to make us wise unto salvation; and perhaps we may be made the honored instruments, in the hands of an all-wise God, in establishing the holy religion of the Protestant Church in that country; and that alone might be a sufficient inducement for the truly pious.

A Colored Female of Philadelphia.
Philadelphia, January 2, 1832.

Source: A Colored Female of Philadelphia, "Emigration to Mexico," *The Liberator*, January 28, 1832, p. 2, Boston Public Library Rare Books Department, in Digital Commonwealth: Massachusetts Collections Online.

In his influential 1852 treatise *The Condition, Elevation, Emigration, and Destiny of the Colored People of the United States*, Martin R. Delany—widely regarded as a pioneer of Black nationalism—makes a powerful case for emigration as a pathway to true freedom and self-determination. Disillusioned by America's systemic racism, Delany calls on African Americans to build an independent future rooted in pride, sovereignty, and global Black unity.

Emigration of the Colored People of the United States.

That there have been people in all ages under certain circumstances, that may be benefited by emigration, will be admitted; and that there are circumstances under which emigration is absolutely necessary to their political elevation, cannot be disputed.

This we see in the Exodus of the Jews from Egypt to the land of Judea; in the expedition of Dido and her followers from Tyre to Mauritania; and not to dwell upon hundreds of modern European examples—also in the ever memorable emigration of the Puritans, in 1620, from Great Britain, the land of their birth, to the wilderness of the New World, at which may be fixed the beginning of emigration to this continent as a permanent residence.

This may be acknowledged; but to advocate the emigration of the colored people of the United States from their native homes, is a new feature in our history, and at first view, may be considered objectionable, as pernicious to our interests. This objection is at once removed, when reflecting on our condition as incontrovertibly shown in a foregoing part of this work. And we shall proceed at once to give the advantages to be derived from emigration, to us as a people, in preference to any other policy that we may adopt. This granted, the question will then be, Where shall we go? This we conceive to be all-important—of paramount consideration, and shall endeavor to show the most advantageous locality; and premise the recommendation, with the strictest advice against any countenance whatever, to the emigration scheme of the so called Republic of Liberia.

Source: Martin R. Delany, *The Condition, Elevation, Emigration, and Destiny of the Colored People of the United States, Politically Considered*, Philadelphia, 1852, pp. 159–188.

"Republic of Liberia."

That we desire the civilization and enlightenment of Africa—the high and elevated position of Liberia among the nations of the earth, may not be doubted, as the writer was among the first, seven or eight years ago, to make the suggestion and call upon the Liberians to hold up their heads like men; take courage, having confidence in their own capacity to govern themselves, and come out from their disparaging position, by formally declaring their Independence.

As our desire is to impart information, and enlighten the minds of our readers on the various subjects herein contained, we present below a large extract from the "First Annual Report of the Trustees of Donations for Education in Liberia." This Extract will make a convenient statistic reference for matters concerning Liberia. We could only wish that many of our readers possessed more historical and geographical information of the world, and there could be little fears of their going anywhere that might be incongenial and unfavorable to their success. We certainly do intend to deal fairly with Liberia, and give the reader every information that may tend to enlighten them. What the colored people most need, is intelligence; give them this, and there is no danger of them being duped into anything they do not desire. This Board was incorporated by the Legislature of Massachusetts, March 19th, 1850—Ensign H. Kellogg, Speaker of the House, Marshall P. Wilder, President of the Senate. Trustees of the Board—Hon. George N. Briggs, LL.D., Hon. Simon Greenleaf, LL.D., Hon. Stephen Fairbanks, Hon. William J. Hubbard, Hon. Joel Giles, Hon. Albert Fearing, Amos A. Lawrence, Esq. Officers of the Board—Hon. G. N. Briggs, President; Hon. S. Fairbanks, Treasurer; Rev. J. Tracy, Secretary. The conclusion of the Report says:—" In view of such considerations, the Trustees cannot doubt the patrons of learning will sustain them in their attempt to plant the first College on the only continent which yet remains without one." In this, the learned Trustees have fallen into a statistical and geographical error, which we design to correct. The continent is not without a College. There are now in Egypt, erected under the patronage of that singularly wonderful man, Mehemet Ali, four colleges conducted on the European principle—Scientific, Medical, Legal, and Military.

These are in successful operation; the Military College having an average of eleven hundred students annually. The continent of Africa then, is not without a college, but though benighted enough, even to an apparent hopeless degeneration, she is still the seat of learning, and must some day rise, in the majesty of ancient grandeur, and vindicate the rights and claims of her own children, against the incalculable wrongs perpetrated through the period of sixty ages by professedly enlightened Christians, against them.

Source: Martin R. Delany, *The Condition, Elevation, Emigration, and Destiny of the Colored People of the United States, Politically Considered*, Philadelphia, 1852, pp. 159–188.

Exile for Survival, Advocacy from Abroad

The Fugitive Slave Acts of 1793 and 1850 rendered even "free" African Americans vulnerable to kidnapping and reenslavement. As a result, prominent activists like **Frederick Douglass** temporarily relocated to Britain and Ireland for safety. From abroad, they continued to denounce slavery, publish antislavery works, and forge transatlantic networks that strengthened the moral and political foundations of the abolition movement.

In his 1857 speech West India Emancipation, delivered on the anniversary of British abolition in the Caribbean, Frederick Douglass reflects on the triumph of emancipation in the West Indies as both a moral victory and a political rebuke to American slavery. He uses the moment to rally continued resistance, famously declaring, "If there is no struggle, there is no progress." Douglass's speech remains a defining articulation of abolitionist courage and the enduring fight for Black liberation.

Let me give you a word of the philosophy of reform. The whole history of the progress of human liberty shows that all concessions yet made to her august claims have been born of earnest struggle. The conflict has been exciting, agitating, all-absorbing, and for the time being, putting all other tumults to silence. It must do this or it does nothing. If there is no struggle there is no progress. Those who profess to favor freedom and yet deprecate agitation are men who want crops without plowing up the ground; they want rain without thunder and lightning. They want the ocean without the awful roar of its many waters.

This struggle may be a moral one, or it may be a physical one, and it may be both moral and physical, but it must be a struggle. Power concedes nothing without a demand. It never did and it never will. Find out just what any people will quietly submit to and you have found out the exact measure of injustice and wrong which will be imposed upon them, and these will continue till they are resisted with either words or blows, or with both. The limits of tyrants are prescribed by the endurance of those whom they oppress. In the light of these ideas, Negroes will be hunted at the North and held and flogged at the South so long as they submit to those devilish outrages and make no resistance, either moral or physical. Men may not get all they pay for in this world, but they must certainly pay for all they get. If we ever get free from the oppressions and wrongs heaped upon us, we must pay for their removal. We must do this by labor, by suffering, by sacrifice, and if needs be, by our lives and the lives of others.

Source: This excerpt is from a speech, West India Emancipation, given by Frederick Douglass on August 4, 1857, and printed in *Two Speeches, by Frederick Douglass; One on West India Emancipation, Delivered at Canandaigua, Aug. 4th, and the Other on the Dred Scott Decision, Delivered in New York, on the Occasion of the Anniversary of the American Abolition Society, May, 1857.* Rochester: C.P. Dewey, 1857, pp. 21–22 (The Gilder Lehrman Institute of American History, GLC07591).

A Nation's Hypocrisy on Display

Anti-emigrationists called attention to the hypocrisy of a nation that celebrated its own revolution while denying basic human rights to millions of Black Americans. On the eve of the Civil War, they critiqued the contradictions at the heart of American democracy—how liberty and justice were weaponized against the very people who had labored to build the country. Their arguments laid the groundwork for future civil rights movements that would continue to demand America live up to its ideals.

TIP

Keep Time in Mind

Aim to spend no more than one minute per MCQ, leaving yourself time to review answers. For FRQs, use the first few minutes to plan, most of the time to write, and the few minutes to review.

Back to Africa? Not So Simple

In the 1800s, some African Americans debated leaving the United States to settle in Africa. Others saw that as giving up their claim to freedom at home. These debates reveal powerful questions: Who gets to belong? Where is home?

You're Practicing: Understanding differing viewpoints within a movement.

Connect This To: Emigration, belonging, and political thought.

Theme: Power and Politics

Practice: Explain the Significance of Historical Developments and Evaluate Competing Perspectives

In the nineteenth century, African Americans engaged in fierce debate over emigration as a strategy for liberation.

(A) Identify one argument used by emigrationists to support leaving the United States.
(B) Describe one counterargument made by anti-emigrationists.
(C) Evaluate how these debates reveal broader tensions about citizenship, identity, and racial justice.

SAMPLE RESPONSES

(A) Emigrationists, such as Martin Delany, argued that African Americans would never achieve true equality or citizenship in the United States due to entrenched racism and white supremacy, so building independent Black nations in Africa or the Caribbean offered a path to self-determination and dignity.

Supporters of the American Colonization Society claimed that establishing colonies like Liberia would provide African Americans with political and economic opportunities free from U.S. discrimination.

(B) Anti-emigrationists, such as Frederick Douglass, argued that African Americans had built the United States through their labor and sacrifices, and therefore had the right to claim citizenship, equality, and freedom within the country rather than abandoning it.

Many believed emigration was a strategy promoted by white elites to remove free Black populations rather than addressing systemic racism, making it a betrayal of the struggle for racial justice at home.

(C) These debates reveal that African Americans were deeply divided over whether liberation could be achieved through integration and reform within the U.S. or through nation-building and autonomy elsewhere.

The tension reflects a larger question of Black identity and belonging: whether African Americans' future was tied to the U.S. as a homeland or to a broader pan-African vision of global freedom and solidarity.

Skills Assessed: Explain historical argument and perspective; comparison of perspectives; argumentation and reasoning.

Topic 2.19 Black Political Thought: Radical Resistance

Key Terms

- David Walker's Appeal (1829)—call for rebellion against oppression
- Henry Highland Garnet—Address to the Slaves of the United States
- Frederick Douglass—radical abolitionist phase
- Self-defense and armed resistance
- Call for immediate emancipation
- Black pride and autonomy
- Moral suasion vs. radical resistance
- Political empowerment through print

Throughout the nineteenth century, Black activists across the African diaspora developed bold and unapologetic strategies to challenge slavery, racial violence, and legal systems that upheld white supremacy. Radical resistance—defined by its moral clarity, confrontational tone, and refusal to compromise on Black humanity—emerged in speeches, manifestos, and organizational efforts that demanded immediate emancipation, citizenship, and dignity. From grassroots organizers to prominent intellectuals, these voices rejected gradualism and reshaped Black political identity through a tradition of resistance rooted in self-determination, justice, and collective liberation.

After engaging with this topic, scholars will be able to:

- Describe the features of nineteenth-century radical resistance strategies promoted by Black activists to demand change.
- Analyze the role of political writing, speech making, and protest in advancing Black liberation.
- Evaluate how radical Black political thought influenced broader social justice movements across the United States and the African diaspora.

Radical Strategies for Freedom

Radical resistance thinkers argued that the daily terror of slavery demanded immediate and forceful action. They rejected gradual emancipation or legal reform as insufficient in the face of systemic brutality. Many embraced the moral legitimacy of revolts, insurrections, and armed resistance as necessary tools to overthrow an institution built on violence. For these leaders, freedom was not a distant ideal—it was an urgent necessity worth fighting for, even at great personal risk.

A Rejection of Moral Suasion

During the 1830s and 1840s, a growing number of Black intellectuals and activists pushed back against the dominant white abolitionist strategy of *moral suasion*—the belief that appealing to the conscience of slaveholders and white Americans would bring about change. Radical Black leaders recognized that logic and morality alone could not dismantle systems of racial violence. Instead, they called instead for bolder, more confrontational methods to secure African American liberation.

The Power of the Pen as a Weapon

Radical resistance activists used printed literature—pamphlets, speeches, and firsthand testimonies—as a form of political warfare. These publications exposed the cruelties of slavery, inspired enslaved readers to resist, and were often distributed covertly throughout the South, despite heavy surveillance. These bold, defiant texts made clear that enslaved people had the right—and, in the eyes of many, the duty—to pursue freedom by any means necessary.

David Walker's *Appeal to the Colored Citizens of the World* (1829) stands as one of the most radical and influential antislavery texts of the nineteenth century. Written by a free Black abolitionist in Boston, the *Appeal* challenged white supremacy and called upon enslaved and free Black people to resist oppression by any means necessary. Its bold language and revolutionary tone helped galvanize resistance across the African diaspora.

ARTICLE II.

OUR WRETCHEDNESS IN CONSEQUENCE OF IGNORANCE.

Ignorance, my brethren, is a mist, low down into the very dark and almost impenetrable abyss in which, our fathers for many centuries have been plunged. The Christians, and enlightened of Europe, and some of Asia, seeing the ignorance and consequent degradation of our fathers, instead of trying to cnlighten them, by teaching them that religion and light with which God had blessed them, they have plunged them into wretchedness ten thousand times more intolerable, than if they had left them entirely to the Lord, and to add to their miseries, deep down into which they have plunged them tell them, that they are an inferior and distinct race of beings, which they will be glad enough to recal and swallow by and by. Fortune and misfortune, two inseparable companions, lay rolled up in the wheel of events, which have from the creation of the world, and will continue to take place among men until God shall dash worlds together.

When we take a retrospective view of the arts and sciences—the wise legislators—the Pyramids, and other magnificent buildings—the turning of the channel of the river Nile, by the sons of Africa or of Ham, among whom learning originated, and was carried thence into Greece, where it was improved upon and refined. Thence among the Romans, and all over the then enlightened parts of the world, and it has been enlightening the dark and benighted minds of men from then, down to this day. I say, when I view retrospectively, the renown of that once mighty people, the children of our great progenitor I am indeed cheered. Yea further, when I view that mighty son of Africa, HANNIBAL, one of the greatest generals of antiquity, who defeated and cut off so many thousands of the white Romans or murderers, and who carried his victorious arms, to the very gate of Rome, and I give it as my candid opinion, that had Carthage been well united and had given him good support, he would have carried that cruel and barbarous city by storm. But they were dis-united, as the coloured people are now, in the United States of America, the reason our natural enemies are enabled to keep their feet on our throats.

Beloved brethren—here let me tell you, and believe it, that the Lord our God, as true as he sits on his throne in heaven, and as true as our Saviour died to redeem the world, will give you a Hannibal, and when the Lord shall have raised him up, and given him to you for your possession, O my suffering brethren! remember the divisions and consequent sufferings of Carthage and of Hayti. Read the history particularly of Hayti, and see how they were butchered by the whites, and do you take warning. The person whom God shall give you, give him your support and let him go his length, and behold in him the salvation of your God. God will indeed, deliver you through him from your deplorable and wretched condition under the Christians of America. I charge you this day before my God to lay no obstacle in his way, but let him go.

Source: David Walker, *Walker's Appeal, in Four Articles; Together with a Preamble, to the Coloured Citizens of the World, but in Particular, and Very Expressly, to Those of the United States of America*, Written in Boston, State of Massachusetts, September 28, 1829, 3rd ed., Boston, 1830.

In 1843, at the National Negro Convention in Buffalo, New York, abolitionist and Presbyterian minister **Henry Highland Garnet** delivered one of the boldest calls for resistance in American history. In An Address to the Slaves of the United States, Garnet urged enslaved African Americans to rise up and claim their freedom through rebellion, making clear that moral persuasion alone would not dismantle slavery. His speech reflects a shift toward radical Black political thought and prefigures the growing militancy of the abolitionist movement.

Address to the Slaves of the U.S.

Brethren and Fellow-Citizens:

Your brethren of the north, east, and west have been accustomed to meet together in National Conventions, to sympathize with each other, and to weep over your unhappy condition. In these meetings we have addressed all classes of the free, but we have never until this time, sent a word of consolation and advice to you. We have been contented in sitting still and mourning over your sorrows, earnestly hoping that before this day, your sacred liberties would have been restored. But, we have hoped in vain. Years have rolled on, and tens of thousands have been borne on streams of blood, and tears, to the shores of eternity. While you have been oppressed, we have also been partakers with you; nor can we be free while you are enslaved. We therefore write to you as being bound with you.

Many of you are bound to us, not only by the ties of a common humanity, but we are connected by the more tender relations of parents, wives, husbands, children, brothers, and sisters, and friends. As such we most affectionately address you.

Slavery has fixed a deep gulf between you and us, and while it shuts out from you the relief and consolation which your friends would willingly render, it afflicts and persecutes you with a fierceness which we might not expect to see in the fiends of hell. But still the Almighty Father of Mercies has left to us a glimmering ray of hope, which shines out like a lone star in a cloudy sky. Mankind are becoming wiser, and better—the oppressor's power is fading, and you, every day, are becoming better informed, and more numerous. Your grievances, brethren, are many. We shall not attempt, in this short address, to present to the world, all the dark catalogue of this nation's sins, which have been committed upon an innocent people. Nor is it indeed, necessary, for you feel them from day to day, and all the civilized world look upon them with amazement.

Two hundred and twenty-seven years ago, the first of our injured race were brought to the shores of America. They came not with glad spirits to select their homes, in the New World. They came not with their own consent, to find an unmolested enjoyment of the blessings of this fruitful soil. The first dealings they had with men calling themselves Christians, exhibited to them the worst features of corrupt and sordid hearts; and convinced them that no cruelty is too great, no villainy, and no robbery too abhorrent for even enlightened men to perform, when influenced by avarice, and lust. Neither did they come flying upon the wings of Liberty, to a land of freedom. But, they came with broken hearts, from their beloved native land, and were doomed to unrequited toil and deep degradation. Nor did the evil of their bondage end at their emancipation by death. Succeeding generations inherited their chains, and millions have come from eternity into time, and have returned again to the world of spirits, cursed, and ruined by American Slavery.

The propagators of the system, or their immediate ancestors very soon discovered its growing evil, and its tremendous wickedness, and secret promises were made to destroy it. The gross inconsistency of a people holding slaves, who had themselves "ferried o'er the wave," for freedom's sake, was too apparent to be entirely overlooked. The voice of Freedom cried, "Emancipate your Slaves." Humanity supplicated with tears, for the deliverance of the children of Africa. Wisdom urged her solemn plea. The bleeding captive plead his innocence, and pointed to Christianity who stood weeping at the cross. Jehovah frowned upon the nefarious institution, and thunderbolts, red with vengeance, struggled to leap forth to blast the guilty wretches who maintained it. But all was vain. Slavery had stretched its dark wings of death over the land, the Church stood silently by—the priests prophesied falsely, and the people loved to have it so. Its throne is established, and now it reigns triumphantly.

We do not advise you to attempt a revolution with the sword, because it would be inexpedient. Your numbers are too small, and moreover the rising spirit of the age, and the spirit of the gospel, are opposed to war and bloodshed. But from this moment cease to labor for tyrants who will not remunerate you. Let every slave throughout the land do this, and the days of slavery are numbered. You cannot be more oppressed than you have been—you cannot suffer greater cruelties than you have already. Rather die freemen, than live to be slaves. Remember that you are THREE MILLIONS.

It is in your power so to torment the God-cursed slaveholders, that they will be glad to let you go free. If the scale was turned, and black men were the masters, and white men the slaves, every destructive agent and element would be employed to lay the oppressor low. Danger and death would hang over their heads day and night. Yes, the tyrants would meet with plagues more terrible than those of Pharaoh. But you are a patient people. You act as though you were made for the special use of these devils. You act as though your daughters were born to pamper the lusts of your masters and overseers. And worse than all, you tamely submit, while your lords tear your wives from your embraces, and defile them before your eyes. In the name of God we ask, are you men? Where is the blood of your fathers? Has it all run out of your veins? Awake, awake; millions of voices are calling you! Your dead fathers speak to you from their graves. Heaven, as with a voice of thunder, calls on you to arise from the dust. Let your motto be resistance! resistance! resistance! No oppressed people have ever secured their liberty without resistance. What kind of resistance you had better make, you must decide by the circumstances that surround you, and according to the suggestion of expediency. Brethren, adieu. Trust in the living God. Labor for the peace of the human race, and remember that you are three millions.

Source: Henry Highland Garnet, "An Address to the Slaves of the United States of America" in Henry Highland Garnet, *Walker's Appeal, with a Brief Sketch of His Life*, New York: J. H. Tobitt, 1848, pp. 89–96.

David Walker's *Appeal* (1829) and Henry Highland Garnet's An Address to the Slaves (1843) represent a defining moment in Black political thought, where radical resistance replaced moral persuasion as a necessary strategy to confront the violence of slavery. Both the written text and the speech powerfully rejected gradualism and demanded immediate liberation, even if it required revolt. Their uncompromising rhetoric laid the foundation for future generations of Black activists who would continue to challenge the moral legitimacy of American slavery and the hypocrisy of its democratic ideals.

Rebellion in Words

David Walker, Maria Stewart, and others used fiery speeches and essays to call out injustice. Their words weren't polite—they were bold, urgent, and defiant. Radical thought wasn't just about dreaming. It was about action.

You're Practicing: Analyzing primary sources with purpose.

Connect This To: Revolutionary rhetoric and freedom philosophies.

Theme: Resistance and Autonomy

Practice: Analyze Primary Sources and Explain the Effects of Historical Developments

Read the excerpt from either David Walker's *Appeal* or Henry Highland Garnet's An Address to the Slaves. Then complete the following.

(A) Describe one major claim the author makes about resistance.
(B) Explain how the author's message challenges dominant abolitionist strategies of the period.
(C) Evaluate how radical Black political thought shaped broader freedom movements in the nineteenth century.

SAMPLE RESPONSES

(A) David Walker's *Appeal* argues that enslaved African Americans have the right—and even the duty—to resist slavery by any means necessary, including violent rebellion, because slavery is a moral crime against God and humanity.

Henry Highland Garnet's Address calls for enslaved people to rise up collectively against their oppressors, declaring that freedom must be seized rather than passively awaited.

(B) Walker and Garnet reject the gradualism and moral persuasion favored by many white abolitionists, such as William Lloyd Garrison, arguing instead for immediate, active resistance.

Their radical stance challenged the notion that freedom would come solely through political compromise or appeals to white morality, demanding self-liberation and direct action from the enslaved.

(C) The uncompromising rhetoric of Walker and Garnet inspired a new generation of abolitionists, including Frederick Douglass and later Harriet Tubman, who embraced armed resistance and direct action.

Radical Black thought also linked abolition to a global freedom struggle, influencing movements for Black emigration, pan-Africanism, and civil rights by centering Black agency and self-determination.

Skills Assessed: Analyze primary sources; contextualization; historical argumentation.

Topic 2.20 Race to the Promised Land: Abolitionism and the Underground Railroad

Key Terms

- Harriet Tubman—conductor, Union scout
- Underground Railroad—secret network to free enslaved people
- William Still—documented escape stories
- Abolitionist press—*The Liberator*, *The North Star*
- Quakers and free Black communities
- Safe houses and coded language
- Resistance through flight
- Black and white cooperation in abolition

In the decades before the Civil War, thousands of African Americans risked everything to escape bondage through a vast, covert network of escape routes and safe houses known as the Underground Railroad. Operating beyond maps and laws, this movement relied on the courage of freedom seekers and the solidarity of allies—Black and white—who defied proslavery statutes to challenge the nation's conscience. Among its most legendary conductors was Harriet Tubman, whose daring missions and unwavering dedication to liberation made her an icon of freedom and resistance.

After engaging with this topic, scholars will be able to:

- Describe the role and scale of the Underground Railroad in providing freedom-seeking routes.
- Explain the significance of Harriet Tubman's contributions to abolitionism and African Americans' pursuit of freedom.

The Underground Railroad: A Covert Network of Liberation

The Underground Railroad was a covert network of routes, safe houses, and abolitionist collaborators—both Black and white—that helped enslaved African Americans escape bondage and reach free territories in the

North, Canada, and Mexico during the nineteenth century. It operated under extraordinary secrecy, using coded language, symbols, and signals to protect both freedom seekers and those who assisted them. Despite the risks of violence, imprisonment, and reenslavement, the Underground Railroad grew into one of the most radical and effective forms of resistance to American slavery.

Historians estimate that more than 30,000 enslaved African Americans reached freedom through the Underground Railroad. Although the exact number may never be known due to the secrecy required for its survival, each successful escape represented a powerful challenge to the legal and economic foundation of slavery. These acts of defiance were not only personal triumphs but also political statements that inspired abolitionist activism, enraged proslavery legislators, and exposed the deep hypocrisy of a nation claiming liberty while upholding human bondage.

The scale and frequency of escapes through the Underground Railroad led to the passage of two Fugitive Slave Acts—first in 1793 and then a more aggressive version in 1850. These federal laws criminalized aiding fugitive slaves and required citizens and officials in free states to participate in their capture and return. The 1850 law, in particular, intensified sectional tensions by nationalizing the institution of slavery, forcing abolitionist communities to choose between civil disobedience and complicity. Black communities responded by strengthening their own vigilance committees and escape networks, reaffirming their commitment to freedom by any means necessary.

Harriet Tubman: Conductor, Strategist, and Revolutionary

Harriet Tubman emerged as the most celebrated conductor of the Underground Railroad. Born into slavery in Maryland, Tubman escaped in 1849 and then made at least 19 daring return trips to the South, risking her life to lead over 80 enslaved people to freedom. She used coded spirituals, disguise, and her deep understanding of local geography to evade capture. Tubman's bravery and strategic genius made her a living legend—called Moses by those she freed. Her work helped expose the moral and political bankruptcy of slavery to broader audiences.

Tubman's expertise in navigation and intelligence extended beyond her work as a conductor. During the Civil War, she served the Union Army as a nurse, scout, and spy, gathering intelligence behind Confederate lines and guiding troops through treacherous Southern terrain. Her service was part of a broader movement in which formerly enslaved people became vital to the Union war effort, not only as laborers and soldiers but as architects of their own liberation.

On June 2, 1863, Harriet Tubman led the Combahee River Raid alongside Union Colonel James Montgomery. During the operation, Tubman helped guide Union gunboats through Confederate mines along the river and liberated over 700 enslaved people from rice plantations in South Carolina. This military feat made her the first woman in U.S. history to lead an armed expedition and marked one of the most successful emancipation raids of the Civil War. Her legacy endures as a symbol of radical Black freedom, military leadership, and unwavering resistance.

Harriet Tubman's reflection, featured in *A North-Side View of Slavery. The Refugee: or The Narratives of Fugitive Slaves in Canada* by Benjamin Drew (1856), offers a rare firsthand account of her motives and unwavering commitment to liberation. In this excerpt, Tubman reflects on her decision to return to the South repeatedly to free others, despite the immense danger. Her words illuminate the moral clarity and revolutionary resolve that defined her role in the Underground Railroad and in Black resistance movements.

> I grew up like a neglected weed,—ignorant of liberty, having no experience of it. Then I was not happy or contented: every time I saw a white man I was afraid of being carried away. I had two sisters carried away in a chain-gang,—one of them left two children. We were always uneasy. Now I've been free, I know what a dreadful condition slavery is. I have seen hundreds of escaped slaves, but I never saw one who was willing to go back and be a slave. I have no opportunity to see my friends in my native land. We would rather stay in our native land, if we could be as free there as we are here. I think slavery is the next thing to hell. If a person would send another into bondage, he would, it appears to me, be bad enough to send him into hell, if he could.

Source: "Harriet Tubman," in *A North-Side View of Slavery. The Refugee: or the Narratives of Fugitive Slaves in Canada*. Related by Themselves, with an Account of the History and Condition of the Colored Population of Upper Canada, edited by Benjamin Drew, Boston: John P. Jewett and Company, 1856, p. 30.

Published over two decades after the Civil War, *Harriet, the Moses of Her People* by Sarah H. Bradford (1886) preserves Harriet Tubman's legacy through vivid storytelling and testimony. In this excerpt, Bradford captures Tubman's bravery and tactical genius during her missions to free enslaved people. The passage underscores Tubman's deep spirituality, strategic use of disguise, and unwavering faith in the promise of Black freedom.

> . . . She held a hurried consultation with her brothers, in which she so wrought upon their fears, that they expressed themselves as willing to start with her that very night, for that far North, where, could they reach it in safety, freedom awaited them. But she must first give some intimation of her purpose to the friends she was to leave behind, so that even if not understood at the time, it might be remembered afterward as her intended farewell. Slaves must not be seen talking together, and so it came about that their communication was often made by singing, and the words of their familiar hymns, telling of the heavenly journey, and the land of Canaan, while they did not attract the attention of the masters, conveyed to their brethren and sisters in bondage something more than met the ear. And so she sang, accompanying the words, when for a moment unwatched, with a meaning look to one and another:
>
> "When dat ar ole chariot comes,
> I'm gwine to lebe you,
> I'm boun' for de promised land,
> Frien's, I'm gwine to lebe you."
>
> Again, as she passed the doors of the different cabins, she lifted up her well-known voice; and many a dusky face appeared at door or window, with a wondering or scared expression; and thus she continued:
>
> "I'm sorry, frien's, to lebe you,
> Farewell! oh, farewell!
> But I'll meet you in de mornin,'
> Farewell! oh, farewell!
>
> "I'll meet you in de mornin,'
> When you reach de promised land;
> On de oder side of Jordan,
> For I'm boun' for de promised land."
>
> The brothers started with her, but the way was strange, the north was far away, and all unknown, the masters would pursue and recapture them, and their fate would be worse than ever before; and so they broke away from her, and bidding her goodbye, they hastened back to the known horrors of slavery, and the dread of that which was worse.
>
> Harriet was now left alone, but after watching the retreating forms of her brothers, she turned her face toward the north, and fixing her eyes on the guiding star, and committing her way unto the Lord, she started again upon her long, lonely journey. Her farewell song was long remembered in the cabins, and the old mother sat and wept for her lost child. No intimation had been given her of Harriet's intention, for the old woman was of a most impulsive disposition, and her cries and lamentations would have made known to all within hearing Harriet's intended escape. And so, with only the North Star for her guide, our heroine started on the way to liberty. "For," said she, "I had reasoned dis out in my mind; there was one of two things I had a right to, liberty, or death; if I could not have one, I would have de oder; for no man should take me alive; I should fight for my liberty as long as my strength lasted, and when de time came for me to go, de Lord would let dem take me." . . .

Source: Sarah H. Bradford, *Harriet: The Moses of Her People*, New York: Geo. R. Lockwood & Son, 1886, pp. 27–29.

The Railroad That Wasn't a Railroad

The Underground Railroad wasn't underground, and it wasn't a train. It was a secret network of people who risked their lives to help enslaved people escape. Codes, songs, and maps stitched into quilts were the tools of liberation.

You're Practicing: Interpreting symbolism and secrecy in history.

Connect This To: Escape, collaboration, and creativity.

Theme: Resistance and Autonomy

Harriet Tubman's heroism on the Underground Railroad reveals how freedom was seized through courage and conviction. In *The Refugee*, Tubman declares, "I had a right to liberty or death," capturing the moral urgency behind her missions. As *Harriet, the Moses of Her People* recounts, her daring leadership helped hundreds escape bondage, making Harriet Tubman a lasting symbol of resistance and liberation.

Practice: Explain the Causes and Effects of Historical Developments

The Underground Railroad was a multifaceted resistance network during the antebellum era.

(A) Describe one feature of the Underground Railroad and how it functioned.

(B) Explain how individuals like Harriet Tubman contributed to both the success and the symbolic power of the Underground Railroad.

(C) Assess the impact of the Underground Railroad on national debates about slavery and law.

SAMPLE RESPONSES

(A) The Underground Railroad was a network of safe houses and secret routes operated by free African Americans, formerly enslaved people, and white abolitionists to help enslaved individuals escape to free states or Canada.

The Underground Railroad relied on covert communication systems, such as coded songs, signals (like lanterns in windows), and assistance from "conductors," to guide freedom seekers safely across hostile territory.

(B) Harriet Tubman, often called "Moses," personally led over a dozen missions, rescuing more than 70 enslaved people, demonstrating remarkable courage and tactical skill in avoiding capture.

Harriet Tubmans success became a symbol of Black resistance and empowerment, inspiring abolitionists and challenging pro-slavery narratives that depicted enslaved people as passive or content with their condition.

(C) The Underground Railroad intensified sectional tensions by undermining the Fugitive Slave Act of 1850, angering Southern slaveholders who saw the network as theft of their "property."

The Underground Railroad fueled debates over the moral legitimacy of slavery and contributed to the growing polarization that led to the Civil War, as Northern abolitionist resistance to federal slave-catching laws highlighted the deep divide over human freedom and states' rights.

Skills Assessed: Describe and explain historical developments; cause-and-effect relationships; develop an argument with historical evidence.

Topic 2.21 Legacies of Resistance in African American Art and Photography

Key Terms

- Daguerreotypes of enslaved people—early photographic documentation
- Art as resistance
- Harriet Powers—story quilts
- David Drake ("Dave the Potter")—enslaved potter with inscribed messages
- Gordon ("Whipped Peter")—powerful image used by abolitionists
- Self-portraiture and dignity
- Cultural memory through material culture
- Black visual archives

Throughout history, African American artists and photographers have captured the dignity, resilience, and political agency of Black communities—often in direct defiance of the dehumanizing visual tropes used to uphold white supremacy. From nineteenth-century portraiture to contemporary reinterpretations, these images did more than preserve likenesses. They told stories, documented resistance, and reshaped how African Americans saw themselves and demanded to be seen.

After engaging with this topic, scholars will be able to:

- Explain the significance of visual depictions of African American leaders in photography and art during and after the era of slavery.
- Analyze how these images challenged racist stereotypes and contributed to historical memory and pride.
- Identify the ways in which art and photography functioned as tools for resistance, self-representation, and cultural preservation.

Portraits of Dignity and Defiance

In the nineteenth century, African American leaders recognized the political power of portrait photography. By carefully curating their images through this emerging technology, these leaders countered racist caricatures and asserted their full humanity. These portraits not only documented their likenesses but also proclaimed their rightful place as citizens deserving of dignity, justice, and equal protection under the law.

Sojourner Truth: Visual Advocacy and Activism

Sojourner Truth used photography as a fundraising and educational tool, selling carte-de-visites inscribed with the caption "I sell the shadow to support the substance." These images financed her abolitionist work, including speaking tours and efforts to recruit Black soldiers during the Civil War. In her portraits, she purposefully presented herself with poise, intellect, and moral authority, making a compelling visual argument for Black womanhood and leadership in the struggle for liberation.

Douglass, Tubman, and the Politics of Representation

Frederick Douglass was the most photographed American of the nineteenth century—not by coincidence but by strategy. He viewed photography as a political act, one that contested dehumanizing images of Black people by presenting a confident, intellectual Black man. Similarly, portraits of Harriet Tubman—dignified, resolute, and free—subverted stereotypes and commemorated her legendary resistance. Together, these visual records marked a revolution in how African Americans demanded to be seen.

Resurrecting Legacy Through Contemporary Art

Today, African American artists such as Kehinde Wiley, Amy Sherald, and Carrie Mae Weems reinterpret historic figures through bold new lenses. Drawing from African aesthetics, Black history, gender politics, and spiritual themes, these creators preserve and elevate the legacies of past leaders. Their work invites modern audiences to reimagine the enduring resistance of Black icons and challenges dominant narratives that have historically excluded them.

This carte-de-visite portrait of Harriet Tubman, taken between 1868 and 1869, captures one of the most iconic freedom fighters in American history during her later years. As both a conductor on the Underground Railroad and a Civil War spy, Tubman's dignified photographic presence challenged dominant stereotypes and asserted Black women's agency. Her image became a powerful symbol of strength, resilience, and the ongoing struggle for liberation.

Carte-de-visite portrait of Harriet Tubman, 1868–1869
(Source: Benjamin F. Powelson, Public domain, via Wikimedia Commons)

This matte collodion print of Harriet Tubman, taken between 1871 and 1876, offers a rare and powerful glimpse of Tubman during the Reconstruction era. By this time, her legacy as a conductor on the Underground Railroad and Union spy had made her a national symbol of resistance. The image reflects her enduring commitment to justice and her role in redefining Black womanhood in postemancipation America.

Matte collodion Print of Harriet Tubman, 1871–1876
(Source: Collection of the National Museum of
African American History and Culture shared with the Library of Congress)

This circa 1908 albumen print captures Harriet Tubman in the final decade of her life, reflecting the quiet dignity of a woman who had reshaped the course of American history. Though aged and frail, her presence in this portrait serves as a living testament to a life of resistance, leadership, and unyielding devotion to freedom. The image preserves Tubman's legacy as a revered elder in the African American freedom tradition.

Albumen print of Harriet Tubman, circa 1908
(Source: Collection of the Smithsonian National Museum of
African American History and Culture, Gift of Charles L. Blockson)

The photographic portraits of Harriet Tubman, from the 1868–1869 carte-de-visite to the matte collodion and albumen prints of the 1870s and early 1900s, offer a rare visual chronology of a freedom fighter's life across decades. These images reflect Tubman's enduring dignity, strength, and evolution from conductor of the Underground Railroad to national icon. As historical artifacts, they resist erasure and affirm Tubman's place as a leader whose legacy was not only lived but also powerfully seen.

TIP

Don't Be Afraid to Make an Educated Guess

There's no penalty for guessing on MCQs. If you're stuck, pick the most plausible answer after eliminating at least one option.

Rebellion in the Frame

Paintings, drawings, and photographs didn't just capture history—they challenged it. Artists used their work to show Black pride, document injustice, and imagine freedom. Art was (and still is) a kind of protest.

You're Practicing: Interpreting visual sources as historical evidence.

Connect This To: Creative resistance and identity.

Theme: Cultural Expression and Resistance

Practice: Explain the Significance of Historical Developments and Analyze Visual Sources

Art and photography played critical roles in documenting and shaping the African American freedom struggle.

(A) Describe one example of how visual media was used to resist racial oppression.
(B) Explain how photography or portraiture challenged dominant narratives about Black life.
(C) Evaluate the role of art in sustaining community, memory, and political activism.

SAMPLE RESPONSES

(A) Abolitionist newspapers like *The Liberator* used political cartoons and illustrations to expose the brutality of slavery and counter pro-slavery propaganda.

(B) Studio portraits of African Americans in formal dress directly contradicted racist caricatures, presenting Black individuals as refined, self-possessed, and worthy of full citizenship.

Frederick Douglass, the most photographed American of the 19th century, used his image to assert Black masculinity, intellect, and equality in contrast to dehumanizing stereotypes.

(C) Art and photography preserved cultural memory and communal pride, offering visual testimony of Black resilience in the face of oppression.

Visual media served as a tool for political mobilization, rallying support for abolition, Reconstruction, and civil rights by showing the humanity and aspirations of Black communities.

Skills Assessed: Analyze visual sources; explain the historical significance; argumentation with evidence.

Topic 2.22 Gender and Resistance in Slave Narratives

Key Terms

- Harriet Jacobs—*Incidents in the Life of a Slave Girl*
- Sexual exploitation and resistance
- Maternal protection and survival strategies
- Narrative silences and coded language
- Enslaved women's voices
- Intersectionality of race, gender, and class
- Fugitive women—unique barriers and paths to freedom
- Resistance through writing and testimony

Throughout the nineteenth century, enslaved Black women authored narratives that revealed how gender shaped their experiences of violence, resistance, and survival. These firsthand accounts were critical to exposing the dual oppressions of slavery and patriarchy. They brought attention to sexual violence and to the complexities of womanhood under enslavement. Narratives by women such as Harriet Jacobs and Sojourner Truth not only challenged white supremacist norms but also laid the foundation for early movements advocating abolition, women's rights, and Black liberation.

After engaging with this topic, scholars will be able to:

- Analyze how enslaved women confronted and resisted sexual violence, using both everyday strategies and testimonial writing as acts of defiance.
- Examine how gender shaped the narrative voices, themes, and political power of nineteenth-century slave narratives authored by Black women.
- Evaluate the influence of Black women's firsthand accounts of slavery on broader abolitionist and women's rights movements during the nineteenth century.

Bodily Autonomy Denied: Gendered Violence and Enslaved Women's Resistance

Enslaved African American women were excluded from legal protections against sexual assault. Their bodies were treated as property, subject to repeated abuse and reproductive exploitation. In defiance of this brutal system, many women resisted in whatever ways they could. They physically fought off attackers, prepared and ingested abortifacients from plants, fled with their children, or in rare but tragic cases, committed infanticide to spare their children from a life in bondage. These acts were desperate but powerful assertions of bodily autonomy and humanity in a system designed to strip away both.

Storytelling as Survival: Slave Narratives as Weapons for Justice

Slave narratives offered direct, personal testimonies that exposed the horrors of slavery while underscoring the intelligence, resilience, and moral agency of the enslaved. These autobiographical accounts often detailed the acquisition of literacy, courageous escapes, and the emotional devastation of family separation. More than just records of experience, they were political tools that challenged racist assumptions and fueled the growing abolitionist movement.

A Gendered Lens: The Distinct Voice of Black Women in Slave Narratives

Narratives written by formerly enslaved Black women were shaped not only by the trauma of slavery but also by societal expectations of femininity in the nineteenth century. These texts often focused on the centrality of family, the struggle to preserve modesty and dignity, and the constant threat of sexual violence. Unlike the narratives of formerly enslaved men, which emphasized individualism and reclaimed masculinity, women's narratives offered insight into the intersection of racial and gendered violence as well as the quiet, daily acts of resistance embedded within caregiving and survival.

Freedom Through Testimony: The Political Power of Black Women's Narratives

Enslaved women's accounts of slavery in both the United States and the Caribbean became foundational to abolitionist and early feminist discourse. Their testimonies provided irrefutable evidence of the cruelty of slavery, particularly its sexual violence, and forced broader political movements to confront the gendered dimensions of racial oppression. These voices became catalysts for change. They influenced public opinion and laid the groundwork for future advocacy on behalf of women and marginalized communities.

Incidents in the Life of a Slave Girl, written by Harriet A. Jacobs under the pseudonym Linda Brent, is one of the most influential and intimate slave narratives published in the nineteenth century. First released in 1860, the work exposes the unique suffering enslaved women endured, especially under the threat of sexual violence. These selected excerpts reveal Jacobs's strategies of resistance and her unwavering fight to protect her children and reclaim her autonomy.

> *Excerpts from Incidents in the Life of a Slave Girl: Written by Herself* by Harriet A. Jacobs, 1860
>
> Such were the unusually fortunate circumstances of my early childhood. When I was six years old, my mother died; and then, for the first time, I learned, by the talk around me, that I was a slave. My mother's mistress was the daughter of my grandmother's mistress. She was the foster sister of my mother; they were both nourished at my grandmother's breast. In fact, my mother had been weaned at three months old, that the babe of the mistress might obtain sufficient food. They played together as children; and, when they became women, my mother was a most faithful servant to her whiter foster sister. On her death-bed her mistress promised that her children should never suffer for any thing; and during her lifetime she kept her word. They all spoke kindly of my dead mother, who had been a slave merely in name, but in nature was noble and womanly. I grieved for her, and my young mind was troubled with the thought who would now take care of me and my little brother. I was told that my home was now to be with her mistress; and I found it a happy one. No toilsome or disagreeable duties were imposed upon me. My mistress was so kind to me that I was always glad to do her bidding, and proud to labor for her as much as my young years would permit. I would sit by her side for hours, sewing diligently, with a heart as free from care as that of any free-born white child. When she thought I was tired, she would send me out to run and jump; and away I bounded, to gather berries or flowers to decorate her room. Those were happy days—too happy to last. The slave child had no thought for the morrow; but there came that blight, which too surely waits on every human being born to be a chattel.
>
> When I was nearly twelve years old, my kind mistress sickened and died. As I saw the cheek grow paler, and the eye more glassy, how earnestly I prayed in my heart that she might live! I loved her; for she had been almost like a mother to me. My prayers were not answered. She died, and they buried her in the little churchyard, where, day after day, my tears fell upon her grave. I was sent to spend a week with my grandmother. I was now old enough to begin to think of the future; and again and again I asked myself what they would do with me. I felt sure I should never find another mistress so kind as the one who was gone. She had promised my dying mother that her children should never suffer for any thing; and when I remembered that, and recalled her many proofs of attachment to me, I could not help having some hopes that she had left me free. My friends were almost certain it would be so. They thought she would be sure to do it, on account of my mother's love and faithful service. But, alas! we all know that the memory of a faithful slave does not avail much to save her children from the auction block.
>
> After a brief period of suspense, the will of my mistress was read, and we learned that she had bequeathed me to her sister's daughter, a child of five years old. So vanished our hopes. My mistress had taught me the

precepts of God's Word: "Thou shalt love thy neighbor as thyself." "Whatsoever ye would that men should do unto you, do ye even so unto them." But I was her slave, and I suppose she did not recognize me as her neighbor. I would give much to blot out from my memory that one great wrong. As a child, I loved my mistress; and, looking back on the happy days I spent with her, I try to think with less bitterness of this act of injustice. While I was with her, she taught me to read and spell; and for this privilege, which so rarely falls to the lot of a slave, I bless her memory. Owing to the boils in my feet, I was unable to wheel the barrow fast through the sand, which got into the sores, and made me stumble at every step; and my master, having no pity for my sufferings from this cause, rendered them far more intolerable, by chastising me for not being able to move so fast as he wished me. Another of our employments was to row a little way off from the shore in a boat, and dive for large stones to build a wall round our master's house. This was very hard work; and the great waves breaking over us continually, made us often so giddy that we lost our footing, and were in danger of being drowned.

Ah, poor me!—my tasks were never ended. Sick or well, it was work—work—work!—After the diving season was over, we were sent to the South Creek, with large bills, to cut up mangoes to burn lime with. Whilst one party of slaves were thus employed, another were sent to the other side of the island to break up coral out of the sea.

When we were ill, let our complaint be what it might, the only medicine given to us was a great bowl of hot salt water, with salt mixed with it, which made us very sick. If we could not keep up with the rest of the gang of slaves, we were put in the stocks, and severely flogged the next morning. Yet, not the less, our master expected, after we had thus been kept from our rest, and our limbs rendered stiff and sore with ill usage, that we should still go through the ordinary tasks of the day all the same.—Sometimes we had to work all night, measuring salt to load a vessel; or turning a machine to draw water out of the sea for the salt-making. Then we had no sleep—no rest—but were forced to work as fast as we could, and go on again all next day the same as usual. Work—work—work—Oh that Turk's Island was a horrible place! The people in England, I am sure, have never found out what is carried on there. Cruel, horrible place! . . .

My old master often got drunk, and then he would get in a fury with his daughter, and beat her till she was not fit to be seen. I remember on one occasion, I had gone to fetch water, and when I was coming up the hill I heard a great screaming; I ran as fast as I could to the house, put down the water, and went into the chamber, where I found my master beating Miss D— dreadfully. I strove with all my strength to get her away from him; for she was all black and blue with bruises. He had beat her with his fist, and almost killed her. The people gave me credit for getting her away. He turned round and began to lick me. Then I said, "Sir, this is not Turk's Island." I can't repeat his answer, the words were too wicked—too bad to say. He wanted to treat me the same in Bermuda as he had done in Turk's Island.

He had an ugly fashion of stripping himself quite naked, and ordering me then to wash him in a tub of water. This was worse to me than all the licks. Sometimes when he called me to wash him I would not come, my eyes were so full of shame. He would then come to beat me. One time I had plates and knives in my hand, and I dropped both plates and knives, and some of the plates were broken. He struck me so severely for this, that at last I defended myself, for I thought it was high time to do so. I then told him I would not live longer with him, for he was a very indecent man—very spiteful, and too indecent; with no shame for his servants, no shame for his own flesh. So I went away to a neighbouring house and sat down and cried till the next morning, when I went home again, not knowing what else to do.

My work there was to attend the chambers and nurse the child, and to go down to the pond and wash clothes. But I soon fell ill of the rheumatism, and grew so very lame that I was forced to walk with a stick. I got the Saint Anthony's fire, also, in my left leg, and became quite a cripple. No one cared much to come near me, and I was ill a long long time; for several months I could not lift the limb. I had to lie in a little old out-house, that was swarming with bugs and other vermin, which tormented me greatly; but I had no other place to lie in. I got the rheumatism by catching cold at the pond side, from washing in the fresh water; in the salt water I never got cold. The person who lived in next yard, (a Mrs. Greene,) could not bear to hear my cries and groans. She was kind, and used to send an old slave woman to help me, who sometimes brought me a little soup. When the doctor found I was so ill, he said I must be put into a bath of hot water. The old slave got the bark of some bush that was good for the pains, which she boiled in the hot water, and every night she came and put me into the bath, and did what she could for me: I don't know what I should have done, or what would have become of me, had it not been for her.—My mistress, it is true, did send me a little food; but no one from our family came near me but the cook, who used to shove my food in at the door, and say, "Molly, Molly, there's your dinner." My mistress did not care to take any trouble about me; and if the Lord had not put it into the hearts of the neighbours to be kind to me, I must, I really think, have lain and died.

It was a long time before I got well enough to work in the house. Mrs. Wood, in the meanwhile, hired a mulatto woman to nurse the child; but she was such a fine lady she wanted to be mistress over me. I thought it very hard for a coloured woman to have rule over me because I was a slave and she was free. Her name was Martha Wilcox; she was a saucy woman, very saucy; and she went and complained of me, without cause, to my mistress, and made her angry with me. Mrs. Wood told me that if I did not mind what I was about, she would get my master to strip me and give me fifty lashes: "You have been used to the whip," she said, "and you shall have it here." This was the first time she threatened to have me flogged; and she gave me the threatening so strong of what she would have done to me, that I thought I should have fallen down at her feet, I was so vexed and hurt by her words. The mulatto woman was rejoiced to have power to keep me down. She was constantly making mischief; there was no living for the slaves—no peace after she came.

Source: Jacobs, Harriet. "Incidents in the Life of a Slave Girl." *Unc.edu*, 1861, docsouth.unc.edu/fpn/jacobs/jacobs.html.

The History of Mary Prince, A West Indian Slave, Related by Herself is a powerful first-person account dictated by Mary Prince and transcribed by an abolitionist ally. Published in 1831 by the London Society for the Abolition of Slavery, it marked the first narrative of an enslaved Black woman to be published in Britain. It offered an unflinching portrayal of slavery's brutality from a woman's perspective.

Excerpt from *The History of Mary Prince, a West Indian Slave, Related by Herself* by Mary Prince, 1831

When I reached the house, I went in directly to Miss Betsey. I found her in great distress; and she cried out as soon as she saw me, "Oh, Mary! my father is going to sell you all to raise money to marry that wicked woman. You are my slaves, and he has no right to sell you; but it is all to please her." She then told me that my mother was living with her father's sister at a house close by, and I went there to see her. It was a sorrowful meeting; and we lamented with a great and sore crying our unfortunate situation. "Here comes one of my poor picaninnies!" she said, the moment I came in, "one of the poor slave-brood who are to be sold to-morrow."

Oh dear! I cannot bear to think of that day,—it is too much.—It recalls the great grief that filled my heart, and the woeful thoughts that passed to and fro through my mind, whilst listening to the pitiful words of my poor mother, weeping for the loss of her children. I wish I could find words to tell you all I then felt and suffered. The great God above alone knows the thoughts of the poor slave's heart, and the bitter pains which follow such separations as these. All that we love taken away from us—Oh, it is sad, sad! and sore to be borne!—I got no sleep that night for thinking of the morrow; and dear Miss Betsey was scarcely less distressed. She could not bear to part with her old playmates, and she cried sore and would not be pacified.

The black morning at length came; it came too soon for my poor mother and us. Whilst she was putting on us the new osnaburgs in which we were to be sold, she said, in a sorrowful voice, (I shall never forget it!)

"See, I am shrouding my poor children; what a task for a mother!"—She then called Miss Betsey to take leave of us. "I am going to carry my little chickens to market," (these were her very words.) "take your last look of them: may be you will see them no more." "Oh, my poor slaves! my own slaves!" said dear Miss Betsey, "you belong to me: and it grieves my heart to part with you."—Miss Betsey kissed us all, and, when she left us, my mother called the rest of the slaves to bid us good bye. One of them, a woman named Moll, came with her infant in her arms. "Ay!" said my mother, seeing her turn away and look at her child with the tears in her eyes, "your turn will come next." The slaves could say nothing to comfort us; they could only weep and lament with us. When I left my dear little brothers and the house in which I had been brought up, I thought my heart would burst.

Our mother, weeping as she went, called me away with the children Hannah and Dinah, and we took the road that led to Hamble Town, which we reached about four o'clock in the afternoon. We followed my mother to the market-place, where she placed us in a row against a large house, with our backs to the wall and our arms folded across our breasts. I, as the eldest, stood first, Hannah next to me, then Dinah; and our mother stood beside, crying over us. My heart throbbed with grief and terror so violently, that I pressed my hands quite tightly across my breast, but I could not keep it still, and it continued to leap as though it would burst out of my body. But who cared for that? Did one of the many by-standers, who were looking at us so carelessly, think of the pain that wrung the hearts of the negro woman and her young ones? No, no! They were not all bad, I dare say, but slavery hardens white people's hearts towards the blacks; and many of them were not slow to make their remarks upon us aloud, without regard to our grief—though their light words fell like cayenne on the fresh wounds of our hearts. Oh those white people have small hearts who can only feel for themselves.

At length the vendue master, who was to offer us for sale like sheep or cattle, arrived, and asked my mother which was the eldest. She said nothing, but pointed to me. He took me by the hand, and led me out into the middle of the street, and, turning me slowly round, exposed me to the view of those who attended the vendue. I was soon surrounded by strange men, who examined and handled me in the same manner that a butcher would a calf or a lamb he was about to purchase, and who talked about my shape and size in like words—as if I could no more understand their meaning than the dumb beasts. I was then put up to sale. The bidding commenced at a few pounds, and gradually rose to fifty-seven, Bermuda currency; about £38 sterling.

When I was knocked down to the highest bidder; and the people who stood by said that I had fetched a great sum for so young a slave. I then saw my sisters led forth, and sold to different owners: so that we had not the sad satisfaction of being partners in bondage. When the sale was over, my mother hugged and kissed us, and mourned over us, begging of us to keep up a good heart, and do our duty to our new masters. It was a sad parting; one went one way, one another, and our poor mammy went home with nothing.

Source: Mary Prince, *The History of Mary Prince, a West Indian Slave. Related by Herself.* With a Supplement by the Editor. To Which Is Added, the *Narrative of Asa-Asa, a Captured African*, Thomas Pringle, ed., London: F. Westley and A. H. Davis, 1831, pp. 10–11 and 13–15.

Slave narratives authored by Black women like Mary Prince and Harriet Jacobs stand as powerful testimonies to gendered resistance within the institution of slavery. These works did more than document brutality. They confronted the legal and cultural erasure of Black womanhood, exposing the sexual violence, family separation, and moral contradictions of a nation built on liberty. By centering their voices, these narratives reshaped political discourse, advancing both abolition and early feminist movements. They continue to inspire critical reflection on justice and dignity across generations.

She Told the Story Differently

Women like Harriet Jacobs gave voice to a kind of resistance that was deeply personal. Their stories revealed how gender shaped slavery and freedom. Listening to women's voices changes how we understand survival and strength.

You're Practicing: Asking who gets to tell the story—and how.

Connect This To: Gender, power, and self-representation.

Theme: Identity and Culture

Practice: Analyze Sources and Explain the Significance of Historical Developments

First-person narratives by formerly enslaved women offered powerful testimony about resistance and identity.

(A) Identify one theme commonly found in women's slave narratives.
(B) Explain how gender shaped the experiences of writers such as Harriet Jacobs and Sojourner Truth.
(C) Evaluate the influence of these narratives on the abolitionist movement and collective memory.

SAMPLE RESPONSES

(A) A common theme is sexual violence and the struggle for bodily autonomy, as seen in Harriet Jacobs's *Incidents in the Life of a Slave Girl*, which exposes the unique vulnerabilities enslaved women faced under slavery.

Another recurring theme is the resilience of Black motherhood, with women emphasizing the emotional pain of family separation and the fierce desire to protect their children.

(B) Harriet Jacobs's narrative centers on how enslaved women endured both racial and sexual exploitation, revealing how slavery operated through the control of both labor and reproduction.

Sojourner Truth challenged prevailing ideas of womanhood by asserting that Black women's strength, labor, and intellect were equal to men's, demanding recognition of both racial and gendered injustice.

(C) These narratives gave the abolitionist movement a moral urgency, showing the specific cruelties faced by Black women and offering irrefutable, firsthand evidence of slavery's horrors.

They helped shape collective memory by centering Black women's voices in the national consciousness, influencing later freedom struggles and feminist movements that drew upon their legacy of resistance and testimony.

Skills Assessed: Source analysis; contextualization and comparison; argumentation.

Topic 2.23 The Civil War and Black Communities

Key Terms

- Contraband camps—early wartime refugee settlements
- United States Colored Troops (USCT)
- Emancipation Proclamation (1863)
- Freedmen's Bureau (1865)—aid to the formerly enslaved
- Black enlistment and military service
- Fort Pillow Massacre (1864)
- Black women's labor and care roles
- Displacement and uncertainty postemancipation

As the nation fractured along the fault lines of slavery and freedom, African Americans—both enslaved and free—rose with strategic urgency and moral clarity to fight for liberation and redefine the meaning of American democracy. Across the warfront and homefront, Black men and women contributed labor, intelligence, advocacy, and military service that would reshape the trajectory of the United States. Their sacrifices challenged the racial hierarchies embedded in the nation's founding and sowed seeds of transformation in Black communities that extended far beyond the battlefield.

After engaging with this topic, scholars will be able to:

- Analyze the various roles that free and enslaved African Americans played in the Civil War effort.
- Explain why African American soldiers enlisted to fight and how they navigated racial discrimination within the Union Army.
- Evaluate the impact of Black military service on African American communities during and after the war, including questions of citizenship, leadership, and collective memory.

The Battle for Freedom and Citizenship

Thousands of free and enslaved African Americans across the North and South enlisted in the Union war effort, viewing military service as a powerful avenue to fight for the abolition of slavery and assert their claim to U.S. citizenship. Their participation was not only an act of defiance against enslavement but a declaration of full belonging in the American democratic project.

Black Men and Women on the Frontlines

African American men served as soldiers, laborers, and engineers, while women played critical roles as nurses, cooks, laundresses, and even spies for Union forces. Despite their exclusion from formal command, Black men and women provided indispensable support to the war effort and often performed these roles while enduring racism, limited rations, and extreme physical conditions.

Refuge, Relief, and Reconstruction

Enslaved people in the South fled plantations to seek refuge behind Union lines, contributing to the collapse of the Confederacy's labor force. Meanwhile, free Black Northerners mobilized to support their Southern brethren, organizing fundraising campaigns and traveling to former Confederate regions to open schools, provide medical aid, and lay the groundwork for postwar Black advancement.

200,000 Reasons for Emancipation

Approximately 200,000 African American men served in the Union forces—50,000 were free men from the North, and nearly 150,000 were formerly enslaved individuals who seized the opportunity to fight for their freedom. Their service embodied the transformative power of emancipation and added moral urgency to the Union cause, forcing the nation to reckon with slavery as incompatible with its founding ideals.

Citizenship Through Combat

For African American men—both free and enslaved—military service represented a bold affirmation of their identity as Americans. Despite facing discrimination and unequal treatment, Black soldiers saw enlistment as a way to prove their loyalty, demand civil rights, and shape the outcome of the war and the nation's future.

Fighting Two Battles: War and Racism

Initially barred from service, African Americans were later recruited due to labor shortages and their demonstrated commitment. They served for unequal pay, with fewer resources, and under threat of death or reenslavement if captured by Confederate forces. Their bravery under such conditions challenged racist ideologies and laid the groundwork for future civil rights struggles.

Resistance from the North

Black participation in the Civil War was met with violent resistance from some segments of Northern society. Anti-Black riots, such as the 1863 New York City Draft Riots, exposed deep racial tensions and resentment toward African American advancement. Despite these challenges, Black communities continued to organize, resist, and contribute to the war effort with resilience and pride.

Preserving Legacy Through Image and Verse

Even though Black soldiers were often denied public recognition, African American artists and writers immortalized their sacrifices. Through photography, poetry, and memoir, they created an enduring archive that honored Black service and challenged the erasure of their contributions, preserving their legacy for future generations. The photograph *Washerwoman for the Union Army in Richmond, VA,* 1860s, highlights the essential role Black women played in sustaining Union forces even as the women remained excluded from formal recognition.

Scholars can view and analyze this image at the Gilder Lehrman Institute of American History online for free, at https://www.gilderlehrman.org/ap-african-american-studies/unit-2/civil-war#par-15036.

Photograph of Charles Remond Douglass, circa 1864, presents the proud image of a Black Union soldier, reflecting the dignity and determination of those who fought for freedom and equality.

Photograph of Charles Remond Douglass, circa 1864
(Source: From the Collection: Simpson, Randolph Linsly, 1927–1992, Beinecke Rare Book and Manuscript Library at Yale University)

In his poem "The Colored Soldiers," Paul Laurence Dunbar honors the courage and sacrifice of African American soldiers during the Civil War. Written by one of the first widely recognized African American poets, this poem highlights themes of patriotism, resilience, and the struggle for equality in the face of systemic racism.

Paul Laurence Dunbar, "The Colored Soldiers" (1895)

If the muse were mine to tempt it
And my feeble voice were strong,
If my tongue were trained to measures,
I would sing a stirring song.

I would sing a song heroic
Of those noble sons of Ham,
Of the gallant colored soldiers
Who fought for Uncle Sam!

In the early days you scorned them,
And with many a flip and flout,
Said "these battles are the white man's
And the whites will fight them out."

Up the hills you fought and faltered,
In the vales you strove and bled,
While your ears still heard the thunder
Of the foes' increasing tread.

Then distress fell on the nation
And the flag was drooping low;
Should the dust pollute your banner?
No! the nation shouted, No!

So when war, in savage triumph,
Spread abroad his funeral pall—
Then you called the colored soldiers,
And they answered to your call.

And like hounds unleashed and eager
For the life blood of the prey,
Sprung they forth and bore them bravely
In the thickest of the fray.

And where'er the fight was hottest—
Where the bullets fastest fell,
There they pressed unblanched and fearless
At the very mouth of hell.

Ah, they rallied to the standard
To uphold it by their might,
None were stronger in the labors,
None were braver in the fight.

At Forts Donelson and Henry
On the plains of Olustee,
They were foremost in the fight
Of the battles of the free.

And at Pillow! God have mercy
On the deeds committed there,
And the souls of those poor victims
Sent to Thee without a prayer.

Let the fullness of thy pity
O'er the hot wrought spirits sway,
Of the gallant colored soldier
Who fell fighting on that day!

Yes, the Blacks enjoy their freedom,
And they won it dearly, too;
For the life blood of their thousands
Did the southern fields bedew.

In the darkness of their bondage,
In their depths of slavery's night;
Their muskets flashed the dawning
And they fought their way to light.

They were comrades then and brothers,
Are they more or less to-day?
They were good to stop a bullet
And to front the fearful fray.

They were citizens and soldiers,
When rebellion raised its head;
And the traits that made them worthy—
Ah! those virtues are not dead.

They have shared your nightly vigils,
They have shared your daily toil;
And their blood with yours commingling
Has made rich the Southern soil.

They have slept and marched and suffered'
Neath the same dark skies as you,
They have met as fierce a foeman,
And have been as brave and true.

And their deeds shall find a record,
In the registry of Fame;
For their blood has cleansed completely
Every blot of Slavery's shame.

So all honor and all glory
To those noble Sons of Ham—
The gallant colored soldiers,
Who fought for Uncle Sam!

Source: Paul [Laurence] Dunbar, "The Colored Soldiers," in Paul Lawrence [Laurence] Dunbar, *Majors and Minors: Poems*, Toledo: Hadley & Hadley, 1895, pp. 38–40.

The photographs of a washerwoman for the Union Army and of Charles Remond Douglass during the Civil War, along with Paul Laurence Dunbar's "The Colored Soldiers," illuminate the multifaceted contributions of African Americans in the fight for freedom and equality. The washerwoman's labor symbolized resilience and determination in supporting Union forces. Douglass's military service represented leadership and valor on the front lines. Dunbar's poem further elevated these sacrifices, highlighting the profound role that Black soldiers played in reshaping the narrative of American democracy. Together, these sources underscore the enduring struggle for dignity, justice, and recognition within the African American experience.

Fighting for More than the Union

For Black soldiers and families, the Civil War wasn't just about preserving the Union—it was about earning freedom. Fighting meant risking everything to claim a future. Black communities organized, enlisted, and demanded justice before, during, and after the war.

You're Practicing: Understanding war through different perspectives.

Connect This To: Citizenship, sacrifice, and strategic resistance.

Theme: Power and Politics

Practice: Explain Significance

African Americans played transformative roles during the Civil War, both on and off the battlefield.

(A) Identify one way African Americans contributed to the Union war effort during the Civil War.

(B) Explain how this contribution influenced national perceptions of African American citizenship and equality.

(C) Evaluate the significance of African American participation in shaping the broader outcomes of the war.

SAMPLE RESPONSES

(A) Over 200,000 African Americans served in the Union Army and Navy, including the famed 54th Massachusetts Infantry Regiment, demonstrating valor and discipline in combat.

African Americans also contributed as laborers, spies, and nurses, providing vital intelligence, building infrastructure, and supporting military logistics behind the lines.

(B) Military service challenged racist assumptions and strengthened calls for full citizenship, as African Americans proved their loyalty and courage on the battlefield.

Their contributions prompted debates in Congress and among abolitionists, leading to key shifts like the passage of the 14th and 15th Amendments, which addressed citizenship and voting rights.

(C) African American soldiers and workers bolstered the Union's manpower and moral cause, transforming the war into a fight for emancipation and Black freedom.

Their participation not only helped secure military victory but laid the foundation for Reconstruction-era civil rights reforms, making African American agency central to the Union's political and moral legacy.

Skills Assessed: Describe and explain historical developments; explain the significance or importance; contextualize developments in broader historical processes.

Topic 2.24 Freedom Days: Commemorating the Ongoing Struggle for Freedom

Key Terms

- Juneteenth (June 19, 1865)—celebration of emancipation in Texas
- Watch Night (December 31, 1862)—vigil for Emancipation Proclamation
- Freedom Day celebrations—across various Black communities
- Black memory and historical commemoration
- Parades, speeches, rituals
- Community resilience and joy
- Fourth of July debates—Frederick Douglass's What to the Slave Is the Fourth of July?
- Intergenerational education and activism

In the aftermath of the Civil War, Black communities across the United States sought to commemorate the formal end of slavery while continuing to fight for true freedom, equality, and recognition. Juneteenth, the most widely recognized Freedom Day, marks not only the delayed announcement of emancipation in Texas but also symbolizes the resilience and ongoing struggle of African Americans to claim the promises of liberty long denied. Across generations, these commemorations have served as acts of remembrance, resistance, and community pride.

After engaging with this topic, scholars will be able to:

- Identify and describe the events that marked the official end of slavery in the United States.
- Explain the historical and cultural importance of Juneteenth in African American communities.
- Reflect on how Freedom Days serve as sites of collective memory, celebration, and activism.

The Emancipation Proclamation: A Wartime Milestone, Not a Final Blow

President Abraham Lincoln's Emancipation Proclamation, issued on January 1, 1863, declared that all enslaved people in Confederate states "in rebellion" were free. However, the order had limited immediate impact as it applied only to areas not under Union control. Enslavement remained legal in border states loyal to the Union (Kentucky, Missouri, Maryland, and Delaware) until later constitutional intervention. Still, the proclamation shifted the purpose of the Civil War toward abolition and allowed for the enlistment of African American soldiers in the Union Army, deepening Black communities' stake in the war's outcome.

The Thirteenth Amendment: Constitutional Abolition with a Carve-Out

Ratified in December 1865, the Thirteenth Amendment permanently abolished slavery and involuntary servitude in the United States—"except as a punishment for crime." This clause would later become a source of legal debate and systemic exploitation. Nevertheless, for nearly 4 million African Americans—nearly a third of the South's population—the amendment represented a seismic shift in status and possibility even as it marked only the beginning of an ongoing fight for civil rights and full citizenship.

Freedom Deferred: Enslavement in Indian Territory

The Thirteenth Amendment did not initially apply to the nearly 10,000 African Americans still enslaved by sovereign Indigenous nations such as the Cherokee, Creek, Choctaw, Chickasaw, and Seminole. These nations had aligned with the Confederacy and maintained slavery within their borders. It was not until 1866 that the U.S. government negotiated treaties with these nations to end slavery. Yet even then, the treaties often failed to recognize the freed people as full tribal citizens, compounding their marginalization in Indian Territory.

Juneteenth: Freedom Announced, Delayed, and Celebrated

Juneteenth marks June 19, 1865, the day Union General Gordon Granger arrived in Galveston, Texas, and publicly read General Order No. 3. This order declared the freedom of all enslaved people in Texas—the last Confederate holdout. The order's language emphasized "absolute equality," a radical assertion at the time. Though enforcement was uneven and delayed, the announcement catalyzed celebrations and marked the symbolic end of slavery in the United States.

Freedom Days: Honoring Abolition from Harlem to Galveston

Juneteenth is part of a broader tradition of African American Freedom Days. Communities across the country commemorated local abolition dates—such as New York's Emancipation Day on July 5, 1827—and engaged in rituals of reflection, joy, and protest. Juneteenth eventually became the most widely celebrated of these, culminating in its designation as a federal holiday in 2021 after more than 150 years of consistent, Black-led observance.

Jubilee Traditions: Clothing, Song, and Communal Joy

Early Juneteenth celebrations included singing spirituals, public readings of the Emancipation Proclamation, sermons, dancing, and the wearing of new clothes to symbolize new beginnings. These gatherings—also called Jubilee Day or Emancipation Day—created space for Black joy, remembrance, and defiance amid ongoing racism and exclusion from the broader American narrative.

More than a Holiday: Juneteenth as a Living History

Juneteenth and other Freedom Days carry deep historical and cultural resonance. They commemorate:

- **The heroic struggles of enslaved ancestors** to win freedom in a hostile legal system.
- **The duality of freedom and oppression** that African Americans continued to face after emancipation.
- **The enduring power of Black cultural expression and resilience** as communities turned remembrance into celebration, even before the nation fully acknowledged their history.

The photograph *Juneteenth Celebration in West Philadelphia,* 2019, captures the enduring legacy and evolving spirit of Black freedom celebrations more than 150 years after emancipation. Vibrant and community centered, the image reflects how Juneteenth continues to serve as both a cultural affirmation and a powerful reminder of the unfinished journey toward justice and equality.

Juneteenth Celebration in West Philadelphia, 2019
(Source: Shutterstock)

General Order No. 3, issued by Union Major General Gordon Granger on June 19, 1865, in Galveston, Texas, proclaimed freedom for enslaved people in the state—more than two years after the Emancipation Proclamation. The order not only declared that "all slaves are free" but also emphasized "absolute equality of personal rights and rights of property." Its reading marked the origin of Juneteenth, one of the most significant commemorations of Black liberation in the United States.

> Headquarters District of Texas, Galveston, Texas, June 19th, 1865. General Order, No. 3.
>
> The people of Texas are informed that in accordance with a proclamation from the Executive of the United States "all slaves are free." This involves an absolute equality of personal rights and rights of property between former masters and slaves, and the connection heretofore existing between them becomes that between employer and hired labor.
>
> The freedmen are advised to remain quietly at their present homes and work for wages. They are informed that they wil[l] not be allowed to collect at military posts, and that they will not be supported in idleness either there or elsewhere. By order of Major General GRANGER. F.W. Emery, Major, A.A. General
>
> Source: Flake's Tri-Weekly Bulletin (Galveston, Tex.), June 20, 1865, p. 2, The Dolph Briscoe Center for American History, accessed on the Portal to Texas History, University of North Texas Libraries.

Freedom Days, Every Day

From Juneteenth to Emancipation Day, Black communities have celebrated freedom—while still fighting for it. These holidays honor the past and renew the call for justice. Celebration is powerful. It's also political.

You're Practicing: Exploring how memory shapes the present.

Connect This To: Commemoration, tradition, and activism.

Theme: Identity and Culture

Practice: Continuities or Changes Over Time

From Juneteenth to Emancipation Day, African American communities have marked freedom through commemorative rituals and celebrations.

(A) Identify one way African Americans have commemorated emancipation or freedom over time.

(B) Explain how these commemorations have changed or have remained consistent from the Reconstruction era to the present.

(C) Assess how these continuities or changes reflect broader developments in the Black freedom struggle.

SAMPLE RESPONSES

(A) African Americans have celebrated Juneteenth with parades, church services, barbecues, and public readings of the Emancipation Proclamation to honor the end of slavery in Texas on June 19, 1865.

In places like Washington, D.C., communities have observed Emancipation Day with political rallies and historical reenactments to honor the abolition of slavery in the district.

(B) While early celebrations often had a strong religious and political tone, emphasizing speeches, sermons, and calls for civil rights, today's commemorations have expanded to include cultural festivals, music, and education, reflecting both continuity and evolution.

Despite shifts in tone and form, these events have consistently served as acts of resistance and remembrance, linking past struggles with present demands for justice.

(C) The enduring nature of these commemorations reflects the ongoing fight for racial justice, with each generation using celebration as a platform for activism, from Reconstruction to Civil Rights to Black Lives Matter.

As Juneteenth became a federal holiday in 2021, the mainstream recognition of Black freedom commemorations signals both a growing national acknowledgment of historical injustice and the power of community-led remembrance to shape public memory and policy.

Skills Assessed: Describe historical developments over time; explain continuities or changes over time; contextualize within broader historical patterns.

KEY TAKEAWAYS

1. **Black Life in Indigenous Territories**
   - Enslaved and free African Americans interacted with Indigenous communities, sometimes finding refuge or forming alliances.
   - These connections shaped cultural exchanges, resistance strategies, and geographic movement across contested frontiers.
2. **Debates Over Emigration and Belonging**
   - Black leaders and communities grappled with the question of staying in the United States or emigrating to places like Liberia or Haiti.
   - Emigration debates highlighted the tension between fighting for inclusion and seeking sovereignty outside a white-dominated society.
3. **Black Political Thought and Radical Resistance**
   - Thinkers like David Walker and Henry Highland Garnet pushed for militant resistance while others emphasized moral persuasion and legal reform.
   - These competing ideologies fueled a broader tradition of Black radical intellectualism.
4. **Abolitionism and the Underground Railroad**
   - Abolitionists, both Black and white, collaborated to challenge slavery through public advocacy, legal cases, and escape networks.
   - The Underground Railroad served as a powerful symbol of collective action and moral courage.
5. **Art and Photography as Resistance**
   - African American artists used visual culture—paintings, daguerreotypes, engravings—to humanize Black subjects and counter racist imagery.
   - This early use of media reshaped public opinion and created enduring legacies in political art.
6. **Gendered Narratives of Enslavement and Freedom**
   - Enslaved women like Harriet Jacobs offered unique perspectives on sexual violence, motherhood, and resistance through their narratives.
   - These works broadened the understanding of oppression and resilience beyond male-centered revolts.
7. **Civil War Participation and Community Transformation**
   - Nearly 200,000 Black soldiers fought for the Union, asserting their right to citizenship and freedom.
   - The war marked a turning point in the pursuit of equality and redefined the role of Black communities in shaping the nation's future.
8. **Commemorating Freedom**
   - Events like Juneteenth and local emancipation celebrations became essential to community memory, identity, and resistance against erasure.
   - These celebrations continue today as acts of remembrance and calls to complete the unfinished struggle for justice.

Practice Multiple-Choice Questions

DIRECTIONS: Pick the letter that best answers the following questions.

Questions 1 through 3 refer to the following.

General Assembly of the State of Arkansas, Petition for Freedmen's Rights to the US Congress (1869)

"To the Honorable Senators and Representatives in the Congress of the United States Representing the State of Arkansas.

Gentlemen,

We the undersigned Petitioners; Members of the General Assembly of the State of Arkansas, do most respectfully represent that information has been received that there are three thousand persons of African descent living and residing in the Choctaw and Chickasaw Nations, who were formerly held in servitude by Said Nations, and who are desirous of remaining in said Nations and enjoying all the rights and privileges of Citizens thereof. Therefore. We request that you use your influence for the passage of an Enabling Act by the Congress of the United States, to allow the Choctaw and Chickasaw Nations to amend or rescind Article III of a Treaty entered into by and between the Government of the United States and the said Choctaw and Chickasaw Nations dated April 26th 1866, so that all persons of African descent may remain in said Nations; select and hold forty (40) acres of Land each—and be entitled to all the rights and privileges of any other class of Citizens in said Nations, including the right of Suffrage.

—Arkansas Petition for Freedmen's Rights (1869)"

Source: General Assembly of the State of Arkansas, Petition for Freedmen's Rights to the US Congress (1869). National Archives, Records of the US Senate.

1. What was the primary purpose of the Arkansas Petition for Freedmen's Rights (1869)?

   (A) To demand reparations from the federal government for labor during enslavement
   (B) To advocate for the removal of native nations from tribal lands
   (C) To secure land rights, suffrage, and citizenship for formerly enslaved people in the Choctaw and Chickasaw Nations
   (D) To protest military occupation by Union troops in Arkansas

2. What does the petition reveal about the legal status of African Americans in the Choctaw and Chickasaw Nations after the Civil War?

   (A) They had already been fully granted citizenship and suffrage rights by the 1866 treaty.
   (B) They were considered citizens by the U.S. government but not by the native nations.
   (C) They remained in legal limbo, with uncertain rights despite emancipation, prompting the call for Congressional intervention.
   (D) They had the same status as white citizens in those territories and sought only economic reparations.

3. The Arkansas Petition for Freedmen's Rights to the US Congress (1869) best reflects which of the following broader trends during Reconstruction?

(A) African American migration to Northern industrial cities to escape violence in the South
(B) Freed people's reliance on federal intervention to secure rights denied by local and tribal authorities
(C) The collapse of Native American sovereignty as a result of Reconstruction policies
(D) The widespread success of land redistribution through the 40 acres and a mule policy

Questions 4 through 6 refer to the following.

General Order No. 3, issued by Union Major General Gordon Granger on June 19, 1865, in Galveston, Texas

"The people of Texas are informed that in accordance with a proclamation from the Executive of the United States 'all slaves are free.' This involves an absolute equality of personal rights and rights of property between former masters and slaves, and the connection heretofore existing between them becomes that between employer and hired labor.

The freedmen are advised to remain quietly at their present homes and work for wages. They are informed that they wil[l] not be allowed to collect at military posts, and that they will not be supported in idleness either there or elsewhere.

By order of Major General GRANGER. F.W. Emery, Major, A.A. General"

Source: Flake's Tri-Weekly Bulletin (Galveston, Tex.), June 20, 1865, p. 2, The Dolph Briscoe Center for American History, accessed on the Portal to Texas History, University of North Texas Libraries.

4. What was the immediate legal significance of General Order No. 3 for the people of Texas?

(A) It officially ended slavery across all Confederate states.
(B) It implemented the Emancipation Proclamation in Texas, where enslaved people had not yet been freed.
(C) It granted voting rights to formerly enslaved people in Texas.
(D) It outlawed racial segregation in Texas.

5. Which of the following best reflects the federal government's expectation for newly freed people as outlined in General Order No. 3?

(A) They should leave plantations immediately to seek opportunities in the North.
(B) They would be granted land and financial reparations to begin their new lives.
(C) They should remain where they were and enter into labor contracts for wages.
(D) They should apply for U.S. citizenship before being allowed to work or travel.

6. Why is General Order No. 3 considered a significant historical moment in the timeline of U.S. emancipation?

(A) It was the first formal statement issued by President Lincoln on slavery.
(B) It signaled the end of slavery in the Union's border states.
(C) It represented the enforcement of emancipation in one of the last Confederate holdouts, leading to the celebration of Juneteenth.
(D) It marked the date when the Thirteenth Amendment was ratified.

Answer Explanations

1. **(C)** The petition explicitly asks Congress to allow the Choctaw and Chickasaw Nations to grant African-descended people the right to remain, own 40 acres of land, and enjoy full citizenship, including voting rights. Choice (A) is incorrect because the petition does not mention reparations for past labor but, rather, focuses on future rights and land access. Choice (B) is incorrect because the petition supports freedmen remaining in native nations. The petition does not advocate for the removal of Indigenous communities. Choice (D) is incorrect because there is no reference to military occupation or protest against federal troops.

2. **(C)** The petition requests Congress to amend or rescind Article III of the 1866 treaty, indicating that the current treaty did not successfully secure the civil and political rights of African Americans in those nations. Choice (A) is incorrect because Article III of the treaty failed to guarantee full rights in practice, which is why the petition exists. Choice (B) is incorrect because the petition does not claim that the U.S. government granted full status—it seeks such action. Choice (D) is incorrect because the petition centers on land rights and suffrage, not economic reparations, and makes clear that Black people were not yet treated equally.

3. **(B)** The petitioners directly ask Congress to intervene and pass an enabling act to secure land and rights. This reflects the broader trend of African Americans appealing to federal power during Reconstruction to protect their rights when local governments or tribal entities resisted. Choice (A) is incorrect because the petition addresses African Americans seeking to remain in Indian Territory—not migrate North. Choice (C) is incorrect because the petition seeks collaboration with tribal nations through treaty amendment, not their collapse or dissolution. Choice (D) is incorrect because the 40 acres and a mule policy was largely unfulfilled. The petitioners are asking for land rights—not citing a successful redistribution.

4. **(B)** General Order No. 3 brought Texas into compliance with the Emancipation Proclamation by announcing the end of slavery in that state, which had delayed enforcement. Choice (A) is incorrect because slavery had already ended in most Confederate states by the Emancipation Proclamation in 1863. Texas was among the last to comply due to geographic distance and resistance. Choice (C) is incorrect because the order granted freedom, not political rights like suffrage. Choice (D) is incorrect because the order did not address segregation. It emphasized labor and civil status, not full civil rights or social equality.

5. **(C)** The order explicitly instructs freedmen to "remain quietly at their present homes and work for wages," signaling the federal push for a transition from slavery to paid labor without a major disruption to the plantation economy. Choice (A) is incorrect because the order discourages freed people from migrating or congregating elsewhere, including at military posts. Choice (B) is incorrect because there is no mention of land redistribution or reparations in the order. Choice (D) is incorrect because citizenship status is not discussed. The focus is on labor relations and maintaining order.

6. **(C)** General Order No. 3 was issued in Galveston, Texas, and announced that slavery had ended—leading to Juneteenth, which commemorates the final enforcement of the Emancipation Proclamation. Choice (A) is incorrect because Lincoln's statements on slavery came years earlier, including the Emancipation Proclamation in 1863. Choice (B) is incorrect because slavery in border states like Kentucky and Delaware ended later, with the ratification of the Thirteenth Amendment. Choice (D) is incorrect because the Thirteenth Amendment was ratified on December 6, 1865—months after this order.

PART 4

Unit 3—The Practice of Freedom

8

From Emancipation to Exclusion: The Legal and Violent Undoing of Reconstruction's Gains

Key Themes

- Legal transformation vs. lived reality—constitutional promises met with state resistance
- Freed people's aspirations for land, family, and education under constant threat
- Systemic exclusion—disenfranchisement, segregation, and judicial betrayal
- Racial violence as policy—used to suppress Black progress and assert white supremacy

TIMELINE

Date/Period	Event/Development	Related Topics
1865	**Thirteenth Amendment ratified**, formally abolishing slavery in the United States	Topic 3.1—The Reconstruction Amendments
1865–1870	Establishment of the **Freedmen's Bureau** to support formerly enslaved people with education, family reunification, and land access	Topic 3.2—Reuniting Families and Freedmen's Bureau
1866	Southern states pass **Black Codes** to restrict Black autonomy, labor mobility, and civil rights	Topic 3.3—Black Codes, Land, and Labor
1868	**Fourteenth Amendment ratified**, granting birthright citizenship and equal protection under the law	Topic 3.1—The Reconstruction Amendments
1869–1877	Ongoing **land struggles**: formerly enslaved people denied 40 acres and a mule	Topic 3.3—Land and Labor
1870	**Fifteenth Amendment ratified**, prohibiting racial discrimination in voting	Topic 3.1—The Reconstruction Amendments
1873	**Slaughterhouse Cases** begin limiting protections of the Fourteenth Amendment	Topic 3.4—The Defeat of Reconstruction

Date/Period	Event/Development	Related Topics
1877	**Compromise of 1877** ends federal military Reconstruction; **Southern Democrats regain power**	Topic 3.4—The Defeat of Reconstruction
1880s–1900s	Rise of **Jim Crow laws**: state-level racial segregation, poll taxes, literacy tests	Topic 3.5—Disenfranchisement and Jim Crow
1896	***Plessy v. Ferguson*** ruling establishes "separate but equal" doctrine	Topic 3.5—Jim Crow Laws
1870s–1920s	Escalation of **white supremacist violence**—KKK, lynchings, and racial massacres	Topic 3.6—White Supremacist Violence
1919	**Red Summer**—dozens of race riots across U.S. cities; white mobs attack Black communities and veterans	Topic 3.6—Red Summer

Topic 3.1 The Reconstruction Amendments: Redefining Citizenship and Power in the Aftermath of Slavery

Key Terms

- Thirteenth Amendment (1865)—abolished slavery
- Fourteenth Amendment (1868)—citizenship and equal protection
- Fifteenth Amendment (1870)—Black male suffrage
- Birthright citizenship
- Due process clause
- Equal protection clause
- Reconstruction Constitution
- Radical Republicans
- Enforcement Acts—laws to protect voting rights

In the wake of the Civil War, the United States entered a bold and contested era of rebuilding—legally, politically, and socially. Central to this transformation were the Reconstruction Amendments: the Thirteenth, Fourteenth, and Fifteenth Amendments. These constitutional changes redefined the boundaries of freedom, citizenship, and suffrage in a nation grappling with its legacy of slavery and racial hierarchy. For African Americans, these amendments represented both hard-won victories and the beginning of new battles to claim and protect their rights.

After engaging with this topic, scholars will be able to:

- Analyze how the Reconstruction Amendments legally abolished slavery and redefined citizenship.
- Evaluate the impact of the Fourteenth Amendment in establishing equal protection and due process for African Americans.
- Explain how the Fifteenth Amendment expanded voting rights and created new political possibilities for Black men while also examining the limits and backlash to Black political participation.

Rebuilding the Nation and Redefining Belonging

During the Reconstruction era (1865–1877), the federal government initiated a series of measures to reintegrate the Southern states and address the legal status of millions of formerly enslaved African Americans. Through constitutional amendments and civil rights legislation, Reconstruction sought to establish a new foundation for citizenship, civil equality, and political participation, reshaping the American legal landscape in the wake of slavery.

The Thirteenth Amendment: Abolishing Slavery, Preserving Injustice

Ratified in 1865, the Thirteenth Amendment formally abolished slavery and involuntary servitude in the United States, "except as a punishment for a crime." Although this amendment marked a legal end to chattel slavery, its exception clause allowed for the rise of new systems of forced labor—particularly the convict leasing system—that continued to target and exploit Black bodies under the guise of criminal justice.

AMENDMENT XIII

Passed by Congress January 31, 1865. Ratified December 6, 1865.

Section 1.
Neither slavery nor involuntary servitude, except as a punishment for crime whereof the party shall have been duly convicted, shall exist within the United States, or any place subject to their jurisdiction.

Section 2.
Congress shall have power to enforce this article by appropriate legislation.

Source: The Constitution: Amendments 13, Founding Documents (National Archives).

The Fourteenth Amendment: Birthright Citizenship and Equal Protection

The Fourteenth Amendment (1868) codified the principle of birthright citizenship, ensuring that all persons born or naturalized in the United States were citizens with equal protection under the law. This amendment directly overturned the Supreme Court's *Dred Scott v. Sandford* (1857) ruling and provided the constitutional basis for challenging discriminatory laws like the Black Codes, laying the groundwork for future civil rights litigation.

AMENDMENT XIV

Passed by Congress June 13, 1866. Ratified July 9, 1868.

Section 1.
All persons born or naturalized in the United States, and subject to the jurisdiction thereof, are citizens of the United States and of the State wherein they reside. No State shall make or enforce any law which shall abridge the privileges or immunities of citizens of the United States; nor shall any State deprive any person of life, liberty, or property, without due process of law; nor deny to any person within its jurisdiction the equal protection of the laws. . . .

Section 3.
No person shall be a Senator or Representative in Congress, or elector of President and Vice-President, or hold any office, civil or military, under the United States, or under any State, who, having previously taken an oath, as a member of Congress, or as an officer of the United States, or as a member of any State legislature, or as an executive or judicial officer of any State, to support the Constitution of the United States, shall have engaged in insurrection or rebellion against the same, or given aid or comfort to the enemies thereof. But Congress may by a vote of two-thirds of each House, remove such disability.

Section 4.
The validity of the public debt of the United States, authorized by law, including debts incurred for payment of pensions and bounties for services in suppressing insurrection or rebellion, shall not be questioned. But neither the United States nor any State shall assume or pay any debt or obligation incurred in aid of insurrection or rebellion against the United States, or any claim for the loss or emancipation of any slave; but all such debts, obligations and claims shall be held illegal and void.

Source: The Constitution: Amendments 14, Founding Documents (National Archives).

The Fifteenth Amendment: Expanding the Electorate, Igniting Resistance

Ratified in 1870, the Fifteenth Amendment declared that no citizen could be denied the right to vote "on account of race, color, or previous condition of servitude." This monumental change granted Black men the legal right to vote. However, it also triggered a swift and violent backlash that would ultimately fuel voter suppression and systemic disenfranchisement for generations.

AMENDMENT XV

Passed by Congress February 26, 1869. Ratified February 3, 1870.

Section 1.
The right of citizens of the United States to vote shall not be denied or abridged by the United States or by any State on account of race, color, or previous condition of servitude—

Section 2.
The Congress shall have power to enforce this article by appropriate legislation.

Source: The Constitution: Amendments 15, Founding Documents (National Archives).

A Surge of Political Power: Black Men and the Ballot

The passage of the Fifteenth Amendment empowered African American men—many of them formerly enslaved—to engage fully in the political process. In the years immediately following its ratification, Black men voted in large numbers, held political rallies, formed grassroots organizations, and helped to redefine what democracy looked like in the postwar South.

From the Senate to City Halls: Black Political Leadership in Reconstruction

Nearly 2,000 African American men held public office at the local, state, and national levels during Reconstruction. Their presence in legislatures and civic institutions symbolized a radical reimagining of power in the postslavery South. Yet, as Reconstruction ended, the rise of Jim Crow laws reversed many of these gains. The fight to reclaim the rights first secured in the 1870s would stretch well into the twentieth century, culminating in the civil rights movements of the 1960s.

The *Engraved Portrait of Five African American Legislators from Reconstruction Congresses*, created in the early 1880s, commemorates the historic participation of Black leaders in the U.S. Congress during Reconstruction. Featuring figures such as Hiram Revels and Blanche K. Bruce, the image symbolizes the transformative impact of the Reconstruction Amendments and the possibilities of Black political power in postemancipation America. It also serves as a visual assertion of dignity, leadership, and the struggle for racial equality in a nation still reckoning with its past.

Engraved Portrait of Five African American Legislators from Reconstruction Congresses, early 1880s (Source: Collection of the Smithsonian National Museum of African American History and Culture)

The Reconstruction Amendments fundamentally redefined American democracy by establishing birthright citizenship, abolishing slavery, and extending voting rights to Black men. Though these constitutional changes ushered in a new era of possibility, they were met with intense backlash and systemic efforts to limit their impact. Still, the Reconstruction era remains a testament to the resilience of African Americans who seized these new rights, organized politically, and helped shape a vision of America rooted in justice and equality. Their legacy laid the constitutional and moral foundation for future civil rights struggles and remains central to the ongoing pursuit of full citizenship and inclusion.

Laws Say One Thing, Life Says Another

The Thirteenth, Fourteenth, and Fifteenth Amendments were supposed to guarantee freedom, citizenship, and voting rights. However, laws can be ignored, bent, or blocked—and many states worked hard to do just that.

You're Practicing: Connecting legal changes to real-life outcomes.

Connect This To: Reconstruction, civil rights, and voter suppression.

Theme: Rights, Citizenship, and Justice

Practice: Explain the Significance or Importance

The Reconstruction Amendments (Thirteenth, Fourteenth, and Fifteenth) marked a constitutional transformation in the aftermath of slavery.

(A) Identify one provision from any of the Reconstruction Amendments.
(B) Explain how that provision sought to redefine citizenship or rights for African Americans.
(C) Assess the significance of the Reconstruction Amendments for African Americans during and after Reconstruction.

SAMPLE RESPONSES

(A) The Thirteenth Amendment abolished slavery and involuntary servitude, except as punishment for a crime.

The Fourteenth Amendment guarantees equal protection under the law and grants citizenship to all persons born or naturalized in the U.S., including formerly enslaved individuals.

(B) The citizenship clause of the Fourteenth Amendment overturned the Dred Scott decision, establishing that African Americans were full U.S. citizens entitled to civil rights.

The Fifteenth Amendment's protection of voting rights aimed to empower Black men politically, giving them a voice in shaping Reconstruction governments and laws.

(C) During Reconstruction, these amendments provided the legal foundation for Black political participation, leading to the election of African American legislators at local, state, and federal levels.

After Reconstruction, while many of these rights were systematically suppressed through Jim Crow laws, the amendments became cornerstones of later civil rights struggles, enabling legal victories during the 20th-century movement for equality.

Skills Assessed: Describe historical developments; explain the significance or importance; use evidence in support of a historical argument.

Topic 3.2 Social Life—Reuniting Black Families and the Freedmen's Bureau

Key Terms

- Freedmen's Bureau (1865–1872)—federal agency for newly freed people
- Marriage records—legitimization of enslaved unions
- Freedmen's schools—education for all ages
- Family reunification efforts—newspaper ads and bureau assistance
- Medical aid and contracts
- Black churches and social life
- Amelia E. Johnson—documentarian of postemancipation social life
- Community building

In the aftermath of the Civil War and the abolition of slavery, African Americans set out to reconstruct not only the nation but the personal bonds that had been torn apart by centuries of enslavement. One of the federal government's first efforts to support this transformation was the creation of the Freedmen's Bureau, an agency designed to provide aid and establish civil order in a society transitioning away from slavery. At the same time, formerly enslaved people launched widespread efforts to reunite with lost loved ones, rebuild households, and affirm the centrality of family and kinship in Black life.

After engaging with this topic, scholars will be able to:

- Describe the mission and functions of the Freedmen's Bureau and its role in aiding African Americans during Reconstruction.
- Explain how African Americans took active steps to restore and preserve family structures after emancipation.
- Analyze how the pursuit of family unity and stability was both a personal and a political act of resistance against the dehumanizing legacies of slavery.

The Bureau of Hope and Transition

Created by Congress in 1865 and operating until 1872, the Bureau of Refugees, Freedmen, and Abandoned Lands—commonly known as the Freedmen's Bureau—was the first federal agency established to provide direct assistance to newly freed African Americans. It played a critical role in the immediate aftermath of the Civil War as the nation grappled with the human cost of slavery and secession.

Rebuilding Lives Through Aid and Education

While the bureau managed confiscated and abandoned Confederate property, its most lasting legacy lay in providing humanitarian relief and civic resources to formerly enslaved people. The agency distributed food and clothing, established hospitals and schools, assisted in labor contracts, legalized marriages, and laid the foundation for Black educational institutions. It served as both a welfare and a rights protection agency during a volatile transition to freedom.

Broken Ties and Enduring Bonds

Slavery tore African American families apart through forced sales, relocations, and the deliberate erasure of names and heritage. Despite these devastating disruptions, Black families nurtured kinship ties by creating new familial networks, godparents, community elders, and fictive kin. These became essential forms of support, resilience, and love both during and after enslavement.

Searching for the Lost: The Long Road to Reunion

After emancipation, many African Americans embarked on emotional and often dangerous journeys to find family members lost to the domestic slave trade. They placed classified ads in Black newspapers, posted flyers, traveled among plantations, and appealed to Freedmen's Bureau agents, hoping for reunions that could restore fractured lineages and heal generational wounds.

Naming Freedom, Legalizing Love

Before emancipation, marriages between enslaved people were not legally recognized. Yet, many formed unions through cultural practices like jumping the broom. After abolition, formerly enslaved couples sought legal recognition of their marriages, viewing it as a declaration of personhood. Many adopted surnames of their choosing, often of admired leaders or family ancestors. This was an expression of their newfound freedom and autonomy.

From Survival to Celebration: The Rise of Black Family Reunions

The tradition of Black family reunions emerged out of these postemancipation quests to reconnect with loved ones. Over time, these gatherings became powerful intergenerational spaces to honor family roots, celebrate cultural resilience, pass down oral histories, and share food, music, and joy. These reunions turned a legacy of loss into one of love and enduring unity.

Published in *The Christian Recorder* in 1864, Elizabeth Brisco's heartfelt advertisement reflects the urgent efforts of formerly enslaved people to reconnect with loved ones after the chaos of slavery and war. Like thousands of African Americans at the time, Brisco turned to Black newspapers to search for lost family members, demonstrating both the trauma of separation and the hope of reunion. Her ad stands as a moving example of Black perseverance and love as well as the power of the Black press during Reconstruction.

paper

INFORMATION WANTED.

Information is wanted of Charles Brisco, who left Virginia, some four or five years ago, to wait upon Lieutenant Fairfax, on a steamer for San Francisco, at the outbreak of this war. Lieutenant Fairfax returned, leaving my husband behind. I am informed that Charles Brisco left San Francisco for Aspinwall, New Grenada, as a cook, or waiter on a family. Any information concerning him may be left at the Book and Christian Recorder office, No. 619 Pine Street, Philadelphia.

(Signed) ELIZABETH BRISCO, his Wife.

N. B.—Charles has a mother and sister in Georgetown, D. C., by the names of Cynthia Brisco and Mrs. Mary A. Dove.

TAR CORDIAL.

Elizabeth Brisco searching for her husband, Charles Brisco, *The Christian Recorder* (Philadelphia, PA), March 26, 1864, last seen: finding family after slavery

The Freedmen's Bureau

In 1865, the U.S. Congress passed an Act to Establish a Bureau for the Relief of Freedmen and Refugees. This created what became known as the Freedmen's Bureau—a federal agency designed to support formerly enslaved people and war refugees in the aftermath of the Civil War. This groundbreaking legislation marked one of the first major federal efforts to provide social services and civil protections for African Americans. The act laid the legal foundation for Reconstruction's promise of freedom, education, and family restoration.

CHAP. XC.–An Act to Establish a Bureau for the Relief of Freedmen and Refugees. March 3, 1865

Be it enacted by the Senate and House of Representatives of the United States of America in Congress assembled, That there is hereby established in the War Department, to continue during the present war of rebellion, and for one year thereafter, a bureau of refugees, freedmen, and abandoned lands, to which shall be committed, as hereinafter provided, the supervision and management of all abandoned lands, and the control of all subjects relating to refugees and freedmen from rebel states, or from any district of country within the territory embraced in the operations of the army, under such rules and regulations as may be prescribed by the head of the bureau and approved by the President. The said bureau shall be under the management and control of a commissioner to be appointed by the President, by and with the advice and consent of the Senate, whose compensation shall be three thousand dollars per annum, and such number of clerks as may be assigned to him by the Secretary of War, not exceeding one chief clerk, two of the fourth class, two of the third class, and five of the first class. And the commissioner and all persons appointed under this act, shall, before entering upon their duties, take the oath of office prescribed in an act entitled "An act to prescribe an oath of office, and for other purposes," approved July second, eighteen hundred and sixty-two, and the commissioner and the chief clerk shall, before entering upon their duties, give bonds to the treasurer of the United States, the former in the sum of fifty thousand dollars, and the latter in the sum of ten thousand dollars, conditioned for the faithful discharge of their duties respectively, with securities to be approved as sufficient by the Attorney-General, which bonds shall be filed in the office of the first comptroller of the treasury, to be by him put in suit for the benefit of any injured party upon any breach of the conditions thereof.

SEC. 2. And be it further enacted, That the Secretary of War may direct such issues of provisions, clothing, and fuel, as he may deem needful for the immediate and temporary shelter and supply of destitute and suffering refugees and freedmen and their wives and children, under such rules and regulations as he may direct.

SEC. 3. And be it further enacted, That the President may, by and with the advice and consent of the Senate, appoint an assistant commissioner for each of the states declared to be in insurrection, not exceeding ten in number, who shall, under the direction of the commissioner, aid in the execution of the provisions of this act; and he shall give a bond to the Treasurer of the United States, in the sum of twenty thousand dollars, in the form and manner prescribed in the first section of this act. Each of said commissioners shall receive an annual salary of two thousand five hundred dollars in full compensation for all his services. And any military officer may be detailed and assigned to duty under this act without increase of pay or allowances. The commissioner shall, before the commencement of each regular session of congress, make full report of his proceedings with exhibits of the state of his accounts to the President, who shall communicate the same to congress, and shall also make special reports whenever required to do so by the President or either house of congress; and the assistant commissioners shall make quarterly reports of their proceedings to the commissioner, and also such other special reports as from time to time may be required.

SEC. 4. And be it further enacted, That the commissioner, under the direction of the President, shall have authority to set apart, for the use of loyal refugees and freedmen, such tracts of land within the insurrectionary states as shall have been abandoned, or to which the United States shall have acquired title by confiscation or sale, or otherwise, and to every male citizen, whether refugee or freedman, as aforesaid, there shall be assigned not more than forty acres of such land, and the person to whom it was so assigned shall be protected in the use and enjoyment of the land for the term of three years at an annual rent not exceeding six per centum upon the value of such land, as it was appraised by the state authorities in the year eighteen hundred and sixty, for the purpose of taxation, and in case no such appraisal can be found, then the rental shall be based upon the estimated value of the land in said year, to be ascertained in such manner as the commissioner may by regulation prescribe. At the end of said term, or at any time during said term, the occupants of any parcels so assigned may purchase the land and receive such title thereto as the United States can convey, upon paying therefor the value of the land, as ascertained and fixed for the purpose of determining the annual rent aforesaid.

SEC. 5. And be it further enacted, That all acts and parts of acts inconsistent with the provisions of this act, are hereby repealed. APPROVED, March 3, 1865.

Source: *U.S. Statutes at Large, Treaties, and Proclamations of the United States of America*, vol. 13 (Boston, 1866), pp. 507–509, Library of Congress. Transcript by Freedmen and Southern Society Project, University of Maryland.

In response to Virginia's 1866 law legalizing the marriages of formerly enslaved couples, the Freedmen's Bureau issued the Bureau of Refugees, Freedmen, and Abandoned Lands, Head Quarters Assistant Commissioner State of Virginia, Circular No. 11. This circular instructed county clerks on how to register "Colored Persons now cohabiting as Husband and Wife." Freedmen's Bureau agents were directed to compile official records recognizing long-standing unions previously denied legal status under slavery. This document reflects how African Americans actively sought to formalize their family ties and assert their rights as citizens in the early Reconstruction period.

In 1883, Clarissa Reed placed this ad in the *Southwestern Christian Advocate*, a weekly African American newspaper published by the Methodist Episcopal Church from 1877 to 1929. Between 1879 and 1896, the paper ran thousands of "Lost Friends" ads from formerly enslaved people seeking to reconnect with loved ones torn apart by slavery. Reed's ad not only recounts the pain of family separation; it also reveals her resilience and determination to reclaim her kin and her story.

DEAR EDITOR—I desire to inquire for my people. Mother was Pearline, stepfather was Sam. Mother had two sets of children. There were five of us, and two died before I left home. The oldest, Sophronia, was sold first; there were Fannie, Morgan, Anderson and myself. Parents belonged to John Ronden. The old man and I was sold to a Mr. Currel, and he died, and mistress married again and carried me to Kentucky. My people were living in St. Charles county, Missouri, when I was sold for cutting off two of my young boss's fingers. It has been about 46 years since I saw or heard from my people. Then I was sold from Kentucky to New Orleans. Last owner was Mrs. Moore. Write to me at Union Chapel M. E. Church, New Orleans, care Rev. S. Priestley.

CLARISSA REED

Source: *Southwestern Christian Advocate* (New Orleans, LA), September 13, 1883. https://informationwanted.org/items/show/2291.

TIP

Stay Focused on the Prompt

Avoid the trap of writing everything you know. Stick to answering what the question is actually asking.

Rebuilding Families from the Ruins

Imagine searching for your children or your spouse after years of separation under slavery. The Freedmen's Bureau helped some families reconnect. It also helped people marry legally for the first time. These moments were joyful but also heartbreaking.

You're Practicing: Exploring how big systems affect personal lives.

Connect This To: Family, freedom, and community repair.

Theme: Kinship and Cultural Survival

Practice: Explain Causality (Effects)

The end of slavery prompted newly freed people to pursue family reunification and access new resources such as those offered by the Freedmen's Bureau.

(A) Describe one goal of the Freedmen's Bureau or a common action taken by African Americans to reunite families.

(B) Explain one way these efforts impacted Black family or community life during Reconstruction.

(C) Evaluate how these efforts shaped long-term cultural or social developments in African American communities.

SAMPLE RESPONSES

(A) One goal of the Freedmen's Bureau was to assist formerly enslaved people in locating and reuniting with separated family members by maintaining records, sending agents into the field, and placing newspaper ads.

African Americans often traveled long distances across the South, placed "Information Wanted" ads in Black newspapers, or enlisted ministers and soldiers to help search for lost relatives.

(B) Family reunification efforts led to the reconstitution of Black households, strengthening kinship ties and allowing families to rebuild a sense of autonomy and dignity after generations of forced separation.

These efforts also fostered the growth of mutual aid networks and churches, which became central to Black community resilience and self-determination during Reconstruction.

(C) The emphasis on family reunification reinforced deep cultural values around kinship, caregiving, and collective responsibility, which remain central in African American communities today.

The work of the Freedmen's Bureau and the grassroots organizing by Black families laid the foundation for institution-building, including the rise of independent Black churches, schools, and civic organizations committed to social uplift and civil rights.

Skills Assessed: Explain the effects of historical developments; use sources and evidence; analyze relationships among developments.

Topic 3.3 Black Codes, Land, and Labor

Key Terms

- Black Codes—restrictive laws limiting the freedom of formerly enslaved people
- Vagrancy laws—used to criminalize unemployment
- Sharecropping—labor system replacing slavery
- Convict leasing—forced labor through imprisonment
- Land redistribution debates—40 acres and a mule
- Freedmen's land claims
- Plantation economy continuity
- Labor contracts—often exploitative

In the aftermath of the Civil War, freedom did not mean equality. Across the South, new laws and labor systems emerged to reassert white control and restrict Black mobility. Known as Black Codes, these oppressive statutes—paired with exploitative labor practices like sharecropping and convict leasing—were designed to maintain a racial and economic order that closely mirrored slavery.

After engaging with this topic, scholars will be able to:

- Analyze how Black Codes curtailed African Americans' freedoms and undermined their rights as newly freed citizens.
- Explain how exploitative labor systems such as sharecropping, tenant farming, and convict leasing restricted African American economic independence.
- Understand how struggles over landownership, labor contracts, and legal protections shaped the post emancipation Black experience in the South.

The Revival of Control: Black Codes and the Ghost of Slavery

In the immediate aftermath of the Civil War, Southern legislatures enacted Black Codes under Presidential Reconstruction (1865–1866) to reassert dominance over African Americans. These laws restricted mobility, access to labor, and civil participation, mirroring the surveillance and coercion of the former slave codes. Despite emancipation, African Americans were systematically criminalized and confined to exploitative economic roles.

Contracted into Servitude: Forced Labor and Economic Suppression

Black Codes demanded that Black individuals sign yearly labor contracts, often under duress. Those who refused or fled could be arrested for vagrancy, imprisoned, or beaten. The contracts frequently yielded poverty wages and reaffirmed white control over Black labor, perpetuating economic dependency under the guise of legality.

The Theft of Black Childhood: Apprenticeships Without Consent

Some of the most damaging Black Codes included provisions that stripped African American parents of their children. States seized Black youths and bound them to white "apprenticeships" without consent, effectively reenslaving the next generation under legal pretenses. This policy devastated families and reinforced the denial of Black parental authority.

The photograph *Juvenile Convicts at Work in the Fields* (1903) captures the haunting legacy of slavery through the system of convict leasing in the Jim Crow South. Featuring young African American boys forced to labor under state control, the image reveals how incarceration became a tool to exploit Black youths long after emancipation. This powerful visual underscores how freedom was repeatedly undermined through new systems of racialized labor and punishment.

Juvenile Convicts at Work in the Fields, 1903
(Source: Detroit Publishing Company photograph collection, Library of Congress)

40 Acres and a Broken Promise: Special Field Orders No. 15

In 1865, General William T. Sherman issued Special Field Orders No. 15, designating over 400,000 acres of Confederate land to be distributed to formerly enslaved people in plots of 40 acres. This vision of landownership was a radical attempt to provide economic independence and restitution to newly freed African Americans. The "Land Order for Richard Brown" (1865) is a historical document issued during Reconstruction under General William T. Sherman's Special Field Orders No. 15, which temporarily redistributed confiscated Confederate land to newly freed African Americans. This specific order granted land to Richard Brown and represented the promise of landownership as a pathway to freedom, self-sufficiency, and dignity. The document embodies the brief moment when reparative justice for formerly enslaved people seemed possible in the post–Civil War South.

No. 118

Office of Superintendent of Freedmen,

Charleston, S. C., April 1st 1865.

In accordance with Major General Sherman's Order, No. 15, permission is hereby granted to Richard Brown to take possession of and occupy forty acres of land, situated in St. Andrews Parish, Island of James and being a part of what was formerly known as Heyward's plantation.

By order of

BREVET MAJOR GENERAL RUFUS SAXTON.

Gilbert Pillsbury
Gov. and General Superintendent of Freedmen.

Land Order for Richard Brown, 1865
(Source: "Select Freedmen's Bureau Records." *National Archives*, 15 Aug. 2016)

Reversal of Freedom: Presidential Pardon and the Return of the Planter Class

President Andrew Johnson overturned Sherman's field orders and returned seized lands to former Confederate owners or allowed them to be purchased by Northern investors. This action forced Black families off land they had begun cultivating. It blocked their path to wealth accumulation and placed them into exploitative labor arrangements like sharecropping.

Sharecropping: A New System of Economic Entrapment

Sharecropping became the dominant agricultural arrangement in the postemancipation South. While landowners provided tools and land, Black farmers received a portion of the crop. In reality, this often translated into economic bondage as high interest rates and manipulated yields kept families in cycles of debt and poverty.

The Crop Lien Trap: Borrowing Against a Future Never Repaid

African Americans and poor white farmers were lured into crop lien systems, borrowing against future harvests to purchase essentials. Merchants and landlords profited, while farmers remained trapped in debt. The system institutionalized economic servitude and hollowed out Black aspirations for generational wealth.

Convict Leasing: Slavery Rebranded Through Incarceration

The South's reliance on forced labor continued through convict leasing. Black men, often arrested on false or minor charges, were leased to private companies and plantations to perform brutal labor without compensation. This system exploited legal loopholes in the Thirteenth Amendment and perpetuated slavery by another name.

The *Picture Postcard of a North Carolina Convict Camp*, circa 1910, offers a stark visual record of the convict leasing system that emerged after the abolition of slavery. The image reveals how Southern states exploited incarcerated Black men—often imprisoned for petty or fabricated charges—as a source of unpaid labor. It serves as a powerful reminder of how racialized systems of control and forced labor persisted well into the twentieth century under the guise of criminal justice.

Picture Postcard of a North Carolina Convict Camp, circa 1910
(Source: Collection of the Smithsonian National Museum of African American History and Culture)

Circular No. 8 from the Bureau of Refugees, Freedmen, and Abandoned Lands (1866) outlines federal efforts to assist freed people in negotiating fair labor contracts during the early years of Reconstruction. Issued just one year after the Civil War ended, the circular reflects how the Freedmen's Bureau sought to protect formerly enslaved individuals from exploitative practices and ensure their transition to wage labor. It represents the federal government's attempt to balance labor demands with emerging rights for African Americans in a racially hostile environment.

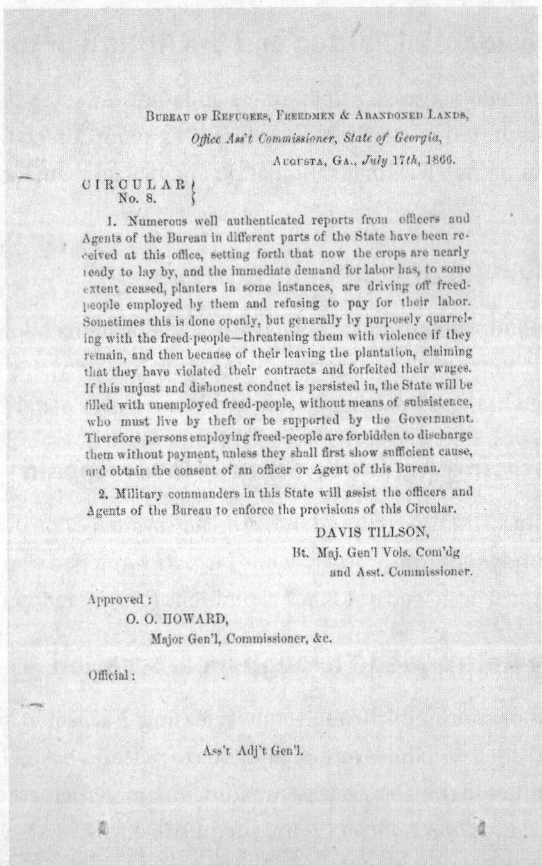

BUREAU OF REFUGEES, FREEDMEN & ABANDONED LANDS,
Office Ass't Commissioner, State of Georgia,
AUGUSTA, GA., *July 17th*, 1866.

CIRCULAR
No. 8.

1. Numerous well authenticated reports from officers and Agents of the Bureau in different parts of the State have been received at this office, setting forth that now the crops are nearly ready to lay by, and the immediate demand for labor has, to some extent ceased, planters in some instances, are driving off freed-people employed by them and refusing to pay for their labor. Sometimes this is done openly, but generally by purposely quarreling with the freed-people—threatening them with violence if they remain, and then because of their leaving the plantation, claiming that they have violated their contracts and forfeited their wages. If this unjust and dishonest conduct is persisted in, the State will be filled with unemployed freed-people, without means of subsistence, who must live by theft or be supported by the Government. Therefore persons employing freed-people are forbidden to discharge them without payment, unless they shall first show sufficient cause, and obtain the consent of an officer or Agent of this Bureau.

2. Military commanders in this State will assist the officers and Agents of the Bureau to enforce the provisions of this Circular.

DAVIS TILLSON,
Bt. Maj. Gen'l Vols. Com'dg
and Asst. Commissioner.

Approved :
O. O. HOWARD,
Major Gen'l, Commissioner, &c.

Official :

Ass't Adj't Gen'l.

Circular No. 8 from the Bureau of Refugees, Freedmen, and Abandoned Lands, 1866
(Source: Collection of the Smithsonian National Museum of African American History and Culture)

Freedom Without Land Isn't Freedom

When slavery ended, many Black families hoped to own land—but most got sharecropping contracts instead. These deals often kept them poor and powerless. The promise of 40 acres and a mule was never kept.

You're Practicing: Identifying economic systems that preserve inequality.

Connect This To: Labor, property, and structural racism.

Theme: Economic Power and Systemic Oppression

The struggle for economic justice and true freedom in the aftermath of slavery was far from over. As this section reveals, Black Codes, exploitative labor systems like sharecropping and convict leasing, and the federal government's failure to fulfill land redistribution promises created new forms of oppression that constrained Black advancement. Yet African Americans continued to resist—negotiating contracts, petitioning for land, and building communities despite the barriers. These efforts laid the foundation for future movements for land justice, civil rights, and labor equity.

Practice: Compare (Similarities)

In the post–Civil War South, labor systems such as sharecropping and convict leasing emerged to replace slavery.

(A) Identify one feature of either sharecropping or convict leasing.
(B) Explain how that feature limited African American freedom or economic advancement.
(C) Compare the two systems in terms of how each functioned to maintain racial and economic hierarchies.

SAMPLE RESPONSES

(A) Sharecropping involved formerly enslaved people renting land from white landowners in exchange for a portion of the crop, often under unfair contracts that kept them in debt.

Convict leasing allowed states to lease incarcerated individuals—mostly African American men—to private companies for labor, often under brutal and deadly conditions.

(B) Sharecropping kept many Black families in cycles of debt peonage, unable to leave the land or accumulate wealth, essentially re-creating economic dependence.

Convict leasing exploited racist policing and vagrancy laws to re-enslave Black men under the guise of criminal punishment, denying them freedom and subjecting them to forced labor.

(C) Both systems replicated slavery by controlling Black labor, restricting mobility, and transferring wealth and productivity to white landowners or corporations.

While sharecropping used deceptive economic contracts, convict leasing used the legal system to criminalize Black life and justify re-enslavement, reinforcing white supremacy through both law and labor.

Skills Assessed: Compare historical developments; explain similarities; describe economic and legal systems.

Topic 3.4 The Defeat of Reconstruction

Key Terms

- Compromise of 1877—ended Reconstruction
- Rutherford B. Hayes—became president in exchange for troop removal
- "Redemption" governments—return of white Democratic rule
- Black officeholders displaced
- Loss of federal protection
- Violent suppression of Black political activity
- Reconstruction fatigue in the North

After the Civil War, the Reconstruction era promised a radical transformation of American society by granting Black citizens legal equality, political participation, and federal protections. But by the end of the nineteenth century, this vision had unraveled under mounting white supremacist backlash, federal withdrawal, and political compromise. The erosion of these gains marked a turning point in African American history, exposing the fragility of progress in the face of racial violence and institutional abandonment.

After engaging with this topic, scholars will be able to:

- Analyze the political, legal, and violent mechanisms used to roll back the progress of Reconstruction.
- Explain how white supremacist ideologies, court rulings, and shifting federal priorities undermined Black civil rights.
- Evaluate the long-term consequences of Reconstruction's failure on African American communities and American democracy.

The Compromise that Ended an Era

The election of 1876 resulted in the Compromise of 1877, in which Rutherford B. Hayes secured the presidency in exchange for the removal of federal troops from the South. This marked the official end of Reconstruction. It allowed Southern states to rewrite their constitutions and implement de jure segregation, paving the way for the Jim Crow era.

Silencing the Black Vote

New laws and local ordinances suppressed African American political power through voter suppression tactics such as poll taxes, literacy tests, and grandfather clauses. These measures targeted Black citizens and effectively disenfranchised generations, undermining the Fifteenth Amendment and halting Black political participation.

Terror and Retaliation as Social Control

The collapse of Reconstruction saw the rise of racial violence across the South. White supremacist groups like the Ku Klux Klan (KKK) waged campaigns of terror, using lynchings, assaults, and intimidation to reassert white dominance and punish African Americans for claiming civil rights and social equality.

Plessy v. Ferguson and the Constitutionalizing of Segregation

In 1896, the Supreme Court ruled in *Plessy v. Ferguson* that racial segregation was constitutional under the doctrine of "separate but equal." This decision validated state laws that enforced racial segregation and gave legal cover to a century of systemic inequality.

Justice Henry Brown of Michigan delivered the majority opinion, which sustained the constitutionality of Louisiana's Jim Crow law. In part, he said:

> We consider the underlying fallacy of the plaintiff's argument to consist in the assumption that the enforced separation of the two races stamps the colored race with a badge of inferiority. If this be so, it is not by reason of anything found in the act, but solely because the colored race chooses to put that construction upon it.... The argument also assumes that social prejudice may be overcome by legislation, and that equal rights cannot be secured except by an enforced commingling of the two races.... If the civil and political rights of both races be equal, one cannot be inferior to the other civilly or politically. If one race be inferior to the other socially, the Constitution of the United States cannot put them upon the same plane.
>
> Source: U.S. Supreme Court, *Plessy vs. Ferguson*, Judgement, Decided May 18, 1896; Records of the Supreme Court of the United States; National Archives.

In the lone dissent, Kentuckian Justice John Marshall Harlan wrote:

> I am of the opinion that the statute of Louisiana is inconsistent with the personal liberties of citizens, white and black, in that State, and hostile to both the spirit and the letter of the Constitution of the United States. If laws of like character should be enacted in the several States of the Union, the effect would be in the highest degree mischievous. Slavery as an institution tolerated by law would, it is true, have disappeared from our country, but there would remain a power in the States, by sinister legislation, to interfere with the blessings of freedom; to regulate civil rights common to all citizens, upon the basis of race; and to place in a condition of legal inferiority a large body of American citizens, now constituting a part of the political community, called the people of the United States, for whom and by whom, through representatives, our government is administrated. Such a system is inconsistent with the guarantee given by the Constitution to each State of a republican form of government, and may be stricken down by congressional action, or by the courts in the discharge of their solemn duty to maintain the supreme law of the land, anything in the Constitution or laws of any State to the contrary notwithstanding.
>
> Source: U.S. Supreme Court, *Plessy vs. Ferguson*, Judgement, Decided May 18, 1896; Records of the Supreme Court of the United States; National Archives.

Separate and Unequal: The Reality of Jim Crow

Though the court claimed facilities for Black Americans would be "equal," in practice they were grossly inferior—underfunded schools, restricted public services, and limited access to transportation and health care. It wasn't until *Brown v. Board of Education* in 1954 that this precedent began to be legally challenged and dismantled.

One Step Forward, Two Steps Back

Black voters and leaders made real gains during Reconstruction—but white supremacists organized to take it all away. With violence, laws, and deals made behind closed doors, the era ended and left many dreams shattered.

You're Practicing: Tracing how power is won—and lost.

Connect This To: Redemption, resistance, and political backlash.

Theme: Power and Politics

Practice: Explain Continuity or Change over Time

The end of Reconstruction ushered in a new era of racial violence, disenfranchisement, and the rollback of civil rights.

(A) Identify one development that contributed to the end of federal Reconstruction policy.
(B) Explain how this development affected African American political rights.
(C) Assess the extent to which the end of Reconstruction marked a significant change or a continuation of earlier patterns of exclusion.

SAMPLE RESPONSES

(A) The Compromise of 1877, which resolved the contested 1876 presidential election, led to the withdrawal of federal troops from the South, effectively ending Reconstruction enforcement.

The declining Northern commitment to racial equality, coupled with rising white supremacist violence, caused Congress to scale back support for Reconstruction policies.

(B) The withdrawal of federal troops allowed Southern states to intimidate Black voters and dismantle Reconstruction governments, ending meaningful Black political participation.

State laws and constitutional amendments in the South imposed literacy tests, poll taxes, and grandfather clauses, leading to widespread Black disenfranchisement.

(C) The end of Reconstruction marked a continuation of white supremacist control, as Southern elites reasserted power through legal and extralegal means, echoing antebellum systems of racial hierarchy.

However, it also represented a change, as the brief period of federal intervention and Black political power during Reconstruction was decisively reversed and replaced by the formalization of Jim Crow segregation and systematic exclusion.

Skills Assessed: Explain continuities or changes over time; evaluate the significance of developments; support an argument using relevant evidence.

Topic 3.5 Disenfranchisement and Jim Crow Laws

Key Terms

- Poll taxes
- Literacy tests
- Grandfather clauses
- White primaries
- Jim Crow segregation laws—enforced racial separation
- *Plessy v. Ferguson* (1896)—"separate but equal" doctrine
- Railcar segregation laws
- De jure segregation—legalized discrimination

In the aftermath of Reconstruction, white supremacist backlash took legislative and violent forms, codifying racial segregation and stripping away African American civil rights. The rise of Jim Crow laws institutionalized inequality across the South and beyond, even as African American leaders and writers pushed back with courage and conviction.

After engaging with this topic, scholars will be able to:

- Analyze how Jim Crow laws suppressed African American rights and dignity in the post-Reconstruction period.
- Evaluate the strategies African American leaders, journalists, and intellectuals used to challenge systemic racism and white mob violence during the nadir of race relations.

From Minstrel to Mandate: The Origins of Jim Crow

The phrase *Jim Crow* began as a racist caricature in minstrel shows of the 1830s but evolved into a legal system of segregation and white dominance. By the late 1800s, **Jim Crow laws** described state and local statutes across the South—and parts of the North—that enforced racial separation and inequality under the Supreme Court's endorsement in *Plessy v. Ferguson* (1896), which upheld the doctrine of "separate but equal."

Segregated by Law, Divided by Design

Jim Crow legislation curtailed Black political and social participation by enforcing voter suppression tactics such as poll taxes, literacy tests, and grandfather clauses. Simultaneously, laws mandated segregated schools, hospitals, cemeteries, and transportation. These laws created separate and unequal systems that remained in place until the Civil Rights Movement launched full-scale challenges in the mid-twentieth century.

The Nadir of American Race Relations

The period from the end of Reconstruction through the early 20th century is known by historians as the *nadir* of American race relations. This time is marked by extreme racial violence, mass disenfranchisement, and legalized segregation. African Americans endured frequent lynchings, mob violence, and public humiliation, often with no legal recourse or protection.

Pen Against the Noose: Black Journalism in the Jim Crow Era

African American journalists and writers, including trailblazers like Ida B. Wells, documented and exposed the false narratives used to justify lynchings and racial terror. Their courageous publications called national and international attention to the brutal realities of white supremacy and racial injustice in the South.

Resistance in the Shadows: Everyday Acts of Defiance

Despite the oppressive conditions of the Jim Crow era, African Americans organized resistance efforts such as streetcar boycotts, protests, and legal challenges. These grassroots movements were supported by a vibrant Black press, which helped circulate stories of abuse and mobilize community response—laying the foundation for the modern civil rights struggle.

Excerpts from *A Red Record*, written by **Ida B. Wells** in 1895, provide a searing, data-driven indictment of racial terror in post-Reconstruction America. In Chapter 1, Wells outlines how lynching became a systemic tool to repress African American advancement and reinforce white supremacy. Her work marks a pivotal moment in the history of investigative journalism and anti-lynching activism.

> THE CASE STATED
>
> The student of American sociology will find the year 1894 marked by a pronounced awakening of the public conscience to a system of anarchy and outlawry which had grown during a series of ten years to be so common, that scenes of unusual brutality failed to have any visible effect upon the humane sentiments of the people of our land.
>
> Beginning with the emancipation of the Negro, the inevitable result of unbribled [sic] power exercised for two and a half centuries, by the white man over the Negro, began to show itself in acts of conscienceless

outlawry. During the slave regime, the Southern white man owned the Negro body and soul. It was to his interest to dwarf the soul and preserve the body. Vested with unlimited power over his slave, to subject him to any and all kinds of physical punishment, the white man was still restrained from such punishment as tended to injure the slave by abating his physical powers and thereby reducing his financial worth. While slaves were scourged mercilessly, and in countless cases inhumanly treated in other respects, still the white owner rarely permitted his anger to go so far as to take a life, which would entail upon him a loss of several hundred dollars. The slave was rarely killed, he was too valuable; it was easier and quite as effective, for discipline or revenge, to sell him "Down South."

But Emancipation came and the vested interests of the white man in the Negro's body were lost. The white man had no right to scourge the emancipated Negro, still less has he a right to kill him. But the Southern white people had been educated so long in that school of practice, in which might makes right, that they disdained to draw. strict lines of action in dealing with the Negro. In slave times the Negro was kept subservient and submissive by the frequency and severity of the scourging, but, with freedom, a new system of intimidation came into vogue; the Negro was not only whipped and scourged; he was killed.

Not all nor nearly all of the murders done by white men, during the past thirty years in the South, have come to light, but the statistics as gathered and preserved by white men, and which have not been questioned, show that during these years more than ten thousand Negroes have been killed in cold blood, without the formality of judicial trial and legal execution. And yet, as evidence of the absolute impunity with which the white man dares to kill a Negro, the same record shows that during all these years, and for all these murders only three white men have been tried, convicted, and executed. As no white man has been lynched for the murder of colored people, these three executions are the only instances of the death penalty being visited upon white men for murdering Negroes.

Naturally enough the commission of these crimes began to tell upon the public conscience, and the Southern white man, as a tribute to the nineteenth-century civilization, was in a manner compelled to give excuses for his barbarism. His excuses have adapted themselves to the emergency, and are aptly outlined by that greatest of all Negroes, Frederick Douglass, in an article of recent date, in which he shows that there have been three distinct eras of Southern barbarism, to account for which three distinct excuses have been made.

The first excuse given to the civilized world for the murder of unoffending Negroes was the necessity of the white man to repress and stamp out alleged "race riots." For years immediately succeeding the war there was an appalling slaughter of colored people, and the wires usually conveyed to northern people and the world the intelligence, first, that an insurrection was being planned by Negroes, which, a few hours later, would prove to have been vigorously resisted by white men, and controlled with a resulting loss of several killed and wounded. It was always a remarkable feature in these insurrections and riots that only Negroes were killed during the rioting, and that all the white men escaped unharmed.

The purpose of the pages which follow shall be to give the record which has been made, not by colored men, but that which is the result of compilations made by white men, of reports sent over the civilized world by white men in the South. Out of their own mouths shall the murderers be condemned. For a number of years the Chicago Tribune, admittedly one of the leading journals of America, has made a specialty of the compilation of statistics touching upon lynching. The data compiled by that journal and published to the world January 1, 1894, up to the present time has not been disputed. In order to be safe from the charge of exaggeration, the incidents hereinafter reported have been confined to those vouched for by the Tribune.

Source: Ida B. Wells, *A Red Record: Tabulated Statistics and Alleged Causes of Lynchings in the United States, 1892–1893–1894*, Chicago: Donohue & Henneberry, 1895.

The photograph *Segregated Water Fountains* captures a stark visual reminder of the daily realities of Jim Crow segregation in the United States. Likely taken during the early-to-mid twentieth century, the image highlights the "separate but equal" doctrine's inherent inequality by juxtaposing facilities designated for "White" and "Colored" citizens. This powerful visual evidence underscores how racism was embedded not just in law but in the architecture of everyday life.

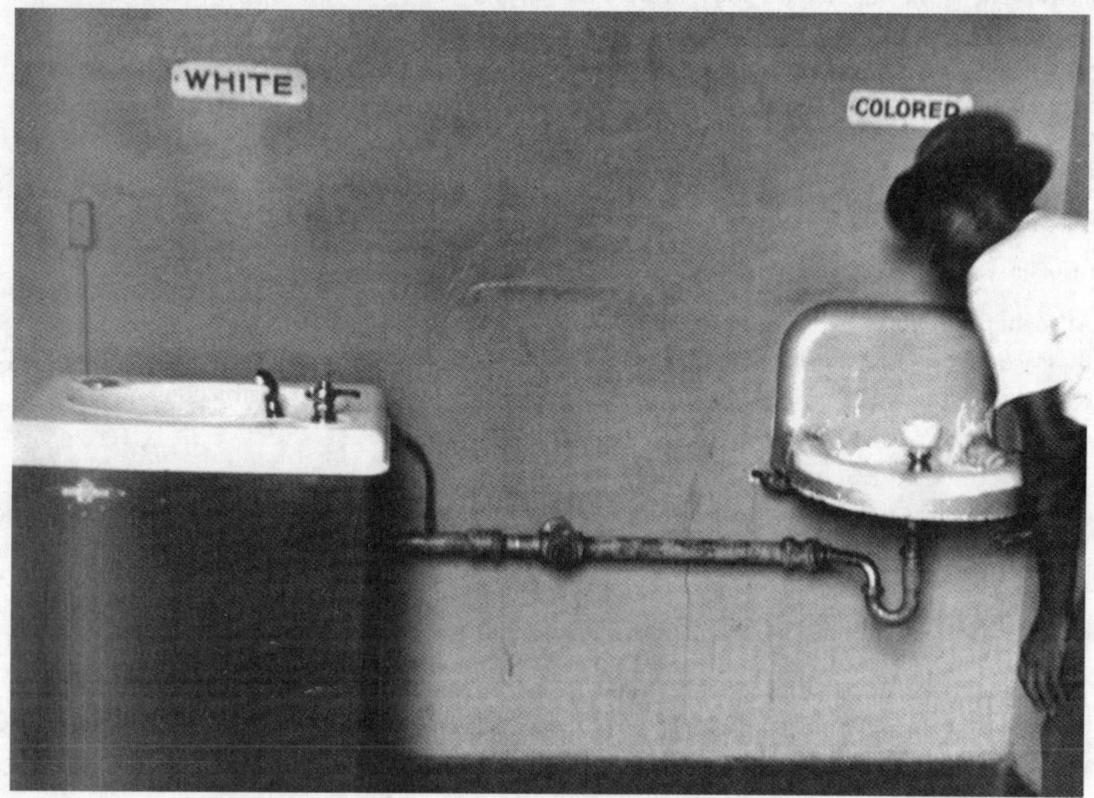

Segregated Water Fountains
(Source: National Museum of American History, CC0, via Wikimedia Commons)

The photograph *Segregated Restrooms,* circa 1960, visually illustrates the legalized racial division entrenched in American society during the Jim Crow era. Captured in the South just before the height of the Civil Rights Movement, this image reflects how segregation extended into basic public facilities, enforcing white supremacy through physical space. Such imagery reveals the humiliation and inequality African Americans endured daily under "separate but equal" laws.

> **TIP**
>
> **Read the Question Before the Source (When Time Allows)**
>
> Reading the question first can help you know what to look for in the stimulus (image, graph, or passage).

Segregated Restrooms, circa 1960
(Source: Photo by Hulton Archive/Getty Images)

Laws That Kept People Out

Literacy tests. Poll taxes. Grandfather clauses. These tools were used to stop Black people from voting—without ever writing the word *Black* in the law. This was segregation by design, not by accident.

You're Practicing: Spotting hidden power in everyday systems.

Connect This To: Voter suppression, legal loopholes, and systemic racism.

Theme: Law and Inequality

Practice: Contextualize

The rise of Jim Crow laws reshaped the racial and legal landscape of the post-Reconstruction South.

(A) Identify one Jim Crow law or practice that targeted African American civil rights.
(B) Place this law or practice in historical context by connecting it to developments from earlier in Reconstruction.
(C) Explain how these laws reflect broader social or political shifts in post-Reconstruction America.

SAMPLE RESPONSES

(A) Segregation laws mandated separate public facilities for Black and white citizens, such as schools, transportation, and restrooms.

Voting restrictions like literacy tests, poll taxes, and grandfather clauses were designed to disenfranchise African American voters.

(B) Jim Crow laws directly reversed gains made during Reconstruction, such as the Fifteenth Amendment, which had briefly enabled African American men to vote and hold office.

The rise of white supremacist groups like the Ku Klux Klan during Reconstruction laid the groundwork for institutionalized racial control through legal and violent means.

(C) Jim Crow laws reflected a national retreat from Reconstruction ideals, as Northern politicians prioritized reconciliation with the South over Black civil rights.

Jim Crow laws emerged alongside the rise of scientific racism and social Darwinism, which provided false intellectual justification for racial segregation and inequality.

Skills Assessed: Contextualize historical developments; explain relationships between legal and social systems; use examples to support a claim.

Topic 3.6 White Supremacist Violence and the Red Summer

Key Terms

- Ku Klux Klan (KKK)—terrorist group targeting Black communities
- Colfax Massacre (1873)
- Wilmington Coup (1898)—overthrow of elected Black leaders
- Red Summer (1919)—widespread race riots
- Elaine Massacre, Chicago Riot, Washington D.C. Riot
- Anti-Black pogroms
- Militant Black self-defense—emergence post-WWI
- Press and propaganda—racialized narratives

At the dawn of the twentieth century, Black Americans continued their pursuit of civil rights and economic independence. However, they faced escalating waves of white supremacist violence. Between 1917 and 1923, racial tensions intensified due to economic competition, the Great Migration, and Black veterans returning from World War I who demanded dignity and equality. These factors converged during the Red Summer of 1919, when dozens of cities erupted into racial terror, including deadly attacks on Black communities in Chicago, Washington, D.C., Knoxville, Tennessee, and Elaine, Arkansas.

After engaging with this topic, scholars will be able to:

- Analyze the structural and societal factors that led to racial violence in the early 1900s.
- Examine how African Americans resisted white supremacist attacks and built organized responses rooted in collective defense, political advocacy, and cultural solidarity.
- Understand the broader implications of the Red Summer as a pivotal moment in the long struggle for civil rights and self-defense.

The Flames of the Red Summer

From 1917 to 1921, white supremacist attacks surged across the United States, culminating in the infamous Red Summer of 1919. This period was marked by widespread racial violence initiated by white mobs targeting African American communities in over 30 cities, including Chicago, Washington D.C., Elaine, Arkansas, and Knoxville, Tennessee. These attacks were often ignored—or enabled—by local authorities, laying bare the violent resistance to Black progress in the early twentieth century.

Crisis in a Time of Pandemic and Return

The Red Summer was fueled by a volatile combination of the post–World War I recession, a deadly global influenza pandemic, and increased racial hostility toward Black veterans returning from the war. Many white Americans perceived Black economic advancement and social demands as threats, leading to intensified racial hatred and the justification of violence under the guise of protecting order.

The Destruction of Black Wall Street

In 1921, the Tulsa Race Massacre became one of the most devastating acts of racial terror in U.S. history. Sparked by a false accusation, white mobs, who were aided by law enforcement and even aerial attacks, destroyed the prosperous Greenwood District—known as *Black Wall Street*. They killed hundreds and erased a thriving Black economic hub in a matter of days.

A Legacy Stolen

White supremacist violence in this era did more than destroy lives. It robbed generations of African Americans of property, wealth, and opportunity. The targeted destruction of Black neighborhoods, homes, and businesses contributed to a long-lasting racial wealth gap and diminished the ability of many families to accumulate and pass down generational assets.

Fighting Back: Black Resistance in Word and Deed

African Americans met white supremacist violence with resilience and resistance. From self-defense groups in cities like Chicago to journalists like Ida B. Wells exposing racial terror, Black communities responded through armed defense, protest, and the written word. These acts of resistance challenged the myth of Black passivity and helped lay the groundwork for future civil rights movements.

Flight for Freedom: The Great Migration Begins

Facing relentless racial violence, political disenfranchisement, and economic exploitation in the South, many African Americans began relocating to cities in the North and West during the Great Migration. This mass movement reshaped Black life in America. It spurred the development of new cultural, political, and economic centers across the country and offered a form of resistance through geographic and community reinvention.

Claude McKay's 1919 poem "If We Must Die" emerged as a defiant literary response to the racial violence of the Red Summer. Written in the wake of widespread white supremacist attacks on Black communities, McKay's sonnet captures the courage, dignity, and unyielding resistance of African Americans determined to fight back. The poem stands as one of the earliest and most powerful examples of radical Black literary resistance in the twentieth century.

If We Must Die

If we must die—let it not be like hogs
Hunted and penned in an inglorious spot,
While round us bark the mad and hungry dogs,
Making their mock at our accursed lot.
If we must die—oh, let us nobly die,
So that our precious blood may not be shed
In vain; then even the monsters we defy
Shall be constrained to honor us though dead!

Oh, kinsmen! We must meet the common foe;
Though far outnumbered, let us still be brave,
And for their thousand blows deal one death-blow!
What though before us lies the open grave?
Like men we'll face the murderous, cowardly pack,
Pressed to the wall, dying, but—fighting back!

Source: The first printing of Claude McKay's poem "If We Must Die," in *The Liberator* 2, no. 7 (July 1919): p. 21.

The photograph of the Greenwood District burning during the Tulsa Race Massacre of 1921 captures one of the most devastating acts of racial violence in U.S. history. Taken as fires engulfed the prosperous Black neighborhood known as Black Wall Street, the image bears witness to the deliberate destruction of more than 1,250 Black-owned homes and businesses by white mobs. This haunting visual record stands as undeniable evidence of the economic and human toll of white supremacist terror.

Photograph of the Greenwood District burning during the Tulsa Race Massacre, 1921
(Source: Collection of the Smithsonian National Museum of African American History and Culture, gift of Cassandra P. Johnson Smith)

This harrowing photograph of Black men with their hands raised during the Tulsa Race Massacre of 1921 reveals the terror and humiliation faced by African Americans as white mobs, often aided by law enforcement, forcibly removed and detained them. Captured in the midst of the destruction of Greenwood, the image underscores the systematic nature of the violence and the vulnerability of even the most successful Black communities in the face of white supremacist aggression. It remains a chilling reminder of how Black dignity and safety were threatened during one of the darkest chapters of American history.

Photograph of Black men with hands raised during the Tulsa Race Massacre, 1921
(Source: Collection of the Smithsonian National Museum of African American History and Culture, gift of Cassandra P. Johnson Smith)

This photograph of the destruction in Greenwood following the Tulsa Race Massacre of 1921 captures the charred remains of what was once a thriving African American business district known as Black Wall Street. The image reflects the devastating impact of white supremacist violence, which obliterated homes, churches, schools, and economic infrastructure in a matter of hours. It stands as a haunting visual testament to both the brutality of the attack and the systemic efforts to erase Black prosperity and self-determination.

Photograph of destruction in Greenwood after the Tulsa Race Massacre, 1921
(Source: Collection of the Smithsonian National Museum of African American History and Culture, gift of Cassandra P. Johnson Smith)

The terror of white supremacist violence that engulfed Black communities during the Red Summer and the Tulsa Race Massacre left scars both physical and psychological. Yet, even amid destruction, resistance and dignity prevailed. Claude McKay's defiant poem "If We Must Die" (1919) captured the determination of African Americans to confront brutality with courage. The poem reflected a spirit that resonated through the images of the Greenwood District in flames, of Black men with hands raised, and of shattered homes and dreams. These primary sources not only bear witness to the violence but also to the resilience and humanity of a people who refused to surrender their right to live, build, and thrive.

When Justice Won't Protect You

When the courts and police refused to stop the violence, Black communities had to defend themselves. From lynchings to deadly riots like the Red Summer of 1919, this was terrorism—and resistance—in the streets.

You're Practicing: Asking how communities respond when institutions fail.

Connect This To: Self-defense, journalism, and organized resistance.

Theme: Violence, Memory, and Survival

Practice: Explain Causality (Causes)

The Red Summer of 1919 and other episodes of white supremacist violence marked a national crisis in racial justice.

(A) Identify one cause of a violent racial conflict during this period.
(B) Explain how this cause was related to broader economic or social tensions.
(C) Evaluate the role of African American resistance in shaping the response to white supremacist violence.

SAMPLE RESPONSES

(A) In Chicago, the murder of a Black teenager, Eugene Williams, who accidentally crossed the color line at a segregated beach, sparked days of deadly racial violence.

In Elaine, Arkansas, Black sharecroppers organizing for better pay and labor rights were met with deadly white mob violence, resulting in a massacre.

(B) The violence was driven by competition over jobs and housing as African Americans migrated North during the Great Migration, leading to white resentment and racial hostility.

White fears of Black political organizing and labor solidarity—especially in places like Elaine—were rooted in broader anxieties about racial hierarchy, economic control, and postwar social change.

(C) In cities like Washington, D.C., Black veterans and citizens organized armed self-defense, challenging the long-standing narrative of Black passivity and signaling a shift toward assertive resistance.

The violence and resistance helped galvanize organizations like the NAACP, which launched national campaigns for federal anti-lynching laws and amplified calls for racial justice through legal, political, and media advocacy.

Skills Assessed: Explain the causes of historical developments; analyze resistance movements and backlash; use historical evidence to support an analysis.

KEY TAKEAWAYS

1. **The Promise and Limits of Reconstruction**
   - The Reconstruction Amendments—the Thirteenth, Fourteenth, and Fifteenth—ushered in sweeping legal reforms, abolishing slavery, establishing birthright citizenship, and granting Black men the right to vote.
   - These amendments marked a revolutionary shift in U.S. constitutional law, but their promise was quickly undermined by Southern resistance and federal retreat.
2. **The Freedmen's Bureau: A Beacon amid Betrayal**
   - Established in 1865, the Freedmen's Bureau provided essential aid, legitimized Black marriages, built schools, and facilitated family reunifications.
   - Despite its successes, it was chronically underfunded and met with widespread white opposition, limiting its long-term effectiveness.
3. **Black Codes and Economic Subjugation**
   - Southern states enacted Black Codes to control Black mobility and labor, enforcing vagrancy laws and compulsory labor contracts.
   - Sharecropping and convict leasing replaced slavery with new systems of economic bondage, ensuring the continuation of racial exploitation.
4. **Land: Promised, Then Revoked**
   - General Sherman's Special Field Orders No. 15 offered formerly enslaved people 40 acres of land, briefly fulfilling a vision of reparative justice.
   - President Andrew Johnson reversed these orders, returning land to white owners and cutting off pathways to Black landownership and wealth accumulation.
5. **The Fall of Reconstruction**
   - The Compromise of 1877 ended federal military support in the South, enabling white "Redemption" governments to dismantle Reconstruction reforms.
   - Judicial rulings like the Slaughterhouse Cases and *Plessy v. Ferguson* further limited constitutional protections for African Americans.
6. **The Jim Crow Era: Legalizing Inequality**
   - Jim Crow laws institutionalized segregation through poll taxes, literacy tests, grandfather clauses, and "separate but equal" policies.
   - The 1896 *Plessy v. Ferguson* ruling legitimized this system, embedding racial discrimination in law for decades to come.

7. **White Supremacist Violence as State Policy**
   - From the Ku Klux Klan to the Wilmington Coup and the Red Summer of 1919, white terror campaigns violently suppressed Black progress.
   - These acts of racial terrorism were rarely prosecuted, revealing complicity from law enforcement and political leaders.
8. **Black Resistance and Resilience**
   - African Americans fought back through political participation, legal challenges, journalism, self-defense, and migration.
   - Figures like Ida B. Wells and Claude McKay chronicled and challenged white violence, while Black families rebuilt through churches, education, and family reunions.
9. **The Enduring Impact**
   - The chapter concludes that Reconstruction's rollback institutionalized systemic racism but also laid the groundwork for future civil rights activism.
   - African Americans' continued resistance preserved the vision of an inclusive democracy, even amid violence and betrayal.

Practice Multiple-Choice Questions

DIRECTIONS: Pick the letter that best answers the following questions.

Questions 1 through 3 refer to the following.

Claude McKay's 1919 Poem "If We Must Die"

If we must die—let it not be like hogs
Hunted and penned in an inglorious spot,
While round us bark the mad and hungry dogs,
Making their mock at our accursed lot.
If we must die—oh, let us nobly die,
So that our precious blood may not be shed
In vain; then even the monsters we defy
Shall be constrained to honor us though dead!

Oh, kinsmen! We must meet the common foe;
Though far outnumbered, let us still be brave,
And for their thousand blows deal one death-blow!
What though before us lies the open grave?
Like men we'll face the murderous, cowardly pack,
Pressed to the wall, dying, but—fighting back!

Source: The first printing of Claude McKay's poem "If We Must Die," in *The Liberator* 2, no. 7 (July 1919): p. 21.

1. Which of the following best describes the central purpose of Claude McKay's poem "If We Must Die"?

   (A) To celebrate the end of World War I and honor fallen soldiers
   (B) To protest racial injustice and encourage dignified resistance against violence
   (C) To mourn the loss of African traditions in the modern world
   (D) To demand political reform through appeals to legislative bodies

2. In "If We Must Die," the speaker most likely uses the metaphor of a "noble death" to emphasize which of the following?

   (A) Revenge is more important than justice.
   (B) Resistance, even when doomed, reclaims dignity.
   (C) Self-destruction is preferable to subjugation.
   (D) War is inevitable and should be embraced.

3. What is the rhetorical effect of the poem's use of collective pronouns like "we" and "us"?

   (A) It distances the speaker from the reader, emphasizing individual struggle.
   (B) It universalizes the poem's message, calling for collective solidarity and resistance.
   (C) It blames a passive audience for not taking action sooner.
   (D) It satirizes the idea of unity in the face of oppression.

Questions 4 through 6 refer to the following.

Engraved Portrait of Five African American Legislators from Reconstruction Congresses

4. What is the primary purpose of the *Engraved Portrait of Five African American Legislators from Reconstruction Congresses*?

   (A) To critique Reconstruction-era policies that excluded African Americans from political office
   (B) To highlight the cultural contributions of African American artists during the Gilded Age
   (C) To Commemorate Black political participation and leadership during the Reconstruction era
   (D) To illustrate the limitations of African American access to voting rights during Jim Crow

5. What does the engraving most clearly suggest about the political landscape for African Americans during Reconstruction?

   (A) African Americans held equal representation in Congress throughout the nineteenth century.
   (B) The period marked a historic, though temporary, expansion of Black political rights.
   (C) Black political leaders consistently faced no opposition from white constituents.
   (D) Congress immediately passed civil rights laws in response to Black political leadership.

6. Why is the creation of this engraving in the early 1880s historically significant?

   (A) It reflects nostalgia for an era of Black political leadership that had largely ended.
   (B) It was used as anti-Reconstruction propaganda by Southern newspapers.
   (C) It marked the beginning of a new era of Black voter enfranchisement.
   (D) It coincided with the founding of the NAACP and the Harlem Renaissance.

Answer Explanations

1. **(B)** McKay's poem was written in response to the racial violence of the Red Summer of 1919. It uses powerful language to promote dignified resistance against oppression and calls for courage in the face of unjust attacks. Choice (A) is incorrect because, although the poem uses militaristic imagery, it is not about either WWI or soldiers. Choice (C) is incorrect because the poem does not focus on African cultural loss but on a collective call to action. Choice (D) is incorrect because the poem is not framed as a political demand directed at lawmakers. Instead, it is a moral appeal to resist dehumanization.

2. **(B)** McKay emphasizes that if death is inevitable, it should be faced with honor and resistance rather than submission. This metaphor elevates the act of resistance into a form of dignity and defiance. Choice (A) is incorrect because revenge is not the poem's main theme. The poem focuses more on moral resistance and dignity. Choice (C) is incorrect because the poem does not promote self-destruction. It is about meaningful resistance. Choice (D) is incorrect because, although the poem uses combat imagery, it does not advocate for war itself but, instead, for resistance against racial violence.

3. **(B)** The repeated use of "we" and "us" serves to unite the speaker with a collective audience, urging communal strength and shared resistance against dehumanizing forces. Choice (A) is incorrect because the use of collective pronouns closes the distance between speaker and audience rather than creating separation. Choice (C) is incorrect because the poem does not place blame but instead issues a call to action. Choice (D) is incorrect because the tone is serious and urgent, not satirical.

4. **(C)** The engraving celebrates the significant breakthrough of Black legislators serving in Congress during Reconstruction—a powerful symbol of political progress during a brief window of expanded civil rights. Choice (A) is incorrect because Reconstruction actually included policies that enabled Black men to vote and hold office, which the engraving honors, not critiques. Choice (B) is incorrect because the engraving is not focused on artistic expression during the Gilded Age but rather on political representation. Choice (D) is incorrect because the engraving predates the widespread disenfranchisement of the Jim Crow era and does not depict voting suppression.

5. **(B)** The engraving reflects the unique moment of Reconstruction when Black political leadership was briefly visible at the federal level—before Jim Crow laws systematically reversed those gains. Choice (A) is incorrect because, although some African Americans served in Congress, they were not proportionally represented and were later excluded. Choice (C) is incorrect because Black leaders faced extreme opposition, including violence, voter suppression, and racism. Choice (D) is incorrect because, although some progress occurred, civil rights laws were limited and often undercut by lack of enforcement.

6. **(A)** By the 1880s, Reconstruction had ended and the rollback of Black civil rights was well underway. The engraving served as a commemorative tribute to Black legislators whose presence in Congress was already becoming rare. Choice (B) is incorrect because the tone of the engraving is celebratory, not satirical or derogatory. Choice (C) is incorrect because this period was marked by increasing disenfranchisement, not expansion. Choice (D) is incorrect because the NAACP and Harlem Renaissance came decades later, in the 1900s and 1920s, respectively.

9

Building a Nation Within a Nation: The Rise of Black Institutions, Double Consciousness, and Cultural Resistance

Key Themes

- Cultural resistance and self-representation in art, literature, and media
- The paradox of American citizenship—belonging yet barred from fully participating
- Empowerment through education, institutions, and mutual aid
- Black women's leadership as foundational to community building
- Photography and media as strategic tools for justice and truth telling

TIMELINE

Date/Period	Event/Development	Related Topics
1895	**Booker T. Washington's Atlanta Compromise Speech** promotes industrial education and racial uplift	Topic 3.8—Uplift Ideologies and Black Women's Leadership
1896	***Plessy v. Ferguson*** ruling codifies segregation, reinforcing the "color line"	Topic 3.7—The Color Line
1903	**W. E. B. Du Bois publishes *The Souls of Black Folk*,** introducing the concept of **double consciousness**	Topic 3.7—Double Consciousness
Late 1800s–early 1900s	Founding of major **Black women's clubs** and organizations (e.g., **National Association of Colored Women, 1896**)	Topic 3.8—Black Women's Rights and Leadership
1909	Formation of the **NAACP** to combat lynching, segregation, and voter suppression	Topic 3.9—Black Organizations
1910–1930s	Expansion of **Black-owned businesses**, mutual aid societies, churches, and community organizations	Topic 3.9—Black Institutions
Post-Civil War–present	Founding and expansion of **HBCUs**—Howard, Tuskegee, Spelman, Morehouse, Fisk	Topic 3.10—HBCUs and Education
1906–1920s	Founding of **Black Greek Letter Organizations**—e.g., Alpha Phi Alpha (1906), Alpha Kappa Alpha (1908), Delta Sigma Theta (1913)	Topic 3.10—Greek Organizations

Date/Period	Event/Development	Related Topics
1910s–1920s	**Harlem Renaissance** flourishes—emergence of Black cultural and political voices in art, music, and literature	Topic 3.11—New Negro Movement
1925	**Alain Locke publishes *The New Negro*,** defining Harlem Renaissance philosophy	Topic 3.11—Harlem Renaissance
Early 1900s–1930s	Rise of **documentary photography** and visual activism (e.g., W. E. B. Du Bois's Paris photo exhibit, 1900)	Topic 3.12—Photography and Social Change
Ongoing	Photography continues to serve as a **tool of resistance and visibility** for African American communities	Topic 3.12—Photography and Cultural Resistance

Topic 3.7 The Color Line and Double Consciousness in American Society

Key Terms

- **Color line—term coined by Frederick Douglass and expanded by W. E. B. Du Bois to describe racial division**
- **Double consciousness—W. E. B. Du Bois's concept of dual identity: being both Black and American**
- **W. E. B. Du Bois—sociologist, cofounder of NAACP**
- ***The Souls of Black Folk* (1903)—foundational text on race and consciousness**
- **Psychological impact of racism**
- **Racialized social structure**
- **The Veil—metaphor for racial exclusion**
- **Black internal conflict vs. external perception**

At the dawn of the twentieth century, African American writers and thinkers crafted powerful critiques of racism and white supremacy while affirming the full humanity and interior lives of Black people. W. E. B. Du Bois famously declared that "the problem of the twentieth century is the problem of the color line." He was articulating the psychological and spiritual toll of navigating a society that viewed Blackness as inferior. In poetry and prose, figures like Paul Laurence Dunbar and Du Bois described what it meant to live behind the veil of race, introducing concepts like double consciousness that continue to shape scholarly and social discourse.

After engaging with this topic, scholars will be able to:

- Analyze how African American intellectuals at the turn of the twentieth century defined the inner struggles of identity, race, and belonging in the United States.
- Examine how literary and philosophical texts like *The Souls of Black Folk* and "We Wear the Mask" conveyed both resistance to racism and a celebration of Black interiority and intellect.
- Explain how concepts such as the color line and double consciousness emerged from and contributed to broader conversations about race, justice, and American democracy.

Behind the Mask and Beyond the Veil

Paul Laurence Dunbar's poem "We Wear the Mask" and W. E. B. Du Bois's book *The Souls of Black Folk* introduced enduring metaphors—the mask and the Veil—to symbolize the psychological burden of racism and exclusion from full citizenship. These images reflect the dual reality faced by African Americans: the public performance of dignity and resilience as well as the private pain of inequality and marginalization. Both works underscore how African Americans navigated their lives while confronting systemic dehumanization and aspiring toward self-determination.

The Color Line as America's Defining Divide

Du Bois famously declared, "The problem of the twentieth century is the problem of the color line," referencing the enduring divide created by racial discrimination and legalized segregation. Even after the abolition of slavery, Black Americans faced structural barriers in housing, education, employment, and justice. The color line symbolized both physical and psychological boundaries enforced by white supremacy, shaping daily life and national identity.

Living in Two Worlds: The Weight of Double Consciousness

Du Bois's theory of double consciousness articulated the internal struggle of African Americans who constantly viewed themselves through both their own eyes and the lens of a racist society. This internal duality created a tension between self-perception and imposed stereotypes, leading to a fractured sense of identity. Yet, by naming this experience, Du Bois empowered African Americans to reflect on their place in the nation critically and to resist the distortions of white supremacy.

Alienation and Agency: Resistance Through Awareness

Although double consciousness emerged from the alienation produced by racism, it also fostered clarity, cultural creativity, and political resistance. This heightened awareness gave rise to critical Black thought, artistic expression, and social activism. Far from being a weakness, the ability to hold two perspectives simultaneously became a source of strength, shaping African American movements for justice throughout the twentieth century and beyond.

Published in 1895, Paul Laurence Dunbar's poem "We Wear the Mask" is a powerful meditation on the emotional and psychological toll of racism. Writing at the dawn of the Jim Crow era, Dunbar used the metaphor of a mask to capture how African Americans concealed their suffering behind a facade of strength and civility. His words reflect a quiet resistance and expose the tension between outward survival and inner truth.

"We Wear the Mask"

We wear the mask that grins and lies,
It hides our cheeks and shades our eyes—
This debt we pay to human guile;
With torn and bleeding hearts we smile
And mouth with myriad subtleties,

Why should the world be over-wise.
In counting all our tears and sighs?
Nay, let them only see us, while
We wear the mask.

We smile, but oh great Christ, our cries
To Thee from tortured souls arise.
We sing, but oh the clay is vile
Beneath our feet, and long the mile,

But let the world dream otherwise,
We wear the mask!

Source: Paul Lawrence [Laurence] Dunbar, "We Wear the Mask," Majors and Minors: Poems. Toledo, Ohio: Hadley & Hadley, 1895, p. 21.

In "The Forethought" to *The Souls of Black Folk*, W. E. B. Du Bois lays the foundation for one of the most influential works in African American intellectual history. He introduces the twin concepts of *the Veil* and *double consciousness* as defining features of the Black experience in the United States. This preface boldly challenges readers to confront the psychological and societal impact of racism, while declaring the dignity, complexity, and humanity of African Americans.

The Forethought

Herein lie buried many things which if read with patience may show the strange meaning of being black here at the dawning of the Twentieth Century. This meaning is not without interest to you, Gentle Reader; for the problem of the Twentieth Century is the problem of the color line. I pray you, then, receive my little book in all charity, studying my words with me, forgiving mistake and foible for sake of the faith and passion that is in me, and seeking the grain of truth hidden there.

I have sought here to sketch, in vague, uncertain outline, the spiritual world in which ten thousand thousand Americans live and strive. First, in two chapters I have tried to show what Emancipation meant to them, and what was its aftermath. In a third chapter I have pointed out the slow rise of personal leadership, and criticized candidly the leader who bears the chief burden of his race to-day. Then, in two other chapters I have sketched in swift outline the two worlds within and without the Veil, and thus have come to the central problem of training men for life. Venturing now into deeper detail, I have in two chapters studied the struggles of the massed millions of the black peasantry, and in another have sought to make clear the present relations of the sons of master and man. Leaving, then, the white world, I have stepped within the Veil, raising it that you may view faintly its deeper recesses,—the meaning of its religion, the passion of its human sorrow, and the struggle of its greater souls. All this I have ended with a tale twice told but seldom written, and a chapter of song.

Some of these thoughts of mine have seen the light before in other guise. For kindly consenting to their republication here, in altered and extended form, I must thank the publishers of the Atlantic Monthly, The World's Work, the Dial, The New World, and the Annals of the American Academy of Political and Social Science. Before each chapter, as now printed, stands a bar of the Sorrow Songs,—some echo of haunting melody from the only American music which welled up from black souls in the dark past. And, finally, need I add that I who speak here am bone of the bone and flesh of the flesh of them that live within the Veil?

W. E. B. Du B. Atlanta, Ga., Feb. 1, 1903.

Source: W. E. Burghardt Du Bois, *The Souls of Black Folk: Essays and Sketches* (Chicago: A. C. McClurg & Co., 1903).

In the opening chapter, "Of Our Spiritual Strivings," Du Bois introduces the powerful metaphor of double consciousness—the sense of looking at oneself through the eyes of a racist society while struggling to affirm a Black identity. He articulates the inner turmoil and resilience of African Americans striving for dignity, freedom, and self-realization in a nation that both marginalizes and depends on them. This foundational text set the stage for twentieth-century discussions of race, identity, and liberation.

Of Our Spiritual Savings

O water, voice of my heart, crying in the sand,
All night long crying with a mournful cry,

As I lie and listen, and cannot understand
The voice of my heart in my side or the voice of the sea,
O water, crying for rest, is it I, is it I?
All night long the water is crying to me.

Unresting water, there shall never be rest
Till the last moon droop and the last tide fail,
And the fire of the end begin to burn in the west;
And the heart shall be weary and wonder and cry like the sea,
All life long crying without avail,
As the water all night long is crying to me.

ARTHUR SYMONS.

Between me and the other world there is ever an unasked question: unasked by some through feelings of delicacy; by others through the difficulty of rightly framing it. All, nevertheless, flutter round it. They approach me in a half-hesitant sort of way, eye me curiously or compassionately, and then, instead of saying directly, How does it feel to be a problem? they say, I know an excellent colored man in my town; or, I fought at Mechanicsville; or, Do not these Southern outrages make your blood boil? At these I smile, or am interested, or reduce the boiling to a simmer, as the occasion may require. To the real question, How does it feel to be a problem? I answer seldom a word.

And yet, being a problem is a strange experience,—peculiar even for one who has never been anything else, save perhaps in babyhood and in Europe. It is in the early days of rollicking boyhood that the revelation first bursts upon one, all in a day, as it were. I remember well when the shadow swept across me. I was a little thing, away up in the hills of New England, where the dark Housatonic winds between Hoosac and Taghkanic to the sea. In a wee wooden schoolhouse, something put it into the boys' and girls' heads to buy gorgeous visiting-cards—ten cents a package—and exchange. The exchange was merry, till one girl, a tall newcomer, refused my card,—refused it peremptorily, with a glance. Then it dawned upon me with a certain suddenness that I was different from the others; or like, mayhap, in heart and life and longing, but shut out from their world by a vast veil. I had thereafter no desire to tear down that veil, to creep through; I held all beyond it in common contempt, and lived above it in a region of blue sky and great wandering shadows. That sky was bluest when I could beat my mates at examination-time, or beat them at a foot-race, or even beat their stringy heads. Alas, with the years all this fine contempt began to fade; for the words I longed for, and all their dazzling opportunities, were theirs, not mine. But they should not keep these prizes, I said; some, all, I would wrest from them. Just how I would do it I could never decide: by reading law, by healing the sick, by telling the wonderful tales that swam in my head,—some way. With other black boys the strife was not so fiercely sunny: their youth shrunk into tasteless sycophancy, or into silent hatred of the pale world about them and mocking distrust of everything white; or wasted itself in a bitter cry, Why did God make me an outcast and a stranger in mine own house? The shades of the prison-house closed round about us all: walls strait and stubborn to the whitest, but relentlessly narrow, tall, and unscalable to sons of night who must plod darkly on in resignation, or beat unavailing palms against the stone, or steadily, half hopelessly, watch the streak of blue above.

After the Egyptian and Indian, the Greek and Roman, the Teuton and Mongolian, the Negro is a sort of seventh son, born with a veil, and gifted with second-sight in this American world,—a world which yields him no true self-consciousness, but only lets him see himself through the revelation of the other world. It is a peculiar sensation, this double-consciousness, this sense of always looking at one's self through the eyes of others, of measuring one's soul by the tape of a world that looks on in amused contempt and pity. One ever feels his twoness,—an Amercan, a Negro; two souls, two thoughts, two unreconciled strivings; two warring ideals in one dark body, whose dogged strength alone keeps it from being torn asunder.

Source: W. E. Burghardt Du Bois, *The Souls of Black Folk: Essays and Sketches* (Chicago: A. C. McClurg & Co., 1903).

In the essay "Of Alexander Crummell," Du Bois offers a poignant reflection on the life and legacy of the pioneering Black minister, scholar, and pan-Africanist. Through lyrical narrative, Du Bois elevates Crummell as a symbol of perseverance and moral vision, portraying his lifelong struggle against racism, isolation, and disappointment as a noble pursuit of racial uplift and intellectual integrity. The essay honors Crummell's unwavering belief in the dignity and destiny of African peoples. An excerpt can be seen here:

Of Alexander Crummell

Then from the Dawn it seemed there came, but faint
As from beyond the limit of the world,
Like the last echo born of a great cry,
Sounds, as if some fair city were one voice
Around a king returning from his wars.

TENNYSON.

This is the story of a human heart,—the tale of a black boy who many long years ago began to struggle with life that he might know the world and know himself. Three temptations he met on those dark dunes that lay gray and dismal before the wonder-eyes of the child: the temptation of Hate, that stood out against the red dawn; the temptation of Despair, that darkened noonday; and the temptation of Doubt, that ever steals along with twilight. Above all, you must hear of the vales he crossed,—the Valley of Humiliation and the Valley of the Shadow of Death.

I saw Alexander Crummell first at a Wilberforce commencement season, amid its bustle and crush. Tall, frail, and black he stood, with simple dignity and an unmistakable air of good breeding. I talked with him apart, where the storming of the lusty young orators could not harm us. I spoke to him politely, then curiously, then eagerly, as I began to feel the fineness of his character,—his calm courtesy, the sweetness of his strength, and his fair blending of the hope and truth of life. Instinctively I bowed before this man, as one bows before the prophets of the world. Some seer he seemed, that came not from the crimson Past or the gray To-come, but from the pulsing Now,—that mocking world which seemed to me at once so light and dark, so splendid and sordid. Fourscore years had he wandered in this same world of mine, within the Veil. He was born with the Missouri Compromise and lay a-dying amid the echoes of Manila and El Caney: stirring times for living, times dark to look back upon, darker to look forward to. The black-faced lad that paused over his mud and marbles seventy years ago saw puzzling vistas as he looked down the world. The slave-ship still groaned across the Atlantic, faint cries burdened the Southern breeze, and the great black father whispered mad tales of cruelty into those young ears. From the low doorway the mother silently watched her boy at play, and at nightfall sought him eagerly lest the shadows bear him away to the land of slaves.

So his young mind worked and winced and shaped curiously a vision of Life; and in the midst of that vision ever stood one dark figure alone,—ever with the hard, thick countenance of that bitter father, and a form that fell in vast and shapeless folds. Thus the temptation of Hate grew and shadowed the growing child,—gliding stealthily into his laughter, fading into his play, and seizing his dreams by day and night with rough, rude turbulence. So the black boy asked of sky and sun and flower the never-answered Why? and loved, as he grew, neither the world nor the world's rough ways.

Strange temptation for a child, you may think; and yet in this wide land to-day a thousand thousand dark children brood before this same temptation, and feel its cold and shuddering arms. For them, perhaps, some one will some day lift the Veil,—will come tenderly and cheerily into those sad little lives and brush the brooding hate away, just as Beriah Green strode in upon the life of Alexander Crummell. And before the bluff, kind-hearted man the shadow seemed less dark. Beriah Green had a school in Oneida County, New York, with a score of mischievous boys. "I'm going to bring a black boy here to educate," said Beriah Green, as only a crank and an abolitionist would have dared to say. "Oho!" laughed the boys. "Ye-es," said his wife; and Alexander came. Once before, the black boy had sought a school, had travelled, cold and hungry, four hundred miles up into free New Hampshire, to Canaan. But the godly farmers hitched ninety yoke of oxen to the abolition schoolhouse and dragged it into the middle of the swamp. The black boy trudged away.

The nineteenth was the first century of human sympathy,—the age when half wonderingly we began to descry in others that transfigured spark of divinity which we call Myself; when clodhoppers and peasants, and tramps and thieves, and millionaires and—sometimes—Negroes, became throbbing souls whose warm pulsing life touched us so nearly that we half gasped with surprise, crying, "Thou too! Hast Thou seen Sorrow and the dull waters of Hopelessness? Hast Thou known Life?" And then all helplessly we peered into those Other-worlds, and wailed, "O World of Worlds, how shall man make you one?"

So in that little Oneida school there came to those schoolboys a revelation of thought and longing beneath one black skin, of which they had not dreamed before. And to the lonely boy came a new dawn of sympathy and inspiration. The shadowy, formless thing—the temptation of Hate, that hovered between him and the world—grew fainter and less sinister. It did not wholly fade away, but diffused itself and lingered thick at the edges. Through it the child now first saw the blue and gold of life,—the sun-swept road that ran 'twixt heaven and earth until in one far-off wan wavering line they met and kissed. A vision of life came to the growing boy,—mystic, wonderful. He raised his head, stretched himself, breathed deep of the fresh new air. Yonder, behind the forests, he heard strange sounds; then glinting through the trees he saw, far, far away, the bronzed hosts of a nation calling,—calling faintly, calling loudly. He heard the hateful clank of their chains; he felt them cringe and grovel, and there rose within him a protest and a prophecy. And he girded himself to walk down the world.

Source: W. E. Burghardt Du Bois, *The Souls of Black Folk: Essays and Sketches* (Chicago: A. C. McClurg & Co., 1903).

In the essay "The Afterthought," Du Bois offers a closing meditation on the spiritual and moral journey traced throughout *The Souls of Black Folk*. He calls for a deeper understanding of African Americans' humanity and cultural contributions, affirming the enduring hope for a future rooted in justice, truth, and shared destiny. The piece serves as both a quiet elegy and a visionary challenge to the nation's conscience.

The Afterthought

Hear my cry, O God the Reader; vouchsafe that this my book fall not still-born into the world wilderness. Let there spring, Gentle One, from out its leaves vigor of thought and thoughtful deed to reap the harvest wonderful. Let the ears of a guilty people tingle with truth, and seventy millions sigh for the righteousness which exalteth nations, in this drear day when human brotherhood is mockery and a snare. Thus in Thy good time may infinite reason turn the tangle straight, and these crooked marks on a fragile leaf be not indeed.

Source: W. E. Burghardt Du Bois, *The Souls of Black Folk: Essays and Sketches* (Chicago: A. C. McClurg & Co., 1903).

The literary and philosophical breakthroughs in this topic reveal how African American thinkers transformed pain into profound insight. Through Paul Laurence Dunbar's haunting metaphor in "We Wear the Mask" and W. E. B. Du Bois's enduring concept of double consciousness in *The Souls of Black Folk*, Black authors gave voice to the tension between visibility and erasure, struggle and strength. Their work shaped the intellectual foundation for future generations of scholars, activists, and artists determined to expose injustice, affirm Black humanity, and redefine American identity.

Two Realities, One Self

W. E. B. Du Bois described double consciousness as the feeling of being torn between how you see yourself and how the world sees you. For African Americans, living in a racist society meant constantly navigating those two identities.

You're Practicing: Interpreting how individuals reflect their social conditions.

Connect This To: Identity, self-perception, and oppression.

Theme: Identity and Culture

Practice: Explain the Significance or Importance

W. E. B. Du Bois introduced the concepts of the color line and double consciousness to describe the psychological and structural dimensions of racism in American society.

(A) Define what Du Bois meant by the color line and double consciousness.

(B) Explain the significance of these concepts in understanding the African American experience at the turn of the twentieth century.

(C) Analyze how these ideas challenged dominant narratives about race and national identity in the United States.

SAMPLE RESPONSES

(A) The color line refers to the racial division that separates Black and white people in society, both legally and socially, and represents the global problem of racism.

Double consciousness describes the internal conflict African Americans feel from seeing themselves through the lens of a racist society while also trying to maintain a true sense of self.

(B) Du Bois's ideas captured the psychological toll of systemic racism, as African Americans navigated being both Black and American in a nation that denied their full humanity.

These concepts explained the conflicted identity many African Americans experienced amid segregation, disenfranchisement, and cultural erasure during the Jim Crow era.

(C) Du Bois's work rejected white supremacist ideologies that portrayed African Americans as inferior, instead framing racism—not Blackness—as the central problem in American democracy.

His ideas challenged the dominant narrative of American unity and progress by exposing the contradictions between the nation's democratic ideals and its racial realities, especially for those excluded from full citizenship.

Skills Assessed: Explain the significance of historical developments; use sources and evidence; analyze relationships among developments.

Topic 3.8 Lifting as We Climb: Uplift Ideologies and Black Women's Rights and Leadership

Key Terms

- Club movement—led by middle-class Black women for social reform
- National Association of Colored Women (NACW)—founded in 1896
- Mary Church Terrell—NACW leader; coined the phrase *lifting as we climb*
- Ida B. Wells-Barnett—anti-lynching crusader and journalist
- Black feminist thought
- Moral and social uplift
- Temperance, education, suffrage
- Intersectionality of race and gender in activism

In the decades after Reconstruction, African Americans confronted the rise of Jim Crow with vision, strategy, and a powerful belief in collective progress. At the heart of this movement stood Black women—teachers, club leaders, writers, and organizers—who called for moral elevation, political representation, and community empowerment. As the nation tried to push African Americans back into second-class status, these leaders built institutions, challenged stereotypes, and gave voice to a philosophy of lifting as we climb—a principle that linked personal achievement to racial advancement.

After engaging with this topic, scholars will be able to:

- Explain the strategies of racial uplift developed by African American educators, reformers, and intellectuals during the late nineteenth and early twentieth centuries.
- Describe how Black women used civic organizations, literary expression, and community leadership to promote African American progress.
- Analyze how uplift ideologies reflected both resistance to white supremacy and intracommunity debates about class, gender, and respectability.

Work with the Hands, Build with the Mind: Washington's Vision for Uplift

Following emancipation, Booker T. Washington rose to prominence as a leading voice for Black advancement. He promoted industrial education, vocational training, and self-help as the keys to racial progress. His founding of the Tuskegee Institute embodied his belief that African Americans should gain economic independence before pursuing civil and political rights.

The Pen and the Plow: Du Bois vs. Washington

Booker T. Washington's Atlanta Exposition Address (1895) urged African Americans to focus on manual labor and remain in the South. In contrast, W. E. B. Du Bois challenged this gradualist approach, advocating for liberal arts education, protest, and political rights. He called for the development of a *Talented Tenth*—a leadership class of educated African Americans dedicated to uplifting the race.

Educate a Woman, Uplift a Nation: Nannie Helen Burroughs and the NACW

Black women leaders like Nannie Helen Burroughs emphasized education as a transformative force. In 1909, she established the National Training School for Women and Girls in Washington, D.C., promoting intellectual growth and self-discipline. As a founding member of the National Association of Colored Women (NACW), she advanced a powerful vision for women's education, moral development, and civic engagement.

"Lift Every Voice": Cultural Pride and Collective Identity

African American creative expression played a vital role in racial uplift. James Weldon Johnson, along with his brother J. Rosamond Johnson, composed "Lift Every Voice and Sing" in 1900. Dubbed the Black National Anthem, the song became a rallying cry for dignity, hope, and resistance—underscoring how culture served as a tool for both healing and organizing.

Our Right to Vote, Our Voice to Raise: Black Women in the Suffrage Movement

Black women participated actively in the women's suffrage movement, even as they were often marginalized by white suffragists. Leaders like Mary Church Terrell, Frances Ellen Watkins Harper, and Ida B. Wells fought not only for women's voting rights but also against lynching, racism, and poverty. They called for an inclusive vision of gender and racial justice.

Backbone of the Race: Black Women and Labor Justice

In the face of economic hardship, Black women played crucial roles in sustaining their families and communities. They entered the labor force in large numbers and created unions and cooperatives to fight for fair wages and humane working conditions, linking racial justice with class solidarity.

Clubwomen and Churchwomen: Building a Nation Within a Nation

From church pulpits to civic halls, Black women formed clubs and institutions that fostered pride and resistance. Organizations like the NACW, women's missionary societies, and sororities created networks that supported education, welfare, and the fight against racial and gender stereotypes. Their work challenged narratives of inferiority by modeling Black excellence in action.

In her groundbreaking 1892 book *A Voice from the South*, educator and activist Anna Julia Cooper offers one of the earliest and most compelling arguments for the central role of Black women in advancing both the race and the nation. In the section titled "Our *Raison d'Être*," Cooper asserts that the moral, intellectual, and civic development of Black women is not only essential for the uplift of African American communities but also foundational to a just and democratic society. Her words continue to resonate as a cornerstone of Black feminist thought.

OUR *RAISON D'ÊTRE*

In the clash and clatter of our American Conflict, it has been said that the South remains Silent. Like the Sphinx she inspires vociferous disputation, but herself takes little part in the noisy controversy. One muffled strain in the Silent South, a jarring chord and a vague and uncomprehended cadenza has been and still is the Negro. And of that muffled chord, the one mute and voiceless note has been the sadly expectant Black Woman,

An infant crying in the night,
An infant crying for the light;
And with no language—but a cry.

The colored man's inheritance and apportionment is still the sombre crux, the perplexing cul de sac of the nation,—the dumb skeleton in the closet provoking ceaseless harangues, indeed, but little understood and seldom consulted. Attorneys for the plaintiff and attorneys for the defendant, with bungling gaucherie have analyzed and dissected, theorized and synthesized with sublime ignorance or pathetic misapprehension of counsel from the black client. One important witness has not yet been heard from. The summing up of the evidence deposed, and the charge to the jury have been made—but no word from the Black Woman.

It is because I believe the American people to be conscientiously committed to a fair trial and ungarbled evidence, and because I feel it essential to a perfect understanding and an equitable verdict that truth from each standpoint be presented at the bar,—that this little Voice, has been added to the already full chorus. The "other side" has not been represented by one who "lives there." And not many can more sensibly realize and more accurately tell the weight and the fret of the "long dull pain" than the open-eyed but hitherto voiceless Black Woman of America.

The feverish agitation, the perfervid energy, the busy objectivity of the more turbulent life of our men serves, it may be, at once to cloud or color their vision somewhat, and as well to relieve the smart and deaden the pain for them. Their voice is in consequence not always temperate and calm, and at the same time radically corrective and sanatory. At any rate, as our Caucasian barristers are not to blame if they cannot quite put themselves in the dark man's place, neither should the dark man be wholly expected fully and adequately to reproduce the exact Voice of the Black Woman.

Delicately sensitive at every pore to social atmospheric conditions, her calorimeter may well be studied in the interest of accuracy and fairness in diagnosing what is often conceded to be a "puzzling" case. If these broken utterances can in any way help to a clearer vision and a truer pulse-beat in studying our Nation's Problem, this Voice by a Black Woman of the South will not have been raised in vain.

TAWAWA CHIMNEY CORNER,
SEPT. 17, 1892.

Source: Anna Julia Cooper, *A Voice from the South: By a Black Woman of the South* (Xenia, OH: The Aldine Printing House, 1892).

Delivered at the 1893 World's Congress of Representative Women, Anna Julia Cooper's speech Womanhood: A Vital Element in the Regeneration and Progress of a Race stands as a seminal statement in African American and feminist thought. In it, Cooper argues that the status of Black women is a critical measure of societal progress and insists that any movement for racial uplift must include the voices, dignity, and leadership of women. Her address boldly challenged both racial and gender exclusion at a time when Black women were often marginalized in national and international reform movements.

WOMANHOOD A VITAL ELEMENT IN THE REGENERATION AND PROGRESS OF A RACE

The two sources from which, perhaps, modern civilization has derived its noble and ennobling ideal of woman are Christianity and the Feudal System.

In Oriental countries woman has been uniformly devoted to a life of ignorance, infamy, and complete stagnation. The Chinese shoe of to-day does not more entirely dwarf, cramp, and destroy her physical powers, than have the customs, laws, and social instincts, which from remotest ages have governed our Sister of the East, enervated and blighted her mental and moral life.

Mahomet makes no account of woman whatever in his polity. The Koran, which, unlike our Bible, was a product and not a growth, tried to address itself to the needs of Arabian civilization as Mahomet with his circumscribed powers saw them. The Arab was a nomad. Home to him meant his present camping place. That deity who, according to our western ideals, makes and sanctifies the home, was to him a transient bauble to be toyed with so long as it gave pleasure and then to be thrown aside for a new one. As a personality, an individual soul, capable of eternal growth and unlimited development, and destined to mould and shape the civilization of the future to an incalculable extent, Mahomet did not know woman. There was no hereafter, no paradise for her. The heaven of the Mussulman is peopled and made gladsome not by the departed wife, or sister, or mother, but by houri—a figment of Mahomet's brain, partaking of the ethereal qualities of angels, yet imbued with all the vices and inanity of Oriental women. The harem here, and—"dust to dust" hereafter, this was the hope, the inspiration, the summum bonum of the Eastern woman's life! With what result on the life of the nation, the "Unspeakable Turk," the "sick man" of modern Europe can to-day exemplify.

Says a certain writer: "The private life of the Turk is vilest of the vile, unprogressive, unambitious, and inconceivably low." And yet Turkey is not without her great men. She has produced most brilliant minds; men skilled in all the intricacies of diplomacy and statesmanship; men whose intellects could grapple with the deep problems of empire and manipulate the subtle agencies which check-mate kings. But these minds were not the normal outgrowth of a healthy trunk. They seemed rather ephemeral excrescencies which shoot far out with all the vigor and promise, apparently, of strong branches; but soon alas fall into decay and ugliness because there is no soundness in the root, no life-giving sap, permeating, strengthening and perpetuating the whole. There is a worm at the core! The homelife is impure! and when we look for fruit, like apples of Sodom, it crumbles within our grasp into dust and ashes.

It is pleasing to turn from this effete and immobile civilization to a society still fresh and vigorous, whose seed is in itself, and whose very name is synonymous with all that is progressive, elevating and inspiring, viz., the European bud and the American flower of modern civilization. And here let me say parenthetically that our satisfaction in American institutions rests not on the fruition we now enjoy, but springs rather from the possibilities and promise that are inherent in the system, though as yet, perhaps, far in the future.

"Happiness," says Madame de Stael, "consists not in perfections attained, but in a sense of progress, the result of our own endeavor under conspiring circumstances toward a goal which continually advances and broadens and deepens till it is swallowed up in the Infinite." Such conditions in embryo are all that we claim for the land of the West. We have not yet reached our ideal in American civilization. The pessimists even declare that we are not marching in that direction. But there can be no doubt that here in America is the arena in which the next triumph of civilization is to be won; and here too we find promise abundant and possibilities infinite.

Now let us see on what basis this hope for our country primarily and fundamentally rests. Can any one doubt that it is chiefly on the homelife and on the influence of good women in those homes? Says Macaulay: "You may judge a nation's rank in the scale of civilization from the way they treat their women." And Emerson, "I have thought that a sufficient measure of civilization is the influence of good women." Now this high regard for woman, this germ of a prolific idea which in our own day is bearing such rich and varied fruit, was ingrafted into European civilization, we have said, from two sources, the Christian Church and the Feudal System. For although the Feudal System can in no sense be said to have originated the idea, yet there can be no doubt that the habits of life and modes of thought to which Feudalism gave rise, materially fostered and developed it; for they gave us chivalry, than which no institution has more sensibly magnified and elevated woman's position in society. Tacitus dwells on the tender regard for woman entertained by these rugged barbarians before they left their northern homes to overrun Europe. Old Norse legends too, and primitive poems, all breathe the same spirit of love of home and veneration for the pure and noble influence there presiding—the wife, the sister, the mother.

And when later on we see the settled life of the Middle Ages "oozing out," as M. Guizot expresses it, from the plundering and pillaging life of barbarism and crystallizing into the Feudal System, the tiger of the field is brought once more within the charmed circle of the goddesses of his castle, and his imagination weaves around them a halo whose reflection possibly has not yet altogether vanished.

It is true the spirit of Christianity had not yet put the seal of catholicity on this sentiment. Chivalry, according to Bascom, was but the toning down and softening of a rough and lawless period. It gave a roseate glow to a bitter winter's day. Those who looked out from castle windows revelled in its "amethyst tints." But God's poor, the weak, the unlovely, the commonplace were still freezing and starving none the less, in unpitied, unrelieved loneliness. Respect for woman, the much lauded chivalry of the Middle Ages, meant what I fear it still means to some men in our own day—respect for the elect few among whom they expect to consort. The idea of the radical amelioration of womankind, reverence for woman as woman regardless of rank, wealth, or culture, was to come from that rich and bounteous fountain from which flow all our liberal and universal ideas—the Gospel of Jesus Christ.

And yet the Christian Church at the time of which we have been speaking would seem to have been doing even less to protect and elevate woman than the little done by secular society. The Church as an organization committed a double offense against woman in the Middle Ages. Making of marriage a sacrament and at the same time insisting on the celibacy of the clergy and other religious orders, she gave an inferior if not an impure character to the marriage relation, especially fitted to reflect discredit on woman. Would this were all or the worst! but the Church by the licentiousness of its chosen servants invaded the household and established too often as vicious connections those relations which it forbade to assume openly and in good faith. "Thus," to use the words of our authority, "the religious corps became as numerous, as searching, and as unclean as the frogs of Egypt, which penetrated into all quarters, into the ovens and kneading troughs, leaving their filthy trail wherever they went." Says Chaucer with characteristic satire, speaking of the Friars:

"Women may now go safely up and doun,
In every bush, and under every tree,
Ther is non other incubus but he,
And he ne will don hem no dishonour."

Henry, Bishop of Liege, could unblushingly boast the birth of twenty-two children in fourteen years. It may help us under some of the perplexities which beset our way in "the one Catholic and Apostolic Church" to-day, to recall some of the corruptions and incongruities against which the Bride of Christ has had to struggle in her past history and in spite of which she has kept, through many vicissitudes, the faith once delivered to the saints. Individuals, organizations, whole sections of the Church militant may outrage the Christ whom they profess, may ruthlessly trample under foot both the spirit and the letter of his precepts, yet not till we hear the voices audibly saying "Come let us depart hence," shall we cease to believe and cling to the promise, "I am with you to the end of the world."

"Yet saints their watch are keeping,
The cry goes up 'How long!'
And soon the night of weeping
Shall be the morn of song."

However much then the facts of any particular period of history may seem to deny it, I for one do not doubt that the source of the vitalizing principle of woman's development and amelioration is the Christian Church, so far as that church is coincident with Christianity. Christ gave ideals not formulæ. The Gospel is a germ requiring millennia for its growth and ripening. It needs and at the same time helps to form around itself a soil enriched in civilization, and perfected in culture and insight without which the embryo can neither be unfolded or comprehended. With all the strides our civilization has made from the first to the nineteenth century, we can boast not an idea, not a principle of action, not a progressive social force but was already mutely foreshadowed, or directly enjoined in that simple tale of a meek and lowly life. The quiet face of the Nazarene is ever seen a little way ahead, never too far to come down to and touch the life of the lowest in days the darkest, yet ever leading onward, still onward, the tottering childish feet of our strangely boastful civilization.

By laying down for woman the same code of morality, the same standard of purity, as for man; by refusing to countenance the shameless and equally guilty monsters who were gloating over her fall,—graciously stooping in all the majesty of his own spotlessness to wipe away the filth and grime of her guilty past and bid her go in peace and sin no more; and again in the moments of his own careworn and footsore dejection, turning trustfully and lovingly, away from the heartless snubbing and sneers, away from the cruel malignity of mobs and prelates in the dusty marts of Jerusalem to the ready sympathy, loving appreciation and unfaltering friendship of that quiet home at Bethany; and even at the last, by his dying bequest to the disciple whom he loved, signifying the protection and tender regard to be extended to that sorrowing mother and ever afterward to the sex she represented;—throughout his life and in his death he has given to men a rule and guide for the estimation of woman as an equal, as a helper, as a friend, and as a sacred charge to be sheltered and cared for with a brother's love and sympathy, lessons which nineteen centuries' gigantic strides in knowledge, arts, and sciences, in social and ethical principles have not been able to probe to their depth or to exhaust in practice.

Source: Anna Julia Cooper, *A Voice from the South: By a Black Woman of the South* (Xenia, OH: The Aldine Printing House, 1892).

Booker T. Washington delivered The Atlanta Exposition Address in 1895 before a predominantly white audience at the Cotton States and International Exposition. In this historic speech, Washington laid out his vision for Black advancement through vocational training, economic self-reliance, and cooperation with Southern whites. While he famously urged African Americans to "cast down your bucket where you are," the address also ignited lasting debate about the balance between accommodation and activism in the struggle for civil rights.

Mr. President and Gentlemen of the Board of Directors and Citizens.

One-third of the population of the South is of the Negro race. No enterprise seeking the material, civil, or moral welfare of this section can disregard this element of our population and reach the highest success. I but convey to you, Mr. President and Directors, the sentiment of the masses of my race when I say that in no way have the value and manhood of the American Negro been more fittingly and generously recognized than by the managers of this magnificent Exposition at every stage of its progress. It is a recognition that will do more to cement the friendship of the two races than any occurrence since the dawn of our freedom.

Not only this, but the opportunity here afforded will awaken among us a new era of industrial progress. Ignorant and inexperienced, it is not strange that in the first years of our new life we began at the top instead of at the bottom; that a seat in Congress or the state legislature was more sought than real estate or industrial skill; that the political convention or stump speaking had more attractions than starting a dairy farm or truck garden.

A ship lost at sea for many days suddenly sighted a friendly vessel. From the mast of the unfortunate vessel was seen a signal, "Water, water; we die of thirst!" The answer from the friendly vessel at once came back, "Cast down your bucket where you are." A second time the signal, "Water, water; send us water!" ran up from the distressed vessel, and was answered, "Cast down your bucket where you are." And a third and fourth signal for water was answered, "Cast down your bucket where you are." The captain of the distressed vessel, at last heading the injunction, cast down his bucket, and it came up full of fresh, sparkling water from the mouth of the Amazon River. To those of my race who depend on bettering their condition in a foreign land or who underestimate the importance of cultivating friendly relations with the Southern white man, who is their next-door neighbour, I would say: "Cast down your bucket where you are"—cast it down in making friends in every manly way of the people of all races by whom we are surrounded.

Cast it down in agriculture, mechanics, in commerce, in domestic service, and in the professions. And in this connection it is well to bear in mind that whatever other sins the South may be called to bear, when it comes to business, pure and simple, it is in the South that the Negro is given a man's chance in the commercial world, and in nothing is this Exposition more eloquent than in emphasizing this chance. Our greatest danger is that in the great leap from slavery to freedom we may overlook the fact that the masses of us are to live by the productions of our hands, and fail to keep in mind that we shall prosper in proportion as we learn to dignify and glorify common labour and put brains and skill into the common occupations of life; shall prosper in proportion as we learn to draw the line between the superficial and the substantial, the ornamental gewgaws of life and the useful. No race can prosper till it learns that there is as much dignity in tilling a field as in writing a poem. It is at the bottom of life we must begin, and not at the top. Nor should we permit our grievances to overshadow our opportunities.

To those of the white race who look to the incoming of those of foreign birth and strange tongue and habits of the prosperity of the South, were I permitted I would repeat what I say to my own race: "Cast down your bucket where you are." Cast it down among the eight millions of Negroes whose habits you know, whose fidelity and love you have tested in days when to have proved treacherous meant the ruin of your firesides. Cast down your bucket among these people who have, without strikes and labour wars, tilled your fields, cleared your forests, builded your railroads and cities, and brought forth treasures from the bowels of the earth, and helped make possible this magnificent representation of the progress of the South. Casting down your bucket among my people, helping and encouraging them as you are doing on these grounds, and to education of head, hand, and heart, you will find that they will buy your surplus land, make blossom the waste places in your fields, and run your factories. While doing this, you can be sure in the future, as in the past, that you and your families will be surrounded by the most patient, faithful, law—abiding, and unresentful people that the world has seen. As we have proved our loyalty to you in the past, nursing your children, watching by the sick-bed of your mothers and fathers, and often following them with tear—dimmed eyes to their graves, so in the future, in our humble way, we shall stand by you with a devotion that no foreigner can approach, ready to lay down our lives, if need be, in defence of yours, interlacing our industrial, commercial, civil, and religious life with yours in a way that shall make the interests of both races one. In all things that are purely social we can be as separate as the fingers, yet one as the hand in all things essential to mutual progress.

There is no defence or security for any of us except in the highest intelligence and development of all. If anywhere there are efforts tending to curtail the fullest growth of the Negro, let these efforts be turned into stimulating, encouraging, and making him the most useful and intelligent citizen. Effort or means so invested will pay a thousand per cent interest. These efforts will be twice blessed—"blessing him that gives and him that takes."

There is no escape through law of man or God from the inevitable:—

The laws of changeless justice bind
Oppressor with oppressed;
And close as sin and suffering joined
We march to fate abreast.

Nearly sixteen millions of hands will aid you in pulling the load upward, or they will pull against you the load downward. We shall constitute one-third and more of the ignorance and crime of the South, or one—third its intelligence and progress; we shall contribute one-third to the business and industrial prosperity of the South, or we shall prove a veritable body of death, stagnating, depressing, retarding every effort to advance the body politic.

Gentlemen of the Exposition, as we present to you our humble effort at an exhibition of our progress, you must not expect overmuch. Starting thirty years ago with ownership here and there in a few quilts and pumpkins and chickens (gathered from miscellaneous sources), remember the path that has led from these to the inventions and production of agricultural implements, buggies, steam-engines, newspapers, books, statuary, carving, paintings, the management of drug-stores and banks, has not been trodden without contact with thorns and thistles. While we take pride in what we exhibit as a result of our independent efforts, we do not for a moment forget that our part in this exhibition would fall far short of your expectations but for the constant help that has come to our education life, not only from the Southern states,

> but especially from Northern philanthropists, who have made their gifts a constant stream of blessing and encouragement.
>
> The wisest among my race understand that the agitation of questions of social equality is the extremest folly, and that progress in the enjoyment of all the privileges that will come to us must be the result of severe and constant struggle rather than of artificial forcing. No race that has anything to contribute to the markets of the world is long in any degree ostracized. It is important and right that all privileges of the law be ours, but it is vastly more important that we be prepared for the exercises of these privileges. The opportunity to earn a dollar in a factory just now is worth infinitely more than the opportunity to spend a dollar in an opera-house.
>
> In conclusion, may I repeat that nothing in thirty years has given us more hope and encouragement, and drawn us so near to you of the white race, as this opportunity offered by the Exposition; and here bending, as it were, over the altar that represents the results of the struggles of your race and mine, both starting practically empty-handed three decades ago, I pledge that in your effort to work out the great and intricate problem which God has laid at the doors of the South, you shall have at all times the patient, sympathetic help of my race; only let this be constantly in mind, that, while from representations in these buildings of the product of field, of forest, of mine, of factory, letters, and art, much good will come, yet far above and beyond material benefits will be that higher good, that, let us pray God, will come, in a blotting out of sectional differences and racial animosities and suspicions, in a determination to administer absolute justice, in a willing obedience among all classes to the mandates of law. This, this, coupled with our material prosperity, will bring into our beloved South a new heaven and a new earth.
>
> Source: Booker T. Washington, "The Atlanta Exposition Address" in *Up from Slavery* (New York: Doubleday, 1901), Chapter 14.

In her powerful 1900 essay "How the Sisters Are Hindered from Helping," educator and activist Nannie Helen Burroughs critiques the barriers faced by Black women seeking to lead within church and community life. Writing at the turn of the twentieth century, Burroughs confronts both racial and gender discrimination while affirming Black women's intellect, spirituality, and potential for leadership. Her words helped lay the foundation for Black women's club movements and broader struggles for inclusion in American religious, educational, and political institutions.

> We come not to usurp thrones nor to sow discord, but to so organize and systematize the work that each church may help through a Woman's Missionary Society and not be made poorer thereby. It is for the utilization of talent and the stimulation to Christian activity in our Baptist churches that prompt us to service. We realize that to allow these gems to lie unpolished longer means a loss to the denomination. For a number of years there has been a righteous discontent, a burning zeal to go forward in his name among the Baptist women of our churches and it will be the dynamic force in the religious campaign at the opening of the 20th century. It will be the spark that shall light the altar fire in the heathen lands. We realize, too, that the work is too great and the laborers too few for us to stand by while like Trojans the brethren at the head of the work under the convention toil unceasingly.
>
> We come now to their rescue. We unfurl our banner upon which is inscribed this motto, "The world for Christ. Woman, arise, He calleth for thee!" Will you as a pastor and friend of missions help by not hindering these women when they come among you to speak and to enlist the women of your church? It has ever been from the time of Miriam, that most remarkable woman, the sister of Moses, that most remarkable man, down to the courageous women that in very recent years have carried the Gospel into Thibet and Africa and proclaimed and taught the truth where no man has been allowed to enter. Surely, women somehow have had a very important part in the work of saving this redeemed earth.

Every religious organization in the world is trying by a special effort to raise a stated sum for the great religious campaign which will mark the opening of the 20th century. This money will be necessary to push forward the work which they must undertake. The Christian world is no longer contented at conquering by piecemeal. They have at last decided to make one grand, triumphant entry into heathen lands, and with one stroke slay the common enemy. The implement to be used is money for the support of men and the purchase of land to build houses of worship. We have decided to help in this campaign, and have apportioned the amounts as follows:

10 woman's conventions to give $25.00 each.
20 woman's associations and district conventions to give $5.00.
1,000 missionary societies to give $2.00 each.
2,000 women to give $1.00.
300 children's bands to give 50 cents each.
15,000 pastors to pray for a great uplift in woman's work at home and abroad.

Praying the Great Head of the Church to bless all the departments of our national work, we are yours for the highest development of Christian womanhood.

Source: Nannie Helen Burroughs, "How the Sisters Are Hindered from Helping," in the *Journal of the Twentieth Annual Session of the National Baptist Convention*. Nashville, TN: National Baptist Publishing Board, 1900, pp. 196–197.

Originally written as a poem by James Weldon Johnson and later set to music by his brother J. Rosamond Johnson, "Lift Every Voice and Sing" debuted in 1900 as part of a celebration of Abraham Lincoln's birthday. Quickly embraced by African American communities, the song became a powerful anthem of hope, resilience, and unity in the face of oppression. Its verses reflect the enduring struggle for freedom and equality, earning it the title of the Black National Anthem in the twentieth century.

"Lift Every Voice and Sing"

Lift every voice and sing
Till earth and heaven ring,
Ring with the harmonies of Liberty;
Let our rejoicing rise
High as the listening skies,
Let it resound loud as the rolling sea.
Sing a song full of the faith that the dark past has taught us,
Sing a song full of the hope that the present has brought us.
Facing the rising sun of our new day begun,
Let us march on till victory is won.
Stony the road we trod,
Bitter the chastening rod,
Felt in the days when hope unborn had died;
Yet with a steady beat,
Have not our weary feet
Come to the place for which our fathers sighed?
We have come over a way that with tears has been watered,
We have come, treading our path through the blood of the slaughtered,
Out from the gloomy past,
Till now we stand at last
Where the white gleam of our bright star is cast.

God of our weary years,
God of our silent tears,
Thou who hast brought us thus far on the way;
Thou who hast by Thy might
Led us into the light,
Keep us forever in the path, we pray.
Lest our feet stray from the places, our God, where we met Thee,
Lest, our hearts drunk with the wine of the world, we forget Thee;
Shadowed beneath Thy hand,
May we forever stand.
True to our God,
True to our native land.

Source: Sheet music for "Lift Every Voice and Sing," which became known as the Black National Anthem, by James Weldon Johnson and J. Rosamond Johnson, New York: Jos. W. Stern & Co., 1900 (Library of Congress).

The strategies of racial uplift at the turn of the twentieth century laid the foundation for future civil rights movements by affirming Black dignity, intellect, and leadership. Figures like Booker T. Washington and W. E. B. Du Bois offered distinct visions for Black advancement. Women such as Anna Julia Cooper, Nannie Helen Burroughs, and the members of the National Association of Colored Women insisted that true liberation required the inclusion of Black women's voices. Through education, political advocacy, artistic expression, and spiritual leadership, they redefined what it meant to lead and to belong—lifting others as they climbed.

TIP

Answer Strategically

Stimulus-based questions often contain visual or textual clues that point directly to the correct answer.

Uplift Together, Not Alone

Leaders like Mary Church Terrell believed that Black advancement wasn't just personal—it had to be collective. Lifting as we climb meant using your education or success to open doors for others, especially women and girls.

You're Practicing: Understanding the relationship between class and justice.

Connect This To: Collective action, gender, and leadership.

Theme: Resistance and Community

Practice: Explain Causality (Effects)

In the late nineteenth and early twentieth centuries, African American women developed powerful ideologies of racial uplift and community service while confronting both racism and sexism.

(A) Identify one major African American woman or organization associated with the uplift movement.
(B) Explain how uplift ideologies shaped the role of Black women in civil rights and reform work.
(C) Analyze the effect these efforts had on perceptions of Black womanhood in broader American society.

SAMPLE RESPONSES

(A) Nannie Helen Burroughs was a key leader who co-founded the National Association of Colored Women (NACW), an organization committed to racial uplift through education, moral reform, and community service.

The NACW adopted the motto "Lifting as We Climb" to reflect its dual commitment to self-help and collective progress for African American communities.

(B) Uplift ideology emphasized respectability, education, and service, which led Black women to become leaders in education, suffrage, anti-lynching campaigns, and public health efforts.

It positioned Black women as moral leaders of the race, empowering them to advocate for civil rights while also addressing issues like poverty, sanitation, and youth development within their communities.

(C) These efforts challenged dominant stereotypes by promoting images of Black women as intelligent, virtuous, and civically engaged, countering racist portrayals of immorality or inferiority.

However, while uplift work gained respect in some reform circles, it also revealed the limits of inclusion, as Black women were often excluded from mainstream (white) feminist and progressive movements despite their leadership and contributions.

Skills Assessed: Explain the effects of historical developments; use sources and evidence; analyze relationships among developments.

Topic 3.9 Black Organizations and Institutions

Key Terms

- Mutual aid societies—support for sick, elderly, or unemployed
- Fraternal orders—Prince Hall Masons, Odd Fellows
- Religious institutions—African Methodist Episcopal (AME) Church
- Black press—*The Chicago Defender, Pittsburgh Courier, The California Eagle*
- YMCA/YWCA for African Americans
- Economic cooperatives—Black-owned banks and insurance firms
- Institution building—a pillar of post emancipation life

What happens when a people are denied access to power, resources, and opportunity? They build their own. In the face of Jim Crow segregation, violence, and exclusion, African Americans did not simply endure. They created institutions that empowered their communities, preserved their dignity, and fueled movements for justice. Throughout the early twentieth century, African Americans responded to racial discrimination by building independent organizations and institutions to meet the spiritual, economic, educational, and social needs of their communities. From mutual aid societies to churches, from fraternal orders to business leagues, Black Americans created networks of care and resistance that uplifted the race. These institutions were not just responses to segregation; they were declarations of Black autonomy, ingenuity, and hope.

After engaging with this topic, scholars will be able to:

- Explain how African Americans built institutions to advance racial pride, education, and economic empowerment.
- Identify key organizations—such as the National Urban League and Black churches—that supported African American communities during the Jim Crow era.

- Analyze how Black mutual aid societies and professional networks laid the foundation for long-term community resilience and political organizing.
- Connect the growth of Black institutions to broader themes of self-determination and collective uplift.

Building Self-Sufficiency: The Rise of Black-Owned Businesses and Organizations

In the face of relentless exclusion from white-dominated institutions and economic markets, African Americans responded by building their own. During the early twentieth century, Black communities across the United States developed businesses and organizations that directly served their needs—barbershops, beauty salons, funeral homes, grocery stores, and banks, among others. These establishments were more than commercial enterprises; they were pillars of self-sufficiency and racial pride. Black business districts like Sweet Auburn in Atlanta and Black Wall Street in Tulsa became economic engines and symbols of communal resilience. By circulating wealth within their own communities, African Americans asserted control over their economic destinies and created a foundation for political and cultural empowerment.

Printing the Truth: The Power of the Black Press

The Black press emerged as a powerful force for truth telling and community cohesion. At a time when mainstream newspapers ignored or distorted Black life, African American publications such as *The Chicago Defender*, *Pittsburgh Courier*, and *The California Eagle* chronicled the realities of racial injustice while also highlighting local achievements and national movements. These papers connected African Americans across geographic boundaries. They offered editorials, coverage of lynchings, updates on civil rights activity, and information on economic opportunities—particularly during the Great Migration. The Black press did more than report news; it inspired action, challenged systemic racism, and became an indispensable tool for political and cultural advocacy.

Faith Reimagined: The Growth of Independent Black Churches

Religion remained a cornerstone of African American life, but Black worship evolved into institutions uniquely shaped by the lived experiences of formerly enslaved people and their descendants. The African Methodist Episcopal (AME) Church, founded in 1816, stood as the first independent Black Christian denomination in the United States. It represented not just spiritual autonomy but political and cultural self-determination. After the fall of Reconstruction, Black churches multiplied across the country, offering worship styles rooted in African traditions and theological interpretations centered on liberation. These institutions were essential in reinforcing a collective identity rooted in faith, resistance, and hope.

Churches as Cultural and Political Powerhouses

More than places of worship, Black churches functioned as safe havens for organizing, cultural expression, and leadership development. Within their walls, African Americans planned boycotts, voter drives, and civil rights campaigns. Churches trained generations of orators, organizers, and artists—from Sunday school teachers to choir directors—who later became influential leaders in politics, music, and grassroots activism. Leaders such as Reverend Dr. Martin Luther King Jr. emerged from these sacred spaces, illustrating the church's unmatched role in developing moral authority, rhetorical skill, and communal trust. In an era of systemic oppression, Black churches were the beating heart of Black liberation and cultural creativity.

Innovation and Influence: Black Inventors, Entrepreneurs, and Philanthropists

African American entrepreneurs shattered ceilings and expanded what was possible for Black economic advancement. Among them was Madam C. J. Walker. She rose to prominence as the first woman in the United States—of any race—to become a self-made millionaire. She built a beauty empire tailored to Black women's needs, affirming their beauty and identity at a time when Eurocentric standards dominated the marketplace. Walker's success extended far beyond personal wealth; she employed thousands of Black women, funded scholarships, and supported civil rights organizations. Like other Black inventors and innovators of her time, Walker demonstrated how entrepreneurship could serve both as personal liberation and a means of collective uplift.

The following advertisement for Madam C. J. Walker Products, 1906–1950, offers a powerful glimpse into how Black entrepreneurship, beauty standards, and racial pride intersected in the early twentieth century. This ad was created by Madam C. J. Walker's company—one of the first major Black-owned businesses in the United States. It not only marketed haircare products tailored to African American women but also promoted a message of self-worth, dignity, and empowerment. In a society that devalued Black beauty, Walker's brand countered mainstream narratives and positioned Black women as deserving of both care and confidence. This source reveals how commercial media became a platform for racial uplift, gendered empowerment, and the growth of Black consumer culture.

An advertisement for Madam C. J. Walker Products, 1906–1950
(Source: Collection of the Smithsonian National Museum of African American History and Culture, gift of A'Lelia Bundles/Madam Walker Family Archives)

Photograph of a Convention of Madam C. J. Walker Agents at Villa Lewaro, 1924 captures a historic gathering of Madam C. J. Walker's sales agents at Villa Lewaro, her luxurious estate in Irvington, New York. More than a business meeting, the convention represented a powerful affirmation of Black economic empowerment, sisterhood, and professional excellence during the Jim Crow era. These women—many of whom had few other economic opportunities—were trained, employed, and inspired by Walker's vision of beauty and independence. Villa Lewaro itself symbolized the heights that African Americans could reach through self-determination and collective effort. This image illustrates how Walker's enterprise was not just about selling products—it was about transforming lives and redefining what was possible for Black women in America.

Photograph of a Convention of Madam C. J. Walker Agents at Villa Lewaro, 1924, in Irvington, New York (Source: Collection of the Smithsonian National Museum of African American History and Culture, gift of A'Lelia Bundles/Madam Walker Family Archives)

The clock used by the Citizens Savings and Trust Company, 1920–2013, stands as both a literal and symbolic marker of Black economic endurance. Displayed prominently by one of the nation's earliest Black-owned financial institutions, this clock served as a public testament to stability, professionalism, and trust within the African American community. Founded to provide banking services to those excluded from white-owned institutions, Citizens Savings and Trust Company reflected a broader movement of Black self-reliance during the twentieth century. The longevity of the clock's use—spanning nearly a century—reminds us of the enduring legacy of Black financial institutions and their role in fostering economic advancement and racial pride.

The clock used by the Citizen's Savings and Trust Company, 1920–2013
(Source: Collection of the Smithsonian National Museum of African American History and Culture; gift of Dr. and Mrs. T. B. Boyd, III and R. H. Boyd Publishing Corporation)

In an era marked by exclusion, violence, and systemic oppression, African Americans built institutions that not only met their immediate needs but also laid the foundation for long-term progress. From churches and newspapers to banks and beauty enterprises, these organizations became engines of self-determination, cultural pride, and economic empowerment. They nurtured leadership, fostered solidarity, and created spaces where Black identity could flourish on its own terms. The legacy of these institutions is not just historical. It continues to shape the strength, resilience, and innovation of Black communities today. Through collective action and visionary leadership, African Americans transformed marginalization into a mandate for building—and defending—their own.

When Institutions Are Built by Us, for Us

Black Americans created schools, churches, businesses, newspapers, and mutual aid societies—spaces where they could lead, learn, and thrive without white control. These institutions became the backbone of Black communities.

You're Practicing: Recognizing the power of self-determination.

Connect This To: Grassroots organizing, survival, and resilience.

Theme: Power and Community

Practice: Explain the Significance or Importance

During the post-Reconstruction era and into the early twentieth century, African Americans built independent organizations and institutions to support community development and political activism.

(A) Identify one prominent Black organization or institution founded during this period.
(B) Explain the purpose of a Black organization or institution, and how it addressed the needs of the African American community.
(C) Analyze the broader significance of a Black organization or institution in shaping Black self-determination and resistance to systemic oppression.

SAMPLE RESPONSES

(A) The National Association for the Advancement of Colored People (NAACP), founded in 1909, became one of the most influential civil rights organizations in U.S. history.

The Tuskegee Institute, founded by Booker T. Washington in 1881, served as a premier educational institution for African Americans in the South.

(B) The NAACP aimed to fight racial injustice through legal challenges, public education, and political advocacy, responding to lynching, segregation, and disenfranchisement.

Tuskegee provided vocational and industrial education, empowering African Americans with skills to achieve economic independence and social respectability in a racist society.

(C) These institutions reflected a strategy of community-led empowerment, allowing African Americans to take control of their futures by building their own schools, newspapers, and advocacy groups.

They served as foundations for long-term resistance, laying the groundwork for future civil rights activism by nurturing Black leadership, fostering collective identity, and challenging white supremacy through organized, sustained efforts.

Skills Assessed: Explain the significance of historical developments; use sources and evidence; analyze relationships among developments.

Topic 3.10 HBCUs, Black Greek Letter Organizations, and Black Education

Key Terms

- Historically Black colleges and universities (HBCUs)—Howard, Fisk, Tuskegee, and others
- Booker T. Washington—vocational education advocate
- Atlanta University, Hampton Institute, Tuskegee Institute
- Du Bois–Washington debate—vocational vs. liberal arts
- Black Greek letter organizations (BGLOs)—Alpha Phi Alpha, Delta Sigma Theta, and others
- Talented Tenth—Du Bois's idea of elite leadership through education
- Educational self-determination
- Black pedagogy and cultural transmission

In a nation that weaponized education as a tool of exclusion, African Americans made it a cornerstone of liberation. From the ashes of slavery and the betrayals of Reconstruction, Black communities built institutions of higher learning that cultivated minds, shaped leaders, and defied the myth of Black inferiority. These institutions were more than campuses; they were acts of resistance and hope.

The founding of historically Black colleges and universities (HBCUs) in the late nineteenth and early twentieth centuries marked a transformative moment in African American history. Created in response to segregation and the denial of educational opportunities, HBCUs provided rigorous academic instruction, professional training, and a space for cultural affirmation. Alongside these institutions, Black Greek letter organizations emerged as powerful networks for leadership development, civic engagement, and social mobility. Together, HBCUs and Black fraternal organizations reshaped what was possible for African Americans in the United States and beyond, producing generations of educators, activists, entrepreneurs, and intellectuals.

After engaging with this topic, scholars will be able to:

- Describe the founding of historically Black colleges and universities (HBCUs) and the historical context that made them necessary.
- Explain how HBCUs advanced the educational and professional aspirations of African Americans nationally and internationally.
- Analyze the emergence of Black Greek letter organizations and their role in leadership development and cultural identity.
- Connect the rise of HBCUs to broader movements for racial self-determination, academic excellence, and global Black solidarity.

Education as Resistance: Founding Black Colleges in the Shadow of Segregation

Following the Civil War, African Americans faced systemic exclusion from white educational institutions due to segregation and racial discrimination. In response, Black leaders, religious communities, and allies established their own colleges and universities. These institutions were designed not only to educate but also to uplift—a direct challenge to the racist belief that African Americans were intellectually inferior or unworthy of formal learning. The postemancipation era gave rise to dozens of institutions committed to academic rigor, moral development, and community service. HBCUs became the backbone of Black higher education in America.

The First HBCUs: A Foundation of Faith and Philanthropy

The earliest historically Black colleges and universities (HBCUs) were primarily private institutions, often founded with the support of religious denominations and white philanthropists. Yet even in these spaces, African Americans asserted agency and vision. Wilberforce University in Ohio, founded in 1856 by the African Methodist Episcopal Church, became the first college to be fully owned and operated by African Americans. Wilberforce set a powerful precedent: that Black institutions could control their governance, curriculum, and cultural mission while cultivating excellence and independence among their students.

Federal Policy and the Birth of Land-Grant HBCUs

The expansion of HBCUs in the late nineteenth century was also shaped by federal legislation. The Second Morrill Act of 1890, which upheld segregated education, required states to provide land-grant institutions for Black students if they did not offer integrated access to white schools. This mandate led to the creation of 18 publicly funded HBCUs across the South. These colleges emphasized agricultural, mechanical, and industrial training, reflecting the era's practical educational needs while also serving as sites of racial uplift and institutional legitimacy in a segregated nation.

Divergent Visions: Liberal Arts vs. Industrial Training

In the formative decades of HBCU development, two dominant educational philosophies emerged. Schools such as Fisk University championed a liberal arts education, aiming to produce critical thinkers, teachers, and leaders versed in literature, philosophy, and the arts. In contrast, institutions like Tuskegee Institute—under the leadership of Booker T. Washington—promoted vocational and industrial training as a path to economic self-reliance. This tension between classical and practical education sparked national debates about the best route to Black progress, reflecting broader struggles over race, labor, and citizenship in the post-Reconstruction era.

The Backbone of Black Higher Education

Until the surge of integration during the Black campus movement of the 1960s, HBCUs served as the primary—and often only—avenues for African Americans to access higher education. These institutions produced the vast majority of Black doctors, lawyers, educators, and clergy in the United States throughout the twentieth century. They were not only centers of academic training but also safe havens where Black identity could be celebrated and leadership could flourish.

A Global and Generational Impact

The founding of HBCUs dramatically expanded access to higher education and professional careers for African Americans. These schools equipped generations of students with the skills, confidence, and credentials needed to rise from poverty and assume positions of influence across every sector of society—from medicine and law to civil rights and the arts. The ripple effects extended beyond U.S. borders as graduates of HBCUs became diplomats, scholars, and change makers throughout the African diaspora.

HBCUs as Cultural and Intellectual Powerhouses

HBCUs were more than academic institutions. They were cultural sanctuaries and ideological battlegrounds. These schools fostered a deep sense of Black pride, provided space for independent Black scholarship, and nurtured activism that challenged racial inequality. Students and faculty alike contributed to the development of African American Studies, participated in civil rights struggles, and created legacies of intellectual resistance that continue to shape public discourse today.

Brotherhood and Sisterhood: The Rise of Black Greek Letter Organizations

Out of the intellectual and cultural vibrancy of HBCUs came the rise of Black Greek letter organizations (BGLOs), which also took root at predominantly white institutions. Beginning with the founding of Alpha Phi Alpha Fraternity, Inc. in 1906 at Cornell University, these fraternities and sororities created tight-knit communities committed to academic excellence, leadership, mutual support, and service.

Among the prestigious members of Alpha Phi Alpha Fraternity, Inc. is the author, Rashad K. Brown—a nationally recognized education reform leader, scholar-practitioner, keynote speaker, strategic advisor on public education policy and equity, and author. He became a proud member while attending Florida A&M University through the historic Beta Nu Chapter, founded in 1932 by original Alpha Jewel Charles Henry Chapman. Other prominent Alpha Phi Alpha men also include civil rights icon Dr. Martin Luther King Jr., scholar Dr. Cornel West, and film producer Will Packer, whose movie *Stomp the Yard* introduced millions to the legacy of the Black Greek letter organizations, known as the Divine Nine.

The Divine Nine: A Legacy of Scholarship, Service, and Leadership

The National Pan-Hellenic Council (NPHC), affectionately known as "The Divine Nine," is a coalition of historically Black fraternities and sororities that have shaped African American collegiate and community life for over a century. Founded in 1930 at Howard University, the NPHC provides a united platform for its member organizations to collaborate in service, leadership, and advocacy. These organizations have nurtured generations of African American leaders, fostering networks that extend from college campuses to the highest levels of public service, business, the arts, and activism.

Member Organizations

The NPHC is composed of nine distinct organizations, each with its own founding date, mission, and traditions, yet all bound by a shared commitment to uplifting African American communities:

Alpha Phi Alpha Fraternity, Inc.—Founded 1906, Cornell University
Alpha Kappa Alpha Sorority, Inc.—Founded 1908, Howard University
Kappa Alpha Psi Fraternity, Inc.—Founded 1911, Indiana University Bloomington
Omega Psi Phi Fraternity, Inc.—Founded 1911, Howard University
Delta Sigma Theta Sorority, Inc.—Founded 1913, Howard University
Phi Beta Sigma Fraternity, Inc.—Founded 1914, Howard University
Zeta Phi Beta Sorority, Inc.—Founded 1920, Howard University
Sigma Gamma Rho Sorority, Inc.—Founded 1922, Butler University
Iota Phi Theta Fraternity, Inc.—Founded 1963, Morgan State University

Historical Significance

The emergence of these organizations must be understood in the context of segregation and limited access to mainstream fraternal networks. They provided African American students with spaces of belonging, leadership training, and academic support. Their existence challenged prevailing racial barriers by producing members who excelled academically, led campus movements, and engaged in direct action to address social inequities.

Service and Activism

The NPHC's influence extends far beyond college campuses. Collectively, its members have:

- Organized voter registration drives during the Civil Rights Movement and beyond.
- Raised millions for scholarships and educational initiatives.
- Advocated for public health awareness, including HIV/AIDS education, cancer prevention, and mental health advocacy.
- Partnered with local, national, and international organizations to address poverty, education inequality, and community development.

Modern Impact

Today, the Divine Nine remains a visible and respected force in African American life. Membership often results in lifelong affiliation, with alumni networks providing mentorship, professional connections, and ongoing opportunities for service. Step shows, stroll competitions, and community projects showcase the vibrancy of these organizations, while their political and philanthropic work continues to shape public policy and civic engagement.

A Global Voice: The Fisk Jubilee Singers and Cultural Diplomacy

The global impact of HBCUs was powerfully demonstrated by the Fisk Jubilee Singers, a student choir from Fisk University. In the late nineteenth and early twentieth centuries, they introduced African American spirituals to audiences across Europe and beyond, challenging stereotypes and raising funds for their school through their talent and discipline. Their performances dignified Black musical traditions and placed African American cultural contributions on the world stage, proving that Black education and Black artistry were inseparable forces of influence and pride.

The picture of the Jubilee Singers of Fisk University, photographed in 1875, offers a rare visual and historical window into one of the most influential cultural and educational ambassadors of the Reconstruction era. Formed at Fisk University, an HBCU founded to educate formerly enslaved people, the Jubilee Singers used their voices to preserve and elevate the spirituals born out of slavery. This image captures the ensemble during their early international tours, where their dignified presence and powerful performances challenged racist assumptions and helped raise funds for their struggling institution. Far more than a choir, the Jubilee Singers were symbols of Black excellence, proof that African American artistry and intellect could captivate the world and transform public perceptions.

The Jubilee Singers of Fisk University, 1875
(Source: National Portrait Gallery, public domain, via Wikimedia Commons)

The image titled *Botanist George Washington Carver with Students in His Laboratory at Tuskegee Institute, 1902* offers a profound snapshot of Black scientific achievement and educational innovation at the turn of the twentieth century. Carver, one of the most respected African American scientists of his era, is shown here not only conducting research but mentoring students at Tuskegee Institute—an HBCU committed to vocational and agricultural excellence. This moment captures the broader mission of Tuskegee: to combine practical skills with intellectual rigor and transform education into a tool of racial uplift. Carver's legacy, as depicted in this image, represents the power of HBCUs to cultivate leadership in fields long denied to African Americans.

Botanist George Washington Carver with Students in His Laboratory at Tuskegee Institute, 1902 (Source: Photograph by Frances Benjamin Johnston, courtesy of the Library of Congress, Prints and Photographs Division)

In 1964, the Tau Psi Chapter of Omega Psi Phi Fraternity, Inc. hosted a widely attended charity dance at North Carolina College (now North Carolina Central University) in Durham, North Carolina. More than 500 students participated in the event, where admission was one canned or packaged food item. As a result, nine baskets of food were collected and distributed to families in need for Thanksgiving. The photograph captures Joseph Williams, basileus of the chapter from Wilson, North Carolina, and Claude Sawyer, keeper of finance from Roper, North Carolina, standing beside the donations. This image reflects the fraternity's deep commitment to community service, brotherhood, and civic responsibility—core values that have long defined the mission of Black Greek letter organizations.

Omega Psi Phi members with baskets of canned food for charity
(Source: Photo by North Carolina Central University via Getty Images)

The photograph titled *Professor Gail Hansberry with Art History Student at North Carolina Central University, 1965* captures a moment of mentorship and intellectual engagement within the HBCU tradition. Taken during a pivotal decade of civil rights activism and educational transformation, this image reflects the vital role historically Black colleges and universities played in cultivating Black scholars, artists, and critical thinkers. Professor Gail Hansberry, an influential educator and cultural historian, exemplifies the academic excellence and individualized instruction that defined HBCU learning environments. The setting underscores how HBCUs provided not just access to education but a nurturing space where Black academic inquiry, creativity, and cultural identity were affirmed and advanced.

Professor Gail Hansberry with Art History Student at North Carolina Central University, 1965
(Source: North Carolina Central University via Getty Images)

The establishment of historically Black colleges and universities, along with the rise of Black Greek letter organizations, represents one of the most powerful legacies of self-determination in African American history. These institutions were born from exclusion but were fueled by vision—spaces where academic excellence, cultural pride, and leadership development thrived against the backdrop of racial segregation. HBCUs equipped generations of African Americans with the tools to transform not only their own lives but also their communities, their professions, and the nation. Likewise, BGLOs fostered lifelong bonds rooted in service, scholarship, and civic responsibility. Together, these educational and fraternal institutions have produced scholars, artists, scientists, educators, and activists whose impact is felt across the globe—and whose legacy continues to shape the Black intellectual tradition.

More than School—a Movement

Historically Black colleges and universities (HBCUs) weren't just places of learning—they were places of resistance. They trained generations of leaders, thinkers, and freedom fighters. Fraternities and sororities helped carry those missions forward.

You're Practicing: Tracing how education builds collective identity.

Connect This To: Institutional memory and leadership development.

Theme: Education and Empowerment

Practice: Explain Causality (Effects)

In response to exclusion from white institutions, African Americans established HBCUs and Black Greek letter organizations as cornerstones of education and leadership development.

(A) Identify one HBCU or Black Greek letter organization established before 1930.
(B) Explain how this institution or organization contributed to Black educational advancement or leadership.
(C) Analyze the long-term effects of these institutions on African American civic and cultural life.

SAMPLE RESPONSES

(A) Howard University, founded in 1867 in Washington, D.C., is one of the most prominent Historically Black Colleges and Universities, producing leaders such as Thurgood Marshall, Toni Morrison, and Kamala Harris.

The university emerged as a leading institution for African American higher education, attracting scholars, activists, and cultural icons from across the nation.

(B) Howard University provided rigorous academic programs in law, medicine, and the liberal arts to African Americans barred from most white institutions, producing leaders like Charles Hamilton Houston, Pauli Murray, and Vernon Jordan.

The university fostered political activism and intellectual leadership by hosting civil rights strategists, NAACP attorneys, and international dignitaries who advanced racial equality worldwide.

Howard University served as the founding site for influential Black Greek letter organizations such as Alpha Kappa Alpha Sorority, Inc. (1908), Omega Psi Phi Fraternity, Inc. (1911), and Delta Sigma Theta Sorority, Inc. (1913), which institutionalized scholarship, leadership development, and service.

(C) Howard University and its affiliated Greek letter organizations created powerful alumni networks that produced civil rights leaders like Stokely Carmichael, Marian Wright Edelman, and Elijah Cummings, who shaped national movements for justice.

Graduates and members from these institutions played central roles in the Civil Rights Movement, from organizing the March on Washington to leading voter registration drives in the South and championing school desegregation cases.

The cultural traditions of HBCUs and the Divine Nine, including step shows, homecoming celebrations, and service projects, have preserved African American pride and unity while inspiring youth leadership in education, politics, and the arts.

Skills Assessed: Explain the effects of historical developments; use sources and evidence; analyze relationships among developments.

Topic 3.11 The New Negro Movement and the Harlem Renaissance

Key Terms

- New Negro—concept of assertive, culturally confident Black identity
- Alain Locke—editor of *The New Negro* anthology (1925)
- Harlem Renaissance—artistic and intellectual flourishing of the 1920s
- Zora Neale Hurston, Langston Hughes, Countee Cullen, Claude McKay
- Jazz and blues—cultural expressions of resistance and joy
- Race pride and racial uplift
- Great Migration—cultural shift northward
- Literature, music, and visual arts as political statements

What happens when a generation refuses to be defined by oppression? In the early twentieth century, African Americans—fueled by migration, modernity, and momentum—declared a new identity: bold, creative, and unapologetically Black. The New Negro was not simply a literary figure or artistic muse—it was a declaration of selfhood, cultural sovereignty, and political awakening.

The New Negro movement, emerging in the aftermath of World War I and during the height of the Great Migration, marked a radical shift in how African Americans saw themselves and how they demanded to be seen by the world. Centered in Harlem but resonating far beyond, this movement gave rise to the Harlem Renaissance—a flourishing of Black cultural production in literature, music, visual art, and thought. Writers, artists, and intellectuals rejected racist caricatures and instead redefined Black identity on their own terms, celebrating African heritage, embracing modernity, and challenging white supremacy through artistic expression. The Harlem Renaissance was more than an artistic movement. It was a cultural revolution rooted in self-definition, racial pride, and collective innovation.

After engaging with this topic, scholars will be able to:

- Describe how the New Negro movement challenged dominant racial narratives and emphasized self-definition.
- Identify the central themes and figures of the Harlem Renaissance across multiple artistic forms.
- Analyze how cultural innovation became a tool for racial pride and political resistance.
- Explain the relationship between migration, urbanization, and the emergence of new Black cultural identities.

Self-Definition in the Shadow of Violence: The Political Roots of the New Negro

Amid the racial terror of the post-Reconstruction era—often referred to as the nadir of American race relations—African Americans began to assert a new vision of identity and resistance. The New Negro movement emerged as a powerful rejection of victimhood. It encouraged Black Americans to define themselves rather than be defined by the legacies of slavery, segregation, and white supremacy. This movement called for political self-advocacy, civic engagement, and a reimagining of Black identity grounded in dignity, intellect, and pride. Influential voices like Alain Locke, Hubert Harrison, and Ida B. Wells articulated the urgency of self-determination in the face of lynching, disenfranchisement, and systemic exclusion.

Forging a New Black Aesthetic

At the heart of the New Negro movement was a bold pursuit of a distinctly Black cultural aesthetic. Artists, writers, and intellectuals sought to craft expressions that were rooted in the lived experiences, spiritual traditions, and historical realities of African Americans. This new aesthetic rejected Eurocentric standards of beauty and artistic value. It instead celebrated Black skin, dialects, music, folklore, and everyday life. In literature, this meant centering Black protagonists and vernacular voices. In visual arts, it meant portraying the strength and elegance of Black subjects. The goal was not simply inclusion in American culture. The goal was to transform it.

Innovation as Resistance: Jazz, Blues, and the Urban Migration

The cultural innovations of the New Negro era—particularly in music, literature, and art—were acts of resistance that challenged prevailing stereotypes and asserted new narratives of Black life.

The rise of blues and jazz, born in the rural South and shaped in the urban North, symbolized the migration of African American culture across geographic and social boundaries. These musical forms captured both the sorrow and the joy of Black life, offering deeply emotional and improvisational counterpoints to white-dominated cultural norms. Likewise, the literature and visual art of the era reflected urban migration, political consciousness, and the dynamic identities emerging in cities like Harlem, Chicago, and Detroit.

The Harlem Renaissance: A Cultural Revolution

The New Negro movement culminated in the Harlem Renaissance, a flourishing of Black literary, artistic, and intellectual life centered in Harlem, New York, during the 1920s and 1930s. Often referred to as a cultural revolution, the Harlem Renaissance produced groundbreaking works by figures such as Langston Hughes, Zora Neale Hurston, Claude McKay, Aaron Douglas, and Duke Ellington. These creators infused their work with themes of racial pride, social critique, and cultural celebration. The Harlem Renaissance was not simply about representation—it was about redefinition. It gave voice to a generation determined to reshape how Blackness was seen, understood, and remembered.

This excerpt from *The New Negro: An Interpretation* by Alain Locke, published in 1925, serves as the intellectual cornerstone of the New Negro movement and the Harlem Renaissance. In this seminal work, Locke argues that African Americans must cast off the old stereotypes imposed by a racist society and instead embrace a renewed sense of selfhood, cultural pride, and creative agency. As editor of the anthology that bears this name, Locke curated essays, poems, and artwork that embodied the vibrant new expressions of Black identity emerging in the early twentieth century. His writing provided a powerful call for African Americans to define themselves—not through the lens of oppression but through the brilliance of their own cultural contributions and intellectual potential.

Excerpt from *The New Negro: An Interpretation* by Alain Locke, 1925

The Younger Generation comes, bringing its gifts. They are the first fruits of the Negro Renaissance. Youth speaks, and the voice of the New Negro is heard. What stirs inarticulately in the masses is already vocal upon the lips of the talented few, and the future listens, however the present may shut its ears. Here we have Negro youth, with arresting visions and vibrant prophecies; forecasting in the mirror of art what we must see and recognize in the streets of reality tomorrow, foretelling in new notes and accents the maturing speech of full racial utterance.

Primarily, of course, it is youth that speaks in the voice of Negro youth, but the overtones are distinctive; Negro youth speaks out of an unique experience and with a particular representativeness. All classes of a people under social pressure are permeated with a common experience; they are emotionally welded as others cannot be. With them, even ordinary living has epic depth and lyric intensity, and this, their material handicap, is their spiritual advantage. So, in a day when art has run to classes, cliques and coteries, and life lacks more and more a vital common background, the Negro artist, out of the depths of his group and personal experience, has to his hand almost the conditions of a classical art.

Negro genius to-day relies upon the race-gift as a vast spiritual endowment from which our best developments have come and must come. Racial expression as a conscious motive, it is true, is fading out of our latest art, but just as surely the age of truer, finer group expression is coming in—for race expression does not need to be deliberate to be vital. Indeed at its best it never is. This was the case with our instinctive and quite matchless folk-art, and begins to be the same again as we approach cultural maturity in a phase of art that promises now to be fully representative. The interval between has been an awkward age, where from the anxious desire and attempt to be representative much that was really unrepresentative has come; we have lately had an art that was stiltedly self-conscious, and racially rhetorical rather than racially expressive. Our poets have now stopped speaking for the Negro—they speak as Negroes. Where formerly they spoke to others and tried to interpret, they now speak to their own and try to express. They have stopped posing, being nearer the attainment of poise.

The younger generation has thus achieved an objective attitude toward life. Race for them is but an idiom of experience, a sort of added enriching adventure and discipline, giving subtler overtones to life, making it more beautiful and interesting, even if more poignantly so. So experienced, it affords a deepening rather than a narrowing of social vision. The artistic problem of the Young Negro has not been so much that of acquiring the outer mastery of form and technique as that of achieving an inner mastery of mood and spirit. That accomplished, there has come the happy release from self-consciousness, rhetoric, bombast, and the hampering habit of setting artistic values with primary regard for moral effect—all those pathetic over-compensations of a group inferiority complex which our social dilemmas inflicted upon several unhappy generations. Our poets no longer have the hard choice between an over-assertive and an appealing attitude. By the same effort they have shaken themselves free from the minstrel tradition and the fowling-nets of dialect, and through acquiring ease and simplicity in serious expression, have carried the folk-gift to the altitudes of art. There they seek and find art's intrinsic values and satisfactions—and if America were deaf, they would still sing.

But America listens—perhaps in curiosity at first; later, we may be sure, in understanding. But—a moment of patience. The generation now in the artistic vanguard inherits the fine and dearly bought achievement of another generation of creative workmen who have been pioneers and path-breakers in the cultural development and recognition of the Negro in the arts. Though still in their prime, as veterans of a hard struggle, they must have the praise and gratitude that is due them. We have had, in fiction, Chestnutt and Burghardt Du Bois; in drama, Du Bois again and Angelina Grimke; in poetry Dunbar, James Weldon Johnson, Fenton and Charles Bertram Johnson, Everett Hawkins, Lucien Watkins, Cotter, Jameson; and in another file of poets, Miss Grimke, Anne Spencer, and Georgia Douglas Johnson; in criticism and belles lettres, Braithwaite and Dr. Du Bois; in painting, Tanner and Scott; in sculpture, Meta Warrick and May Jackson; in acting, Gilpin and Robeson; in music, Burleigh. Nor must the fine collaboration of white American artists be omitted; the work of Ridgeley Torrence and Eugene O'Neill in drama, of Stribling, and Shands and Clement Wood in fiction, all of which has helped in the bringing of the materials of Negro life out of the shambles of conventional polemics, cheap romance and journalism into the domain of pure and unbiassed art.

Then, rich in this legacy, but richer still, I think, in their own endowment of talent, comes the youngest generation of our Afro-American culture: in music Diton, Dett, Grant Still, and Roland Hayes; in fiction, Jessie Fauset, Walter White, Claude McKay (a forthcoming book); in drama, Willis Richardson; in the field of the short story, Jean Toomer, Eric Walrond, Rudolph Fisher; and finally a vivid galaxy of young Negro poets, McKay, Jean Toomer, Langston Hughes and Countée Cullen.

These constitute a new generation not because of years only, but because of a new aesthetic and a new philosophy of life. They have all swung above the horizon in the last three years, and we can say without disparagement of the past that in that short space of time they have gained collectively from publishers, editors, critics and the general public more recognition than has ever before come to Negro creative artists in an entire working lifetime. First novels of unquestioned distinction, first acceptances by premier journals whose pages are the ambition of veteran craftsmen, international acclaim, the conquest for us of new provinces of art, the development for the first time among us of literary coteries and channels for the contact of creative minds, and most important of all, a spiritual quickening and racial leavening such as no generation has yet felt and known. It has been their achievement also to bring the artistic advance of the Negro sharply into stepping alignment with contemporary artistic thought, mood and style. They are thoroughly modern, some of them ultra-modern, and Negro thoughts now wear the uniform of the age.

Source: Alain Locke, "Negro Youth Speaks" in *The New Negro: An Interpretation*, edited by Alain Locke, New York: Albert and Charles Boni, 1925, pp. 47–53.

In his influential 1926 essay "The Negro Artist and the Racial Mountain," Langston Hughes issues a bold challenge to Black artists to embrace their cultural heritage rather than aspire to white artistic standards. While writing at the height of the Harlem Renaissance, Hughes critiques the internalized racism that led some Black artists to distance themselves from Black culture and expression. Instead, he celebrates the beauty, rhythm, and resilience of everyday Black life as the true foundation for artistic greatness. This essay stands as both a manifesto and a call to action, urging Black creatives to find power in their authenticity and to shape a cultural future rooted in pride, not assimilation.

"The Negro Artist and the Racial Mountain" (1926)

One of the most promising of the young Negro poets said to me once, "I want to be a poet—not a Negro poet," meaning, I believe, "I want to write like a white poet"; meaning subconsciously, "I would like to be a white poet"; meaning behind that, "I would like to be white." And I was sorry the young man said that, for no great poet has ever been afraid of being himself. And I doubted then that, with his desire to run away spiritually from his race, this boy would ever be a great poet. But this is the mountain standing in the way of any true Negro art in America—this urge within the race toward whiteness, the desire to pour racial individuality into the mold of American standardization, and to be as little Negro and as much American as possible.

But let us look at the immediate background of this young poet. His family is of what I suppose one would call the Negro middle class: people who are by no means rich yet never uncomfortable nor hungry—smug, contented, respectable folk, members of the Baptist church. The father goes to work every morning. He is a chief steward at a large white club. The mother sometimes does fancy sewing or supervises parties for the rich families of the town. The children go to a mixed school. In the home they read white papers and magazines. And the mother often says "Don't be like niggers" when the children are bad. A frequent phrase from the father is, "Look how well a white man does things." And so the word white comes to be unconsciously a symbol of all virtues. It holds for the children beauty, morality, and money. The whisper of "I want to be white" runs silently through their minds. This young poet's home is, I believe, a fairly typical home of the colored middle class. One sees immediately how difficult it would be for an artist born in such a home to interest himself in interpreting the beauty of his own people. He is never taught to see that beauty. He is taught rather not to see it, or if he does, to be ashamed of it when it is not according to Caucasian patterns.

For racial culture the home of a self-styled "high-class" Negro has nothing better to offer. Instead there will perhaps be more aping of things white than in a less cultured or less wealthy home. The father is perhaps a doctor, lawyer, landowner, or politician. The mother may be a social worker, or a teacher, or she may do nothing and have a maid. Father is often dark but he has usually married the lightest woman he could find. The family attend a fashionable church where few really colored faces are to be found. And they themselves draw a color line. In the North they go to white theaters and white movies. And in the South they have at least two cars and house "like white folks." Nordic manners, Nordic faces, Nordic hair, Nordic art (if any), and an Episcopal heaven. A very high mountain indeed for the would-be racial artist to climb in order to discover himself and his people.

But then there are the low-down folks, the so-called common element, and they are the majority—may the Lord be praised! The people who have their nip of gin on Saturday nights and are not too important to themselves or the community, or too well fed, or too learned to watch the lazy world go round. They live on Seventh Street in Washington or State Street in Chicago and they do not particularly care whether they are like white folks or anybody else. Their joy runs, bang! into ecstasy. Their religion soars to a shout. Work maybe a little today, rest a little tomorrow. Play awhile. Sing awhile. O, let's dance! These common people are not afraid of spirituals, as for a long time their more intellectual brethren were, and jazz is their child. They furnish a wealth of colorful, distinctive material for any artist because they still hold their own individuality in the face of American standardizations. And perhaps these common people will give to the world its truly great Negro artist, the one who is not afraid to be himself. Whereas the better-class Negro would tell the artist what to do, the people at least let him alone when he does appear. And they are not ashamed of him—if they know he exists at all. And they accept what beauty is their own without question.

Certainly there is, for the American Negro artist who can escape the restrictions the more advanced among his own group would put upon him, a great field of unused material ready for his art. Without going outside his race, and even among the better classes with their "white" culture and conscious American manners, but still Negro enough to be different, there is sufficient matter to furnish a black artist with a lifetime of creative work. And when he chooses to touch on the relations between Negroes and whites in this country, with their innumerable overtones and undertones, surely, and especially for literature and the drama, there is an inexhaustible supply of themes at hand. To these the Negro artist can give his racial individuality, his heritage of rhythm and warmth, and his incongruous humor that so often, as in the Blues, becomes ironic laughter mixed with tears. But let us look again at the mountain.

A prominent Negro clubwoman in Philadelphia paid eleven dollars to hear Raquel Meller sing Andalusian popular songs. But she told me a few weeks before she would not think of going to hear "that woman," Clara Smith, a great black artist, sing Negro folksongs. And many an upper-class Negro church, even now, would not dream of employing a spiritual in its services. The drab melodies in white folks' hymnbooks are much to be preferred. "We want to worship the Lord correctly and quietly. We don't believe in 'shouting.' Let's be dull like the Nordics," they say, in effect. The road for the serious black artist, then, who would produce a racial art is most certainly rocky and the mountain is high. Until recently he received almost no encouragement for his work from either white or colored people. The fine novels of Chesnutt go out of print with neither race noticing their passing. The quaint charm and humor of Dunbar's dialect verse brought to him, in his day, largely the same kind of encouragement one would give a sideshow freak (A colored man writing poetry! How odd!) or a clown (How amusing!).

The present vogue in things Negro, although it may do as much harm as good for the budding colored artist, has at least done this: it has brought him forcibly to the attention of his own people among whom for so long, unless the other race had noticed him beforehand, he was a prophet with little honor. I understand that Charles Gilpin acted for years in Negro theaters without any special acclaim from his own, but when Broadway gave him eight curtain calls, Negroes, too, began to beat a tin pan in his honor. I know a young colored writer, a manual worker by day, who had been writing well for the colored magazines for some years, but it was not until he recently broke into the white publications and his first book was accepted by a prominent New York publisher that the "best" Negroes in his city took the trouble to discover that he lived there. Then almost immediately they decided to give a grand dinner for him. But the society ladies were careful to whisper to his mother that perhaps she'd better not come. They were not sure she would have an evening gown.

The Negro artist works against an undertow of sharp criticism and misunderstanding from his own group and unintentional bribes from the whites. "O, be respectable, write about nice people, show how good we are," say the Negroes. "Be stereotyped, don't go too far, don't shatter our illusions about you, don't amuse us too seriously. We will pay you," say the whites. Both would have told Jean Toomer not to write "Cane." The colored people did not praise it. The white people did not buy it. Most of the colored people who did read "Cane" hate it. They are afraid of it. Although the critics gave it good reviews the public remained indifferent. Yet (excepting the work of Du Bois) "Cane" contains the finest prose written by a Negro in America. And like the singing of Robeson, it is truly racial.

But in spite of the Nordicized Negro intelligentsia and the desires of some white editors we have an honest American Negro literature already with us. Now I await the rise of the Negro theater. Our folk music, having achieved world-wide fame, offers itself to the genius of the great individual American Negro composer who is to come. And within the next decade I expect to see the work of a growing school of colored artists who paint and model the beauty of dark faces and create with new technique the expressions of their own soul-world. And the Negro dancers who will dance like flame and the singers who will continue to carry our songs to all who listen—they will be with us in even greater numbers tomorrow.

Most of my own poems are racial in theme and treatment, derived from the life I know. In many of them I try to grasp and hold some of the meanings and rhythms of jazz. I am as sincere as I know how to be in these poems and yet after every reading I answer questions like these from my own people: Do you think Negroes should always write about Negroes? I wish you wouldn't read some of your poems to white folks. How do you find anything interesting in a place like a cabaret? Why do you write about black people? You aren't black. What makes you do so many jazz poems?

But jazz to me is one of the inherent expressions of Negro life in America: the eternal tom-tom beating in the Negro soul—the tom-tom of revolt against weariness in a white world, a world of subway trains, and work, work, work; the tom-tom of joy and laughter, and pain swallowed in a smile. Yet the Philadelphia clubwoman is ashamed to say that her race created it and she does not like me to write about it, The old subconscious "white is best" runs through her mind. Years of study under white teachers, a lifetime of white books, pictures, and papers, and white manners, morals, and Puritan standards made her dislike the spirituals. And now she turns up her nose at jazz and all its manifestations—likewise almost everything else distinctly racial. She doesn't care for the Winold Reiss portraits of Negroes because they are "too Negro." She does not want a true picture of herself from anybody. She wants the artist to flatter her, to make the white world believe that all Negroes are as smug and as near white in soul as she wants to be. But, to my mind, it is the duty of the younger Negro artist, if he accepts any duties at all from outsiders, to change through the force of his art that old whispering "I want to be white," hidden in the aspirations of his people, to "Why should I want to be white? I am a Negro—and beautiful!"

So I am ashamed for the black poet who says, "I want to be a poet, not a Negro poet," as though his own racial world were not as interesting as any other world. I am ashamed, too, for the colored artist who runs from the painting of Negro faces to the painting of sunsets after the manner of the academicians because he fears the strange un-whiteness of his own features. An artist must be free to choose what he does, certainly, but he must also never be afraid to do what he might choose.

Let the blare of Negro jazz bands and the bellowing voice of Bessie Smith singing the Blues penetrate the closed ears of the colored near-intellectuals until they listen and perhaps understand. Let Paul Robeson singing Water Boy, and Rudolph Fisher writing about the streets of Harlem, and Jean Toomer holding the heart of Georgia in his hands, and Aaron Douglas drawing strange black fantasies cause the smug Negro middle class to turn from their white, respectable, ordinary books and papers to catch a glimmer of their own beauty. We younger Negro artists who create now intend to express our individual dark-skinned selves without fear or shame. If white people are pleased we are glad. If they are not, it doesn't matter. We know we are beautiful. And ugly too. The tom-tom cries and the tom-tom laughs. If colored people are pleased we are glad. If they are not, their displeasure doesn't matter either. We build our temples for tomorrow, strong as we know how, and we stand on top of the mountain, free within ourselves.

Source: Langston Hughes, "The Negro Artist and the Racial Mountain," *The Nation*, June 23, 1926, pp. 692–93.

The New Negro Movement and the Harlem Renaissance marked a defining chapter in African American history—one in which art, literature, and music became tools of both resistance and reimagination. In rejecting imposed stereotypes and asserting cultural agency, Black artists and intellectuals redefined what it meant to be African American in the modern world. From the philosophical writings of Alain Locke to the poetic declarations of Langston Hughes, this era gave voice to a generation determined to create on its own terms. The Harlem Renaissance was not simply a moment of artistic achievement. It was a cultural revolution that celebrated Black life, affirmed Black humanity, and laid the intellectual and creative foundations for future movements for justice and liberation.

TIP

Address All Parts of the FRQ

Free-response questions are often divided into multiple parts—labeled A, B, C, and D. To earn full credit, be sure to respond to each part separately and clearly, directly addressing what each subquestion is asking. Skipping even one section can lower your overall score.

A New Voice in Harlem

The Harlem Renaissance gave rise to the New Negro—bold, proud, creative, and unapologetically Black. Writers, musicians, and artists used their talents to rewrite how America saw Black life.

You're Practicing: Exploring how art challenges dominant narratives.

Connect This To: Expression, pride, and cultural power.

Theme: Cultural Expression and Identity

Practice: Contextualize

The Harlem Renaissance of the 1920s marked a flourishing of Black cultural, intellectual, and political expression, often framed as part of the broader New Negro movement.

(A) Define the term New Negro in the context of the Harlem Renaissance.
(B) Explain how the Harlem Renaissance reflected broader historical developments in African American life, including migration, urbanization, and activism.
(C) Contextualize how this cultural moment reshaped ideas about Black identity and racial pride in the United States.

SAMPLE RESPONSES

(A) The term New Negro referred to a confident, self-assertive African American identity that rejected the subservient stereotypes of the past and demanded full social, political, and cultural equality, as articulated by intellectuals like Alain Locke in *The New Negro* (1925), activist W. E. B. Du Bois, and poet Claude McKay.

This concept embraced racial pride, artistic achievement, and political activism, emphasizing the dignity and potential of African Americans in contrast to racist caricatures that had dominated mainstream culture since Reconstruction.

(B) The Harlem Renaissance emerged from the Great Migration, when hundreds of thousands of African Americans moved from the rural South to northern cities like New York, Chicago, and Detroit in search of jobs, safety from racial violence, and greater political participation.

Harlem became a vibrant cultural hub where intellectuals, artists, and activists—such as Langston Hughes, Zora Neale Hurston, and Marcus Garvey—interacted in salons, theaters, and political organizations to advance the cause of racial equality.

The period also coincided with a surge in African American activism, from the NAACP's legal campaigns against disenfranchisement and lynching to A. Philip Randolph's labor organizing for Black workers in northern industries.

(C) The Harlem Renaissance fostered a renewed sense of racial pride by celebrating African heritage, promoting the beauty of Black life, and rejecting assimilationist ideals, as seen in the works of Aaron Douglas, Bessie Smith, and Countee Cullen.

This cultural flowering challenged mainstream American perceptions of African Americans by elevating Black voices in literature, music, and art, leading to the global recognition of jazz, blues, and African-inspired visual aesthetics.

The movement laid the intellectual and cultural groundwork for later civil rights struggles by demonstrating the power of cultural expression as a form of activism, inspiring mid-20th-century leaders like James Baldwin, Nina Simone, and the organizers of the Black Arts Movement.

Skills Assessed: Contextualize historical developments; use sources and evidence; analyze relationships among developments.

Topic 3.12 Photography and Social Change

Key Terms

- Visual activism
- James Van Der Zee—Harlem Renaissance photographer
- Daguerreotypes of Black abolitionists
- *Whipped Peter* image—abolitionist iconography
- Du Bois's Paris Exposition photo collection (1900)
- Photographs as counternarrative
- Dignity and beauty in representation
- Black identity and visual culture

What can a photograph do that a speech cannot? In the twentieth century, African Americans wielded the lens as both a mirror and a weapon—documenting truth, challenging injustice, and reshaping public consciousness. In a society that distorted Black life, photography became a means of reclaiming it. Throughout the twentieth century, African Americans used photography and other visual media as powerful tools for advocacy, resistance, and cultural affirmation. In the face of racist propaganda and mainstream misrepresentation, Black photographers and documentarians captured the dignity, struggle, and everyday humanity of their communities. From studio portraits to photojournalism, visual media exposed the harsh realities of segregation, racial violence, and poverty while simultaneously elevating Black beauty, resilience, and joy. These images did not merely reflect the times. These images reshaped them, helping to mobilize public opinion and energize movements for civil rights and social transformation.

After engaging with this topic, scholars will be able to:

- Explain how African Americans used photography and visual media to advocate for civil rights and social justice.
- Analyze the cultural and political impact of photographs in shaping the public understanding of Black life.
- Identify key Black photographers, photojournalists, and visual artists who contributed to twentieth-century movements for change.
- Evaluate how photography challenged racist imagery and redefined the visual narrative of African American identity.

Reclaiming the Image: Photography as a Tool of Resistance

In response to a media landscape saturated with racist caricatures and dehumanizing imagery, African American scholars, artists, and activists turned to photography as a tool of self-representation and political resistance. Visual media offered a way to directly confront the lies of white supremacy and the visual narratives that upheld Jim Crow segregation. By producing their own images—dignified, deliberate, and authentic—African Americans challenged the pseudoscience of racial inferiority and the mainstream media's role in justifying Black oppression. Whether used in pamphlets, newspapers, or exhibition spaces, these photographs offered undeniable evidence of Black humanity, complexity, and worth.

A New Visual Aesthetic: Celebrating Black Life and Heritage

During the New Negro movement, African American photographers helped forge a distinctly Black aesthetic grounded in cultural pride and the beauty of everyday life. Their work rejected the gaze of white voyeurism and instead reflected a community-centered perspective, where Black families, traditions, and spaces were celebrated. Drawing from African heritage, folk culture, and the vibrant life of urban Black America, these artists captured their subjects with elegance and intimacy. Their photographs became visual affirmations—statements of self-love, cultural depth, and artistic control at a time when visual representation was a political act.

James Van Der Zee and the Portrait of a People

As one of the most influential photographers of the Harlem Renaissance, James Van Der Zee played a pivotal role in reshaping how African Americans were seen by both themselves and the wider world. Through carefully composed portraits, Van Der Zee documented Black life in Harlem during the early twentieth century—capturing weddings, church gatherings, family milestones, artistic performances, and scenes of everyday leisure. His work highlighted the sophistication, style, and dignity of Black urban life and embodied the ideals of the New Negro. By presenting African Americans not as caricatures but as fully human—cultured, proud, and beautiful—Van Der Zee's photography contributed to a global reimagining of Black identity.

Selections from James Van Der Zee's Portfolio of Eighteen Photographs, 1905–1938

These selected photographs from James Van Der Zee's influential *Portfolio of Eighteen Photographs* offer a striking visual narrative of African American life in Harlem during the early twentieth century. Van Der Zee's lens captured not only the physical likenesses of his subjects but also their aspirations, identities, and social context during a period of intense cultural transformation.

Taken in 1915, *Miss Suzie Porter, Harlem* is one of James Van Der Zee's early portraits that captures the elegance, poise, and self-assurance of Black womanhood during the formative years of the New Negro era. Suzie Porter, shown in formal attire and composed with intention, stands as a symbol of dignity and upward mobility within Harlem's growing middle class. Van Der Zee's photographic choices—careful lighting, graceful composition, and refined setting—challenge prevailing stereotypes and offer a counternarrative to dominant portrayals of African American women at the time. This portrait exemplifies how Black photographers used their craft to affirm beauty, pride, and self-definition in a society intent on denying all three.

Garveyite Family, Harlem (1924) situates its subjects within the backdrop of Marcus Garvey's Black nationalist movement, signaling the rise of political consciousness and diasporic pride within the community. *Swimming Team, Harlem* (1925) showcases African American youth engaged in an organized sport—an image of physical discipline, teamwork, and leisure that countered narratives of Black pathology. Finally, *Couple, Harlem* (1932) captures intimacy, dignity, and love in a moment of shared connection. It reflects Van Der Zee's consistent emphasis on portraying the interior lives and emotional depth of Black subjects.

Together, these photographs function as visual counternarratives—refinements of the New Negro ideal and powerful correctives to the dehumanizing images that often dominated mainstream media. Van Der Zee's work not only documented the aesthetics of Harlem life but also offered a celebration of Black pride, prosperity, and cultural complexity during the Harlem Renaissance.

Throughout the twentieth century, photography emerged as one of the most powerful instruments in the struggle for African American self-representation and social transformation. Black photographers like James Van Der Zee did more than document—they redefined the visual language of dignity, family, resistance, and cultural pride. In an era marked by dehumanizing imagery and systemic erasure, these artists turned the lens inward, creating archives that honored the full humanity of Black life. Their images confronted injustice, celebrated community, and shaped public memory. By reclaiming the right to be seen on their own terms, African Americans used photography not only as art, but as activism—forever altering the way history sees them.

For a more in-depth analysis of these images and their historical significance, scholars are encouraged to view them online at the Gilder Lehrman Institute of American History for free at: https://www.gilderlehrman.org/ap-african-american-studies/unit-3/black-organizing-early-twentieth-century#par-16559.

Snapping Back at Injustice

From everyday portraits to protest photography, Black photographers used the camera to show truth. They documented beauty, family, poverty, and racism—and reminded the world that every image tells a story.

You're Practicing: Reading visuals as primary sources.

Connect This To: Representation, dignity, and activism.

Theme: Media and Memory

Practice: Explain the Significance or Importance

In the early twentieth century, photography became a powerful tool for documenting Black life and exposing racial injustice.

(A) Identify one prominent African American photographer or photographic project from this period.
(B) Explain how photography was used to challenge racial stereotypes or promote social change.
(C) Analyze the significance of photography in shaping public perception and advancing African American civil rights.

SAMPLE RESPONSES

(A) James Van Der Zee, a leading Harlem Renaissance photographer, documented Black urban life through portraits such as *Miss Suzie Porter, Harlem* (1915), *Garveyite Family, Harlem* (1924), and *Couple, Harlem* (1932), each capturing elegance, political consciousness, and dignity.

His *Portfolio of Eighteen Photographs* (1905–1938) celebrated weddings, family milestones, and community gatherings, challenging the dehumanizing stereotypes of African Americans in mainstream media.

(B) Van Der Zee's refined portraits, including *Swimming Team, Harlem* (1925) and images of Marcus Garvey's followers, countered prevailing images of African Americans as poor, unrefined, or dangerous by depicting sophistication, leisure, and political pride.

Du Bois's curated photo collection for the 1900 Paris Exposition presented African Americans in professional dress, academic settings, and respectable domestic environments, challenging pseudoscientific racism and promoting a counternarrative of Black progress.

Abolitionist and civil rights movements also used photography as political evidence, as seen in the *Whipped Peter* image during the 1860s, which exposed the brutality of slavery and served as an early example of visual activism influencing public opinion.

(C) Photography served as visual activism, humanizing African Americans for audiences at home and abroad, much like Van Der Zee's Harlem portraits, Du Bois's Paris Exposition collection, and Gordon Parks's later *Life* magazine photo essays on segregation and poverty.

By creating visual archives that celebrated Black beauty, family, and community pride, photographers like Van Der Zee helped define the New Negro ideal and fostered racial pride that would fuel later civil rights and Black Arts movements.

These images became lasting cultural touchstones, shaping public memory and offering undeniable proof of African American dignity, resilience, and cultural complexity during an era dominated by racist caricatures.

Skills Assessed: Explain the significance of historical developments; use sources and evidence; analyze relationships among developments.

KEY TAKEAWAYS

1. **Double Consciousness and the Tension of Identity**
   - W. E. B. Du Bois's concept of double consciousness describes the internal conflict of being both Black and American in a racially segregated society.
   - This theme reflects the psychological and cultural balancing act required for African Americans to navigate systemic racism while asserting full personhood.
2. **Institutional Power and Community Autonomy**
   - In response to exclusion, African Americans built an array of institutions—churches, schools, newspapers, hospitals, and civic organizations—to foster self-reliance.
   - These spaces served as both protective enclaves and launching pads for broader activism and empowerment.
3. **Black Women as Movement Architects**
   - Black women were key organizers and thought leaders, from suffrage and temperance to education and mutual aid.
   - Figures like Mary Church Terrell, Anna Julia Cooper, and Frances Ellen Watkins Harper advanced gender justice within broader freedom struggles.
4. **HBCUs and Black Intellectualism**
   - Historically Black colleges and universities (HBCUs) cultivated generations of educators, activists, and professionals.
   - These institutions embodied the power of education as a liberatory tool and a site of cultural production.
5. **Fraternal Organizations and Social Networks**
   - Black Greek letter organizations and fraternal lodges fostered leadership, mutual aid, and solidarity.
   - They filled social, political, and economic gaps left by white exclusion and provided platforms for resistance and advocacy.
6. **The New Negro Movement: Cultural and Political Assertion**
   - The New Negro philosophy embraced assertiveness, pride, and self-definition, challenging earlier portrayals of Black passivity.
   - This movement catalyzed the Harlem Renaissance and promoted political activism, artistic expression, and economic independence.
7. **Photography as Social Documentation**
   - Black photographers used their art to capture dignity, joy, resistance, and struggle in African American life.
   - These visual narratives countered racist imagery and chronicled everyday Black resilience in an era of segregation.

Practice Multiple-Choice Questions

DIRECTIONS: Pick the letter that best answers the following questions.

Questions 1 through 3 refer to the following.

An Advertisement for Madam C. J. Walker Products, 1906–1950

1. The advertisement for Madam C. J. Walker Products (1906–1950) is most useful for understanding which of the following developments in early twentieth-century African American life?

   (A) The rise of interracial business partnerships in the beauty industry
   (B) The reliance on European beauty standards by African American entrepreneurs
   (C) The use of consumer culture to promote racial pride and economic self-sufficiency
   (D) The decline of Black-owned businesses due to Jim Crow restrictions

2. Which of the following best explains how Madam C. J. Walker's advertisement challenged dominant cultural narratives of the time?

   (A) It portrayed African American women as independent, desirable consumers and producers in a society that often denied them agency.
   (B) It offered humorous caricatures of Black life as a means of softening racial tensions in national markets.
   (C) It promoted the idea of racial integration through shared beauty standards.
   (D) It used scientific arguments to appeal to white investors and mainstream beauty salons.

3. Which broader historical context helps explain the significance of Madam C. J. Walker's advertising efforts?

   (A) The formation of Black Greek letter organizations and their influence on educational leadership
   (B) The Second Morrill Act and the development of land-grant HBCUs
   (C) The New Negro movement's emphasis on self-definition and cultural pride
   (D) The Harlem Renaissance's government-funded public art programs

Questions 4 through 6 refer to the following.

The Clock Used by the Citizen's Savings and Trust Company (1920–2013)

4. What does the clock used by the Citizens Savings and Trust Company (1920–2013) best symbolize in the context of African American history?

   (A) The decline of Black banking institutions during the early twentieth century due to federal restrictions
   (B) The rise of Black consumerism driven by the Harlem Renaissance
   (C) The long-standing commitment to Black economic autonomy and financial self-reliance
   (D) The integration of African Americans into white-owned financial institutions during the postwar period

5. Which of the following historical developments provides the most relevant context for interpreting the significance of the Citizens Savings and Trust Company clock?

   (A) The creation of New Deal–era social welfare programs in the 1930s
   (B) The emergence of Black-owned financial institutions as a response to segregation and economic exclusion
   (C) The desegregation of public schools following *Brown v. Board of Education*
   (D) The growth of multinational corporations and their influence on American consumer banking

6. What does the longevity of the clock used by the Citizens Savings and Trust Company (1920–2013) suggest about Black community institutions during the twentieth century?

   (A) They often relied on short-term charitable donations and had difficulty surviving past the 1950s.
   (B) They lacked legitimacy and struggled to gain the support of African American consumers.
   (C) They were built on grassroots support and reflected a deep investment in racial self-determination.
   (D) They were quickly absorbed by white institutions once integration was legally mandated.

Answer Explanations

1. **(C)** Madam C. J. Walker used advertising not only to sell products but to advance racial pride and economic empowerment. Her ads often included positive imagery of African American women, encouraging self-care, professionalism, and financial success. This approach aligned with a broader trend in the Black community of using commerce and image making as tools for racial uplift. Choice (A) is incorrect because the beauty brand was independently Black-owned and operated. Madam C. J. Walker did not rely on interracial partnerships. Rather, her work represented a significant moment in Black entrepreneurship, especially for Black women in business. Choice (B) is incorrect because, although beauty advertisements in the early twentieth century often promoted Eurocentric features, Madam C. J. Walker's products emphasized hair care and beauty specifically designed for African American women. Although some elements of her branding may have reflected contemporary aesthetics, her broader mission celebrated Black beauty and independence. Choice (D) is incorrect because the advertisement itself reflects the growth and success of a Black-owned business during segregation—not decline. Madam C. J. Walker's enterprise flourished in spite of Jim Crow and became a model of Black economic resilience.

2. **(A)** The advertisement reframed the image of Black women during an era when dominant media often portrayed them as inferior, invisible, or caricatured. Madam C. J. Walker's brand presented African American women as confident, professional, and deserving of luxury and care. The ad also positioned Black women not just as consumers but as agents of economic progress—as sales agents, entrepreneurs, and community leaders. Choice (B) is incorrect because there is no evidence that Walker's advertisements relied on caricature or humor. In fact, her ads were notable for their dignified tone and deliberate rejection of racist visual tropes commonly seen in mainstream media. Choice (C) is incorrect because Madam C. J. Walker's products were created specifically for African American hair and beauty needs. The brand celebrated distinctively Black features and aesthetics rather than promoting assimilation to white beauty standards. Choice (D) is incorrect because, although Walker was an effective businesswoman, her advertisements were directed at Black consumers—not white investors or white-owned salons. Her appeal was rooted in community uplift, not scientific authority or cross-racial marketing.

3. **(C)** The New Negro movement emphasized reclaiming cultural identity, promoting Black pride, and rejecting degrading stereotypes. Madam C. J. Walker's advertisements reflected and reinforced these values by celebrating Black beauty and financial independence. Her business model, imagery, and philanthropy were all expressions of the movement's ethos of self-definition and racial uplift. Choice (A) is incorrect because, although Black Greek letter organizations played a vital role in developing Black leadership, especially within higher education, they are not the most relevant context for interpreting a commercial advertisement rooted in beauty, self-image, and entrepreneurship. Choice (B) is incorrect because the Second Morrill Act of 1890 focused on the creation of land-grant institutions for Black students. This legislative development pertains more to higher education access than to Black business and visual culture. Choice (D) is incorrect because, although the Harlem Renaissance was part of this broader cultural awakening, most artists during that era operated without substantial government funding. Public art programs tied to federal support were more typical of the New Deal era, which began in the 1930s—well after Walker had established her brand.

4. **(C)** The clock, which was visible to the public for nearly a century, represents the endurance of a Black-owned financial institution and the broader commitment to Black economic independence. It literally measured time, but symbolically it measured progress and resilience. Choice (A) is incorrect because the clock represents endurance, not decline. Although Black banks did face challenges, this clock marked a lasting and stable presence in the community, not a collapse due to policy. Choice (B) is incorrect because, although the Harlem Renaissance fostered cultural pride and increased consumer engagement, this clock predates and outlasts that era. Its meaning is tied more to institutional stability than to cultural trends. Choice (D) is incorrect because this artifact commemorates a Black institution serving Black communities, not integration into white-owned financial systems. It reflects self-sufficiency, not assimilation.

5. **(B)** Black-owned banks like Citizens Savings and Trust were established precisely because African Americans were denied equitable access to white-owned financial institutions. These banks emerged to support community lending, savings, and business growth in the face of systemic exclusion. Choice (A) is incorrect because, although New Deal programs addressed poverty and economic reform, they often excluded or marginalized African Americans. The founding of Citizens Savings and Trust predates the New Deal and was not directly tied to those federal reforms. Choice (C) is incorrect because this question focuses on financial institutions, not education. *Brown v. Board of Education* is significant but unrelated to the clock's symbolism. Choice (D) is incorrect because the rise of multinational banks occurred much later and was not a factor in the founding of this institution. The Citizens Savings and Trust Company served local Black communities, not global markets.

6. **(C)** The clock's long-standing presence reflects how deeply Black communities invested in their own institutions. These institutions were not temporary or symbolic. They were the economic backbone of many neighborhoods, representing the ethos of self-help, solidarity, and economic agency. Choice (A) is incorrect because Citizens Savings and Trust lasted nearly a century—far beyond the 1950s—and was sustained through sound financial practices and community support, not short-term charity. Choice (B) is incorrect because the very existence and longevity of the clock and the institution it represents disproves the claim that such institutions lacked community support. In fact, they thrived because of it. Choice (D) is incorrect because many Black institutions, including Citizens Savings and Trust, remained independent even after integration. They were not quickly absorbed. In fact, many continued to serve specific community needs well into the twenty-first century.

10

Africa in the Imagination: Black Artistry, Movement, and Global Liberation

Key Themes

- Africa as both a symbol and a destination of identity, pride, and liberation
- Cultural production (poetry, performance, film) as a site of activism
- Migration as transformation—urbanization reshapes politics and expression
- Global Black solidarity through education and mass movements
- UNIA as a milestone in international Black nationalism and diasporic vision

TIMELINE

Date/Period	Event/Development	Related Topics
1910s–1930s	**Harlem Renaissance poets** like **Langston Hughes**, **Claude McKay**, and **Georgia Douglas Johnson** explore Africa as a source of identity, pride, and historical connection	Topic 3.13—Envisioning Africa in Poetry
1921	**Langston Hughes travels to West Africa**, strengthening diasporic literary themes	Topic 3.13—Harlem Renaissance Poetry
Early 1900s–1930s	**Black musicians and performers** (e.g., Duke Ellington, Paul Robeson, Josephine Baker) influence global culture and challenge stereotypes	Topic 3.14—Black Performance in Music and Theater
1920s	**Race films** and theater—produced by and for Black audiences—emerge as forms of cultural resistance	Topic 3.14—Film and Theater
Early 1900s onward	**Carter G. Woodson** founds **Negro History Week** in 1926 (precursor to Black History Month)	Topic 3.15—Black History Education
Late 20th century	**African American Studies departments** established after student protests (e.g., at San Francisco State, 1968)	Topic 3.15—African American Studies
1916–1970	**The Great Migration**—over 6 million African Americans relocate from the rural South to the urban North and West	Topic 3.16—The Great Migration
1910s–1940s	**Afro-Caribbean migration** increases to U.S. cities like New York, Boston, and Miami; fuels Harlem Renaissance	Topic 3.17—Afro-Caribbean Migration

Date/Period	Event/Development	Related Topics
1914	**Marcus Garvey founds the Universal Negro Improvement Association (UNIA)** in Jamaica	Topic 3.18—UNIA
1916–1927	UNIA expands globally after Garvey relocates to the United States; promotes **pan-Africanism**, Black self-determination, and the Back to Africa movement	Topic 3.18—Garveyism and Global Liberation
1920	UNIA holds the **International Convention of the Negro Peoples of the World**; introduces a Black nationalist flag	Topic 3.18—UNIA and Nationhood

Topic 3.13 Envisioning Africa in Harlem Renaissance Poetry

Key Terms

- Cultural reclamation—Africa as ancestral homeland and symbol of pride
- Pan-African identity
- Harlem Renaissance poets—Langston Hughes, Claude McKay, Georgia Douglas Johnson, Anne Spencer
- Romanticized vs. politicized Africa
- Spiritual connection to Africa
- Literary nationalism
- "The Negro Speaks of Rivers"—Langston Hughes
- Symbolism of the Nile, Congo, and pyramids

What does it mean to remember a homeland you have never seen? For many Harlem Renaissance poets, Africa was more than a continent—it was a symbol of ancestral pride, historical longing, and cultural reclamation. Through verse, they reached across the Atlantic to reimagine connections severed by slavery and sustained through memory, art, and identity.

During the Harlem Renaissance, a number of African American poets turned to Africa as a central motif in their work. They imagined the continent not only as a place of origin but as a source of cultural strength and artistic inspiration.

In the aftermath of enslavement, forced migration, and systemic erasure, these writers used poetry to reclaim ties to African heritage and to resist the historical dehumanization of Black identity. Africa became a poetic landscape for exploring themes of displacement, diaspora, resistance, and spiritual connection. Although interpretations of Africa varied—from romanticized visions of a lost homeland to critiques of colonialism—the desire to reconstruct a sense of historical rootedness unified much of this literary expression.

After engaging with this topic, scholars will be able to:

- Explain how Harlem Renaissance poets used Africa as a symbol of identity, pride, and historical memory.
- Analyze the different poetic strategies used to express connections to the African continent.
- Evaluate how the poetic reimagining of Africa served as a tool for resisting racism and affirming Black cultural heritage.
- Interpret selected poems that reflect diasporic consciousness and the impact of pan-African thought.

Diasporic Longing and Historical Disconnection

Harlem Renaissance writers, artists, and scholars frequently wrestled with both connection to and detachment from Africa as they confronted the enduring legacies of colonialism and the transatlantic slave trade. For African

Americans—descendants of people forcibly uprooted from their homelands—the question of belonging was complicated by generational distance, cultural loss, and the violence of displacement. Poetry became a means of navigating this dual consciousness: of being rooted in America yet spiritually and imaginatively tethered to Africa. In exploring this tension, Harlem Renaissance poets framed Africa as both a symbolic homeland and a site of historical disruption, using their work to reimagine what had been violently obscured.

Reframing the Image of Africa

In an era when dominant narratives depicted Africa as primitive, uncivilized, or lacking historical value, Harlem Renaissance poets used imagery to challenge and subvert these stereotypes. Through their verses, they presented Africa as a land of majesty, depth, and cultural richness. Writers such as Countee Cullen and Langston Hughes depicted African landscapes, kingdoms, and traditions not as relics of savagery but as sources of dignity and spiritual beauty. These poetic choices served to restore agency to African people and counteract the colonial gaze that had long distorted the continent's global image.

Personal Reflection and Pan-African Identity

For many Harlem Renaissance poets, Africa was not simply a geographic reference. Instead, it was a deeply personal symbol woven into questions of identity, memory, and heritage. Poems often reflect an inward journey, a search for meaning and belonging in the face of historical rupture. Writers like Claude McKay and Georgia Douglas Johnson used poetic reflection to express feelings of yearning, alienation, and rediscovery, situating Africa within the evolving contours of African American selfhood. In doing so, their work contributed to a broader diasporic consciousness and laid the cultural groundwork for emerging pan-African movements that sought solidarity across the African world.

Published in 1922, "Heritage" by Gwendolyn Bennett is a powerful meditation on ancestral memory, diasporic identity, and the spiritual pull of Africa. Writing at the height of the Harlem Renaissance, Bennett explores the emotional and cultural complexities of being African American, born in the United States yet bound by an invisible lineage to a distant, often romanticized homeland. Through vivid sensory imagery and rhythmic verse, she conveys both the pain of historical dislocation and the longing to reclaim a sense of origin and belonging. "Heritage" reflects how Harlem Renaissance poets infused their work with personal reflection and collective memory, using poetry to bridge the gap between past and present, Africa and America.

"Heritage" by Gwendolyn Bennett, 1922

I want to see the slim palm-trees,
Pulling at the clouds
With little pointed fingers. . . .

I want to see lithe Negro girls,
Etched dark against the sky
While sunset lingers.

I want to hear the silent sands,
Singing to the moon
Before the Sphinx-still face. . . .

I want to hear the chanting
Around a heathen fire
Of a strange black race.

I want to breathe the Lotus flow'r,
Sighing to the stars
With tendrils drinking at the Nile. . . .

I want to feel the surging
Of my sad people's soul
Hidden by a minstrel-smile.

Source: Gwendolyn B. Bennett, "Heritage," *Opportunity* 1, no. 12 (December 1923): 371.

Countee Cullen's 1925 poem "Heritage" is a landmark work of Harlem Renaissance literature that grapples with the tension between ancestral connection and cultural alienation. Written in a moment of rising pan-African consciousness, the poem reflects Cullen's personal struggle to reconcile his African heritage with his Christian upbringing and Western education. Through vivid imagery and conflicted introspection, Cullen presents Africa as both a spiritual inheritance and a source of emotional dissonance—yearned for yet unfamiliar.

"Heritage" embodies the complexity of diasporic identity. It captures the internal contradictions many African Americans faced as they sought to define themselves in a world shaped by racial displacement and historical rupture. The poem stands as a profound example of how Harlem Renaissance poets used verse to navigate the psychological and cultural legacies of slavery and colonialism.

"Heritage" by Countee Cullen, 1925

What is Africa to me:
Copper sun or scarlet sea,
Jungle star or jungle track,
Strong bronzed men, or regal black
Women from whose loins I sprang
When the birds of Eden sang?
One three centuries removed
From the scenes his fathers loved,
Spicy grove, cinnamon tree,
What is Africa to me?

So I lie, who all day long
Want no sound except the song
Sung by wild barbaric birds
Goading massive jungle herds,
Juggernauts of flesh that pass
Trampling tall defiant grass
Where young forest lovers lie,
Plighting troth beneath the sky.
So I lie, who always hear,
Though I cram against my ear
Both my thumbs, and keep them there,
Great drums throbbing through the air.
So I lie, whose fount of pride,
Dear distress, and joy allied,
Is my somber flesh and skin,
With the dark blood dammed within
Like great pulsing tides of wine
That, I fear, must burst the fine
Channels of the chafing net
Where they surge and foam and fret.

Africa? A book one thumbs
Listlessly, till slumber comes.
Unremembered are her bats
Circling through the night, her cats
Crouching in the river reeds,
Stalking gentle flesh that feeds
By the river brink; no more
Does the bugle-throated roar
Cry that monarch claws have leapt
From the scabbards where they slept.
Silver snakes that once a year
Doff the lovely coats you wear,
Seek no covert in your fear
Lest a mortal eye should see;
What's your nakedness to me?
Here no leprous flowers rear
Fierce corollas in the air;

Here no bodies sleek and wet,
Dripping mingled rain and sweat,
Tread the savage measures of
Jungle boys and girls in love.
What is last year's snow to me,
Last year's anything? The tree
Budding yearly must forget
How its past arose or set—
Bough and blossom, flower, fruit,
Even what shy bird with mute
Wonder at her travail there,
Meekly labored in its hair.
One three centuries removed
From the scenes his fathers loved,
Spicy grove, cinnamon tree,
What is Africa to me?

So I lie, who find no peace
Night or day, no slight release
From the unremittent beat
Made by cruel padded feet
Walking through my body's street.
Up and down they go, and back,
Treading out a jungle track.
So I lie, who never quite
Safely sleep from rain at night—
I can never rest at all
When the rain begins to fall;
Like a soul gone mad with pain
I must match its weird refrain;
Ever must I twist and squirm,

Writhing like a baited worm,
While its primal measures drip
Through my body, crying, "Strip!
Doff this new exuberance.
Come and dance the Lover's Dance!"
In an old remembered way
Rain works on me night and day.

Quaint, outlandish heathen gods
Black men fashion out of rods,
Clay, and brittle bits of stone,
In a likeness like their own,
My conversion came high-priced;
I belong to Jesus Christ,
Preacher of humility;
Heathen gods are naught to me.

Father, Son, and Holy Ghost,
So I make an idle boast;
Jesus of the twice-turned cheek,
Lamb of God, although I speak
With my mouth thus, in my heart
Do I play a double part.

Ever at Thy glowing altar
Must my heart grow sick and falter,
Wishing He I served were black,
Thinking then it would not lack
Precedent of pain to guide it,
Let who would or might deride it;
Surely then this flesh would know
Yours had borne a kindred woe.
Lord, I fashion dark gods, too,
Daring even to give You
Dark despairing features where,

Crowned with dark rebellious hair,
Patience wavers just so much as
Mortal grief compels, while touches
Quick and hot, of anger, rise
To smitten cheek and weary eyes.
Lord, forgive me if my need
Sometimes shapes a human creed.
All day long and all night through,
One thing only must I do:
Quench my pride and cool my blood,
Lest I perish in the flood.
Lest a hidden ember set
Timber that I thought was wet
Burning like the dryest flax,

Melting like the merest wax,
Lest the grave restore its dead.
Not yet has my heart or head
In the least way realized
They and I are civilized.

Source: Countee Cullen, "Heritage," *Color*. New York: Harper & Bros., 1925, pp. 36–41.

Africa as Inspiration, Not Stereotype

Writers in the Harlem Renaissance didn't just look to Africa as a faraway land—they saw it as a source of strength and identity. Through poetry, they reimagined Africa as vibrant, historic, and deeply connected to the Black experience.

You're Practicing: Interpreting symbols in literature.

Connect This To: Cultural memory and pride.

Theme: Identity and Cultural Expression

Practice: Explain Continuities or Changes over Time

Harlem Renaissance poets often invoked Africa as a cultural and historical reference point to affirm Black identity and heritage.

(A) Identify one Harlem Renaissance poet who wrote about Africa.

(B) Explain how that poet's representation of Africa reflected a shift in African American cultural expression compared with earlier periods.

(C) Analyze how these poetic visions of Africa contributed to evolving ideas of diasporic consciousness and pride.

SAMPLE RESPONSES

(A) Langston Hughes, one of the most celebrated Harlem Renaissance poets, wrote works such as *The Negro Speaks of Rivers* (1921) and *African Dance* (1926), which directly invoked Africa as a source of cultural and historical pride.

His poetry connected African American identity to African heritage, drawing imagery from the Nile, Congo, and other African landscapes to root Black identity in an ancient and noble lineage.

(B) Hughes's celebration of Africa marked a shift from the 19th-century tendency to downplay African heritage in favor of assimilation into white American norms, instead embracing African roots as a central element of Black identity.

Unlike earlier works that sometimes portrayed Africa as distant or primitive, Hughes presented it as a source of spiritual depth and historical legitimacy, linking it to pride, resilience, and shared heritage across the diaspora.

His portrayal paralleled the New Negro movement's rejection of racial inferiority narratives, echoing the ideas of thinkers like Alain Locke and Marcus Garvey, who championed African pride and pan-African unity.

(C) By invoking Africa as a shared ancestral homeland, Hughes and other poets like Countee Cullen (*Heritage*, 1925) helped foster a sense of global Black unity and diasporic consciousness that transcended national boundaries.

These works encouraged African Americans to see themselves as part of a larger pan-African community engaged in a collective struggle for dignity, freedom, and cultural affirmation.

The poetic visions of Africa inspired subsequent generations of Black artists and activists, influencing movements from the Negritude literary movement in Francophone Africa and the Caribbean to the Black Arts Movement in the United States.

Skills Assessed: Explain continuities or changes over time; use sources and evidence; analyze relationships among developments.

Topic 3.14 *Symphony in Black*: Black Performance in Music, Theater, and Film

Key Terms

- Duke Ellington—*Symphony in Black* (1935)
- Paul Robeson—actor, singer, and civil rights activist
- Race films—movies with Black casts for Black audiences
- Oscar Micheaux—pioneering Black filmmaker
- *Shuffle Along* (1921)—landmark all-Black Broadway musical
- Minstrelsy and resistance—reclaiming performance space
- Cotton Club—segregated venue showcasing Black artists
- Cultural diplomacy through performance

In the shadows of segregation, African American artists lit the stage, screen, and concert hall with brilliance. Although denied full participation in American democracy, Black performers reshaped American culture. They elevated the everyday, resisted caricature, and turned rhythm, drama, and voice into powerful forms of expression and protest. During the 1930s and 1940s, African Americans made transformative contributions to American music, theater, and film, often redefining the genres they entered.

In music, jazz and blues evolved into sophisticated art forms that carried the weight of Black life—its joys, sorrows, and hopes—into clubs, across radio waves, and into concert halls across the nation. At the same time, African American playwrights and performers challenged the racial constraints of the stage, while pioneering Black filmmakers and actors disrupted Hollywood's stereotypical portrayals with complex characters and bold storytelling. The period was marked by both institutional exclusion and creative innovation. African American performers used their artistry to affirm identity, humanize their experiences, and shape national culture on their own terms.

After engaging with this topic, scholars will be able to:

- Describe how African American musicians influenced the development of jazz, blues, and other popular musical forms in the 1930s and 1940s.
- Analyze the contributions of African Americans to theater and film during the same period, including their efforts to challenge stereotypes and broaden representation.
- Evaluate how Black performers navigated and resisted racial limitations in performance industries.
- Connect Black artistic achievements to broader cultural and political movements for racial justice and creative autonomy.

The Rise of the Black Soundscape: Blues, Jazz, and the Broadcast Age

In the early twentieth century, African American musicians and entrepreneurs found new pathways to reach national audiences through the rise of the Harlem Renaissance, the Jazz Age, and radio broadcasting. As jazz clubs thrived in cities like New York and Chicago, Black-owned record labels began producing music that carried the voices of African American vocalists and instrumentalists beyond segregated venues. For the first time, genres like blues, gospel, and jazz, which were all rooted in Black cultural traditions, were broadcast across the country, reshaping American popular music. These genres became vehicles for storytelling, emotional depth, and spiritual expression, allowing Black artists to assert their creative authority in an industry that often exploited them.

Blues as Memory and Migration

Emerging from the spirituals and work songs of the enslaved, the blues served as both historical record and emotional outlet for African Americans in the post emancipation South. Initially performed with acoustic instruments and steeped in local vernacular, the blues evolved during the Great Migration when Black communities brought their sounds north. This migration gave rise to electrified blues, amplifying its themes of sorrow, resilience, love, and survival. Stylistic elements such as repetition, call and response, and improvisation created a dynamic musical form that honored ancestral memory while adapting to urban life. The blues offered more than entertainment. It conveyed a psychological and cultural truth about the Black experience in America.

Jazz as Cultural Innovation and American Art Form

Born in the streets of New Orleans and shaped by African American musical ingenuity, jazz emerged as one of the most original contributions to global culture. Drawing from blues, ragtime, and African rhythmic traditions, jazz evolved as a genre of complexity and improvisation. As African Americans migrated to cities like Chicago, New York, Detroit, and Los Angeles, new styles emerged—from swing and bebop to cool jazz and free jazz. Artists such as Duke Ellington, Count Basie, and Charlie Parker helped transform jazz into an international art form that maintained deep roots in Black cultural expression. Jazz was not only music. It was a declaration of freedom, artistry, and intellectual sophistication that stood in defiance of racial hierarchies.

Released in 1943, Duke Ellington's "It Don't Mean a Thing (If It Ain't Got That Swing)" is a defining anthem of the swing era and a testament to African American innovation in jazz. Blending sophisticated orchestration with infectious rhythm, the song captures the energy and improvisational spirit that made swing music a cultural force. With its iconic refrain, the piece not only popularized a new musical style but also affirmed Black artistry at the center of American popular music. Ellington's work helped elevate jazz from entertainment to high art, challenging racial barriers in the music industry.

> Scholars can listen Duke Ellington's song "It Don't Mean a Thing (If It Ain't Got That Swing)," recorded in 1943, on YouTube by going to https://youtu.be/qDQpZT3GhDg.

Even in an industry shaped by exclusion, African American performers carved out spaces of visibility and artistry on stages and screens. Black talent flourished in Harlem's cabarets, on Broadway, and increasingly in film. Productions like *Cabin in the Sky* (1943) showcased all-Black casts in major studio releases, while actors like Ethel Waters broke new ground in television, becoming the first African American to lead her own show in 1939. These breakthroughs occurred alongside persistent typecasting and limited roles. However, Black performers used every opportunity to portray complex characters and challenge dominant narratives. Whether through musicals, drama, or comedy, African American artists redefined what was possible in American entertainment—setting the stage for future generations of Black excellence in performance.

This image of Katherine Dunham in *Cabin in the Sky* (1940) captures the brilliance of one of the most influential African American performers and choreographers of the twentieth century. Dunham, known for blending African diasporic dance traditions with classical ballet and modern technique, brought both innovation and dignity to the Broadway stage. Her performance in *Cabin in the Sky*—a groundbreaking all-Black musical—helped redefine Black representation in American theater. It showcased the depth, grace, and complexity of Black movement and storytelling. Dunham's artistry embodied the cultural sophistication of African American performance during an era of profound racial limitation and creative resistance.

Ethel Waters's performance in *Cabin in the Sky* (1943) marked a historic moment in American film and Black performance. As one of the first African American women to star in a Hollywood studio film with an all-Black cast, Waters brought emotional depth, vocal power, and dramatic nuance to a role that challenged prevailing stereotypes. Her portrayal reflected the broader ambitions of the Harlem Renaissance generation: to assert the complexity of Black life on stage and screen. In doing so, Waters not only broke barriers in the entertainment industry but also helped pave the way for future generations of Black actresses and vocalists in American cinema.

Actress Katherine Dunham performing with others in the play *Cabin in the Sky*, 1940 (Source: Photo by George Karger/Getty Images)

The 1943 film *Cabin in the Sky* brought together an extraordinary cast of African American performers, including Ethel Waters, Lena Horne, Eddie "Rochester" Anderson, and Louis Armstrong. This ensemble production marked a significant moment in Hollywood history because it featured an all-Black cast in a major studio release at a time when African Americans were largely excluded from complex or leading roles. The film challenged industry norms by highlighting the talents of Black actors, musicians, and dancers in roles that, although still shaped by the limitations of the era, allowed for greater depth and humanity than most mainstream portrayals. The cast of *Cabin in the Sky* exemplifies how Black performers used their artistry to expand visibility and redefine representation on the American screen.

Cast of *Cabin in the Sky*, 1943
(Source: Unknown (MGM), public domain, via Wikimedia Commons)

In the 1930s and 1940s, African American artists transformed the cultural landscape of the United States through music, theater, and film. Despite facing systemic racism and exclusion, Black performers asserted their creative agency in spaces that had long marginalized their voices. From the innovation of jazz and blues to groundbreaking performances on Broadway and in Hollywood, African American artists redefined what it meant to be both Black and American in the performing arts. Their work not only challenged racial stereotypes but also laid the cultural foundation for future movements in civil rights, Black artistic expression, and American popular culture.

Black Sound on the Global Stage

Black musicians, actors, and dancers didn't just entertain. They told stories, challenged stereotypes, and reshaped American culture. Whether in jazz clubs or on Broadway, their work transformed the stage.

You're Practicing: Evaluating artistic impact.

Connect This To: Expression, resistance, and innovation.

Theme: Cultural Power and Representation

Practice: Explain the Significance or Importance

During the early twentieth century, African American artists reshaped American culture through innovations in music, theater, and film, asserting creative control and challenging racial stereotypes.

(A) Identify one prominent African American performer or production from this era.

(B) Explain how the work reflected or resisted dominant cultural narratives.

(C) Analyze the broader significance of Black performance in shaping public discourse and advancing racial pride.

SAMPLE RESPONSES

(A) Katherine Dunham, a pioneering dancer, choreographer, and anthropologist, blended African diasporic dance traditions with ballet and modern technique, revolutionizing American concert dance. Her performance in the groundbreaking all-Black Broadway musical *Cabin in the Sky* (1940) displayed the grace, cultural depth, and technical mastery of African American performance on a national stage.

Alternatively, *Cabin in the Sky* (1943 film) itself was a landmark production featuring an extraordinary all-Black cast including Ethel Waters, Lena Horne, Eddie "Rochester" Anderson, and Louis Armstrong, making it one of the few major Hollywood films of its era to showcase Black performers in complex and leading roles.

(B) Dunham's choreography resisted the demeaning caricatures of Black movement common in vaudeville and minstrelsy, instead presenting African American dance as a sophisticated, world-class art form that commanded respect on Broadway and in Hollywood.

The 1943 film adaptation of *Cabin in the Sky* resisted dominant film industry stereotypes by giving African American performers space to portray characters with emotional complexity and dignity, even within the constraints of segregation-era Hollywood.

These performances paralleled earlier cultural resistance seen in *Shuffle Along* (1921), which broke barriers as one of the first Broadway hits written, produced, and performed by African Americans, introducing romance and artistry into portrayals of Black life.

(C) Productions such as *Cabin in the Sky*, along with the careers of artists like Katherine Dunham and Ethel Waters, redefined the possibilities for African American representation in mainstream entertainment by replacing stereotypes with artistry, sophistication, and cultural authenticity.

These performances played a role in shaping public discourse by proving that Black performers could succeed on the most prestigious stages and in major Hollywood productions, laying groundwork for later achievements by figures such as Harry Belafonte, Sidney Poitier, and Josephine Baker.

By asserting creative control and celebrating Black identity through music, theater, and film, African American performers of the 1930s and 1940s not only challenged racism in the arts but also inspired a generation of artists whose work became intertwined with the civil rights and Black cultural nationalism movements of the mid-20th century.

Skills Assessed: Explain the significance of historical developments; use sources and evidence; analyze relationships among developments.

Topic 3.15 Black History Education and African American Studies

Key Terms

- Carter G. Woodson—Father of Black History; founded Negro History Week (1926)
- Association for the Study of Negro Life and History (ASNLH)
- *Negro History Bulletin*
- Black history as counternarrative
- Institutional racism in education
- Inclusive curriculum movements
- Early Black Studies curricula in Black schools
- Activist scholarship

What happens when a people are systematically erased from the story of a nation? In the face of this erasure, African American educators, writers, and intellectuals refused silence. Instead, they built a tradition of truth telling—recovering the past to empower the present. During and after the New Negro movement, Black scholars, artists, and educators launched an urgent effort to research, write, and teach African American history. Denied visibility in mainstream curricula and textbooks, they recognized that education could be both a tool of oppression and a path to liberation. Leaders like Carter G. Woodson, Anna Julia Cooper, and W. E. B. Du Bois worked tirelessly to preserve Black historical memory and challenge the dominant narratives that dismissed or distorted the Black experience.

Their work laid the foundation for what would become African American Studies—a formal academic discipline that emerged in the mid-twentieth century but was built on a much older Black intellectual tradition. This tradition combined rigorous scholarship with racial justice advocacy, cultural affirmation, and a deep belief in the power of history to transform the future.

After engaging with this topic, scholars will be able to:

- Explain why New Negro movement leaders prioritized the teaching and preservation of Black history.
- Identify key figures in the early Black intellectual tradition and their contributions to historical education.
- Describe the development of African American Studies as a field and its connection to earlier movements for educational justice.
- Analyze how the act of studying Black history became a form of resistance and cultural empowerment.

Education as Empowerment: The New Negro's Call to Reclaim History

New Negro movement writers, artists, and educators recognized that the American school system had long reinforced the myth that Black people had contributed nothing of cultural or historical value. In response, they challenged Black students and communities to become agents of their own intellectual liberation. By encouraging the study of African and African American history, they sought not only to correct historical inaccuracies but to affirm the humanity, creativity, and resilience of Black people. Education became both a means of cultural recovery and a strategy for racial advancement, transforming classrooms into spaces of resistance and self-definition.

Literature as Curriculum: Making Black History Visible

Rejecting the notion that African Americans were a people without history or culture, New Negro movement leaders built an enduring body of literature, scholarship, and artistic production that elevated the African American past. Their efforts helped bring Black history into schools and libraries—reaching Black students of all ages and inspiring pride in cultural identity. Figures like Alain Locke, Langston Hughes, and Nella Larsen used literature and the arts as educational tools, while others collaborated with schools and community centers to develop curricula centered on the Black experience. These early initiatives laid the groundwork for a more inclusive educational landscape.

The Roots of a Tradition: Black Intellectual Life Before African American Studies

Long before African American Studies became a formal academic field in the late 1960s, a vibrant Black intellectual tradition had already been thriving for centuries. Educators, clergy, writers, and activists labored to document and interpret the lives of Black people in a world that sought to erase them. These thinkers combined scholarship with advocacy, insisting that Black experiences were not only worthy of study but central to understanding the history of the United States and the world. This tradition valued oral histories, archival work, lived experiences, and critical theory, offering a powerful foundation for future scholarship.

The African Free School and Early Black Educational Leadership

Established in the late eighteenth century in New York City, the African Free School provided a rare opportunity for Black children—both free and formerly enslaved—to receive an education. The school became a critical institution in the early Black educational movement, producing some of the nation's first Black abolitionist leaders. Its graduates went on to play key roles in the fight for emancipation, civil rights, and Black education, showing that the relationship between learning and liberation was recognized even in the earliest years of the Black intellectual tradition.

Arturo Schomburg and the Recovery of Global Black History

Afro-Puerto Rican scholar and bibliophile Arturo Schomburg devoted his life to collecting documents that proved the richness of African diasporic culture and history. His expansive collection—later donated to the New York Public Library—formed the basis of the Schomburg Center for Research in Black Culture. Schomburg's work directly countered the myth of Black historical absence and inspired generations of scholars to recover and preserve African diasporic knowledge. His legacy remains foundational in both Black Studies and public history institutions around the world.

In his seminal 1925 essay "The Negro Digs Up His Past," Arturo A. Schomburg asserts the urgent necessity of historical recovery for African-descended people across the diaspora. Published in *The New Negro: An Interpretation*, Schomburg's contribution challenged the myth that Black people were without history. Instead, it highlighted a long and global legacy of Black achievement in literature, science, politics, and the arts. He urged African Americans to take ownership of their historical narrative and to reject the colonial distortions that had rendered Black contributions invisible in Western education. The essay became a foundational text in the Black intellectual tradition.

It shaped how future scholars, educators, and institutions—like the Schomburg Center for Research in Black Culture—would frame African diasporic history as a source of pride, empowerment, and scholarly inquiry. Here is an excerpt of the essay.

"The Negro Digs Up His Past" by Arturo A. Schomburg, in *The New Negro: An Interpretation* edited by Alain Locke, 1925

THE American Negro must remake his past in order to make his future. Though it is orthodox to think of America as the one country where it is unnecessary to have a past, what is a luxury for the nation as a whole becomes a prime social necessity for the Negro. For him, a group tradition must supply compensation for persecution, and pride of race the antidote for prejudice. History must restore what slavery took away, for it is the social damage of slavery that the present generations must repair and offset. So among the rising democratic millions we find the Negro thinking more collectively, more retrospectively than the rest, and apt out of the very pressure of the present to become the most enthusiastic antiquarian of them all.

Vindicating evidences of individual achievement have as a matter of fact been gathered and treasured for over a century: Abbé Gregoire's liberal-minded book on Negro notables in 1808 was the pioneer effort; it has been followed at intervals by less known and often less discriminating compendiums of exceptional men and women of African stock. But this sort of thing was on the whole pathetically over-corrective, ridiculously over-laudatory; it was apologetics turned into biography. A true historical sense develops slowly and with difficulty under such circumstances. But to-day, even if for the ultimate purpose of group justification, history has become less a matter of argument and more a matter of record. There is the definite desire and determination to have a history, well documented, widely known at least within race circles, and administered as a stimulating and inspiring tradition for the coming generations.

Gradually as the study of the Negro's past has come out of the vagaries of rhetoric and propaganda and become systematic and scientific, three outstanding conclusions have been established: First, that the Negro has been throughout the centuries of controversy an active collaborator, and often a pioneer, in the struggle for his own freedom and advancement. This is true to a degree which makes it the more surprising that it has not been recognized earlier. Second, that by virtue of their being regarded as something "exceptional," even by friends and well-wishers, Negroes of attainment and genius have been unfairly disassociated from the group, and group credit lost accordingly. Third, that the remote racial origins of the Negro, far from being what the race and the world have been given to understand, offer a record of credible group achievement when scientifically viewed, and more important still, that they are of vital general interest because of their bearing upon the beginnings and early development of human culture.

With such crucial truths to document and establish, an ounce of fact is worth a pound of controversy. So the Negro historian to-day digs under the spot where his predecessor stood and argued. Not long ago, the Public Library of Harlem housed a special exhibition of books, pamphlets, prints and old engravings, that simply said, to skeptic and believer alike, to scholar and school-child, to proud black and astonished white, "Here is the evidence." Assembled from the rapidly growing collections of the leading Negro book-collectors and research societies, there were in these cases, materials not only for the first true writing of Negro history, but for the rewriting of many important paragraphs of our common American history. Slow though it be, historical truth is no exception to the proverb.

Here among the rarities of early Negro Americana was Jupiter Hammon's Address to the Negroes of the State of New York, edition of 1787, with the first American Negro poet's famous "If we should ever get to Heaven, we shall find nobody to reproach us for being black, or for being slaves." Here was Phyllis Wheatley's Mss. poem of 1767 addressed to the students of Harvard, her spirited encomiums upon George Washington and the Revolutionary Cause, and John Marrant's St. John's Day eulogy to the "Brothers of African Lodge No. 459" delivered at Boston in 1789. Here too were Lemuel Haynes' Vermont commentaries on the American Revolution and his learned sermons to his white congregation in Rutland, Vermont, and the sermons of the year 1808 by the Rev. Absalom Jones of St. Thomas Church, Philadelphia, and Peter Williams of St. Philip's, New York, pioneer Episcopal rectors who spoke out in daring and influential ways on the Abolition of the Slave Trade. Such things and many others are more than mere items of curiosity: they educate any receptive mind.

Reinforcing these were still rarer items of Africana and foreign Negro interest, the volumes of Juan Latino, the best Latinist of Spain in the reign of Philip V, incumbent of the chair of Poetry at the University of Granada, and author of Poems printed there in 1573 and a book on the Escurial published 1576; the Latin and Dutch treatises of Jacobus Eliza Capitein, a native of West Coast Africa and graduate of the University of Leyden, Gustavus Vassa's celebrated autobiography that supplied so much of the evidence in 1796 for Granville Sharpe's attack on slavery in the British colonies, Julien Raymond's Paris exposé of the disabilities of the free people of color in the then (1791) French colony of Hayti, and Baron de Vastey's Cry of the Fatherland, the famous polemic by the secretary of Christophe that precipitated the Haytian struggle for independence. The cumulative effect of such evidences of scholarship and moral prowess is too weighty to be dismissed as exceptional.

But weightier surely than any evidence of individual talent and scholarship could ever be, is the evidence of important collaboration and significant pioneer initiative in social service and reform, in the efforts toward race emancipation, colonization and race betterment. From neglected and rust-spotted pages comes testimony to the black men and women who stood shoulder to shoulder in courage and zeal, and often on a parity of intelligence and talent, with their notable white benefactors. There was the already cited work of Vassa that aided so materially the efforts of Granville Sharpe, the record of Paul Cuffee, the Negro colonization pioneer, associated so importantly with the establishment of Sierra Leone as a British colony for the occupancy of free people of color in West Africa; the dramatic and history-making exposé of John Baptist Phillips, African graduate of Edinburgh, who compelled through Lord Bathhurst in 1824 the enforcement of the articles of capitulation guaranteeing freedom to the blacks of Trinidad. There is the record of the pioneer colonization project of Rev. Daniel Coker in conducting a voyage of ninety expatriates to West Africa in 1820, of the missionary efforts of Samuel Crowther in Sierra Leone, first Anglican bishop of his diocese, and that of the work of John Russwurm, a leader in the work and foundation of the American Colonization Society.

When we consider the facts, certain chapters of American history will have to be reopened. Just as black men were influential factors in the campaign against the slave trade, so they were among the earliest instigators of the abolition movement. Indeed there was a dangerous calm between the agitation for the suppression of the slave trade and the beginning of the campaign for emancipation. During that interval colored men were very influential in arousing the attention of public men who in turn aroused the conscience of the country. Continuously between 1808 and 1845, men Prince Saunders, Peter Williams, Absalom Jones, Nathaniel Paul, and Bishops Varick and Richard Allen, the founders of the two wings of African Methodism, spoke out with force and initiative, and men like Denmark Vesey (1822), David Walker (1828) and Nat Turner (1831) advocated and organized schemes for direct action. This culminated in the generally ignored but important conventions of Free People of Color in New York, Philadelphia and other centers, whose platforms and efforts are to the Negro of as great significance as the nationally cherished memories of Faneuil and Independence Halls. Then with Abolition comes the better documented and more recognized collaboration of Samuel R. Ward, William Wells Brown, Henry Highland Garnett, Martin Delaney, Harriet Tubman, Sojourner Truth, and Frederick Douglass with their great colleagues, Tappan, Phillips, Sumner, Mott, Stowe and Garrison.

Source: Arthur [Arturo] A. Schomburg, "The Negro Digs Up His Past" in *The New Negro: An Interpretation*, edited by Alain Locke (New York: Albert and Charles Boni, 1925), pp. 231–237.

Du Bois, Hurston, and the Foundations of Black Social Science

W. E. B. Du Bois, one of the most influential Black intellectuals of the twentieth century, conducted pioneering sociological research that challenged racist pseudoscience and documented the lived realities of African Americans. His early work, including *The Philadelphia Negro* (1899), set a new standard for empirical research grounded in racial justice. Similarly, Zora Neale Hurston, who trained as an anthropologist, conducted fieldwork in the American South and the Caribbean, preserving Black folk culture, dialects, and oral traditions. Together, their scholarship demonstrated that the Black experience was not marginal but central to understanding human society.

Carter G. Woodson and the Institutionalization of Black History

Often referred to as the "father of Black history," Carter G. Woodson recognized the urgent need to institutionalize the study of African American life. He founded the Association for the Study of Negro Life and History in 1915, launched the *Journal of Negro History*, and created what would become Black History Month. Through these initiatives, Woodson ensured that Black perspectives and experiences were not only recorded but celebrated. His legacy remains central to African American Studies and continues to influence curriculum development across the country.

Published in 1933, Carter G. Woodson's *The Mis-Education of the Negro* is a foundational work in the history of Black educational thought and a powerful critique of systemic erasure in American schooling. Woodson argued that African Americans had been deliberately miseducated: trained to internalize inferiority and disconnected from their own history and cultural legacy. He insisted that true liberation required an education rooted in Black historical consciousness and critical self-awareness. More than a critique, the book served as a call to action. It urged African Americans to reclaim their minds, their histories, and their institutions. Its enduring relevance continues to shape the core philosophy of African American Studies and Black educational advocacy. Here is an excerpt of the Preface to Carter Woodson's *The Mis-Education of the Negro.*

Excerpt of the Preface to Carter Godwin Woodson's *The Mis-Education of the Negro* (1933)

> Herein are recorded not opinions but the reflections of one who for forty years has participated in the education of the Black, brown, yellow and white races in both hemispheres and in tropical and temperate regions. Such experience, too, has been with students in all grades from the kindergarten to the university. The author, moreover, has traveled around the world to observe not only modern school systems in various countries but to study the special systems set up by private agencies and governments to educate the natives in their colonies and dependencies. Some of these observations, too, have been checked against more recent studies on a later tour.
>
> Discussing herein the mistakes made in the education of the Negro, the writer frankly admits that he has committed some of these errors himself. In several chapters, moreover, he specifically points out wherein he himself has strayed from the path of wisdom. This book, then, is not intended as a broadside against any particular person or class, but it is given as a corrective for methods which have not produced satisfactory results.
>
> The author does not support the once popular views that in matters of education Negroes are rightfully subjected to the will of others on the presumption that these poor people are not large taxpayers and must be content with charitable contributions to their uplift. The author takes the position that the consumer pays the tax, and as such every individual of the social order should be given unlimited opportunity make the most of himself. Such opportunity, too, should not be determined from without by forces set to direct the proscribed element in a way to redound solely to the good of others but should be determined by the make-up of the Negro himself and by what his environment requires of him.

This new program of uplift, the author contends, should not be decided upon by the trial and error method in the application of devices used in dealing with others in a different situation and at another epoch. Only by careful study of the Negro himself and the life which he is forced to lead can we arrive at the proper procedure in this crisis. The mere imparting of information is not education. Above all things, the effort must result in making a man think and do for himself just as the Jews have done in spite of universal persecution.

In thus estimating the results obtained from the so-called education of the Negro the author does not go to the census figures to show the progress of the race. It may be of no importance to the race to be able to boast today of many times as many "educated" members as it had in 1865. If they are of the wrong kind the increase in numbers will be a disadvantage rather than an advantage. The only question which concerns us here is whether these "educated" persons are actually equipped to face the ordeal before them or unconsciously contribute to their own undoing by perpetuating the regime of the oppressor. Herein, however, lies no argument for the oft-heard contention that education for the white man should mean one thing and for the Negro a different thing. The element of race does not enter here. It is merely a matter of exercising common sense in approaching people through their environment in order to deal with conditions as they are rather than as you would like to see them or imagine that they are. There may be a difference in method of attack, but the principle remains the same.

"Highly educated" Negroes denounce persons who advocate for the Negro a sort of education different in some respects from that now given the white man. Negroes who have been so long inconvenienced and denied opportunities for development are naturally afraid of anything that sounds like discrimination. They are anxious to have everything the white man has even if it is harmful. The possibility of originality in the Negro, therefore, is discounted one hundred per cent to maintain a nominal equality. If the whites decide to take up Mormonism the Negroes must follow their lead. If the whites neglect such a study, then the Negroes must do likewise.

The author, however, does not have such an attitude. He considers the educational system as it has developed both in Europe and America an antiquated process which does not hit the mark even in the case of the needs of the white man himself. If the white man wants to hold on to it, let him do so; but the Negro, so far as he is able, should develop and carry out a program of his own. The so-called modern education, with all its defects, however, does others so much more good than it does the Negro, because it has been worked out in conformity to the needs of those who have enslaved and oppressed weaker peoples. For example, the philosophy and ethics resulting from our educational system have justified slavery, peonage, segregation, and lynching. The oppressor has the right to exploit, to handicap, and to kill the oppressed. Negroes daily educated in the tenets of such a religion of the strong have accepted the status of the weak as divinely ordained, and during the last three generations of their nominal freedom they have done practically nothing to change it. Their pouting and resolutions indulged in by a few of the race have been of little avail.

No systematic effort toward change has been possible, for, taught the same economics, history, philosophy, literature and religion which have established the present code of morals, the Negro's mind has been brought under the control of his oppressor. The problem of holding the Negro down, therefore, is easily solved. When you control a man's thinking you do not have to worry about his actions. You do not have to tell him not to stand here or go yonder. He will find his "proper place" and will stay in it. You do not need to send him to the back door. He will go without being told. In fact, if there is no back door, he will cut one for his special benefit. His education makes it necessary.

The same educational process which inspires and stimulates the oppressor with the thought that he is everything and has accomplished everything worthwhile, depresses and crushes at the same time the spark of genius in the Negro by making him feel that his race does not amount to much and never will measure up to the standards of other peoples. The Negro thus educated is a hopeless liability of the race.

The difficulty is that the "educated Negro" is compelled to live and move among his own people whom he has been taught to despise. As a rule, therefore, the "educated Negro" prefers to buy his food from a white grocer because he has been taught that the Negro is not clean. It does not matter how often a Negro washes his hands, then, he cannot clean them, and it does not matter how often a white man uses his hands he cannot soil them. The educated Negro, moreover, is disinclined to take part in Negro business, because he has been taught in economics that Negroes cannot operate in this particular sphere. The "educated Negro" gets less and less pleasure out of the Negro church, not on account of its primitiveness and increasing corruption, but because of his preference for the seats of "righteousness" controlled by his oppressor. This has been his education, and nothing else can be expected of him.

If the "educated Negro" could go off and be white he might be happy, but only a mulatto now and then can do this. The large majority of this class, then, must go through life denouncing white people because they are trying to run away from the Blacks and decrying the Blacks because they are not white.

Source: Carter Godwin Woodson, "Preface," *The Mis-Education of the Negro* (Washington, DC: Associated Publishers, 1933).

The effort to research, teach, and preserve Black history has always been more than an academic pursuit. It has been an act of resistance, reclamation, and cultural survival. Long before African American Studies became a formal discipline, Black intellectuals, educators, and activists built a powerful tradition of historical inquiry rooted in the belief that truth telling could liberate the mind and transform the future. From the early work of Carter G. Woodson and Arturo Schomburg to the enduring legacy of institutions like the African Free School, this tradition insisted that Black experiences, knowledge, and contributions are central to any honest understanding of history. By confronting erasure and affirming identity, Black history education laid the foundation for generations of scholars, artists, and students to see themselves not as marginal to the American story but as essential to its meaning.

Learning Our Own History

For a long time, Black stories weren't told in textbooks. So Black scholars and activists built their own ways to study the past—from community teach-ins to college programs that challenged the status quo.

You're Practicing: Investigating who gets to shape the narrative.

Connect This To: Historical interpretation and education justice.

Theme: Knowledge, Power, and Agency

Practice: Explain Causality (Effects)

In the twentieth century, African Americans led efforts to institutionalize Black history education and develop African American Studies as a formal academic discipline.

(A) Identify one major figure or organization that promoted Black history education.

(B) Explain how efforts to teach Black history were connected to broader struggles for civil rights and cultural recognition.

(C) Analyze the effects of these educational movements on American curricula and intellectual life.

SAMPLE RESPONSES

(A) Carter G. Woodson, often called the "Father of Black History," founded the Association for the Study of Negro Life and History (ASNLH) in 1915 and launched the Journal of Negro History in 1916 to advance research on African American life.

In 1926, he created Negro History Week, which evolved into today's Black History Month, to ensure Black history was celebrated in schools and public institutions.

Through publications like the Negro History Bulletin (1937), Woodson provided teachers and students with accessible materials that countered the whitewashed narratives dominating American textbooks.

(B) Woodson's campaign for Black history education directly challenged institutional racism in education, which portrayed African Americans as historically insignificant or absent from the national narrative.

This intellectual activism aligned with the New Negro movement and the work of contemporaries like W. E. B. Du Bois and Arturo Schomburg, who used scholarship to assert the dignity and global contributions of people of African descent.

Teaching Black history became a form of cultural resistance and civil rights advocacy, anticipating later demands of the Civil Rights Movement for inclusive curricula that validated African American identity and historical agency.

(C) The institutionalization of Black history education inspired the development of African American Studies as a formal discipline in the late 1960s, with programs emerging at San Francisco State University and Cornell University following student protests led by the Black Student Union.

Public school systems gradually expanded curricula to include African American history, literature, and cultural contributions, reshaping how U.S. history was taught and broadening historical consciousness among all students.

The growth of Black history scholarship influenced the rise of related academic fields such as Africana Studies and African Diaspora Studies, while also inspiring community institutions like the Schomburg Center for Research in Black Culture, which continues to preserve and promote global Black history.

Skills Assessed: Explain the effects of historical developments; use sources and evidence; analyze relationships among developments.

Topic 3.16 The Great Migration

Key Terms

- **1910–1940 (first wave); 1940–1970 (second wave)**
- **Push factors—Jim Crow laws, violence, sharecropping**
- **Pull factors—industrial jobs, Northern freedom**
- **Chicago, Detroit, New York, Philadelphia—key destinations**
- **Cultural impact—growth of urban Black middle class**
- **White backlash and housing segregation**
- **Black newspapers as migration guides—*The Chicago Defender***
- **Changing political power (urban Black vote)**

What happens when millions of people decide that staying is no longer an option? Beginning in the early twentieth century, African Americans launched one of the largest internal migrations in U.S. history. They left behind the racial terror of the South in search of safety, opportunity, and dignity in the urban North and West. However, they didn't just move—they transformed the nation.

The Great Migration refers to the mass movement of over 6 million African Americans from the rural South to cities in the North, Midwest, and West between roughly 1910 and 1970. This migration was driven by a complex set of push and pull factors, including Jim Crow segregation, racial violence, economic exploitation, and the promise of industrial jobs and greater freedom in urban centers.

As African Americans relocated, they reshaped the cultural, political, and economic fabric of American cities. From the development of vibrant Black urban neighborhoods to the birth of new art forms and political movements, the Great Migration stands as a defining chapter in African American history—one rooted in the pursuit of liberation and the refusal to be confined by racial oppression.

After engaging with this topic, scholars will be able to:

- Describe the historical causes and conditions that led to the Great Migration.
- Explain how this movement reshaped Black communities and urban life across the United States.
- Analyze the cultural and political consequences of the Great Migration, including its influence on music, literature, and civil rights activism.
- Connect the migration to broader themes of resistance, resilience, and transformation in African American history.

A Movement of Millions: The Scope of the Great Migration

The Great Migration was one of the largest internal migrations in American history, with more than 6 million African Americans relocating from the South to the North, Midwest, and West between the 1910s and the 1970s. Occurring in two major waves—before and after World War II—this mass movement was a turning point in African American history. For many, migration offered the hope of escaping the rigid boundaries of Jim Crow segregation and forging a new life rooted in economic opportunity, dignity, and safety. The migration was not simply demographic. It was transformative, reshaping both the Black experience and the American urban landscape.

War and Work: Industrial Opportunities in the Urban North

Labor shortages caused by World War I and World War II opened new economic doors for African Americans in northern industrial centers. As white workers were drafted into military service, Black Southerners were recruited—sometimes aggressively—to fill positions in factories, steel mills, railroads, and meatpacking plants. For many Black families, these jobs represented their first real chance to earn livable wages and begin accumulating generational wealth. Though discrimination persisted in the North, the promise of economic mobility helped fuel this historic relocation and changed the class structure of Black America.

Environmental Hardship and Rural Displacement

Environmental degradation in the South played a critical role in driving Black migration. Natural disasters like floods and agricultural crises—such as the destruction of cotton crops by the boll weevil—left many Black farmers destitute. These hardships compounded the burdens of racial discrimination, tenant farming, and sharecropping, making life in the South both economically unsustainable and socially oppressive. The Great Migration thus became a flight not only from violence but also from environmental and economic devastation.

Flight from Terror: Escaping Racial Violence

The Great Migration was also a response to the existential threat posed by Jim Crow laws, lynching, and everyday racial terror. In many Southern communities, Black families lived under constant threat of mob violence, with little to no legal recourse. Seeking physical safety and legal protection, many African Americans left in hopes of finding greater personal security in Northern cities. Although racism existed in the North, the absence of legalized segregation and the presence of growing Black institutions created a relatively safer environment for Black life and progress.

Trains, Newspapers, and the Mechanics of Movement

The infrastructure of the Great Migration was shaped by innovation and information. Expanding railroad networks provided accessible transportation routes out of the South. At the same time, the Black press—particularly newspapers like *The Chicago Defender*—encouraged migration by offering firsthand accounts, job listings, and advice for resettlement. These papers painted the North as a "Promised Land," helping to build a collective vision of freedom and mobility. In this way, transportation and communication technology were essential tools of both literal and psychological escape.

Transforming Cities and Culture: The Impact of Migration

The effects of the Great Migration were deeply felt in cities such as Chicago, New York, Detroit, Pittsburgh, and Los Angeles, where new Black neighborhoods blossomed into cultural, political, and economic hubs. Migrants brought Southern traditions—religious, culinary, musical—and adapted them to urban life, creating a shared national Black identity. This movement directly fueled major cultural renaissances, including the Harlem Renaissance and the rise of jazz and blues as dominant art forms, marking the migration as a turning point in American cultural history.

Urbanization and New Black Relationships with the Land

As a result of the migration, African Americans shifted from being a predominantly rural population to one that was increasingly urban. This new geography reshaped their relationship to land and labor. No longer tied primarily to agriculture, many Black families engaged with natural environments through parks, leisure, and recreation rather than subsistence farming. This change fostered new notions of citizenship, belonging, and cultural participation in America's growing cities.

Southern Resistance to Black Mobility

Not all responded favorably to the Great Migration. Many white Southern employers and authorities saw the departure of Black laborers as a direct threat to the regional economy and power structure. In some cases, local officials resorted to coercion—arresting Black migrants on fabricated charges or threatening violence to prevent their departure. This resistance underscored the broader systemic control that the migration disrupted and the desperation with which white elites sought to maintain their grip on the racial and economic order.

Uplift and Transition: The Role of the National Urban League

Founded in New York City in 1910, the National Urban League played a pivotal role in supporting African Americans during the Great Migration. As an interracial organization, it provided newly arrived migrants with critical resources such as job placement assistance, housing referrals, and urban acclimation support. The league's broader mission aligned with the ethos of racial uplift, helping Black families navigate new challenges in the North. In later decades, it would continue to play an important role in the Civil Rights Movement. The National Urban League supported initiatives like A. Philip Randolph's March on Washington and worked alongside organizations such as the Southern Christian Leadership Conference (SCLC).

Published in *The Messenger* in March 1920, this anonymous letter serves as a firsthand expression of the urgency and hope that defined the Great Migration. Written in the voice of a Southern Black resident urging others to escape the oppressive conditions of the Jim Crow South, the letter appeals to shared experiences of racial violence, poverty, and limited opportunity. Its message is both emotional and strategic, describing the North as a place of dignity, fair wages, and safety for Black families. This document reflects the grassroots communications that accompanied formal campaigns by the Black press and migration networks. It offers a poignant glimpse into the personal motivations and communal calls to action that fueled one of the most significant mass movements in African American history.

Anonymous editorial, "Negroes, Leave the South!" The Messenger, March 1920

Fellow Negroes of the South, leave there. Go North, East, and West—anywhere—to get out of that hell hole. There are better schools here for your children, higher wages for yourselves, votes if you are twenty-one, better housing and more liberty. All is not rosy here, by any means, but it is Paradise compared with Georgia, Arkansas, Texas, Mississippi and Alabama. Besides, you make it better for those you leave behind. Labor becomes scarce, so that the Bourbons of Dixie are compelled to pay your brothers back home more wages. They will give them more schools and privileges, too, to try to get them to come back and, secondly, to try to keep you from leaving.

Stop buying property in the South, to be burned down and run away from over night. Sell out your stuff quietly, saying nothing to the Negro lackeys, and leave! Come into the land of at least incipient civilization!

Source: "Negroes, Leave the South!" *The Messenger*, March 1920, p. 2 (public domain).

Jacob Lawrence's *The Migration Series* is a groundbreaking visual narrative that chronicles the causes, experiences, and consequences of the Great Migration. Completed between 1940 and 1941, the series uses bold color, simplified forms, and captioned text to tell a collective story of African American movement from the South to the North. Panel No. 1, which declares, "During the World War there was a great migration North by Southern Negroes," sets the tone for the series by linking Black migration to larger historical forces. This panel—and the series as a whole—distills complex social realities into vivid imagery that centers Black agency, struggle, and resilience.

For a deeper analysis of *The Migration Series* and its historical significance, scholars are encouraged to view it online for free at the Gilder Lehrman Institute of American History at, https://www.gilderlehrman.org/ap-african-american-studies/unit-3/twentieth-century-black-migration.

The map of the Great Migration visually illustrates the massive internal relocation of African Americans from the rural South to urban centers in the North, Midwest, and West between 1910 and 1970. Highlighting the geographic scope and direction of this movement, the map reveals key departure states such as Mississippi, Georgia, and Alabama as well as major destination cities like Chicago, Detroit, New York, and Los Angeles. This visual representation underscores how migration patterns were shaped by economic opportunity, racial violence, and transportation networks. By tracing these routes, the map allows scholars to understand better how regional Black cultures converged, urban Black communities expanded, and the national landscape of African American life was forever transformed.

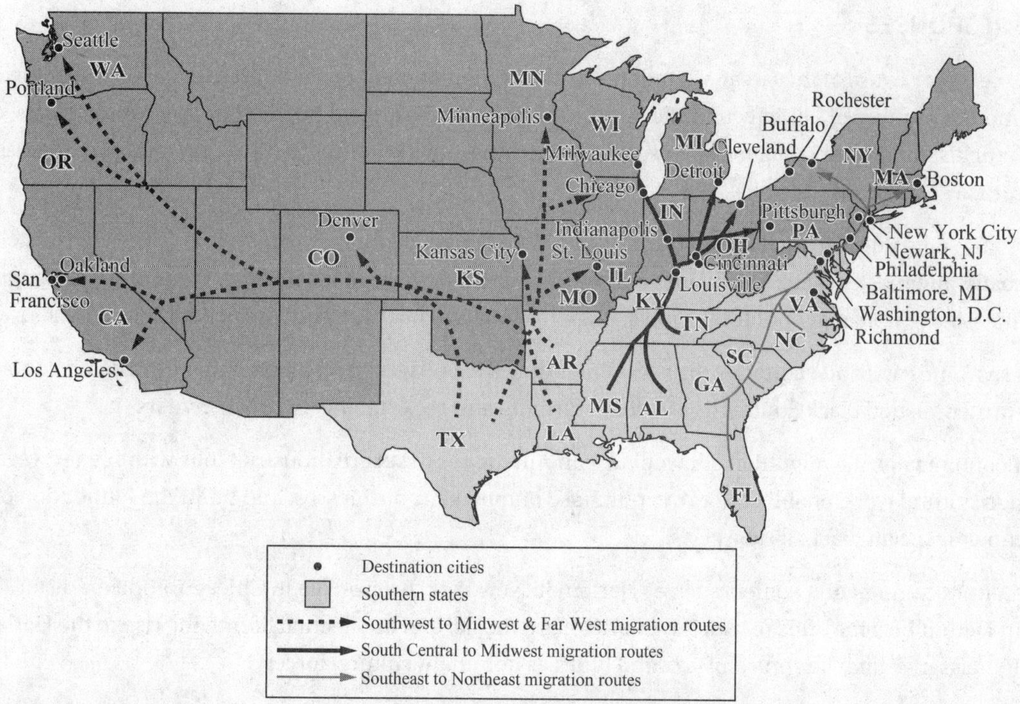

Map of the Great Migration

The Great Migration was not merely a relocation of bodies. It was a redefinition of Black life in America. As millions of African Americans fled the racial terror and economic marginalization of the Jim Crow South, they reshaped the cultural, political, and economic contours of the nation. From the birth of vibrant urban communities to the rise of national Black cultural movements and political activism, the migration gave rise to new forms of identity, resistance, and solidarity. It was, at its core, a collective assertion of freedom—proof that African Americans would not wait to be liberated but would move boldly toward liberation on their own terms.

TIP

Pace Yourself

Don't spend too much time on a single question. If you're stuck, move on to the next one and come back later if you have time.

A Journey North, A New Life Begins

Between 1910 and 1970, millions of Black families left the South for cities in the North and West. They were searching for jobs, freedom, and safety. They brought Southern culture with them and reshaped entire cities in the process.

You're Practicing: Connecting movement to culture.

Connect This To: Migration, opportunity, and community change.

Theme: Migration and Urban Life

Practice: Explain Causality (Causes and Effects)

Between 1910 and 1940, the Great Migration transformed African American life as millions moved from the rural South to urban centers in the North and West.

(A) Identify one major cause of the Great Migration.
(B) Explain how the migration changed the economic, cultural, or political lives of African Americans.
(C) Analyze both the immediate and long-term effects of the Great Migration on American society.

SAMPLE RESPONSES

(A) One major cause of the Great Migration was the combination of racial oppression in the Jim Crow South and the promise of better economic opportunities in the industrial North. Rigid segregation laws, disenfranchisement, and racial terror—especially lynching—made Southern life dangerous and oppressive for African Americans.

At the same time, labor shortages during World War I opened jobs in Northern industries such as steel, railroads, and meatpacking. Companies actively recruited Southern Black workers, with Black newspapers like The Chicago Defender publishing job listings, personal testimonies, and instructions for relocation.

Environmental and economic disasters, including the boll weevil infestation that devastated cotton crops, further pushed Black Southerners to leave farming and seek stability in urban centers.

(B) Economically, the migration allowed African Americans to secure industrial jobs with higher wages than agricultural work, enabling many to purchase homes, start businesses, and build the foundation of a growing urban Black middle class.

Culturally, migration centers such as Harlem in New York, Bronzeville in Chicago, and Paradise Valley in Detroit became hubs of African American art, music, and intellectual life, giving rise to the Harlem Renaissance and the spread of jazz and blues as dominant cultural forces.

Politically, African Americans in Northern cities gained voting rights denied in the South, influencing elections, supporting civil rights organizations like the NAACP and the National Urban League, and laying the groundwork for future political power in municipal and national politics.

(C) Immediately, the migration transformed the demographics of cities, creating vibrant Black neighborhoods that became centers of cultural production, community institutions, and political activism. In cities like Chicago and Detroit, the Black vote began to shape local elections and challenge white political dominance.

In the long term, the migration reshaped the national political landscape, contributing to the mid-20th-century realignment of African American voters toward the Democratic Party and bolstering the base for the Civil Rights Movement.

The cultural impact was profound: African American literature, visual art, and music gained national prominence through figures such as Langston Hughes, Louis Armstrong, and Jacob Lawrence, whose *Migration Series* documented the journey and transformed it into a defining narrative of resilience, freedom, and self-determination.

Skills Assessed: Explain the causes and effects of historical developments; use sources and evidence; analyze relationships among developments.

Topic 3.17 Afro-Caribbean Migration

Key Terms

- West Indian immigrants—from Jamaica, Barbados, Trinidad
- Cultural exchange in Harlem and other cities
- Marcus Garvey and the Universal Negro Improvement Association (UNIA)
- Labor migration—Panama Canal, sugar plantations, urban labor
- Tensions and solidarity—cultural differences with African Americans
- Creole identity and pan-Africanism
- Political radicalism and activism

While millions of African Americans in the United States migrated to the North from the South, another wave of movement reshaped Black life in the twentieth century: Afro-Caribbean migration. Arriving with distinct cultural traditions, political ideologies, and diasporic identities, Black Caribbean migrants brought new energy—and new tensions—to African American communities already in transformation. Afro-Caribbean migration to the United States increased significantly in the early twentieth century, especially from islands such as Jamaica, Barbados, Haiti, and Trinidad. Many migrants were drawn by economic opportunity, political refuge, and educational advancement, particularly as U.S. imperial and commercial interests expanded in the Caribbean region.

Afro-Caribbean migrants settled primarily in northeastern cities like New York, where they contributed to the growing Black urban population alongside African Americans from the Great Migration. These migrants brought with them unique cultural practices, strong diasporic consciousness, and vibrant political traditions—many influenced by anti-colonial movements and pan-Africanism. Their arrival enriched African American cultural and intellectual life. However, it also sparked debates over class, identity, and belonging within Black communities navigating American racism and segregation.

After engaging with this topic, scholars will be able to:

- Explain the economic, political, and social factors that contributed to increased Afro-Caribbean migration to the United States in the early twentieth century.
- Describe how Afro-Caribbean migrants influenced African American cultural, political, and intellectual movements.
- Analyze the similarities and tensions between Afro-Caribbean and African American communities in urban centers in the North.
- Connect Afro-Caribbean migration to broader patterns of Black internationalism and diasporic exchange.

Causes of Afro-Caribbean Migration: Empire, Economy, and Education

Afro-Caribbean migration to the United States in the early twentieth century was shaped by both push and pull factors. The decline of Caribbean economies during World War I, including the collapse of agricultural markets and limited employment opportunities, prompted many Afro-Caribbean people to seek better prospects abroad. At the same time, the expansion of U.S. imperial and economic interests in the region—such as the 1903 acquisition of the Panama Canal and increased military and commercial influence—opened migration routes and forged closer connections between the Caribbean and the United States. Migrants came seeking not only work but also educational advancement and political freedom. Their arrival added a new diasporic dimension to the Black experience in America.

Settlement Patterns and Urban Presence

Between 1899 and 1937, more than 140,000 Afro-Caribbean immigrants arrived in the United States. Many settled in Florida and New York, particularly in urban centers like Miami and Harlem. These communities often lived alongside African American populations already reshaped by the Great Migration. Although they shared a common African ancestry and experiences with racial discrimination, Afro-Caribbean migrants brought with them distinct national identities, customs, and dialects. This added further complexity to the racial and cultural dynamics of Black urban life in the early twentieth century.

Cultural Exchange and Community Tensions

The arrival of Afro-Caribbean migrants created both cultural enrichment and social tension within African American communities. At times, cultural misunderstandings and class-based assumptions fueled divisions. Some African Americans perceived Caribbean immigrants as aloof or overly assimilationist, and some migrants viewed African Americans as too entrenched in domestic racial struggles. Over time, these interactions also gave rise to new cultural syntheses in music, food, fashion, and community organization—contributing to a richer and more diverse Black American identity. Afro-Caribbean influence was particularly strong in Harlem, where Caribbean immigrants helped shape the politics and aesthetics of the Harlem Renaissance.

Expanding Religious and Linguistic Diversity

Afro-Caribbean migration introduced new forms of religious expression and linguistic diversity into Black communities in the United States. Many migrants practiced Catholicism, Anglicanism, or Episcopalianism—differing from the predominantly Baptist and Methodist traditions in African American communities. Additionally, immigrants from non-English-speaking islands brought languages such as Spanish, French Creole, and Patois into the mix, further broadening the cultural and linguistic landscape. These differences challenged rigid definitions of Blackness and helped shape a more globalized understanding of the African diaspora in the United States.

Intellectual Influence and Political Radicalism

Afro-Caribbean intellectuals played a key role in shaping radical Black thought in the United States during the twentieth century. Influenced by anti-colonial struggles and pan-Africanist ideas, figures such as Marcus Garvey, Claudia Jones, and Hubert Harrison brought a global perspective to Black liberation politics. Their experiences with colonialism and Black self-governance in the Caribbean informed their critiques of American racism and capitalism, helping to radicalize African American social movements. Afro-Caribbean thinkers were instrumental in building bridges between African American struggles and global movements for racial and economic justice, laying the groundwork for Black internationalism.

Published in the October 1924 issue of *Opportunity*, Wilfred A. Domingo's essay "Restricted West Indian Immigration and the American Negro" offers a pointed critique of U.S. immigration policy and its impact on Black unity across national lines. A Jamaican-born journalist and pan-Africanist, Domingo defends Afro-Caribbean immigrants against growing nativist sentiment and warns that restrictions on West Indian migration threaten to divide Black communities in the United States. He calls for solidarity between African Americans and Afro-Caribbean migrants, arguing that shared ancestry and common struggles against racism should unite rather than divide them. Domingo's essay reflects early tensions within the Black diaspora in the United States while also envisioning a broader, transnational Black identity rooted in mutual respect, political consciousness, and collective liberation.

"Restricted West Indian Immigration and the American Negro," *Opportunity*, October 1924

The Immigration Act of 1924, "to limit the immigration of aliens into the United States, and for other purposes," which came into force July 1, has achieved the object of its framers and sponsors who were mainly concerned about excluding undesirable racial strains. Not only was this accomplished by securing a reduction of non-Nordic Europeans in favor of Nordics, but what is of vital importance to American Negroes, by a palpable discrimination which singled out for quota restriction only those sections of the New World from which any appreciable number of Negroes had come and was likely to come in the future. That this latter achievement is among the "other purposes" of the Act seems of little doubt when the facts are studied and a comparison is made between the present Act and its predecessor of 1921.

The Act of 1921, entitled "An Act to limit the immigration of aliens into the United States," made a perpendicular distinction between immigrants who were eligible to enter the country without special treaty regulations. Those from the Old World were restricted to 3 per cent of their number in the United States in 1910, while those from the New World were admitted on a non-quota basis. In neither case were the immigrants affected by the political status of the country or colony from which they came.

Section 2 of the 1921 Act, dealing with "excepted classes" or non-quota immigrants, included aliens from "the Dominion of Canada, Newfoundland, the Republic of Cuba, the Republic of Mexico, countries of Central and South America, or adjacent islands." Under this provision immigrants from all parts of the Americas were on an equal non-quota basis.

The Act of 1924, section 4 (c), defines the term "non-quota immigrant" as "an immigrant who was born in the Dominion of Canada, Newfoundland, the Republic of Haiti, the Republic of Mexico, the Republic of Cuba, the Dominican Republic, the Canal Zone, or an independent country of Central and South America." By specifically naming Canada and Newfoundland for exemption from quota, placing the word "independent" before countries, and omitting the words "adjacent islands," the framers of the Act very adroitly excluded from the non-quota classes those European colonies in the Caribbean Sea from which American Negroes had been receiving any numerical increase. Conclusive proof that the Act, which was passed by the present Republican Administration, was intended to erect a barrier against the comparatively slight immigration of people of African descent from the West Indies is found in President Coolidge's Proclamation of June 30. Subdivision 6 of the Proclamation states: "In contrast with the law of 1921 the Immigration Act of 1924 provides that persons born in the colonies or dependencies of European countries situated in Central America and South Ameri[c]a or the islands adjacent to the American continents . . . will be charged to the quota of the country to which such colony or dependency belongs." The language is clear and unmistakable. It makes a horizontal distinction between British North America and other European colonial possessions in the New World. The distinction is significant in view of the reason that inspired the Act and the racial stock of immigrants from both groups of colonies.

The law to limit immigration into the United States was agitated for and defended on two main grounds: race and culture of recent immigrants and inability of the country to absorb the huge number seeking admission from Europe. The grounds were qualitative and quantitative. To achieve both ends the Census of 1890 was used as the basis to determine the 2 per cent to be admitted yearly until 1927, after which the maximum will be 150,000 annually. Whether or not a colony is self-governing does not affect the issue. In Europe, England, the Mother Country, the Irish Free State, whose status is similar to that of Canada, Malta, having a form of government like that of Jamaica or Barbados, and Gibraltar, a Crown Colony like Antigua and St. Kitts, are subject to a 2 per cent quota, regardless of their varying degrees of autonomy. The same equality of quota exists between truly independent and powerful countries like England and France and vassal states like Hungary and Poland. In the Western World the law makes no distinction between independent countries like Brazil and Argentina and nominally independent countries like Cuba and Costa Rica. It is only when colonial possessions are dealt with that a distinction is made. All British North American possessions are on a non-quota basis, while other European possessions are subject to restriction. In practice this means that only those places in the Western World from which any noticeable number of Negro immigrants had been coming are singled out for quota restrictions! With the uniform treatment accorded to British subjects in Europe it cannot be successfully contended that "self-government" inspired the in- equality of treatment given to British subjects in the New World. Nor can it be seriously claimed that the number of immigrants coming from the restricted colonies, compared with the number from Canada and Newfoundland, justified restricting the former and not the latter. The contrary is the truth.

According to the World Almanac (1924) the principal sources of immigrants from the New World in 1923 were British North America, 117,011; Mexico, 63,768; and the West Indies, 13,181 (mostly Negroes). If number constitutes a reason for restriction then Canada, rather than the West Indies, furnished the justification. Stating it differently, of the 199,972 immigrants from the American continents who entered the United States in 1923, only 13,181 or less than 7 per cent were from countries with Negro majorities. And as not an inconsiderable portion of the 13,181 were Caucasians, it is clear that the proportion of Negro immigrants who remain in America is less than the proportion that American Negroes bear to the total population. More white immigrants came from Canada and Newfoundland in 1923 than the total number of foreign-born Negroes in the United States that year! Despite this fact and the further fact that while 4,183 West Indians left the United States that year only 2,775 British North Americans and 2,660 Mexicans departed, the former are restricted while the latter are not.

It is nowhere claimed that language or culture constituted the reason for exempting all other American peoples while restricting West Indians. With the exception of English-speaking Canadians, there are no people in the Western World more culturally and linguistically akin to Americans than British West Indians. The great difference between the West Indies and the favored British possessions of North America is that a majority of the inhabitants of the former colonies are of African descent. And this difference explains why the comparatively slight stream of immigration from these islands called for restriction.

Allied by blood to the 12,000,000 Negroes of this country, who have a deep interest in keeping the door of Negro immigration open in these days of discussion of the population question; when everything is being done to make America approximate the Ku Klux ideal of a white man's country by keeping Negroes in a hopeless minority, West Indians can only look to their brothers "of the mainland to emulate the late Booker T. Washington who, in 1914, succeeded with the cooperation of other far-sighted leaders in defeating the attempt made at the time to exclude from entry people of African descent. The present law, less frank than the one of ten years ago, has nevertheless achieved the same end, for it means in effect that while the number of immigrants coming from countries that formerly sent a few Negroes will be limited to a couple of hundred yearly, white immigrants will come from Europe to the extent of half a million annually until 1927, and 150,000 after then, while those from Canada and other parts of the American continent will be unlimited. In such a situation, if Negroes are not by their silence to acquiesce in racial discrimination by the Federal government, they will use their influence to see that all immigrants in the Western World are placed upon a quota or none; that the principle of equality among colonies in Europe be applied to colonies in the Americas.

Regardless of explanations and apologies, the bald fact stands out that the present Immigration Act, which is designed to be selective racially, by deliberate discrimination against those countries in the New World from which Negroes had been coming to any extent, while exempting those from which Caucasians are still coming without limit, places Negro blood in despite and serves notice upon American Negroes that they cannot hope to increase their number by immigration. In so many words, they are told that against their natural increase will be pitted not only the natural increase of white America but a constant entry of European immigrants. Such an outlook should engage the serious consideration of the best minds of the Negro race in America.

Source: Wilfred A. Domingo, "Restricted West Indian Immigration and the American Negro," *Opportunity* 2, no. 22 (October 1924): pp. 298–299 (public domain).

Afro-Caribbean migration in the early twentieth century significantly reshaped the cultural, political, and intellectual contours of Black life in the United States. While the arrival of Caribbean migrants introduced tensions within African American communities, it also expanded the richness of Black identity, expression, and global consciousness. Through religious diversity, linguistic influence, and political radicalism, Afro-Caribbean thinkers and communities deepened the diasporic connections that linked Black struggles across national boundaries. Their contributions challenged narrow definitions of Blackness and helped forge a more expansive vision of freedom—one rooted in solidarity, cultural exchange, and transnational resistance to white supremacy.

Caribbean Currents in Black America

Caribbean immigrants brought new rhythms, politics, and ideas to Black communities in the United States. From Marcus Garvey to calypso music, they added to the richness of the African diaspora experience.

You're Practicing: Comparing different expressions of Black identity.

Connect This To: Diaspora, activism, and cultural blending.

Theme: Global Blackness

Practice: Compare (Explain Similarities or Differences)

During the early twentieth century, Afro-Caribbean migrants arrived in the United States and contributed to the social, political, and cultural life of Black communities, particularly in cities like New York.

(A) Identify one key similarity or difference between the experiences of Afro-Caribbean migrants and African Americans during this period.

(B) Explain how Afro-Caribbean migrants contributed to or challenged existing Black institutions and ideologies in the United States.

(C) Compare how race, nationality, and class shaped Afro-Caribbean and African American identities and activism.

SAMPLE RESPONSES

(A) One major cause of Afro-Caribbean migration to the United States was the economic downturn in the Caribbean during World War I, which was marked by the collapse of agricultural markets and limited job opportunities in islands such as Jamaica, Barbados, and Trinidad.

The expansion of U.S. imperial and commercial influence in the region—including the construction of the Panama Canal and increased American investment—created new travel and employment routes that facilitated migration.

Afro-Caribbean migrants were also drawn by opportunities for education and political refuge, particularly in Northern cities like New York's Harlem, which had growing Black cultural and political communities.

(B) Afro-Caribbean migrants enriched African American urban communities by introducing distinct cultural traditions, including Caribbean music, foodways, and religious practices such as Anglicanism, Catholicism, and African-influenced spiritual traditions.

In Harlem, Afro-Caribbean intellectuals and activists such as Marcus Garvey, founder of the Universal Negro Improvement Association (UNIA), advanced a vision of pan-Africanism that connected African Americans to global anti-colonial struggles.

Caribbean immigrants brought a strong tradition of political activism and labor organizing, influencing African American labor movements and contributing to radical publications like The Messenger and Negro World, which encouraged political consciousness and solidarity across the diaspora.

(C) Immediately, Afro-Caribbean migration expanded the cultural diversity of African American neighborhoods, contributing to the intellectual and artistic vibrancy of the Harlem Renaissance while also creating moments of tension over differences in class background, national identity, and approaches to racial activism.

Over the long term, Afro-Caribbean thinkers such as Hubert Harrison and Claudia Jones deepened the tradition of Black radicalism in the United States, linking civil rights to global movements for independence, socialism, and anti-colonial liberation.

The migration strengthened a transnational Black identity in the United States, fostering connections between African Americans and people of African descent throughout the Americas, and laying an intellectual foundation for later movements in Black internationalism and diasporic solidarity.

Skills Assessed: Explain the similarities and differences between historical developments; use sources and evidence; analyze relationships among developments.

Topic 3.18 The Universal Negro Improvement Association (UNIA)

Key Terms

- Marcus Garvey—Jamaican-born leader of pan-African movement
- UNIA—founded in 1914; expanded to the United States in 1916
- Back-to-Africa movement
- Black Star Line—steamship company to connect global diaspora
- Race first philosophy
- Self-determination and racial pride
- *Negro World* newspaper
- Red, black, and green flag—symbol of Black nationalism
- Largest mass Black organization in U.S. history

What if freedom meant more than integration? What if it meant self-rule, economic power, and global unity among people of African descent? In the early twentieth century, Marcus Garvey and the Universal Negro Improvement Association (UNIA) ignited one of the largest mass movements in Black history by asking just that. Founded in 1914 by Jamaican-born activist Marcus Garvey, the Universal Negro Improvement Association (UNIA) became a global force for Black pride, economic independence, and pan-African unity. By the 1920s, the UNIA had grown into a transnational organization with millions of followers, branches across the world, and its own flag, anthem, newspaper (*Negro World*), and shipping company (Black Star Line).

Garvey's message of race-first solidarity, self-determination, and a return to Africa resonated with African-descended people facing colonialism, segregation, and systemic oppression. The UNIA empowered Black communities to build their own schools, businesses, and institutions, and it left an indelible mark on political movements throughout the African diaspora. Although controversial, Garvey's legacy continues to influence global Black political thought, pan-Africanism, and nationalist ideology.

After engaging with this topic, scholars will be able to:

- Describe the mission, methods, and structure of the Universal Negro Improvement Association (UNIA).
- Analyze Marcus Garvey's leadership and his vision of Black nationalism and pan-Africanism.
- Evaluate the UNIA's influence on Black political consciousness and mass organizing across the diaspora.
- Explain how the UNIA shaped future movements for Black empowerment and cultural pride.

A Global Black Movement: The Rise of the UNIA

Founded by Marcus Garvey in 1914 and expanded in the United States after 1916, the Universal Negro Improvement Association (UNIA) became the largest pan-African organization in African American history. Garvey envisioned a mass movement that would unite all people of African descent under a shared banner of pride, self-determination, and global solidarity. At its height, the UNIA had hundreds of branches and thousands of members throughout the Caribbean, Latin America, Africa, and North America. Through speeches, conventions, and publications like *Negro World*, Garvey mobilized a transnational Black public and challenged the colonial and racist systems that oppressed African peoples worldwide.

"Africa for the Africans": Garvey's Repatriation Vision and the Black Star Line

A central tenet of Garvey's political ideology was the Back-to-Africa movement, which called for the repatriation of African Americans and other members of the African diaspora to their ancestral homeland. Garvey believed that Black people could never be free under white-dominated governments and instead should return to Africa to build a sovereign Black nation. To support this vision, he founded the Black Star Line—a steamship company intended to facilitate commerce and migration between the diaspora and the African continent. Although the company ultimately collapsed under financial and political pressure, the vision of "Africa for the Africans" became a rallying cry for global Black liberation.

Black Pride, Economic Power, and Institutional Independence

Garvey's message resonated deeply with African Americans who had endured Jim Crow segregation, racial violence, and economic marginalization. Through the UNIA, he promoted industrial, educational, and political advancement by urging Black people to build their own institutions—schools, businesses, newspapers, and political structures. Garvey's vision of Black separatism was not based on racial hatred but on empowerment: a belief that Black people should not wait for acceptance or equality within white society but instead should define and control their own destiny. His emphasis on African heritage and collective self-worth laid the cultural foundation for later Black nationalist and Afrocentric movements.

Lasting Legacy: From Pan-Africanism to Global Black Nationalism

Garvey's influence extended far beyond his lifetime. His emphasis on anti-colonial struggle, diaspora unity, and racial pride helped shape Black political thought across the globe. The UNIA's red, black, and green flag—symbolizing the blood, skin, and land of African peoples—has endured as a global emblem of Black liberation. Garvey's ideas inspired countless movements, including the Nation of Islam, the Rastafari movement, and various African independence struggles in the mid-twentieth century. Though controversial and often criticized by his contemporaries, Garvey's legacy remains central to understanding the evolution of pan-Africanism and the global dimensions of Black nationalism.

Delivered at the Second UNIA Convention in 1921, Marcus Garvey's Address to the Second UNIA Convention captures the bold rhetoric and sweeping vision that defined his leadership of the global pan-African movement. Speaking before thousands of supporters, Garvey articulated the goals of the Universal Negro Improvement Association: racial pride, Black self-governance, economic independence, and the unification of all people of African descent. His call to action—"Africa for the Africans, at home and abroad"—served not only as a demand for liberation from colonial rule but also as a rallying cry for Black solidarity across the diaspora. This speech stands as a defining moment in twentieth-century Black political thought. It offers scholars direct insight into the ideals and urgency that fueled one of the largest mass movements in African diasporic history.

Excerpt from Marcus Garvey's Address to the Second UNIA Convention

> . . . We have been here, sent here by the good will of the 400,000,000 Negroes of the world to legislate in their interests, and in the time allotted to us we did our best to enact laws and to frame laws that in our judgment, we hope, will help solve the great problem that confronts us universally. The Universal Negro Improvement Association seeks to emancipate the Negro everywhere, industrially, educationally, politically and religiously. It also seeks a free and redeemed Africa. It has a great struggle ahead; it has a gigantic task to face. Nevertheless, as representatives of the Negro people of the world we have undertaken the task of freeing the 400,000,000 of our race, and of freeing our bleeding Motherland, Africa. We counseled with each other during the thirty-one days....and out of all we did, and out of all we said, we have come to the

one conclusion – that speedily Africa must be redeemed! We have come to the conclusion that speedily there must be an emancipated Negro race everywhere; and on going back to our respective homes we go with our determination to lay down, if needs be, the last drop of our blood for the defense of Africa and for the emancipation of our race.

The handwriting is on the wall. You see it as plain as daylight; you see it coming out of India, the tribes of India rising in rebellion against their overlords. You see it coming out of Africa, our dear motherland, Africa; the Moors rising in rebellion against their overlords, and defeating them at every turn. (Applause.) According to the last report flashed to this country from Morocco by the Associated Press, the Moors have again conquered and subdued the Spanish hordes. The same Associated Press flashes to us the news that there is a serious uprising in India, and the English people are marshaling their troops to subdue the spirit of liberty, of freedom, which is now permeating India. The news has come to us, and I have a cable in my pocket that comes from Ireland that the Irish are determined to have liberty and nothing less than liberty. (Applause.)

The League of Nations

The handwriting is on the wall, and as we go back to our respective homes we shall serve notice upon the world that we are also coming; coming with a united effort; coming with a united determination, a determination that Africa shall be free from coast to coast. (Applause) I have before me the decision of the League of Nations. Immediately after the war a Council of the League of Nations was called, and at that Council they decided that the territories wrested from Germany in West Africa, taken from her during the conflict, should be divided between France and England—608,000 square miles—without even asking the civilized Negroes of the world what disposition shall be made of their own homeland, of their own country. An insult was hurled at the civilized Negroes of the world when they thus took upon themselves the right to parcel out and apportion as they pleased 608,000 square miles of our own land; for we never gave it up; we never sold it. It is still our[s]. They parceled it out between these two nations—England and France—gave away our property without consulting us, and we are aggrieved, and we desire to serve notice on civilization and on the world that 400,000,000 Negroes are aggrieved. (Cries of "Yes!" And applause)

And we are the more aggrieved because of the lynch rope, because of segregation, because of the Jim Crowism that is used, practiced and exercised here in this country and in other parts of the world by the white nations of the earth, wherever Negroes happen accidentally or otherwise to find themselves. If there is no safety for Negroes in the white world, I cannot see what right they have to parcel out the homeland, the country of Negroes, without consulting Negroes and asking their permission so to do. Therefore, we are aggrieved. This question of prejudice will be the downfall of civilization, (applause) and I warn the white race of this, and of their doom. I hope they will take heed, because the handwriting is on the wall. (Applause.) No portion of humanity, no group of humanity, has an abiding right, an everlasting right, an eternal right to oppress other sections or portions of humanity. God never gave them the right, and if there is such a right, man arrogated it to himself, and God in all ages has been displeased with the arrogance of man. I warn those nations that believe themselves above human justice. You cannot long ignore the laws of God; you cannot long ignore the commandments of God; you cannot long ignore human justice, and exist. Your arrogance will destroy you, and I warn the races and the nations that have arrogated to themselves the right to oppress, the right to circumscribe, the right to keep down other races. I warn them that the hour is coming when the oppressed will rise in their might, in their majesty, and throw off the yoke of ages.

The world ought to understand that the Negro has come to life, possessed with a new conscience and a new soul. The old Negro is buried, and it is well the world knew it. It is not my purpose to deceive the world. I believe in righteousness; I believe in truth; I believe in honesty. That is why I warn a selfish world of the outcome of their actions towards the oppressed. There will come a day, Josephus Daniels wrote about it, a white statesman, and the world has talked about it, and I warn the world of it, that the day will come when the races of the world will marshal themselves in great conflict for the survival of the fittest. Men of the Universal Negro Improvement Association, I am asking you to prepare yourselves, and prepare your race the world over, because the conflict is coming, not because you will it, not because you desire it, but because you will be forced into it. The conflict between the races is drawing nearer and nearer. You see it; I see it; I see it in the handwriting on the wall, as expressed in the uprising in India. You see the handwriting on the wall of Africa; you see it, the handwriting on the wall of Europe. It is coming; it is drawing nearer and nearer. Four hundred million Negroes of the world, I am asking you to prepare yourselves, so that you will not be found wanting when that day comes. What a sorry day it will be. I hope it will never come. But my hope, my wish, will not prevent its coming. All that I can do is to warm humanity everywhere, so that humanity may change its tactics, and warn them of the danger. I repeat: I warn the white world against the prejudice they are practicing against Negroes; I warn them against the segregation and injustice they mete out to us, for the perpetuation of these things will mean the ultimate destruction of the present civilization, and the building up of a new civilization founded upon mercy, justice and equality.

I know that we have good men in all races living at the present time. We have good men of the black race, we have good men of the white race, good men of the yellow race, who are endeavoring to do the best they can to ward off this coming conflict. White men who have the vision, go ye back and warn your people of this coming conflict! Black men of vision, go ye to the four corners of the earth, and warn your people of this coming conflict. Yellow men, go ye out and warn your people of this coming conflict, because it is drawing nearer and nearer; nearer and nearer. Oh! If the world will only listen to the heart-throbs, to the soul-beasts of those who have the vision, those who have God's love in their hearts.

I see before me white men, black men and yellow men working assiduously for the peace of the world; for the bringing together of this thing called human brotherhood; I see them working through their organizations. They have been working during the last fifty. years. Some worked to bring about the emancipation, because they saw the danger of perpetual slavery. They brought about the liberation of 4,000,000 black people. They passed away, and the others started to work, but the opposition against them is too strong; the opposition against them is weighing them down. The world has gone mad; the world has become too material; the world has lost its spirit of kinship with God, and man can see nothing else but prejudice, avarice and greed. Avarice and greed will destroy the world and I am appealing to white, black and yellow whose hearts, whose souls are touched with the true spirit of humanity, with the true feeling of human brotherhood, to preach the doctrine of human love, more, to preach it louder, to preach it longer, because there is great need for it in the world at this time. Ah! If they could but see the danger – the conflict between the races – races fighting against each other. What a destruction, what a holocaust it will be! Can you imagine it?

Just take your idea from the last bloody war, wherein a race was pitted against itself (for the whole white races united as one from a common origin), the members of which, on both sides, fought so tenaciously that they killed off each other in frightful, staggering numbers. If a race pitted against itself could fight so tenaciously to kill itself without mercy, can you imagine the fury, can you imagine the mercilessness, the terribleness of the war that will come when all the races of the world will be on the battlefield, engaged in deadly combat for the destruction or overthrow of the one or the other, when beneath it and as a cause of it lies prejudice and hatred? Truly, it will be an ocean of blood; that is all it will be. So that if I can sound a note of warning now that will echo and reverberate around the world and thus prevent such conflict, God help me to do it; for Africa, like Europe, like Asia, is preparing for the day.

Africa's Possibilities

You may ask yourselves if you believe Africa is still asleep. Africa has been slumbering; but she was slumbering for a purpose. Africa still possesses her hidden mysteries; Africa has unused talents, and we are unearthing them now for the coming conflict. Oh, I hope it will never come therefore, I hope the white world will change its attitude towards the weaker races of the world, for we shall not be weak everlastingly. Ah, history teaches us of the rise and fall of nations, races, and empires. Rome fell in her majesty; Greece fell in her triumph; Babylon, Assyria, Carthage, Prussia, the German Empire – all fell in their pomp and power; the French Empire fell from the sway of the great Napoleon, for the dominion of the indomitable Corsican soldier. As they fell in the past, so will nations fall in the present age, and so will they fall in the future ages to come, the result of their unrighteousness.

I repeat, I warn the world, and I trust you will receive this warning as you go into the four corners of the earth. The white race should teach humanity. Out there is selfishness in the world. Let the white race teach humanity first, because we have been following the cause of humanity for three hundred years, and we have suffered much. If a change must come, it must not come from Negroes; it must come from the white race, for they are the ones who have brought about this estrangement between the races. The Negro never hated; at no time within the last five hundred years can they point to one single instance of Negro hatred. The Negro has loved even under the severest punishment. In slavery the Negro loved his master; he protected his master; he safeguarded his master's home. "Greater love hath no man than that he should lay down his life for another." We gave not only our services, our unrequited labor; we gave also our souls, we gave our hearts, we gave our all, to our oppressors.

But, after all, we are living in a material world, even though it is partly spiritual, and since we have been very spiritual in the past, we are going to take a part of the material now, and will give others the opportunity to practice the spiritual side of life. Therefore, I am not telling you to lead in humanity; I am not telling you to lead in the bringing about of the turning of humanity, because you have been doing that for three hundred years, and you have lost. But the compromise must come from the dominant races. We are warning them. We are not preaching a doctrine of hatred, and I trust you will not go back to your respective homes and preach such a doctrine. We are preaching, rather, a doctrine of humanity, a doctrine of human love. But we say love begins at home; "charity begins at home."

We are aggrieved because of this partitioning of Africa, because it seeks to deprive Negroes of the chance of higher national development; no chance, no opportunity, is given to us to prove our fitness to govern, to dominate in our own behalf. They impute so many bad things against Haiti and against Liberia, that they themselves circumvented Liberia so as to make it impossible for us to demonstrate our ability for self-government. Why not be honest? Why not be straightforward? Having desired the highest development, as they avowed and professed, of the Negro, why not give him a fair chance, an opportunity to prove his capacity for governing? What better opportunity ever presented itself than the present, when the territories of Germany in Africa were wrested from her control by the Allies in the last war—what better chance ever offered itself for trying out the higher ability of Negroes to govern themselves than to have given those territories to the civilized Negroes, and thus give them a trial to exercise themselves in a proper system of government? Because of their desire to keep us down, because of their desire to keep us apart, they refuse us a chance. The chance that they did give us is the chance that we are going to take. (Great applause.) Hence tonight, before I take my seat, I will move a resolution, and I think it is befitting at this time to pass such a resolution as I will move, so that the League of Nations and the Supreme Council of the Nations will understand that Negroes are not asleep; that Negroes are not false to themselves; that Negroes are wide awake, and that Negroes intend to take a serious part in the future government of this world; that God Almighty created him and placed him in it. This world owes us a place, and we are going to occupy that place.

We have a right to a large part in the political horizon, and I say to you that we are preparing to occupy that spot. Go back to your respective corners of the earth and preach the real doctrine of the Universal Negro Improvement Association—the doctrine of universal emancipation for Negroes, the doctrine of a free and a redeemed Africa!

Resolution

Be it Resolved, That we, the duly elected representatives of the Negro peoples of the world, assembled in the Second Annual Convention, do protest against the distribution of the land of Africa by the Supreme Council and the League of Nations among the white nations of the world. Africa, by right of heritage, is the property of the African races, and those at home and those abroad are now sufficiently civilized to conduct the affairs of their own homeland. This convention believes in the right of Europe for the Europeans; Asia for the Asiatics, and Africa for the Africans, those at home and those abroad. We believe, further, that only a close and unselfish application of this principle will prevent threatening race wars that may cast another gloom over civilization and humanity. At this time humanity everywhere is determined to reach a common standard of nationhood. Hence 400,000,000 Negroes demand a place in the political sun of the world.

Source: Marcus Garvey, "Address to the Second UNIA Convention," *Negro World*, September 10, 1921, pp. 3 and 6.

The photograph *Marcus Garvey at His Desk, 1924* offers a compelling visual representation of Garvey not only as a charismatic orator and movement leader but also as a disciplined administrator and architect of Black institutional power. While seated at his desk, Garvey is surrounded by the papers, symbols, and structure of the Universal Negro Improvement Association (UNIA), underscoring the organization's global reach and organizational ambition. The image conveys his commitment to building an independent Black infrastructure—complete with newspapers, businesses, and governing bodies—intended to rival the political and economic systems that excluded African people worldwide. This photograph stands as a powerful reminder that Garvey's vision was not merely rhetorical but operational: a blueprint for global Black self-determination.

Marcus Garvey at His Desk, 1924
(Source: Library of Congress Prints and Photographs Division)

The photograph *Marcus Garvey in Harlem, 1924* captures the magnetic presence of one of the most influential Black leaders of the twentieth century at the height of his global movement. Harlem, then the epicenter of Black cultural and political life in the United States, served as the UNIA's headquarters and the staging ground for Garvey's mass rallies, parades, and conventions. In this image, Garvey stands adorned in military regalia—emblematic of his vision of Black sovereignty and structured leadership. The public spectacle of Garvey in Harlem reflected more than pageantry. It represented a bold assertion of Black pride and unity as well as a global mission to dismantle white supremacy through organized pan-African solidarity.

Scholars can view and analyze this image at the Gilder Lehrman Institute of American History online for free, at https://www.gilderlehrman.org/ap-african-american-studies/additional-resources/resource-library?modal=/ap-african-american-studies/unit-2/organizing-for-freedom/west-india-emancipation-1857&f%5B0%5D=units%3A3299877&f%5B1%5D=units%3A3299878&page=5

The Universal Negro Improvement Association, under the leadership of Marcus Garvey, ignited a global movement rooted in Black pride, economic independence, and pan-African unity. At a time when white supremacy and colonial domination defined much of the world order, the UNIA offered a bold alternative: self-determination for people of African descent, at home and abroad. Though Garvey's strategies were debated, his message of racial uplift, institutional autonomy, and global Black solidarity reshaped political consciousness across the diaspora. His legacy endures in the symbols, movements, and philosophies that continue to inspire struggles for freedom and self-definition throughout the African world.

One Vision, Millions of Followers

Marcus Garvey's movement wasn't small. It was international. With powerful speeches, newspapers, and parades, he inspired Black pride and called for economic independence and unity across the African diaspora.

You're Practicing: Understanding mass movements.

Connect This To: Leadership, nationalism, and transnational organizing.

Theme: Autonomy and Pan-Africanism

Practice: Explain the Significance or Importance

Founded by Marcus Garvey, the Universal Negro Improvement Association (UNIA) emerged as a major global Black nationalist movement in the early twentieth century.

(A) Identify one central goal or belief of the UNIA.
(B) Explain how the UNIA's vision of Black pride, economic independence, or pan-African unity differed from or aligned with other Black political ideologies of the era.
(C) Analyze the significance of the UNIA's impact on African American identity, global Black consciousness, or later movements for Black empowerment.

SAMPLE RESPONSES

(A) A central goal of the Universal Negro Improvement Association (UNIA) was to promote Black pride, economic self-sufficiency, and global unity among people of African descent, which Marcus Garvey described as the vision of a "United States of Africa."

Garvey encouraged African Americans and Afro-Caribbean people to develop their own businesses, schools, and institutions, exemplified by the Black Star Line steamship company, which aimed to foster economic independence and facilitate trade between Africa and the diaspora.

The UNIA also sought to challenge white supremacy by celebrating African heritage and rejecting the idea that liberation for Black people should come solely through integration into white-dominated societies.

(B) The UNIA's emphasis on separatism and global African unity contrasted with the NAACP's integrationist strategy, which focused on using the U.S. legal system to secure equal rights within American society.

Garvey's vision aligned more closely with the pan-African Congresses organized by W. E. B. Du Bois in its recognition of global Black solidarity, but diverged in strategy—Du Bois emphasized elite leadership and political advocacy, while Garvey stressed mass mobilization and economic enterprise.

Unlike the more accommodationist approach of leaders such as Booker T. Washington, who advocated industrial education and gradual economic advancement, Garvey's movement called for an immediate reclamation of African identity and the eventual establishment of a sovereign Black nation.

(C) The UNIA fostered a global sense of Black identity by linking African Americans, Afro-Caribbean migrants, and Africans in a shared vision of liberation and self-determination, influencing later movements in Black internationalism and African independence struggles.

Garvey's message of Black pride and self-reliance laid ideological groundwork for mid-twentieth-century movements such as the Nation of Islam and the Black Power movement, which similarly emphasized economic autonomy and cultural nationalism.

Even after the decline of the UNIA in the late 1920s, its legacy persisted through the symbolism of the red, black, and green Pan-African flag, which became a lasting emblem of African unity and resistance against white supremacy.

Skills Assessed: Explain the significance of historical developments; use sources and evidence; analyze relationships among developments.

KEY TAKEAWAYS

1. **Africa as Symbol and Site of Return**
   - During the Harlem Renaissance and beyond, Africa functioned as both a real and an imagined homeland for African Americans.
   - Poets and artists invoked Africa as a source of cultural pride, historical depth, and political solidarity.
2. **Migration and Diasporic Identity Formation**
   - The Great Migration of African Americans from the rural South to urban centers reshaped Black cultural life, politics, and identity.
   - Simultaneously, Afro-Caribbean migration brought new religious, linguistic, and artistic influences, fostering vibrant diasporic networks in places like Harlem.
3. **Black History as a Tool for Liberation**
   - Black educators, historians, and public intellectuals developed African American Studies to reclaim the narrative of Black experiences and contributions.
   - The institutionalization of Black history was itself an act of resistance against cultural erasure and misrepresentation.
4. **Performing Blackness on Global Stages**
   - Black performers transformed global music, theater, and dance through innovations rooted in African diasporic tradition.
   - Works like Josephine Baker's performances and Paul Robeson's multilingual concerts combined artistry with political commentary.
5. **The Universal Negro Improvement Association (UNIA) and Pan-Africanism**
   - Led by Marcus Garvey, the UNIA promoted Black pride, economic independence, and a vision of returning to Africa.
   - The movement's bold aesthetics, mass appeal, and unapologetic pan-Africanism inspired future liberation movements globally.

Practice Multiple-Choice Questions

DIRECTIONS: Pick the letter that best answers the following questions.

Questions 1 through 3 refer to the following.

Anonymous Letter Beckoning African Americans to Leave the South, published in *The Messenger*, March 1920

"Fellow Negroes of the South, leave there. Go North, East, and West—anywhere—to get out of that hell hole. There are better schools here for your children, higher wages for yourselves, votes if you are twenty-one, better housing and more liberty. All is not rosy here, by any means, but it is Paradise compared with Georgia, Arkansas, Texas, Mississippi and Alabama. Besides, you make it better for those you leave behind. Labor becomes scarce, so that the Bourbons of Dixie are compelled to pay your brothers back home more wages. They will give them more schools and privileges, too, to try to get them to come back and, secondly, to try to keep you from leaving.

Stop buying property in the South, to be burned down and run away from over night. Sell out your stuff quietly, saying nothing to the Negro lackeys, and leave! Come into the land of at least incipient civilization!"

Source: "Negroes, Leave the South!" *The Messenger*, March 1920, p. 2.

1. What was the main purpose of the editorial "Negroes, Leave the South!"?

   (A) To promote reconciliation between Black and white Southerners through industrial cooperation
   (B) To encourage African Americans to migrate to the North in pursuit of safety and opportunity
   (C) To criticize the rise of labor unions for excluding African American workers
   (D) To advocate for the reestablishment of African American-owned plantations in the South

2. Which of the following best describes the tone of the editorial "Negroes, Leave the South!"?

   (A) Cautiously optimistic about the potential for Southern reform
   (B) Indifferent and detached from the urgency of Black migration
   (C) Urgent and confrontational, calling for immediate action
   (D) Nostalgic for antebellum Southern traditions

3. The editorial "Negroes, Leave the South!" provides historical evidence for which of the following developments?

   (A) The political success of Reconstruction-era African American leaders
   (B) The collapse of agricultural markets during the Great Depression
   (C) The grassroots motivations behind the Great Migration
   (D) The expansion of Black voting rights in the Jim Crow South

Questions 4 through 6 refer to the following.

Photograph *Marcus Garvey at His Desk, 1924*

4. The photograph *Marcus Garvey at His Desk, 1924* is most useful to historians studying which of the following?
   (A) The collapse of Black-led organizations during the Harlem Renaissance
   (B) The administrative and institutional foundations of Black nationalist movements
   (C) The political integration of African Americans into the U.S. federal government
   (D) The migration of African Americans from the rural South to urban centers

5. Which of the following best explains the significance of Garvey's desk setting in the 1924 photograph?
   (A) It symbolizes the UNIA's role as a global organization with newspapers, businesses, and governance structures.
   (B) It reflects Garvey's assimilation into mainstream white political institutions.
   (C) It demonstrates the decline of his movement and the disorganization of the UNIA by the mid-1920s.
   (D) It shows Garvey's turn away from politics toward religious and spiritual leadership.

6. What does Garvey's posture and placement in the 1924 photograph most clearly convey about his leadership style?
   (A) His emphasis on discipline, order, and the construction of independent Black institutions
   (B) His rejection of administrative leadership in favor of grassroots activism alone
   (C) His reliance on European allies and white political figures to support his movement
   (D) His retreat from international organizing to focus only on Harlem community issues

Answer Explanations

1. **(B)** The editorial is a direct appeal to African Americans to leave the South due to its entrenched racial oppression, including lynching, voter suppression, and economic exploitation. It promotes migration to the North as a means to escape and seek a better life. Choice (A) is incorrect because the editorial does not promote reconciliation or industrial cooperation. It highlights racial violence, injustice, and the systemic denial of opportunity in the South, arguing that these conditions make reconciliation impossible. Choice (C) is incorrect because, although labor conditions are relevant to the context of the Great Migration, this editorial does not focus on labor unions or their treatment of Black workers. Choice (D) is incorrect because the editorial explicitly rejects the idea that the South is redeemable for African Americans; it does not suggest returning to agricultural life or landownership in the South as a solution.

2. **(C)** The editorial is forceful in its language, emphasizing the urgency of leaving the South. It seeks to awaken readers to the life-threatening dangers of staying and encourages mass migration as a form of resistance and survival. Choice (A) is incorrect because the editorial expresses no hope for Southern reform; it condemns the South as violently racist and hostile to Black life. Choice (B) is incorrect because the tone is impassioned and direct, not indifferent or detached. The writer urges immediate migration as a survival tactic. Choice (D) is incorrect because the editorial firmly rejects Southern traditions, particularly those associated with white supremacy and racial violence.

3. **(C)** The editorial serves as primary source evidence for why many African Americans participated in the Great Migration. It reveals the grassroots, emotional, and political motivations—especially the desire to escape racial violence and pursue opportunity in the North. Choice (A) is incorrect because the editorial was published long after Reconstruction and does not reflect on that era's political gains. Choice (B) is incorrect because, although economic hardship is mentioned, the Great Depression had not yet occurred in 1920. The editorial focuses more on racial violence and social conditions than on national economic collapse. Choice (D) is incorrect because the editorial documents the suppression of Black voting rights in the South, not their expansion. It condemns disenfranchisement as a key reason for leaving.

4. **(B)** The photograph is most useful for studying the administrative and institutional foundations of Black nationalist movements. Garvey is shown at his desk, surrounded by organizational materials, which underscores his role as a builder of institutions like the *Negro World* newspaper, the Black Star Line, and the UNIA's governing bodies. Choice (A) is incorrect because the UNIA was at its height in 1924, not in decline. Choice (C) is incorrect because Garvey's focus was on separatism and self-determination, not integration into U.S. government systems. Choice (D) is incorrect because while the Great Migration shaped Harlem's demographics, this photo highlights Garvey's administrative leadership, not migration patterns.

5. **(A)** Garvey's desk setting symbolizes the UNIA's global scope and infrastructure, including its press, businesses, and administrative framework. The setting conveys that Garvey's leadership extended beyond speeches and parades to include practical governance and institution-building. Choice (B) is incorrect because Garvey resisted assimilation and instead created independent Black systems. Choice (C) is incorrect because the UNIA remained a significant force in 1924; its decline came later. Choice (D) is incorrect because Garvey did not abandon politics—he maintained his focus on economic and political autonomy.

6. **(A)** Garvey's posture and placement convey discipline, order, and a commitment to building independent Black institutions. His seated position at the center of organizational activity reflects a leader deeply engaged in the operational aspects of his movement. Choice (B) is incorrect because the photo emphasizes his role as an administrator, not just a grassroots activist. Choice (C) is incorrect because Garvey's focus was on Black self-reliance, not dependence on European allies. Choice (D) is incorrect because his movement remained global in scope, not confined to Harlem.

PART 5

Unit 4—Movements and Debates

11

Freedom in the Global Arena: Black Resistance, Radical Thought, and the Civil Rights Movement

Key Themes

- Global Black consciousness forged through literature, revolution, and shared anti-colonial struggles
- Wartime contradictions of democracy denied to Black Americans
- Housing and education discrimination as key battlegrounds for civil rights
- Grassroots organizing and women's leadership as the foundation of the movement
- Intersection of cultural pride and political activism across the diaspora

TIMELINE

Date/Period	Event/Development	Related Topics
1930s–1950s	**Négritude movement** emerges among francophone African and Caribbean writers like **Aimé Césaire** and **Léopold Senghor**, celebrating Black identity and rejecting colonial assimilation	Topic 4.1—Négritude and *Negrismo* Movements
1930s–1940s	***Negrismo*** in Latin America promotes Afro-Caribbean culture and challenges racial hierarchies	Topic 4.1—*Negrismo* Movements
1945–1960s	**Anticolonial revolutions** gain momentum across Africa and the Caribbean (e.g., Ghana, Algeria, Kenya)	Topic 4.2—Anticolonialism and Black Thought
1942–1945	**Double V Campaign** launched by Black newspapers during WWII—victory abroad against fascism and at home against racism	Topic 4.3—WWII and Double V Campaign
1944	**G.I. Bill** enacted but benefits often denied to African American veterans through discriminatory implementation	Topic 4.3—G.I. Bill and Black Veterans
1940s–1950s	**Segregation in schools, public life, and housing** persists; sparks early legal and grassroots challenges	Topic 4.4—Segregation and Early Civil Rights
1930s–1970s	Practice of **redlining** by federal agencies and banks denies mortgages and investment in Black communities	Topic 4.5—Redlining and Housing Discrimination

Date/Period	Event/Development	Related Topics
1954	***Brown v. Board of Education*** Supreme Court decision declares school segregation unconstitutional	Topic 4.4—Civil Rights Origins
1955–1965	Growth of **major civil rights organizations**: NAACP, SCLC, SNCC, CORE, Urban League	Topic 4.6—Civil Rights Organizations
1955	**Montgomery Bus Boycott** begins, led by Rosa Parks and **Jo Ann Robinson**—supported by **Women's Political Council**	Topic 4.7—Black Women's Leadership
1960s	Black women like **Ella Baker**, **Fannie Lou Hamer**, and **Septima Clark** lead grassroots activism and voter registration campaigns	Topic 4.7—Women's Leadership and Organizing

Topic 4.1 The Négritude and *Negrismo* Movements

Key Terms

- Négritude—Black consciousness literary and political movement
- Aimé Césaire, Léopold Sédar Senghor—founding thinkers
- Black identity and solidarity
- Colonialism and resistance
- Afro-Caribbean and Francophone thought
- *Negrismo*—Afro-Cuban literary movement
- Nicolás Guillén—poet of *Negrismo*
- Cultural pride and pan-Africanism

What does it mean to write yourself back into history? In the first half of the twentieth century, Black writers and intellectuals across the French-and Spanish-speaking world responded to colonization not only with protest but with poetry, essays, and art that celebrated Black identity, language, and resistance.

The Négritude and *Negrismo* movements emerged as two powerful literary and cultural responses to European colonialism and anti-Black racism in the early twentieth century. While rooted in different linguistic and geographic contexts—Négritude in the Francophone world (notably among intellectuals from Senegal, Martinique, and Haiti), and *Negrismo* in Latin America and the Caribbean (especially Cuba and Puerto Rico)—both movements sought to reclaim Black cultural identity and challenge the Eurocentric foundations of empire.

Writers such as Aimé Césaire, Léopold Sédar Senghor, and Nicolás Guillén used poetry and prose to critique colonial domination, elevate African heritage, and redefine what it meant to be Black in a global context. These movements helped lay the intellectual foundation for later Black nationalist, pan-Africanist, and decolonial thought.

After engaging with this topic, scholars will be able to:

- Describe the historical and political contexts that gave rise to the Négritude and *Negrismo* movements.
- Identify key figures, texts, and themes associated with each movement.
- Analyze how both movements critiqued colonialism and celebrated Black identity.
- Evaluate the broader connections between Black cultural production and anti-colonial resistance across the African diaspora.

Diasporic Awakening: The Rise of Négritude and *Negrismo*

In the early to mid-twentieth century, the Négritude and *Negrismo* movements emerged as powerful literary and political responses to colonialism, racial hierarchy, and cultural erasure. Though geographically and linguistically distinct—Négritude emerging among French-speaking African and Caribbean intellectuals and *Negrismo* arising in the Spanish-speaking Caribbean—both movements affirmed the enduring influence of African heritage and aesthetics in the lives of African descendants. Heavily inspired by the cultural pride and political consciousness of the New Negro movement in the United States, both movements sought to reclaim Black identity through poetry, art, and resistance to assimilation. Their simultaneous emergence illustrates the shared urgency across the African diaspora to define Blackness on its own terms.

Shared Goals, Divergent Visions

While the Négritude, *Negrismo*, and New Negro movements all centered around cultural pride and Black political liberation, they approached Blackness and Africa from different perspectives. Négritude emphasized a pan-African vision rooted in common ancestral ties and spiritual kinship with Africa, often rejecting European colonial influence entirely. *Negrismo*, by contrast, focused on the celebration of African contributions to Caribbean life—particularly in music, dance, folklore, and literature—while sometimes operating within mestizo and creole cultural frameworks that blurred racial lines. Despite these distinctions, both movements highlighted the necessity of elevating Black voices and traditions as a form of resistance to white supremacy and colonial domination.

Négritude: Black Consciousness and Anti-Colonial Critique

Négritude, which translates to *Blackness* in French, was a literary and political movement that took shape in the 1930s among Francophone African and Caribbean writers such as Aimé Césaire (Martinique), Léopold Sédar Senghor (Senegal), and Léon Damas (French Guiana). These thinkers condemned colonialism not only for its political violence but also for its attempt to erase African culture through forced assimilation. In their poetry and prose, they rejected European ideals of civilization and instead exalted African identity, spiritual depth, and historical continuity. Négritude was deeply intellectual and philosophical, offering a vision of Black liberation that embraced African epistemologies while attacking the psychological and material violence of empire.

Negrismo: Cultural Affirmation in the Spanish-Speaking Caribbean

At the same time that Négritude emerged, *Negrismo* developed across the Spanish-speaking Caribbean—particularly in Cuba, Puerto Rico, and the Dominican Republic—as a literary and artistic celebration of African heritage. Writers such as Nicolás Guillén (Cuba) and Luis Palés Matos (Puerto Rico) used poetry to highlight African rhythms, vernacular speech, and spiritual traditions embedded in Caribbean culture. *Negrismo* was often adopted by Black and mixed-race intellectuals who sought to affirm African cultural contributions while challenging the marginalization of Black identity in Latin American societies. Though sometimes critiqued for romanticizing or commodifying African culture, *Negrismo* helped bring Black life and artistry to the center of national cultural narratives.

Critiques of Colonialism and Racial Ideology

Proponents of both Négritude and *Negrismo*—including figures like Aimé Césaire—fiercely rejected the colonial justification that European empires had "civilized" African peoples. Instead, they exposed colonialism as a brutal system of exploitation built on racial ideologies that dehumanized the colonized and justified coerced labor, land theft, and cultural domination. Their literary work served as both creative expression and revolutionary critique, connecting the struggle against colonization with a broader fight for psychological, spiritual, and political liberation.

Transnational Solidarity and Shared Struggles

African American writers and activists engaged deeply with the Négritude and *Negrismo* movements, identifying shared struggles against global racism, imperialism, and economic exploitation. Figures like Jessie Redmon Fauset—editor of *The Crisis*, the NAACP's official magazine—amplified voices from across the diaspora and articulated a critique of colonialism that mirrored Black American opposition to Jim Crow and racial capitalism. These transnational exchanges strengthened pan-African solidarity and forged intellectual and cultural alliances that would influence Black internationalist thought throughout the twentieth century.

Les Fétiches by Loïs Mailou Jones, 1938

Loïs Mailou Jones's *Les Fétiches* (1938) is a striking visual declaration of Black identity and diasporic heritage. Painted during her time in Paris, the work synthesizes African artistic traditions with modernist techniques. It depicts five stylized African masks layered across a vivid and abstract background. Drawing on African sculpture, cubist influence, and African American cultural pride, Jones's composition reflects her belief that African aesthetics were not primitive relics but sources of beauty, power, and artistic innovation. The painting emerged at the intersection of the Harlem Renaissance and Négritude movements, both of which celebrated Africa as a wellspring of cultural strength.

The Jungle (La Jungla) by Wifredo Lam, 1943

Wifredo Lam's *The Jungle* (1943) is a dense and enigmatic painting that blends Afro-Cuban spirituality, surrealism, and anticolonial symbolism. Created during Lam's return to Cuba, the work critiques the racial and economic exploitation of Afro-Caribbean people under colonial sugar economies. Elongated human-animal figures, reminiscent of Santería deities and African masks, occupy a compressed sugarcane field—confronting viewers with themes of identity, labor, and resistance. Lam, of Afro-Cuban and Chinese descent, sought to "paint the drama of his country" while also engaging in global conversations about race, colonialism, and modern art.

Excerpt from *Discourse on Colonialism* by Aimé Césaire, 1955

Aimé Césaire's *Discourse on Colonialism* (1955) is one of the most influential anti-colonial texts of the twentieth century. In this excerpt, Césaire dismantles the myth that colonialism was a civilizing mission, arguing instead that it dehumanized both colonizers and the colonized. He denounces Europe's moral hypocrisy, comparing colonialism to fascism, and asserts that Europe cannot claim superiority while maintaining global systems of domination. Césaire's work, deeply rooted in the Négritude movement, bridges poetry and political theory, blending searing critique with lyrical force. His writings provided ideological foundations for global decolonization movements in Africa, the Caribbean, and beyond.

To further explore the themes presented in the image of *Les Fétiches*, *The Jungle*, or Aimé Césaire's *Discourse on Colonialism*, scholars are encouraged to visit the Gilder Lehrman Institute of American History's AP African American Studies resource online: https://www.gilderlehrman.org/ap-african-american-studies/unit-4/anticolonialism-transatlantic-black-political-thought#par-16942.

Freedom in More than One Language

Black writers and artists from Africa, the Caribbean, and Latin America found common ground in celebrating Blackness. Their words resisted racism and colonialism—and reminded the world that Black pride has no borders.

You're Practicing: Comparing movements across the Black diaspora.

Connect This To: Poetry, pride, and global solidarity.

Theme: Global Black Identity

Practice: Explain the Significance or Importance

In the early twentieth century, the Négritude and *Negrismo* movements emerged as literary and cultural responses to colonialism, European racism, and Black identity.

(A) Identify one central figure or text from either the Négritude or *Negrismo* movement.
(B) Explain how the movement you selected responded to colonial oppression or shaped Black cultural identity.
(C) Analyze the significance of these movements in promoting pan-African consciousness and challenging dominant European narratives.

SAMPLE RESPONSES

(A) A central figure in the Négritude movement was Aimé Césaire, a Martinican poet, playwright, and politician whose 1939 work *Cahier d'un retour au pays natal* (*Notebook of a Return to the Native Land*) fused surrealist imagery with African cultural affirmation to critique colonialism.

Césaire's ideas were developed alongside Léopold Sédar Senghor of Senegal and Léon Damas of French Guiana, whose poetry and essays elevated African heritage and spiritual traditions as sources of strength for the global African diaspora.

In the Negrismo movement, a parallel figure was Nicolás Guillén, the Cuban poet whose *Motivos de son* (1930) integrated Afro-Cuban rhythms, vernacular speech, and musical traditions into modern poetry, placing African heritage at the center of Cuban identity.

(B) The Négritude movement arose as a direct rejection of the French colonial policy of assimilation, which sought to erase African and Afro-Caribbean cultural practices in favor of European norms. Césaire and Senghor responded by affirming African cultural values as equal, if not superior, to European traditions.

In their writings, Négritude poets reclaimed African aesthetics, oral traditions, and philosophies, framing them as vital to human civilization rather than as "primitive" or obsolete, as colonial narratives claimed.

This work paralleled the Negrismo movement's embrace of African cultural roots in the Caribbean, where writers like Guillén used music, dance, and folklore to challenge anti-Black stereotypes and assert the centrality of African traditions in national culture.

(C) The Négritude and *Negrismo* movements advanced pan-African consciousness by linking the struggles of African-descended peoples in Africa, the Caribbean, and the Americas into a shared narrative of resilience and cultural pride.

By centering Africa and the African diaspora as sources of artistic, spiritual, and philosophical richness, these movements dismantled colonial ideologies that positioned Europe as the sole source of civilization.

Their influence extended far beyond literature: Négritude inspired anti-colonial leaders such as Kwame Nkrumah and Frantz Fanon, while *Negrismo*'s cultural nationalism informed later movements for Black cultural sovereignty in Latin America. Together, they forged a transnational cultural front against white supremacy that resonated throughout the twentieth century.

Skills Assessed: Explain the significance of historical developments; use sources and evidence; analyze relationships among developments.

Topic 4.2 Anticolonialism and Black Political Thought

Key Terms

- Kwame Nkrumah, Frantz Fanon, Amílcar Cabral
- Pan-African Congresses
- Decolonization of Africa and the Caribbean
- Fanon's *The Wretched of the Earth*
- Solidarity with African independence movements
- U.S. Black activists and global liberation
- Nonalignment and anti-imperialism
- Malcolm X's visits to Africa

What connects Black freedom struggles in Mississippi, Accra, Havana, and Johannesburg? In the twentieth century, Black political thinkers and activists across the globe came to see their fights not as isolated but as linked by common systems of racism, colonialism, and economic exploitation—and by a shared vision of liberation. Throughout the twentieth century, the global Black Freedom movement was shaped by a deep and evolving tradition of anti-colonial political thought. As African nations fought to liberate themselves from European rule and as African Americans confronted segregation and systemic racism, a transnational network of solidarity emerged across the African diaspora.

Activists, writers, and intellectuals exchanged ideas, collaborated on strategies, and framed their local struggles within a broader global context of racial justice and decolonization. From pan-African congresses and anti-apartheid protests to the influence of leaders like Kwame Nkrumah, Malcolm X, and Angela Davis, this era witnessed the rise of a distinctly diasporic political consciousness. Anti-colonial thought did not just critique empire. It called for the creation of new Black futures built on self-determination, unity, and revolutionary change.

After engaging with this topic, scholars will be able to:

- Describe the goals and strategies of the Black Freedom movement in the twentieth century.
- Identify major expressions of diasporic solidarity and collaboration across African-descended communities.
- Explain how anti-colonial and pan-African ideas influenced Black politics in the United States, Africa, the Caribbean, and beyond.
- Analyze how transnational connections reshaped activism and resistance within local and global Black communities.

The Black Freedom Movement as a Transnational Struggle

The Black Freedom movement, spanning from the mid-1940s through the 1970s, was not confined to the borders of the United States. It encompassed a global wave of activism rooted in the dismantling of racist, colonial, and imperialist systems. In the United States, it included the Civil Rights Movement, which challenged and overturned Jim Crow laws through nonviolent resistance and legal reform, and the Black Power movement, which emphasized racial pride, cultural affirmation, and self-determination. Abroad, anti-colonial revolutions surged across Africa and the Caribbean, forming a broader context in which Black liberation movements mutually influenced and reinforced each other. These struggles shared not only a common enemy—white supremacy and colonial domination—but also a vision of Black autonomy and global solidarity.

African Americans and the Rise of Pan-African Solidarity

In the 1950s and 1960s, African American intellectuals, activists, and artists increasingly turned their gaze toward Africa—not only as an ancestral homeland but as a living site of revolutionary transformation. Many traveled to newly independent or decolonizing nations to express solidarity and participate in the broader pan-African project. These encounters deepened political consciousness and expanded the geographic imagination of the Black Freedom movement. Figures such as Malcolm X and Maya Angelou championed the idea that the fate of African Americans was tied to the liberation of all African people and that Black unity across borders was essential to dismantling racism globally.

Ghana as a Beacon of Liberation

The Republic of Ghana's independence from British colonial rule in 1957 served as a major symbolic and strategic turning point for global Black political thought. African American leaders including Dr. Martin Luther King Jr., Malcolm X, Pauli Murray, Maya Angelou, and W. E. B. Du Bois traveled to Ghana to witness and celebrate this historic achievement. For many, Ghana became a touchstone for diasporic solidarity and pan-African aspiration—a living example of what a liberated African state could symbolize for the rest of the Black world. Du Bois, who died and was buried in Ghana, embodied the full circle of diasporic commitment to African sovereignty.

Black Diplomacy and Resistance through Travel

Beyond the African continent, African Americans also looked to other parts of the Global South to establish alliances against white supremacy and segregation. In 1960, famed boxer Joe Louis joined a largely African American delegation to Cuba, where they promoted the island as a destination free from the racial segregation that still gripped the U.S. South. These forms of Black diplomacy blurred the lines between tourism, politics, and resistance—using travel as a means of challenging the legitimacy of Jim Crow and fostering connections with other nations pursuing racial and economic justice.

Diasporic Solidarity and the Global Reach of Black Resistance

As African Americans and Africans identified shared experiences of colonial exploitation and racial violence, they forged bonds of solidarity that extended the influence of the Black Freedom movement beyond U.S. borders. These connections enriched both African American civil rights organizing and African anti-colonial struggles, creating a reciprocal network of support, strategy, and inspiration. The transnational dialogue allowed Black activists to reimagine liberation as a global project, not merely a national one.

The Year of Africa and Its Lasting Legacy

The impact of this diasporic solidarity became especially visible in 1960—designated the Year of Africa—when 17 African nations declared their independence from European colonial powers. This surge in African sovereignty was both celebrated and amplified by African American activists, journalists, and organizations. It signaled a moment of global reckoning with imperialism and inspired renewed commitments to racial justice in the United States. Though colonialism in its formal sense has declined, the legacy of pan-African and anti-colonial solidarity continues to shape Black political thought into the present day—linking contemporary movements for justice across borders.

In March 1957, Dr. Martin Luther King Jr. and his wife, Coretta Scott King, traveled to Accra, Ghana, to attend the nation's independence celebrations at the invitation of Prime Minister Kwame Nkrumah. This historic event marked Ghana as the first sub-Saharan African country to gain independence from colonial rule, symbolizing a significant milestone in the global movement against imperialism. During his visit, Dr. King participated in a radio interview conducted by Etta Moten Barnett in which he reflected on the profound significance of Ghana's independence.

Dr. King's observations underscored the interconnectedness of global struggles for freedom and justice. He perceived Ghana's emergence from colonial rule as a beacon of hope for oppressed peoples worldwide, including African Americans fighting against segregation and racial injustice in the United States. This interview exemplifies the transnational solidarity that characterized the Black Freedom movement in the twentieth century.

Dr. King's experience in Ghana reinforced his commitment to nonviolent resistance and deepened his understanding of the global dimensions of the struggle for civil rights. The insights he gained during this visit influenced his subsequent speeches and writings, wherein he increasingly linked the African American civil rights movement to broader global movements for decolonization and human rights.

For scholars seeking to explore this interview further, the full transcript can be accessed by conducting an online search for "Martin Luther King Jr. Interview During Visit to Newly Independent Ghana on Invitation from Kwame Nkrumah, 1957," available through the Martin Luther King, Jr. Research and Education Institute at Stanford University: https://kinginstitute.stanford.edu/king-papers/documents/interview-etta-moten-barnett#ftnref5.

In 1960, former heavyweight boxing champion Joe Louis participated in a historic delegation of African American business and media leaders who traveled to Havana, Cuba, during the early years of the Cuban Revolution. The visit aimed to explore economic and cultural partnerships and to promote Cuba as a destination free from the segregation and racial violence that African Americans faced in the Jim Crow South. As a globally recognized sports icon, Louis's presence lent visibility and credibility to the delegation's mission, symbolizing a form of Black diplomacy rooted in dignity, self-determination, and solidarity with oppressed peoples in the Global South. This moment reflected a broader trend of African Americans engaging in international travel and activism to critique U.S. racial policies and build diasporic alliances during the Cold War era.

Scholars can view and analyze a photograph by Robert Abbott Sengstacke of American boxer Joe Louis (1914–1981) and Cuban leader Fidel Castro (1926–2016) during a visit by the Joe Louis Commission, a delegation composed predominantly of African American business and media leaders, to Havana, Cuba, January 1960 at the Gilder Lehrman Institute of American History online for free at https://www.gilderlehrman.org/ap-african-american-studies/unit-4/anticolonialism-transatlantic-black-political-thought/joe-louis-fidel-castro-1960

This 1963 photograph captures Maya Angelou, Julian Mayfield, and a group of African American expatriates demonstrating outside the U.S. Embassy in Accra, Ghana, in protest of racial violence and injustice in the United States. Occurring during the height of the Civil Rights Movement, this act of public petitioning abroad reflected the growing urgency among African Americans to internationalize the Black Freedom struggle. Many African American intellectuals, artists, and activists had relocated to Ghana during Kwame Nkrumah's presidency, drawn by the promise of pan-African unity and postcolonial possibility. Their protest in Accra symbolized diasporic solidarity and a rejection of American racial hypocrisy on a global stage. By taking their grievances to the steps of their own government while standing on African soil, these figures reframed civil rights as a matter of international human rights.

Petitioners Julian Mayfield, Alphaeus Hunton, Alice Windom, W. A. Jeanpierre, and Maya Angelou Make, outside the U.S. Embassy in Accra, Ghana, 1963 (Source: Schomburg Center for Research in Black Culture, Manuscripts, Archives and Rare Books Division, The New York Public Library)

The anti-colonial struggles of the twentieth century reshaped Black political thought by forging powerful connections among African Americans and people of African descent across the globe. From Accra to Havana, Black writers, activists, and leaders envisioned liberation not as an isolated national project but as a shared global imperative. Through pan-African alliances, cultural exchange, and transnational protest, the Black Freedom movement extended beyond the borders of the United States and became a model of diasporic solidarity. This era of political awakening revealed that the fight against white supremacy, colonialism, and racial capitalism was a collective struggle—one rooted in shared histories and united by a vision of freedom that spanned continents.

Freedom Isn't Just an American Dream

The fight for civil rights in the United States was deeply connected to anti-colonial movements in Africa and the Caribbean. Leaders like Kwame Nkrumah and Malcolm X saw themselves as part of the same global fight for liberation.

You're Practicing: Seeing U.S. history as part of world history.

Connect This To: Liberation movements and global power shifts.

Theme: Power and Resistance

Practice: Explain Causality (Causes or Effects)

During the twentieth century, Black political thinkers and activists developed ideologies that connected the fight against racism in the United States with anti-colonial struggles around the world.

(A) Identify one Black intellectual, leader, or movement that contributed to anti-colonial political thought.

(B) Explain how global systems of imperialism and colonialism influenced the development of Black political ideologies.

(C) Analyze one effect of anti-colonial thought on African American activism or international solidarity movements.

SAMPLE RESPONSES

(A) Kwame Nkrumah, the first president of independent Ghana, was a central figure in anti-colonial political thought and pan-Africanism, advocating for the liberation of Africa from European rule and for global Black unity.

Nkrumah hosted African American leaders such as Martin Luther King Jr., Malcolm X, and W. E. B. Du Bois in Ghana, turning the country into a symbolic and strategic hub for global Black solidarity.

His writings, including *Africa Must Unite* (1963), emphasized that African independence was inseparable from the freedom of African-descended people worldwide, influencing movements for racial justice in the United States and beyond.

(B) European colonialism in Africa and the Caribbean operated through racial hierarchy, economic exploitation, and cultural erasure, paralleling Jim Crow segregation and racial oppression in the United States.

Recognizing these shared structures, African American activists such as Malcolm X and Angela Davis reframed U.S. racial injustice as part of a global struggle against imperialism, aligning themselves with anti-colonial movements in Africa, Asia, and Latin America.

The pan-African Congresses (1919–1945) and later solidarity visits to decolonizing nations deepened the belief that liberation movements were interconnected, and that dismantling white supremacy required both local civil rights action and global anti-imperialist alliances.

(C) Anti-colonial thought inspired African American activists to internationalize the Civil Rights Movement, framing it as part of a larger human rights struggle. This shift influenced leaders such as Dr. Martin Luther King Jr., who, after attending Ghana's 1957 independence celebration, linked the fight against segregation to global decolonization in his speeches.

It also fostered direct participation in global liberation struggles, as seen when African American expatriates such as Maya Angelou and Julian Mayfield relocated to Ghana in the 1960s to work alongside newly independent African nations and to protest U.S. racial violence on an international stage.

By forging alliances with anti-colonial movements, African American activists strengthened Black internationalism, laying the intellectual and organizational groundwork for later movements such as the Black Power era and the anti-apartheid solidarity campaigns of the 1970s and 1980s.

Skills Assessed: Explain the effects of historical developments; use sources and evidence; analyze relationships among developments.

Topic 4.3 African Americans and the Second World War: The Double V Campaign and the G.I. Bill

Key Terms

- Double V Campaign—victory against fascism abroad and racism at home
- *Pittsburgh Courier*—newspaper that launched Double V
- Tuskegee Airmen; 6888th Central Postal Battalion
- Segregated military units
- G.I. Bill of Rights (1944)—postwar education and housing aid
- Disparities in G.I. Bill access for Black veterans
- Postwar racial unrest

How could a nation fight for freedom abroad while denying it at home? For African Americans serving during World War II, this contradiction sparked a movement that demanded victory not only over fascism overseas but also over racism within the United States. African Americans played a vital role in the Second World War, serving in segregated military units, working in defense industries, and supporting the war effort through community mobilization and activism. Yet even as they wore the uniform of a nation committed to democracy, they faced systemic discrimination, racial violence, and exclusion from many of the very freedoms they were defending.

This contradiction gave rise to the Double V Campaign—an urgent call for "victory abroad and victory at home"—which galvanized Black newspapers, veterans, and civil rights organizations. After the war, the G.I. Bill promised to expand access to education, housing, and economic security for returning veterans. However, Black service members often faced discriminatory barriers that limited their ability to benefit from these programs. Together, African Americans' wartime service, political demands, and postwar struggles reveal how World War II became a turning point in the long fight for racial justice in America.

After engaging with this topic, scholars will be able to:

- Describe the contributions and experiences of African Americans during World War II.
- Analyze the origins and impact of the Double V Campaign as a strategy of wartime resistance.
- Evaluate how racial discrimination shaped African Americans' access to the benefits of the G.I. Bill.
- Connect wartime activism to the broader momentum of the postwar Civil Rights Movement.

Segregated Service and Widespread Participation

Despite the continuation of racially segregated units in the United States Armed Forces during World War II, more than 2 million African Americans either volunteered for or were drafted into military service. Black service members contributed in every branch of the military, from frontline combat roles to logistics and labor battalions. While they trained and served under discriminatory conditions—including inferior accommodations, unequal pay, and exclusion from leadership positions—many Black Americans saw military service as both a patriotic duty and a pathway to greater rights. Their participation marked a critical moment in the long fight for full citizenship and challenged the moral legitimacy of American democracy under segregation.

The Tuskegee Airmen and the Battle Against Fascism and Racism

Among the most celebrated units of Black service members were the Tuskegee Airmen—the first African American military pilots in U.S. history. Trained at Tuskegee Army Air Field in Alabama, these aviators flew combat missions in Europe and North Africa as part of the U.S. Army Air Corps. Despite facing intense racial prejudice at home and within the military, the Tuskegee Airmen earned widespread respect for their skill, discipline, and courage. Their excellence undermined racist assumptions about Black inferiority and helped lay the groundwork for the eventual desegregation of the military in 1948, ordered by President Harry S. Truman.

The Double V Campaign: A Demand for Dual Liberation

As African Americans fought for the United States abroad, they also launched a political movement to demand equal treatment at home. The Double V Campaign—short for "victory abroad and victory at home"—emerged in 1942 after James G. Thompson, a Black veteran and journalist, wrote a letter to the *Pittsburgh Courier* calling for Black Americans to claim victory against fascism overseas and against Jim Crow segregation within U.S. borders. This campaign galvanized support among Black newspapers, veterans, and civil rights organizations. It reflected the growing demand for racial justice as part of the war effort. It also exposed the hypocrisy of a nation promoting freedom abroad while denying basic rights to millions at home.

The Promise and Unequal Reality of the G.I. Bill

Passed in 1944, the Servicemen's Readjustment Act—commonly known as the G.I. Bill—was intended to provide returning World War II veterans with a range of benefits, including tuition for higher education, low-interest home loans, and support for starting businesses. On paper, the program was race neutral and applied to all veterans, including the 1.2 million Black service members who had served their country honorably. These benefits represented a potential turning point in Black economic advancement and access to the American middle class.

Local Discrimination and Systemic Exclusion

In practice, however, the implementation of the G.I. Bill was subject to local control—especially in the South—where Jim Crow laws and racist institutions actively limited Black access to its benefits. Many Black veterans were denied home loans by racist banks and real estate agents, turned away from predominantly white colleges, and steered toward vocational or underfunded institutions. These structural barriers prevented Black families from building generational wealth at the same rate as white veterans. The unequal distribution of G.I. Bill benefits contributed to the widening of the racial wealth gap and reinforced patterns of housing segregation and educational disparity that persist to this day.

Published in the *Pittsburgh Courier* in January 1942, James G. Thompson's letter to the editor—titled "Should I Sacrifice to Live 'Half-American'?"—served as the catalyst for what would become the Double V Campaign. A 26-year-old African American service member in Wichita, Kansas, Thompson wrote in response to the outbreak of World War II, questioning how he could be expected to risk his life abroad when he remained a second-class citizen at home. In the letter, he posed a searing moral challenge to the nation, questioning if he should sacrifice his life to live half American.

Thompson's powerful appeal demanded a "double victory"—victory against fascism abroad and victory against racism at home. His words resonated across the Black press and galvanized African American communities to demand full democratic rights while supporting the war effort. The *Pittsburgh Courier*, one of the most influential Black newspapers of the era, adopted Thompson's framing as the foundation for its Double V Campaign, which became a national symbol of African American patriotism and protest.

Thompson's letter reflects the growing political consciousness among African Americans during World War II. It exposes the contradiction between American democratic ideals and the realities of racial segregation. It serves as a primary source that bridges wartime service and civil rights advocacy, laying the groundwork for the postwar movement for racial equality.

For a deeper exploration of James G. Thompson's pivotal letter "Should I Sacrifice to Live 'Half-American'?," scholars are encouraged to access the Gilder Lehrman Institute of American History's AP African American Studies online resource: *https://www.gilderlehrman.org/ap-african-american-studies/unit-4/black-organizing-twentieth-century*.

This 1945 photograph captures Major Charity E. Adams and Captain Mary Kearney, two pioneering African American officers, inspecting members of the 6888th Central Postal Directory Battalion—the only all-Black, all-women battalion deployed overseas during World War II. Stationed in England and later in France, the unit was tasked with clearing a massive backlog of mail to ensure morale and communication for U.S. troops abroad. Facing both the pressures of wartime service and the dual burdens of racism and sexism, the "Six Triple Eight," as the battalion was known, operated with exceptional efficiency and discipline under Adams's leadership. This image is not only a record of military service. It is a testament to African American women's critical contributions to the war effort, their leadership under adversity, and their refusal to be written out of American military history.

Major Charity E. Adams and Captain Mary Kearney, two pioneering African American officers, inspecting members of the 6888th Central Postal Directory Battalion in England, 1945 (Source: National Archives)

This 1945 photograph of the flight instructor staff at Tuskegee Army Airfield offers a powerful visual record of the highly trained African American officers who prepared the famed Tuskegee Airmen for combat during World War II. As the first program to train Black military pilots in the segregated U.S. Army Air Corps, the Tuskegee Army Airfield became a symbol of both Black excellence and resistance to institutional racism. The flight instructors, often overlooked in popular narratives, played a critical role in shaping one of the most successful air units of the war. Their presence in uniform, captured in this image, challenged white supremacist assumptions about Black intellectual capacity, discipline, and patriotism. This photograph is more than a snapshot of wartime instruction. It is a portrait of quiet defiance and institutional transformation within a military still entrenched in segregation.

The flight instructor staff at Tuskegee Army Airfield, late Second World War, 1945 (Source: National Air and Space Museum Archives, Smithsonian Institution)

World War II was a turning point in African American history—not only because of the scale of Black military service but because of the political awakening it catalyzed. African Americans fought bravely abroad while demanding full citizenship at home, as captured in the rallying cry of the Double V Campaign. Their sacrifices laid the foundation for the postwar Civil Rights Movement even as systemic racism limited their access to the very benefits—like the G.I. Bill—that promised generational uplift. The war years exposed the contradictions of American democracy and made clear that the struggle for Black freedom was inseparable from the nation's definition of justice. Through military service, activism, and protest, African Americans redefined patriotism on their own terms—one that demanded not just loyalty to the flag but loyalty to the ideals it claimed to represent.

TIP

Consider Context

Consider the historical context in which the question is framed. Think about the time period, location, and events surrounding the topic. This can provide valuable clues for selecting the correct answer.

Double V for Victory—At Home and Abroad

Black soldiers fought in World War II for a country that didn't give them full rights. The Double V Campaign demanded victory over fascism abroad and over racism at home.

You're Practicing: Identifying irony and contradiction in history.

Connect This To: Citizenship, sacrifice, and civil rights activism.

Theme: Service and Struggle

Practice: Explain Causality (Causes or Effects)

World War II marked a pivotal period in African American history as Black communities mobilized for civil rights at home while serving in the military abroad.

(A) Identify one major development or outcome of the Double V campaign or the G.I. Bill for African Americans.
(B) Explain how World War II influenced African American demands for civil rights and equality.
(C) Analyze one effect of wartime service or postwar policy on African American political activism, social mobility, or systemic inequality.

SAMPLE RESPONSES

(A) The Double V Campaign, launched by the *Pittsburgh Courier* in 1942 after James G. Thompson's powerful letter, became a national rallying cry demanding victory over fascism abroad and victory over racism at home, uniting African Americans in a dual struggle for democracy.

Black military service in units such as the Tuskegee Airmen and the 6888th Central Postal Directory Battalion symbolized this dual fight, proving Black capability and patriotism even while challenging military segregation.

The G.I. Bill of Rights (1944) promised tuition aid, home loans, and job training to all veterans, including African Americans, but discriminatory implementation in banks, colleges, and real estate markets severely restricted Black access, especially in the Jim Crow South.

(B) Military service for over 1.2 million African Americans, despite being in segregated units, heightened awareness of the hypocrisy of fighting for democracy overseas while being denied it at home, intensifying demands for civil rights.

Activists like A. Philip Randolph leveraged wartime labor needs to secure the Fair Employment Practices Committee (FEPC) in 1941, prohibiting discrimination in defense industries and marking a rare federal intervention against employment discrimination.

The rhetoric of democracy used by President Franklin D. Roosevelt and Allied leaders inspired African Americans to insist that the fight against fascism must include dismantling Jim Crow, fueling postwar desegregation lawsuits and grassroots civil rights activism.

(C) Wartime service fostered a generation of politically conscious veterans who became leaders in postwar civil rights struggles, such as Medgar Evers, who served in World War II before becoming an NAACP field secretary.

Although some Black veterans used the G.I. Bill to attend historically Black colleges and build professional careers, systemic racism in loan approvals and college admissions largely excluded African Americans from the bill's full benefits, widening the racial wealth gap.

Denial of equal G.I. Bill access entrenched residential segregation through redlining, limiting African American home ownership in emerging suburbs and restricting opportunities for generational wealth accumulation—a structural inequality that still shapes racial economic disparities today.

Skills Assessed: Explain the effects of historical developments; use sources and evidence; analyze relationships among developments.

Topic 4.4 Discrimination, Segregation, and the Origins of the Civil Rights Movement

Key Terms

- Jim Crow laws—legalized racial segregation
- Lynching and racial terror
- Great Migration and Black urbanization
- NAACP Legal Defense Fund
- Charles Hamilton Houston—architect of civil rights legal strategy
- Thurgood Marshall—*Brown v. Board of Education* lawyer
- World War II activism spillover
- Montgomery Bus Boycott (1955)—early mass protest

How long can a nation survive when it promises equality under law but delivers injustice by design? For African Americans in the early twentieth century, the daily realities of segregation, disenfranchisement, and racial violence revealed that the fight for freedom would require not just patience but organized resistance. Despite constitutional amendments and promises of liberty after the Civil War, African Americans in the first half of the twentieth century continued to face deeply entrenched forms of racial segregation and discrimination. From unequal schools and segregated public facilities to voter suppression and mob violence, the system of Jim Crow reinforced white supremacy in both law and custom.

These injustices set the stage for the modern Civil Rights Movement, which began to take organized form well before the 1950s. A pivotal turning point came in 1954 when the U.S. Supreme Court issued its decision in *Brown v. Board of Education*, declaring that segregation in public schools violated the Equal Protection Clause of the Fourteenth Amendment. The decision challenged the legal foundation of "separate but equal" and sparked nationwide resistance, organizing, and eventual federal intervention. This topic explores the daily realities of segregation, the legal strategy to dismantle it, and the powerful responses—both for and against—school integration in the post-*Brown* era.

After engaging with this topic, scholars will be able to:

- Describe the persistent patterns of racial segregation and discrimination African Americans faced in the early 1900s.
- Analyze the legal reasoning behind the Supreme Court's *Brown v. Board of Education* decision and its rejection of "separate but equal."
- Evaluate how various individuals, institutions, and communities responded to school integration in the wake of the *Brown* decision.
- Understand how the legal and lived realities of segregation catalyzed the broader Civil Rights Movement.

Living Under Jim Crow: Segregation and Racial Violence in Daily Life

Through the mid-twentieth century, African Americans faced pervasive racial segregation and discrimination in virtually every area of life—regardless of whether they lived in the South under Jim Crow laws or in the North under more subtle, yet equally damaging, forms of racial exclusion. Segregated schools, public transportation, restaurants, theaters, hospitals, and neighborhoods were enforced by custom, legislation, and violence. African Americans were denied access to quality housing through redlining, blocked from the ballot box by literacy tests and poll taxes, and threatened by mob violence when they resisted. In this context, the Civil Rights Movement emerged not simply as a reaction to legal injustice but as a response to generations of social, political, and economic oppression that violated the very rights guaranteed by the Reconstruction Amendments and the Civil Rights Act of 1875.

A Legal Turning Point: *Brown v. Board of Education* and the End of "Separate but Equal"

In 1954, the Supreme Court issued its landmark decision in *Brown v. Board of Education of Topeka*, ruling that racial segregation in public schools was unconstitutional. The court found that segregation violated the Equal Protection Clause of the Fourteenth Amendment, effectively overturning the precedent of *Plessy v. Ferguson* (1896), which had legitimized "separate but equal" policies for more than half a century. *Brown* was the product of years of strategic litigation by the NAACP Legal Defense Fund, led by Thurgood Marshall and other civil rights attorneys who marshaled evidence to show that separate facilities were inherently unequal and psychologically damaging to Black children.

U.S. Supreme Court, *Brown v. Board of Education of Topeka* Opinion (1954)

MR. CHIEF JUSTICE WARREN delivered the opinion of the Court.

These cases come to us from the States of Kansas, South Carolina, Virginia, and Delaware. They are premised on different facts and different local conditions, but a common legal question justifies their consideration together in this consolidated opinion.

In each of the cases, minors of the Negro race, through their legal representatives, seek the aid of the courts in obtaining admission to the public schools of their community on a nonsegregated basis. In each instance, they had been denied admission to schools attended by white children under laws requiring or permitting segregation according to race. This segregation was alleged to deprive the plaintiffs of the equal protection of the laws under the Fourteenth Amendment. In each of the cases other than the Delaware case, a three-judge federal district court denied relief to the plaintiffs on the so-called "separate but equal" doctrine announced by this Court in *Plessy* v. *Ferguson*, 163 U.S. 537. Under that doctrine, equality of treatment is accorded when the races are provided substantially equal facilities, even though these facilities be separate. In the Delaware case, the Supreme Court of Delaware adhered to that doctrine, but ordered that the plaintiffs be admitted to the white schools because of their superiority to the Negro schools.

The plaintiffs contend that segregated public schools are not "equal" and cannot be made "equal," and that hence they are deprived of the equal protection of the laws. Because of the obvious importance of the question presented, the Court took jurisdiction. Argument was heard in the 1952 Term, and reargument was heard this Term on certain questions propounded by the Court. Reargument was largely devoted to the circumstances surrounding the adoption of the Fourteenth Amendment in 1868. It covered exhaustively consideration of the Amendment in Congress, ratification by the states, then-existing practices in racial segregation, and the views of proponents and opponents of the Amendment.

This discussion and our own investigation convince us that, although these sources cast some light, it is not enough to resolve the problem with which we are faced. At best, they are inconclusive. The most avid proponents of the post-War Amendments undoubtedly intended them to remove all legal distinctions among "all persons born or naturalized in the United States." Their opponents, just as certainly, were antagonistic to both the letter and the spirit of the Amendments and wished them to have the most limited effect. What others in Congress and the state legislatures had in mind cannot be determined with any degree of certainty.

An additional reason for the inconclusive nature of the Amendment's history with respect to segregated schools is the status of public education at that time. In the South, the movement toward free common schools, supported by general taxation, had not yet taken hold. Education of white children was largely in the hands of private groups. Education of Negroes was almost nonexistent, and practically all of the race were illiterate. In fact, any education of Negroes was forbidden by law in some states. Today, in contrast, many Negroes have achieved outstanding success in the arts and sciences, as well as in the business and professional world. It is true that public school education at the time of the Amendment had advanced further in the North, but the effect of the Amendment on Northern States was generally ignored in the congressional debates. Even in the North, the conditions of public education did not approximate those existing today. The curriculum was usually rudimentary; ungraded schools were common in rural areas; the school term was but three months a year in many states, and compulsory school attendance was virtually unknown. As a consequence, it is not surprising that there should be so little in the history of the Fourteenth Amendment relating to its intended effect on public education.

In the first cases in this Court construing the Fourteenth Amendment, decided shortly after its adoption, the Court interpreted it as proscribing all state-imposed discriminations against the Negro race. The doctrine of "separate but equal" did not make its appearance in this Court until 1896 in the case of *Plessy* v. *Ferguson*, supra, involving not education but transportation. American courts have since labored with the doctrine for over half a century. In this Court, there have been six cases involving the "separate but equal" doctrine in the field of public education. In *Cumming* v. *County Board of Education*, 175 U.S. 528, and *Gong Lum* v. *Rice*, 275 U.S. 78, the validity of the doctrine itself was not challenged. In more recent cases, all on the graduate school level, inequality was found in that specific benefits enjoyed by white students were denied to Negro students of the same educational qualifications. Missouri ex rel. *Gaines* v. *Canada*, 305 U.S. 337; *Sipuel* v. *Oklahoma*, 332 U.S. 631; *Sweatt* v. *Painter*, 339 U.S. 629; *McLaurin* v. *Oklahoma State Regents*, 339 U.S. 637. In none of these cases was it necessary to reexamine the doctrine to grant relief to the Negro plaintiff. And in *Sweatt* v. *Painter*, supra, the Court expressly reserved decision on the question whether *Plessy* v. *Ferguson* should be held inapplicable to public education.

In the instant cases, that question is directly presented. Here, unlike *Sweatt* v. *Painter*, there are findings below that the Negro and white schools involved have been equalized, or are being equalized, with respect to buildings, curricula, qualifications and salaries of teachers, and other "tangible" factors. Our decision, therefore, cannot turn on merely a comparison of these tangible factors in the Negro and white schools involved in each of the cases. We must look instead to the effect of segregation itself on public education.

In approaching this problem, we cannot turn the clock back to 1868, when the Amendment was adopted, or even to 1896, when *Plessy* v. *Ferguson* was written. We must consider public education in the light of its full development and its present place in American life throughout the Nation. Only in this way can it be determined if segregation in public schools deprives these plaintiffs of the equal protection of the laws.

Today, education is perhaps the most important function of state and local governments. Compulsory school attendance laws and the great expenditures for education both demonstrate our recognition of the importance of education to our democratic society. It is required in the performance of our most basic public responsibilities, even service in the armed forces. It is the very foundation of good citizenship. Today it is a principal instrument in awakening the child to cultural values, in preparing him for later professional training, and in helping him to adjust normally to his environment. In these days, it is doubtful that any child may reasonably be expected to succeed in life if he is denied the opportunity of an education. Such an opportunity, where the state has undertaken to provide it, is a right which must be made available to all on equal terms.

We come then to the question presented: Does segregation of children in public schools solely on the basis of race, even though the physical facilities and other "tangible" factors may be equal, deprive the children of the minority group of equal educational opportunities? We believe that it does.

In *Sweatt* v. *Painter*, supra, in finding that a segregated law school for Negroes could not provide them equal educational opportunities, this Court relied in large part on "those qualities which are incapable of objective measurement but which make for greatness in a law school." In *McLaurin* v. *Oklahoma State Regents*, supra, the Court, in requiring that a Negro admitted to a white graduate school be treated like all other students, again resorted to intangible considerations: ". . . his ability to study, to engage in discussions and exchange views with other students, and, in general, to learn his profession." Such considerations apply with added force to children in grade and high schools. To separate them from others of similar age and qualifications solely because of their race generates a feeling of inferiority as to their status in the community that may affect their hearts and minds in a way unlikely ever to be undone. The effect of this separation on their educational opportunities was well stated by a finding in the Kansas case by a court which nevertheless felt compelled to rule against the Negro plaintiffs:

Segregation of white and colored children in public schools has a detrimental effect upon the colored children. The impact is greater when it has the sanction of the law, for the policy of separating the races is usually interpreted as denoting the inferiority of the negro group. A sense of inferiority affects the motivation of a child to learn. Segregation with the sanction of law, therefore, has a tendency to [retard] the educational and mental development of negro children and to deprive them of some of the benefits they would receive in a racial[ly] integrated school system.

Whatever may have been the extent of psychological knowledge at the time of *Plessy* v. *Ferguson*, this finding is amply supported by modern authority. Any language in *Plessy* v. *Ferguson* contrary to this finding is rejected.

We conclude that, in the field of public education, the doctrine of "separate but equal" has no place. Separate educational facilities are inherently unequal. Therefore, we hold that the plaintiffs and others similarly situated for whom the actions have been brought are, by reason of the segregation complained of, deprived of the equal protection of the laws guaranteed by the Fourteenth Amendment. This disposition makes unnecessary any discussion whether such segregation also violates the Due Process Clause of the Fourteenth Amendment.

Because these are class actions, because of the wide applicability of this decision, and because of the great variety of local conditions, the formulation of decrees in these cases presents problems of considerable complexity. On reargument, the consideration of appropriate relief was necessarily subordinated to the primary question—the constitutionality of segregation in public education. We have now announced that such segregation is a denial of the equal protection of the laws. In order that we may have the full assistance of the parties in formulating decrees, the cases will be restored to the docket, and the parties are requested to present further argument on Questions 4 and 5 previously propounded by the Court for the reargument this Term The Attorney General of the United States is again invited to participate. The Attorneys General of the states requiring or permitting segregation in public education will also be permitted to appear as amici curiae upon request to do so by September 15, 1954, and submission of briefs by October 1, 1954.

It is so ordered.

Source: *Brown v. Board of Education of Topeka*, Opinion; May 17, 1954; Records of the Supreme Court of the United States; Record Group 267; National Archives.

Social Science and the Doll Test

A significant factor in the Supreme Court's landmark decision in *Brown v. Board of Education of Topeka* was the citation of psychological research conducted by Drs. Mamie and Kenneth Clark, known as the doll test. Their studies revealed that many Black children, when presented with white and Black dolls, often assigned positive attributes to the white dolls and negative ones to the Black dolls. This research demonstrated the psychological harm caused by segregation and supported the argument that separate educational environments undermined children's self-worth. The court's recognition of this evidence shifted the legal discourse from physical inequality to the deeper, lasting impacts on human dignity and emotional development.

Photographed in Harlem in 1947 by renowned photojournalist Gordon Parks, *Clark Doll Test, Harlem* captures a moment from the Clarks' research: a young African American girl choosing between dolls. With quiet power, the image visualizes the internalized effects of systemic racism. Gordon Parks's photograph transforms the study's findings into a deeply human portrait, reinforcing the moral urgency of dismantling segregation.

In his series of photographs, Gordon Parks in 1947 documents a pivotal moment in the psychological study that helped shape the legal and moral framework of the Civil Rights Movement. The photograph shows Dr. Kenneth Clark conducting the now-famous "doll test" with a young African American child, part of a series of experiments he and his wife, Dr. Mamie Clark, designed to assess how segregation affected Black children's self-image. This intimate image captures more than a scientific procedure; it reflects the emotional toll of systemic racism and the vulnerability of childhood shaped by societal bias. Parks's lens frames Dr. Clark not only as a scientist but also as a figure of empathy, engaged in revealing the quiet, internalized effects of segregation.

To view the photographs taken by Gordon Parks of the *Clark Doll Test*, visit the *Gordon Parks Foundation* https://www.gordonparksfoundation.org/gordon-parks/photography-archive/doll-test-19472.

Resistance and Retrenchment: The Struggle over Implementation

Although *Brown v. Board of Education* was a legal victory, it did not bring immediate or uniform change. In many parts of the South—and even in some cities in the North—white officials and citizens resisted integration through tactics ranging from legal obstruction to outright violence. Some states diverted funds away from public schools that attempted to integrate, while others subsidized all-white private academies. White flight to the suburbs and the creation of exclusionary zoning laws ensured that many African American children remained in underfunded, segregated schools. In the most extreme cases, entire school systems were shut down to avoid compliance with federal desegregation orders, and police forces were used to intimidate or block Black students from entering newly integrated schools.

Courage in the Classroom: The Role of Black Students

Despite hostility and danger, Black students across the South and beyond became frontline participants in the struggle to integrate American schools. One of the most iconic examples is the Little Rock Nine—nine African American teenagers who, in 1957, integrated Little Rock Central High School in Arkansas under the protection of federal troops ordered in by President Dwight D. Eisenhower. Their bravery inspired national attention and global scrutiny, placing the fight for civil rights within the moral spotlight of the Cold War era. These students, and countless others whose names may never be widely known, faced harassment, physical threats, and isolation to claim their constitutional right to equal education.

The persistence of segregation and systemic discrimination in the early twentieth century exposed the deep contradictions at the heart of American democracy. For African Americans, daily encounters with inequality—in schools, public spaces, housing, and the justice system—fueled a growing demand for civil rights rooted in both legal challenge and grassroots resistance. The *Brown v. Board of Education* decision marked a decisive break with the legal precedent of "separate but equal," affirming the dignity and humanity of Black children and families. Yet the path to integration was met with fierce resistance. This revealed that the end of legal segregation was only the beginning of a broader fight for equity and inclusion. This period laid the moral and legal foundations of the modern Civil Rights Movement, where African Americans—through courage, intellect, and activism—refused to accept a nation that denied them full citizenship.

Segregation by Design

Separate schools. Redlined neighborhoods. Poll taxes. These weren't just accidents—they were systems built to keep power out of Black hands.

You're Practicing: Tracing the roots of inequality.

Connect This To: Policy, protest, and long-term injustice.

Theme: Structural Racism

Practice: Explain Continuities or Changes over Time

The post–World War II period witnessed persistent racial discrimination and segregation, yet it also saw the emergence of grassroots efforts that laid the foundation for the Civil Rights Movement.

(A) Identify one form of racial discrimination or segregation that persisted after World War II.
(B) Explain how African Americans responded to these conditions in ways that signaled the early development of the modern Civil Rights Movement.
(C) Analyze the continuity or change in strategies used to challenge racial inequality between the 1940s and early 1950s.

SAMPLE RESPONSES

(A) The Brown v. Board of Education of Topeka (1954) Supreme Court decision marked a major legal turning point by overturning *Plessy v. Ferguson* and ruling that segregated public schools violated the Equal Protection Clause of the Fourteenth Amendment.

This victory was the product of years of strategic litigation led by the NAACP Legal Defense Fund, under the leadership of Charles Hamilton Houston and Thurgood Marshall, which built a precedent through earlier graduate-school cases such as *Sweatt v. Painter* (1950) and *McLaurin v. Oklahoma State Regents* (1950).

The Court's reasoning incorporated social science evidence such as the Clark Doll Test, demonstrating that segregation inflicted psychological harm on Black children and reinforced a sense of inferiority.

(B) Civil rights attorneys—most notably Charles Hamilton Houston, called the "architect of the civil rights legal strategy"—systematically dismantled the *separate but equal* doctrine by targeting inequities in higher education before confronting public school segregation directly.

Grassroots activism also gained momentum through community-based challenges, such as the Montgomery Bus Boycott (1955–1956), which demonstrated the power of mass, sustained protest in challenging segregation in public transportation.

This dual approach, combining courtroom victories with public protest, laid the groundwork for the broader Civil Rights Movement by uniting legal precedent with mass mobilization.

(C) Brown inspired a surge in African American activism by affirming that legal segregation had no constitutional basis, encouraging students, parents, and civil rights organizations to demand equal educational access nationwide.

At the same time, segregationists organized massive resistance campaigns, including the creation of segregation academies, legislative obstruction, and white flight to suburban school districts to avoid integration.

In extreme cases—such as the integration of Little Rock Central High School (1957)—state officials attempted to block Black students from entering schools, prompting federal intervention and highlighting that dismantling Jim Crow required both judicial enforcement and federal protection of civil rights.

Skills Assessed: Explain continuities or changes over time; use sources and evidence; analyze relationships among developments.

Topic 4.5 Redlining and Housing Discrimination

Key Terms

- Federal Housing Administration (FHA)—discriminatory loan policies
- Home Owners' Loan Corporation (HOLC) maps
- Redlining—denial of mortgages in Black neighborhoods
- Restrictive covenants—clauses barring home sales to nonwhites
- Urban renewal—"Negro removal"
- Blockbusting—exploiting white fear to flip neighborhoods
- Public housing segregation
- Racial wealth gap

What happens when a zip code determines the value of your life, your health, and your future? For generations of African Americans, where one could—and could not—live was shaped not by choice but by policy. In the second half of the twentieth century, African Americans faced persistent and systemic housing discrimination that limited where they could live, build wealth, and access opportunity. One of the most damaging practices was redlining. This was a federally sanctioned system that denied loans and investment to neighborhoods deemed high-risk, typically because they were home to African Americans or other communities of color.

These discriminatory practices were enforced by banks, real estate agents, and federal agencies. Their long-term effects rippled through every aspect of Black life: underfunded schools, limited access to health care, crumbling infrastructure, and a massive racial wealth gap. Even after legal barriers were challenged during the Civil Rights Movement, the legacy of redlining continued to shape patterns of segregation and inequality into the present. This topic explores how housing became both a tool of exclusion and a central battleground in the struggle for racial justice.

After engaging with this topic, scholars will be able to:

- Explain the historical development of redlining and housing discrimination.
- Analyze how these practices created and sustained racial segregation.
- Describe the long-term economic, educational, and health consequences of housing discrimination for African American communities.
- Connect housing injustice to broader patterns of structural racism and civil rights resistance.

Homeownership and the Racial Wealth Gap

Throughout the twentieth century, African Americans faced systemic barriers to homeownership—one of the most critical means of building generational wealth in the United States. Denied access to fair mortgages, insurance, and property in growing suburban markets, many Black families were forced to rent in overcrowded, segregated urban neighborhoods. This exclusion prevented African Americans from benefiting from the postwar housing boom that helped millions of white Americans accumulate equity and pass down assets. As a result, housing discrimination became a central driver of the racial wealth gap, depriving generations of Black families of the economic security and upward mobility homeownership often provides.

Codified Segregation: The Role of Federal Policy

The architecture of modern housing discrimination was constructed not just through individual bias but through official federal policy. The 1938 Federal Housing Administration (FHA) underwriting manual explicitly instructed lenders to avoid investing in areas where African Americans lived, effectively legalizing residential segregation. These policies, often enforced through racially restrictive covenants and zoning laws, made it illegal or financially impossible for African Americans to live in many suburban communities. In response, civil rights organizations such as the NAACP fought to dismantle these policies, culminating in the passage of the Fair Housing Act of 1968, which sought to outlaw housing discrimination—but did not erase its deep, systemic legacy.

Redlining and Mortgage Discrimination

At the heart of housing discrimination was the practice of redlining, named after the red lines, drawn on government-backed maps to designate neighborhoods deemed high-risk for mortgage lending. These areas were overwhelmingly populated by African Americans and other communities of color. Under the pretense of protecting investment, banks and mortgage lenders systematically denied loans, devalued properties, and starved these neighborhoods of investment. While white families secured low-interest government loans to build homes and accumulate wealth, Black families were locked out of opportunity by design. Redlining reinforced patterns of racial segregation and ensured that Black neighborhoods remained underdeveloped and underserved.

The 1937 "residential security" map of Philadelphia and Camden, created by the Home Owners' Loan Corporation (HOLC), offers a visual representation of how federal policy codified racial and economic segregation during the mid-twentieth century. Developed as part of a broader effort to stabilize the housing market during the Great Depression, the HOLC produced color-coded maps that graded neighborhoods based on perceived lending risk. Predominantly Black and immigrant communities were marked in red—designated as hazardous—and deemed unworthy of investment, regardless of residents' income or creditworthiness.

The Philadelphia-Camden map reflects the broader national pattern. Investment was funneled into white, suburban neighborhoods while communities of color were intentionally disinvested. These maps became a blueprint for decades of housing inequality, the effects of which are still visible in contemporary patterns of segregation and wealth disparity.

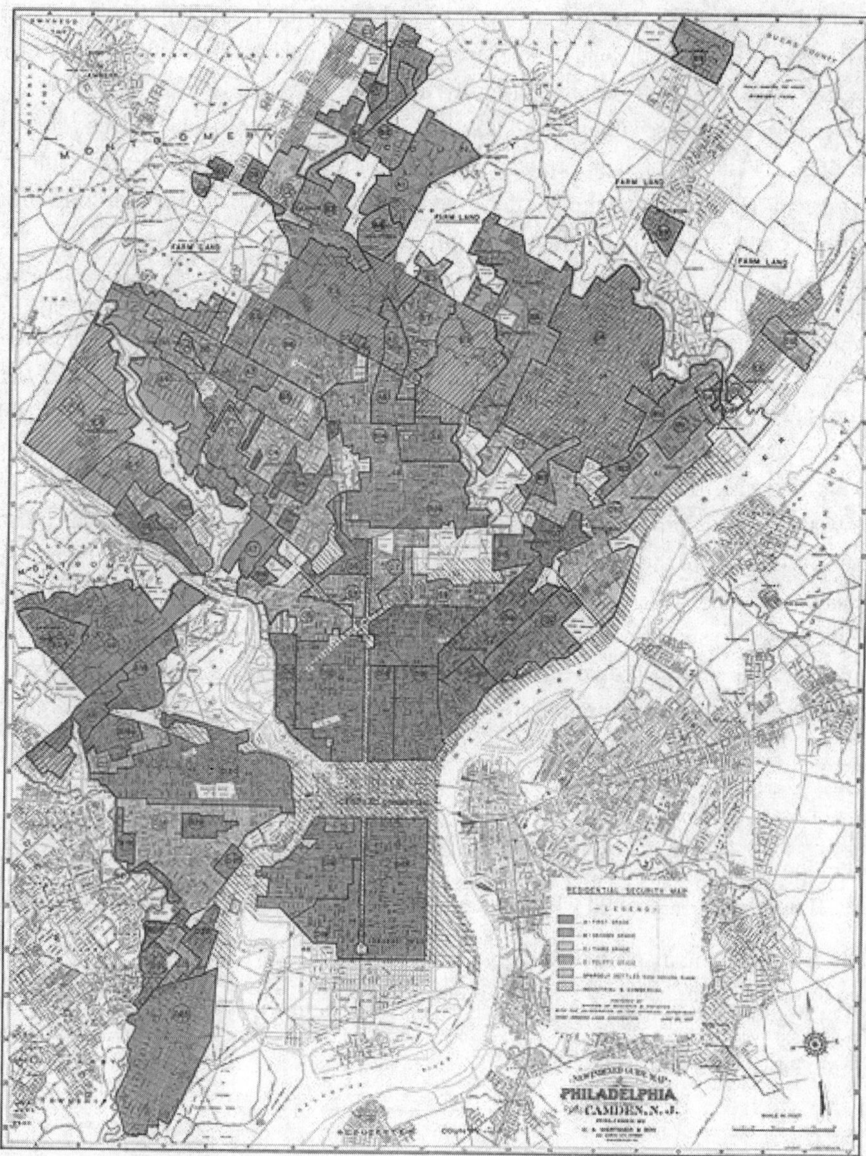

Home Owners' Loan Corporation "residential security" map of Philadelphia and Camden, 1937

Racial Violence in Integrated Communities

Even when African American families managed to move into well-resourced or predominantly white neighborhoods, they often faced violent backlash. Across the country—from Chicago and Los Angeles to Philadelphia and Detroit—Black homeowners were targeted by angry white mobs and subjected to threats, vandalism, and physical attacks. These acts of racial terror were meant to enforce the boundaries of segregation and intimidate Black families seeking equal access to housing. The violence revealed that housing discrimination was not only about policy. It was also about the defense of white social and economic dominance through fear and intimidation.

Excerpt from *A Raisin in the Sun* by Lorraine Hansberry, 1959

Lorraine Hansberry's *A Raisin in the Sun* (1959) is a landmark of American theater and a profound exploration of housing discrimination, generational dreams, and the pursuit of dignity within a racially segregated society. The play follows the Younger family, a working-class Black household in Chicago, as they confront the emotional and structural challenges of trying to purchase a home in a white neighborhood. The excerpt commonly studied in African American literature and history courses reveals the tension between hope and systemic exclusion as family members debate whether to accept a buyout from a white neighborhood association that seeks to block their move. Hansberry dramatizes not just the legal and economic constraints of redlining and restrictive covenants but also the psychological toll of racism on ambition, identity, and intergenerational unity.

Through characters like Walter Lee Younger and Lena "Mama" Younger, Hansberry gives voice to the aspirations and frustrations of Black Americans denied access to the American Dream. The play's title, drawn from Langston Hughes's poem "Harlem," asks whether deferred dreams inevitably "dry up like a raisin in the sun"—a question deeply rooted in the realities of housing discrimination.

For a more in-depth analysis of this source, scholars are encouraged to search online for Excerpt from A Raisin in the Sun by Lorraine Hansberry, 1959, which is widely available through educational and literary archives.

Housing discrimination was not merely a reflection of individual prejudice. It was a deliberate and institutionalized system that shaped the physical and economic landscape of the United States. Through redlining, restrictive covenants, and state-sanctioned segregation, African Americans were systematically excluded from homeownership, wealth accumulation, and access to high-quality education and health care. These policies not only deepened racial inequality in the twentieth century but continue to influence disparities in the present day. The struggle against housing injustice, from the courtroom to the stage in works like *A Raisin in the Sun*, revealed how central the fight for space, security, and dignity was—and remains—to the broader Black Freedom movement. Understanding this history is essential to understanding the structures of inequality that civil rights activists sought to dismantle and the enduring power of community resistance.

Red Lines, Real Lives

In the mid-1900s, banks and the government literally drew red lines around Black neighborhoods, refusing to give loans there. These decisions shaped where people could live and how wealth was passed down.

You're Practicing: Connecting maps to inequality.

Connect This To: Wealth gaps, urban planning, and racial segregation.

Theme: Economic Power and Place

Practice: Explain the Effects of Historical Developments

Following World War II, federal and local housing policies institutionalized racial discrimination and created long-term barriers to homeownership and wealth accumulation for African Americans.

(A) Identify one policy or practice that contributed to housing discrimination in the mid-twentieth century.
(B) Explain how redlining or similar practices reinforced segregation and economic inequality.
(C) Analyze one long-term effect of housing discrimination on African American communities.

SAMPLE RESPONSES

(A) The Federal Housing Administration (FHA) adopted underwriting guidelines in the 1930s that explicitly discouraged loans in racially mixed or predominantly African American neighborhoods, a practice known as redlining.

Private banks and real estate agents reinforced this discrimination through racially restrictive covenants, legal agreements prohibiting the sale of property to nonwhite buyers.

The G.I. Bill of Rights (1944) promised home loans to returning veterans but, when administered locally, often excluded African American veterans through discriminatory lending and appraisal practices.

(B) Redlining maps, created by the federal Home Owners' Loan Corporation, marked African American neighborhoods as "high-risk" for mortgage lending, which denied residents access to low-interest, long-term home loans that white families received.

This lack of access forced African Americans into overcrowded urban areas with inflated rents, while white families moved to federally subsidized suburbs such as Levittown, New York—whose developers openly barred Black buyers.

By concentrating disinvestment in Black neighborhoods, redlining entrenched racial segregation and created a two-tier housing market in which property values in African American areas stagnated or declined while white suburbs accumulated wealth.

(C) Housing discrimination widened the racial wealth gap by preventing African Americans from acquiring equity through homeownership—a key driver of intergenerational wealth in postwar America.

Disinvestment in redlined areas led to declining property values, underfunded schools tied to local property taxes, and fewer business and employment opportunities, perpetuating cycles of poverty.

The spatial segregation established by mid-twentieth-century housing policies persists today, shaping patterns of school segregation, unequal access to public services, and health disparities in African American communities.

Skills Assessed: Explain the effects of historical developments; use sources and evidence; analyze relationships among developments.

Topic 4.6 Major Civil Rights Organizations

Key Terms

- NAACP (1909)—legal strategy for racial justice
- SCLC (Southern Christian Leadership Conference)—nonviolent protest; led by MLK
- CORE (Congress of Racial Equality)—Freedom Rides, sit-ins
- SNCC (Student Nonviolent Coordinating Committee)—grassroots youth activism
- Nation of Islam—religious and Black nationalist movement
- Urban League—economic and social welfare
- Freedom Summer (1964)—voter registration campaign
- Leadership diversity and tactics

Movements do not succeed through passion alone; they require vision, structure, and strategy. From courtroom battles to lunch counter sit-ins, the mid-twentieth-century Civil Rights Movement was powered by a constellation of organizations that transformed grassroots energy into lasting change. The Civil Rights Movement of the mid-twentieth century was shaped by the leadership, coordination, and strategic direction of several major organizations. They each had distinct approaches but a shared goal: dismantling systemic racism and securing full citizenship for African Americans. Groups such as the NAACP, SCLC, SNCC, CORE, and the Urban League deployed a range of tactics—from legal challenges and mass mobilization to grassroots organizing and voter registration drives.

At the heart of many of these efforts was a commitment to nonviolent resistance, a philosophy that drew from both Christian theology and global anticolonial movements and that proved powerful in exposing the moral failures of segregation. These organizations not only helped catalyze public support for racial justice but also played a crucial role in pressuring Congress to pass landmark federal legislation, including the Civil Rights Act of 1964 and the Voting Rights Act of 1965. Together, they helped redefine American democracy through coordinated struggle and unyielding activism.

After engaging with this topic, scholars will be able to:

- Identify and describe the major civil rights organizations and their roles in advancing racial justice.
- Analyze the strategic use of nonviolent resistance in civil rights campaigns.
- Explain how organized activism influenced public opinion and led to major federal legislative reforms.
- Understand the interplay between local movements and national leadership in shaping the Civil Rights Movement's successes.

Building a Unified Movement: The Big Four Civil Rights Organizations

The mid-twentieth-century Civil Rights Movement was led by a coalition of major national organizations, each contributing distinct strengths to the shared struggle for racial justice. Known as the Big Four, the NAACP (National Association for the Advancement of Colored People), SCLC (Southern Christian Leadership Conference), CORE (Congress of Racial Equality), and SNCC (Student Nonviolent Coordinating Committee) united African Americans from a range of backgrounds, regions, and philosophies. While the NAACP focused on legal strategy, SNCC emphasized grassroots youth activism, SCLC prioritized nonviolent mass mobilization under faith-based leadership, and CORE engaged in direct-action protest campaigns. Despite their differences, these organizations coordinated efforts to confront racial inequality in housing, education, employment, and voting rights.

Strategic Nonviolence and Grassroots Action

Civil rights organizations employed nonviolent resistance as a transformative method of protest. Local branches became hubs of community organizing, implementing sit-ins, freedom rides, voter registration drives, and legal challenges. These forms of direct action—often peaceful and racially inclusive—were designed to provoke public awareness and expose the brutality of segregation. When met with violence, these protests often generated national sympathy and catalyzed support for federal intervention. Yet in some communities, the continual threat of white supremacist retaliation also led activists to consider and debate the role of self-defense, revealing the movement's evolving complexity.

Mobilizing the Nation: The Power of Demonstration and Media

In 1963, civil rights leaders turned the national spotlight on Birmingham, Alabama, where the SCLC and local activists launched a series of protests culminating in the Children's Crusade. Strategically involving school-aged youth, organizers aimed to protect adult protesters from job loss while emphasizing the moral urgency of the cause. The televised images of Black children being attacked with fire hoses and police dogs by Birmingham police shocked audiences worldwide and pressured President John F. Kennedy to act. That same year, an interracial and interfaith coalition led by A. Philip Randolph and Bayard Rustin organized the March on Washington for Jobs and Freedom. More than 250,000 people gathered at the Lincoln Memorial to demand economic justice and civil rights. There, Martin Luther King Jr. delivered his iconic "I Have a Dream" speech, which became a defining moment in American political history.

Grassroots Education and the Mississippi Freedom Summer

The Mississippi Freedom Summer of 1964 further revealed the dangers and determination of civil rights activism in the Deep South. Organized by SNCC, CORE, SCLC, and the NAACP, the project aimed to register African American voters and combat the literacy tests, intimidation, and violence that suppressed Black political participation. Volunteers also established Freedom Schools to teach Black history, constitutional rights, and community organizing skills. The murder of three young activists—James Chaney, Andrew Goodman, and Michael Schwerner—exposed the lethal resistance to racial equality and drew national outrage. Their sacrifice helped catalyze the formation of the Mississippi Freedom Democratic Party, which challenged the legitimacy of the state's all-white Democratic delegation at the 1964 Democratic National Convention.

Legislative Breakthroughs: From Protest to Policy

The coordinated efforts of these organizations directly contributed to historic legislative victories. In 1964, Congress passed the Civil Rights Act, which outlawed segregation in public accommodations and banned employment discrimination based on race, color, religion, sex, or national origin. One year later, the Voting Rights Act of 1965 targeted the disenfranchisement of African Americans by outlawing literacy tests, poll taxes, and other discriminatory practices used to suppress the Black vote. These achievements marked the culmination of decades of organizing, legal strategy, and moral appeal—and affirmed the central role of civil rights organizations in reshaping the American legal and political landscape.

"Nonviolence and Racial Justice" by Martin Luther King Jr., 1957

Published in 1957 in *The Christian Century*, Martin Luther King Jr.'s essay "Nonviolence and Racial Justice" articulates the foundational philosophy that would guide the Civil Rights Movement. Drawing from Christian ethics and the teachings of Mahatma Gandhi, King presents nonviolence not merely as a tactic but as a moral imperative and a way of life. He argues that nonviolent resistance is the most potent weapon available to oppressed people in their struggle for freedom and human dignity.

King emphasizes that nonviolence seeks to win friendship and understanding, aiming for redemption and reconciliation rather than defeat of an adversary. He underscores the importance of resisting injustice without resorting to violence, stating that violence leads only to temporary victories and breeds more social problems. Instead, nonviolence confronts evil itself, not the individuals perpetrating it, allowing for the possibility of transforming opponents through love and understanding.

This essay marks a significant moment in King's development as a leader and thinker, laying the groundwork for the strategies employed during the Montgomery Bus Boycott and subsequent civil rights campaigns. It encapsulates the ethical and strategic dimensions of nonviolent resistance, highlighting its role in achieving lasting social change.

For a deeper exploration of Dr. Martin Luther King Jr.'s foundational ideas on peaceful resistance, scholars are encouraged to read "Nonviolence and Racial Justice" by visiting the Martin Luther King, Jr. Research and Education Institute's King Papers Project online at: *https://kinginstitute.stanford.edu/king-papers/documents/nonviolence-and-racial-justice*. This free resource offers valuable insights into Dr. King's philosophy and its impact on the struggle for civil rights.

JoŸ Lewis and Colleagues, Prayer Demonstration at a Segregated Swimming Pool, Cairo, Illinois by Danny Lyon, 1962

Photographed by civil rights photographer Danny Lyon in 1962, *JoŸ Lewis and Colleagues, Prayer Demonstration at a Segregated Swimming Pool, Cairo, Illinois* captures a moment of disciplined nonviolent protest against racial segregation in public accommodations. The image shows Student Nonviolent Coordinating Committee (SNCC) activist John Lewis and fellow demonstrators kneeling in prayer outside a whites-only swimming pool, confronting a local symbol of exclusion with spiritual resolve and moral clarity.

For an in-depth exploration of the *Prayer Demonstration at a Segregated Swimming Pool in Cairo, Illinois* led by John Lewis and his colleagues, as photographed by Danny Lyon in 1962, scholars are encouraged to access the Gilder Lehrman Institute of American History's AP African American Studies online resource: https://www.gilderlehrman.org/ap-african-american-studies/unit-4/black-organizing-twentieth-century. This free platform offers rich historical context and primary sources to enhance your understanding of Black organizing during the twentieth century.

"The Revolution Is at Hand" by John Lewis, 1963

Originally drafted for delivery at the March on Washington for Jobs and Freedom on August 28, 1963, John Lewis's speech "The Revolution Is at Hand" stands as a powerful testament to the radical energy and generational urgency that youth activists brought to the Civil Rights Movement. As the 23-year-old chairman of the Student Nonviolent Coordinating Committee (SNCC), Lewis was the youngest speaker at the march. He represented a growing faction within the movement that called for bold, uncompromising action against systemic racism.

In his original draft, Lewis criticized the Kennedy administration's proposed civil rights bill for not going far enough, declaring, "We want our freedom, and we want it now." He condemned the slow pace of federal change and warned that the movement would not wait for justice to be delivered through cautious negotiation. Though SNCC leaders ultimately revised portions of the speech in response to requests from other organizers, the final version still captured Lewis's core message: that the movement was not merely about reform but about revolutionary transformation grounded in moral urgency.

Lewis's speech highlighted the growing impatience among younger activists with the slow pace of institutional change and the persistence of racial injustice in the North and South. It affirmed that the struggle for civil rights was not simply a legal battle. It was a human rights revolution.

> Scholars interested in reading the full version of "The Revolution Is at Hand" by John Lewis can access it for free through the SNCC Digital Gateway at: *https://snccdigital.org/inside-sncc/policy-statements/march-washington-speech/*.

The Civil Rights Movement's success was not accidental. It was the result of coordinated vision, collective sacrifice, and the disciplined efforts of major civil rights organizations that mobilized communities across the nation. From legal battles in courtrooms to acts of civil disobedience in city streets, these organizations helped turn moral outrage into legislative transformation. Through strategic nonviolence, grassroots education, mass media, and public protest, they exposed the violence of segregation and made racial justice a national imperative. The legacy of the NAACP, SCLC, SNCC, and CORE endure not only in the legal victories they helped secure but also in their enduring blueprint for how organized movements can challenge injustice, shift public consciousness, and reshape democracy itself.

Marching Together, Organizing for Change

The NAACP, SCLC, SNCC, CORE, and others didn't just hold protests—they trained, strategized, and fought in court. Each group had a different approach, but all demanded justice.

You're Practicing: Comparing tactics in social movements.

Connect This To: Legal change, grassroots power, and coalition building.

Theme: Activism and Institutional Change

Practice: Compare (Explain Similarities or Differences)

In the mid-twentieth century, a range of civil rights organizations emerged with distinct strategies and leadership styles in the struggle for racial justice.

(A) Identify two major civil rights organizations active during the Civil Rights Movement.
(B) Explain one similarity and one difference in their approaches to achieving racial equality.
(C) Analyze how their strategies reflected broader goals within the Civil Rights Movement.

SAMPLE RESPONSES

(A) NAACP (National Association for the Advancement of Colored People)—Focused on legal challenges to segregation and discrimination, winning landmark cases such as *Brown v. Board of Education* (1954).

SCLC (Southern Christian Leadership Conference)—Led by Martin Luther King Jr., used nonviolent mass protest and moral persuasion rooted in Christian theology and Gandhian philosophy to mobilize communities and gain national attention.

(B) The NAACP's legal victories directly dismantled segregation laws and provided constitutional precedent for later reforms, increasing public awareness of legal inequality.

SCLC's nonviolent protests, such as the Birmingham Campaign (1963), generated televised images of brutality against peaceful demonstrators, creating public outrage that pressured Congress to pass the Civil Rights Act of 1964.

(C) Tactical diversity allowed the movement to operate on multiple fronts—legal challenges (NAACP), grassroots mobilization (SNCC), nonviolent demonstrations (SCLC), and direct action campaigns (CORE).

Leadership diversity united different segments of the Black community, balancing courtroom strategy, youth activism, and mass protest, which amplified national impact and sustained momentum for legislative victories like the Voting Rights Act of 1965.

Skills Assessed: Compare developments; use sources and evidence; analyze relationships among developments.

Topic 4.7 Black Women's Leadership and Grassroots Organizing in the Civil Rights Movement

Key Terms

- Ella Baker—SNCC advisor, community-based leadership
- Fannie Lou Hamer—Mississippi Freedom Democratic Party
- Septima Clark—citizenship schools
- Diane Nash—Nashville sit-ins, Freedom Rides
- Jo Ann Robinson—Women's Political Council, Montgomery Bus Boycott
- Bridge leadership—grassroots, behind-the-scenes organizing
- Intersection of race, gender, and class
- Undervalued contributions of women

Behind every mass march, voter registration drive, and courtroom victory of the Civil Rights Movement were Black women whose organizing power shaped the course of American democracy—often without national recognition or headlines. Black women were the backbone of the Civil Rights Movement. As strategists, educators, fundraisers, protest organizers, and political theorists, they advanced both the goals of major civil rights organizations and the transformative work of grassroots activism. Leaders such as Ella Baker, Septima Clark, Fannie Lou Hamer, and Diane Nash helped shift the movement's center of gravity from courtroom litigation to community-based resistance, emphasizing collective leadership and empowerment from the bottom up.

While some worked within national organizations like the NAACP, SCLC, and SNCC, many others built power through local churches, citizenship schools, unions, and neighborhood associations. Beyond the South, Black women organized rent strikes in the North, protested police violence in urban centers, and linked civil rights to broader struggles for housing, labor, and education equity. Their leadership demonstrated that freedom was not simply won on national stages. It was cultivated in living rooms, churches, classrooms, and front porches.

After engaging with this topic, scholars will be able to:

- Describe the central role of Black women leaders in advancing civil rights through both national organizations and local efforts.
- Analyze the grassroots strategies employed by women in the South and beyond to challenge segregation and inequality.
- Understand how grassroots organizing shaped the broader goals, methods, and reach of the Civil Rights Movement.
- Recognize the often-overlooked contributions of Black women to the movement's leadership, vision, and legacy.

Centering Black Women in the Movement

Black women were essential architects of the Civil Rights Movement, leading voter registration drives, citizenship schools, national organizations, and local protests. Yet despite their indispensable contributions, many faced gender discrimination within major civil rights institutions. Leaders such as Ella Baker and Fannie Lou Hamer not only challenged racial injustice but also confronted the marginalization of women within movement spaces. Drawing from a long legacy of Black women's activism stretching back to the nineteenth century, they advanced a vision of liberation that accounted for both racial and gender justice—a dual commitment that foreshadowed later developments in intersectional activism.

Ella Baker and the Power of Grassroots Leadership

Often referred to as the "mother of the Civil Rights Movement," Ella Baker transformed the movement's structure by advocating for decentralized, community-driven leadership. Unlike many male leaders who embodied charismatic, top-down leadership models, Baker emphasized participatory democracy and collective decision-making. She mentored young activists in SNCC (Student Nonviolent Coordinating Committee), encouraging them to reject hierarchy and embrace grassroots power. Baker's philosophy helped shape a more inclusive movement culture, one that empowered students, women, and working-class people to become frontline leaders in the struggle for racial justice.

Reframing Protest: Beyond Lunch Counters

At SNCC's founding conference in 1960, Ella Baker delivered a keynote address that reframed the meaning of student sit-ins. She argued that the fight for access to lunch counters was not simply about food service—it symbolized a broader demand for full citizenship and the dismantling of racial exclusion in every sector of American life. Baker's framing helped SNCC evolve beyond protest actions and into a comprehensive grassroots organization focused on education, economic justice, political empowerment, and youth leadership.

SNCC Position Paper: Women in the Movement, 1964

The *SNCC Position Paper: Women in the Movement* (1964) is one of the earliest internal critiques of gender inequality within the Civil Rights Movement. Though written anonymously by a member of the Student Nonviolent Coordinating Committee (SNCC), the document is widely recognized as a foundational feminist text that highlighted the contradictions between the movement's fight for racial justice and its often patriarchal internal dynamics.

In the paper, the author compares the status of women in SNCC to the position of Black people in society. Both groups were asked to support and uplift others but were rarely empowered with decision-making authority or given credit for their leadership. The paper challenged male-dominated leadership structures and called for full inclusion of women in every aspect of movement organizing. The paper did not deny the importance of collective struggle; rather, it insisted that liberation must be comprehensive, not partial.

Circulated within SNCC's ranks, the document sparked intense debate and helped lay the intellectual groundwork for later expressions of Black feminism and intersectional thought. It also served as an early critique of sexism in progressive spaces, insisting that the Civil Rights Movement had to live up to its own democratic ideals.

For a deeper understanding of the role of women in the Civil Rights Movement, scholars are encouraged to read the *SNCC Position Paper: Women in the Movement* (1964) by visiting the Gilder Lehrman Institute of American History's AP African American Studies online resource: *https://www.gilderlehrman.org/ap-african-american-studies/unit-4/black-organizing-twentieth-century*. This free resource offers valuable insights into gender dynamics and the contributions of women to Black organizing in the twentieth century.

Dorothy Height and Sustained Institutional Leadership

Dorothy Height served as president of the National Council of Negro Women (NCNW) for four decades. As president, she led initiatives addressing issues ranging from Black women's political empowerment to voter education, childcare, and housing. Height was often one of the few women at the table during critical civil rights events, including the March on Washington. Though she worked behind the scenes, her strategic vision and institutional leadership ensured that Black women's voices, needs, and perspectives remained central to national organizing efforts.

Northern Organizing and the Coordinating Council of Community Organizations (CCCO)

Though much attention has focused on civil rights battles in the South, powerful grassroots organizing also occurred in cities like Chicago. In the mid-1960s, the Coordinating Council of Community Organizations (CCCO) mobilized residents to challenge deeply entrenched school segregation, inadequate housing, and discriminatory hiring practices in Chicago. CCCO served as a bridge between local Black communities and national civil rights leaders, demonstrating that the struggle for racial justice required confronting liberalism in the North as well as apartheid in the South.

The 1964 New York City School Boycott

The *New York Times* article "Boycott Cripples City Schools; Absences 360,000 Above Normal, Negroes and Puerto Ricans Unite," published on February 4, 1964, documents the unprecedented mass school boycott led by Black and Puerto Rican parents, students, and civil rights activists in New York City to protest racial segregation and systemic inequality in the public school system. The article reported that more than 460,000 students—nearly half of the city's total enrollment—refused to attend school, marking the largest single-day civil rights protest in U.S. history. The action challenged the notion that segregation was only a problem in the South and highlighted the urgency of addressing educational injustice in cities in the North. It also underscored how grassroots activism—often led by women—could reshape public discourse and policy on a massive scale.

The boycott was organized by a coalition of civil rights organizations and grassroots leaders, including the NAACP, the Congress of Racial Equality (CORE), and local parent-teacher associations. Protesters demanded immediate action to address the unequal distribution of resources, the concentration of Black and Puerto Rican students in overcrowded, underfunded schools, and the lack of integration in one of the nation's most diverse cities. The article provides a contemporaneous record of the scale and impact of the protest, highlighting the coordinated efforts of marginalized communities to expose and disrupt structural racism outside the South. It also illustrates how the Civil Rights Movement extended into cities in the North and tackled issues of educational injustice that still resonate today.

For a detailed account of the 1964 New York City school boycott, students are encouraged to read "Boycott Cripples City Schools; Absences 360,000 Above Normal, Negroes and Puerto Ricans Unite" published by *The New York Times*. This pivotal source is available at the Gilder Lehrman Institute of American History's AP African American Studies online resource: *https://www.gilderlehrman.org/ap-african-american-studies/unit-4/black-organizing-twentieth-century#par-19783*. The article highlights the powerful coalition between Black and Puerto Rican communities in advocating for educational equality.

Black women were not only the lifeblood of the Civil Rights Movement—they were its visionaries, strategists, and community builders. From Ella Baker's philosophy of participatory democracy to the mobilization of school boycotts and neighborhood protests in cities like Chicago and New York, Black women led with a commitment to justice that was both intersectional and deeply rooted in lived experience. Their work expanded the scope of the movement beyond national organizations and southern landmarks, embedding the fight for civil rights in classrooms, churches, unions, and city streets across the country. Although often denied recognition in male-dominated leadership structures, their transformative leadership left an indelible impact—reshaping not only the Civil Rights Movement but also the very meaning of American democracy.

She Was a Leader—Even Without the Mic

Women like Fannie Lou Hamer, Ella Baker, and Septima Clark didn't always get credit—but they were the soul of the movement. They led voter drives, trained leaders, and kept the momentum going.

You're Practicing: Noticing who history often leaves out.

Connect This To: Gender, leadership, and grassroots strategy.

Theme: Intersectionality and Power

Practice: Explain the Significance or Importance

Although often underrecognized, Black women were central to grassroots organizing and leadership in the Civil Rights Movement.

(A) Identify one Black woman who played a leadership role in civil rights organizing.
(B) Explain how her work advanced the goals of the Civil Rights Movement.
(C) Analyze the broader significance of Black women's leadership and organizing for the movement's success and legacy.

SAMPLE RESPONSE

(A) Ella Baker, a veteran civil rights strategist and community organizer, played a central role in the Civil Rights Movement as an advisor to the Student Nonviolent Coordinating Committee (SNCC), where she championed grassroots, community-based leadership over top-down, charismatic leadership models.

Ella Baker drew on her experience in the NAACP and the Southern Christian Leadership Conference (SCLC) to mentor young activists, helping to bridge national civil rights organizations with local community struggles.

Ella Baker's leadership style emphasized participatory democracy, empowering ordinary people—especially students, women, and working-class African Americans—to take ownership of the fight for racial justice.

(B) Ella Baker advanced the goals of the Civil Rights Movement by reframing the 1960 student sit-ins as part of a larger demand for full citizenship rights, thereby connecting isolated acts of protest to a sustained movement for racial equality.

Ella Baker strengthened the Civil Rights Movement by guiding SNCC from spontaneous direct actions toward long-term grassroots strategies, including voter registration, political education, and community organizing in rural and urban areas.

Ella Baker expanded the movement's reach by developing young leaders who could operate outside traditional male-dominated leadership structures, ensuring that the Civil Rights Movement reflected the lived experiences and leadership potential of ordinary Black Americans.

(C) Black women leaders such as Ella Baker, Fannie Lou Hamer, Septima Clark, Diane Nash, and Jo Ann Robinson shaped the success and legacy of the Civil Rights Movement by linking racial justice to broader struggles for voting rights, education equity, fair housing, and gender equality.

Black women's leadership, as demonstrated by Ella Baker's emphasis on grassroots empowerment, ensured that the Civil Rights Movement was grounded in community-based organizing rather than relying solely on high-profile national campaigns.

Black women organizers helped define the movement's legacy by leading transformative actions such as the 1964 New York City school boycott, which mobilized hundreds of thousands to protest educational inequality in the North, proving that systemic racism was a national problem that demanded national solutions.

Skills Assessed: Explain the significance of historical developments; use sources and evidence; analyze relationships among developments.

KEY TAKEAWAYS

1. **Transnational Black Consciousness**
   - Movements like Négritude and *Negrismo* connected African diasporic writers and intellectuals through themes of anticolonialism, cultural pride, and solidarity.
   - These literary and political movements fostered a global sense of Black identity, rooted in shared resistance to white supremacy and imperialism.
2. **Anticolonialism and African American Thought**
   - African American leaders like W. E. B. Du Bois and Paul Robeson engaged with anti-colonial struggles in Africa, Asia, and the Caribbean.
   - Black political thought during this era emphasized internationalism, linking domestic civil rights to global liberation.
3. **WWII and the Double V Campaign**
   - African Americans fought in WWII while experiencing racism at home, prompting the Double V Campaign: victory over fascism abroad and racism at home.
   - The G.I. Bill offered postwar benefits but was applied unequally, further entrenching economic disparities.
4. **Segregation, Discrimination, and the Civil Rights Spark**
   - The contradiction between American democratic ideals and racial segregation inspired a new generation of civil rights activism.
   - Legal challenges, community organizing, and mass protests targeted segregation in schools, transportation, and housing.
5. **Redlining and Housing Inequality**
   - Federal policies like redlining denied Black communities access to mortgages and homeownership, reinforcing racial wealth gaps.
   - Housing discrimination shaped segregated neighborhoods and deepened structural inequality.
6. **Civil Rights Organizations as Catalysts**
   - Groups like the NAACP, SCLC, and CORE organized protests, legal challenges, and voter registration drives to confront systemic racism.
   - Their work laid the foundation for landmark legislation like the Civil Rights Act (1964) and Voting Rights Act (1965).
7. **Black Women's Leadership**
   - Women like Ella Baker, Fannie Lou Hamer, and Septima Clark led grassroots campaigns and voter education initiatives.
   - Their often-overlooked contributions were essential to the success and direction of the movement.

Practice Multiple-Choice Questions

DIRECTIONS: Pick the letter that best answers the following questions.

Questions 1 through 3 refer to the following.

Petitioners Julian Mayfield, Alphaeus Hunton, Alice Windom, W. A. Jeanpierre, and Maya Angelou Make, outside the U.S. Embassy in Accra, Ghana, 1963

1. The photograph of Maya Angelou and Julian Mayfield in Accra is most useful to historians studying which of the following developments in the 1960s?

   (A) The rise of Black nationalist movements exclusively within the United States
   (B) The ways African American activists framed civil rights as part of global human rights struggles
   (C) The decline of African American participation in international affairs after World War II
   (D) The U.S. government's successful containment of racial protests abroad

2. Why was Ghana, under Kwame Nkrumah's presidency, a significant location for African American activists such as Maya Angelou in the early 1960s?

   (A) Ghana was the only African nation to officially fund the U.S. Civil Rights Movement.
   (B) Ghana's independence and Nkrumah's pan-African vision made it a hub for diasporic intellectuals and activists.
   (C) Ghana's geographic location allowed African Americans to avoid Cold War scrutiny.
   (D) Ghana was directly governed by the United States during the early 1960s.

3. The photograph most directly illustrates which broader historical trend of the mid-twentieth century?

   (A) The retreat of colonial powers in Africa and the global resonance of decolonization struggles
   (B) The decline of international solidarity among African-descended peoples after the Harlem Renaissance
   (C) The U.S. government's expansion of Jim Crow segregation into African colonies
   (D) The withdrawal of African American leaders from transnational politics after World War II

Questions 4 through 6 refer to the following.

Major Charity E. Adams and Captain Mary Kearney Inspect Members of the 6888th Central Postal Directory Battalion in England, 1945

4. The photograph of Major Charity E. Adams and Captain Mary Kearney inspecting the 6888th Battalion is most significant because it highlights which of the following?

   (A) The complete integration of the U.S. military during World War II
   (B) The use of African American women in frontline combat operations
   (C) The presence and leadership of African American women in overseas military service during World War II
   (D) The mass protest against segregation led by women soldiers during the war

5. What was the primary mission of the 6888th Central Postal Directory Battalion during World War II?

   (A) To serve as nurses and provide medical aid to wounded soldiers
   (B) To carry out espionage work behind enemy lines
   (C) To sort and deliver backlogged mail for U.S. service members overseas
   (D) To manage troop deployments and battlefield logistics

6. The military service of the 6888th Battalion during World War II is most significant for demonstrating which broader historical theme?

   (A) The elimination of racism and sexism from American institutions during wartime
   (B) The increased visibility of Black women's leadership in national and global arenas
   (C) The decline of African American enlistment due to segregation policies
   (D) The lack of meaningful contributions by African American women to the war effort

Answer Explanations

1. **(B)** The photograph shows African American expatriates in Ghana using public protest to connect U.S. racial injustice with international human rights, directly reflecting how the Black Freedom struggle became globalized. Choice (A) is incorrect because Garvey-era separatism and domestic Black nationalism were not the main point of this protest; the context here is transnational. Choice (C) is incorrect because, far from declining, African American international engagement grew in the 1960s. Choice (D) is incorrect since the U.S. government struggled to contain racial protest at home and abroad—this photograph proves its global visibility.

2. **(B)** Ghana, having won independence in 1957 under Kwame Nkrumah, became a beacon of pan-Africanism and postcolonial optimism. Many African American expatriates—including Maya Angelou, W. E. B. Du Bois, and Julian Mayfield—saw it as a site for diasporic unity and a model for Black liberation worldwide. Choice (A) is incorrect because Ghana did not directly fund the Civil Rights Movement. Choice (C) is inaccurate; activists in Ghana often faced Cold War scrutiny, especially from U.S. intelligence. Choice (D) is factually false, as Ghana was fully independent in the 1960s.

3. **(A)** The protest in Accra highlights how African American struggles were tied to global anti-colonial and decolonization movements. Ghana's independence symbolized the retreat of colonial powers and inspired African Americans to link their own freedom struggle with worldwide liberation efforts. Choice (B) is incorrect because this moment represents expanded solidarity, not decline. Choice (C) is incorrect; Jim Crow segregation was confined to the United States and was not exported into African colonies. Choice (D) is incorrect because African Americans increased international activism during the Cold War, often framing civil rights as part of global human rights.

4. **(C)** This image documents the leadership of Major Adams and Captain Kearney as part of the only all-Black, all-women military unit to serve abroad, symbolizing a breakthrough in both race and gender barriers within a segregated military. Choice (A) is incorrect because the U.S. military was still segregated during World War II. The 6888th's formation was an exception, not a reflection of full integration. Choice (B) is incorrect because the 6888th Battalion was not a combat unit. Its members were assigned to process mail for troops overseas. Choice (D) is incorrect because, although the women faced discrimination, this image does not represent a protest but, instead, formal inspection and service under military orders.

5. **(C)** The 6888th's key assignment was processing and distributing a massive backlog of mail for American troops in Europe, which was critical for morale and military efficiency. Choice (A) is incorrect because the 6888th was not composed of either nurses or medical personnel. Choice (B) is incorrect because members of the battalion were not trained or tasked with espionage or intelligence operations. Choice (D) is incorrect because, although their work was logistical in nature, battalion members were not responsible for managing troop movements or combat deployments.

6. **(B)** The leadership of Major Adams and Captain Kearney, along with the deployment of their battalion, showcased African American women in active, visible roles abroad—challenging stereotypes and setting precedent. Choice (A) is incorrect because racism and sexism persisted within the military and broader society. The 6888th's existence is notable precisely because it broke through barriers, not because those barriers were eliminated. Choice (C) is incorrect because African American enlistment remained high, despite discriminatory treatment. Choice (D) is incorrect because this battalion's formation and overseas deployment represent a powerful example of Black women's vital and meaningful contributions to the war effort.

12

Radical Imagination: Black Power, Politics, and the Reshaping of Identity

Key Themes

- Art as political expression—liberation through culture
- Radical shifts in identity and self-definition—from Afrocentric aesthetics to feminist frameworks
- Community empowerment models that challenged state neglect
- Global Black consciousness rooted in self-determination, not assimilation
- Understanding how race, gender, class, and sexuality intersect in systemic oppression and resistance

TIMELINE

Date/Period	Event/Development	Related Topics
1950s–1970s	Emergence of **freedom music, protest poetry, and political theater** linking the arts to liberation struggles	Topic 4.8—Arts, Music, and Politics of Freedom
1965	**Malcolm X's influence grows posthumously**, shaping **Black religious nationalism** and global anti-imperial critiques	Topic 4.9—Black Religious Nationalism
1966	**Black Power movement** gains momentum with **Stokely Carmichael's (Kwame Ture's)** speech at the March Against Fear	Topic 4.9—Black Power Movement
1965–1975	The **Black Arts movement**—founded by **Amiri Baraka** and others—emphasizes self-determination in cultural production	Topic 4.10—Black Arts Movement
1966	Founding of the **Black Panther Party for Self-Defense** by Huey Newton and Bobby Seale in Oakland, CA	Topic 4.11—Black Panther Party
Late 1960s–1970s	**Black Panther free breakfast programs, health clinics, and educational outreach** gain national attention	Topic 4.11—Community Programs
Late 1960s–1970s	Rise of the **Black Is Beautiful movement**, embracing natural hair, African dress, and cultural pride	Topic 4.12—Black Is Beautiful and Afrocentricity
1970s–1980s	Development of **Afrocentric curricula** and **Black Studies departments** at universities	Topic 4.12—Afrocentricity

Date/Period	Event/Development	Related Topics
1977	**Combahee River Collective** issues groundbreaking statement on **Black feminist thought and intersectionality**	Topic 4.13—Black Feminist Movement
1980s–present	Continued activism by **Black women scholars and organizers** challenges racism, sexism, and classism together	Topic 4.13—Womanism and Intersectionality
Late 20th century	Term ***interlocking systems of oppression*** coined to explain overlapping structural inequalities	Topic 4.14—Systems of Oppression

Topic 4.8 The Arts, Music, and Politics of Freedom

Key Terms

- Freedom songs—adapted spirituals used in protests (e.g., "We Shall Overcome")
- Jazz and blues—cultural expressions of resilience and protest
- Nina Simone, John Coltrane, Max Roach—artists who blended music and activism
- Poetry of resistance—Amiri Baraka, Gil Scott-Heron
- Cultural nationalism
- Spoken word and performance
- Black aesthetic—valuing Black cultural expression as inherently political
- Art as protest and liberation

How do you silence a movement when its message is carried in a song, spoken in poetry, and painted across the walls of history? For African Americans, artistic expression has always been more than performance. It has been protest, prayer, and power. Throughout the Civil Rights Movement, Black artists, poets, musicians, and performers served in the cultural front lines in the global struggle for racial justice. Their work transcended barriers, giving voice to the oppressed and exposing the hypocrisies of American democracy. Whether through the soul-stirring rhythms of gospel, the resolute poetry of resistance, or the revolutionary performances on stage and screen, African-descended artists used their platforms to challenge injustice, amplify the call for equality, and inspire international solidarity.

At the same time, faith traditions—particularly those rooted in the Black church—intertwined with music to sustain communities through collective worship, protest, and hope. This topic explores how creativity became a weapon of liberation and how the arts and music of freedom not only chronicled the movement but moved it forward.

After engaging with this topic, scholars will be able to:

- Explain how African American artists, poets, and musicians brought visibility and urgency to the Black Freedom struggle.
- Analyze the global and domestic impact of Black cultural expression on the Civil Rights Movement.
- Describe how faith traditions and freedom songs inspired and sustained African American activism.
- Evaluate how artistic and spiritual expression advanced the goals of political and social liberation.

Artistic Expression as Global Protest

During the Black Freedom movement of the twentieth century, African American artists used their creative platforms to resist racial injustice and project the struggle for equality onto the global stage. Visual artists, dancers, playwrights, and musicians infused their work with political critique, highlighting the realities of segregation, police violence, and systemic inequality. These cultural interventions resonated across the African diaspora, inspiring parallel movements among Afro-descendants in Latin America, the Caribbean, and Africa. Through their art, Black creators forged a transnational language of liberation that crossed borders and challenged the moral legitimacy of white supremacy worldwide.

Black Poets and International Solidarity

Poets such as Nicolás Guillén, a leading voice of the Cuban *Negrismo* movement, forged literary bridges between the Americas. Guillén's poetry not only celebrated African heritage and identity but also denounced the racial hierarchies that persisted in both the United States and Latin America. His work made clear that anti-Black racism was not confined to one country; it was a global structure of oppression. By connecting the violence of U.S. segregation with racial injustice across the hemisphere, poets like Guillén helped internationalize the moral urgency of the Civil Rights Movement.

"Little Rock" by Nicolás Guillén, 1958

Nicolás Guillén's 1958 poem "Little Rock" offers a searing poetic response to the violent backlash against school desegregation in the United States—specifically the crisis surrounding the Little Rock Nine in Arkansas in 1957. Guillén, a Cuban poet of African descent and a central figure in the *Negrismo* movement, uses verse to condemn the hypocrisy of a nation that claimed to champion democracy abroad while denying basic rights to Black children at home.

In "Little Rock," Guillén depicts the young students not as isolated figures but as global symbols of dignity and resistance in the face of hatred. His tone is both mournful and defiant as he calls out the irony of white mobs terrorizing children for attempting to attend school. By addressing American racism from outside U.S. borders, Guillén positions himself as part of a broader Afro-diasporic tradition of solidarity, critiquing imperialism and white supremacy through a poetic lens.

The poem exemplifies how Black and Afro-descended writers across the Americas used art to connect their own struggles to those unfolding in the U.S. South. Guillén's words reflect not only a condemnation of segregation but also a commitment to transnational justice, amplifying the global dimensions of the Civil Rights Movement.

For a more in-depth analysis of this source and access to the full poem, scholars are encouraged to visit the Gilder Lehrman Institute online at: https://www.gilderlehrman.org/ap-african-american-studies/unit-4/black-power-politics-culture/little-rock-1958.

Musicians like Charles Mingus used jazz—a genre deeply rooted in African American cultural traditions—as a vehicle for protest. Drawing on techniques like call and response, improvisation, and blues-infused harmonies, Mingus composed politically charged pieces that challenged listeners to confront racism and state violence. Charles Mingus's "Original Faubus Fables" (1960) stands as one of the most direct and unapologetic musical critiques of American racism in the modern jazz era. Composed in response to Arkansas Governor Orval Faubus's use of the National Guard to block the integration of Little Rock Central High School in 1957, the piece blends sharp satire, political commentary, and jazz improvisation into a powerful protest composition. In the original studio recording, which was released on the album *Charles Mingus Presents Charles Mingus*, Mingus and drummer Dannie Richmond vocalize biting, mocking lyrics that ridicule Faubus's white supremacist stance and call out the cowardice of segregationist politics.

Unlike the earlier 1959 version released by Columbia Records—where lyrics were omitted due to censorship concerns—this version restores the raw, satirical text that Mingus intended. The result is a work that fuses the urgency of the Civil Rights Movement with the expressive power of Black musical resistance. Using jazz idioms like call and response, free improvisation, and blues-based phrasing, Mingus transforms his ensemble into a vehicle for political dissent, rooted in both cultural pride and social outrage.

The 9-minute video recording of "Original Faubus Fables" not only showcases Mingus's musical brilliance but also invites audiences to consider how art can serve as a weapon against injustice. Through rhythm, melody, and wordplay, the performance exposes the absurdity and violence of segregation while reinforcing the role of Black musicians as cultural activists.

Scholars interested in further analyzing this protest performance can find the full video by searching "Original Faubus Fables Charles Mingus 1960" on YouTube at *https://youtu.be/m2nBE0PHaDM*.

Faith, Song, and Spiritual Resistance

During the Civil Rights Movement of the 1950s and 1960s, faith and music were powerful forces of inspiration and community mobilization. Many of the era's most enduring freedom songs emerged from the Black church, drawing from hymns, spirituals, gospel music, and labor chants. These songs were not only expressions of faith but also tools of political resistance—infusing the movement with moral clarity and unshakable resolve. Churches served as both spiritual sanctuaries and strategic centers, where music unified communities and prepared them for protest.

"Can't Turn Me Around"

"Can't Turn Me Around" exemplifies the spirit of resilience that defined the Civil Rights era. Performed during marches, in mass meetings, and behind bars, the song—rooted in gospel and call and response traditions—functioned as both a rallying cry and a source of collective strength in the face of systemic injustice.

At just over three minutes, this rendition captures the emotional endurance of activists who stood firm against violence and repression. Its repetitive, affirming lyrics reinforced solidarity and reminded participants that their cause was both just and unstoppable. The simplicity of the melody made it accessible to all, while its message carried profound weight: the movement would not back down.

Freedom songs like "Can't Turn Me Around" were far more than background music. They were instruments of protest, sources of courage, and expressions of dignity. As a cultural artifact, the song offers deep insight into how music sustained the emotional and spiritual infrastructure of the Black Freedom struggle.

Scholars may view the performance by searching "Can't Turn Me Around Civil Rights Movement song" on YouTube.

The Unifying Power of Freedom Songs

Freedom songs were more than symbolic—they were functional. As activists risked their lives in the face of police brutality and white supremacist violence, songs provided cohesion, comfort, and clarity. Lyrics gave direction and purpose, while the communal act of singing reinforced solidarity and defiance. Whether sung in churches, on buses, or in jail cells, freedom songs articulated a vision of a more just and inclusive future and reminded participants that they were part of a moral tradition far larger than themselves.

"We Shall Overcome" as a Movement Anthem

No song captured the spirit of the Civil Rights Movement more profoundly than "We Shall Overcome." Often sung during marches, protests, and imprisonment, the anthem became a sonic symbol of collective endurance. Dr. Martin Luther King Jr. recognized its power, referencing the song in his 1966 speech of the same name. The song's simple structure and powerful message made it easy to learn and difficult to ignore. As voices rose in unison, "We Shall Overcome" transformed protest into prophecy, declaring that freedom was not only possible but inevitable.

Why We Can't Wait

In the book *Why We Can't Wait* (1964), Dr. Martin Luther King Jr. offers a vivid account of the Birmingham Campaign, one of the most strategically significant and morally compelling moments in the Civil Rights Movement. Chapter 4, titled "A New Day in Birmingham," recounts the transformative events of the spring of 1963 when local activists, youth, clergy, and national leaders converged in Birmingham, Alabama, to confront the entrenched system of Jim Crow segregation.

In the excerpt from page 48, King emphasizes the moral clarity and courage of young protesters—many of them schoolchildren—who faced down police dogs, firehoses, and arrest with remarkable dignity. He describes a new spirit of resistance rising from the Black community in Birmingham, noting that even children had become "foot soldiers" in a larger battle for human rights. King's language reveals both the brutality of the state's response and the spiritual power of nonviolent protest. He portrays Birmingham not only as a battleground but as a proving ground for a new phase of disciplined, faith-inspired activism that would shape national consciousness.

This chapter exemplifies King's ability to combine strategic insight, historical narrative, and moral vision. It situates Birmingham as a turning point in the movement—one that galvanized federal action and inspired similar efforts across the nation.

> For an in-depth exploration of Dr. Martin Luther King Jr.'s powerful analysis of the Civil Rights Movement's urgency, scholars are encouraged to read *Why We Can't Wait* (1964). This influential text offers insight into the necessity of direct action and the moral imperative of justice.

The Civil Rights Movement was not only a political struggle. It was a cultural revolution powered by the voices, visions, and convictions of Black artists, musicians, poets, and faith leaders. Through song, verse, and performance, African Americans communicated resistance, restored dignity, and inspired collective action. These creative expressions reached beyond borders, resonating across the African diaspora and galvanizing global solidarity. Whether through a freedom song or a jazz composition condemning state violence, the arts served as a vital force in shaping public consciousness and sustaining the movement's moral authority. In every note, lyric, and brushstroke, the politics of freedom lived.

Art with a Message

Black creativity didn't just entertain—it exposed injustice and gave people hope. From jazz musicians to protest poets, artists made their work part of the movement.

You're Practicing: Thinking about how culture can challenge power.

Connect This To: Music, performance, and protest.

Theme: Cultural Expression and Resistance

Practice: Explain the Significance or Importance

Artists and musicians played a vital role in shaping and spreading messages of liberation during the Civil Rights Movement and beyond.

(A) Identify one example of an artist or musical work associated with Black freedom struggles.
(B) Explain how this artistic expression communicated political or social messages.
(C) Analyze the significance of arts and music in unifying, mobilizing, or sustaining movements for justice.

SAMPLE RESPONSES

(A) One example of an artist associated with Black freedom struggles is Nicolás Guillén, whose 1958 poem "Little Rock" condemned racial segregation in the United States and expressed solidarity with the African American students integrating Central High School. Guillén used his art to align the U.S. Civil Rights Movement with global struggles for racial justice.

Another example is the freedom song "Can't Turn Me Around," which activists sang during marches, jailhouse protests, and mass meetings. The song drew from Black church traditions and gospel call-and-response styles to inspire resilience and unify communities in the fight for racial equality.

(B) "Little Rock" communicated a powerful political message by portraying U.S. segregation as a violation of democracy and human rights. Guillén used poetry to amplify the voices of the Little Rock Nine and highlight their courage, framing the integration crisis as part of a global fight for equality and dignity.

The freedom song "We Shall Overcome" communicated messages of hope, unity, and perseverance during the Civil Rights Movement. By declaring that eventual triumph was inevitable, the song's simple melody and collective singing inspired activists, mobilized support, and provided an enduring moral vision for the movement.

(C) Arts and music were significant in sustaining movements for justice because they created shared spaces of identity and hope. In *Why We Can't Wait* (1964), Dr. Martin Luther King Jr. highlights how churches became strategic centers where freedom songs like "Can't Turn Me Around" unified communities, boosted morale, and prepared activists for nonviolent resistance during campaigns like Birmingham.

Poetry sustained movements for justice by elevating local struggles into global narratives. Guillén's "*Little Rock*" linked the U.S. Civil Rights Movement to anti-colonial and anti-racist struggles worldwide, showing that artistic expression could mobilize international solidarity and reshape public consciousness beyond U.S. borders.

Skills Assessed: Explain the significance of historical developments; use sources and evidence; analyze relationships among developments.

Topic 4.9 Black Religious Nationalism and the Black Power Movement

Key Terms

- Nation of Islam (NOI)—founded by Wallace Fard Muhammad, led by Elijah Muhammad
- Malcolm X—key figure advocating Black self-determination and critique of nonviolence
- Black theology—merging Black liberation with Christianity
- James Cone—*A Black Theology of Liberation*
- Spiritual nationalism—empowerment through religious identity
- Moorish Science Temple
- "By any means necessary"—Malcolm X slogan
- Sacred and secular Black power

What happens when the demand is no longer for inclusion but for independence, self-determination, and control of one's destiny? In the late 1960s, the Black Freedom struggle evolved from calls for civil rights to a louder, more radical assertion: **Black Power**. As the Civil Rights Movement faced mounting resistance and internal limitations, a new wave of political and cultural activism emerged, led by voices that called not only for justice but for self-determination. This shift was deeply informed by Black religious nationalism, particularly the teachings of the **Nation of Islam**, which offered a powerful critique of white supremacy while promoting racial pride, economic independence, and spiritual renewal. Leaders such as **Elijah Muhammad** and **Malcolm X** challenged the moral and political assumptions of integration and encouraged African Americans to reclaim control over their communities, institutions, and identities.

The emergence of the Black Power movement in the mid- to late-1960s reflected this broader ideological transition. Advocates of Black Power—many of whom had roots in civil rights activism—called for political sovereignty, cultural affirmation, and resistance by any means necessary. This movement reshaped the landscape of Black activism by centering Black consciousness, celebrating African heritage, and rejecting narratives that cast nonviolence as the only legitimate form of resistance. Topic 4.9 explores the religious and political ideologies that informed this shift and the leaders who made them central to the next phase of the Black Freedom struggle.

After engaging with this topic, scholars will be able to:

- Describe the founding, beliefs, and influence of the Nation of Islam within the Black Freedom movement.
- Analyze the philosophical and strategic shift from civil rights to Black Power.
- Evaluate the roles of key figures such as Elijah Muhammad, Malcolm X, and Stokely Carmichael in advancing Black nationalist thought.
- Understand the cultural and political significance of Black Power in reshaping African American identity and resistance.

Origins and Beliefs of the Nation of Islam

The Nation of Islam (NOI) was founded in Detroit in 1930. It combined basic Islamic beliefs and practices—such as devotion to Allah and study of the Qur'an—with mythology and Black nationalist ideology. Its teachings emphasized self-reliance, racial pride, and separation from the structures of white supremacy. The NOI positioned itself not merely as a religious movement but as a vehicle for the moral, political, and economic uplift of African Americans during an era of intense racial oppression.

The Honorable Elijah Muhammad and the Reclamation of Identity

The Honorable Elijah Muhammad led the Nation of Islam from 1934 until his death in 1975, establishing its national headquarters in Chicago and growing its influence across the United States. Under his guidance, the NOI encouraged followers to reject their "slave names" and reclaim their identities through Islamic naming practices. Many members adopted the letter "X" to symbolize the lost names of their ancestors—an act of resistance against the legacy of enslavement and an assertion of autonomy. This symbolic renaming represented a deeper ideological shift: a break from assimilation and a commitment to cultural and spiritual sovereignty.

Nation of Islam Members with Bundles of *Muhammad Speaks* Newspapers

This 1965 photograph, taken in Chicago, Illinois, captures members of the Nation of Islam (NOI) distributing bundles of *Muhammad Speaks*, the official newspaper of the organization. Published from its Chicago headquarters under the leadership of the Honorable Elijah Muhammad, the newspaper served as both a communication tool and an ideological platform for the NOI's teachings. It featured content on racial injustice, international Black solidarity, economic self-sufficiency, and critiques of integrationist politics, offering a worldview grounded in Black nationalism and religious conviction.

The image documents the grassroots efforts of NOI members who not only distributed literature but also embodied the movement's discipline, self-reliance, and community outreach. By selling *Muhammad Speaks* in urban neighborhoods across the country, these individuals extended the NOI's influence beyond religious spaces and into the public square—reaching everyday African Americans with a message of dignity, resistance, and transformation.

Nation of Islam members stand on the steps of Muhammad's Temple in Chicago, carrying bundles of *Muhammad Speaks*
(Source: Photo by Robert Abbott Sengstacke/Getty Images)

The Honorable Elijah Muhammad Addressing Black Muslims in Chicago

This 1966 photograph captures Elijah Muhammad, the longtime leader of the Nation of Islam (NOI), delivering an address to a congregation of Black Muslims in Chicago. As the central figure of the NOI since 1934, the Honorable Elijah Muhammad played a formative role in shaping the organization's message of Black self-reliance, religious discipline, and separation from white-dominated institutions. Speaking from the movement's national headquarters, Muhammad's leadership in this image reflects both spiritual authority and ideological clarity during a period of growing national attention to Black religious nationalism.

Elijah Muhammad delivering an address to a congregation of Black Muslims in Chicago
(Source: Bettmann/Contributor/Getty)

The photograph underscores the Nation of Islam's structured hierarchy, formal presentation, and mass appeal during the height of the Black Power era. Gatherings like this served not only as religious events but also as forums for disseminating the NOI's vision of Black identity, autonomy, and moral reform.

From Civil Rights to Black Power

By the mid-1960s, a growing number of African Americans began to question the efficacy and limits of the Civil Rights Movement's emphasis on integration and nonviolence. In response to ongoing violence, economic inequality, and systemic neglect, the Black Power movement emerged as a new ideological and strategic phase of the Black Freedom struggle. Advocates of Black Power promoted self-determination, community control, and the right to self-defense. The movement also emphasized the transformation of Black consciousness, encouraging pride in African heritage, political independence, and cultural expression that rejected white normative standards.

Malcolm X and Dr. Martin Luther King Jr. at the United States Capitol

This historic photograph taken after a press conference captures a brief but symbolic moment between two of the most prominent figures of the Black Freedom movement: Malcolm X and Dr. Martin Luther King Jr. Taken at the United States Capitol in 1964 following a Senate debate on the Civil Rights Act, this image marks the only documented meeting between the two leaders. Although their strategies differed—King advocated nonviolent civil disobedience and Malcolm X emphasized Black autonomy and self-defense—both were deeply committed to securing dignity, justice, and full citizenship for African Americans.

The photograph serves as a visual testament to the ideological breadth and complexity of the movement. It reminds scholars that although these leaders sometimes disagreed publicly, they were ultimately united in their pursuit of liberation. The convergence of their paths in this moment underscores the historical urgency of 1964 and the growing national and global pressure to confront racial injustice in the United States.

Martin Luther King and Malcolm X after King's press conference at the U.S. Capitol about the senate debate on the Civil Rights Act of 1964 (Source: Library of Congress)

Malcolm X and the Call for Autonomy

Malcolm X, one of the most influential ministers within the Nation of Islam, played a pivotal role in articulating the principles of Black nationalism to a national and global audience. He urged African Americans to build their own institutions—schools, businesses, and political structures—rather than seek validation through integration. Malcolm's vision of freedom was rooted in dignity, discipline, and independence. He critiqued both racial injustice and the limitations of traditional civil rights frameworks, pushing for a more radical and unapologetic model of Black liberation.

Self-Defense and Constitutional Rights

Unlike other Civil Rights leaders who promoted nonviolence as a moral and strategic imperative, Malcolm X asserted the right of African Americans to defend themselves "by any means necessary." He argued that if the government failed to protect Black citizens from racial terror, Black citizens themselves had both the moral and constitutional right to defend their lives and property. This position resonated with many African Americans living under daily threat of violence. It also directly influenced later groups like the Black Panther Party, which explicitly embraced the principle of armed self-defense and community protection.

Malcolm X—The Ballot or the Bullet

Delivered in April 1964 shortly after his departure from the Nation of Islam, Malcolm X's speech The Ballot or the Bullet marks a pivotal moment in the Black Freedom struggle. In this address, Malcolm X urged African Americans to exercise their right to vote judiciously, emphasizing that political engagement was essential for achieving racial justice. He cautioned, however, that if the government continued to deny African Americans full equality, more assertive measures might become necessary.

Malcolm X highlighted the importance of Black political unity and self-determination. He criticized both major political parties for failing to address the needs of Black Americans and advocated for the establishment of independent Black political organizations. The speech underscored the urgency of the moment, suggesting that 1964 was a critical year for African Americans to leverage their voting power effectively.

This speech is significant for its articulation of Black nationalism and its emphasis on the right to self-defense. Malcolm X's rhetoric empowered African Americans to take control of their political destiny and challenged the status quo of racial oppression.

Scholars interested in experiencing Malcolm X's powerful speech, The Ballot or the Bullet, are encouraged to search for the full speech on YouTube by typing "Malcolm X—The Ballot or the Bullet" or by visiting YouTube https://www.youtube.com/watch?v=CRNciryImqg.

Malcolm X's Evolution and Global Vision

Malcolm X's thinking evolved significantly in the final years of his life. After leaving the Nation of Islam in 1964 and embracing orthodox Islam, he began to advocate for a global human rights agenda that connected the struggles of African Americans with those of oppressed people around the world. He supported pan-African solidarity, denounced colonialism, and sought to bring international pressure to bear on U.S. racial policies. In doing so, Malcolm reframed the Black Freedom Movement not only as a fight for civil rights but as part of a worldwide campaign for human dignity and justice.

Black religious nationalism and the rise of the Black Power movement marked a pivotal shift in the Black Freedom struggle. The Nation of Islam, under the Honorable Elijah Muhammad, offered a theological and cultural framework that emphasized pride, discipline, and separation from oppressive systems. Through figures like Malcolm X, this ideology helped catalyze a broader movement rooted in self-determination, autonomy, and an uncompromising demand for dignity. As the limitations of integration became increasingly visible, Black Power emerged as both a political and cultural response—reshaping how African Americans defined liberation, challenged white supremacy, and envisioned their future in the United States and beyond.

TIP

Be Clear and Concise

Write clearly and concisely. Avoid using vague or overly complex language. Your points should be easy for the reader to understand.

Faith Meets Freedom

Religious beliefs inspired resistance, which ranged from Christian churches to the Nation of Islam. Faith helped organize people and gave meaning to the fight for justice.

You're Practicing: Linking spiritual ideas to political action.

Connect This To: Religion, identity, and organizing.

Theme: Belief and Resistance

Practice: Contextualize

During the mid-twentieth century, Black religious movements offered spiritual and political alternatives to mainstream civil rights approaches, contributing to the rise of Black Power ideologies.

(A) Identify one Black religious nationalist organization or leader active during the Black Power era.

(B) Explain how their religious beliefs shaped their views on Black identity, self-determination, or liberation.

(C) Contextualize their role within broader shifts in Black political thought during the 1960s and 1970s.

SAMPLE RESPONSES

(A) The Nation of Islam, led by Elijah Muhammad during the mid-twentieth century, was one of the most influential Black religious nationalist organizations, promoting a theology centered on Black self-determination, moral discipline, and independence from white society.

Minister Malcolm X, as the Nation of Islam's most visible spokesperson in the early 1960s, brought the group's message of Black pride, economic self-sufficiency, and spiritual renewal to a national and international audience.

The Moorish Science Temple of America, founded earlier by Noble Drew Ali but influential during the Black Power era, also advanced a religious nationalist vision connecting African Americans to a Moorish Muslim identity and emphasizing sovereignty and self-definition.

(B) Elijah Muhammad's teachings in the Nation of Islam framed Black identity as divinely chosen and distinct from white society, shaping the belief that true liberation required separation from systems of white control and the building of independent Black institutions.

Malcolm X, while in the Nation of Islam, used the group's religious framework to argue that African Americans must embrace their African and Islamic heritage, reject assimilation into white culture, and achieve self-determination through economic, political, and spiritual autonomy.

The Moorish Science Temple of America used its religious philosophy to instill pride in a distinct Moorish-American identity, teaching that reclaiming African heritage and rejecting imposed racial categories were essential steps toward liberation.

(C) The Nation of Islam played a pivotal role in the shift from the integrationist focus of the early Civil Rights Movement to the separatist and self-determination ethos of the Black Power era, influencing groups such as the Black Panther Party and activists seeking community control.

Malcolm X's public speeches, especially after leaving the Nation of Islam and embracing Sunni Islam, connected African American liberation to global anti-colonial struggles, reinforcing the era's growing emphasis on international solidarity and pan-Africanism.

Black religious nationalist organizations provided an alternative to nonviolent civil rights activism, helping to shape the ideological foundation of the Black Power movement by blending spirituality, cultural pride, and calls for political independence.

Skills Assessed: Contextualize historical developments; use sources and evidence; analyze relationships among developments.

Topic 4.10 The Black Arts Movement

Key Terms

- Amiri Baraka (LeRoi Jones)—founder of the movement
- Black Is Beautiful ethos
- Political poetry, theater, and visual arts
- Art as revolutionary expression
- Black cultural institutions—theaters, publishing houses
- Self-representation and aesthetic autonomy
- Connection to Black Power
- Theatrical protest and community workshops

During the height of the Black Freedom struggle, a powerful question emerged: What should Black art do? In the 1960s and 1970s, the answer came through a cultural revolution that demanded art serve the people and reflect their fight for liberation.

The Black Arts movement (BAM) redefined the role of cultural expression in African American life. Emerging in the 1960s alongside the rise of Black Power, BAM called for literature, performance, and visual art that centered Black experiences, uplifted Black pride, and directly confronted systemic injustice. It rejected Eurocentric artistic standards and instead promoted a distinctly Black aesthetic grounded in self-determination, political resistance, and cultural affirmation.

Beyond its influence on artistic production, the Black Arts movement had a lasting impact on education. Its emphasis on reclaiming and affirming Black identity helped fuel the development of African American Studies as an academic discipline. Students and educators, inspired by the cultural shift, pushed for the institutionalization of Black history, literature, and thought in classrooms and curricula across the nation.

After engaging with this topic, scholars will be able to:

- Explain how the Black Arts movement influenced Black cultural expression in the 1960s and 1970s.
- Describe how the movement supported the emergence of African American Studies in higher education.
- Analyze the connection between artistic expression and political self-determination within the context of the Black Freedom struggle.

Black Art as a Tool for Liberation

The Black Arts movement (BAM), which spanned from 1965 to 1975, mobilized Black artists, writers, musicians, and dramatists to create works that directly contributed to the goal of Black liberation. Although BAM participants did not all share a single vision of what Black art should look or sound like, they were unified by the belief that Black art had its own unique inspiration, aesthetic, and purpose. Art was not neutral; it was political. In the context of the Black Freedom struggle, art was expected to serve and reflect the realities of Black life.

Building on Historical Foundations

Much like the Harlem Renaissance of the 1920s, which had introduced the idea of a New Negro consciousness, the Black Arts movement reimagined the role of culture in shaping political identity. It provided a new foundation for

Black artistic expression by emphasizing continuity with the long tradition of Black cultural production. Through literature, music, theater, and visual arts, BAM connected contemporary creative voices to the legacy of Black artistic resistance, highlighting the ongoing role of culture in shaping liberation movements.

Cultural Innovation and Academic Impact

The influence of the Black Arts movement extended beyond the realm of artistic production. It led to the creation of Black-owned magazines, publishing houses, art centers, and scholarly journals. These institutions fostered independent Black cultural expression and helped preserve a wide range of creative works. At the same time, BAM played a crucial role in establishing African American Studies as an academic field. The flourishing of Black cultural forms during this period demonstrated the value of interdisciplinary study and contributed to the creation of some of the earliest African American Studies programs in universities.

Negro es Bello II by Elizabeth Catlett

Elizabeth Catlett, the granddaughter of formerly enslaved people, was an African American artist whose work explored themes of race, gender, class, and historical memory through painting, sculpture, and printmaking. After relocating to Mexico in the 1940s and later becoming a Mexican citizen, Catlett developed a style that reflected the influences of African, African American, and Mexican modernist traditions.

Her print *Negro es Bello II* (1969) captures the diasporic and transnational dimensions of the Black Power and Black Is Beautiful movements. The artwork features two stylized faces in the form of African masks and images of black panthers, encircled by the phrase "Black Is Beautiful." Through this composition, Catlett engages with the cultural affirmation and political urgency of the era, positioning her work within a global dialogue on Black pride and liberation.

To explore the rich cultural legacy of the Black Power era, scholars are encouraged to examine *Negro es Bello II* (1969) by Elizabeth Catlett. This iconic artwork celebrates Black identity, pride, and resilience. You can find this piece and further contextual resources at the Gilder Lehrman Institute of American History's AP African American Studies online resource: https://www.gilderlehrman.org/ap-african-american-studies/unit-4/black-power-politics-culture.

When Art Became a Weapon

The Black Arts movement used poetry, theater, and visual art to speak truth to power. Artists showed the world what Black pride and pain looked like—unfiltered.

You're Practicing: Interpreting art as activism.

Connect This To: Black pride and cultural revolution.

Theme: Expression and Self-Definition

Practice: Explain the Effects of Historical Developments

The Black Arts movement emerged as the cultural counterpart to the Black Power movement, aiming to produce art rooted in Black experiences and political consciousness.

(A) Identify one poet, playwright, or visual artist associated with the Black Arts movement.
(B) Explain how that artist's work reflected the political and cultural goals of the era.
(C) Analyze one specific effect the Black Arts movement had on African American identity, education, or community organization.

SAMPLE RESPONSES

(A) Amiri Baraka (formerly LeRoi Jones), founder of the Black Arts Movement, was a poet, playwright, and cultural theorist whose work fused political activism with a revolutionary vision for Black artistic self-determination.

Elizabeth Catlett, an African American and later Mexican citizen, created politically charged visual art such as *Negro es Bello II* (1969) that celebrated Black identity and aligned with the Black Is Beautiful ethos of the Black Arts Movement.

Sonia Sanchez, a leading poet of the Black Arts Movement, used her verse to celebrate African American cultural pride while urging political resistance to systemic racism.

(B) Amiri Baraka's plays and essays reflected the Black Arts Movement's goal of creating art that served the Black community by rejecting Eurocentric standards and centering Black cultural and political liberation.

Elizabeth Catlett's *Negro es Bello II* reflected the Black Arts Movement's call for cultural affirmation and political self-representation by blending African mask imagery with the symbolic power of the Black Panther iconography.

Sonia Sanchez's poetry reflected the Black Arts Movement's political and cultural goals by using African American speech rhythms and themes of resistance to affirm Black pride and challenge white cultural dominance.

(C) The Black Arts Movement transformed African American identity by popularizing the "Black Is Beautiful" ethos, which encouraged self-love, pride in African heritage, and the rejection of white beauty standards.

The Black Arts Movement influenced education by helping to institutionalize African American Studies programs in universities, embedding Black literature, history, and culture into higher education curricula.

The Black Arts Movement strengthened community organization by fostering the creation of independent Black theaters, publishing houses, and art centers that nurtured self-determined Black cultural expression.

Skills Assessed: Explain the effects of historical developments; use sources and evidence; analyze relationships among developments.

Topic 4.11 The Black Panther Party for Self-Defense

Key Terms

- Huey P. Newton and Bobby Seale—cofounders
- Ten-Point Program—political demands and community focus
- Police patrols and self-defense
- Free Breakfast for Children Program
- Health clinics, education, and housing activism
- COINTELPRO—FBI surveillance and infiltration
- Militant image vs. community service
- Alliances with global revolutionary movements

What does it mean to demand justice not just through protest but through organized, community-based action? In the late 1960s, the Black Panther Party for Self-Defense offered an answer rooted in both protection and empowerment. Formed in response to police brutality and systemic racial oppression, the Black Panther Party for Self-Defense emerged as a powerful political and social force in the twentieth century. Although often misrepresented solely as a militant group, the organization pursued a wide range of reforms aimed at addressing the political, economic, and social needs of Black communities.

Through a combination of direct action, public education, and community survival programs, the party sought to confront injustice while building alternatives to institutions that had historically failed African Americans. The party's vision extended beyond protest. It included health clinics, food distribution, education programs, and legal advocacy, reflecting a comprehensive approach to liberation. This topic explores how the Black Panther Party translated the demands of the Black Freedom struggle into structured, community-based strategies for reform and empowerment.

After engaging with this topic, scholars will be able to:

- Explain how the Black Panther Party for Self-Defense addressed issues of political disenfranchisement, economic inequality, and social injustice.
- Analyze how the party's community programs reflected broader goals of the Black Freedom movement.
- Understand the party's place within the larger context of twentieth-century struggles for racial justice and self-determination.

Political Platform and Vision

The Black Panther Party for Self-Defense was a revolutionary Black Power organization shaped by the ideas of Malcolm X. Its foundational **Ten-Point Program** outlined demands for freedom from systemic oppression and imprisonment along with demands for access to housing, health care, education, and employment. The party viewed these demands as essential rights—not privileges—and rooted its vision in confronting structural inequality through organized political action.

The Black Panther Party, Ten-Point Program (1966)

The Ten-Point Program, published in 1966, served as the foundational platform of the Black Panther Party for Self-Defense. It outlined the party's core demands and political vision, calling for freedom, full employment, decent housing, education that reflects the true history of Black people, and an end to police brutality and unjust imprisonment. Framed as both a declaration of rights and a list of grievances, the document identified systemic racism, economic inequality, and state violence as interconnected forces that demanded immediate redress.

This program reflected the party's belief that liberation required structural transformation—not reform alone. Each point connected daily injustices to broader demands for self-determination and dignity. The Ten-Point Program became a rallying framework for the party's organizing efforts nationwide and remains one of the most important political documents of the Black Power era.

Black Panther Platform

WHAT WE WANT

1. We want freedom. We want power to determine the destiny of our black community.
2. We Want Full Employment for Our People.
3. We Want An End to the Robbery By the Capitalists of Our Black Community.
4. We Want Decent Housing Fit For The Shelter of Human Beings.
5. We Want Education for Our People That Exposes The True Nature Of This Decadent American Society. We Want Education That Teaches Us Our True History And Our Role in the Present-Day Society.
6. We Want All Black Men To Be Exempt From Military Service.
7. We Want An Immediate End to Police Brutality and the Murder of Black People.
8. We Want Freedom For All Black Men Held in Federal, State, County and City Prisons and Jails.
9. We Want All Black People When Brought to Trial To Be Tried In Court By A Jury Of Their Peer Group Or People From Their Black Communities, As Defined By the Constitution of the United States.
10. We Want Land, Bread, Housing, Education, Clothing, Justice And Peace.

WHAT WE BELIEVE

1. We believe that Black people will not be free until we are able to determine our destiny.
2. We believe that the federal government is responsible and obligated to give every man employment or a guaranteed income. We believe that if the White American businessmen will not give full employment, then the means of production should be taken from the businessmen and placed in the community so that the people of the community can organize and employ all of its people and give a high standard of living.
3. We believe that this racist government has robbed us, and now we are demanding the overdue debt of forty acres and two mules. Forty acres and two mules were promised 100 years ago as restitution for slave labor and mass murder of Black people. We will accept the payment in currency which will be distributed to our many communities. The Germans are now aiding the Jews in Israel for the genocide of the Jewish people. The Germans murdered six million Jews. The American racist has taken part in the slaughter of over fifty million Black people; therefore, we feel that this is a modest demand that we make.
4. We believe that if the White Landlords will not give decent housing to our Black community, then the housing and the land should be made into cooperatives so that our community, with government aid, can build and make decent housing for its people.
5. We believe in an educational system that will give to our people a knowledge of self. If a man does not have knowledge of himself and his position in society and the world then he has little chance to relate to anything else.
6. We believe that Black people should not be forced to fight in the military service to defend a racist government that does not protect us. We will not fight and kill other people of color in the world who, like Black people, are being victimized by the White racist government of America. We will protect ourselves from the force and violence of the racist police and the racist military by whatever means necessary.
7. We believe we can end police brutality in our Black community by organizing Black self-defense groups that are dedicated to defending our Black community from racist police oppression and brutality. The Second Amendment to the Constitution of the United States gives a right to bear arms. We therefore believe that all Black people should arm themselves for self-defense.
8. We believe that all Black People should be released from the many jails and prisons because they have not received a fair and impartial trial.
9. We believe that the courts should follow the United States Constitution so that Black people will receive fair trials. The Fourteenth Amendment of the U.S. Constitution gives a man a right to be tried by his peer group. A peer is a person from a similar economic, social, religious, geographical, environmental, historical, and racial background. To do this the court will be forced to select a jury from the Black community from which the Black defendant came. We have been, and we are being, tried by all-White juries that have no understanding of the "average reasoning man" of the Black community.
10. When, in the course of human events, it becomes necessary for one people to dissolve the political bands which have connected them with another, and to assume, among the powers of the earth, the separate and equal station to which the laws of nature and nature's God entitle them, a decent respect of the opinions of mankind requires that they should declare the causes which impel them to the separation.

We hold these truths to be self-evident, that all men are created equal; that they are endowed by their Creator with certain inalienable rights; that among these are life, liberty, and the pursuit of happiness. That, to secure these rights, governments are instituted among men, deriving their just powers from the consent of the governed; that, whenever any form of government becomes destructive of these ends, it is the right of the people to alter or abolish it, and to institute a new government, laying its foundation on such principles, and organizing its powers in such form, as to them shall seem most likely to effect their safety and happiness. Prudence, indeed, will dictate that governments long established should not be changed for light and transient causes; and, accordingly, all experience hath shown that mankind are more disposed to suffer, while evils are sufferable, than to right themselves by abolishing the forms to which they are accustomed. But, when a long train of abuses and usurpations, pursing invariably the same object, evinces a design to reduce them under absolute despotism, it is their right, it is their duty, to throw off such government, and to provide new guards for their future security.

Source: The Black Panther Party, "Ten-Point Program" (October 15, 1966), *Helix* 3, no. 7 (May 9, 1968): 14. (The Seattle Public Library; Seattle Room Digital Collections.)

Armed Self-Defense and State Surveillance

The Black Panther Party cited the Second Amendment to assert the right of African Americans to bear arms in self-defense. Their calls for armed resistance to racial oppression led to confrontations with law enforcement and were often framed by the media as violent extremism. In response, the FBI targeted the Panthers. It used counterintelligence programs (COINTELPRO)—including surveillance, infiltration, and disruption campaigns—and classified the Panthers as a threat to national security.

Women's Leadership and Community Programs

Women comprised nearly half of the party's membership and frequently held leadership positions in local chapters. The organization quickly expanded to cities across the United States and implemented a wide range of social reform initiatives. These included "survival programs" such as the Free Breakfast for School Children Program, free legal aid offices, and community relief services offering medical care and clothing. These programs were central to the Black Panther Party's mission to uplift and protect low-income Black communities.

Black Panther Women in Oakland, CA, 1968

This black-and-white photograph captures a defining moment at a Black Panther rally in Oakland, California in 1968. Six African American women stand in a row with their left fists raised—a powerful gesture of solidarity and resistance associated with the Black Power movement. The women pictured include Mary Ann Carlton, Delores Henderson, Joyce Lee, Joyce Means, Paula Hill, and one unidentified woman. Their presence and posture reflect the central yet often underrecognized role that women played in the leadership, organization, and public representation of the Black Panther Party.

The image offers visual evidence of the Party's gender dynamics as well as the ways in which Black women embodied the principles of political defiance and community strength. Their raised fists signal both unity and resolve, underscoring how women were not only participants in the movement but leaders in advancing its mission.

For more in-depth analysis, scholars can view the image by searching "Black Panther Women in Oakland, CA, 1968" at the Gilder Lehrman Institute of American History: *https://www.gilderlehrman.org/ap-african-american-studies/unit-4/black-power-politics-culture/black-panther-women-oakland-california-1968.*

Black Panther Free Food Program, 1972

This black-and-white photograph, *Black Panther Free Food Program, 1972*, documents children participating in the Black Panther Party's Free Food Program during the Community Survival Conference held in Oakland, California, in 1972. In the image, four children—two boys and two girls—are seen carefully placing bags of puffed wheat cereal into rows of brown paper grocery bags being prepared for community distribution. The photograph offers a compelling view of how the party's survival programs were not only community based but intergenerational, involving youth in the broader mission of mutual aid and empowerment.

The Free Food Program was one of the party's most well-known initiatives. It was designed to meet the immediate needs of low-income families while exposing the failure of public institutions to provide basic services. This image captures the everyday work of community care that defined the party's approach to social reform—rooted in dignity, self-determination, and practical action.

For deeper analysis, scholars are encouraged to view the image *Black Panther Free Food Program, 1972* by visiting the Gilder Lehrman Institute of American History's AP African American Studies online resource at *https://www.gilderlehrman.org/ap-african-american-studies/unit-4/black-power-politics-culture/black-panther-free-food-program-1972*. This image highlights the community-focused initiatives of the Black Panther Party during the Black Power era.

The Black Panther Party for Self-Defense redefined the landscape of Black political activism in the twentieth century by pairing radical critique with direct community engagement. Rooted in a demand for liberation, the party's Ten-Point Program laid out a clear vision for political, economic, and social reform. Through armed self-defense, community survival programs, and a national organizing network that often relied on the leadership of women, the Party challenged systemic inequality while offering practical resources to underserved communities. Its legacy endures as a powerful example of how grassroots activism can confront oppression and build alternative systems of care and empowerment.

More than Just Self-Defense

The Black Panther Party wasn't just about carrying weapons—it was about feeding kids, educating communities, and standing up for Black dignity.

You're Practicing: Understanding how protest can also mean protection.

Connect This To: Safety, survival, and care.

Theme: Power and Community

Practice: Explain Causality (Causes or Effects)

The Black Panther Party for Self-Defense emerged in response to systemic injustices and became a symbol of militant resistance and community empowerment.

(A) Identify one major cause that led to the formation of the Black Panther Party.
(B) Explain how the party's Ten-Point Program addressed the needs of Black communities.
(C) Analyze one effect of the Black Panther Party's activities on local or national responses to racial inequality.

SAMPLE RESPONSES

(A) The Black Panther Party for Self-Defense was founded in 1966 in Oakland, California, by Huey P. Newton and Bobby Seale in direct response to systemic police brutality and racial oppression faced by African Americans in urban communities.

The Black Panther Party for Self-Defense emerged in 1966 as a response to the persistent economic inequality, racial discrimination, and state violence that mainstream civil rights strategies had failed to fully address.

The Black Panther Party for Self-Defense was formed in 1966 when Huey P. Newton and Bobby Seale recognized that African Americans in Oakland and across the nation faced ongoing police harassment, inadequate housing, and limited economic opportunities under entrenched systemic racism.

(B) The Black Panther Party's Ten-Point Program addressed the needs of Black communities by demanding full employment, decent housing, quality education that taught true African American history, and an end to police brutality and state violence.

The Black Panther Party's Ten-Point Program served as a blueprint for self-determination by calling for community control over institutions, economic justice through guaranteed jobs, and the right to self-defense against police oppression.

The Black Panther Party's Ten-Point Program directly responded to systemic inequities by linking demands for economic, educational, and political rights with the broader struggle for liberation from racial and class oppression.

(C) The Black Panther Party's community survival programs, such as the Free Breakfast for Children Program, pressured local and federal agencies to expand food assistance and social welfare services for low-income communities.

The Black Panther Party's grassroots organizing and militant stance on self-defense heightened national awareness of police brutality, prompting both government crackdowns through COINTELPRO and increased public debate over systemic racism in law enforcement.

The Black Panther Party's emphasis on community self-empowerment inspired the creation of similar grassroots movements nationwide, influencing both radical Black activism and broader conversations on racial justice and social policy.

Skills Assessed: Explain the causes and effects of historical developments; use sources and evidence; analyze relationships among developments.

Topic 4.12 Black Is Beautiful and Afrocentricity

Key Terms

- Black Is Beautiful—cultural pride campaign starting in the 1960s
- Natural hair movement—afros as political statements
- Afrocentric curriculum—prioritizing African and Black diasporic history
- Kwanzaa—created by Maulana Karenga to affirm African heritage
- Pan-African pride
- Redefining standards of beauty
- Black fashion and aesthetics
- Cultural renaissance grounded in identity

In a world that taught Black people to reject their features, heritage, and history, a bold cultural affirmation emerged: Black Is Beautiful. This declaration was more than a slogan. It was a movement to reclaim identity, pride, and truth. In the mid-twentieth century, the Black Is Beautiful movement and the rise of Afrocentricity challenged long-standing Eurocentric standards that had shaped everything from education to beauty ideals. These cultural shifts affirmed that African heritage, history, and aesthetics were not only valid but worthy of celebration. Through natural hairstyles, African-inspired fashion, and artistic expression rooted in Black history and identity, African Americans redefined how they saw themselves and how they demanded to be seen by the world.

Afrocentricity called for centering African people and their contributions within global history, pushing back against narratives that erased or marginalized the African experience. Together, the Black Is Beautiful movement and Afrocentric thinking reshaped Black culture in the 1960s and 1970s and laid a foundation for lasting academic and political change. They also played a pivotal role in the development of African American Studies and ethnic studies, embedding cultural pride and historical reclamation at the heart of educational inquiry.

After engaging with this topic, scholars will be able to:

- Describe the emergence of the Black Is Beautiful movement and Afrocentricity in the mid-twentieth century.
- Explain how these movements influenced Black cultural expression in the 1960s, 1970s, and beyond.
- Analyze how Black Is Beautiful and Afrocentric thought contributed to the formation of African American Studies and ethnic studies in academic institutions.

Origins and Core Beliefs

The Black Is Beautiful movement and Afrocentricity emerged in the 1960s and 1970s as cultural responses to long-standing narratives of Black inferiority. These movements encouraged African Americans to reject conformity to mainstream beauty standards and instead embrace Black identity, well-being, and a deeper connection to African heritage. Both movements sought to affirm the value and dignity of Black culture on its own terms.

Cultural Practices and Aesthetic Expression

The Black Is Beautiful movement promoted Afrocentric aesthetics through natural hairstyles such as afros and cornrows, African-inspired fashion like dashikis and head wraps, and non-Western naming practices rooted in African and Islamic traditions. Cultural expressions also included the celebration of holidays like Kwanzaa (established in 1966) and the embrace of African symbols such as the Akan adinkra symbol of the Sankofa bird, which represents learning from the past to inform the future.

Afrocentric Historical Perspective

Afrocentricity is an approach that centers the experiences, perspectives, and contributions of people of African descent in history and culture. This framework places Africa at the core of historical understanding and emerged alongside efforts in the 1960s to establish African American Studies. Afrocentricity served as both an academic and a cultural tool for affirming pride in African heritage and challenging historical exclusion.

Influence on Ethnic Studies Movements

The Black Is Beautiful movement's rejection of cultural assimilation contributed to the foundation of multicultural and ethnic studies initiatives. By emphasizing cultural pride and challenging dominant norms, the movement helped open space for a broader recognition of diverse histories and identities in education and public discourse.

Limitations and Critiques of Afrocentricity

While Afrocentricity elevates Africa as a central reference point for people of African descent, some critics argue that it can blur distinctions within the African diaspora, such as ethnic, national, or cultural differences. Others contend that Afrocentric frameworks may unintentionally mirror the limitations of Eurocentrism if applied without critical reflection on internal diversity or power dynamics.

Kathleen Cleaver on Natural Hair, 1968

In a brief yet powerful video clip from 1968, *Kathleen Cleaver on Natural Hair*, legal scholar and activist Kathleen Cleaver speaks to the cultural significance of natural hair within the Black Power movement. As a member of the Black Panther Party, Cleaver emphasizes the importance of rejecting imposed beauty standards and embracing natural Black features. Her words encourage African Americans to become comfortable in their own skin and recognize that natural hairstyles are not only expressions of personal identity but affirmations of pride and self-worth.

Cleaver's message reflects the broader goals of the Black Is Beautiful movement, which sought to redefine beauty through an Afrocentric lens and dismantle cultural narratives of inferiority.

Scholars can view the video by visiting the Gilder Lehrman Institute of American History at: *https://www.gilderlehrman.org/ap-african-american-studies/unit-4/black-power-politics-culture#par-17276*.

Naturally '68 Photo Shoot in the Apollo Theater

This color photograph, taken in 1968, captures a powerful visual expression of Afrocentric pride and cultural affirmation during the Naturally '68 photo shoot at the historic Apollo Theater. Featured in the image are ten Grandassa models—African American women who promoted natural hairstyles and Afrocentric fashion—alongside five founding members of the African Jazz Art Society and Studios (AJASS). The models are arranged by order of height in the back row and are wearing brightly colored garments with African-inspired designs. The men, including Kletus Smith, Frank Adu, Bob Gumbs, Elombe Brath, and Ernest Baxter, are crouched in the front row dressed in dashikis and trousers.

AJASS was founded by artists and jazz musicians who drew inspiration from Marcus Garvey and Black nationalist thought. Through its annual Naturally fashion shows, the group promoted community-based celebrations of Black beauty, emphasizing natural hair and African aesthetics. This photograph documents one of the most iconic visual representations of the Black Is Beautiful movement, affirming the connection between cultural pride, self-determination, and public performance.

For a deeper analysis, scholars are encouraged to view the photograph of the Naturally '68 Photo Shoot in the Apollo Theater featuring Grandassa models and AJASS members in dashikis, 1968 online at the Gilder Lehrman Institute of American History's AP African American Studies resource: *https://www.gilderlehrman.org/ap-african-american-studies/unit-4/black-power-politics-culture/apollo-theater-ca1968*. This image highlights the cultural pride and aesthetic empowerment of the Black Power movement.

"Still I Rise" by Maya Angelou, 1978

Published in 1978, "Still I Rise" by Maya Angelou is a landmark poem that affirms Black resilience, dignity, and self-worth in the face of historical and ongoing oppression. Written in a voice that is both defiant and celebratory, the poem echoes the core principles of the Black Is Beautiful movement by declaring confidence in Black identity and pride in African heritage. Its repeated refrain—"I rise"—reinforces a sense of unshakable strength and determination shaped by ancestral struggle and collective memory.

Angelou's poem resonates as a cultural anthem, articulating an unwavering belief in liberation through self-definition and self-love. It remains one of the most widely studied and recited poems in American literature, serving as both a personal declaration and a communal call to rise above injustice.

For deeper analysis, scholars are encouraged to listen to Maya Angelou's full recitation of "Still I Rise" by searching the title on YouTube or by visiting *https://www.youtube.com/watch?v=vOO2LmyGILg*. This powerful poem reflects themes of resilience, dignity, and empowerment central to African American experiences.

The Black Is Beautiful movement and Afrocentricity redefined how African Americans understood themselves, their culture, and their place in history. By rejecting imposed standards of beauty and reclaiming African identity, these movements empowered individuals to see Blackness as a source of pride, creativity, and strength. From natural hairstyles and traditional clothing to naming practices and educational reform, their influence reshaped cultural norms and laid the groundwork for African American Studies and ethnic studies programs. Although not without critique, both movements left a lasting legacy—elevating Africa as a cultural and historical anchor and reaffirming that liberation begins with how one sees the self.

Black Is Beautiful

Wearing an Afro. Celebrating African culture. Teaching Black history. These were powerful ways to fight back against racism and to love yourself out loud.

You're Practicing: Reclaiming identity and heritage.

Connect This To: Pride, culture, and resistance.

Theme: Identity and Liberation

Practice: Explain the Significance or Importance

The Black Is Beautiful movement and the rise of Afrocentric thought reshaped cultural and intellectual expressions of Black identity during the late 1960s and 1970s.

(A) Identify one key feature or slogan associated with the Black Is Beautiful movement.
(B) Explain the significance of Afrocentricity as an approach to history, culture, or education.
(C) Analyze how these movements challenged dominant narratives about race and appearance in American society.

SAMPLE RESPONSES

(A) The Black Is Beautiful movement challenged Eurocentric beauty standards by encouraging African Americans to wear natural hairstyles such as afros and cornrows as visible symbols of pride in Black identity.

Afrocentricity disrupted Western fashion ideals by promoting African-inspired clothing like dashikis and head wraps as expressions of cultural heritage and self-determination.

(B) The embrace of Afrocentric thinking led to the creation of African American Studies and ethnic studies programs in schools and universities, centering African heritage and Black diasporic history in academic spaces.

The cultural affirmation of Blackness energized community activism by inspiring cultural festivals, grassroots programs, and political movements that celebrated African identity as a foundation for liberation.

(C) The Black Is Beautiful and Afrocentric movements reflected a broader shift in the Black freedom struggle toward cultural self-determination, linking personal identity to collective liberation.

These movements embodied the pan-African and Black Power emphasis on rejecting assimilation, affirming global Black solidarity, and redefining beauty, history, and culture on African-centered terms.

Skills Assessed: Explain the significance of historical developments; use sources and evidence; analyze relationships among developments.

Topic 4.13 The Black Feminist Movement, Womanism, and Intersectionality

Key Terms

- **Combahee River Collective—foundational Black feminist statement**
- **Audre Lorde, bell hooks, Barbara Smith, Angela Davis**
- **Intersectionality—term coined by Kimberlé Crenshaw**
- **Womanism—Alice Walker's term to center Black women's experience**
- **Critique of racism in feminism and sexism in Civil Rights Movement**
- **Double burden—racism and sexism**
- **Black women's intellectual labor and leadership**
- **Collective liberation**

What happens when voices long pushed to the margins step forward to reshape the conversation? The Black feminist movement of the twentieth century emerged to center the lived experiences of Black women and confront the overlapping forces of racism and sexism. Drawing strength from generations of Black women's activism, the Black feminist movement of the twentieth century built upon a legacy of resistance, advocacy, and community care. While earlier Black women had challenged racism, sexism, and class inequality through abolitionism, suffrage, education, and labor organizing, the modern movement gave language to the specific ways these oppressions intersected in the lives of Black women. Black feminists rejected being silenced in movements that prioritized either race or gender, instead insisting on an approach that accounted for both.

The emergence of womanism and intersectionality provided frameworks for understanding the complex realities that shape Black women's lives. These concepts deepened the Black Freedom struggle by challenging movements and institutions to see how multiple systems of power operate simultaneously. Topic 4.13 explores how Black feminism both honored earlier traditions and advanced new strategies for justice rooted in the fullness of Black womanhood.

After engaging with this topic, scholars will be able to:

- Explain how the Black feminist movement of the twentieth century was informed by the activism of earlier generations of Black women.
- Analyze the development of womanism and intersectionality as responses to the limitations of traditional feminist and civil rights frameworks.
- Understand how Black feminism has shaped broader conversations about equity, identity, and justice.

Historical Foundations of Black Feminism

Black women have played central roles in struggles for racial and gender equality throughout U.S. history. In the eighteenth and nineteenth centuries, figures such as Jarena Lee, Sojourner Truth, and Harriet Tubman resisted injustice as both enslaved and free people. Their activism laid the foundation for future generations. In the 1970s, the Black feminist movement drew inspiration from these women and others who highlighted the ways Black women experienced both racism and sexism simultaneously.

Womanism and the Expansion of Black Feminist Thought

In the 1980s, author Alice Walker introduced the term *womanist* to describe a framework that builds on earlier Black women's activism. Womanism emerged in response to racism within mainstream feminist circles and sexism within Black communities. It affirmed the need for a perspective that embraced the full cultural, spiritual, and political lives of Black women.

Intersectionality and Black Feminist Scholarship

In the 1990s, legal scholar Kimberlé Crenshaw introduced the concept of intersectionality as a framework to analyze how systems of inequality affect individuals with multiple, overlapping identities. Intersectionality emphasized how Black women's social, political, and economic experiences are shaped by the interaction of race, gender, class, and other factors. This concept helped connect contemporary Black feminist scholarship to the legacy of earlier Black women's activism.

The Combahee River Collective Statement, 1977

Published in 1977, *The Combahee River Collective Statement* is a foundational document in the history of Black feminism. Authored by a Boston-based Black feminist and lesbian organization, the statement articulates a political framework that centers the unique experiences of Black women. It emphasizes that the liberation of Black women necessitates the dismantling of all systems of oppression, including racism, sexism, classism, and homophobia. The collective argued that addressing these interlocking oppressions would lead to the freedom of all marginalized groups.

The statement draws inspiration from earlier Black women activists and underscores the importance of identity politics, asserting that the most profound and potentially radical politics come directly from one's own identity and lived experiences. It remains a critical text for understanding the intersections of race, gender, sexuality, and class in the struggle for social justice.

Scholars can view the full statement online at the Gilder Lehrman Institute of American History: *https://www.gilderlehrman.org/ap-african-american-studies/unit-4/black-power-politics-culture/combahee-river-collective-statement-1977*.

The Black feminist movement of the twentieth century built upon the legacy of earlier Black women who had long resisted both racial and gender-based oppression. By naming and confronting the overlapping systems that shaped their experiences, Black feminists introduced powerful new frameworks—such as womanism and intersectionality—that deepened the struggle for justice. These frameworks called attention to the ways race, gender, class, and sexuality intersect, making it clear that the fight for liberation must be inclusive and multidimensional. Grounded in historical continuity and guided by lived experience, the movement continues to influence scholarship, activism, and policy today.

TIP

Stay Relevant

Stick to the topic and avoid going off on tangents. Every sentence in your response should directly contribute to answering the prompt.

Fighting on All Fronts

Black women fought racism, sexism, classism—often all at once. They helped movements understand that you can't fight one kind of injustice without fighting them all.

You're Practicing: Seeing how systems of oppression overlap.

Connect This To: Intersectionality, gender, and power.

Theme: Equity and Inclusion

Practice: Explain the Significance or Importance

The rise of Black feminism, womanism, and intersectionality reshaped understandings of gender, race, and power within both the Civil Rights Movement and feminist movement.

(A) Identify one foundational text or figure associated with Black feminism or womanism.
(B) Explain the significance of intersectionality as a framework for analyzing systems of oppression.
(C) Analyze how the emergence of Black feminist thought expanded the goals of broader social justice movements.

SAMPLE RESPONSES

(A) The Combahee River Collective Statement (1977) is a foundational text of the Black feminist movement that explicitly articulated how racism, sexism, classism, and homophobia intersect in the lives of Black women, calling for the dismantling of all systems of oppression.

Kimberlé Crenshaw, a legal scholar, is a foundational figure who introduced the term intersectionality in the late 1980s to describe how overlapping systems of power—such as racism and sexism—compound the discrimination Black women face.

Alice Walker is a foundational womanist thinker whose definition of *womanism* expanded Black feminist thought by centering the cultural, spiritual, and political experiences of Black women while responding to both racism in feminism and sexism in Black liberation movements.

(B) Intersectionality, as defined by Kimberlé Crenshaw, is significant because it reveals how Black women's experiences of oppression are shaped by the simultaneous and interconnected effects of racism, sexism, classism, and other forms of marginalization, rather than by any single factor alone.

The significance of intersectionality lies in its ability to expand civil rights and feminist analysis, demonstrating that legal, social, and political remedies must address the combined effects of multiple oppressions to effectively advance justice for Black women.

Intersectionality is significant because it shifts the focus of social justice work toward a more inclusive approach, ensuring that the needs of those who experience multiple layers of discrimination—such as Black women—are addressed in both policy and movement strategies.

(C) The emergence of Black feminist thought expanded the goals of broader social justice movements by insisting that the liberation of Black women requires dismantling all systems of oppression—racism, sexism, classism, and homophobia—thereby broadening the Civil Rights Movement's focus beyond race alone.

Black feminist thought, as exemplified in the Combahee River Collective Statement, expanded feminist movements by demanding that they confront racism within their ranks and acknowledge the lived realities of women of color, thus making feminism more inclusive and intersectional.

The rise of womanism, intersectionality, and Black feminist scholarship expanded social justice goals by linking struggles for racial and gender equality to movements for LGBTQ+ rights, economic justice, and cultural affirmation, influencing later activism such as reproductive justice campaigns and Black Lives Matter.

Skills Assessed: Explain the significance of historical developments; use sources and evidence; analyze relationships among developments.

Topic 4.14 Interlocking Systems of Oppression

Key Terms

- Intersectionality theory—interconnected nature of race, gender, class, and more
- Patricia Hill Collins—*Black Feminist Thought*
- Matrix of domination—framework of overlapping forms of power and exclusion
- Structural racism
- Heteropatriarchy
- Class exploitation
- Disability justice, queer Black studies—inclusive liberation movements
- Systemic and institutional analysis

What if the struggle against injustice is not one battle but many happening at once? Black feminist thought introduced a vital framework for understanding how racism, sexism, classism, and other forms of discrimination do not operate separately. They operate together. The concept of *interlocking systems of oppression* emerged from the work of Black feminists who recognized that their experiences could not be explained by racism or sexism alone. Instead, they argued that multiple systems of power—such as white supremacy, patriarchy, capitalism, and heteronormativity—operate simultaneously, reinforcing one another. This framework challenged movements that treated race, gender, or class in isolation and demanded a more inclusive, intersectional approach to justice.

Grounded in the legacy of earlier Black women's activism, this concept deepened the understanding of social inequality and reshaped scholarship, organizing, and cultural production. Black writers and theorists have used their work to expose and challenge these interlocking systems, revealing how personal experiences of oppression are tied to broader structures of power. Topic 4.14 explores the origins of this concept and examines how it continues to shape the language and strategies of resistance today.

After engaging with this topic, scholars will be able to:

- Describe the concept of interlocking systems of oppression and its connection to Black feminist activism.
- Analyze how Black writers have represented the complexities of intersecting oppressions in their creative and theoretical work.
- Evaluate how this framework has influenced movements for equity and justice across disciplines and communities.

Defining Interlocking Systems of Oppression

The concept of interlocking systems of oppression explains how categories such as race, gender, class, sexuality, and ability are interconnected and shape individuals' experiences in relation to social systems. These overlapping categories interact within institutions—such as education, health care, housing, the criminal legal system, and the economy—to produce unequal outcomes. This framework highlights how individuals can experience multiple, compounding forms of discrimination or privilege depending on their social identities.

Scholarly Origins and Framework

The concept was first formally articulated by sociologist Patricia Hill Collins and is widely used in sociological research. It builds on a long-standing tradition of Black feminist thought that critiques the treatment of race, gender, class, and sexuality as separate and independent categories. Instead, Black feminist scholars, activists, and writers have emphasized the importance of analyzing how these categories operate together within systems of power.

Literary Representations of Intersecting Identities

Writers such as Gwendolyn Brooks and Audre Lorde represent the lived experiences of Black individuals by exploring how race, gender, and class affect how people are perceived, the roles they are expected to perform, and their access to economic opportunity. Their works demonstrate how social identities are not experienced in isolation but within a broader structure of interrelated oppressions.

Navigating Identity Through Literature

In literary works such as *Maud Martha*, Gwendolyn Brooks portrays the complexity of African American life by examining how individuals negotiate multiple aspects of identity. The text reveals how factors such as race, gender, and social class shape daily life and interpersonal relationships, both within Black communities and in wider society.

"We're the Only Colored People Here" by Gwendolyn Brooks

In 1953, Gwendolyn Brooks published her only novel, *Maud Martha*, a series of vignettes that follow the life of Maud Martha Brown from childhood to adulthood on Chicago's South Side. The vignette titled "We're the Only Colored People Here" captures a moment of isolation and subtle exclusion, reflecting the layered realities of race, gender, and class that shape Maud's everyday experiences.

Through this brief but powerful episode, Brooks reveals how African Americans navigate predominantly white spaces and internalize social boundaries. The narrative demonstrates how systems of oppression are not always overt but can be deeply embedded in everyday interactions. Brooks's work exemplifies how literature can portray the complexities of identity and the interlocking structures that shape perception, belonging, and self-worth.

For deeper analysis, scholars can access the excerpt online at the Gilder Lehrman Institute of American History: *https://www.gilderlehrman.org/ap-african-american-studies/unit-4/black-power-politics-culture/only-colored-people-here-1945*.

The framework of interlocking systems of oppression offers a vital lens for understanding how multiple forms of inequality—such as racism, sexism, and classism—interact to shape lived experiences. Grounded in Black feminist thought and advanced by scholars like Patricia Hill Collins, this concept challenges approaches that isolate identity categories. Through literature and theory alike, Black writers have illustrated how individuals must navigate overlapping systems of power that affect their roles, perceptions, and access to opportunity. By naming these interconnections, the framework continues to inform scholarship, activism, and efforts to build more inclusive and equitable societies.

Systems Don't Work Alone

Racism. Sexism. Classism. Homophobia. They all reinforce each other—and that's why real freedom means breaking them all down together.

You're Practicing: Connecting the dots between different injustices.

Connect This To: Systems thinking and social change.

Theme: Structural Justice

Practice: Explain Causality (Effects)

The concept of interlocking systems of oppression highlights how race, gender, class, sexuality, and other identities intersect to shape experiences of inequality.

(A) Define the idea of interlocking systems of oppression and identify a scholar or activist associated with its development.
(B) Explain how this framework helps reveal the limitations of single-axis approaches to social justice.
(C) Analyze one way that interlocking systems of oppression have influenced activism or policy advocacy in the United States.

SAMPLE RESPONSES

(A) The concept of interlocking systems of oppression explains how categories such as race, gender, class, sexuality, and ability are interconnected and shape individuals' experiences in relation to social systems. Patricia Hill Collins, in *Black Feminist Thought*, developed the framework and described it as a matrix of domination that shows how these overlapping forms of power and exclusion operate together.

This framework builds on the tradition of Black feminist thought, which critiques the treatment of race, gender, class, and sexuality as separate categories and instead analyzes how they function together within systems of power.

(B) The interlocking systems of oppression framework shows that focusing on only one axis of inequality, such as race or gender, fails to capture the full reality of people's experiences.

For example, the discrimination experienced by a Black woman cannot be fully explained by racism alone or sexism alone, because both forms of oppression operate together in her life.

By analyzing how multiple categories of identity interact, this framework reveals the limits of single-axis approaches and underscores the need for justice movements to address race, gender, class, sexuality, and ability together.

(C) The interlocking systems of oppression framework has influenced activism by showing that struggles for racial justice must also address gender, class, sexuality, and other intersecting forms of inequality. Writers such as Gwendolyn Brooks and Audre Lorde have illustrated through literature how race, gender, and class intersect to shape identity, belonging, and access to opportunity.

This perspective has also influenced organizing and advocacy that challenges structural racism, heteropatriarchy, and class exploitation as interconnected systems that must be confronted together to achieve meaningful liberation.

Skills Assessed: Explain the effects of historical developments; use sources and evidence; analyze relationships among developments.

KEY TAKEAWAYS

1. **Art as Political Liberation**
   - Black artists in the 1960s and 1970s redefined cultural expression as a tool of political resistance.
   - Music, poetry, theater, and visual arts became central to liberation struggles, exemplified by artists like Nina Simone, Gil Scott-Heron, and Amiri Baraka.
2. **Black Power and Cultural Nationalism**
   - The Black Power movement emphasized self-determination, economic justice, and pride in African heritage.
   - Groups like the Black Panther Party implemented survival programs—free breakfasts, health clinics, and education—modeling community-based empowerment.
3. **Afrocentricity and Identity Transformation**
   - The Black Is Beautiful movement encouraged pride in natural hair, African clothing, and cultural heritage as acts of resistance to white standards.
   - Afrocentric worldviews recentered Black histories, traditions, and values in education, art, and public discourse.
4. **Intersections of Race, Gender, and Power**
   - Black feminists and womanists—like bell hooks, Audre Lorde, and the Combahee River Collective—challenged both racial and gender hierarchies.
   - They introduced the concept of intersectionality, exploring how systems of oppression overlap and reinforce one another.
5. **Black Religious Nationalism**
   - Movements like the Nation of Islam and Moorish Science Temple merged religion, Black pride, and political autonomy.
   - These traditions critiqued white supremacy, emphasized self-discipline, and offered alternative spiritual frameworks for liberation.
6. **The Black Arts Movement**
   - This cultural movement demanded art that reflected Black experiences and served political aims.
   - Rooted in the ethos Art for the People, it fostered radical theater, literature, and music that validated Black lives and histories.
7. **Systemic Oppression and the Need for Structural Change**
   - Activists and thinkers critiqued capitalism, patriarchy, and state violence as interconnected systems requiring radical transformation.
   - Emphasis was placed on collective liberation, healing, and the envisioning of alternative futures beyond white supremacy.

Practice Multiple-Choice Questions

DIRECTIONS: Pick the letter that best answers the following questions.

Questions 1 through 3 refer to the following.

Photograph of the Honorable Elijah Muhammad Addressing Black Muslims in Chicago (1966)

1. The photograph of Elijah Muhammad addressing Black Muslims in Chicago in 1966 most directly reflects which of the following broader goals of the Nation of Islam (NOI)?
   (A) Promoting cultural assimilation through integration into mainstream religious institutions
   (B) Advocating for Black self-reliance and spiritual discipline grounded in an alternative religious framework
   (C) Supporting nonviolent civil disobedience modeled after the Southern Christian Leadership Conference
   (D) Encouraging African Americans to abandon organized religion altogether

2. Which of the following aspects of the 1966 photograph best illustrates the Nation of Islam's emphasis on community structure and discipline?
   (A) The presence of women in religious head coverings seated beside men
   (B) The Honorable Elijah Muhammad's formal attire and elevated speaking position
   (C) The lack of written materials or religious texts visible in the scene
   (D) The use of public protest banners and signs in the background

3. The photograph is most useful to historians as evidence of which of the following developments during the Black Freedom movement?
   (A) The widespread adoption of mainstream Christian ideologies among African American activists
   (B) The growing support for violent rebellion as the primary method of achieving civil rights
   (C) The rise of alternative religious and cultural institutions that emphasized Black autonomy
   (D) The legal dismantling of segregation laws across the American South

Questions 4 through 6 refer to the following.

Malcolm X and Dr. Martin Luther King Jr. After Press Conference at U.S. Capitol, 1964

4. What is most historically significant about the 1964 photograph of Malcolm X and Dr. Martin Luther King Jr. together at the U.S. Capitol?
   (A) It marks the beginning of a formal alliance between the Nation of Islam and the Southern Christian Leadership Conference (SCLC).
   (B) It demonstrates the convergence of different philosophies within the Black Freedom movement at a pivotal legislative moment.
   (C) It signals Malcolm X's endorsement of nonviolent civil disobedience as the most effective strategy for Black liberation.
   (D) It documents the final meeting between the two leaders before both transitioned into elected political office.

5. At the time this photograph was taken, both Malcolm X and Dr. King were responding to which of the following developments in the Black Freedom struggle?
   (A) The signing of the Voting Rights Act of 1965
   (B) The passage of the Civil Rights Act of 1964
   (C) The conclusion of the Montgomery Bus Boycott
   (D) The Supreme Court ruling in *Brown v. Board of Education*

6. Which of the following best describes the contrasting public philosophies represented by Malcolm X and Dr. Martin Luther King Jr. at the time of the photograph?
   (A) Both advocated for armed revolution and the establishment of an all-Black political party.
   (B) Dr. King emphasized moral persuasion and nonviolence, while Malcolm X promoted self-defense and Black autonomy.
   (C) Malcolm X sought federal office, while Dr. King campaigned for the separation of church and state.
   (D) Dr. King supported cultural assimilation, while Malcolm X opposed all forms of education reform.

Answer Explanations

1. **(B)** Elijah Muhammad's leadership promoted Black self-reliance, moral reform, and discipline through a distinct interpretation of Islam, separate from mainstream religious frameworks. Choice (A) is incorrect because the Nation of Islam explicitly rejected cultural assimilation and did not seek integration into mainstream institutions, especially not religious ones. Choice (C) is incorrect because, although nonviolence was associated with the Southern Christian Leadership Conference (SCLC), the Nation of Islam (NOI) did not promote nonviolent civil disobedience as a primary tactic. Choice (D) is incorrect because the NOI did not reject religion; rather, it offered an alternative religious structure rooted in Islamic teachings and Black nationalism.

2. **(B)** The Honorable Elijah Muhammad's formal appearance and positioning at the front of the congregation underscore the NOI's emphasis on discipline, respectability, and hierarchical leadership. Choice (A) is incorrect because, although modest dress was important, the key feature here is the leader's central position and authoritative role in the community. Choice (C) is incorrect because the absence of texts is not a defining feature of NOI structure or doctrine. Choice (D) is incorrect because the Nation of Islam was known more for structured indoor gatherings and religious instruction than for the protest tactics used by civil rights organizations.

3. **(C)** The photograph documents the Nation of Islam as a religious and cultural institution that offered an autonomous space for African American spiritual, social, and political life. Choice (A) is incorrect because the Nation of Islam provided a religious alternative to Christianity, not an endorsement of it. Choice (B) is incorrect because, although the NOI supported self-defense and separation, it did not promote widespread violent rebellion. Choice (D) is incorrect because the photo relates to religious and cultural identity, not to legal decisions or Southern segregation laws.

4. **(B)** The image captures a rare moment when two influential leaders, representing different philosophies, stood together during a key moment in the Civil Rights Movement, underscoring the broad spectrum of Black political thought. Choice (A) is incorrect because the Nation of Islam and the SCLC maintained distinct approaches and did not form a formal alliance. Choice (C) is incorrect because Malcolm X did not endorse nonviolence as his primary strategy, though his views were evolving at the time. Choice (D) is incorrect because neither leader transitioned into elected political office.

5. **(B)** In 1964, both leaders were engaged with ongoing debates and activism surrounding the Civil Rights Act, which aimed to end segregation and workplace discrimination. Choice (A) is incorrect because the Voting Rights Act was signed in 1965, after this photograph was taken. Choice (C) is incorrect because the Montgomery Bus Boycott ended in 1956 and predates this meeting. Choice (D) is incorrect because *Brown v. Board of Education* was decided in 1954 and does not align chronologically with this image.

6. **(B)** Dr. King emphasized nonviolent civil disobedience rooted in Christian ethics, while Malcolm X—especially during this period—advocated for Black self-determination and the right to self-defense. Choice (A) is incorrect because neither man promoted armed revolution or a political party at this time. Choice (C) is incorrect because neither figure was campaigning for elected office or focusing on church-state separation in this context. Choice (D) is incorrect because both advocated for education reform, though from different philosophical frameworks.

13

Black Excellence and Innovation: Cultural Power, Political Progress, and Futures Reimagined

Key Themes

- Resilience and creativity as engines of progress and possibility
- Diverse cultural expressions across music, art, and media as tools for identity and resistance
- Black excellence in science, politics, and sports breaks barriers and redefines leadership
- Afrofuturism and Black Studies center radical hope, reparation, and transformation for the future

TIMELINE

Date/Period	Event/Development	Related Topics
1965–present	Post–Voting Rights Act era leads to increases in **Black political representation** at local, state, and national levels (e.g., **Shirley Chisholm, Barack Obama**)	Topic 4.15—Economic Growth and Political Representation
1980s–2000s	**Black mayors**, governors, and congressional leaders rise across U.S. cities; Black wealth and middle-class growth expands unevenly	Topic 4.15—Economic Progress
21st century	**Contemporary Black communities** reflect growing **religious, ethnic, and cultural diversity**, including Afro-Caribbean, African immigrant, and multiracial populations	Topic 4.16—Demographic and Religious Diversity
1700s–present	**African American music** evolves from **spirituals, gospel, blues, jazz, and soul** to **hip-hop and rap**, expressing both resistance and innovation	Topic 4.17—Evolution of Music
1980s–present	Rise of **hip-hop as global cultural force**—artists like Public Enemy, Lauryn Hill, Kendrick Lamar challenge injustice	Topic 4.17—Hip-Hop as Political Commentary
1960s–present	**Black actors, filmmakers, and playwrights** reshape film and theater—e.g., **August Wilson, Ava DuVernay, Jordan Peele**	Topic 4.18—Theater, TV, and Film

Date/Period	Event/Development	Related Topics
2000s–present	Successes of **Black-led films and shows**—*Black Panther, Insecure, When They See Us*—reach global audiences	Topic 4.18—Representation in Media
20th–21st centuries	African Americans transform **sports history**—from **Jackie Robinson** and **Wilma Rudolph** to **Serena Williams** and **LeBron James**	Topic 4.19—African Americans and Sports
Recent decades	Ongoing activism in sports (e.g., **Colin Kaepernick, WNBA protests**) spotlights systemic injustice	Topic 4.19—Sports as Protest
20th–21st centuries	Black leaders and innovators in **STEM fields**—e.g., **Katherine Johnson, Dr. Kizzmekia Corbett**	Topic 4.20—Science, Medicine, and Technology
Contemporary era	Focus on **health equity, environmental justice, and tech access** in Black communities	Topic 4.20—Equity in Innovation
Late 20th century–now	Growth of **Black Studies as an academic discipline** rooted in community activism and interdisciplinary inquiry	Topic 4.21—Black Studies and Futures
21st century	Rise of **Afrofuturism**—imagining Black futures through science fiction, technology, art, and liberation (e.g., **Octavia Butler, Janelle Monáe,** *Black Panther*)	Topic 4.21—Afrofuturism

Topic 4.15 Economic Growth and Black Political Representation

Key Terms

- Post–Civil Rights economic mobility
- Black middle-class growth
- Affirmative action policies
- Wealth gap—persistent disparities in income and asset ownership
- Black mayors and political leadership—Shirley Chisholm, Harold Washington, and others
- Congressional Black Caucus (CBC)—established in 1971
- Voting Rights Act (1965) and its erosion
- Barack Obama's presidency—symbolic and structural impacts

What happens when political access expands while economic justice remains uneven? The story of Black life in the late twentieth century is shaped by simultaneous advances in leadership and persistent struggles for economic equity. In the decades following the Civil Rights Movement, African American communities experienced both progress and continued barriers in the pursuit of economic stability and political power. Discriminatory practices such as redlining, unequal employment opportunities, and disinvestment continued to hinder growth in many Black neighborhoods. However, other efforts—including affirmative action, minority-owned business initiatives, and increased access to public resources—sought to close long-standing racial economic gaps.

The passage of the Voting Rights Act of 1965 marked a turning point in Black political representation. By removing discriminatory barriers to the ballot box, the legislation paved the way for a significant increase in Black elected officials at the local, state, and federal levels. This transformation contributed to a new era of political leadership that extended into the twenty-first century, with historic advancements in federal representation and public service. Topic 4.15 explores the intersection of economic and political change, examining how access to wealth and power has been both expanded and obstructed in post–Civil Rights America.

After engaging with this topic, scholars will be able to:

- Explain how Black economic growth was both promoted and hindered in the late twentieth century.
- Analyze the impact of the Voting Rights Act of 1965 on Black political participation and representation.
- Describe major developments in Black political leadership at the federal level in the late twentieth and early twenty-first centuries.

Economic Disparities and Limited Wealth Accumulation

Although the Black middle class grew in the second half of the twentieth century, significant disparities in wealth between Black and white Americans persisted. Structural barriers in housing and employment throughout the early twentieth century limited African Americans' ability to build and transfer generational wealth. These historical inequities remained evident decades later. By 2016, the median wealth for Black families was $17,150, compared with $171,000 for white families.

Educational Advancement and Economic Mobility

Desegregation efforts in the 1950s and 1960s helped expand access to higher education for African Americans. As a result, the number of Black college graduates increased steadily. By 2019, 23 percent of African American adults had earned a bachelor's degree or higher, contributing to greater representation in professional fields and a more robust Black middle class.

Urbanization and the Growth of Black-Owned Businesses

Urbanization created new opportunities for employment and entrepreneurship in Black communities. Black-owned businesses—ranging from restaurants and banks to publishing houses—were established to serve the needs of Black consumers and foster economic independence. Many of these enterprises contributed significantly to local economies and, in some cases, continue to operate today.

The Voting Rights Act and Political Empowerment

The Voting Rights Act of 1965 prohibited local and state governments from implementing laws or procedures that produced racial discrimination in voting. This legislation expanded Black political participation and representation, particularly as the Black middle class grew. In the decades that followed, African Americans increasingly served as members of Congress, local legislators, judges, and federal officials.

Increases in Black Elected Officials

From 1970 to 2006, the number of Black elected officials in the United States increased from approximately 1,500 to 9,000. The most significant annual increase occurred in 1971, reflecting the momentum of the Black Freedom movement and the transformative impact of the Voting Rights Act on political representation at all levels of government.

Shirley Chisholm and the Rise of Federal Leadership

In 1968, Shirley Chisholm became the first Black woman elected to Congress. A staunch advocate for women's rights and political inclusion, she cofounded the Congressional Black Caucus in 1971. The caucus worked to expand Black political influence by supporting Black candidates and advancing policy reforms in areas such as health care, employment, and social services.

General Colin Powell's Commencement Address at Howard University

In 1994, **General Colin Powell** delivered the commencement address at Howard University, offering a message of unity, service, and optimism. Drawing from his experiences as a military leader and public servant, Powell emphasized the importance of character, civic responsibility, and the strength found in America's diversity. His speech underscored the idea that, despite challenges, the United States remains a nation of promise and opportunity. Powell's address resonated with graduates, encouraging them to contribute positively to society and uphold the values of integrity and perseverance.

For a more in-depth analysis, scholars can listen to General Colin Powell's 1994 commencement address at Howard University through the Gilder Lehrman Institute of American History: https://www.gilderlehrman.org/ap-african-american-studies/unit-4/business-culture-20th-21st-centuries/commencement-address-general-colin-powell-1994.

First Lady Michelle Obama by Amy Sherald, 2018

Unveiled in 2018, the portrait *First Lady Michelle Obama* (originally titled *Michelle LaVaughn Robinson Obama*) by artist Amy Sherald offers a modern and stylized interpretation of one of the most visible figures of the twenty-first century. Known for her use of grayscale skin tones and bold, symbolic patterns, Sherald presents Michelle Obama seated against a sky-blue background, dressed in a flowing geometric gown that references African American cultural aesthetics and modern art.

Sherald's portrait departs from traditional representational norms and centers a vision of dignity, intellect, and self-possession. It challenges conventions of first lady portraiture while affirming the historical significance of Michelle Obama's presence and legacy. The work invites viewers to reflect on how race, gender, and cultural expression shape national identity.

First Lady Michelle Obama (originally titled *Michelle LaVaughn Robinson Obama*) by Amy Sherald, oil on linen, 2018 (Source: Smithsonian's National Portrait Gallery)

Portrait of Former President Barack Obama by Kehinde Wiley, 2018

Unveiled in 2018, the official portrait of former President Barack Obama by artist Kehinde Wiley broke with traditional presidential portraiture by combining realist technique with vibrant, symbolic background imagery. Wiley, known for his reimagining of classical European portraiture with African American subjects, presents Obama seated against a lush backdrop of botanical elements, each chosen to reflect aspects of his heritage and personal history. The portrait's bold composition and layered symbolism reflect a blending of cultural traditions, political achievement, and individual identity.

The work is significant not only as a representation of the first African American president but also as a statement about visibility, legacy, and the evolving aesthetic of power. Wiley's portrait situates Obama within a long history of Black excellence and creative expression while challenging viewers to reconsider the visual language of leadership.

For a deeper analysis, scholars are encouraged to view the portrait *Barack Obama* (2018) online at the Gilder Lehrman Institute of American History's AP African American Studies resource: https://www.gilderlehrman.org/ap-african-american-studies/unit-4/business-culture-20th-21st-centuries/portrait-barack-obama-2018. This artwork captures a significant moment in contemporary African American political and cultural history.

Charts from The Black Middle Class Needs Political Attention, Too

These charts, taken from the 2020 Brookings Institution report by Andre M. Perry and Carl Romer titled The Black Middle Class Needs Political Attention, Too, offer data-driven insight into the status and challenges of the Black middle class in the United States. The visualizations highlight persistent wealth gaps, housing disparities, and uneven access to public investment—issues that continue to shape economic outcomes for Black Americans despite rising educational attainment and income levels.

The report argues that while the Black middle class has grown in size and influence, it remains politically overlooked and economically vulnerable due to historic and systemic inequities. These charts serve as valuable tools for understanding the limitations of traditional economic indicators and emphasize the need for targeted policy interventions that address racial disparities in wealth and opportunity.

Black Metros Are Concentrated in the South and Mid-Atlantic

When political leaders invoke the needs of the middle class without addressing the racial wealth gap or Black homeownership rates, they are signaling that their message is not meant for everyone. In doing so, they erase the distinct economic realities of Black Americans whose class status and political interests are shaped by centuries of systemic exclusion. As scholars Richard V. Reeves and Camille Busette observed in a 2018 Brookings Institution report, although the term "American middle class" is rarely framed explicitly in racial terms, it has long operated as a coded reference to whiteness. This rhetorical exclusion reinforces a narrative that centers white economic experience while marginalizing Black middle-class communities—many of which are geographically concentrated in the South and mid-Atlantic regions.

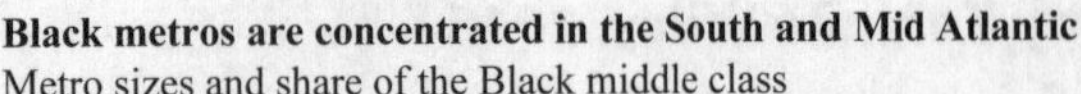

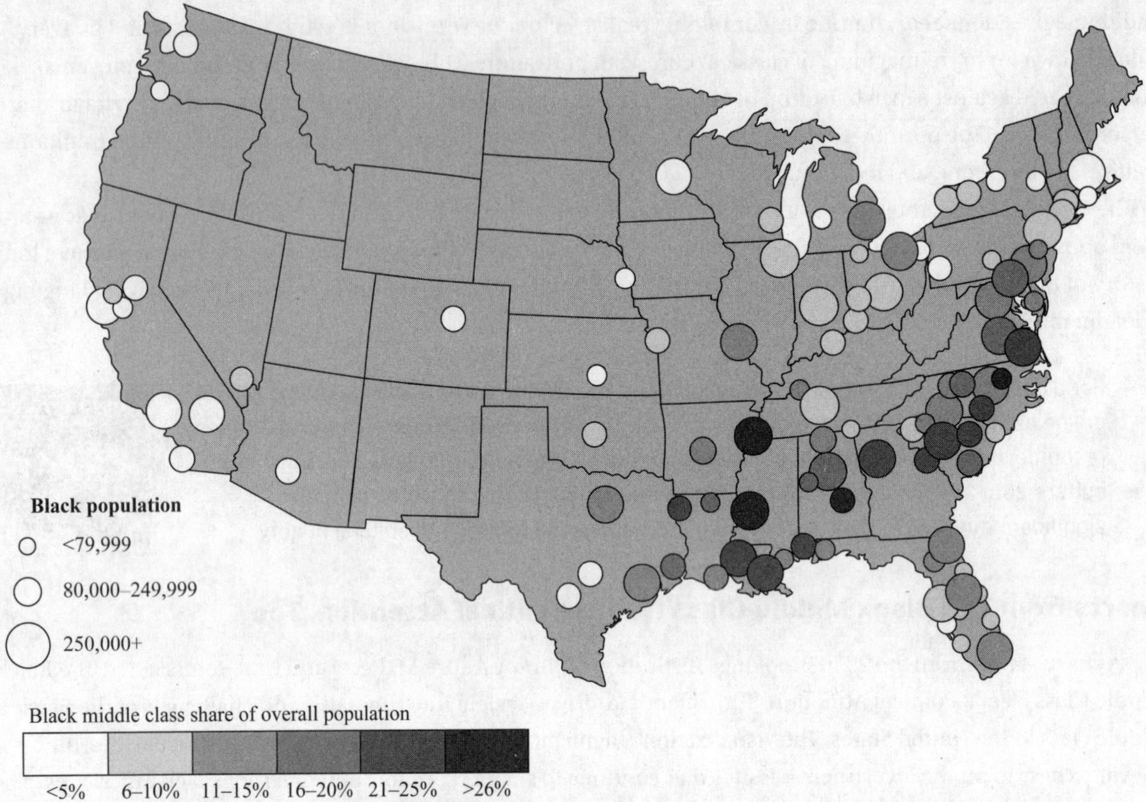

From "The Black Middle Class Needs Political Attention, Too" by Andre M. Perry and Carl Romer, February 27, 2020, Brookings Institution

While Lower and Middle Classes Increase, Black Upper Class Declines

From 2008 to 2017, the Black middle class expanded nationwide as a share of the overall population. This growth, however, was accompanied by a simultaneous rise in the Black working class and a decline in the Black upper class. These shifts challenge dominant political narratives that suggest full employment alone will yield upward mobility for Black communities. The data reveal a more complex picture. While more Black Americans are entering the middle class, fewer are reaching or maintaining elite economic status.

Geographically, the Black middle class is concentrated in the South and in major metropolitan areas. These regions are often left out of the national conversation around middle-class identity, which typically centers around small, predominantly white towns in the rural Midwest. As such, any serious effort to strengthen the Black middle class must begin with policies that invest in the South. Although metro areas like Detroit, Cleveland, and St. Louis—which are outside the South and mid-Atlantic—have sizable Black populations, they remain exceptions. These three cities are the only non-Southern metros where the Black middle class comprises more than 10 percent of the overall population.

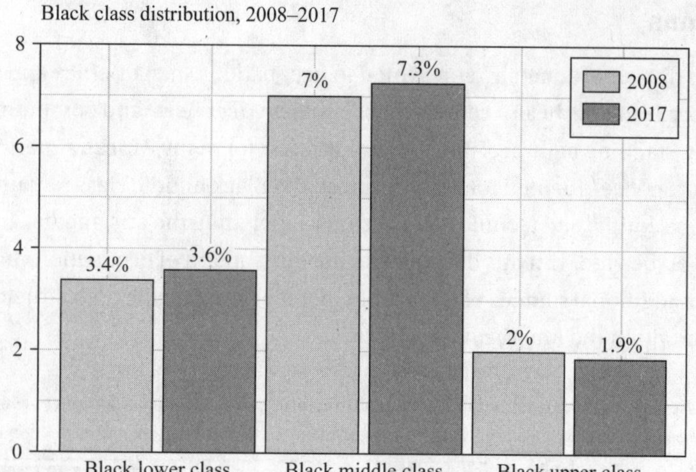

From "The Black Middle Class Needs Political Attention, Too" by Andre M. Perry and Carl Romer, February 27, 2020, Brookings Institution

Where the Black Middle Class Works

Approximately one in four middle-class workers across racial groups are employed in office administration or sales-related occupations.

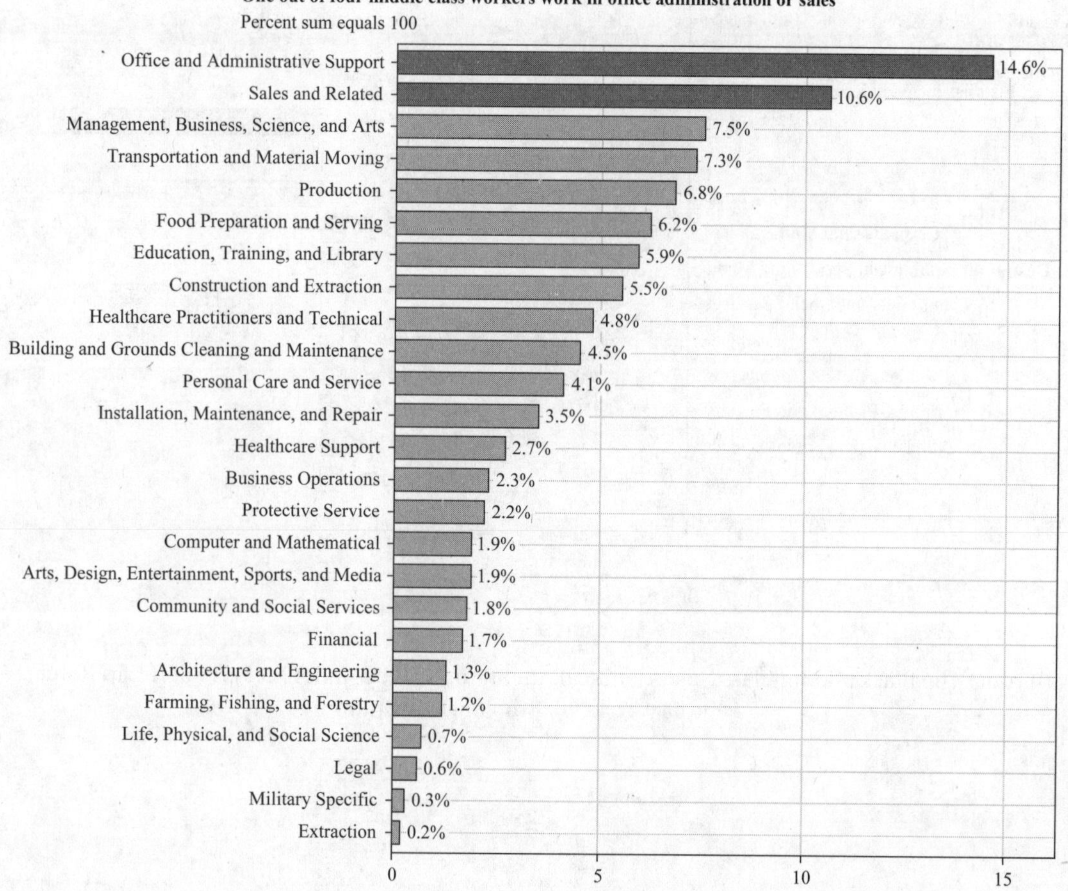

From "The Black Middle Class Needs Political Attention, Too" by Andre M. Perry and Carl Romer, February 27, 2020, Brookings Institution

Black Middle Class Overrepresented in Office, Transportation, and Health Care Support Occupations

The Black middle class is disproportionately represented in occupations such as office and administrative support, transportation and material moving, health care support, protective services, and community and social services. These sectors reflect long-standing pathways into the middle class for many African Americans, who are often rooted in public-facing or service-oriented roles. By contrast, the Black middle class remains underrepresented in managerial, business, scientific, and technical professions—including the arts, media, architecture, and engineering fields. The chart associated with this data reflects the distribution of occupations held by middle-class individuals, regardless of additional sources of household income. It highlights both structural opportunity and occupational segregation within the American workforce.

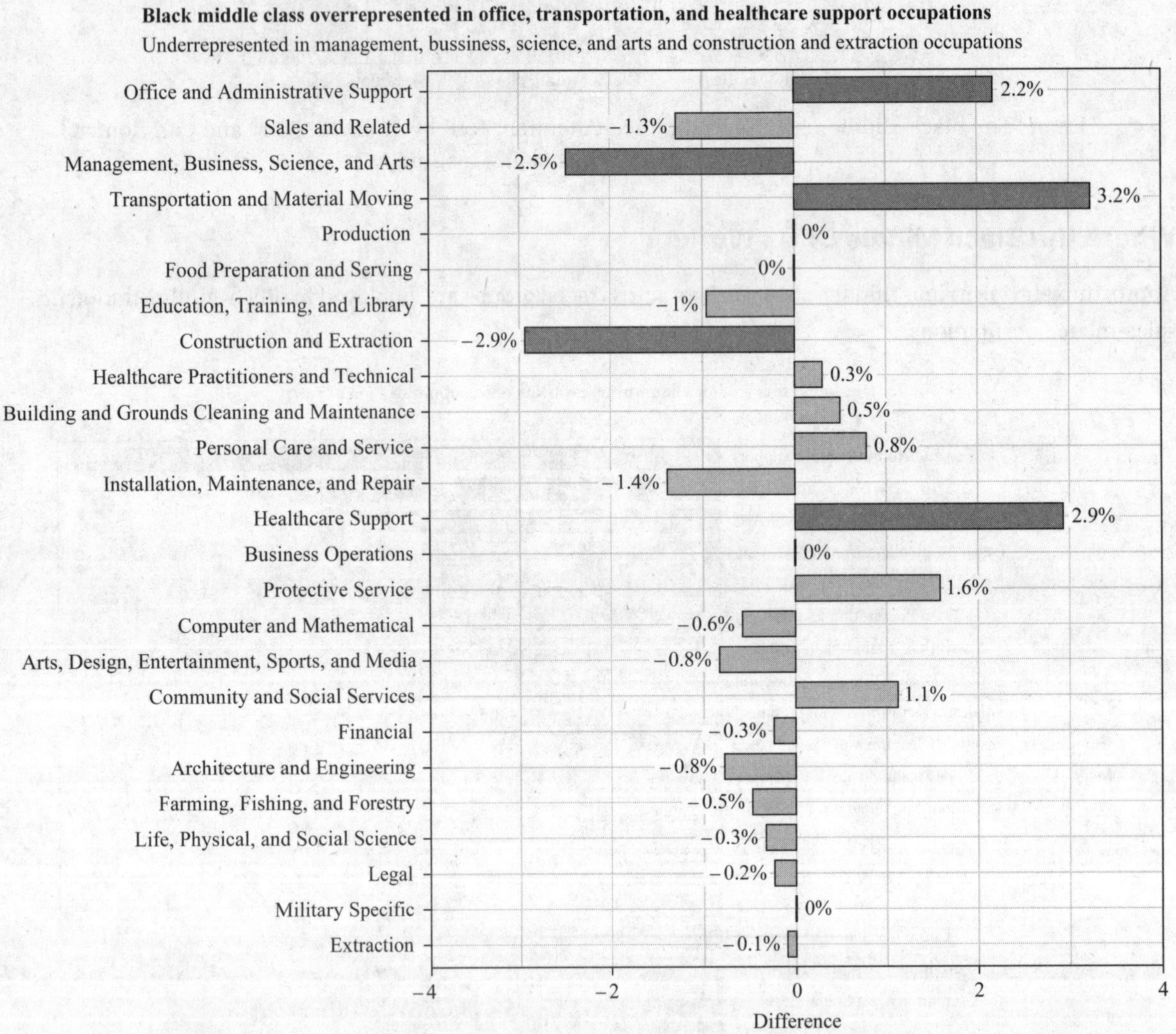

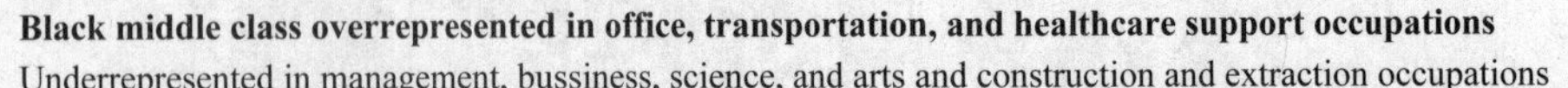

From "The Black Middle Class Needs Political Attention, Too" by Andre M. Perry and Carl Romer, February 27, 2020, Brookings Institution

The Black Middle Class Is Less Likely to Be Homeowners

One of the most visible indicators of the racial wealth gap is the disparity in homeownership rates. Despite achieving middle-class status, only about half of Black middle-class households own their homes, compared with 69 percent of their non-Black middle-class peers. This gap underscores how systemic barriers to generational wealth—such as redlining, lending discrimination, and housing segregation—continue to constrain wealth-building opportunities for Black families, even among those with comparable incomes and education levels.

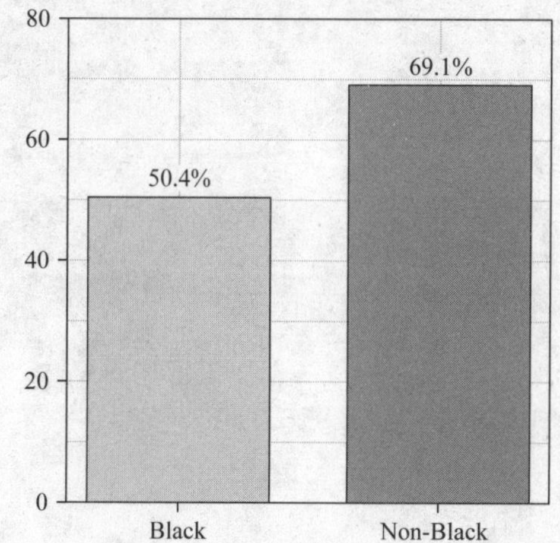

From "The Black Middle Class Needs Political Attention, Too"
by Andre M. Perry and Carl Romer, February 27, 2020, Brookings Institution

Black Homeownership Is Also Concentrated in the South

Homeownership rates among Black middle-class families differ by region, but a consistent trend emerges in the South. Across Southern metro areas, Black middle-class households tend to have higher homeownership rates than their counterparts in other parts of the country. This regional concentration reflects both historical settlement patterns and the relative affordability of housing in the South, even as national disparities in wealth and access to credit persist.

Progress at the Polls

More Black Americans began running for office after the Voting Rights Act—and winning. Leaders like Shirley Chisholm and Barack Obama showed what representation could look like on a national scale.

You're Practicing: Tracing long-term effects of legislation.

Connect This To: Civic leadership and political change.

Theme: Representation and Power

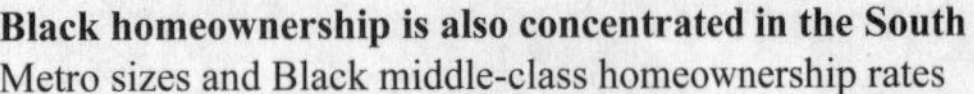

Black homeownership is also concentrated in the South
Metro sizes and Black middle-class homeownership rates

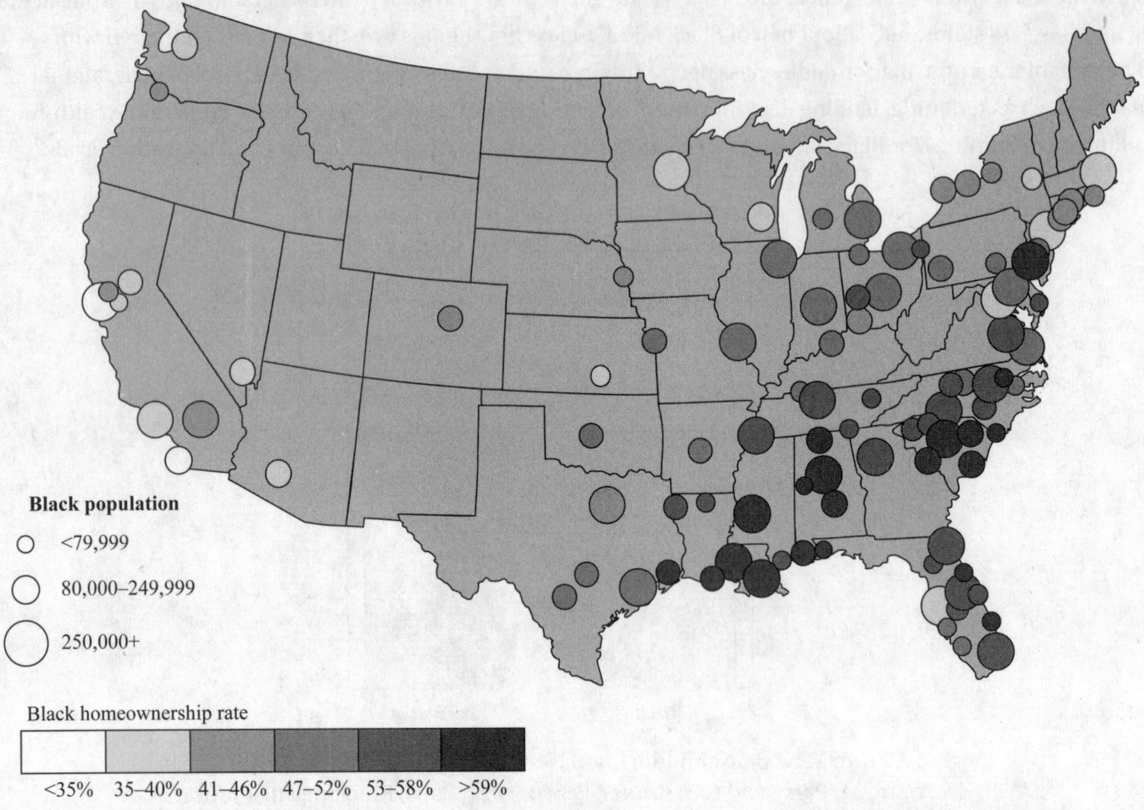

From "The Black Middle Class Needs Political Attention, Too" by Andre M. Perry and Carl Romer, February 27, 2020, Brookings Institution

The economic and political evolution of the Black middle class in the late twentieth and early twenty-first centuries reflects both progress and persistent inequities. Although desegregation, urbanization, and educational advancement expanded pathways into the middle class and entrepreneurship, structural barriers—particularly in wealth accumulation and homeownership—have limited full economic equity. The Voting Rights Act of 1965 was pivotal in strengthening Black political representation, leading to a significant increase in elected officials and the rise of influential leaders in federal office. Yet, as economic disparities remain and political inclusion continues to evolve, the experiences of the Black middle class remind us that true equity requires intentional policy, institutional accountability, and sustained civic engagement.

Practice: Explain Continuities or Changes over Time

From the 1970s onward, African Americans made significant gains in economic sectors and political offices across local, state, and national levels.

(A) Identify one milestone in Black political representation since the Civil Rights era.
(B) Explain how economic growth among segments of the Black population influenced opportunities for political leadership.
(C) Analyze whether these changes reflected a lasting shift in systemic equity or continuity in structural barriers.

SAMPLE RESPONSES

(A) A major milestone in Black political representation since the Civil Rights era was the founding of the Congressional Black Caucus (CBC) in 1971, which gave African American members of Congress a unified platform to advocate for policy reforms in health care, employment, education, and social services.

The establishment of the CBC reflected the political empowerment made possible by the Voting Rights Act of 1965, which removed many discriminatory barriers to voting and allowed a record number of Black elected officials to serve at the local, state, and federal levels.

Leaders such as Shirley Chisholm, the first Black woman elected to Congress in 1968 and a cofounder of the CBC, symbolized the growing influence of African Americans in shaping national policy and political discourse.

(B) Economic growth among segments of the Black population after the Civil Rights era, driven by desegregation, expanded higher education access, and affirmative action policies, created a larger Black middle class with the resources to participate more fully in politics.

The growth of Black-owned businesses, increased professional employment, and higher college graduation rates strengthened the economic base that supported campaigns for public office and civic leadership roles.

This economic advancement allowed more African Americans to run for and win positions such as mayors of major cities—Maynard Jackson in Atlanta in 1973 and Harold Washington in Chicago in 1983—marking a new era of Black political visibility and influence.

(C) The post–Civil Rights era brought historic gains in Black political representation and middle-class growth, but persistent systemic inequities revealed a continuity of structural barriers.

Despite higher educational attainment and greater political access, African Americans continued to face a racial wealth gap, lower rates of homeownership, and occupational segregation that limited generational wealth-building.

The experience of the Black middle class shows that while political representation expanded—culminating in milestones such as Barack Obama's presidency—true economic and social equity remained constrained by deep-rooted institutional and structural inequalities.

Skills Assessed: Explain the continuities or changes over time; use sources and evidence; analyze relationships among developments.

Topic 4.16 Demographic and Religious Diversity in Contemporary Black Communities

Key Terms

- Black immigrants—from Africa, the Caribbean, and Latin America
- Intragroup diversity—ethnic, linguistic, national distinctions
- Religious pluralism—Christianity, Islam, traditional African religions
- Black atheism and spiritualism
- Black church—enduring social/political center
- Intersection of faith and activism
- Denominational diversity—AME, Baptist, Pentecostal, Sunni, and Nation of Islam
- Transnational Black identities

What does it mean to speak of *the Black community* in the twenty-first century? Since 2000, the African American population has not only grown but has also become more culturally, ethnically, and religiously diverse, reshaping the meanings of identity, solidarity, and community. The African American population in the United States has experienced significant demographic shifts in the early twenty-first century. Immigration from Africa, the Caribbean, and Latin America has contributed to a broader spectrum of cultural experiences and national origins within Black communities. This diversity has expanded conversations about Black identity, citizenship, and belonging while also presenting new challenges and opportunities for political unity and social cohesion.

Faith and religion continue to serve as powerful forces in African American life, evolving alongside this demographic complexity. From traditional Black churches to emergent forms of spiritual expression, religion has remained central to social justice movements, community building, education, and mutual aid. Topic 4.16 explores how Black communities today reflect an increasingly global and multifaceted identity while affirming the enduring role of religion as a source of cultural strength, activism, and resilience.

After engaging with this topic, scholars will be able to:

- Describe the ways in which the African American population has grown and diversified since the year 2000.
- Explain how religious institutions and faith practices continue to shape the social, educational, and cultural lives of African American communities.
- Evaluate the relationship between demographic change and community formation in contemporary Black life.

The Growing Diversity of Black America by Christine Tamir

Published in 2021 by the Pew Research Center, Christine Tamir's report The Growing Diversity of Black America offers a comprehensive analysis of the evolving demographics within Black communities in the United States. Drawing on data from the U.S. Census Bureau and the American Community Survey, the report highlights significant trends that have reshaped the Black American experience since 2000.

Expanding Demographics of the Black Population

Between 2000 and 2019, the Black-identifying population in the United States grew by 30 percent, reaching approximately 47 million people—nearly 14 percent of the total population. This growth reflects not only increasing numbers but also a more complex demographic makeup that challenges monolithic conceptions of Black identity.

Among the U.S. Black population, both multiracial and Hispanic numbers have grown sharply since 2000

U.S. Black population

U.S. Black population 36.2 million
1.0 million
1.5 million
33.7 million

U.S. Black population 42.1 million
1.7 million
2.5 million
37.9 million

U.S. Black population 47.2 million

Black Hispanic 2.8 million

Multiracial (Non-Hispanic) 5.2 million

Single race (Non-Hispanic) 39.3 million

50 million
40
30
20
10
0

2000 2006 2010 2015 2021

Note: Populations rounded to nearest 100,000. Populations may not sum to total for a given year due to rounding. "U.S. Black population" refers to all people who self-identify as Black, inclusive of single-race Black, multiracial Black and Black Hispanic people. "Single race" refers to people who self-identify as Black alone and do not identify as Hispanic or Latino. "Multiracial" refers to people who self-identify as Black and one or more races in combination, but do not identify as Hispanic or Latino. "Black Hispanic" refers to people who self-identify as Hispanic or Latino and as Black (multiracial or otherwise).

From "The Growing Diversity of Black America" by Christine Tamir, 2021, Pew Research Center

One in Four Black Americans Are Members of Generation Z

This chart demonstrates how the age profile of the Black population in the United States has shifted notably since 2000. For example, it shows how by 2019, the median age of single-race, non-Hispanic Black Americans had risen to 35—up from 30 in 2000. Although this reflects a maturing demographic, the Black population remains younger on average than single-race, non-Hispanic white Americans (median age 43) and Asian Americans (38) and is only slightly older than Hispanic Americans (29). Notably, approximately one in four Black Americans belongs to Generation Z, underscoring the significance of youth voices in shaping the future of Black political, cultural, and civic life.

In 2019, most multiracial Black people in U.S. were members of Gen Z or younger, reflecting their youth

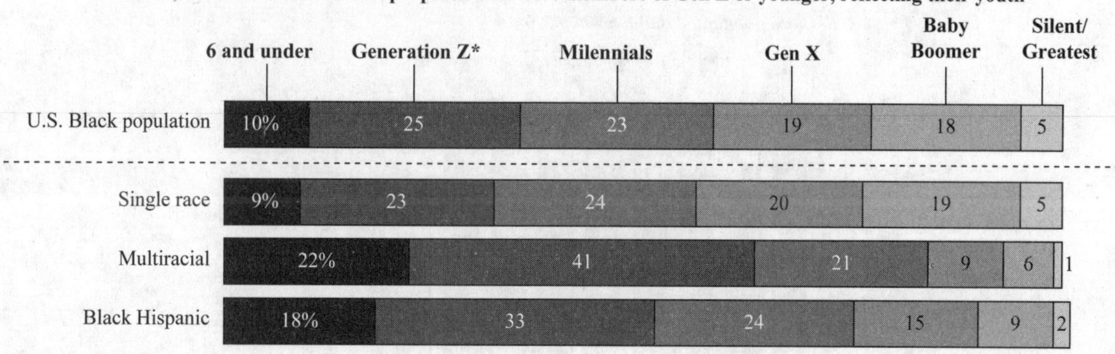

* No chronological endpoint has been set for this group. For this analysis, Generation Z is defined as those ages 7 to 22 in 2019.

Note: Figures may not add to 100% due to rounding. "U.S. Black population" refers to all people who self-identify as Black, inclusive of single-race Black, multiracial Black and Black Hispanic people. "Single race" refers to people who self-identify as Black alone and do not identify as Hispanic or Latino. "Multiracial" refers to people who self-identify as Black and one or more races in combination, but do not identify as Hispanic or Latino. "Black Hispanic" refers to people who self-identify as Hispanic or Latino and as Black (multiracial or otherwise).

From "The Growing Diversity of Black America" by Christine Tamir, 2021, Pew Research Center

Over Half of the Black Population Lives in the South

This chart demonstrates how, in 2019, the South remained home to the largest share of the nation's Black population, with 56 percent residing in the region. The Midwest and Northeast each accounted for 17 percent, while the West was home to approximately 10 percent of Black Americans.

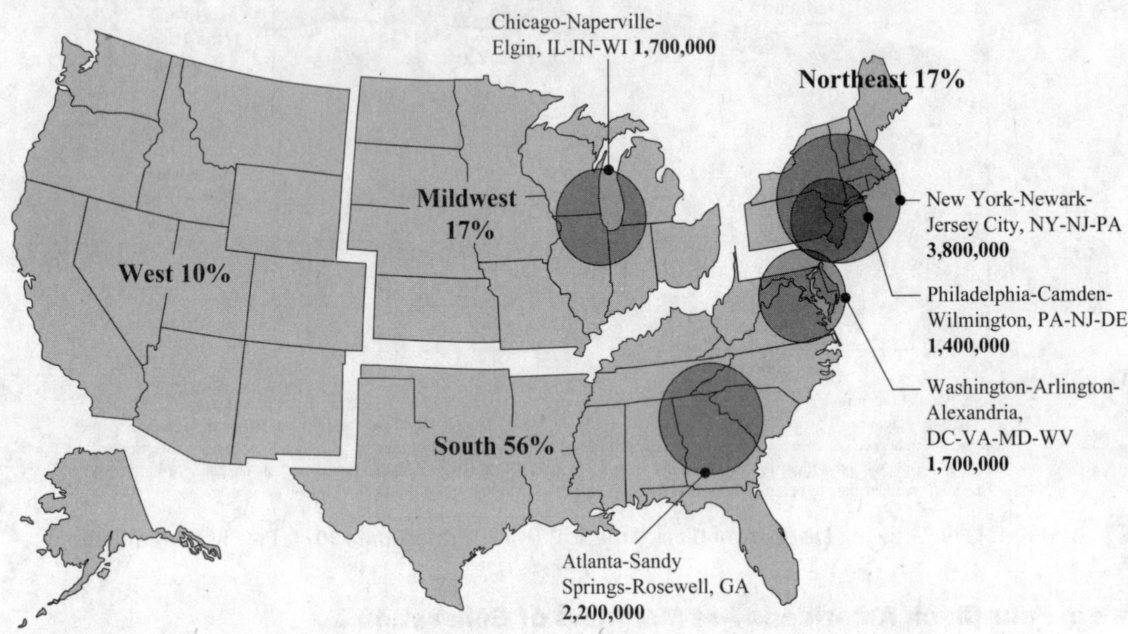

From "The Growing Diversity of Black America" by Christine Tamir, 2021, Pew Research Center

This chart demonstrates how the growth of the Black population in the South reflects a reversal of earlier migration patterns, signaling a renewed return to the region that many once left during the Great Migration.

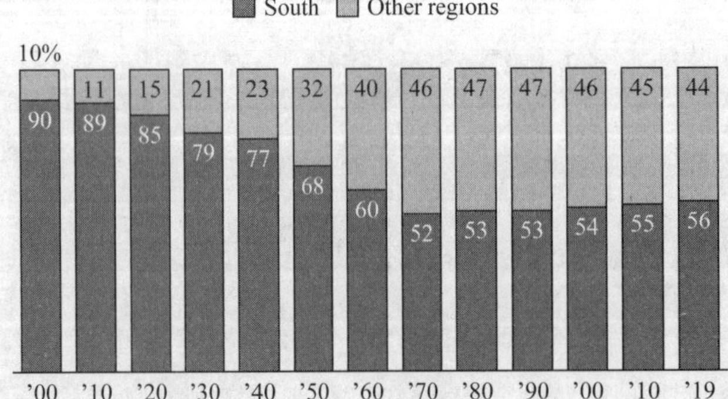

From "The Growing Diversity of Black America" by Christine Tamir, 2021, Pew Research Center

Texas Has the Largest Black State Population

This chart demonstrates how the top states of residence vary across Black racial and ethnic subgroups. For example, it shows that Texas has the largest population of non-Hispanic single-race Black Americans, followed by Georgia, Florida, New York, and North Carolina. Among non-Hispanic multiracial Black individuals, California ranks first, followed by Texas, Florida, Ohio, and New York. For Black Hispanics, New York leads, followed by Florida, California, Texas, and New Jersey. Notably, Texas, New York, and Florida appear among the top five states for all three subgroups, underscoring their demographic significance across the broader Black population.

Top five states of residence for the U.S. Black population in 2019
U.S. Black population

	All		Single race		Multiracial		Black Hispanic	
	State	Population	State	Population	State	Population	State	Population
1	Texas	3,900,000	Texas	3,400,000	California	350,000	New York	450,000
2	Florida	3,800,000	Georgia	3,300,000	Texas	250,000	Florida	260,000
3	Georgia	3,600,000	Florida	3,300,000	Florida	245,000	California	240,000
4	New York	3,400,000	New York	2,800,000	Ohio	208,000	Texas	210,000
5	California	2,800,000	North Carolina	2,200,000	New York	206,000	New Jersey	130,000

Note: Numbers are rounded to the nearest 100,000 if over 1 million and to the nearest 10,000 if below 1 million. "U.S. Black population" refers to all people who self-identify as Black, inclusive of single-race Black, multiracial Black and Black Hispanic people. "Single race" refers to people who self-identify only as Black and do not identify as Hispanic or Latino. "Multiracial" refers to people who self-identify as Black and one or more races in combination, but do not identify as Hispanic or Latino. "Black Hispanic" refers to people who self-identify as Hispanic or Latino and as Black (multiracial or otherwise).
Source: Pew Research Center tabulations of the 2019 American Community Survey (1% IPUMS).

From "The Growing Diversity of Black America" by Christine Tamir, 2021, Pew Research Center

Which Metropolitan Area Has the Largest Black Urban Population?

This chart demonstrates how, as of 2019, the New York metropolitan area had the largest Black population of any U.S. metro region, home to approximately 3.8 million Black residents.

Largest metropolitan areas by Black population, 2019 U.S. Black population				
		Black Americans Non-Hispanic		
	All	Single race	Multiracial	Black Hispanic
1	New York-Newark-Jersey City, NY-NJ-PA **3,800,000**	New York-Newark-Jersey City, NY-NJ-PA **3,100,000**	New York-Newark-Jersey City, NY-NJ-PA **160,000**	New York-Newark-Jersey City, NY-NJ-PA **510,000**
2	Atlanta-Sandy Springs-Roswell, GA **2,200,000**	Atlanta-Sandy Springs-Roswell, GA **2,100,000**	Washington-Arlington-Alexandria, DC-VA-MD-WV **100,000**	Miami-Fort Lauderdale-West Palm Beach, FL **100,000**
3	Washington-Arlington-Alexandria, DC-VA-MD-WV **1,700,000**	Washington-Arlington-Alexandria, DC-VA-MD-WV **1,600,000**	Los Angeles-Long Beach-Anaheim, CA **100,000**	Boston-Cambridge-Newton, MA-NH **100,000**
4	Chicago-Naperville-Elgin, IL-IN-WI **1,700,000**	Chicago-Naperville-Elgin, IL-IN-WI **1,500,000**	Philadelphia-Camden-Wilmington, PA-NJ-DE **100,000**	Los Angeles-Long Beach-Anaheim, CA **70,000**
5	Philadelphia-Camden-Wilmington, PA-NJ-DE **1,400,000**	Philadelphia-Camden-Wilmington, PA-NJ-DE **1,200,000**	Chicago-Naperville-Elgin, IL-IN-WI **90,000**	Philadelphia-Camden-Wilmington, PA-NJ-DE **70,000**

Note: Numbers are rounded to the nearest 100,000 if over 1 million and over and to the nearest 10,000 if below 1 million. "U.S. Black population" refers to all people who self-identify as Black, inclusive of single-race Black, multiracial Black and Black Hispanic people. "Single race" refers to people who self-identify only as Black and do not identify as Hispanic or Latino. "Multiracial" refers to people who self-identify as Black and one or more races in combination, but do not identify as Hispanic or Latino. "Black Hispanic" refers to people who self-identify as both Hispanic or Latino and as Black (multiracial or otherwise).
Source: Pew Research Center tabulations of the 2019 American Community Survey (1% IPUMS).

From "The Growing Diversity of Black America" by Christine Tamir, 2021, Pew Research Center

Growth in Education and Population Diversity

Since 2000, the number of Black Americans earning college degrees has more than doubled, signaling increased access to higher education and shifting socioeconomic dynamics within Black communities. At the same time, Black communities have become more diverse due to immigration and changing patterns of racial identification. The number of Black immigrants—particularly from Africa and the Caribbean—has nearly doubled. More individuals now identify as Black and Hispanic or as multiracial, reflecting broader intersections of racial and ethnic identity.

This chart demonstrates how the number of Black adults with a college degree or more education has more than doubled since 2000.

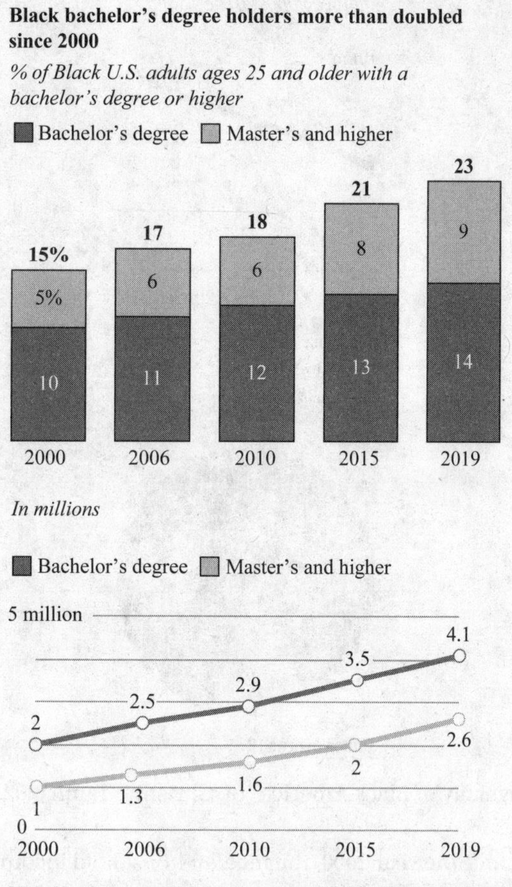

From "The Growing Diversity of Black America" by Christine Tamir, 2021, Pew Research Center

A Shared Identity amid Diversity

The term *Black* functions as a unifying identity rooted in shared African heritage and collective historical experience. Yet within this category exists significant diversity, including the descendants of enslaved people in the United States who may use the term *African American*, recent immigrants who may identify with both race and nationality (e.g., use the term *Afro-Colombian*), and multiracial individuals with substantial Black ancestry. This broad coalition reflects a range of cultural, historical, and geographic experiences within a shared political and social framework.

This chart demonstrates how immigrants represent a growing segment of the nation's Black population.

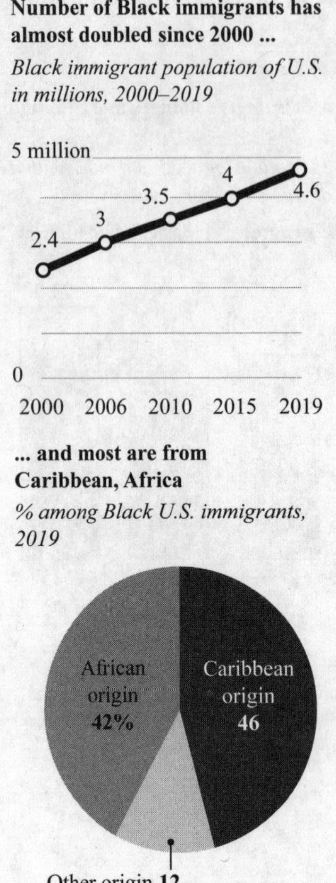

From "The Growing Diversity of Black America" by Christine Tamir, 2021, Pew Research Center

This chart demonstrates that since the year 2000, the median household income for the U.S. Black population has seen only modest gains, reflecting persistent economic disparities.

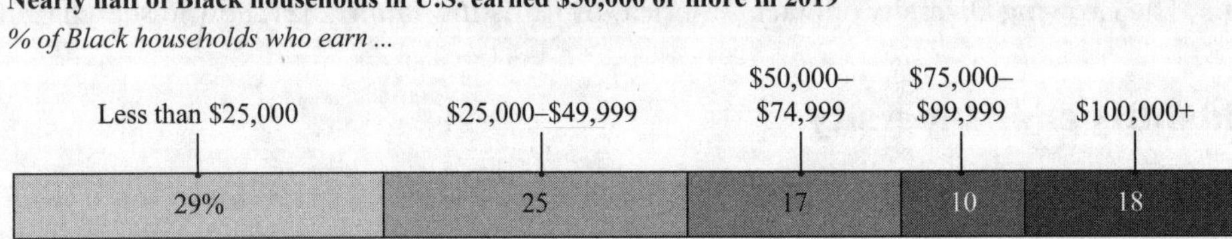

From "The Growing Diversity of Black America" by Christine Tamir, 2021, Pew Research Center

Contemporary Religious Affiliation

In the early twenty-first century, religion continues to play a central role in Black community life. Approximately two-thirds of African American adults identify as Protestant, while approximately 20 percent report no religious affiliation. This spectrum reflects both continuity with historical religious traditions and evolving trends in secular identification.

Young Black adults less Protestant than their elders % of Black Americans who identify religiously as ...					
	Protestant	Catholic	Other Christians	Non-Christian faiths	Unaffiliated
	%	%	%	%	%
All Black adults	66	6	3	3	21
Men	60	7	3	3	26
Women	70	5	3	3	18
Generation Z	52	9	4	5	28
Millennial	55	6	3	4	33
Generation X	67	6	3	3	21
Baby Boomer	76	6	4	2	11
Silent Generation*	83	6	4	1	5
U.S. born	68	5	3	3	22
African born	55	20	8	10	6
Caribbean born	57	15	2	3	23
Some college or less	66	5	4	3	22
College graduate	68	9	2	4	18
Black, non-Hispanic	69	5	3	3	19
Multiracial	41	11	4	6	38
Black Hispanic	35	24	2	6	33
All U.S. adults	42	21	3	6	27

*This includes a very small number of those in the Greatest Generation (born before 1928).
Note: Those who did not answer are not shown.
Source: Survey conducted Nov. 19, 2019-June 3, 2020, among U.S. adults.
"Faith Among Black Americans"

Survey conducted November 9, 2019–June 3, 2020, from Besheer Mohamed and Kiana Cox, "Young Black adults less Protestant than their elders," in *Faith Among Black Americans*, Pew Research Center, February 16, 2021

Faith-Based Advocacy and Social Justice

Black religious leaders and institutions have long been central to the fight for civil rights and continue to engage in social justice advocacy. Faith communities have mobilized around political, social, and economic issues—not only those impacting Black Americans directly but also broader concerns of equity, justice, and human rights.

The Black Church as a Cultural and Intellectual Anchor

The Black church remains a foundational institution for articulating and debating core values related to education, racial justice, community uplift, and diasporic identity. It has served as a space for cultural formation, language development, intergenerational leadership, and the negotiation of identity across diverse Black experiences.

Since 2000, the African American population has grown in both size and complexity, reflecting increased immigration, rising multiracial identification, and broader geographic dispersion—especially within the South. This demographic expansion has challenged narrow definitions of Black identity, emphasizing a shared heritage alongside diverse cultural, national, and generational experiences. Amid these changes, religion and faith traditions have continued to serve as foundational institutions—advancing social justice, cultivating leadership, and sustaining community life. Together, these evolving demographic and religious dynamics underscore the resilience and adaptability of Black communities in the twenty-first century.

A Tapestry of Black Identity

Black identity is many things—Afro-Caribbean, African immigrant, multiracial, Christian, Muslim, secular, and more. Understanding that diversity helps us better understand what brings people together.

You're Practicing: Exploring internal diversity within a community.

Connect This To: Diaspora, migration, and culture.

Theme: Identity and Community

Practice: Contextualize

Contemporary Black communities in the United States are characterized by a wide range of cultural, national, and religious identities.

(A) Describe two significant sources of demographic or religious diversity within contemporary African American communities.
(B) Contextualize how global migration, interfaith dynamics, or cultural exchange have shaped these developments.
(C) Analyze how this diversity complicates or enriches discussions of Black identity and solidarity.

SAMPLE RESPONSES

(A) One significant source of demographic diversity within contemporary African American communities is the growing number of Black immigrants from Africa, the Caribbean, and Latin America, which has expanded the cultural, linguistic, and national origins represented within the Black population in the United States.

Another significant source of diversity is religious pluralism, with African Americans identifying across a range of faith traditions including historically Black Protestant denominations such as AME, Baptist, and Pentecostal churches, as well as Islam, traditional African religions, and secular or spiritualist identities.

(B) Global migration since 2000, particularly from countries in Africa, the Caribbean, and Latin America, has significantly reshaped African American demographics by introducing new cultural traditions, languages, and national identities into Black communities.

Interfaith dynamics, including the coexistence of historically Black Protestantism with Islam, traditional African religions, and nonreligious or spiritualist perspectives, have created a richer religious landscape and fostered cultural exchange within African American communities.

These changes reflect the rise of transnational Black identities, in which individuals embrace both a shared African heritage and distinct cultural or national experiences that shape their place within the broader African American community.

(C) The demographic and religious diversity within contemporary African American communities enriches discussions of Black identity by incorporating a wide range of national origins, faith traditions, and cultural perspectives into a shared framework rooted in African heritage and historical experience.

This diversity can also complicate solidarity efforts, as differences in immigration history, generational background, and religious affiliation may shape political priorities, community organizing strategies, and understandings of cultural identity.

Ultimately, the presence of diverse cultural and religious voices within the African American population challenges narrow definitions of Blackness while offering opportunities to build inclusive solidarity that reflects the complex realities of twenty-first-century Black life.

Skills Assessed: Contextualize historical developments; use sources and evidence; analyze relationships among developments.

Topic 4.17 The Evolution of African American Music—from Spirituals to Hip-Hop

Key Terms

- Spirituals—rooted in African traditions and enslaved resistance
- Blues, jazz, gospel, R&B, soul, funk, hip-hop
- Cultural lineage and transformation
- Sampling and storytelling in hip-hop
- Civil Rights–era music—protest and consciousness
- Political hip-hop—Public Enemy, Kendrick Lamar, and others
- Commercialization vs. resistance
- Afrofuturism in music—Sun Ra, Janelle Monáe, and others

What do a field holler, a gospel hymn, a jazz solo, and a hip-hop cypher all have in common? They each reflect the enduring power of African American music to carry history, shape identity, and transform global culture. African American music is one of the most influential and enduring cultural contributions in world history. Rooted in African rhythmic and performative traditions, Black musical expression in the United States has evolved across centuries—from spirituals and work songs to gospel, blues, jazz, soul, funk, and ultimately, hip-hop. Each genre preserves a record of resistance, resilience, and reinvention.

The rise of hip-hop in the 1970s signaled a new era in Black cultural expression. Informed by the political and cultural movements of the 1960s and 1970s, hip-hop became a dynamic force that blended music, poetry, dance, fashion, and social commentary. This topic examines the deep African roots of African American music, its shaping of American and global soundscapes, and the emergence of hip-hop as a revolutionary cultural movement.

African American music has evolved into one of the most powerful cultural forces in the world, rooted in African performative traditions and continuously reimagined through each generation's lived experiences. From spirituals to blues, to gospel, to jazz, and ultimately to hip-hop, these sonic forms have served as vehicles for storytelling, resistance, cultural pride, and political expression. The rise of hip-hop in the late twentieth century reflects both continuity and innovation, blending inherited rhythms with new technologies, aesthetics, and global influence. Together, these genres reveal how African American communities have used music to affirm identity, confront injustice, and transform the soundscape of both America and the world.

After engaging with this topic, scholars will be able to:

- Describe how African American music incorporates performative and rhythmic traditions from Africa.
- Explain the influence of African American music on American and global genres.
- Identify the origins, elements, and cultural significance of hip-hop.
- Analyze how the Black Freedom and cultural movements of the 1960s and 1970s laid the foundation for hip-hop's emergence.

African Foundations in Sound and Movement

Since their forced arrival in the Americas, African Americans have drawn on musical and performative traditions rooted in West and Central African cultures. Core elements such as improvisation, call and response, syncopation, storytelling, and the integration of music with dance formed the foundation of African American music. These techniques allowed enslaved and free Black communities to preserve cultural memory, foster collective identity, and express resistance through rhythm, voice, and movement.

"The Evolution of African American Music" by Portia K. Maultsby

In her foundational essay "The Evolution of African American Music," ethnomusicologist Portia K. Maultsby examines how African musical elements—such as rhythm, improvisation, call and response, and communal participation—have shaped the development of African American music across centuries. Published in the 1980 volume *Africanisms in African American Music*, Maultsby's work traces a continuous cultural lineage from African traditions to spirituals, blues, jazz, gospel, and soul. Her analysis emphasizes both continuity and transformation, positioning Black musical expression as a form of cultural retention, resistance, and innovation within the African diaspora.

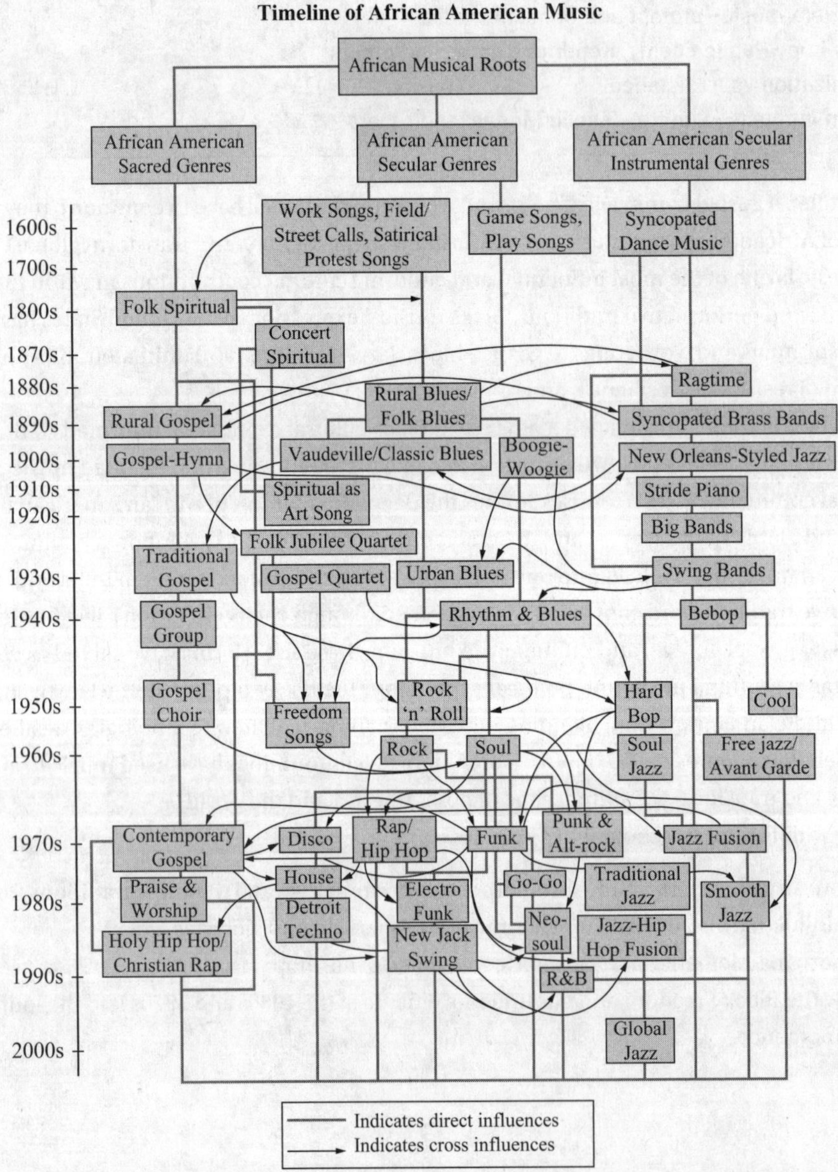

From "The Evolution of African American Music" by Portia K. Maultsby

Transformative Influence on American and Global Music

African American music has generated and reshaped some of the most influential genres in both American and global music history. From spirituals, blues, and gospel to jazz, rhythm and blues, and hip-hop, this tradition has provided the sonic backbone for genres such as rock and roll and Latin jazz. Performers like Sister Rosetta Tharpe, Bo Diddley, and Little Richard pioneered the electric, rhythmic styles that laid the foundation for rock and roll. At its core, African American music is a creative response to oppression—channeling joy, pain, critique, and hope in ways that continue to resonate worldwide.

Hip-Hop as a Cultural Movement

Emerging in the Bronx, New York, during the 1970s, hip-hop began as a grassroots cultural movement among Black and Latino youths. Music became its most prominent and enduring element. Influenced by African American artists like James Brown, early DJs such as Grandmaster Flash experimented with innovative turntable techniques like mixing, scratching, and extending *the break*—the part of the song used by dancers to showcase movement. These breaks gave rise to breakdancing and elevated b-boys and b-girls into cultural icons of hip-hop expression.

Breakdancers in New York, 1984

Captured during the early years of hip-hop culture's rise, the photograph *Breakdancers in New York* (1984) offers a vivid glimpse into one of the foundational elements of hip-hop: breakdancing. This photograph documents young dancers—often referred to as b-boys and b-girls—performing dynamic and improvised moves during a street performance. Emerging from the Bronx and other New York neighborhoods in the 1970s and early 1980s, breakdancing reflected a fusion of athleticism, musicality, and cultural expression. This image underscores the importance of movement, competition, and creativity in hip-hop's evolution as a global artistic and cultural force.

Breakdancers in New York, 1984
(Source: Photo by Michael Ochs Archives/Getty Images)

Visual Expression and Artistic Innovation

Alongside music and dance, graffiti became a vital artistic element of hip-hop culture. Emerging even before the musical aspects of the movement, graffiti—often created by "writers" on subway cars, buildings, and public infrastructure—gave rise to visual storytelling and protest art. Artists like Jean-Michel Basquiat emerged from this scene, turning street art into celebrated and politically charged commentary.

Political Roots and the Legacy of Black Movements

Hip-hop was born in the shadow of the Black Freedom movements and the Black Arts movement of the 1960s and 1970s. It inherited a political consciousness shaped by Black nationalism, Afrocentric aesthetics, and revolutionary thought. Drawing from the fashion, poetry, and resistance strategies of groups like the Black Panthers, hip-hop became a new language for articulating Black experience in urban America.

Cultural Memory and Global Impact

Following the decline of the Black Power movement, hip-hop filled the cultural void by vocalizing the ongoing political and social struggles of African Americans. Artists from Queen Latifah to Kendrick Lamar have continued this legacy, using their platforms to raise awareness about systemic injustice, state violence, and racial inequality. Hip-hop has grown into a global force—amplifying the voices of Black communities and reshaping political discourse through rhythm, lyricism, and cultural innovation.

"Hey Mama, He Treats Your Daughter Mean" (Live)

Ruth Brown, often referred to as the Queen of R&B, was a pioneering figure in the evolution of rhythm and blues (R&B) in the mid-twentieth century. Her 1953 hit "Hey Mama, He Treats Your Daughter Mean" became a defining anthem of early R&B, blending blues traditions with gospel-influenced vocal stylings and a dynamic stage presence. Her live performance captures not only Brown's powerful delivery but also the genre's growing influence on American popular music and Black expressive culture during the postwar era.

For a deeper insight into the evolution of early rhythm and blues, scholars are encouraged to listen to Ruth Brown's live performance of "Hey Mama, He Treats Your Daughter Mean." This performance captures the vibrant energy and cultural significance of early R&B music. The video is available at: https://www.youtube.com/watch?v=BqmGZRGvKC8.

From Spirituals to Hip-Hop

Black music has always been more than sound—it's a reflection of struggle, hope, and joy. From field chants to trap beats, artists continue to innovate and resist.

You're Practicing: Tracing cultural evolution across time.

Connect This To: Resistance through art and legacy.

Theme: Cultural Expression and Continuity

Practice: Explain the Significance or Importance

African American musical traditions have evolved from spirituals to blues, jazz, soul, funk, and hip-hop—each genre reflecting cultural resilience and innovation.

(A) Identify two distinct musical genres that emerged from African American communities and describe the historical context of their development.

(B) Explain how these musical forms functioned as both cultural expression and political commentary.

(C) Analyze the significance of African American music as a vehicle for shaping national and global conversations on identity, resistance, and belonging.

SAMPLE RESPONSES

(A) Spirituals emerged during slavery in the United States, rooted in West and Central African traditions and infused with Christian themes, serving as both coded resistance and a means of preserving cultural memory.

Hip-hop developed in the Bronx during the 1970s as a grassroots cultural movement blending DJing, MCing, breakdancing, and graffiti, shaped by the political consciousness of the Black Freedom and Black Arts movements.

(B) Spirituals expressed the pain, hope, and resilience of enslaved African Americans while covertly communicating messages of escape and solidarity in the face of oppression.

Hip-hop provided a platform for marginalized Black and Latino youth to address systemic racism, police brutality, and economic inequality through rhythm, lyricism, and visual artistry.

(C) African American music has influenced national debates about race and equality by foregrounding the lived experiences of Black communities and challenging dominant narratives through sound and performance.

Hip-hop has become a global cultural force that amplifies voices of resistance, fosters cross-cultural solidarity, and redefines concepts of identity and belonging on an international stage.

Skills Assessed: Explain the significance of cultural developments; use sources and evidence; analyze relationships among developments.

Topic 4.18 Black Life in Theater, TV, and Film

Key Terms

- Oscar Micheaux—early Black filmmaker
- Sidney Poitier, Cicely Tyson, Ruby Dee, Spike Lee
- Blaxploitation—1970s genre with complex legacy
- Tyler Perry, Shonda Rhimes, Ava DuVernay, Jordan Peele—modern visionaries
- Representation and stereotype—Mammy, Jezebel, Buck, Magical Negro
- Black independent cinema
- Black creatives and ownership—reclaiming narratives
- Cultural authenticity in media

From Broadway stages to Hollywood screens, African American artists have long used performance to challenge stereotypes, reclaim narratives, and reflect the depth and complexity of Black life in America. Throughout the twentieth and twenty-first centuries, African American playwrights, directors, actors, and filmmakers have reshaped how Black life is portrayed in theater, television, and film. Their work has pushed back against caricatures and limited roles, offering instead a fuller representation of African American identity, culture, and resilience. These creators have illuminated the beauty, pain, humor, and political struggles of Black communities—on their own terms.

The migration of Black Americans to urban centers and the rise of the Black middle class during the Great Migration and beyond played a pivotal role in expanding opportunities in the performing arts. As African Americans gained economic power and broader cultural visibility, new platforms emerged for storytelling that honored Black voices and perspectives.

After engaging with this topic, scholars will be able to:

- Describe how African American artists have represented Black life on stage and screen across the twentieth and twenty-first centuries.
- Explain how patterns of migration and economic progress influenced the expansion and evolution of African American representation in film, television, and theater.
- Recognize the significance of self-representation in shaping public perception and cultural power.

Oscar Micheaux and the Foundations of Black Cinema

In the early twentieth century, African American filmmaker Oscar Micheaux emerged as a groundbreaking voice in cinema. His work directly challenged the racist portrayals that dominated mainstream film by creating complex, multidimensional Black characters and narratives. Between the 1920s and 1940s, Micheaux produced nearly 50 films, providing opportunities for all-Black casts and redefining how Black life was represented on screen. His pioneering efforts laid a foundation for future generations of Black directors, producers, and performers in both film and television.

Lobby Card for *The Betrayal* by Oscar Micheaux, 1948

This 1948 lobby card advertises *The Betrayal*, one of the final films directed and produced by pioneering African American filmmaker Oscar Micheaux. As the first Black filmmaker to produce full-length feature films, Micheaux used cinema as a tool for social commentary, offering multidimensional Black characters and narratives that directly countered the racist caricatures of mainstream Hollywood. *The Betrayal*—a film focused on themes of love, racial identity, and social mobility—reflects Micheaux's enduring commitment to portraying African American life with realism and dignity. The lobby card serves as both a marketing tool and a visual artifact of early independent Black cinema.

Lobby card for *The Betrayal*, by Oscar Micheaux (1948)
(Source: Astor Pictures/Oscar Micheaux, public domain, via Wikimedia Commons)

Soul Train and the Celebration of Black Culture on Screen

Launched in 1971 by Don Cornelius, *Soul Train* was a landmark African American dance and music television program modeled after *American Bandstand*. Unlike its predecessor, however, *Soul Train* centered on Black performers, dancers, and cultural aesthetics. It became a vital space for celebrating Black style, music, and creativity while providing national exposure for artists across genres and generations.

Staple Singers on *Soul Train*
(Source: Public domain, via Wikimedia Commons)

Soul Train It's a Vibe: The Best Soul Train Line Dances

Soul Train, created by Don Cornelius in 1971, became one of the most iconic showcases of Black music, fashion, and dance on American television. This video compilation, *Soul Train It's a Vibe: The Best Soul Train Line Dances,* highlights the show's famous *Soul Train* line, where individual dancers took turns improvising along a corridor of cheering peers. The clip captures the creativity, confidence, and style that defined the program—and made it a cultural institution. Beyond entertainment, *Soul Train* served as a national stage for African American expression during a time when Black representation in media was still limited.

Scholars can explore the full video by searching the title on YouTube or by visiting the following link: https://www.youtube.com/watch?v=0iUJzQ5svaE.

Black Theater and the Influence of Migration

The Great Migration brought millions of African Americans to urban centers, which soon became hubs of Black cultural production. In these cities, professional and community-based Black theater companies flourished, producing plays that addressed pressing political, economic, and social issues. These performances often depicted the full spectrum of Black life—grappling with struggles while also expressing joy, resilience, and imagination through both dramatic and musical forms.

Diverse Representations in Late-Twentieth-Century Television

Since the 1970s, African American representation on television has grown more varied and multidimensional. Shows like *The Jeffersons* (1975–1985) and *The Fresh Prince of Bel-Air* (1990–1996) portrayed upward mobility and the aspirations of the Black middle and upper classes. Meanwhile, series like *Good Times* (1974–1979) and *Black-ish* (2014–2022) emphasized strong family dynamics and intergenerational themes, challenging earlier one-dimensional portrayals and reflecting the expanding range of African American experiences.

Playbill for *Fences* by August Wilson, 1987

The Playbill for *Fences* (1987), written by Pulitzer Prize–winning playwright August Wilson, represents one of the most acclaimed works in African American theater. *Fences*, part of Wilson's ten-play *Pittsburgh Cycle*, explores the complexities of Black life in mid-twentieth-century America through the character of Troy Maxson, a former Negro League baseball player grappling with disillusionment, family tensions, and the lingering effects of systemic racism. The Playbill not only documents a landmark moment in American theater history but also signals Wilson's broader contribution to expanding Black representation on stage with nuance, dignity, and cultural depth.

For a deeper analysis, scholars can view the original Playbill online at the Gilder Lehrman Institute of American History: https://www.gilderlehrman.org/ap-african-american-studies/unit-4/business-culture-20th-21st-centuries/playbill-fences-1987.

African American contributions to theater, television, and film have transformed cultural landscapes by centering on authentic portrayals of Black life, struggle, and joy. From Oscar Micheaux's pioneering films to contemporary shows that reflect the diversity and complexity of Black experiences, African American artists have used performance to challenge stereotypes, affirm identity, and push for broader social change. These representations have been shaped by historical forces such as migration, economic growth, and cultural movements. They continue to serve as powerful platforms for storytelling, resistance, and self-definition.

Black Voices on Screen

Shows like *Black-ish* and movies like *Black Panther* do more than entertain—they change who gets to tell stories and how Black life is seen.

You're Practicing: Analyzing media and representation.

Connect This To: Storytelling, power, and perception.

Theme: Visibility and Self-Definition

Practice: Explain the Effects of Historical Developments

Throughout the twentieth and twenty-first centuries, portrayals of Black life in theater, television, and film have reflected and shaped societal understandings of race, culture, and identity.

(A) Identify one major development in the representation of Black life in theater, television, or film.

(B) Explain how this development influenced public perception of African American communities or contributed to broader social or political movements.

(C) Analyze how evolving media portrayals have either challenged or reinforced racial stereotypes over time.

SAMPLE RESPONSES

(A) Oscar Micheaux's pioneering independent films in the early twentieth century created complex Black characters and narratives that directly countered the racist caricatures dominating mainstream Hollywood.

Don Cornelius's *Soul Train*, launched in 1971, brought Black music, dance, and style into millions of American homes, offering a consistent national platform for celebrating African American culture.

(B) Micheaux's work expanded public understanding of African American life by portraying dignity, ambition, and complexity, laying the foundation for future Black filmmakers to tell authentic stories.

Soul Train positively influenced public perception by normalizing Black cultural expression on national television and amplifying the visibility of African American artistry during an era of limited representation.

(C) Landmark works such as August Wilson's *Fences* and television shows like *Black-ish* have challenged racial stereotypes by centering multidimensional characters, authentic narratives, and intergenerational Black family experiences.

At the same time, some genres, such as certain Blaxploitation films of the 1970s, reinforced problematic stereotypes by relying on exaggerated depictions of violence, hypersexuality, or criminality, even while expanding opportunities for Black actors and filmmakers.

Skills Assessed: Explain the effects of historical developments; use sources and evidence; analyze relationships among developments.

Topic 4.19 African Americans and Sports

Key Terms

- Jackie Robinson—broke the MLB color barrier in 1947
- Wilma Rudolph, Muhammad Ali, Bill Russell, Serena Williams, Colin Kaepernick
- Racial integration and backlash
- Athletes as activists—from Muhammad Ali to LeBron James
- NCAA exploitation debates
- Endorsement and representation
- Title IX and Black women athletes
- Black excellence vs. structural inequality

On the field, the court, and the track, African American athletes have not only broken records—they've broken barriers. They have redefined excellence and have used their platforms to challenge racial injustice. From the nineteenth century to the present day, African American athletes have shaped the landscape of American and global sports. Although their achievements in performance are undeniable, their legacy goes far beyond competition. Black athletes have historically confronted racism, segregation, and exclusion, transforming sports into arenas of protest, empowerment, and cultural expression.

In the face of institutional discrimination, many used their visibility to advocate for civil rights, social justice, and equity, becoming symbols of both resistance and resilience. Their influence continues in the twenty-first century as a new generation of athletes expands the legacy of protest and pride across every level of play.

After engaging with this topic, scholars will be able to:

- Describe the contributions of Black athletes to sports from the nineteenth century forward.
- Explain how African American athletes have contested discrimination and advocated for racial equality across generations.
- Analyze how sports have served as a stage for both performance and protest in the Black Freedom struggle.

Pioneers in the Post–Civil War Era

During Reconstruction, African American athletes began asserting their presence and excellence in competitive sports despite racial segregation. In 1875, Oliver Lewis became the first winner of the Kentucky Derby. In 1877, William "Billy" Walker followed in his footsteps. Their victories marked the early dominance of Black jockeys in horse racing, setting a precedent that lasted into the early twentieth century before exclusionary practices emerged.

Jockeys Compete at the Washington Races, 1840

This 1840 image, *Jockeys Compete at the Washington Races*, offers a rare visual glimpse into the early participation of African American athletes in organized sports during the antebellum era. Black jockeys, many of whom were enslaved or formerly enslaved, played a dominant role in horse racing—a sport that held widespread popularity in the nineteenth century. Their skill, discipline, and courage on the track laid the foundation for future generations of Black athletes even as racial segregation and exclusion would later bar many from competing at the highest levels.

Jockeys Compete at the Washington Races, 1840
(Source: Library Company of Philadelphia)

Early Black Athletic Institutions

In 1895, Black athletes in Halifax, Nova Scotia, founded the Colored Hockey League of the Maritimes—an all-Black league that predated the National Hockey League (NHL). With teams established across Canada's Maritime provinces, the league highlighted the innovation and athleticism of Black players in a sport rarely associated with African diasporic history.

Negro Leagues and the Integration of Baseball

Facing systemic exclusion from white-controlled sports, African Americans built their own athletic institutions, including baseball leagues known as the *Negro leagues*, which thrived from the post–Civil War period through the 1960s. These leagues not only showcased elite talent but also fostered community pride. A turning point came in

1947 when Jackie Robinson broke Major League Baseball's color barrier, becoming the first Black player in the league and symbolizing the beginning of sports integration.

Olympic Triumphs and Racial Realities

African American athletes have long brought honor to the United States in the Olympic Games, even while confronting discrimination at home. Jesse Owens's four gold medals at the 1936 Berlin Olympics challenged Nazi racial ideology, yet his return to America was met with the same segregation and racism he had defied abroad.

Tommie Smith and John Carlos Raise Clenched Fists During XIX Summer Olympics, 1968

This iconic photograph from the 1968 Mexico City Olympics captures U.S. athletes Tommie Smith and John Carlos standing on the medal podium during the national anthem, each with a black-gloved fist raised in the air. Their silent protest was a powerful act of defiance against racial discrimination and a bold expression of solidarity with the Black Freedom movement. This powerful act of nonviolent protest aligned their athletic success with the broader Black Freedom movement and signaled the growing fusion of sports and political activism.

U.S. athletes Tommie Smith and John Carlos raised clenched fists during the XIX Summer Olympics, 1968 (Source: Angelo Cozzi (Mondadori Publishers), public domain, via Wikimedia Commons)

Sports as a Platform for Racial Equality: Muhammad Ali and the Vietnam War

Across generations, African American athletes have used their platforms to challenge racism and advocate for justice. Their visibility on the world stage has allowed them to speak out against systemic inequality while excelling in their respective sports. In 1967, heavyweight boxing champion Muhammad Ali refused induction into the U.S. Army during the Vietnam War, citing religious beliefs and racial injustice in America. His bold stance against the war and declaration, "The real enemy of my people is right here," transformed him into a global symbol of principled resistance.

Taking a Knee: Modern Protests Against Injustice

In 2016, NFL quarterback Colin Kaepernick began kneeling during the national anthem to protest police brutality and racial injustice. His peaceful protest sparked a national conversation and inspired athletes across sports to engage in similar acts of solidarity, bringing renewed focus to the role of athletes in the fight for civil rights.

Athletes, including Colin Kaepernick, take a knee during a game between the Seattle Seahawks and the San Francisco 49ers, 2017 (Source: Photo by Michael Zagaris/San Francisco 49ers/Getty Images)

From the racetracks of the nineteenth century to the global arenas of today, African American athletes have continually shaped the world of sports while challenging structures of racial inequality. Their achievements have broken records and barriers, and their platforms have served as catalysts for broader social change. Whether founding segregated leagues, dominating Olympic podiums, or leading protests against injustice, Black athletes have exemplified resilience, excellence, and activism. Their legacy affirms that sports are not merely games. They are powerful stages for demanding dignity, equity, and transformation.

More than a Game

From Muhammad Ali to Colin Kaepernick, athletes have used their platforms to protest injustice and spark conversation about race, power, and equity.

You're Practicing: Connecting culture to activism.

Connect This To: Visibility, protest, and performance.

Theme: Public Influence and Resistance

Practice: Explain the Significance or Importance

From segregated leagues to Olympic podiums, African American athletes have shaped American sports and challenged broader social injustices.

(A) Describe two ways African Americans have historically used sports as platforms for resistance or advocacy.

(B) Explain how key individuals or events in sports history contributed to broader cultural or political shifts in the United States.

(C) Analyze the significance of sports as a space for both visibility and contestation of racial inequality.

SAMPLE RESPONSES

(A) In 1947, Jackie Robinson broke Major League Baseball's color barrier, using his athletic success to challenge segregation and open the door for racial integration in professional sports.

At the 1968 Mexico City Olympics, Tommie Smith and John Carlos raised black-gloved fists during the national anthem to protest racial discrimination and show solidarity with the Black Freedom movement.

(B) Muhammad Ali's refusal to be drafted into the Vietnam War in 1967 brought global attention to racial injustice in America and made him a lasting symbol of principled resistance.

Colin Kaepernick's decision to kneel during the national anthem in 2016 sparked a national debate on police brutality and racial inequality, inspiring similar acts of protest by athletes across sports.

(C) Sports have provided African American athletes with a visible platform to challenge systemic racism and advocate for social justice on a national and global stage.

At the same time, sports have been contested spaces where acts of protest have often been met with backlash, revealing ongoing tensions between racial equity and institutional resistance.

Skills Assessed: Explain the significance of cultural and political developments; use sources and evidence; analyze relationships among developments.

Topic 4.20 Science, Medicine, and Technology in Black Communities

Key Terms

- Medical racism—e.g., Tuskegee Syphilis Study
- Henrietta Lacks—HeLa cells and bioethics
- Underrepresentation in STEM fields
- Black medical institutions—e.g., Meharry Medical College, Howard University College of Medicine
- Health disparities—maternal mortality, chronic disease
- Environmental racism—Flint water crisis
- Black innovators in tech and science—George Washington Carver, Mae Jemison
- Community health activism

Behind the stethoscopes, the lab benches, and the inventions that shaped modern America are African American minds whose innovations, breakthroughs, and resilience often went unrecognized—until now. African Americans have made transformative contributions to science, medicine, and technology despite persistent exclusion from institutions and recognition. From pioneering researchers and medical trailblazers to inventors and engineers, Black innovators have expanded the boundaries of knowledge while often operating within segregated environments or without the necessary resources.

Yet as they contributed to the health and progress of the nation, Black communities also faced multiple forms of discrimination in health care, research, and disability rights. This topic explores the achievements of African Americans in these fields while also confronting the structural barriers that have historically limited access and equity in medicine and technology.

After engaging with this topic, scholars will be able to:

- Describe African Americans' contributions to scientific and technological advancements.
- Identify the roles African Americans have played in shaping American medical care and education.
- Explain the intersecting forms of discrimination faced by Black people with disabilities and assess governmental responses to these inequalities.

Scientific Innovation and Agricultural Genius

African American contributions to science and technology have had global impact. Born enslaved, George Washington Carver became one of the most respected agricultural scientists of his time. As a botanist and professor, Carver developed innovative methods to prevent soil depletion and introduced crop rotation techniques that improved farming efficiency. His counsel was sought by President Theodore Roosevelt, and his work helped transform agricultural practices throughout the South and beyond.

Black Women in Space and Aeronautics

African American women have played vital and often overlooked roles in shaping the space and aeronautics programs in the United States. Mathematician Katherine Johnson, whose career at NASA spanned over three decades, was instrumental in calculating flight trajectories, orbital mechanics, and reentry paths that enabled the successful launch, orbit, and return of astronauts during the height of the space race. Her work on missions such as John Glenn's orbital flight helped secure American leadership in space exploration and laid the foundation for future achievements in aerospace engineering.

Mae Jemison Works at Zero Gravity, 1992

This 1992 photograph captures Dr. Mae Jemison—physician, engineer, and astronaut—conducting work aboard the space shuttle *Endeavour* in zero gravity. As the first African American woman to travel in space, Jemison's mission represented a historic breakthrough in both science and representation. Her presence aboard the shuttle symbolized not only a triumph of individual excellence but also the cumulative progress of African Americans in STEM fields. This image exemplifies the critical contributions Black women have made to space exploration and challenges long-standing barriers in science, technology, and engineering.

Mae Jemison poses in Spacelab-Japan, 1992
(Source: "Mae Jemison Poses in Spacelab-Japan (SLJ)." *Archives.gov*, 2025, catalog.archives.gov/id/22725970)

Mary Jackson at Work, 1977

This 1977 photograph captures Mary Jackson, the first Black female engineer at NASA, working in her element during a pivotal era for both civil rights and scientific advancement. Beginning her career as a *human computer* at the National Advisory Committee for Aeronautics (later NASA), Jackson overcame systemic barriers to become an aerospace engineer and advocate for equity in the workplace. Her contributions to aeronautics helped shape the development of space technology, while her later work in equal opportunity efforts at NASA paved the way for more inclusive hiring and promotion practices. This image stands as a powerful testament to both her scientific brilliance and her dedication to institutional change.

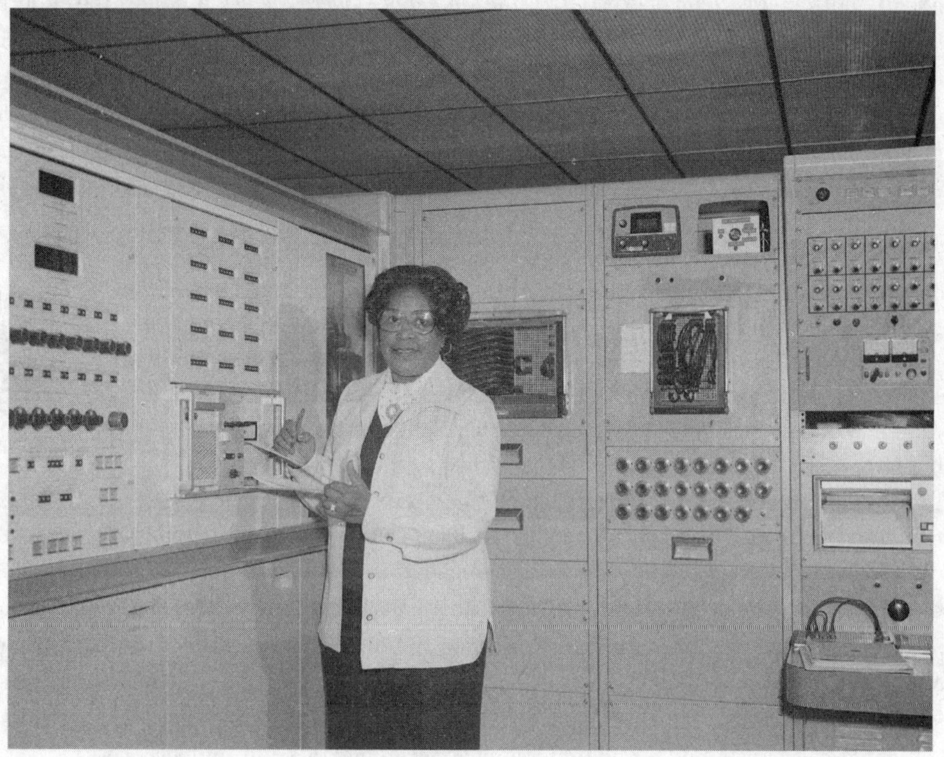

Mathematician Mary Jackson, the first black woman engineer at NASA, 1977
(Source: NASA, public domain, via Wikimedia Commons)

Black Medical Leadership and Community Health

African Americans have long contributed to the advancement of health care in the United States, particularly through community-based medical efforts. Black physicians were instrumental in providing free health services, promoting early diagnosis, and establishing the country's first nonsegregated hospitals in the late 1800s and during the Black hospital movement of the mid-twentieth century. These efforts reflected a commitment to public health and racial equity in medical care.

Training the Next Generation of Black Medical Professionals

In response to exclusion from white-led medical institutions, African Americans established their own schools and professional organizations. Institutions such as Meharry Medical College, Howard University, and Morehouse College played a critical role in educating generations of Black physicians. The founding of the National Medical Association provided a professional network to support Black doctors and advocate for racial equity in medicine, especially as the American Medical Association excluded them for decades.

Pioneering Contributions to Medical Breakthroughs

Black individuals have driven major advances in medical history. Onesimus, an enslaved man in colonial Boston, introduced the practice of variolation—a method that helped reduce the impact of smallpox. In 1891, Dr. Daniel Hale Williams founded Provident Hospital, the first Black-owned hospital in the United States. In 1893, Dr. Williams performed the first successful open-heart surgery. More recently, Dr. Kizzmekia Corbett played a leading role in developing the Moderna COVID-19 vaccine, continuing the legacy of Black medical innovation.

Kadir Nelson, *Henrietta Lacks (HeLa): The Mother of Modern Medicine*, 2017

Kadir Nelson's 2017 portrait, *Henrietta Lacks (HeLa): The Mother of Modern Medicine*, honors the enduring legacy of Henrietta Lacks, an African American woman whose cancer cells transformed modern science. In 1951, without her consent or knowledge, physicians at Johns Hopkins University Hospital extracted cells from Lacks's cervix during treatment for an aggressive form of cancer. These cells—later known as HeLa cells—became the first immortal human cell line and have been used globally in the development of the polio vaccine, COVID-19 vaccines, and treatments for diseases including AIDS and Parkinson's. Nelson's artwork pays tribute to the life behind science, foregrounding the ethical issues surrounding consent and medical exploitation in Black communities.

For a deeper exploration of the life and legacy of Henrietta Lacks, known as the Mother of Modern Medicine, scholars are encouraged to visit the Gilder Lehrman Institute of American History's **AP African American Studies** resource: https://www.gilderlehrman.org/ap-african-american-studies/unit-4/business-culture-20th-21st-centuries/henrietta-lacks-mother-modern-medicine-2017. This source highlights the lasting impact of her contribution to medical research and the ethical issues surrounding her story.

The contributions of African Americans to science, medicine, and technology are foundational to the advancement of modern society. Despite systemic exclusion, segregation, and unethical treatment—particularly in the fields of medical research and disability rights—African Americans have pioneered breakthroughs, established institutions, and redefined innovation in the face of adversity. From agricultural science and aerospace engineering to community health care and disability justice, Black excellence in these fields not only transformed American life but also challenged the very structures that once denied access. Their enduring legacy continues to inspire new generations of scholars, scientists, and health professionals committed to equity and discovery.

Disability, Eugenics, and Systemic Injustice

Throughout the twentieth century, Black people with disabilities faced compounding forms of discrimination. The rise of eugenics fueled stigmatizing beliefs that combined racism and ableism, resulting in widespread institutionalization, social exclusion, and coercive practices such as forced sterilization. These injustices were often justified through pseudoscience and deeply embedded in medical and public policy systems.

Science and Service

Whether creating life-saving vaccines or fighting environmental racism, Black scientists are shaping the future and demanding justice in the process.

You're Practicing: Linking innovation with equity.

Connect This To: Health, ethics, and representation in STEM.

Theme: Equity and Innovation

Civil Rights and the Americans with Disabilities Act

Building on the momentum of the Civil Rights Movement, the Americans with Disabilities Act (ADA) of 1990 marked a significant legal milestone. It prohibited discrimination based on disability in employment, housing, education, and access to public services. Although not a perfect solution, the ADA represented a step forward in dismantling some of the structural inequities experienced by people with disabilities—including Black Americans who have long been marginalized at the intersection of race and disability.

Practice: Explain the Effects of Historical Developments

African American communities have long navigated unequal access to science, medicine, and technological advancements while also contributing meaningfully to these fields.

(A) Identify one historical barrier to equitable health care or scientific opportunity for African Americans.

(B) Explain how Black communities have responded to or resisted these inequities through grassroots innovation, advocacy, or institutional creation.

(C) Analyze the broader impact of African American contributions to medicine, science, or technology on U.S. society.

SAMPLE RESPONSES

(A) The Tuskegee Syphilis Study, in which Black men were denied treatment without their consent, exemplified systemic medical racism that eroded trust in public health systems.

The exclusion of African Americans from white-led medical schools and professional organizations during segregation severely limited access to medical training and scientific careers.

(B) African Americans established their own medical institutions, such as Meharry Medical College and Howard University College of Medicine, to train Black physicians and expand access to quality care in their communities.

Black scientists and medical pioneers, such as Dr. Daniel Hale Williams, created hospitals like Provident Hospital to provide inclusive medical treatment and advance professional opportunities for Black health care providers.

(C) Scientific innovators such as George Washington Carver revolutionized agricultural practices through crop rotation and soil preservation, influencing farming worldwide.

Breakthroughs by African American scientists, including Dr. Kizzmekia Corbett's work on the Moderna COVID-19 vaccine, have advanced global health and demonstrated the essential role of Black expertise in medical innovation.

Skills Assessed: Explain the effects of historical developments; use sources and evidence; analyze relationships among developments.

Topic 4.21 Black Studies, Black Futures, and Afrofuturism

Key Terms

- Black Studies departments—founded after student protests in late 1960s
- Afrofuturism—blending African diaspora culture with technology and imagination
- Octavia Butler, Sun Ra, Janelle Monáe, *Black Panther* (film)
- Speculative fiction and liberation
- Diasporic time and identity
- Reparative imagination
- Interdisciplinarity in Black Studies
- Visioning Black futures beyond trauma

What happens when Black history, culture, and imagination are placed at the center of scholarly inquiry and speculative creation? The result is a powerful vision of the past, present, and future shaped by African American intellectual traditions and radical possibilities. Born out of student-led protests and community demands for educational justice, African American Studies emerged in the late 1960s as a transformative academic discipline. Since then, it has evolved into an interdisciplinary field that draws from history, literature, sociology, political science, cultural studies, and the arts to explore the full scope of Black experiences.

At the same time, Afrofuturism has grown as a cultural and intellectual movement that blends science fiction, African cosmologies, technology, and Black liberation to imagine new futures rooted in Black identity. Together, Black Studies and Afrofuturism expand the boundaries of what it means to study, dream, and live Blackness—academically, artistically, and futuristically.

After engaging with this topic, scholars will be able to:

- Explain how African American Studies contributes to interdisciplinary knowledge and critical inquiry.
- Describe how Afrofuturism reimagines Black lives in futuristic, technological, and speculative contexts.
- Recognize how both fields advance Black intellectual and creative traditions while challenging dominant historical narratives.

African American Studies and Interdisciplinary Innovation

African American Studies serves as a central platform for examining the global impact of Black expression and confronting the persistence of racial inequities. As an academic discipline, it moves beyond the limitations of traditional fields by centering Black experiences—past and present—in history, literature, politics, sociology, and cultural studies. The field continues to evolve, integrating new methodologies and theoretical frameworks to better understand the complexity of Black life across time and space.

Afrofuturism and the Reimagining of Black Realities

Afrofuturism is an artistic and intellectual movement that reimagines Black pasts and envisions liberated futures shaped by Afrocentric perspectives, technology, and speculative thinking. It challenges dominant narratives by exploring worlds where Black people thrive free from historical oppression, blending science fiction with cultural memory and innovation. Afrofuturism comes alive in literature, visual art, music, architecture, and fashion, creating a multidimensional space to explore what freedom, identity, and power might look like in imagined Black futures.

Early Visions of Afrofuturism

Although the term *Afrofuturism* was coined in the late twentieth century, its spirit can be traced back to early Black intellectuals and artists. The poetry of Phillis Wheatley envisioned future mobility and liberation in the aftermath of abolition, offering speculative hope grounded in her lived reality. Likewise, Benjamin Banneker—a mathematician and astronomer—charted the cosmos in his *Almanac and Ephemeris*, using science and imagination to project a vision of Black excellence and autonomy in a nation still grappling with slavery.

Afrofuturism from the 1970s to the Present

Afrofuturism took on its modern shape in the 1970s with the avant-garde music of Sun Ra, who combined cosmic themes, jazz, and Black liberation theology to imagine alternate realities. This tradition expanded through the decades in works like *Black Panther*, which captured global attention by visualizing a technologically advanced African nation untouched by colonialism. From sound to cinema, Afrofuturist works have become essential tools for exploring Black identity, resistance, and possibility in the twenty-first century and beyond.

Let's Talk About Black Panther *and Afrofuturism* (Video)

This concise video, *Let's Talk About* Black Panther *and Afrofuturism*, offers an accessible overview of Afrofuturism through the lens of Marvel's *Black Panther*. It explores how the film reimagines African identity and culture by blending advanced technology with traditional African aesthetics, presenting a vision of a future unburdened by colonial history. The video discusses the significance of Wakanda as a symbol of Black excellence and self-determination, highlighting how Afrofuturism serves as a medium for envisioning empowered Black futures.

Scholars interested in *Let's Talk* About Black Panther *and Afrofuturism* are encouraged to watch the full video on YouTube: https://www.youtube.com/watch?v=QqtD2HbDfew.

Photograph of Nichelle Nichols as Uhura in *Star Trek*

This iconic photograph of Nichelle Nichols as Lieutenant Uhura in the 1968 *Star Trek* episode "A Piece of the Action" captures more than a fictional character. It reflects a transformative moment in American media and representation. As one of the first Black women featured in a major television role that portrayed dignity, intelligence, and authority, Nichols broke racial barriers in science fiction. Although she considered resigning due to racism in the entertainment industry, Dr. Martin Luther King Jr., a devoted fan of the show, convinced her to stay, emphasizing the cultural impact of her presence on screen. Beyond acting, Nichols went on to play a critical role in diversifying the U.S. space program by recruiting African American, Asian American, and women astronaut candidates. Her portrayal inspired generations, including Dr. Mae Jemison, who later became the first African American woman in space.

Nichelle Nichols as Uhura in the *Star Trek* episode "A Piece of the Action," 1968
(Source: Photo by CBS via Getty Images)

Walter Mosley, "Culture Zone; Black to the Future"

In his 1998 essay "Culture Zone; Black to the Future," published in *The New York Times Magazine* on November 1, 1988, acclaimed author Walter Mosley explores the intersection of African American identity and speculative fiction. Mosley delves into how science fiction and Afrofuturism provide a framework for reimagining Black experiences, allowing for narratives that transcend historical oppression and envision empowered futures. He emphasizes the importance of Black voices in shaping these genres, arguing that speculative storytelling can serve as a tool for cultural critique and transformation.

Scholars interested in the role of Afrofuturism in literature and cultural studies can access the full article through the Gilder Lehrman Institute: https://www.gilderlehrman.org/ap-african-american-studies/unit-4/business-culture-20th-21st-centuries#par-17765.

Poster for the Film *Space Is the Place*

This poster for the film *Space Is the Place* (circa 1974) reflects the visionary work of Sun Ra, a pioneering musician and philosopher whose contributions helped shape the foundations of Afrofuturism. Blending science fiction, Black liberation theology, and avant-garde jazz, the film presents a cosmic journey in which Sun Ra seeks to relocate African Americans to a utopian planet free from racism and oppression. The poster visually captures the film's central themes—space as refuge, music as liberation, and imagination as a revolutionary act. As an Afrofuturist artifact, the poster invites viewers to consider how speculative narratives and aesthetics can be used to critique systemic injustice and envision radical Black futures.

Poster for the film *Space Is the Place*, circa 1974
(Source: Collection of the Smithsonian National Museum of African American History and Culture)

African American Studies continues to expand the boundaries of academic inquiry by centering Black voices, histories, and cultural contributions that have often been excluded from traditional disciplines. At the same time, Afrofuturism challenges the limitations of the present by reimagining Black futures through the lenses of science, technology, and creativity. Together, these frameworks empower scholars and artists to draw from the past while envisioning bold new possibilities for liberation, identity, and global Black expression.

Imagining a Liberated Future

Afrofuturism asks: What does a world without oppression look like? Through books, music, and art, Black creators envision freedom that hasn't yet arrived but could.

You're Practicing: Using imagination as a tool for justice.

Connect This To: Liberation, futurism, and creativity.

Theme: Vision and Transformation

Practice: Explain the Significance or Importance

Black Studies and Afrofuturism offer tools for reclaiming historical narratives and imagining liberated futures for Black communities.

(A) Explain how the development of Black Studies as an academic discipline has transformed approaches to history and cultural knowledge.

(B) Describe the role of Afrofuturism in envisioning alternative futures for Black people through literature, art, or media.

(C) Analyze why the rise of Afrofuturist themes has particular significance in the context of both historical and ongoing struggles for racial justice.

SAMPLE RESPONSES

(A) Black Studies, founded in the late 1960s through student protests and community advocacy, transformed historical inquiry by centering Black voices, histories, and cultural traditions that were long excluded from mainstream academia.

As an interdisciplinary field, Black Studies integrates history, literature, sociology, political science, and cultural studies to produce holistic understandings of Black life, identity, and resistance across time and space.

(B) Afrofuturism blends African diasporic culture, science fiction, technology, and speculative imagination to create visions of liberated Black futures unbound by historical oppression.

Works such as Sun Ra's *Space Is the Place*, Octavia Butler's speculative novels, and Marvel's *Black Panther* present empowered narratives that merge cultural heritage with futuristic innovation.

(C) Afrofuturism reclaims the right for Black people to imagine themselves as central to global progress, countering centuries of exclusion from dominant visions of the future.

By envisioning worlds where systemic racism is dismantled, Afrofuturist narratives provide both hope and strategic inspiration for ongoing movements seeking racial equity and liberation.

Skills Assessed: Explain the significance of intellectual and cultural developments; use sources and evidence; analyze relationships among developments.

KEY TAKEAWAYS

1. **Political Representation and Economic Growth in the Post–Civil Rights Era**
   - Following the Voting Rights Act of 1965, Black political representation expanded significantly at all levels of government.
   - Leaders like Shirley Chisholm, Harold Washington, and members of the Congressional Black Caucus advanced racial equity and civic engagement.
   - Despite gains, economic disparities remained pronounced due to systemic obstacles like redlining, wage gaps, and disinvestment.
2. **Expanding Cultural Power Across Media and Performance**
   - Black artists, musicians, filmmakers, and writers have shaped U.S. and global culture, challenging stereotypes and offering transformative narratives.
   - From hip-hop and jazz to Hollywood cinema and Black theater, cultural production has been a powerful tool of identity, education, and resistance.
3. **Black Excellence in Science, Medicine, and Sports**
   - African Americans have excelled in fields historically closed to them—breaking barriers in medicine, technology, athletics, and innovation.
   - Figures like Dr. Kizzmekia Corbett (COVID-19 vaccine research) and Serena Williams symbolize excellence and global impact.
4. **Faith, Diversity, and Community Evolution**
   - Black communities encompass a wide array of religious identities—including Christianity, Islam, African spiritualities, and secular traditions.
   - This diversity reflects a broader evolution of Black identity in the twenty-first century, shaped by migration, generational change, and global connection.
5. **Afrofuturism and the Vision of Black Futures**
   - Afrofuturism imagines liberated futures through speculative fiction, visual art, and cultural theory.
   - Artists like Sun Ra, Janelle Monáe, and authors like Octavia Butler blend science fiction with African diasporic themes to reclaim narrative space and envision justice-forward societies.
6. **The Enduring Relevance of Black Studies**
   - Black Studies continues to grow as a scholarly field and community force, connecting historical inquiry with contemporary activism and imaginative possibility.
   - It serves as a foundation for understanding both the long arc of African American history and the radical potential of Black futures.

Practice Multiple-Choice Questions

DIRECTIONS: Pick the letter that best answers the following questions.

Questions 1 through 3 refer to the following.

Photograph of *Soul Train*, circa 1970

1. The *Soul Train* photograph most directly reflects which of the following cultural developments in the 1970s?

    (A) The emergence of hip-hop as a form of protest and social commentary
    (B) The commercialization and celebration of Black cultural expression through mass media
    (C) The integration of African American performers into mainstream television programming for the first time
    (D) The decline of rhythm and blues as a central form of Black musical expression

2. Which of the following best explains the broader historical context of *Soul Train*'s popularity in the 1970s?

    (A) The rise of African American political power following the Civil Rights Act of 1964
    (B) A renewed focus on Black nationalism and self-determination movements
    (C) The increasing visibility and influence of Black culture in mainstream American media
    (D) The immediate aftermath of the Watts Rebellion and urban unrest of the 1960s

3. Which of the following best describes how *Soul Train* contributed to the cultural empowerment of African Americans?

    (A) By providing a platform that combined entertainment with direct political activism
    (B) By promoting the idea of multicultural harmony and interracial unity
    (C) By showcasing African American performers and styles as well as affirming cultural pride and identity
    (D) By introducing African American cultural traditions to international audiences

Questions 4 through 6 refer to the following.

Mae Jemison Works in Zero Gravity, 1992

4. Mae Jemison's work in zero gravity during her space mission in 1992 most directly reflects which of the following developments?

    (A) The expansion of opportunities for women and minorities in STEM fields
    (B) The initial stages of American space exploration
    (C) The privatization of space travel and the emergence of commercial space enterprises
    (D) The Cold War space race between the United States and the Soviet Union

5. Which broader historical trend is reflected by Mae Jemison's career in the early 1990s?

    (A) The decline of government support for science and space exploration
    (B) The ongoing exclusion of minority women from leadership positions in science and technology
    (C) The gradual dismantling of racial and gender barriers in professional fields
    (D) The shift of NASA's focus from human spaceflight to robotic missions

6. Mae Jemison's contributions to the space program can best be seen as part of which broader theme in African American history?

    (A) The rise of Black nationalism in the late twentieth century
    (B) African American leadership in grassroots civil rights organizing
    (C) The integration of African Americans into previously exclusionary institutions
    (D) The push for reparations for historical injustices

Answer Explanations

1. **(B)** *Soul Train* commercialized and celebrated Black cultural expression through national television, making it a platform for showcasing African American music, dance, and style. Choice (A) is incorrect because hip-hop began to emerge in the late 1970s but was not the focus of *Soul Train*, which primarily showcased R&B, soul, and funk music. Choice (C) is incorrect because, although *Soul Train* was significant for Black representation, African American performers had appeared on mainstream television before, including on variety shows like *The Ed Sullivan Show*. Choice (D) is incorrect because rhythm and blues did not decline in the 1970s. Rather, it was thriving, especially through shows like *Soul Train*.

2. **(C)** The 1970s saw a growing mainstream appreciation for Black culture, with *Soul Train* serving as a key platform showcasing this visibility and influence. Choice (A) is incorrect because, although political gains were important, *Soul Train*'s popularity was more directly tied to cultural rather than political shifts. Choice (B) is incorrect because, although the Black Power movement promoted self-determination, *Soul Train* focused on entertainment and cultural pride, not explicitly nationalist ideology. Choice (D) is incorrect because, although the Watts Rebellion and urban unrest preceded *Soul Train*, the show's success was not a direct reaction to those events.

3. **(C)** *Soul Train* affirmed Black cultural pride by highlighting African American music, fashion, and dance. It provided positive representation in mass media. Choice (A) is incorrect because *Soul Train* focused primarily on entertainment and did not incorporate explicit political activism into its format. Choice (B) is incorrect because, although *Soul Train* was accessible to a broad audience, its focus was on celebrating Black culture rather than promoting multicultural or interracial unity. Choice (D) is incorrect because *Soul Train* targeted primarily domestic audiences in the United States, although its cultural influence did extend internationally over time.

4. **(A)** Mae Jemison's 1992 mission aboard the Space Shuttle Endeavour represents the increasing inclusion of women and African Americans in science and technology careers. Choice (B) is incorrect because the initial stages of American space exploration occurred decades earlier, beginning in the late 1950s and 1960s. Choice (C) is incorrect because privatization and commercial space enterprises emerged later; Jemison's mission was conducted by NASA. Choice (D) is incorrect because the Cold War space race was most prominent in the 1960s and was not directly related to Jemison's 1992 mission.

5. **(C)** Mae Jemison's career illustrates progress in overcoming racial and gender barriers, marking an important moment in American professional history. Choice (A) is incorrect because, although budgetary shifts occurred, NASA's missions continued. Additionally, Jemison's inclusion reflected expansion, not decline. Choice (B) is incorrect because Jemison's role actually represents the breaking of barriers, not ongoing exclusion. Choice (D) is incorrect because, although robotic missions increased, human spaceflight was still a significant part of NASA's work in the early 1990s.

6. **(C)** Mae Jemison's achievements illustrate the broader trend of African Americans breaking barriers in elite and professional spaces. Choice (A) is incorrect because Black nationalism emphasizes political and cultural movements rather than integration into institutions like NASA. Choice (B) is incorrect because Jemison's contributions were in science and technology, not in grassroots civil rights organizing. Choice (D) is incorrect because, although reparations debates existed, they were not directly connected to Jemison's achievements in space exploration.

PART 6
Practice Tests

ANSWER SHEET
Practice Test 1

Section 1: Multiple-Choice

1. Ⓐ Ⓑ Ⓒ Ⓓ	16. Ⓐ Ⓑ Ⓒ Ⓓ	31. Ⓐ Ⓑ Ⓒ Ⓓ	46. Ⓐ Ⓑ Ⓒ Ⓓ
2. Ⓐ Ⓑ Ⓒ Ⓓ	17. Ⓐ Ⓑ Ⓒ Ⓓ	32. Ⓐ Ⓑ Ⓒ Ⓓ	47. Ⓐ Ⓑ Ⓒ Ⓓ
3. Ⓐ Ⓑ Ⓒ Ⓓ	18. Ⓐ Ⓑ Ⓒ Ⓓ	33. Ⓐ Ⓑ Ⓒ Ⓓ	48. Ⓐ Ⓑ Ⓒ Ⓓ
4. Ⓐ Ⓑ Ⓒ Ⓓ	19. Ⓐ Ⓑ Ⓒ Ⓓ	34. Ⓐ Ⓑ Ⓒ Ⓓ	49. Ⓐ Ⓑ Ⓒ Ⓓ
5. Ⓐ Ⓑ Ⓒ Ⓓ	20. Ⓐ Ⓑ Ⓒ Ⓓ	35. Ⓐ Ⓑ Ⓒ Ⓓ	50. Ⓐ Ⓑ Ⓒ Ⓓ
6. Ⓐ Ⓑ Ⓒ Ⓓ	21. Ⓐ Ⓑ Ⓒ Ⓓ	36. Ⓐ Ⓑ Ⓒ Ⓓ	51. Ⓐ Ⓑ Ⓒ Ⓓ
7. Ⓐ Ⓑ Ⓒ Ⓓ	22. Ⓐ Ⓑ Ⓒ Ⓓ	37. Ⓐ Ⓑ Ⓒ Ⓓ	52. Ⓐ Ⓑ Ⓒ Ⓓ
8. Ⓐ Ⓑ Ⓒ Ⓓ	23. Ⓐ Ⓑ Ⓒ Ⓓ	38. Ⓐ Ⓑ Ⓒ Ⓓ	53. Ⓐ Ⓑ Ⓒ Ⓓ
9. Ⓐ Ⓑ Ⓒ Ⓓ	24. Ⓐ Ⓑ Ⓒ Ⓓ	39. Ⓐ Ⓑ Ⓒ Ⓓ	54. Ⓐ Ⓑ Ⓒ Ⓓ
10. Ⓐ Ⓑ Ⓒ Ⓓ	25. Ⓐ Ⓑ Ⓒ Ⓓ	40. Ⓐ Ⓑ Ⓒ Ⓓ	55. Ⓐ Ⓑ Ⓒ Ⓓ
11. Ⓐ Ⓑ Ⓒ Ⓓ	26. Ⓐ Ⓑ Ⓒ Ⓓ	41. Ⓐ Ⓑ Ⓒ Ⓓ	56. Ⓐ Ⓑ Ⓒ Ⓓ
12. Ⓐ Ⓑ Ⓒ Ⓓ	27. Ⓐ Ⓑ Ⓒ Ⓓ	42. Ⓐ Ⓑ Ⓒ Ⓓ	57. Ⓐ Ⓑ Ⓒ Ⓓ
13. Ⓐ Ⓑ Ⓒ Ⓓ	28. Ⓐ Ⓑ Ⓒ Ⓓ	43. Ⓐ Ⓑ Ⓒ Ⓓ	58. Ⓐ Ⓑ Ⓒ Ⓓ
14. Ⓐ Ⓑ Ⓒ Ⓓ	29. Ⓐ Ⓑ Ⓒ Ⓓ	44. Ⓐ Ⓑ Ⓒ Ⓓ	59. Ⓐ Ⓑ Ⓒ Ⓓ
15. Ⓐ Ⓑ Ⓒ Ⓓ	30. Ⓐ Ⓑ Ⓒ Ⓓ	45. Ⓐ Ⓑ Ⓒ Ⓓ	60. Ⓐ Ⓑ Ⓒ Ⓓ

Practice Test 1

Section I: Multiple-Choice

TIME: 1 HOUR AND 10 MINUTES—60 QUESTIONS

DIRECTIONS: Each question or incomplete statement is followed by four answer choices. Select the one choice that best answers the question or completes the statement.

Questions 1 through 4 refer to the following.

A Black Student Union Leader in Front of a Crowd of Demonstrators at San Francisco State College in December 1968

1. What is the most likely claim being made by the students depicted in the photo?

    (A) Black students were demanding increased funding for athletics.

    (B) The curriculum at San Francisco State adequately represented Black experiences.

    (C) There was a need for the establishment of African American Studies programs in higher education.

    (D) Integration into predominantly white institutions had eliminated educational inequity.

2. Which of the following developments best provides historical context for the protest seen in the image?

    (A) The rise of African independence movements following World War II

    (B) Student-led activism influenced by the Civil Rights and Black Power movements

    (C) Reconstruction-era Black Codes limiting Black education

    (D) The Harlem Renaissance's literary and artistic contributions

3. What is the most reasonable interpretation of the source's purpose?

    (A) To portray the benefits of racial integration in higher education

    (B) To call for greater student involvement in campus governance

    (C) To highlight student-led efforts to institutionalize African American knowledge and history

    (D) To document the end of educational discrimination in California

4. What broader historical development is best exemplified by the student protest shown in the image?

   (A) The end of the Cold War and the expansion of global democracy
   (B) The growing demand for educational inclusion and cultural representation in U.S. institutions
   (C) The return of African American veterans from World War II demanding civil rights
   (D) The integration of historically Black colleges and universities into predominantly white institutions

Questions 5 through 8 refer to the following map.

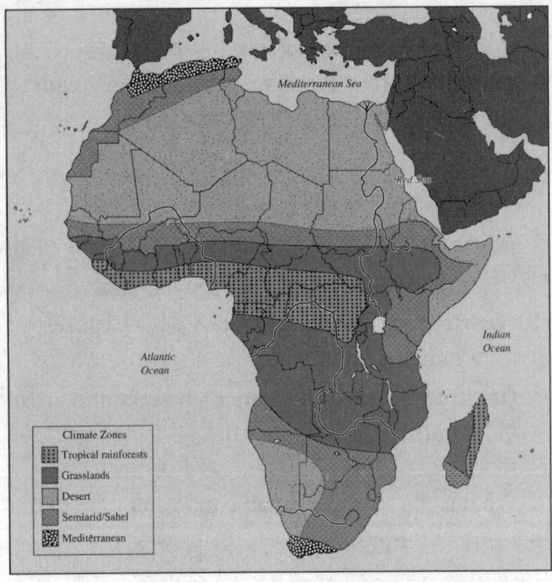

Map Showing the Major Climate Regions of Africa

5. According to the map, which of the following best explains why population centers emerged in the Sahel and savannah regions?

   (A) The Sahel and savannah had harsh desert conditions that prevented settlement.
   (B) These areas were remote and far from any trade routes or water sources.
   (C) The presence of fertile land and proximity to trade routes encouraged agricultural development and livestock trade.
   (D) The Mediterranean zone was more conducive to agriculture, so the Sahel and savannah remained uninhabited.

6. Based on the patterns shown in the map, what conclusion can be drawn about Africa's trade networks in early history?

   (A) Geographic diversity and proximity to water sources enabled extensive trade among climate zones.
   (B) All African trade occurred along the Atlantic coast because of colonization.
   (C) Deserts blocked trade routes entirely, isolating the interior of Africa.
   (D) Trade was mostly local and unconnected to external regions or empires.

7. What can be inferred from the map about the significance of Africa's rivers to the development of civilizations?

   (A) The rivers created barriers between societies and limited exchange.
   (B) The rivers were used primarily for military conquest rather than commerce.
   (C) The rivers acted as inland highways, connecting regions and supporting trade and population growth.
   (D) Rivers were important only in the tropical rainforest zones and were irrelevant elsewhere.

8. Which climate zone likely supported gold and yam production, based on the map and essential knowledge?

   (A) Desert
   (B) Savannah grasslands
   (C) Semiarid zone
   (D) Tropical rainforest

Questions 9 through 12 refer to the following.

Excerpt of Letter from Nzinga Mbemba to Portuguese King João III

"And we cannot reckon how great the damage is, since the mentioned merchants are taking every day our natives, sons of the land and the sons of our noblemen and vassals and our relatives, because the thieves and men of bad conscience grab them wishing to have the things and wares of this Kingdom which they are ambitious of, they grab them and get them to be sold; and so great, Sir, is the corruption and licentiousness that our country is being completely depopulated, and Your Highness should not agree with this nor accept it as in your service. And to avoid it we need from those Kingdoms no more than some priests and a few people to reach in schools, and no other goods except wine and flour for the holy sacrament. That is why we beg of Your Highness to help and assist us in this matter, commanding your factors that they should nor send here either merchants or wares, because it is our will that in these Kingdoms there should not be any trade of slaves nor outlet for them."

Source: Excerpt of Letter from Nzinga Mbemba to Portuguese King João III | World History Commons, 202.

9. What concern is most clearly expressed by King Nzinga Mbemba in the letter?

(A) The Portuguese are refusing to bring missionaries to the Kongo.
(B) The slave trade is destabilizing Kongo society and depleting its population.
(C) Kongo has banned Christianity and its associated rituals.
(D) The Portuguese are enriching Kongo's economy through fair trade.

10. Which of the following best explains the relationship between Kongo's adoption of Christianity and its economic challenges, based on the excerpt?

(A) Christianity made slavery more widespread and accepted across all of Africa.
(B) Christianity undermined the authority of the Kongo monarchy and replaced it with European missionaries.
(C) The Kingdom of Kongo accepted Christianity but opposed the economic exploitation tied to the transatlantic slave trade.
(D) Christian beliefs led to the rejection of all forms of foreign trade.

11. Which broader historical pattern is illustrated by the interaction described in the letter?

(A) African resistance to European cultural influences
(B) Conflict between Islamic and Christian rulers in Africa
(C) The decline of Indigenous African belief systems due to conquest
(D) African leaders attempting to manage European trade relationships to preserve sovereignty

12. What conclusion can be drawn about the long-term cultural impact of the Kingdom of Kongo's Christian identity?

(A) Christian beliefs were abandoned once Portuguese trade relations ended.
(B) Christianity was violently imposed on the population through military conquest.
(C) Kongo's Christian heritage influenced religious practices among enslaved Africans in the Americas.
(D) Christian communities in the Kongo had no lasting influence beyond the 1500s.

Questions 13 through 16 refer to the following two sources.

Source 1: Map of Africa's Kingdoms and Empires

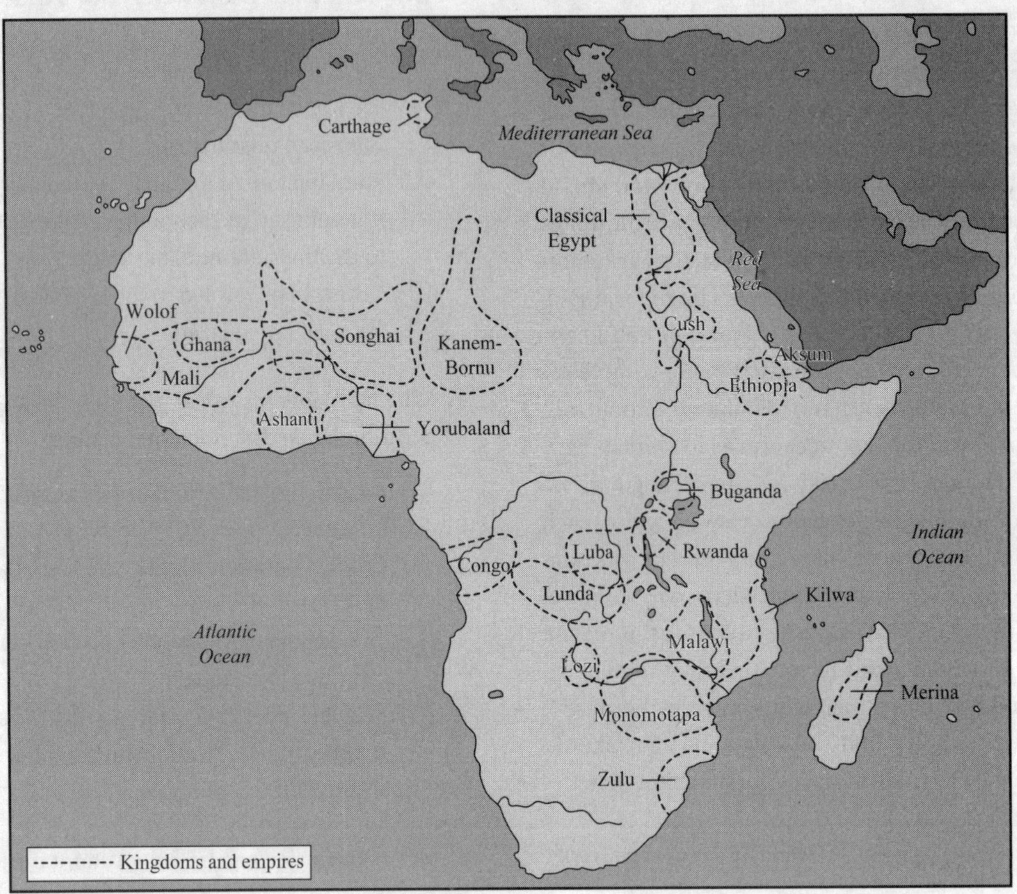

Source 2: *Catalan Atlas* by Abraham Cresques, 1375

13. Which claim is best supported by both the map and the *Catalan Atlas*?
    (A) Mali's influence was primarily limited to its local region.
    (B) Gold was a central factor in the global visibility and power of West African empires.
    (C) The empire of Ghana was the only African kingdom known outside of Africa.
    (D) The *Catalan Atlas* downplays Mali's role in trade and power in medieval times.

14. What does the *Catalan Atlas* suggest about European perceptions of the Mali Empire?
    (A) Mali was viewed as a land of immense wealth and powerful leadership.
    (B) Europeans were unaware of Mali's existence during the medieval period.
    (C) Mali's leaders were considered poor but spiritually wise.
    (D) Europeans considered Mali culturally inferior despite its riches.

15. Which claim best explains the Mali Empire's ability to establish regional and global influence?
    (A) Its location in the desert allowed for easy isolation and protection from outsiders.
    (B) Its access to gold and trade networks enabled political expansion and international prestige.
    (C) Its leaders prioritized military conquest over trade or religion.
    (D) Its agricultural base was stronger than that of any neighboring society.

16. What connection can be drawn between the Sudanic empires and early generations of African Americans?
    (A) The Sudanic empires had no lasting cultural influence on the Atlantic world.
    (B) Most African Americans descended from desert nomadic communities.
    (C) The legacy of Islamic scholarship and West African wealth influenced African cultural memory in the Americas.
    (D) The Sudanic empires were rejected by enslaved people as irrelevant to their experience.

Questions 17 through 20 refer to the following.

Source 1: Photographs of Great Zimbabwe's Walls and Stone Enclosures, Twelfth to Fifteenth Centuries

Source 2: Map Showing Indian Ocean Trade Routes from the Swahili Coast

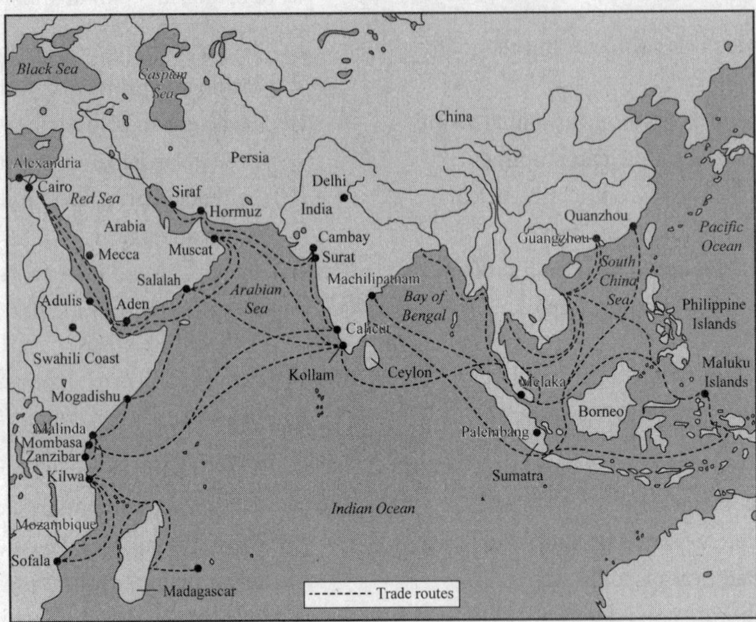

17. Which claim is best supported by the stone architecture seen in the photographs of Great Zimbabwe?

    (A) The structures were decorative but held no cultural or economic significance.
    (B) The massive stone enclosures reflected the region's military, administrative, and religious strength.
    (C) Great Zimbabwe was modeled entirely on Islamic design and architecture.
    (D) The Shona had little knowledge of agriculture or long-distance trade.

18. Which conclusion is best supported by the map of Indian Ocean trade routes?

    (A) The Swahili Coast was isolated from inland African communities.
    (B) The Swahili city-states traded primarily with the Atlantic world.
    (C) East African trade networks connected African societies to Arab, Indian, and Chinese merchants.
    (D) The trade routes shown were used only during the era of European colonization.

19. Which claim best explains how Great Zimbabwe and the Swahili Coast were connected?

    (A) Both regions spoke identical languages and shared the same religion.
    (B) Both were only agricultural communities with little exposure to outside cultures.
    (C) Both benefited from long-distance trade routes that linked African resources to foreign markets.
    (D) Neither region had contact with Indian Ocean traders until after the eighteenth century.

20. What broader conclusion can be drawn about early African societies based on both sources?

    (A) Early African societies were culturally isolated and lacked urban infrastructure.
    (B) African kingdoms like Zimbabwe and Swahili city-states built complex economies through internal trade only.
    (C) African societies developed advanced architecture, religion, and trade networks well before the arrival of Europeans.
    (D) African political structures were weak and dependent on foreign leadership.

Questions 21 through 24 refer to the following.

Source 1: Excerpt of Letter from Nzinga Mbemba to Portuguese King João III

"And we cannot reckon how great the damage is, since the mentioned merchants are taking every day our natives, sons of the land and the sons of our noblemen and vassals and our relatives, because the thieves and men of bad conscience grab them wishing to have the things and wares of this Kingdom which they are ambitious of, they grab them and get them to be sold; and so great, Sir, is the corruption and licentiousness that our country is being completely depopulated, and Your Highness should not agree with this nor accept it as in your service. And to avoid it we need from those Kingdoms no more than some priests and a few people to reach in schools, and no other goods except wine and flour for the holy sacrament. That is why we beg of Your Highness to help and assist us in this matter, commanding your factors that they should nor send here either merchants or wares, because it is our will that in these Kingdoms there should not be any trade of slaves nor outlet for them."

Source: Letter from Nzinga Mbemba to Portuguese King João III | World History Commons, 2024.

Source 2: Image of *Triple Crucifix*, Sixteenth to Nineteenth Centuries

21. Which conclusion is best supported by both the letter and the crucifix?
    (A) Kongo resisted all foreign religious influence.
    (B) Christianity in Kongo was imposed through conquest and forced conversion.
    (C) Kongo's Christian identity blended Catholic traditions with local aesthetics and beliefs.
    (D) The *Triple Crucifix* was created in Portugal and had no African cultural elements.

22. What pattern is revealed by Nzinga Mbemba's letter regarding Kongo's relationship with Portugal?
    (A) Political alliances were based solely on religious ideals, not trade.
    (B) Portuguese traders respected all local laws established by the Kongo monarchy.
    (C) Economic dependency on European goods weakened the monarchy's authority over the slave trade.
    (D) The Portuguese strictly limited the number of enslaved people exported from the Kongo.

23. How does the crucifix symbolize broader cultural continuities across the Atlantic?
    (A) It represents how Christian iconography disappeared during enslavement.
    (B) It reveals the survival of African Catholic traditions among early African American communities.
    (C) It was rejected by enslaved people due to its European origins.
    (D) It had no symbolic meaning and served only as decoration.

24. What comparison can be made between the letter and the crucifix?
    (A) Both reflect the fusion of political resistance and architectural engineering.
    (B) Both sources highlight the rejection of Christianity by African nobility.
    (C) Both show how Kongo leaders navigated foreign influence while shaping a distinct African Christian identity.
    (D) Both reveal how European missionaries controlled all aspects of the Kongo's religious life.

Questions 25 through 28 refer to the following.

Source 1: Illustration of Queen Njinga, Seventeenth Century

Source 2: Queen Mother Pendant Mask: *Iyoba*

25. What is the most likely purpose of the ivory pendant mask depicting Queen Idia?
    (A) To intimidate rival European powers through symbolism
    (B) To portray her as a spiritual and political figure central to royal power
    (C) To mock African matriarchs and deny their political legitimacy
    (D) To serve as a decorative trade item for the Portuguese

26. What is the best interpretation of Queen Njinga's image within its historical context?
    (A) It was intended to diminish her authority by comparing her to male rulers.
    (B) It emphasizes her role as a submissive subject of Portuguese colonial rule.
    (C) It portrays her as a powerful and strategic leader resisting European influence.
    (D) It shows her as a religious leader with no political involvement.

27. Which claim best compares the leaderships of Queen Idia and Queen Njinga?
    (A) Both women inherited their positions and ruled during times of peace.
    (B) Both used political wisdom and either spiritual or military strategies to lead and defend their people.
    (C) Neither engaged in warfare or strategic diplomacy.
    (D) Both relied entirely on European alliances to maintain their rule.

28. What can be inferred about the audience of both sources?
    (A) The sources were produced solely for Portuguese merchants.
    (B) They were designed to elevate the legacies of African queens among African and diasporic audiences.
    (C) The images were primarily meant to criticize female authority.
    (D) Both sources were created as religious icons used in Catholic ceremonies.

Questions 29 through 32 refer to the following.

Source 1: The Opening of Juan Garrido's Probanza (Petitionary Proof of Merit) of September 27, 1538

"I, Juan Garrido, black in color, resident of this city [Mexico], appear before Your Mercy and state that I am in need of providing evidence to the perpetuity of the king [a perpetuidad rey], a report on how I served Your Majesty in the conquest and pacification of this New Spain, from the time when the Marqués del Valle [Cortés] entered it; and in his company I was present at all the invasions and conquests and pacifications which were carried out, always with the said Marqués, all of which I did at my own expense without being given either salary or allotment of natives [repartimiento de indios] or anything else. As I am married and a resident of this city, where I have always lived; and also as I went with the Marqués del Valle to discover the islands which are in that part of the southern sea [the Pacific] where there was much hunger and privation; and also as I went to discover and pacify the islands of San Juan de Buriquén de Puerto Rico; and also as I went on the pacification and conquest of the island of Cuba with the adelantado Diego Velázquez; in all these ways for thirty years have I served and continue to serve Your Majesty—for these reasons stated above do I petition Your Mercy. And also because I was the first to have the inspiration to sow wheat here in New Spain and to see if it took; I did this and experimented at my own expense."

Source: The opening of Juan Garrido's probanza (petitionary proof of merit) of September 27, 1538 (Archivo General de Indias, Seville, México 204), f.1. Transcription in Ricardo Alegría, Juan Garrido, el conquistador negro en las Antillas, Florida, México y California, 1503–1540 (Centro de Estudios Avanzados de Puerto Rico y el Caribe, 1990). Translated by Matthew Restall, in "Black Conquistadors: Armed Africans in Early Spanish America," The Americas 57 no. 2 (October 2000): 171.

Source 2: Image of Juan Garrido on a Spanish Expedition, Sixteenth Century

29. What is the most likely purpose of Juan Garrido's 1538 petition?
    (A) To reject Spanish identity and align with Indigenous resistance
    (B) To request recognition and compensation for his military service
    (C) To establish a legal code for enslaved Africans in New Spain
    (D) To deny African involvement in colonization

30. What does the image of Juan Garrido on a Spanish expedition suggest about his historical role?
    (A) He was a marginalized observer with no political or military significance.
    (B) He was portrayed as a leader and participant in colonial conquest.
    (C) He served only as an agricultural laborer in Caribbean colonies.
    (D) He was an enslaved person with no chance of social mobility.

31. How do the petition and image together reflect the context of ladinos in early colonial America?
    (A) They show that ladinos held no special roles in the Americas.
    (B) They demonstrate how ladinos blended African and European identities to gain agency.
    (C) They indicate that Africans arrived in the Americas only through chattel slavery.
    (D) They prove that all ladinos were born in the Americas.

32. What does the audience of Garrido's petition tell us about his strategy?

(A) He was appealing to Indigenous leaders for land.
(B) He was demanding reparations from Portuguese slavers.
(C) He was addressing Spanish authorities in hopes of securing rights and recognition.
(D) He was writing for an African audience to inspire rebellion.

Questions 33 through 36 refer to the following.

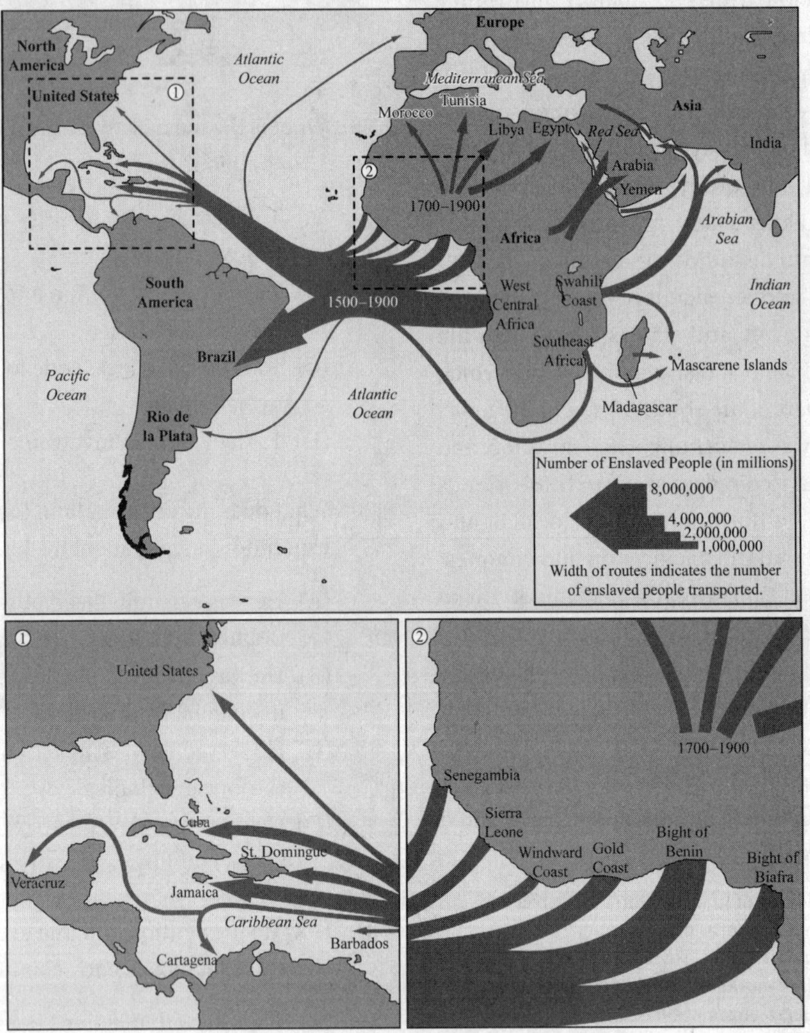

Map Showing an Overview of the Slave Trade out of Africa

33. What does the map most clearly show about the scale of the transatlantic slave trade?

(A) Most enslaved Africans were taken to the present-day United States.
(B) The vast majority of captives were transported to Brazil and the Caribbean.
(C) Only a small number of Africans were ever forcibly removed from the continent.
(D) The transatlantic slave trade lasted fewer than 100 years.

34. Which conclusion is best supported by the geographic distribution shown in the map?

    (A) Enslaved Africans were taken only from East Africa.
    (B) Nearly half of the enslaved Africans who came to mainland North America were from Senegambia and Angola.
    (C) Most enslaved Africans were taken from North Africa.
    (D) South Africa was the most common departure zone for enslaved captives.

35. What trend can be inferred from the presence of multiple African regions along the slave trade routes?

    (A) The enslaved population in the Americas became culturally homogenous over time.
    (B) The slave trade involved only a few African ethnic groups.
    (C) African American communities in the United States developed from a mix of diverse African ethnic backgrounds.
    (D) The United States received enslaved Africans only from Ghana and Nigeria.

36. What limitations does the map present for understanding the full cultural impact of the transatlantic slave trade?

    (A) It does not show the languages, religions, or cultural practices of African ethnic groups.
    (B) It overrepresents the number of enslaved people taken to South America.
    (C) It explains how African political systems participated in the trade.
    (D) It shows how enslaved people resisted capture across Africa.

Questions 37 through 39 refer to the following.

"On Being Brought from Africa to America," Phillis Wheatley

'Twas mercy brought me from my Pagan land,
Taught my benighted soul to understand
That there's a God, that there's a Saviour too:
Once I redemption neither sought nor knew.
Some view our sable race with scornful eye,
"Their colour is a diabolic die."
Remember, Christians, Negros, black as Cain,
May be refined and join the angelic train.

Source: "On Being Brought from Africa to America." Learning for Justice, 7 July 2014, www.learningforjustice.org/classroom-resources/texts/on-being-brought-from-africa-to-america.

37. What is the central claim of Wheatley's poem?

    (A) Enslavement permanently severed her connection to Africa.
    (B) Her arrival in America introduced her to Christianity and a spiritual transformation.
    (C) She believed slavery was morally justified by religion.
    (D) She rejected all elements of European culture, including religion.

38. How does the poem reflect characteristics of early African American narratives?

    (A) It blends literary skill with spiritual and political commentary to assert Black humanity.
    (B) It focuses solely on glorifying African kings and noble life.
    (C) It was written as an autobiography detailing physical labor on a plantation.
    (D) It promotes the continuation of the transatlantic slave trade.

39. What reasoning does Wheatley offer to challenge societal views of African-descended people?

    (A) She asserts that even "Negroes, black as Cain, may be refined" and included in Christian salvation.
    (B) She emphasizes that African traditions are superior to European ones.
    (C) She warns Europeans of divine punishment for participating in the slave trade.
    (D) She describes the trauma of the Middle Passage as her main concern.

Questions 40 through 43 refer to the following.

Source 1: Excerpt from *Twelve Years a Slave: Narrative of Solomon Northup, a Citizen of New-York, Kidnapped in Washington City in 1841, and Rescued in 1853*

"'It Was a Mournful Scene Indeed: Solomon Northup Remembers the New Orleans Slave Market,' recounting his personal experience:

> The slave auction was one of the most barbaric practices of the harsh system of slavery. The slave trade within the United States destroyed families and tore apart communities, especially after 1840 when slavery was extended into the newer lands of the lower South and Southwest. Planters in the older settled areas of the upper South could realize substantial profits selling enslaved people, and New Orleans became the center of the trade. The resulting forced migration involved hundreds of thousands of African Americans. Some moved with their masters, but the migration also tore apart slave families residing on different plantations. Others were sold on the block, as Solomon Northup described in his Twelve Years a Slave. Narrative of Solomon, a Citizen of New-York, Kidnapped in Washington City in 1841."
>
> Source: Solomon Northup, *Twelve Years a Slave: Narrative of Solomon Northup, a Citizen of New-York, Kidnapped in Washington City in 1841, and Rescued in 1853, from a Cotton Plantation near the Red River, in Louisiana* (Auburn, NY: Derby and Miller, 1853), 78–82.

Source 2: Broadside for an Auction of Enslaved Persons at the Charleston Courthouse, 1859

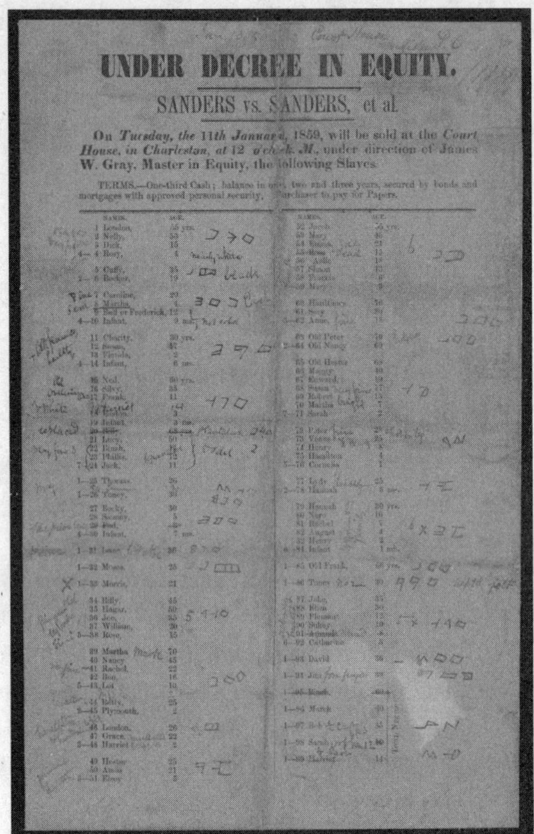

UNDER DECREE IN EQUITY.

SANDERS vs. SANDERS, et al.

On *Tuesday, the 11th January*, 1859, will be sold at the *Court House, in Charleston, at 12 o'clock M.*, under direction of James W. Gray, Master in Equity, the following Slaves.

TERMS.—One-third Cash; balance in one, two and three years, secured by bonds and mortgages with approved personal security. Purchaser to pay for Papers.

40. What does Solomon Northup's perspective as the author reveal about the experience of slave auctions?

    (A) He viewed the auction system as orderly and justified.
    (B) He emphasized the emotional trauma and inhumanity of being sold and separated from loved ones.
    (C) He presented the auction as beneficial to enslaved families.
    (D) He wrote about auctions from the perspective of an enslaver.

41. What is the intended purpose of the auction broadside?

    (A) To humanize enslaved individuals through poetry and storytelling
    (B) To advertise enslaved persons as property to potential buyers
    (C) To protest the cruelty of the cotton economy
    (D) To advocate for gradual emancipation

42. What does the contrast between Northup's narrative and the auction broadside reveal about historical context?

    (A) Both sources promote the expansion of the cotton industry.
    (B) Northup seeks to expose cruelty, while the broadside reflects the commodification of human beings for profit.
    (C) Both were written by abolitionists trying to end slavery.
    (D) Northup's writing ignores the institution of slavery entirely.

43. What can be inferred about the audience for Northup's narrative?

    (A) It was intended for Southern plantation owners to guide auction etiquette.
    (B) It was written for enslaved people to read and share.
    (C) It was aimed at Northern readers to build sympathy for abolition and expose slavery's brutality.
    (D) It was published as a legal defense for slave traders.

Questions 44 through 47 refer to the following.

Source 1: Article IV, Section 2 of the United States Constitution, 1787

"Article IV

Section 2

The Citizens of each State shall be entitled to all Privileges and Immunities of Citizens in the several States. A Person charged in any State with Treason, Felony, or other Crime, who shall flee from Justice, and be found in another State, shall on Demand of the executive Authority of the State from which he fled, be delivered up, to be removed to the State having Jurisdiction of the Crime.

No Person held to Service or Labour in one State, under the Laws thereof, escaping into another, shall, in Consequence of any Law or Regulation therein, be discharged from such Service or Labour, but shall be delivered up on Claim of the Party to whom such Service or Labour may be due."

Source: United States Constitution, 1787. See the full transcription on the National Archives website (National Archives).

Source 2: Excerpts from Dred Scott's Plea and Chief Justice Roger B. Taney's Opinion in *Dred Scott* v. *Sandford*, 1857

"The question is simply this: Can a negro, whose ancestors were imported into this country, and sold as slaves, become a member of the political community formed and brought into existence by the Constitution of the United States, and as such become entitled to all the rights, and privileges, and immunities, guarantied by that instrument to the citizen? One of which rights is the privilege of suing in a court of the United States in the cases specified in the Constitution....

We think [people of African ancestry] are not, and that they are not included, and were not intended to be included, under the word "citizens" in the Constitution, and can therefore claim none of the rights and privileges which that instrument provides for and secures to citizens of the United States....

They had for more than a century before been regarded as beings of an inferior order, and altogether unfit to associate with the white race, either in social or political relations; and so far inferior, that they had no rights which the white man was bound to respect; and that the negro might justly and lawfully be reduced to slavery.... He was bought and sold, and treated as an ordinary article of merchandise and traffic, whenever a profit could be made by it. This opinion was at that time fixed and universal in the civilized portion of the white race."

Dred Scott v. Sandford. LII/Legal Information Institute, 2019, www.law.cornell.edu/supremecourt/text/60/393.

44. What is the central claim made in Chief Justice Roger B. Taney's opinion in *Dred Scott v. Sandford*?
    (A) All enslaved people were automatically granted citizenship when brought to free states.
    (B) The Constitution guaranteed freedom to anyone held in slavery for over ten years.
    (C) African Americans were not and could not be citizens under the Constitution.
    (D) The Dred Scott case was decided in favor of emancipation and equal rights.

45. What was Dred Scott's argument in his plea to the court?
    (A) He sought compensation for forced labor in the cotton industry.
    (B) He claimed that having lived in free territories made him legally free.
    (C) He requested the repeal of the slave codes in Missouri.
    (D) He argued that enslaved people should be permitted to testify in court.

46. How does Article IV, Section 2 of the Constitution relate to the Dred Scott case?
    (A) It supports Dred Scott's claim by guaranteeing freedom in all states.
    (B) It mandates that enslaved individuals who escape to another state must be returned to their enslavers.
    (C) It directly bans slavery in all new U.S. territories.
    (D) It explicitly grants citizenship to African Americans.

47. How does the Dred Scott decision reflect the broader purpose of slave codes and racialized legal systems in the eighteenth and nineteenth centuries?
    (A) It shows how legal systems institutionalized the denial of rights to Black people regardless of status.
    (B) It confirmed that Black and white Americans had equal access to citizenship.
    (C) It prioritized state laws over federal law in all matters.
    (D) It offered protections for enslaved people seeking legal emancipation.

Questions 48 thorough 51 refer to the following.

Source 1: "If We Must Die" by Claude McKay (1919)

If we must die—let it not be like hogs
Hunted and penned in an inglorious spot,
While round us bark the mad and hungry dogs,
Making their mock at our accursed lot.
If we must die—oh, let us nobly die,
So that our precious blood may not be shed
In vain; then even the monsters we defy
Shall be constrained to honor us though dead!
Oh, kinsmen! We must meet the common foe;
Though far outnumbered, let us still be brave,
And for their thousand blows deal one death-blow!
What though before us lies the open grave?
Like men we'll face the murderous, cowardly pack,
Pressed to the wall, dying, but—fighting back!

Source: The first printing of Claude McKay's poem "If We Must Die," in *The Liberator* 2, no. 7 (July 1919): p. 21.

Source 2: Photograph of the Greenwood District Burning During the Tulsa Race Massacre (1921)

48. What is the central purpose of McKay's poem "If We Must Die"?

 (A) To justify submission in the face of white supremacist violence
 (B) To encourage silent endurance of racism to avoid further violence
 (C) To call for dignified resistance and self-defense against racial injustice
 (D) To mourn the loss of Black soldiers after World War I

49. How does the photograph of Greenwood during the Tulsa Race Massacre reflect the context of McKay's poem?

 (A) It visually confirms the government's efforts to protect Black communities.
 (B) It illustrates the devastating violence that Black communities like Greenwood faced during the Red Summer and after.
 (C) It celebrates the resilience of Greenwood's economy after the fire.
 (D) It shows the successful evacuation of Greenwood's residents before destruction.

50. How does the audience and tone of McKay's poem contrast with the photograph?

 (A) The photograph was for protest, while the poem was for entertainment.
 (B) The poem spoke defiantly to Black communities, while the photograph was used to document destruction for broader awareness.
 (C) The photograph was meant to inspire pride in white supremacy, while the poem was a private letter.
 (D) Both were intended to justify the actions of white mobs.

51. What broader conclusion can be drawn from the two sources about African American responses to racial violence?

 (A) African Americans quietly accepted oppression to avoid escalation.
 (B) Literary expression and community documentation were key methods of resistance and remembrance.
 (C) Most African Americans fled the country after such events.
 (D) The events had no lasting effect on African American political movements.

Questions 52 through 54 refer to the following.

Source 1: Botanist George Washington Carver with Students at Tuskegee Institute, 1902

Source: Library of Congress Prints and Photographs Division.

Source 2: Professor Gail Hansberry with Art History Student at North Carolina Central University, 1965

52. What historical development best explains the founding of Tuskegee Institute as seen in the 1902 photograph?
    (A) The Second Morrill Act required desegregated education in the South.
    (B) African Americans established separate educational institutions in response to systemic exclusion from white colleges.
    (C) Tuskegee was built to provide theological education exclusively.
    (D) HBCUs like Tuskegee were designed to replace white industrial training schools.

53. What broader historical process connects the 1902 and 1965 photographs?
    (A) The decline in educational access for African Americans over time
    (B) Federal bans on private Black institutions
    (C) The sustained role of HBCUs in developing African American professionals across generations
    (D) The resegregation of HBCUs after the Civil Rights Movement

54. What impact of HBCUs is best reflected by the presence of educators like Professor Hansberry in 1965?
    (A) HBCUs contributed to the rise of Black intellectuals and academic leadership in the United States.
    (B) HBCUs abandoned the liberal arts in favor of military training.
    (C) HBCUs failed to enroll African American women in higher education.
    (D) HBCUs closed during the Cold War due to lack of funding.

Questions 55 through 57 refer to the following.

Source: Maya Angelou, Julian Mayfield, and Others Petition Outside the U.S. Embassy in Accra, Ghana (1963)

55. The 1963 photograph of Maya Angelou, Julian Mayfield, and others petitioning outside the U.S. Embassy in Ghana is most useful to historians for illustrating which of the following patterns in the mid-twentieth-century Black Freedom movement?

(A) African Americans became less involved in international political efforts.
(B) Black leaders and cultural figures increasingly engaged in transnational activism and solidarity.
(C) African American elites were primarily interested in tourism and leisure abroad.
(D) Diasporic engagement in the 1960s reduced global interest in U.S. civil rights issues.

56. What does Maya Angelou's participation in a protest outside the U.S. Embassy in Accra most clearly reveal about the character of Black Freedom activism in the early 1960s?

(A) That African American activists sought to frame racial injustice as an international human rights issue.
(B) That African American expatriates in Ghana rejected any involvement in U.S. civil rights struggles.
(C) That African Americans abroad primarily limited their activism to cultural exchange and performance.
(D) That U.S. diplomats encouraged African American activists to participate in local political protests.

57. How does the protest in Accra exemplify continuity within the broader Black Freedom movement?

(A) It reflects a retreat from international engagement and diasporic solidarity.
(B) It demonstrates how activists extended civil rights struggles into global forums, linking U.S. racism to broader anti-colonial and human rights campaigns.
(C) It illustrates a focus exclusively on domestic African politics, separate from American issues.
(D) It shows how divisions between African Americans and African governments prevented collaboration.

Questions 58 through 60 refer to the following.

Major Charity E. Adams and Captain Mary Kearney Inspect Members of the 6888th Central Postal Directory Battalion in England, 1945

58. What does the image of the 6888th Battalion in 1945 reveal about African American participation in World War II?

(A) African Americans were excluded from overseas military service.
(B) Black women served in key logistical and support roles even while the military remained segregated.
(C) The U.S. military was fully integrated during WWII.
(D) African American units were restricted to nonmilitary labor in the United States only.

59. How does the service of the 6888th Battalion connect to the Double V Campaign?

(A) It demonstrates African American support for fascism in Europe.
(B) It reflects African American contributions to the war effort abroad while also demanding equal treatment at home.
(C) It promoted segregation in military leadership.
(D) It was unrelated to African American civil rights goals.

60. What long-term issue did many African American women face after World War II despite their military service?

(A) They were fully embraced by white colleges due to the G.I. Bill.
(B) They received equal access to housing, education, and loans.
(C) They were often excluded from G.I. Bill benefits due to discriminatory local policies.
(D) They were offered free land in states in the South.

Section II: Free-Response

TIME: 85 MINUTES—4 QUESTIONS

This section includes three short-answer questions (SAQs) and one document-based question (DBQ). You will have 85 minutes to complete all four questions.

Your responses should be written in complete sentences and paragraph form. Bullet points, outlines, or note fragments will not receive credit. Organize your ideas clearly, and support your responses with specific examples and historical reasoning.

Suggested time management:

- 40 minutes for the three short-answer questions (SAQ)
- 45 minutes for the document-based question (DBQ)

You may answer the questions in any order and revisit them as needed within the time limit.

NOTE: Although you may use scratch paper or planning space for outlines and notes, only your typed or written final responses will be scored. Make sure to review your work and submit your answers before time expires.

1. Short-Answer Question, Visual Source

Malcolm X and Dr. Martin Luther King Jr. After Press Conference at U.S. Capitol, 1964

This historic photograph captures a brief but symbolic moment between two of the most prominent figures of the Black Freedom Movement. Taken at the U.S. Capitol in 1964 following a Senate debate on the Civil Rights Act, this image marks the only documented meeting between the two leaders.

DIRECTIONS: Respond to parts A, B, C, and D. Each response should be in complete sentences and paragraph form, demonstrating historical understanding, clarity, and critical thinking.

(A) Describe one difference in the philosophies or tactics of Dr. Martin Luther King Jr. and Malcolm X during the early 1960s.

(B) Identify one key event, organization, or speech associated with either Dr. Martin Luther King Jr. or Malcolm X that reflects their respective approaches to civil rights.

(C) Explain how the contrasting strategies of Dr. Martin Luther King Jr. and Malcolm X contributed to the broader goals of the Black Freedom movement.

(D) Apply your understanding of the historical context by evaluating how the symbolism of this 1964 meeting continues to inform present-day discussions about Black leadership and activism.

2. Short-Answer Question, Text-Based Source

Excerpt from *Twelve Years a Slave: Narrative of Solomon Northup, a Citizen of New-York, Kidnapped in Washington City in 1841, and Rescued in 1853*

"The slave auction was one of the most barbaric practices of the harsh system of slavery. The slave trade within the United States destroyed families and tore apart communities, especially after 1840 when slavery was extended into the newer lands of the lower South and Southwest. Planters in the older settled areas of the upper South could realize substantial profits selling enslaved people, and New Orleans became the center of the trade. The resulting forced migration involved hundreds of thousands of African Americans. Some moved with their masters, but the migration also tore apart slave families residing on different plantations. Others were sold on the block, as Solomon Northup described in his Twelve Years a Slave. Narrative of Solomon, a Citizen of New-York, Kidnapped in Washington City in 1841."

Source: Solomon Northup, *Twelve Years a Slave: Narrative of Solomon Northup, a Citizen of New-York, Kidnapped in Washington City in 1841, and Rescued in 1853, from a Cotton Plantation near the Red River, in Louisiana* (Auburn, NY: Derby and Miller, 1853), 78–82.

DIRECTIONS: Respond to parts A, B, and C. Each response should be written in complete sentences and demonstrate historical understanding, analysis, and contextual reasoning.

(A) Describe the nature of slave auctions in the nineteenth-century Southern United States, using evidence from the excerpt.

(B) Identify one economic or agricultural development that contributed to the forced migration of enslaved African Americans, and explain how it contributed to the breakup of enslaved families.

(C) Explain how Northup's narrative reflects a specific perspective or purpose that advanced the cause of abolition and influenced public understanding of slavery.

3. Short-Answer Question, No Source

DIRECTIONS: Respond to parts A, B, and C. Each response should be written in complete sentences and demonstrate deep understanding of historical and cultural developments.

(A) Describe one way ancient African civilizations such as Egypt or Nubia have influenced cultural pride or identity among African Americans.

(B) Identify one way the Black diaspora has preserved or reimagined elements of African heritage in the Americas, and describe how it shaped African American cultural development.

(C) Using a specific example, explain how African Americans in the twentieth or twenty-first century have drawn upon ancient African history or symbolism to inspire social or political change over time.

4. Document-Based Question

Explain how African Americans have used diverse forms of activism—such as protests, legal challenges, cultural movements, and collective actions—to fight for freedom, justice, and equality, from the nineteenth century to the present.

In your response, you should do the following:

- Craft a defensible thesis or claim that directly responds to the prompt and establishes a clear line of reasoning.
- Describe a broader historical or disciplinary context that frames your argument and demonstrates understanding of the prompt's significance.
- Support your argument with evidence from at least three of the sources provided.
- Incorporate at least one additional piece of specific evidence beyond the provided sources to strengthen your argument.
- For at least two of the sources, explain how or why the source's perspective, purpose, context, and/or audience is relevant to your argument.
- Cite the sources you reference in your response by letter, title, or author to ensure clarity and attribution.

Source 1: "Am I Not a Woman and a Sister?" from *The Liberator*, 1849

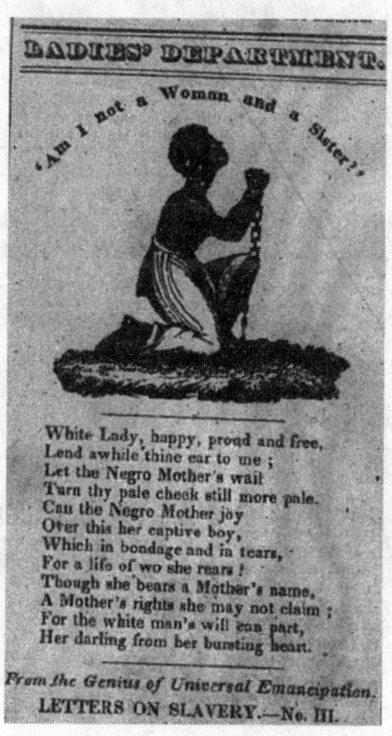

LADIES' DEPARTMENT.

'Am I not a Woman and a Sister?'

White Lady, happy, proud and free,
Lend awhile thine ear to me;
Let the Negro Mother's wail
Turn thy pale cheek still more pale.
Can the Negro Mother joy
Over this her captive boy,
Which in bondage and in tears,
For a life of wo she rears!
Though she bears a Mother's name,
A Mother's rights she may not claim;
For the white man's will can part,
Her darling from her bursting heart.

From the Genius of Universal Emancipation.

LETTERS ON SLAVERY.—No. III.

Source 2: Editorial Letter, The Messenger, African American Magazine, March 1920

"Fellow Negroes of the South, leave there. Go North, East, and West—anywhere—to get out of that hell hole. There are better schools here for your children, higher wages for yourselves, votes if you are twenty-one, better housing and more liberty. All is not rosy here, by any means, but it is Paradise compared with Georgia, Arkansas, Texas, Mississippi and Alabama. Besides, you make it better for those you leave behind. Labor becomes scarce, so that the Bourbons1 of Dixie are compelled to pay your brothers back home more wages. They will give them more schools and privileges, too, to try to get them to come back, and, secondly, to try to keep you from leaving."

Source: "Negroes, Leave the South!" The Messenger, March 1920, p. 2.

Source 3: Photo of Harriet Tubman: Matte Collodion Print of Harriet Tubman, 1871–1876

Source 4: U.S. Supreme Court, *Brown v. Board of Education of Topeka* Opinion (1954)

"**MR. CHIEF JUSTICE WARREN** delivered the opinion of the Court. To separate them from others of similar age and qualifications solely because of their race generates a feeling of inferiority as to their status in the community that may affect their hearts and minds in a way unlikely ever to be undone. The effect of this separation on their educational opportunities was well stated by a finding in the Kansas case by a court which nevertheless felt compelled to rule against the Negro plaintiffs: Segregation of white and colored children in public schools has a detrimental effect upon the colored children. The impact is greater when it has the sanction of the law, for the policy of separating the races is usually interpreted as denoting the inferiority of the negro group. A sense of inferiority affects the motivation of a child to learn. Segregation with the sanction of law, therefore, has a tendency to [retard] the educational and mental development of negro children and to deprive them of some of the benefits they would receive in a racial[ly] integrated school system.

Whatever may have been the extent of psychological knowledge at the time of Plessy v. Ferguson, this finding is amply supported by modern authority. Any language in Plessy v. Ferguson contrary to this finding is rejected. We conclude that, in the field of public education, the doctrine of 'separate but equal' has no place. Separate educational facilities are inherently unequal. Therefore, we hold that the plaintiffs and others similarly situated for whom the actions have been brought are, by reason of the segregation complained of, deprived of the equal protection of the laws guaranteed by the Fourteenth Amendment. This disposition makes unnecessary any discussion whether such segregation also violates the Due Process Clause of the Fourteenth Amendment.

Because these are class actions, because of the wide applicability of this decision, and because of the great variety of local conditions, the formulation of decrees in these cases presents problems of considerable complexity. On re-argument, the consideration of appropriate relief was necessarily subordinated to the primary question—the constitutionality of segregation in public education. We have now announced that such segregation is a denial of the equal protection of the laws. In order that we may have the full assistance of the parties in formulating decrees, the cases will be restored to the docket, and the parties are requested to present further argument on Questions 4 and 5 previously propounded by the Court for the re-argument this Term The Attorney General of the United States is again invited to participate. The Attorneys General of the states requiring or permitting segregation in public education will also be permitted to appear as amici curiae upon request to do so by September 15, 1954, and submission of briefs by October 1, 1954.

It is so ordered."

Source: *Brown v. Board of Education of Topeka*, Opinion; May 17, 1954; Records of the Supreme Court of the United States; Record Group 267; National Archives.

Source 5: NFL Quarterback Colin Kaepernick Takes a Knee During a Game Between the Seattle Seahawks and the San Francisco 49ers, 2017

Answer Explanations

Section I: Multiple-Choice

1. **(C)** The image captures student protestors demanding the creation of Black Studies programs—a direct reflection of their claim for institutional reform. (A) is incorrect. There is no visual or contextual evidence suggesting athletics were the focus of the protest. (B) is incorrect. The protest itself challenges the adequacy of the curriculum, not affirms it. (D) is incorrect. The signs and demonstration reveal dissatisfaction with ongoing inequality, not a celebration of its resolution.

   Skill: 2A: Identify and explain a source's claim(s), evidence, and reasoning

   Learning Objective: LO 1.1.B: Describe the developments that led to the incorporation of African American Studies into United States colleges and universities in the 1960s and 1970s

   Topic: 1.1: What Is African American Studies?

2. **(B)** The Black Student Union strike was directly influenced by broader Black freedom struggles, especially the Black Power movement and Student Nonviolent Coordinating Committee (SNCC) organizing, which emphasized self-determination and educational justice. (A) is incorrect. African independence movements shaped global Black consciousness but were not the immediate catalyst for U.S. campus protests. (C) is incorrect. Black Codes are a Reconstruction-era phenomenon that precedes the 1968 photo by nearly a century. (D) is incorrect. Although important, the Harlem Renaissance predates the student strike and doesn't explain the specific call for Black academic programs.

   Skill: 2A: Identify and explain a source's claim(s), evidence, and reasoning

   Learning Objective: LO 1.1.B: Describe the developments that led to the incorporation of African African American Studies into U.S. colleges and universities in the 1960s and 1970s

   Topic: 1.1: What Is African American Studies?

3. **(C)** The protest reflects a push to legitimize African American history, culture, and political thought through formal academic departments. (A) is incorrect. The image centers on protest and activism, not successful integration. (B) is incorrect. Although student agency is evident, the focus is specifically on curricular change, not general governance. (D) is incorrect. The visual message contradicts the notion that discrimination had ended. Instead, the image documents resistance to its persistence.

   Skill: 2A: Identify and explain a source's claim(s), evidence, and reasoning

   Learning Objective: LO 1.1.B: Describe the developments that led to the incorporation of African American Studies into United States colleges and universities in the 1960s and 1970s

   Topic: 1.1: What Is African American Studies?

4. **(B)** The protest reflects a national movement to demand institutional inclusion, the creation of Black Studies departments, and representation of African American histories and voices. (A) is incorrect. The Cold War's conclusion occurred decades later and is unrelated to domestic educational reform. (C) is incorrect. Although World War II veterans played a role in early civil rights advocacy, this image specifically ties to 1960s student activism and curriculum reform. (D) is incorrect. The protest occurred at a predominantly white institution and focused on creating new academic programs, not integrating HBCUs.

   Skill: 2A: Identify and explain a source's claim(s), evidence, and reasoning

   Learning Objective: LO 1.1.B: Describe the developments that led to the incorporation of African American Studies into United States colleges and universities in the 1960s and 1970s

   Topic: 1.1: What Is African American Studies?

5. **(C)** The Sahel and savannah regions supported trade, agriculture, and livestock herding due to fertile land and their position along major trade routes. (A) is incorrect. Although the Sahel and savannah can have dry seasons, they were not as harsh as deserts and did support population growth. (B) is incorrect. These regions were

trade hubs, not remote or isolated. (D) is incorrect. These regions were well-inhabited, while Mediterranean zones were smaller and not central to early trade routes.

Skill: 2D: Describe and draw conclusions from patterns, trends, and limitations in data, making connections to relevant course content

Learning Objective: LO 1.2.B: Explain how Africa's varied landscape affected patterns of settlement and trade between diverse cultural regions

Topic: 1.2: The African Continent: A Varied Landscape

6. **(A)** The map highlights Africa's rivers, varied climates, and proximity to seas and oceans, all of which facilitated cross-regional and global trade. (B) is incorrect. Atlantic-based colonization occurred centuries later and doesn't explain the ancient trade patterns. (C) is incorrect. Trade routes traversed deserts with camel caravans and linked distant regions. (D) Historical evidence shows active, complex trade across the continent and beyond.

Skill: 2D: Describe and draw conclusions from patterns, trends, and limitations in data, making connections to relevant course content

Learning Objective: LO 1.2.B: Explain how Africa's varied landscape affected patterns of settlement and trade between diverse cultural regions

Topic: 1.2: The African Continent: A Varied Landscape

7. **(C)** Africa's major rivers helped form trade routes and enabled communication between inland regions. (A) is incorrect. Rivers connected regions and supported, rather than blocked, movement. (B) is incorrect. Although military use may have occurred, rivers primarily supported economic development and population expansion. (D) is incorrect. Rivers such as the Nile and Niger played roles across multiple climate zones, not just in the rainforest.

Skills: 2D: Describe and draw conclusions from patterns, trends, and limitations in data, making connections to relevant course content

Learning Objective: LO 1.2.B: Explain how Africa's varied landscape affected patterns of settlement and trade between diverse cultural regions

Topic: 1.2: The African Continent: A Varied Landscape

8. **(D)** Tropical rainforests supported the cultivation of kola trees, yams, and the gold trade, as shown in the map and essential knowledge. (A) is incorrect. Deserts were inhospitable to gold and yam production. (B) is incorrect. While savannahs supported grain crops and livestock, gold and yams were more prominent in rainforest zones. (C) is incorrect. Semiarid zones were suited for the salt trade and nomadic herding, not tropical crops.

Skill: 2D: Describe and draw conclusions from patterns, trends, and limitations in data, making connections to relevant course content

Learning Objective: LO 1.2.A: Describe the geographic features of the African continent

Topic: 1.2: The African Continent: A Varied Landscape

9. **(B)** Nzinga Mbemba is deeply concerned that merchants and corrupt actors are depleting the Kongo population through an unregulated slave trade. (A) is incorrect. The letter does not express a complaint about the absence of missionaries. (C) is incorrect. The letter reaffirms Kongo's Christian beliefs and does not mention banning Christianity. (D) is incorrect. The letter condemns, rather than praises, the economic impact of Portuguese trade.

Skill: 1C: Identify and explain patterns, connections, or other relationships (causation, changes, continuities, comparison)

Learning Objective: LO 1.9.B: Explain how the Kingdom of Kongo's political relations with Portugal affected the kingdom's participation in the transatlantic slave trade

Topic: 1.9: West Central Africa: The Kingdom of Kongo

10. **(C)** Nzinga Mbemba emphasizes the need for religious goods and clergy while condemning the economic damage caused by the slave trade. (A) is incorrect. The excerpt criticizes the spread of slavery, not the spread of Christianity. (B) is incorrect. Nzinga Mbemba remains in power and is appealing to the Portuguese king, not being replaced by missionaries. (D) is incorrect. The letter does not oppose trade entirely, only the destructive aspects linked to human trafficking.

    Skill: 1C: Identify and explain patterns, connections, or other relationships (causation, changes, continuities, comparison)
    Learning Objective: LO 1.9.A: Explain how the adoption of Christianity affected economic and religious aspects of the Kingdom of Kongo

    Topic: 1.9: West Central Africa: The Kingdom of Kongo

11. **(D)** Nzinga Mbemba is appealing diplomatically to maintain trade on his terms while opposing exploitation. (A) is incorrect. Nzinga Mbemba embraces Christianity and Portuguese ties but seeks reform. (B) is incorrect. The conflict here is not religious but economic and political. (C) is incorrect. There is no mention of religious conquest or the destruction of traditional beliefs.

    Skill: 1C: Identify and explain patterns, connections, or other relationships (causation, changes, continuities, comparison)
    Learning Objective: LO 1.9.B: Explain how the Kingdom of Kongo's political relations with Portugal affected the kingdom's participation in the transatlantic slave trade

    Topic: 1.9: West Central Africa: The Kingdom of Kongo

12. **(C)** The Kingdom of Kongo's adoption of Christianity contributed to the religious traditions that enslaved Africans carried to the Americas. (A) is incorrect. Christian traditions continued and were preserved even during enslavement. (B) is incorrect. Christianity was adopted voluntarily and strategically by the monarchy. (D) is incorrect. The letter reflects a deeply rooted Christian identity with long-term influence.

    Skill: 1C: Identify and explain patterns, connections, or other relationships (causation, changes, continuities, comparison)

    Learning Objective: LO 1.9.C: Explain how the Kingdom of Kongo's Christian culture influenced early generations of African Americans

    Topic: 1.9: West Central Africa: The Kingdom of Kongo

13. **(B)** Both sources highlight Mali's prominence and wealth, especially symbolized by Mansa Musa and gold. (A) is incorrect. The map and atlas suggest broad influence, not any limitation. (C) is incorrect. Mali, not just Ghana, gained international attention, particularly through Islamic and Mediterranean trade routes. (D) is incorrect. The *Catalan Atlas* elevates Mali's status by visually emphasizing its ruler and wealth.

    Skill: 3A: Formulate a defensible claim

    Learning Objective: LO 1.5.A: Explain how the influence of gold and trade shaped the political, economic, and religious development of the ancient West African empires of Ghana, Mali, and Songhai

    Topic: 1.5: The Sudanic Empires: Ghana, Mali, and Songhai

14. **(A)** The *Catalan Atlas* shows Mansa Musa with a golden orb, signaling wealth and political power admired across the Mediterranean. (B) is incorrect. The *Catalan Atlas* is direct evidence that Europeans knew of Mali. (C) is incorrect. There is no mention of Mali's leaders being viewed as spiritually wise but poor. (D) is incorrect. The *Catalan Atlas* depicts Mali as culturally important and rich in resources.

    Skill: 3A: Formulate a defensible claim
    Learning Objective: LO 1.5.B: Explain how Mali's wealth and power created opportunities for the empire to expand its reach to other societies within Africa and across the Mediterranean

    Topic: 1.5: The Sudanic Empires: Ghana, Mali, and Songhai

15. **(B)** The Mali Empire's access to trans-Saharan trade and gold fueled political strength and recognition abroad. (A) is incorrect. The Mali Empire's geographic location supported trade, not isolation. (C) is incorrect. Trade and religion were central to Mali's influence, not conquest alone. (D) is incorrect. Agricultural productivity was important but was not the main driver of Mali's global reach.

    Skill: 3A: Formulate a defensible claim

    Learning Objective: LO 1.5.B: Explain how Mali's wealth and power created opportunities for the empire to expand its reach to other societies within Africa and across the Mediterranean

    Topic: 1.5: The Sudanic Empires: Ghana, Mali, and Songhai

16. **(C)** West African Islamic traditions, scholarship, and economic systems left cultural imprints that survived in the Americas. (A) is incorrect. The Sudanic empires contributed to cultural memory and identity in the Atlantic world. (B) is incorrect. Although some nomads lived in Africa, most African Americans descended from regions influenced by the Sudanic states. (D) is incorrect. Enslaved Africans carried cultural knowledge, including pride in African empires like Mali and Songhai.

    Skill: 3A: Formulate a defensible claim

    Learning Objective: LO 1.5.C: Explain the connection between the Sudanic empires and early generations of African Americans

    Topic: 1.5: The Sudanic Empires: Ghana, Mali, and Songhai

17. **(B)** The massive stone walls reflect the Shona's wealth, centralized authority, religious practice, and trade connections. (A) is incorrect. The structures had significant political, spiritual, and economic meaning. They were not just decoration. (C) is incorrect. Great Zimbabwe developed independently of Islamic architectural traditions. (D) is incorrect. The Shona had sophisticated agricultural and trade systems.

    Skill: 3A: Formulate a defensible claim

    Learning Objective: LO 1.8.A: Describe the function and importance of Great Zimbabwe's stone architecture

    Topic: 1.8: Culture and Trade in Southern and East Africa

18. **(C)** The trade routes connected African coastal cities to merchants from Arabia, India, and China. (A) is incorrect. The map shows direct connections from inland Africa to Indian Ocean ports. (B) is incorrect. Atlantic trade is not depicted; this map emphasizes East Africa's Indian Ocean networks. (D) is incorrect. Atlantic trade is not depicted; this map emphasizes East Africa's Indian Ocean networks.

    Skill: 3A: Formulate a defensible claim

    Learning Objective: LO 1.8.B: Explain how geographic, cultural, and political factors contributed to the rise and fall of the city-states on the Swahili Coast

    Topic: 1.8: Culture and Trade in Southern and East Africa

19. **(C)** Both were part of a long-distance trading ecosystem connecting African goods like gold and ivory to international markets. (A) is incorrect. Although Swahili city-states shared Islamic culture, Great Zimbabwe did not. (B) is incorrect. Both had extensive trade networks and were not in isolation. (D) is incorrect. Trade between these regions and Indian Ocean networks began well before the eighteenth century.

    Skill: 3A: Formulate a defensible claim

    Learning Objective: LO 1.8.B: Explain how geographic, cultural, and political factors contributed to the rise and fall of the city-states on the Swahili Coast

    Topic: 1.8: Culture and Trade in Southern and East Africa

20. **(C)** Both sources demonstrate the complexity and advancement of African societies long before European colonization. (A) is incorrect. The sources show thriving trade, infrastructure, and global connections. (B) is incorrect. Trade was not solely internal; external networks were vital. (D)

is incorrect. These were powerful, self-governing kingdoms and city-states.

Skill: 3A: Formulate a defensible claim

Learning Objective: LO 1.8.A Describe the function and importance of Great Zimbabwe's stone architecture; LO 1.8.B: Explain how the Swahili Coast rose and fell

Topic: 1.8: Culture and Trade in Southern and East Africa

21. **(C)** The crucifix's design and the letter both reflect the synthesis of African traditions with Catholic beliefs. (A) is incorrect. The Kingdom of Kongo voluntarily adopted Christianity. (B) is incorrect. Christianity was not forced. It was adopted through diplomacy and alliance. (D) is incorrect. The crucifix shows distinctly African craftsmanship and cultural expression.

    Skill: 1C: Identify and explain patterns, connections, or other relationships (causation, changes, continuities, comparison)

    Learning Objective: LO 1.9.A: Explain how the adoption of Christianity affected economic and religious aspects of the Kingdom of Kongo

    Topic: 1.9: West Central Africa: The Kingdom of Kongo

22. **(C)** The letter reveals a power imbalance where the Portuguese exploited their position, straining Kongo's control over trade and sovereignty. (A) is incorrect. Alliances were deeply tied to trade, not to purely spiritual motives. (B) is incorrect. Nzinga Mbemba's letter expresses frustration with Portuguese lawlessness. (D) is incorrect. The Portuguese exploited Kongo's slave markets with little restriction.

    Skill: 1C: Identify and explain patterns, connections, or other relationships (causation, changes, continuities, comparison)

    Learning Objective: LO 1.9.B: Explain how the Kingdom of Kongo's political relations with Portugal affected the kingdom's participation in the transatlantic slave trade

    Topic: 1.9: West Central Africa: The Kingdom of Kongo

23. **(B)** The *Triple Crucifix* embodies the spiritual and cultural blending that influenced enslaved Central Africans and their descendants. (A) is incorrect. Christian iconography endured in various African American religious traditions. (C) is incorrect. African Catholics preserved and adapted these traditions rather than reject them. (D) The crucifix had deep religious and cultural meaning.

    Skill: 1C: Identify and explain patterns, connections, or other relationships (causation, changes, continuities, comparison)

    Learning Objective: LO 1.9.C: Explain how the Kingdom of Kongo's Christian culture influenced early generations of African Americans

    Topic: 1.9: West Central Africa: The Kingdom of Kongo

24. **(C)** The letter and crucifix both reflect how Kongo leaders balanced foreign influence with local adaptations, shaping a unique African Christian identity. (A) is incorrect. Neither source addresses architecture or engineering. (B) is incorrect. Both sources show that Kongo embraced Christianity rather than reject it. (D) is incorrect. Kongo maintained religious autonomy and shaped its own practices.

    Skill: 1C: Identify and explain patterns, connections, or other relationships (causation, changes, continuities, comparison)

    Learning Objective: LO 1.9.A: Explain how the adoption of Christianity affected economic and religious aspects of the Kingdom of Kongo; LO 1.9.B: Explain how the Kingdom of Kongo's political relations with Portugal affected the kingdom's participation in the transatlantic slave trade; LO 1.9.C: Explain how the Kingdom of Kongo's Christian culture influenced early generations of African Americans

    Topic: 1.9: West Central Africa: The Kingdom of Kongo

25. **(B)** The mask was designed to honor Queen Idia's role as a spiritual advisor and political leader in Benin. (A) is incorrect. The pendant was not intended for foreign intimidation. (C) is incorrect. The mask celebrates, not mocks, female power. (D) is incorrect. The mask held deep royal and

symbolic significance within Benin; it was not a trade good.

Skill: 2B: Describe a source's perspective, purpose, context, and audience

Learning Objective: LO 1.10.A: Describe the function of kinship along with the varied roles women played in early West and Central African societies

Topic: 1.10: Kinship and Political Leadership

26. **(C)** The image highlights Queen Njinga's strategic resistance, leadership, and power. (A) is incorrect. Njinga's authority was affirmed, not diminished, through comparison with male rulers. (B) is incorrect. Njinga was an opponent, not a subject, of Portuguese rule. (D) is incorrect. Njinga had direct political and military involvement.

Skill: 2B: Describe a source's perspective, purpose, context, and audience

Learning Objective: LO 1.10.B: Compare the political and military leadership of Queen Idia of Benin and Queen Njinga of Ndongo-Matamba

Topic: 1.10: Kinship and Political Leadership

27. **(B)** Queen Idia used spiritual and medicinal powers, while Queen Njinga led military campaigns and negotiated diplomatically. (A) is incorrect. Both ruled during times of conflict and were appointed through unique circumstances. (C) is incorrect. Both were deeply involved in warfare and diplomacy. (D) is incorrect. Both led from within, not through dependence on European alliances.

Skill: 2B: Describe a source's perspective, purpose, context, and audience

Learning Objective: LO 1.10.B: Compare the political and military leadership of Queen Idia of Benin and Queen Njinga of Ndongo-Matamba

Topic: 1.10: Kinship and Political Leadership

28. **(B)** The imagery affirms their legacies, celebrating female leadership across generations, both in Africa and in the diaspora. (A) is incorrect. These sources were rooted in African cultural traditions. (C) is incorrect. Neither source was meant to criticize. (D) is incorrect. These are political-cultural symbols, not religious artifacts for Catholic rituals.

Skill: 2B: Describe a source's perspective, purpose, context, and audience

Learning Objective: LO 1.10.C: Describe the legacy of Queen Idia and Queen Njinga's leadership

Topic: 1.10: Kinship and Political Leadership

29. **(B)** The petition aims to secure rewards and acknowledgment for Garrido's service as a free African conquistador. (A) is incorrect. Garrido's petition does not reject Spanish identity. Instead, he sought recognition within it. (C) is incorrect. The petition is personal, not legislative. (D) is incorrect. Garrido's writings affirm African contributions to colonization.

Skill: 2B: Describe a source's perspective, purpose, context, and audience

Learning Objective: LO 2.1.B: Describe the diverse roles Africans played during colonization of the Americas in the sixteenth century

Topic: 2.1: African Explorers in the Americas

30. **(B)** Garrido is shown in armor, indicating his role in military and exploration efforts. (A) is incorrect. The image depicts Garrido as actively participating in Spanish expeditions. (C) is incorrect. Garrido's role extended beyond labor to conquest and exploration. (D) is incorrect. Garrido was a free man with military rank and social mobility.

Skill: 2B: Describe a source's perspective, purpose, context, and audience

Learning Objective: LO 2.1.B: Describe the diverse roles Africans played during colonization of the Americas in the sixteenth century

Topic: 2.1: African Explorers in the Americas

31. **(B)** Both sources reflect how ladinos blended cultural fluency and military service to secure mobility and status. (A) is incorrect. Ladinos like Garrido played essential early roles. (C) is incorrect. The narrative of chattel slavery emerged later; Garrido arrived as a free man. (D) is incorrect. Garrido was born in Africa and came to the Americas via Europe.

Skill: 2B: Describe a source's perspective, purpose, context, and audience

Learning Objective: LO 2.1.A: Explain the significance of the roles ladinos played as the first Africans to arrive in the territory that became the United States

Topic: 2.1: African Explorers in the Americas

32. **(C)** Garrido's audience was the Spanish Crown, seeking recognition, support, and possibly a pension. (A) is incorrect. Garrido directed his petition to Spanish colonial authorities. (B) is incorrect. There's no reference to Portuguese reparations. (D) is incorrect. Garrido was not writing for an African audience.

Skill: 2B: Describe a source's perspective, purpose, context, and audience

Learning Objective: LO 2.1.A: Explain the significance of the roles ladinos played as the first Africans to arrive in the territory that became the United States

Topic: 2.1: African Explorers in the Americas

33. **(B)** The majority of enslaved Africans were transported to Brazil and the Caribbean, not to the present-day United States. (A) is incorrect. The present-day United States received only a small percentage of enslaved Africans. (C) is incorrect. Over 12.5 million people were forcibly removed. (D) is incorrect. The trade spanned more than 350 years.

Skill: 2D: Describe and draw conclusions from patterns, trends, and limitations in data, making connections to relevant course content

Learning Objective: LO 2.2.A: Describe the scale and geographic scope of the transatlantic slave trade

Topic: 2.2: Departure Zones in Africa and the Slave Trade to the United States

34. **(B)** The map supports that Senegambia and Angola were leading departure zones for enslaved Africans sent to mainland North America. (A) is incorrect. West and Central Africa were the most significant regions, not just East Africa. (C) is incorrect. North Africa was not the primary region involved in the transatlantic trade. (D) is incorrect. South Africa played a minor role in the transatlantic slave trade.

Skill: 2D: Describe and draw conclusions from patterns, trends, and limitations in data, making connections to relevant course content

Learning Objective: LO 2.2.B: Identify the primary slave trading zones in Africa from which Africans were forcibly taken

Topic: 2.2: Departure Zones in Africa and the Slave Trade to the United States

35. **(C)** The presence of diverse African groups led to the formation of culturally rich African American communities. (A) is incorrect. The diversity of African ethnic groups created cultural variety, not uniformity. (B) is incorrect. Dozens of groups were involved across multiple regions. (D) is incorrect. Africans arrived from a broad range of West and Central African regions.

Skill: 2D: Describe and draw conclusions from patterns, trends, and limitations in data, making connections to relevant course content

Learning Objective: LO 2.2.C: Explain how the distribution of distinct African ethnic groups during the era of slavery shaped the development of African American communities in the United States

Topic: 2.2: Departure Zones in Africa and the Slave Trade to the United States

36. **(A)** The map doesn't convey cultural depth—such as religion, language, or beliefs—limiting understanding of the cultural impact. (B) is incorrect. The map accurately reflects high traffic to South America. (C) is incorrect. The map doesn't explain African political dynamics. (D) is incorrect. The map does not depict resistance movements or capture methods.

Skill: 2D: Describe and draw conclusions from patterns, trends, and limitations in data, making connections to relevant course content

Learning Objective: LO 2.2.C: Explain how the distribution of distinct African ethnic groups during the era of slavery shaped the development of African American communities in the United States

Topic: 2.2: Departure Zones in Africa and the Slave Trade to the United States

37. **(B)** Wheatley's poem expresses gratitude for her Christian awakening in America, despite her forced journey. (A) is incorrect. Wheatley's poem does not emphasize permanent disconnection but, instead, spiritual transformation. (C) is incorrect. Wheatley uses faith as a lens for personal growth, not to justify enslavement. (D) is incorrect. Wheatley acknowledges Christianity and suggests it can unify across racial lines.

Skill: 2A: Identify and explain a source's claim(s), evidence, and reasoning

Learning Objective: LO 2.3.C: Describe the key features and purposes of narratives written by formerly enslaved Africans

Topic: 2.3: Capture and the Impact of the Slave Trade on West African Societies

38. **(A)** Wheatley's poem integrates religious themes and poetic form to assert dignity and intellect in defense of Black humanity. (B) is incorrect. The poem does not glorify African nobility; its focus is spiritual. (C) is incorrect. It is a poem, not an autobiography, and does not describe plantation labor. (D) is incorrect. Wheatley's writing advocates moral uplift, not support for slavery.

Skill: 2A: Identify and explain a source's claim(s), evidence, and reasoning

Learning Objective: LO 2.3.C: Describe the key features and purposes of narratives written by formerly enslaved Africans

Topic: 2.3: Capture and the Impact of the Slave Trade on West African Societies

39. **(A)** Wheatley uses biblical allusion ("black as Cain") to argue that people of African descent are spiritually redeemable and worthy of inclusion. (B) is incorrect. The poem focuses on universal salvation through Christianity, not cultural superiority. (C) is incorrect. The poem is hopeful and reflective, not accusatory. (D) is incorrect. Although Wheatley experienced enslavement, the poem's focus is on spiritual insight rather than trauma.

Skill: 2A: Identify and explain a source's claim(s), evidence, and reasoning

Learning Objective: LO 2.3.C: Describe the key features and purposes of narratives written by formerly enslaved Africans

Topic: 2.3: Capture and the Impact of the Slave Trade on West African Societies

40. **(B)** Northup's firsthand account underscores the brutal separation of families and the dehumanizing violence of auctions. (A) is incorrect. Northup condemns, rather than justifies, the auction system. (C) is incorrect. There is no evidence Northup believed auctions were beneficial. (D) is incorrect. Northup wrote as a formerly enslaved man, not as an enslaver.

Skill: 2C: Explain the significance of a source's perspective, purpose, context, and audience

Learning Objective: LO 2.5.A: Describe the nature of slave auctions in the nineteenth century United States South

Topic: 2.5: Slave Auctions and the Domestic Slave Trade

41. **(B)** The broadside is a commercial advertisement treating people as property to attract buyers. (A) is incorrect. Broadsides were neither poetic nor reflective. (C) is incorrect. The broadside was not designed to protest slavery. (D) is incorrect. There is no advocacy in this source—only commodification.

Skill: 2C: Explain the significance of a source's perspective, purpose, context, and audience

Learning Objective: LO 2.5.A: Describe the nature of slave auctions in the nineteenth-century United States South

Topic: 2.5: Slave Auctions and the Domestic Slave Trade

42. **(B)** The contrast reflects how Northup's abolitionist narrative exposed injustice while the broadside coldly presents human beings as chattel. (A) is incorrect. Northup's narrative critiques slavery while the broadside supports the institution economically. (C) is incorrect. The broadside is not abolitionist. (D) is incorrect. Northup's writing directly addresses the horrors of slavery.

Skill: 2C: Explain the significance of a source's perspective, purpose, context, and audience

Learning Objective: LO 2.5.B: Explain how African American authors advanced the causes of abolition and equality in their writings about slave auctions

Topic: 2.5: Slave Auctions and the Domestic Slave Trade

43. **(C)** Northup's book was written for Northern and abolitionist audiences to expose the cruelty of slavery and call for reform. (A) is incorrect. Southern planters were not the intended audience. (B) is incorrect. Most enslaved people could not legally read. (D) is incorrect. The narrative was not a defense of traders but a condemnation of the system.

Skill: 2C: Explain the significance of a source's perspective, purpose, context, and audience

Learning Objective: LO 2.5.B: Explain how African American authors advanced the causes of abolition and equality in their writings about slave auctions

Topic: 2.5: Slave Auctions and the Domestic Slave Trade

44. **(C)** Taney ruled that African Americans were not U.S. citizens and had no standing to sue. (A) is incorrect. The ruling denied the idea that free states automatically granted freedom. (B) is incorrect. No constitutional provision guaranteed freedom after time served. (D) is incorrect. The decision upheld slavery and limited legal rights.

Skill: 2A: Identify and explain a source's claim(s), evidence, and reasoning

Learning Objective: LO 2.7.A: Explain how American law affected the lives and citizenship rights of enslaved and free African Americans between the seventeenth and nineteenth centuries

Topic: 2.7: Slavery and American Law: Slave Codes and Landmark Cases

45. **(B)** Scott argued that his residence in free territories made him legally free. (A) is incorrect. Northup, not Scott, labored on cotton plantations. (C) is incorrect. The case challenged federal law, not state slave codes. (D) is incorrect. Testifying in court was not the core issue in his plea.

Skill: 2A: Identify and explain a source's claim(s), evidence, and reasoning

Learning Objective: LO 2.7.A: Explain how American law affected the lives and citizenship rights of enslaved and free African Americans between the seventeenth and nineteenth centuries

Topic: 2.7: Slavery and American Law: Slave Codes and Landmark Cases

46. **(B)** Article IV, Section 2 mandated the return of fugitives to bondage, shaping the court's logic. (A) is incorrect. Article IV, Section 2 did not support emancipation. (C) is incorrect. Article IV, Section 2 did not abolish or ban slavery in new territories. (D) is incorrect. Article IV, Section 2 never mentioned African American citizenship.

Skill: 2A: Identify and explain a source's claim(s), evidence, and reasoning

Learning Objective: LO 2.7.A: Explain how American law affected the lives and citizenship rights of enslaved and free African Americans between the seventeenth and nineteenth centuries

Topic: 2.7: Slavery and American Law: Slave Codes and Landmark Cases

47. **(A)** The Dred Scott decision denied African Americans legal standing, aligning with slave codes that codified racial oppression. (B) is incorrect. The Dred Scott decision reaffirmed racial exclusion, not equality. (C) is incorrect. The Dred Scott decision focused on federal power limiting state emancipation policies. (D) is incorrect. The Dred Scott decision rejected legal protections for enslaved people.

Skill: 2A: Identify and explain a source's claim(s), evidence, and reasoning

Learning Objective: LO 2.7.B: Explain how slave codes developed in response to African Americans' resistance to slavery

Topic: 2.7: Slavery and American Law: Slave Codes and Landmark Cases

48. **(C)** McKay called for noble resistance in the face of violence and injustice, especially amid 1919's racial attacks. (A) is incorrect. McKay rejected submission. (B) is incorrect. The tone is defiant and urgent, not passive. (D) is incorrect. The poem is about community survival; it is not a eulogy.

Skill: 2C: Explain the significance of a source's perspective, purpose, context, and audience

Learning Objective: LO 3.6.B: Explain how African Americans responded to white supremacist attacks in the early twentieth century

Topic: 3.6: White Supremacist Violence and the Red Summer

49. **(B)** The image documents the destruction of Black Wall Street during the Tulsa Massacre, part of the broader racial violence McKay alludes to. (A) is incorrect. The photo shows devastation, not protection. (C) is incorrect. The destruction decimated the community; this was not a celebration of recovery. (D) is incorrect. The photo documents tragedy, not evacuation.

Skill: 2C: Explain the significance of a source's perspective, purpose, context, and audience

Learning Objective: LO 3.6.A: Describe the causes of heightened racial violence in the early twentieth century

Topic: 3.6: White Supremacist Violence and the Red Summer

50. **(B)** McKay's poem empowered Black communities to resist, while the photograph visually preserved the impact of white supremacist violence for the historical record. (A) is incorrect. McKay's poem is a political and literary call to action, not entertainment. (C) is incorrect. The photo was not intended to promote white supremacy. Additionally, McKay's work was published poetry, not a private letter. (D) is incorrect. Neither source supports white mob violence.

Skill: 2C: Explain the significance of a source's perspective, purpose, context, and audience

Learning Objective: LO 3.6.B: Explain how African Americans responded to white supremacist attacks in the early twentieth century

Topic: 3.6: White Supremacist Violence and the Red Summer

51. **(B)** Literature like McKay's and historical documentation like the Tulsa photograph were key tools of resistance, memory, and advocacy. (A) is incorrect. McKay and the photograph reflect defiance and resilience, not submission. (C) is incorrect. The Great Migration did occur, but this claim is unrelated to the sources. (D) is incorrect. These events spurred activism and cultural expression in the civil rights struggle.

Skill: 2C: Explain the significance of a source's perspective, purpose, context, and audience

Learning Objective: LO 3.6.B: Explain how African Americans responded to white supremacist attacks in the early twentieth century

Topic: 3.6: White Supremacist Violence and the Red Summer

52. **(B)** The HBCU in Tuskegee was created in response to educational exclusion, exemplifying African American self-determination. (A) is incorrect. The Morrill Act required separate institutions if states didn't desegregate, but Tuskegee was founded earlier. (C) is incorrect. Tuskegee offered vocational training, not solely theological education. (D) is incorrect. HBCUs supplemented—not replaced—white industrial schools.

Skill: 1B: Identify and explain the context of a specific event, development, or process

Learning Objective: LO 3.10.A: Describe the founding of historically Black colleges and universities (HBCUs) in the late nineteenth and early twentieth centuries

Topic: 3.10: HBCUs, Black Greek Letter Organizations, and Black Education

53. **(C)** The images reflect generational continuity in HBCUs' commitment to producing Black leaders and scholars. (A) is incorrect. Educational access expanded over time. (B) is incorrect. No such federal ban existed. (D) is incorrect. HBCUs expanded rather than resegregated after the Civil Rights era.

 Skill: 1B: Identify and explain the context of a specific event, development, or process

 Learning Objective: 3.10.B: Explain how the creation of historically Black colleges and universities (HBCUs) in the United States impacted the educational and professional lives of African Americans nationally and internationally

 Topic: 3.10: HBCUs, Black Greek Letter Organizations, and Black Education

54. **(A)** The presence of Black faculty mentoring students reflects the role of HBCUs in cultivating African American professionals and scholars. (B) is incorrect. Liberal arts remained central to many HBCUs. (C) is incorrect. African American women have historically enrolled in and graduated from HBCUs. (D) is incorrect. HBCUs faced funding challenges but remained open and influential.

 Skill: 1B: Identify and explain the context of a specific event, development, or process

 Learning Objective: LO 3.10.B: Explain how the creation of historically Black colleges and universities (HBCUs) in the United States impacted the educational and professional lives of African Americans nationally and internationally

 Topic: 3.10: HBCUs, Black Greek Letter Organizations, and Black Education

55. **(B)** The photograph illustrates African American intellectuals and artists actively engaging in transnational activism by petitioning the U.S. Embassy in Ghana, directly connecting U.S. civil rights struggles to global human rights campaigns. This reflects a key pattern of the mid-twentieth century, where Black leaders sought solidarity with African independence movements. Choice (A) is incorrect because the protest shows increased, not decreased, international engagement. Choice (C) is incorrect because the image depicts political activism, not leisure. Choice (D) is incorrect because diasporic activism in the 1960s amplified, rather than reduced, global attention to U.S. racial injustice.

 Skill: 1C: Identify and explain patterns, connections, or other relationships (causation, changes, continuities, comparison)

 Learning Objective: LO 4.2.A: Describe the Black Freedom movement in the twentieth century

 Topic: 4.2: Anticolonialism and Black Political Thought

56. **(A)** Maya Angelou's protest in Ghana shows how African American activists abroad reframed civil rights as part of a global human rights struggle. By petitioning the U.S. Embassy, these activists highlighted U.S. racial injustice before an international audience, strengthening diasporic solidarity. Choice (B) is incorrect because Angelou and others did not abandon U.S. struggles—they internationalized them. Choice (C) is incorrect because the protest clearly demonstrates political engagement, not cultural performance alone. Choice (D) is incorrect because U.S. officials did not encourage such protests; instead, these demonstrations often embarrassed the American government.

 Skill: 1C: Identify and explain patterns, connections, or other relationships (causation, changes, continuities, comparison)

 Learning Objective: LO 4.2.B: Describe examples of diasporic solidarity that emerged across the African diaspora in the twentieth century

 Topic: 4.2: Anticolonialism and Black Political Thought

57. **(B)** The Accra protest reflects continuity within the Black Freedom movement by showing how activists connected the domestic civil rights struggle to broader global campaigns against colonialism and racism. This continuity demonstrates that the fight for Black liberation was never confined to national borders but was instead part of a global tradition of resistance. Choice (A) is incorrect because the protest affirms internationalism rather than a retreat from it. Choice (C) is incorrect because the demonstration was explicitly tied to U.S. injustice, not only African politics. Choice (D) is incorrect because the photo shows

collaboration between African Americans and Ghanaians, not division.

Skill: 1C: Identify and explain patterns, connections, or other relationships (causation, changes, continuities, comparison)

Learning Objective: LO 4.2.C: Explain how diasporic solidarity between African Americans and Africans impacted Black politics in the United States and abroad in the twentieth century and beyond

Topic: 4.2: Anticolonialism and Black Political Thought

58. **(B)** Black women in the 6888th managed vital logistics and mail delivery under segregated conditions. (A) is incorrect. The 6888th served overseas in England and France. (C) is incorrect. The military was not desegregated until after the war (1948). (D) is incorrect. The 6888th served abroad in direct support of combat forces.

    Skill: 1C: Identify and explain patterns, connections, or other relationships (causation, changes, continuities, comparison)

    Learning Objective: LO 4.3.A: Describe African Americans' involvement in the Second World War

    Topic: 4.3: African Americans and the Second World War: The Double V Campaign and the G.I. Bill

59. **(B)** The service of the 6888th Battalion embodied the "double victory" goal: defeating fascism overseas while demanding justice at home. (A) is incorrect. African Americans opposed fascism abroad. (C) is incorrect. The 6888th Battalion and other units advanced integration, not segregation. (D) is incorrect. The 6888th Battalion aligned directly with the civil rights goals of the Double V Campaign.

    Skill: 1C: Identify and explain patterns, connections, or other relationships (causation, changes, continuities, comparison)

    Learning Objective: LO 4.3.B: Explain how the Double V Campaign emerged during the Second World War

    Topic: 4.3: African Americans and the Second World War: The Double V Campaign and the G.I. Bill

60. **(C)** Discriminatory state-level administration of federal benefits limited Black veterans' access to housing, education, and capital. (A) is incorrect. Many African American veterans faced barriers at predominantly white institutions. (B) is incorrect. G.I. Bill benefits were often unequally distributed. (D) is incorrect. No such land distribution occurred for Black women.

    Skill: 1C: Identify and explain patterns, connections, or other relationships (causation, changes, continuities, comparison)

    Learning Objective: LO 4.3.C: Describe African Americans' access to the benefits of the G.I. Bill

    Topic: 4.3: African Americans and the Second World War: The Double V Campaign and the G.I. Bill

Section II: Free-Response

1. **Acceptable responses for Part A:**

    - Dr. King promoted nonviolence and civil disobedience, influenced by Gandhi.
    - Malcolm X promoted Black nationalism and self-defense, initially aligned with Nation of Islam ideology.
    - Dr. King focused on integration; Malcolm X initially advocated separation from white society.

    Skill: 1B: Identify and explain the context of a specific event, development, or process.

    Learning Objective: LO 4.9.B: Explain how Black Freedom movement strategies transitioned from civil rights to Black Power.

    Topic: 4.9: Black Religious Nationalism and the Black Power Movement

    Acceptable responses for Part B:

    - Dr. King's "I Have a Dream" speech at the 1963 March on Washington
    - Malcolm X's "The Ballot or the Bullet" speech in 1964
    - Dr. King's leadership in the Southern Christian Leadership Conference (SCLC)
    - Malcolm X's role in the Nation of Islam and later the Organization of Afro-American Unity

    Skill: 1B: Identify and explain the context of a specific event, development, or process.

Learning Objective: LO 4.9.B: Explain how Black Freedom movement strategies transitioned from civil rights to Black Power.

Topic: 4.9: Black Religious Nationalism and the Black Power Movement

Acceptable responses for Part C:

- Dr. King's nonviolent protests garnered sympathy and federal support.
- Malcolm X's rhetoric empowered Black communities and highlighted systemic racism.
- Together, they broadened the scope and appeal of the Civil Rights Movement.

Skill: 2A: Identify and explain a source's claim(s), evidence, and reasoning.

Learning Objective: LO 4.9.B: Explain how Black Freedom movement strategies transitioned from civil rights to Black Power.

Topic: 4.9: Black Religious Nationalism and the Black Power Movement

Acceptable responses for Part D:

- The image symbolizes a potential unity among diverse Black leaders.
- Modern movements like Black Lives Matter reflect both nonviolent protest and calls for systemic change.
- This meeting demonstrates that strategic diversity can coexist within shared goals for racial justice.

Skill: 1B: Identify and explain the context of a specific event, development, or process.

Learning Objective: LO 4.9.B: Explain how Black Freedom movement strategies transitioned from civil rights to Black Power.

Topic: 4.9: Black Religious Nationalism and the Black Power Movement

2. **Acceptable responses for Part A:**

- Slave auctions were dehumanizing public events where individuals, including children, were sold like property.
- Enslaved families were regularly separated during sales, often without notice.
- Northup's description emphasizes the sorrow, fear, and emotional devastation of those being sold.

Skill: 1B: Identify and explain the context of a specific event, development, or process.

Learning Objective: LO 2.5.A: Describe the nature of slave auctions in the nineteenth century United States South.

Topic: 2.5: Slave Auctions and the Domestic Slave Trade

Acceptable responses for Part B:

- The expansion of cotton cultivation in the Deep South created increased demand for enslaved labor.
- Planters in the upper South sold enslaved people to buyers in states like Louisiana and Mississippi.
- This economic incentive resulted in the displacement and destruction of enslaved families.

Skill: 1B: Identify and explain the context of a specific event, development, or process.

Learning Objective: LO 2.5.C: Explain how the growth of the cotton industry in the United States displaced enslaved African American families.

Topic: 2.5: Slave Auctions and the Domestic Slave Trade

Acceptable responses for Part C:

- Northup's narrative offers a firsthand account of slavery's brutality, countering proslavery propaganda.
- His work was published and circulated in the North, influencing the abolitionist movement.
- The detailed emotional perspective was aimed at generating empathy and mobilizing antislavery support.

Skill: 2C: Explain the significance of a source's perspective, purpose, context, and audience.

Learning Objective: LO 2.5.B: Explain how African American authors advanced the causes of abolition and equality in their writings about slave auctions.

Topic: 2.5: Slave Auctions and the Domestic Slave Trade

3. **Acceptable responses for Part A:**

- Ancient African civilizations like Egypt and Nubia inspire pride and cultural identity among African Americans.
- Symbols such as pyramids, the Sphinx, and Nubian queens are used in art, fashion, and media.
- These civilizations demonstrate a legacy of strength, leadership, and cultural richness, challenging historical stereotypes.

Skill: 1A: Identify and explain course concepts, developments, and processes.

Learning Objective: LO 4.8.A: Explain how artists, performers, poets, and musicians of African descent advocated for racial equality and brought international attention to the Black Freedom movement.

Topic: 4.8: The Arts, Music, and the Politics of Freedom

Acceptable responses for Part B:

- The Black diaspora has preserved African heritage through music, dance, oral storytelling, and spiritual practices.
- Traditions such as drumming, call and response singing, and folklore maintain connections to African origins.
- These cultural continuities shape African American identity and community solidarity.

Skill: 1C: Identify and explain patterns, connections, or other relationships (causation, changes, continuities, comparison).

Learning Objective: LO 3.11.A: Describe ways the New Negro movement emphasized self-definition, racial pride, and cultural innovation, and LO 4.8.A: Explain how artists, performers, poets, and musicians of African descent advocated for racial equality and brought international attention to the Black Freedom movement.

Topic: 3.11: The New Negro Movement and the Harlem Renaissance and 4.8: The Arts, Music, and the Politics of Freedom

Acceptable responses for Part C:

- The 1960s Black Power movement invoked images of African kings and queens to promote racial pride.
- Pan-African symbols and colors (red, black, green) are used to signify unity and liberation.
- Modern movements like Afrocentric education and fashion reclaim African heritage to inspire activism.

Skill: 1C: Identify and explain patterns, connections, or other relationships (causation, changes, continuities, comparison).

Learning Objective: LO 4.10.A: Explain how the Black Arts movement (BAM) influenced Black culture in the 1960s and 1970s, and LO 3.11.A: Describe ways the New Negro movement emphasized self-definition, racial pride, and cultural innovation.

Topic: 3.11: The New Negro Movement and the Harlem Renaissance and 4.10: The Black Arts Movement

DBQ Scoring Guide: African American Activism

Reporting Category	Scoring Criteria	Decision Rules and Scoring Notes	Examples That Do Not Earn This Point	Examples That Earn This Point
Thesis/Claim (0–1 pt)	Responds to the prompt with a historically defensible thesis/claim that establishes a line of reasoning. Additional Note: The thesis must appear as one or more sentences in a single location—either in the introduction or conclusion—and be clearly identifiable.	To earn this point, the thesis must make a claim that responds to the prompt rather than restating or rephrasing it. The claim must establish a line of reasoning that directly addresses the question of how African Americans have used diverse forms of activism to fight for freedom, justice, and equality from the nineteenth century to the present.	Restates the prompt without making a claim. Lists activism types without connecting them to a historical argument. Makes an overly vague claim. States an opinion without historical grounding.	Establish a line of reasoning that evaluates the topic of the prompt: "From the nineteenth century to the present, African Americans have advanced the fight for freedom, justice, and equality through evolving forms of activism—combining legal challenges, mass protests, cultural movements, and symbolic acts to confront systemic racism and expand democratic ideals." Establish a line of reasoning with analytic categories: "African American activism has developed through three major strategies: direct resistance to oppression through liberation networks and migration, legal battles to dismantle discriminatory laws, and cultural and symbolic protest to redefine public perception and demand equality." Establish a line of reasoning (minimally acceptable): ▪ "African Americans have fought for freedom in many different ways over time."

DBQ Scoring Guide: African American Activism (*Continued*)

Reporting Category	Scoring Criteria	Decision Rules and Scoring Notes	Examples That Do Not Earn This Point	Examples That Earn This Point
Contextualization (0–1 pt)	Describes a broader historical context relevant to the prompt.	To earn this point, the response must relate the topic of the prompt to broader historical events, developments, or processes that occur before, during, or continue after the time frame of the question.	Mentions historical events without linking them to African American activism. Provides only a brief, vague reference. Includes unrelated facts.	Place activism in the post-Civil War racial order: ▪ "Following Reconstruction, the rise of Jim Crow laws and systemic disenfranchisement forced African Americans to seek justice outside of mainstream political institutions, laying the groundwork for grassroots activism, self-help organizations, and independent Black institutions." Link to national demographic and political shifts: ▪ "The Great Migration, highlighted in *The Messenger* (Source 2), moved millions of African Americans from the rural South to urban centers in the North and West, creating new communities that became hubs for cultural expression, labor organizing, and political mobilization." Include relevant cultural/intellectual context: ▪ "The Harlem Renaissance encouraged cultural pride and demonstrated the power of literature, music, and art as activism, influencing later protest traditions from the Civil Rights Movement to Kaepernick's use of sports as a political stage (Source 5)."

DBQ Scoring Guide: African American Activism (*Continued*)

Reporting Category	Scoring Criteria	Decision Rules and Scoring Notes	Examples That Do Not Earn This Point	Examples That Earn This Point
Evidence (0–3 pts)	Uses evidence from the documents and beyond to support an argument.	To earn the evidence points, responses must use at least three of the provided sources, integrate outside historical evidence, and explain how that evidence supports the argument.	Summarizes sources without connecting them to the argument. Mentions outside events but fails to explain their relevance. Quotes documents without analysis.	Use sources to support the argument: ▪ Am I Not a Woman and a Sister? (Source 1) reflects how African Americans used abolitionist imagery to humanize enslaved people and challenge racial and gender oppression." ▪ The Messenger editorial (Source 2) shows how migration was framed as a deliberate act of resistance to Southern racial violence and economic exploitation." ▪ "Harriet Tubman (Source 3) embodies direct resistance, using the Underground Railroad to free enslaved people and undermine the slave economy." ▪ "The Brown v. Board opinion (Source 4) illustrates the power of legal activism to dismantle the constitutional basis for segregation." ▪ "Kaepernick's kneeling (Source 5) demonstrates modern symbolic protest drawing on earlier traditions of visibility and moral confrontation."

DBQ Scoring Guide: African American Activism (*Continued*)

Reporting Category	Scoring Criteria	Decision Rules and Scoring Notes	Examples That Do Not Earn This Point	Examples That Earn This Point
				Outside evidence beyond the sources: ▪ "The March on Washington in 1963 combined mass protest with a legislative push that contributed to the Civil Rights Act of 1964." ▪ "Student sit-ins organized by SNCC in 1960 exemplified youth-led direct action that reshaped public opinion and forced desegregation of public spaces." Explain how the evidence supports the argument: ▪ "By combining symbolic protest, legal strategy, and collective migration, African Americans developed a multifaceted activism that adapted to each era's challenges while remaining focused on freedom and equality."

DBQ Scoring Guide: African American Activism (*Continued*)

Reporting Category	Scoring Criteria	Decision Rules and Scoring Notes	Examples That Do Not Earn This Point	Examples That Earn This Point
Source Use (0–1 pt)	For at least 2 sources, explains how or why the source's perspective, purpose, historical situation, or audience is relevant to the argument.	To earn this point, the response must explain—not just state how a source's perspective, purpose, historical situation, or audience is relevant to the argument.	Simply states "This source shows..." without analysis. Identifies perspective/purpose inaccurately. Provides context but fails to connect it to the argument.	Explain perspective, purpose, and historical situation: ▪ The Messenger editorial (Source 2), written in 1920 for a Black readership, reflects the perspective of African American intellectuals urging migration as a path to economic and political empowerment during the height of Jim Crow." ▪ "The *Brown v. Board* opinion (Source 4), delivered by Chief Justice Earl Warren, carried the authority of the Supreme Court and was intended to compel compliance from segregated school districts nationwide." ▪ "Kaepernick's protest (Source 5), performed during a nationally televised NFL game, strategically used the mass audience of American football to draw attention to systemic racism and police brutality." Tie sourcing to the argument: ▪ "Recognizing that these sources were created for specific audiences under specific historical pressures shows how African Americans used every available platform—from abolitionist newspapers to the Supreme Court to professional sports—to advance their cause."

DBQ Scoring Guide: African American Activism (*Continued*)

Reporting Category	Scoring Criteria	Decision Rules and Scoring Notes	Examples That Do Not Earn This Point	Examples That Earn This Point
Reasoning (0–1 pt)	Uses historical reasoning (continuity/change, comparison, causation) to frame the argument.	To earn this point, the response must use a reasoning skill to organize and connect the argument across time and types of activism.	Lists events without linking them. Makes vague claims without specifics. Uses reasoning words but without analytical substance.	Show continuity and change over time: ▪ "The liberation work of Harriet Tubman (Source 3) and the symbolic imagery of Am I Not a Woman and a Sister?* (Source 1) share the same goal as Kaepernick's protest (Source 5)—publicly confronting racial injustice—though their strategies reflect different historical contexts." Explain causation: ▪ "The violence and economic oppression of the Jim Crow South drove the Great Migration (Source 2), which in turn expanded African American political influence in Northern cities, enabling legal victories like Brown v. Board (Source 4)." Make comparisons: ▪ "Symbolic activism, such as the 19th-century abolitionist imagery (Source 1), can be compared to modern symbolic acts like kneeling during the anthem (Source 5), while legal challenges like Brown v. Board (Source 4) parallel earlier use of the courts to fight discrimination in housing and transportation."

DBQ Scoring Breakdown

This chart summarizes the document-based question (DBQ) scoring rubric for AP African American Studies. Use it to understand how your response will be evaluated and how you can earn all possible points.

Scoring Category	Points Available	Key Elements
Thesis/Claim	1	▪ Write a clear, defensible thesis or claim directly addressing the prompt.
Contextualization	1	▪ Provide a roader historical or disciplinary context. ▪ Go beyond prompt details.
Evidence from Documents	2	▪ Use at least 6 pieces of evidence from documents. ▪ Support argument clearly.
Additional Evidence	1	▪ Include at least 1 specific piece of evidence beyond the documents.
Analysis and Reasoning	2	▪ Analyze connections, patterns, or nuances. ▪ Explain perspective, purpose, context, or audience for at least 2 sources.
Total Points	7	**Maximum score available**

DBQ Success Checklist—Maximize Your Score

Checklist Item	Actionable Tips
Thesis/Claim	Craft a clear thesis that directly addresses the prompt and establishes a line of reasoning.
Contextualization	Describe a broader historical or disciplinary context to situate your argument.
Evidence from Documents	Use at least 6 pieces of evidence from documents and support your argument clearly.
Additional Evidence	Include 1 or more pieces of evidence beyond the provided documents.
Analysis and Reasoning	Analyze connections, patterns, or nuances, and explain the perspective, purpose, context, or audience of at least 2 sources.
Structure and Time Management	Structure your essay with clear paragraphs, and manage your time effectively.
Source Citation	Cite sources by letter, author, or title to integrate evidence smoothly and clearly.

ANSWER SHEET
Practice Test 2

Section 1: Multiple-Choice

1.	Ⓐ Ⓑ Ⓒ Ⓓ	16.	Ⓐ Ⓑ Ⓒ Ⓓ	31.	Ⓐ Ⓑ Ⓒ Ⓓ	46.	Ⓐ Ⓑ Ⓒ Ⓓ
2.	Ⓐ Ⓑ Ⓒ Ⓓ	17.	Ⓐ Ⓑ Ⓒ Ⓓ	32.	Ⓐ Ⓑ Ⓒ Ⓓ	47.	Ⓐ Ⓑ Ⓒ Ⓓ
3.	Ⓐ Ⓑ Ⓒ Ⓓ	18.	Ⓐ Ⓑ Ⓒ Ⓓ	33.	Ⓐ Ⓑ Ⓒ Ⓓ	48.	Ⓐ Ⓑ Ⓒ Ⓓ
4.	Ⓐ Ⓑ Ⓒ Ⓓ	19.	Ⓐ Ⓑ Ⓒ Ⓓ	34.	Ⓐ Ⓑ Ⓒ Ⓓ	49.	Ⓐ Ⓑ Ⓒ Ⓓ
5.	Ⓐ Ⓑ Ⓒ Ⓓ	20.	Ⓐ Ⓑ Ⓒ Ⓓ	35.	Ⓐ Ⓑ Ⓒ Ⓓ	50.	Ⓐ Ⓑ Ⓒ Ⓓ
6.	Ⓐ Ⓑ Ⓒ Ⓓ	21.	Ⓐ Ⓑ Ⓒ Ⓓ	36.	Ⓐ Ⓑ Ⓒ Ⓓ	51.	Ⓐ Ⓑ Ⓒ Ⓓ
7.	Ⓐ Ⓑ Ⓒ Ⓓ	22.	Ⓐ Ⓑ Ⓒ Ⓓ	37.	Ⓐ Ⓑ Ⓒ Ⓓ	52.	Ⓐ Ⓑ Ⓒ Ⓓ
8.	Ⓐ Ⓑ Ⓒ Ⓓ	23.	Ⓐ Ⓑ Ⓒ Ⓓ	38.	Ⓐ Ⓑ Ⓒ Ⓓ	53.	Ⓐ Ⓑ Ⓒ Ⓓ
9.	Ⓐ Ⓑ Ⓒ Ⓓ	24.	Ⓐ Ⓑ Ⓒ Ⓓ	39.	Ⓐ Ⓑ Ⓒ Ⓓ	54.	Ⓐ Ⓑ Ⓒ Ⓓ
10.	Ⓐ Ⓑ Ⓒ Ⓓ	25.	Ⓐ Ⓑ Ⓒ Ⓓ	40.	Ⓐ Ⓑ Ⓒ Ⓓ	55.	Ⓐ Ⓑ Ⓒ Ⓓ
11.	Ⓐ Ⓑ Ⓒ Ⓓ	26.	Ⓐ Ⓑ Ⓒ Ⓓ	41.	Ⓐ Ⓑ Ⓒ Ⓓ	56.	Ⓐ Ⓑ Ⓒ Ⓓ
12.	Ⓐ Ⓑ Ⓒ Ⓓ	27.	Ⓐ Ⓑ Ⓒ Ⓓ	42.	Ⓐ Ⓑ Ⓒ Ⓓ	57.	Ⓐ Ⓑ Ⓒ Ⓓ
13.	Ⓐ Ⓑ Ⓒ Ⓓ	28.	Ⓐ Ⓑ Ⓒ Ⓓ	43.	Ⓐ Ⓑ Ⓒ Ⓓ	58.	Ⓐ Ⓑ Ⓒ Ⓓ
14.	Ⓐ Ⓑ Ⓒ Ⓓ	29.	Ⓐ Ⓑ Ⓒ Ⓓ	44.	Ⓐ Ⓑ Ⓒ Ⓓ	59.	Ⓐ Ⓑ Ⓒ Ⓓ
15.	Ⓐ Ⓑ Ⓒ Ⓓ	30.	Ⓐ Ⓑ Ⓒ Ⓓ	45.	Ⓐ Ⓑ Ⓒ Ⓓ	60.	Ⓐ Ⓑ Ⓒ Ⓓ

Practice Test 2

Section I: Multiple-Choice

TIME—1 HOUR AND 10 MINUTES—60 QUESTIONS

DIRECTIONS: Each question or incomplete statement is followed by four answer choices. Select the one choice that best answers the question or completes the statement.

Questions 1 through 4 refer to the following.

Source 1: Juan Garrido's Petition, 1538

"I, Juan Garrido, black in color, resident of this city [Mexico], appear before Your Mercy and state that I am in need of providing evidence to the perpetuity of the king [a perpetuidad rey], a report on how I served Your Majesty in the conquest and pacification of this New Spain, from the time when the Marqués del Valle [Cortés] entered it; and in his company I was present at all the invasions and conquests and pacifications which were carried out, always with the said Marqués, all of which I did at my own expense without being given either salary or allotment of natives [repartimiento de indios] or anything else. As I am married and a resident of this city, where I have always lived; and also as I went with the Marqués del Valle to discover the islands which are in that part of the southern sea [the Pacific] where there was much hunger and privation; and also as I went to discover and pacify the islands of San Juan de Buriquén de Puerto Rico; and also as I went on the pacification and conquest of the island of Cuba with the adelantado Diego Velázquez; in all these ways for thirty years have I served and continue to serve Your Majesty—for these reasons stated above do I petition Your Mercy. And also because I was the first to have the inspiration to sow wheat here in New Spain and to see if it took; I did this and experimented at my own expense."

Source: The opening of Juan Garrido's probanza (petitionary proof of merit) of September 27, 1538 (Archivo General de Indias, Seville, México 204), f.1. Transcription in Ricardo Alegría, Juan Garrido, el conquistador negro en las Antillas, Florida, México y California, 1503–1540 (Centro de Estudios Avanzados de Puerto Rico y el Caribe, 1990). Translated by Matthew Restall, in "Black Conquistadors: Armed Africans in Early Spanish America," The Americas 57 no. 2 (October 2000): 171.

Source 2: Juan Garrido on a Spanish Expedition, Sixteenth Century

1. What does Juan Garrido's petition reveal about the roles Africans played in early Spanish expeditions?
   (A) It highlights their forced labor in mining operations only.
   (B) It shows how Africans like Garrido voluntarily participated in conquest and petitioned for recognition.
   (C) It suggests that Africans were only translators with limited social mobility.
   (D) It implies that Africans remained enslaved with no legal rights or military involvement.

2. How does Juan Garrido's experience as a ladino reflect the status of Atlantic creoles?
   (A) It shows they lacked the ability to integrate into European society.
   (B) It exemplifies their multilingualism and ability to serve as cultural intermediaries.
   (C) It limits them to agricultural labor roles.
   (D) It shows they were mostly unskilled and uninfluential in colonization.

3. What is the significance of Juan Garrido's presence in the Americas in 1513?
   (A) He was the first African enslaved in the American South.
   (B) His military service helped him avoid enslavement and gain social standing.
   (C) He represented the majority of Africans who came through the Middle Passage.
   (D) His presence was limited to religious conversion efforts.

4. Which of the following best describes the historical contribution of ladinos like Juan Garrido?
   (A) They were passive subjects in European colonization.
   (B) They introduced Christianity to Indigenous communities.
   (C) They actively shaped early American history through exploration and skilled labor.
   (D) They remained isolated from both African and European societies.

Questions 5 through 8 refer to the following.

Source: *Marcus Garvey at His Desk, 1924*

PRACTICE TEST 2

5. What best explains the mission of Marcus Garvey's Universal Negro Improvement Association (UNIA)?
   (A) To promote integration between Black and white Americans
   (B) To support civil rights litigation through the U.S. court system
   (C) To unite people of African descent globally through Black self-determination and independence
   (D) To promote Black pride, economic self-sufficiency, and transnational unity across the African diaspora

6. Why did Marcus Garvey's Back-to-Africa movement and the Black Star Line gain widespread attention in the 1920s?
   (A) They symbolized a bold effort to repatriate African Americans and unite the diaspora through pan-African nationalism.
   (B) They were created to encourage African Americans to seek civil rights within the U.S. legal system.
   (C) They were sponsored by mainstream civil rights organizations of the time.
   (D) They were intended to challenge European powers directly in Africa.

7. How did Garvey's vision of Black nationalism differ from that of other civil rights leaders of the era?
   (A) He focused exclusively on legal reforms through the U.S. Supreme Court.
   (B) He promoted multiracial coalitions and social integration.
   (C) He encouraged industrial collaboration with white-owned corporations.
   (D) He rejected integration, advocating instead for self-reliance and separate Black institutions globally.

8. What was a long-term impact of the UNIA on political thought in the African diaspora?
   (A) It became the legal foundation of the NAACP's court cases.
   (B) It inspired desegregation efforts in public schools.
   (C) It established a model for later Black nationalist movements advocating global Black solidarity.
   (D) It focused on religious revivalism more than political change.

Questions 9 through 12 refer to the following.

Source 1: Engraved Portrait of Five African American Legislators from Reconstruction Congresses, Early 1880

Source 2: The Fifteenth Amendment to the United States Constitution (1870)

"AMENDMENT XV

Passed by Congress February 26, 1869. Ratified February 3, 1870.

Section 1.

The right of citizens of the United States to vote shall not be denied or abridged by the United States or by any State on account of race, color, or previous condition of servitude—

Section 2.

The Congress shall have power to enforce this article by appropriate legislation."

Source: The Constitution: Amendments 13–15, Founding Documents (National Archives).

9. What was one major impact of the Fifteenth Amendment during Reconstruction?
   (A) It guaranteed women's suffrage alongside Black men's voting rights.
   (B) It repealed the Black Codes and ended racial segregation in the South.
   (C) It gave African American men the right to own land in every state.
   (D) It granted Black men the right to vote, which expanded their participation in American politics.

10. What pattern is best illustrated by the portrait of African American legislators from the 1880s?
   (A) The federal government excluded Black political leaders during Reconstruction.
   (B) Black officeholding was symbolic but lacked any real legislative power.
   (C) Black men gained political representation during Reconstruction, but many of these gains were later reversed under Jim Crow laws.
   (D) The number of Black legislators increased steadily from Reconstruction through the 1950s.

11. How did the Reconstruction Amendments collectively reshape citizenship in the United States?
   (A) They abolished slavery, established birthright citizenship, and expanded voting rights regardless of race.
   (B) They granted land and reparations to all freed people.
   (C) They eliminated all state-level restrictions on civil rights.
   (D) They prioritized economic reforms over political representation.

12. How does the passage of the Fifteenth Amendment compare with the impact of the Fourteenth Amendment?
   (A) Both amendments focused only on criminal justice reform.
   (B) The Fourteenth Amendment defined citizenship and equal protection, while the Fifteenth Amendment expanded voting rights to Black men.
   (C) The Fifteenth Amendment repealed the Fourteenth Amendment in Southern states.
   (D) Both amendments were created to prevent foreign immigration.

Questions 13 through 16 refer to the following.

Source 1: *Juvenile Convicts at Work in the Fields*, 1903

PRACTICE TEST 2

Source 2: Picture Postcard of a North Carolina Convict Camp, circa 1910

13. What do these images most clearly reveal about labor systems in the post-Reconstruction South?

(A) They show the growing influence of Black landowners across the South.
(B) They depict racial equality emerging within industrial labor systems.
(C) They demonstrate how convict leasing was used to reenslave African Americans through forced labor.
(D) They suggest Southern states transitioned to wage-based labor after Reconstruction.

14. What is the significance of the visual portrayal of child laborers in the 1903 image?

(A) It highlights the role of children in organizing early labor unions.
(B) It shows an increase in apprenticeship programs after emancipation.
(C) It reflects how Black Codes allowed children to be forced into unpaid labor without parental consent.
(D) It captures the rise of free public education for all children regardless of race.

15. How did Black Codes impede the economic advancement of African Americans after the Civil War?

(A) By protecting their property from confiscation and ensuring voting rights
(B) By offering loans for land purchases and business development
(C) By restricting landownership and forcing African Americans into low-paid or unpaid labor contracts
(D) By integrating African Americans into urban industrial jobs

16. What pattern do the two visual sources reflect regarding postemancipation labor practices in the South?

(A) Despite the end of slavery, African Americans were subjected to exploitative labor systems like sharecropping and convict leasing.
(B) Black workers were integrated into industries in the North at high wages.
(C) Enslaved labor was fully abolished, resulting in economic mobility.
(D) The Freedmen's Bureau established landownership for most freedpeople.

Questions 17 through 20 refer to the following.

Source 1: *Plessy v. Ferguson* Supreme Court Ruling, 1896—Majority Opinion by Justice Henry Brown

"Justice Henry Brown of Michigan delivered the majority opinion, which sustained the constitutionality of Louisiana's Jim Crow law. In part, he said:

> We consider the underlying fallacy of the plaintiff's argument to consist in the assumption that the enforced separation of the two races stamps the colored race with a badge of inferiority. If this be so, it is not by reason of anything found in the act, but solely because the colored race chooses to put that construction upon it.... The argument also assumes that social prejudice may be overcome by legislation, and that equal rights cannot be secured except by an enforced commingling of the two races... If the civil and political rights of both races be equal, one cannot be inferior to the

other civilly or politically. If one race be inferior to the other socially, the Constitution of the United States cannot put them upon the same plane."

Source: U.S. Supreme Court, *Plessy vs. Ferguson*, Judgement, Decided May 18, 1896; Records of the Supreme Court of the United States; National Archives.

Source 2: *Plessy v. Ferguson* Supreme Court Ruling, 1896—Dissenting Opinion by Justice John Marshall Harlan

"In the lone dissent, Kentuckian Justice John Marshall Harlan wrote:

I am of the opinion that the statute of Louisiana is inconsistent with the personal liberties of citizens, white and black, in that State, and hostile to both the spirit and the letter of the Constitution of the United States. If laws of like character should be enacted in the several States of the Union, the effect would be in the highest degree mischievous. Slavery as an institution tolerated by law would, it is true, have disappeared from our country, but there would remain a power in the States, by sinister legislation, to interfere with the blessings of freedom; to regulate civil rights common to all citizens, upon the basis of race; and to place in a condition of legal inferiority a large body of American citizens, now constituting a part of the political community, called the people of the United States, for whom and by whom, through representatives, our government is administrated. Such a system is inconsistent with the guarantee given by the Constitution to each State of a republican form of government, and may be stricken down by congressional action, or by the courts in the discharge of their solemn duty to maintain the supreme law of the land, anything in the Constitution or laws of any State to the contrary notwithstanding."

Source: U.S. Supreme Court, *Plessy vs. Ferguson*, Judgement, Decided May 18, 1896; Records of the Supreme Court of the United States; National Archives.

17. What claim did the majority opinion in *Plessy v. Ferguson* seek to justify?

(A) That segregation was unconstitutional under the Fourteenth Amendment
(B) That African Americans could vote freely and equally
(C) That segregated facilities were inherently unequal and damaging
(D) That racial segregation was legal if the separate facilities were "equal" in quality

18. What argument did Justice Harlan make in his dissenting opinion in *Plessy v. Ferguson*?

(A) That states had the right to determine their own definitions of citizenship
(B) That the Constitution is color-blind and all citizens are equal before the law
(C) That segregation was justified by precedent from Reconstruction courts
(D) That African Americans should be granted separate facilities based on social customs

19. Based on both sources, which development best represents the long-term impact of the majority decision?

(A) The desegregation of all public institutions in the early 1900s
(B) The widespread legalization of racial segregation under the "separate but equal" doctrine
(C) The immediate federal enforcement of equal facilities for all citizens
(D) The expansion of African American voting rights and legal protections

20. Which of the following would most effectively support Justice Harlan's claim that segregation violated the U.S. Constitution?

(A) A Reconstruction-era literacy test used to disenfranchise Black voters
(B) A photograph of segregated train cars that appear identical in condition
(C) A legal analysis demonstrating that separate facilities systematically denied African Americans equal access to public goods and services
(D) A political cartoon that mocks the U.S. Supreme Court

Questions 21 through 24 refer to the following.

Source 1: ***Segregated Water Fountains*** **(date unknown)**

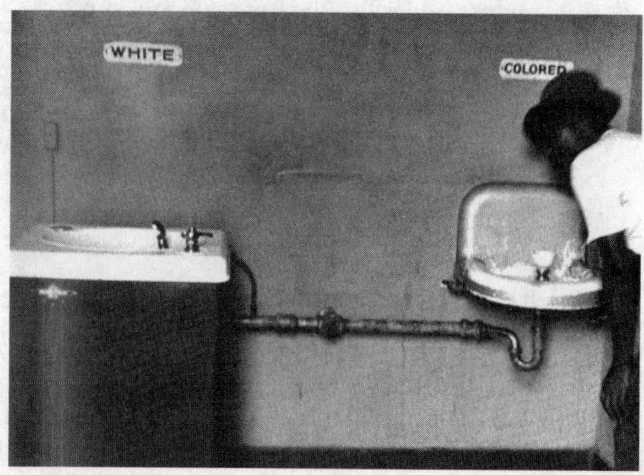

Source 2: ***Segregated Restrooms,*** **Circa 1960**

21. Which claim is best supported by both photographic sources?
   (A) Segregation created equal public spaces for African Americans and white Americans.
   (B) Jim Crow laws were limited to Southern states and private institutions.
   (C) Racial segregation during the Jim Crow era created visibly unequal and humiliating public accommodations for African Americans.
   (D) The government guaranteed access to separate but equal facilities for Black citizens.

22. What historical development do these images most clearly reflect?
   (A) The early integration of public schools following *Brown v. Board of Education*
   (B) The efforts of the Freedmen's Bureau to protect African American rights
   (C) The enforcement of de jure segregation laws following *Plessy v. Ferguson*
   (D) The success of New Deal programs in eliminating discriminatory policies

23. Which form of resistance best aligns with African American responses to the conditions seen in these images?
   (A) Boycotts and organized campaigns to expose the inequality and humiliation of segregation
   (B) Emigration from the South to establish all-Black cities in the Midwest
   (C) Lawsuits defending white business owners' rights to segregate public facilities
   (D) Protests led exclusively by white liberal allies of Black communities

24. Which piece of evidence would best support the claim that segregation was part of a larger system of racial oppression during the nadir?
   (A) A textbook showing different restroom designs in urban and rural areas
   (B) An excerpt from Ida B. Wells's writings condemning mob violence and legal inequality
   (C) A political cartoon advocating racial harmony through separation
   (D) A state law mandating integrated cemeteries in New England

Questions 25 through 28 refer to the following.

Source 1: Advertisement for Madam C. J. Walker Products, 1906–1950

Source 2: *Photograph of a Convention of Madam C. J. Walker Agents at Villa Lewaro, 1924*

25. Which claim is best supported by the two sources about Madam C. J. Walker?
    (A) Her success was limited by mainstream beauty standards of the time.
    (B) Her primary contributions were philanthropic rather than economic.
    (C) She focused her career on integrating Black and white corporate industries.
    (D) She empowered Black women through entrepreneurship and the development of beauty and wellness products.

26. How did Madam C. J. Walker's business model contribute to the well-being of Black communities in the early twentieth century?
    (A) It provided employment and leadership opportunities for Black women and supported local communities through economic independence.
    (B) It encouraged industrial jobs in predominantly white-owned factories.
    (C) It relied on federal loans granted during Reconstruction.
    (D) It primarily promoted beauty ideals from white-owned publications.

27. Which broader development do the sources reflect in early-twentieth-century African American life?
    (A) The decline of independent Black-owned businesses during the nadir
    (B) The adoption of European cultural norms in Black communities
    (C) The migration of African Americans into rural agricultural spaces
    (D) The rise of Black economic self-sufficiency and institutions outside white society

28. What kind of evidence would most strongly support a claim about the legacy of Madam C. J. Walker?
    (A) A political cartoon criticizing New Deal labor laws
    (B) An article highlighting how Walker's agents became community leaders and business owners
    (C) A timeline showing migration patterns during the Great Depression
    (D) A textbook excerpt on Black church music in the Harlem Renaissance

PRACTICE TEST 2

Questions 29 through 31 refer to the following.

"Heritage" by Gwendolyn Bennett, 1922

I want to see the slim palm-trees,
Pulling at the clouds
With little pointed fingers....

I want to see lithe Negro girls,
Etched dark against the sky
While sunset lingers.

I want to hear the silent sands,
Singing to the moon
Before the Sphinx-still face....

I want to hear the chanting
Around a heathen fire
Of a strange black race.

I want to breathe the Lotus flow'r,
Sighing to the stars
With tendrils drinking at the Nile....
I want to feel the surging
Of my sad people's soul
Hidden by a minstrel-smile.

Source: Gwendolyn B. Bennett, "Heritage," *Opportunity* 1, no. 12 (December 1923): 371. The ellipsis points in this poem are in the original and do not indicate missing text.

29. What is the significance of Gwendolyn Bennett's perspective in the poem "Heritage"?

(A) She rejects African ancestry in favor of European traditions.
(B) She critiques African American culture as disconnected from global identity.
(C) She romanticizes the institution of slavery as a means of cultural preservation.
(D) She expresses a longing and personal connection to Africa as part of her identity.

30. Which best describes the purpose of Bennett's use of imagery in "Heritage"?

(A) To promote a return to rural Southern life as a source of heritage
(B) To counter stereotypes and elevate Africa as a place of beauty and cultural richness
(C) To explain the legal injustices faced by African Americans in the 1920s
(D) To promote industrialization as a form of progress in Black communities

31. What element of the Harlem Renaissance does "Heritage" most clearly reflect?

(A) Advocacy for desegregation through legal petitions
(B) A reflective exploration of African heritage and its significance to African American identity
(C) Support for Americanization of immigrant communities
(D) A campaign to eliminate jazz and blues from African American art forms

Question 32 through 35 refer to the following.

Source 1: Anonymous Letter Beckoning African Americans to Leave the South, published in *The Messenger*, March 1920

"Fellow Negroes of the South, leave there. Go North, East, and West—anywhere—to get out of that hell hole. There are better schools here for your children, higher wages for yourselves, votes if you are twenty-one, better housing and more liberty. All is not rosy here, by any means, but it is Paradise compared with Georgia, Arkansas, Texas, Mississippi and Alabama. Besides, you make it better for those you leave behind. Labor becomes scarce, so that the Bourbons of Dixie are compelled to pay your brothers back home more wages. They will give them more schools and privileges, too, to try to get them to come back and, secondly, to try to keep you from leaving.

Stop buying property in the South, to be burned down and run away from over night. Sell out your stuff quietly, saying nothing to the Negro lackeys, and leave! Come into the land of at least incipient civilization!"

Source: "Negroes, Leave the South!" *The Messenger*, March 1920, p. 2.

PRACTICE TEST 2

Source 2: Map of the Great Migration

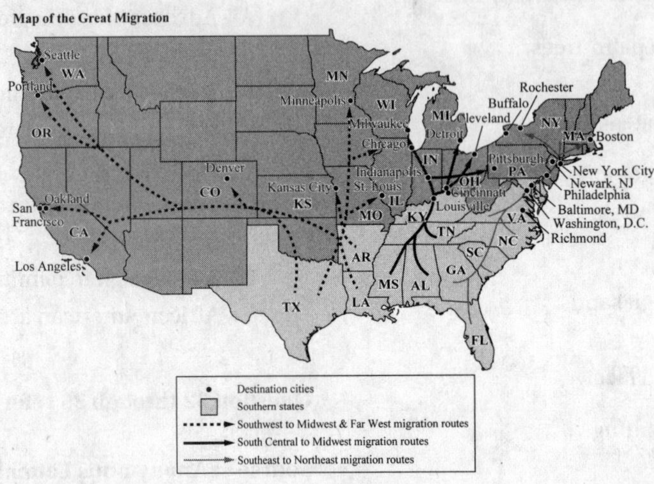

32. What was the most likely purpose of the anonymous letter in Source 1?

(A) To document the legal reforms in the Southern Black Codes
(B) To call on African Americans to protest publicly in Southern courthouses
(C) To encourage African Americans to seek freedom and opportunity by migrating North
(D) To warn African Americans of the dangers of industrial labor in the North

33. Based on the letter's tone and content, what can best be inferred about its audience?

(A) The audience was white laborers who sought job security during wartime.
(B) The audience was African Americans enduring racial terror and poverty in the Jim Crow South.
(C) The audience was Southern politicians sympathetic to anti-lynching legislation.
(D) The audience was industrial leaders seeking to recruit Southern workers.

34. What trend is most clearly represented in the map of the Great Migration?

(A) African Americans migrated in large numbers from the rural South to urban centers in the North, Midwest, and West.
(B) White populations declined in cities in the North as a result of racial violence.
(C) The migration was primarily from cities in the North to farms in the South.
(D) African Americans moved primarily for educational opportunities in the South.

35. Which conclusion is best supported by combining the insights of both sources?

(A) The Great Migration led to the permanent end of racism in cities in the North.
(B) A combination of racial violence and economic opportunity motivated African Americans to relocate, reshaping American cities and culture.
(C) African Americans primarily moved for agricultural opportunities and landownership.
(D) Southern leaders widely supported the goals of the Great Migration.

PRACTICE TEST 2

Questions 36 through 39 refer to the following.

Source: Excerpt from *Brown v. Board of Education of Topeka*, Opinion, May 17, 1954

"MR. CHIEF JUSTICE WARREN delivered the opinion of the Court.

These cases come to us from the States of Kansas, South Carolina, Virginia, and Delaware. They are premised on different facts and different local conditions, but a common legal question justifies their consideration together in this consolidated opinion.

We conclude that, in the field of public education, the doctrine of 'separate but equal' has no place. Separate educational facilities are inherently unequal. Therefore, we hold that the plaintiffs and others similarly situated for whom the actions have been brought are, by reason of the segregation complained of, deprived of the equal protection of the laws guaranteed by the Fourteenth Amendment. This disposition makes unnecessary any discussion whether such segregation also violates the Due Process Clause of the Fourteenth Amendment.

Because these are class actions, because of the wide applicability of this decision, and because of the great variety of local conditions, the formulation of decrees in these cases presents problems of considerable complexity. On reargument, the consideration of appropriate relief was necessarily subordinated to the primary question—the constitutionality of segregation in public education. We have now announced that such segregation is a denial of the equal protection of the laws. In order that we may have the full assistance of the parties in formulating decrees, the cases will be restored to the docket, and the parties are requested to present further argument on Questions 4 and 5 previously propounded by the Court for the reargument this Term The Attorney General of the United States is again invited to participate. The Attorneys General of the states requiring or permitting segregation in public education will also be permitted to appear as amici curiae upon request to do so by September 15, 1954, and submission of briefs by October 1, 1954.

It is so ordered."

Source: *Brown v. Board of Education of Topeka*, Opinion; May 17, 1954; Records of the Supreme Court of the United States; Record Group 267; National Archives.

36. According to the Source, what was the primary constitutional basis for the Court's decision in *Brown v. Board of Education*?

(A) The First Amendment's guarantee of free speech
(B) The Fourteenth Amendment's Equal Protection Clause
(C) The Fifth Amendment's protection against self-incrimination
(D) The Tenth Amendment's reservation of powers to the states

37. What procedural step did the Supreme Court take after announcing its decision in *Brown v. Board of Education*?

(A) It immediately ordered all schools to integrate without further hearings.
(B) It sent the case back to the lower courts for retrial.
(C) It restored the case to the docket to hear further arguments on how to implement the decision.
(D) It dismissed the case because states refused to comply.

38. What broader historical context best explains why the *Brown v. Board of Education* ruling was necessary?

(A) African Americans continued to face daily segregation and legal discrimination in schools, housing, and public spaces.
(B) Public schools were mostly integrated by the 1940s.
(C) The Reconstruction Amendments had been repealed by mid-century.
(D) Voter suppression was the only civil rights concern in the 1950s.

39. Which of the following best describes one response to the *Brown v. Board of Education* ruling?

(A) Public support for integration was immediate and widespread across the South.
(B) Many school districts voluntarily integrated without incident.
(C) Some states resisted by cutting funding to integrated schools or closing them altogether.
(D) Federal troops refused to support integration efforts due to local opposition.

Questions 40 through 43 refer to the following.

Source: Home Owners' Loan Corporation "Residential Security" Map of Philadelphia and Camden, 1937

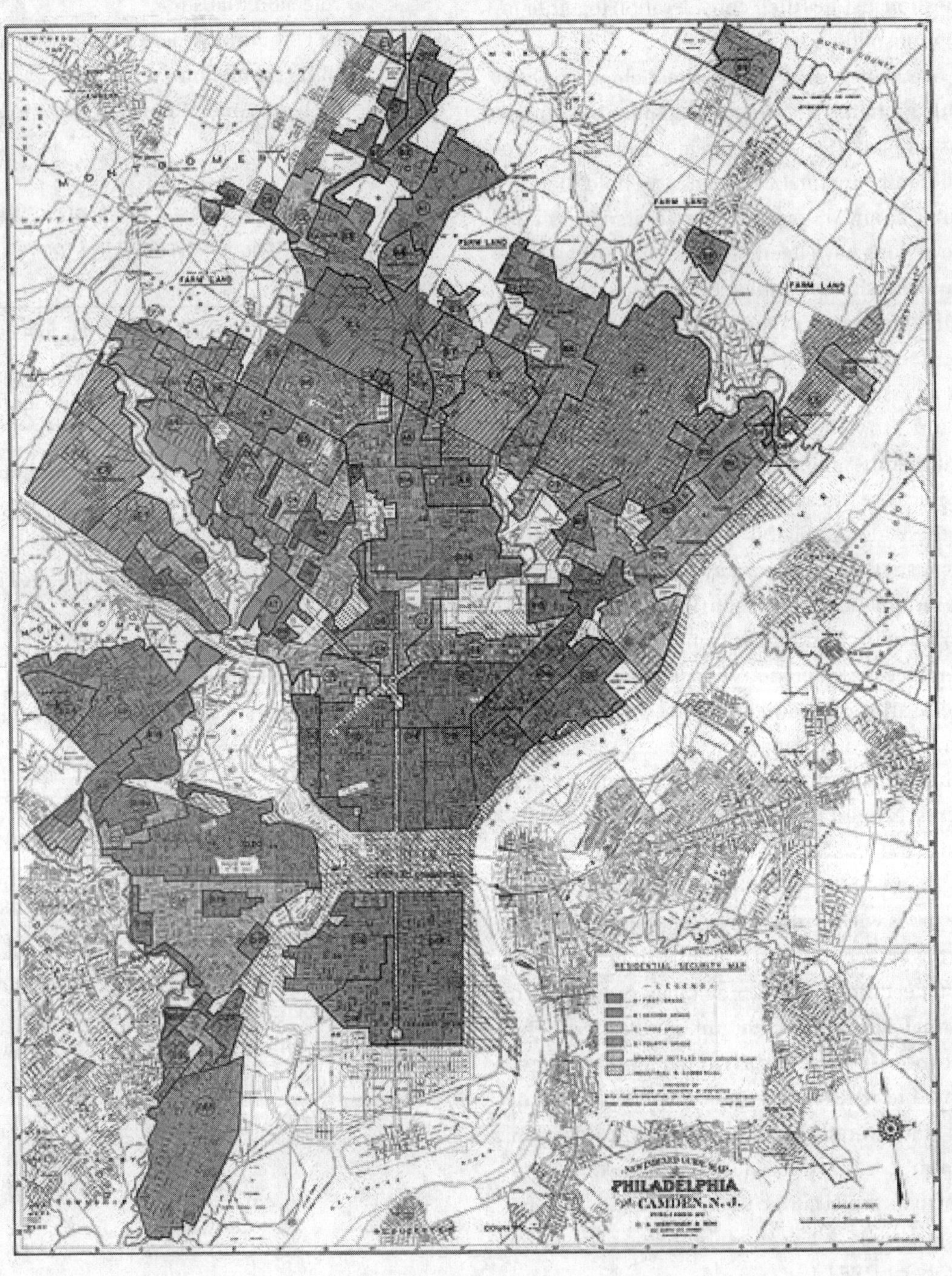

PRACTICE TEST 2

40. What pattern is most clearly revealed by the 1937 "residential security" map of Philadelphia and Camden?
    (A) Equal mortgage access for both Black and white residents across all neighborhoods
    (B) Institutionalized racial discrimination that denied loans to Black communities labeled as "hazardous"
    (C) The concentration of African Americans in high-income urban housing zones
    (D) A shift toward racial integration in housing as supported by federal programs

41. What does the term *redlining* refer to as evidenced by the source?
    (A) A banking initiative that ensured fair lending practices in minority neighborhoods
    (B) A New Deal program that prioritized desegregation of public housing
    (C) A government-backed policy of denying home loans based on racially coded neighborhood risk
    (D) A process by which real estate developers reinvested in underserved communities

42. Which long-term effect did redlining have on African American communities?
    (A) It prevented many Black families from building generational wealth through homeownership.
    (B) It eliminated racial wealth gaps through public-housing vouchers.
    (C) It expanded transportation options in underserved neighborhoods.
    (D) It increased environmental protections in redlined communities.

43. What conclusion can be drawn by comparing the Home Owners' Loan Corporation (HOLC) map to present-day patterns of racial inequality?
    (A) HOLC maps no longer influence modern housing or health disparities.
    (B) Segregated housing was resolved entirely after the passage of the Civil Rights Act of 1964.
    (C) Redlining contributed to entrenched inequities in housing, health, and infrastructure that persist today.
    (D) Urban planning has since prioritized reinvestment in formerly redlined Black neighborhoods.

Questions 44 through 47 refer to the following.

Source 1: Elijah Muhammad Addressing Black Muslims at Convention, 1966

Source 2: Malcolm X and Martin Luther King Jr. After Press Conference at U.S. Capitol, 1964

44. Based on Source 1, what belief most defined Elijah Muhammad's leadership of the Nation of Islam?

    (A) The rejection of all Islamic traditions in favor of Christian theology
    (B) The promotion of complete racial integration in both public and private life
    (C) The emphasis on self-determination, Islamic faith, and racial pride within Black communities
    (D) The encouragement of immediate political party formation by Black voters

45. What symbolic act was encouraged by Elijah Muhammad to represent breaking from the legacy of slavery?

    (A) Publicly burning the American flag during protests
    (B) Refusing to pay federal taxes to a racist government
    (C) Replacing enslavers' surnames with the letter "X" until a Muslim name was received
    (D) Converting to Christianity as a rejection of African traditional religions

46. Based on Source 2, what strategic shift within the Black Freedom movement is illustrated by the interaction of Malcolm X and Martin Luther King Jr.?

    (A) A merging of the Civil Rights Movement with the labor movement
    (B) A commitment by both leaders to launch a new political party
    (C) A growing conversation between integrationist and nationalist strategies within the Black Freedom struggle
    (D) A mutual agreement to avoid any future interaction for strategic clarity

47. How did Malcolm X's philosophy evolve in the years following his break with the Nation of Islam?

    (A) He renounced Islam and supported full assimilation into white society.
    (B) He joined the U.S. military and became a Republican senator.
    (C) He embraced pan-Africanism and global human rights, advocating for African Americans on an international stage.
    (D) He moved to Canada and stopped engaging in political activism.

Questions 48 through 51 refer to the following.

Source 1: Schedule of Courses for Black and Puerto Rican Studies, Hunter College, 1972

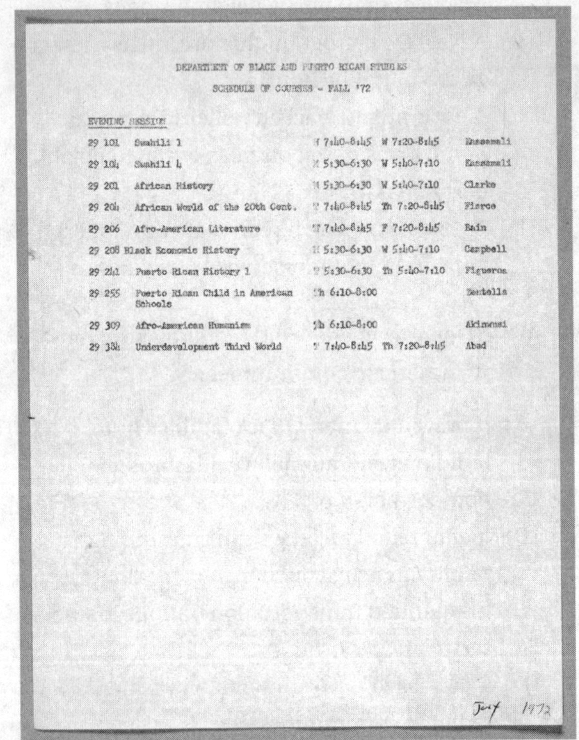

DEPARTMENT OF BLACK AND PUERTO RICAN STUDIES

SCHEDULE OF COURSES - FALL '72

EVENING SESSION

29 101	Swahili 1	M 7:40-8:45	W 7:20-8:45	Kassamali
29 104	Swahili 4	M 5:30-6:30	W 5:40-7:10	Kassamali
29 201	African History	M 5:30-6:30	W 5:40-7:10	Clarke
29 204	African World of the 20th Cent.	T 7:40-8:45	Th 7:20-8:45	Pierce
29 206	Afro-American Literature	T 7:40-8:45	F 7:20-8:45	Bain
29 208	Black Economic History	M 5:30-6:30	W 5:40-7:10	Campbell
29 241	Puerto Rican History 1	T 5:30-6:30	Th 5:40-7:10	Figueroa
29 255	Puerto Rican Child in American Schools	Th 6:10-8:00		Zentella
29 309	Afro-American Humanism	Th 6:10-8:00		Akinnasi
29 334	Underdevelopment Third World	T 7:40-8:45	Th 7:20-8:45	Abad

1972

Source 2: Bulletin Program for the First National Council for Black Studies Annual Conference, 1975

48. What do the courses listed in Source 1 reveal about the goals of early African American Studies programs?
    (A) They were designed exclusively to teach ancient African civilizations with no connection to modern issues.
    (B) They focused on general humanities without specific reference to race or culture.
    (C) They aimed to explore the history, culture, and political realities of Black and Afro-Caribbean peoples through an interdisciplinary lens.
    (D) They were created solely to fulfill diversity requirements at predominantly white institutions.

49. What claim is best supported by the creation of the National Council for Black Studies as shown in Source 2?
    (A) That African American Studies had become irrelevant by the mid-1970s
    (B) That the field had gained national momentum and institutional support from scholars, students, and activists
    (C) That only HBCUs participated in the founding of Black Studies departments
    (D) That the primary focus of Black Studies was to promote political campaigns

50. What broader historical development led to the creation of the Black and Puerto Rican Studies program at Hunter College?
    (A) The decline of interest in race-based curriculum following the Civil Rights Act of 1964
    (B) Passage of the Voting Rights Act in 1965
    (C) Student-led protests during the Black Campus movement that demanded inclusive curriculum and representation
    (D) Federal mandates requiring all colleges to offer African American history courses

51. How does African American Studies, as demonstrated by both sources, enhance the study of early Africa and its global connections?
    (A) By rejecting all Western scholarly frameworks in favor of oral storytelling alone
    (B) By focusing solely on the transatlantic slave trade as the beginning of African history
    (C) By using interdisciplinary methods to document early African societies' contributions and their influence across the diaspora
    (D) By teaching that Africa remained isolated from global history until European colonization

Questions 52 through 54 refer to the following.

Source 1: Image of Aksumite Coin Showing King Ezana, Circa 340–400

Source 2: Image of Nok Sculpture, Circa 900 BCE–200 CE

52. What historical feature of the Aksumite Empire is reflected in Source 1?

 (A) A lack of political centralization or urbanization
 (B) Isolation from global trade routes and cultural exchange
 (C) A sovereign African society that minted its own currency and adopted Christianity independently
 (D) A civilization dependent solely on oral history and without any written language

53. How does Source 2 challenge stereotypes about ancient African societies?

 (A) It shows that African societies developed art only after European contact.
 (B) It illustrates a European influence on African sculpture and design.
 (C) It presents African societies as isolated and unskilled in creative expression.
 (D) It demonstrates the Nok society's complex artistry and cultural sophistication through terracotta sculpture.

54. Why are ancient African civilizations like Aksum and Nok significant to the discipline of African American Studies?

 (A) They provide proof that African societies contributed little to early global history.
 (B) They confirm that ancient African communities avoided international contact until the slave trade.
 (C) They serve as historical evidence of African civilizations' complexity and legacy, countering colonial stereotypes and enriching diasporic identity.
 (D) They are included in African American Studies only to compare with European empires.

Questions 55 through 57 refer to the following.

Source: Image of Mali Equestrian Figure, Thirteenth to Fifteenth Century

55. What does the equestrian figure from the Mali Empire most directly suggest about the empire's political and military power?
    (A) Horses were exclusively used for agriculture and had no military significance.
    (B) Wealth from trans-Saharan trade allowed Mali to acquire horses and weapons, solidifying military dominance over rival groups.
    (C) Horses were symbolic pets of elite families but not used in battle.
    (D) Horses and riders were mainly featured in ceremonial parades without any military utility.

56. Which claim about the Mali Empire is best supported by this visual source?
    (A) Mali remained largely isolated from external trade and cultural influence.
    (B) Mali's leadership utilized cavalry to secure trade routes and expand influence across West Africa.
    (C) Mali relied solely on seafaring power to connect to Mediterranean markets.
    (D) Mali's rulers prohibited Islamic cultural practices in their military traditions.

57. How can the image of the equestrian figure serve as credible evidence in understanding Mali's significance in African and African American Studies?
    (A) It verifies that Mali was the only ancient African empire with documented architecture.
    (B) It visually supports written accounts of Mali's militaristic and economic sophistication, which counters stereotypes of precolonial African societies.
    (C) It proves Mali was uninfluenced by Islam or external trade relations.
    (D) It shows that Mali collapsed due to excessive spending on horses and armor.

Questions 58 through 60 refer to the following.

Source: Map Showing the Movement of Bantu Peoples, Languages, and Technologies

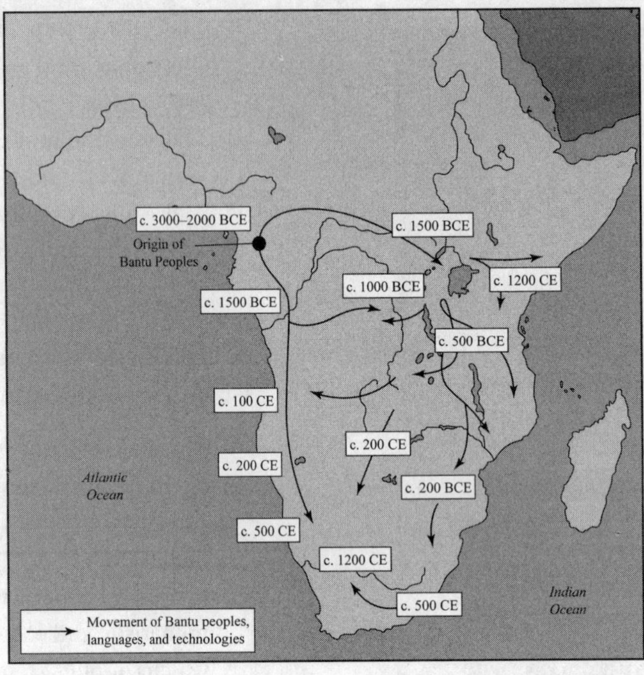

58. What was one primary cause of the Bantu expansion shown in the source map?
    (A) A decline in agricultural productivity forced migration to the North.
    (B) Increased conflict with European empires led to forced relocation.
    (C) Agricultural and technological innovations supported population growth and migration across Africa.
    (D) Bantu-speaking peoples migrated solely to escape enslavement by coastal traders.

59. Based on the source, which statement best explains the long-term impact of the Bantu migrations?
    (A) The migrations led to a decline in linguistic diversity due to language loss.
    (B) The Bantu peoples settled exclusively in North Africa and had limited cultural diffusion.
    (C) The Bantu peoples introduced European languages across Africa during the Iron Age.
    (D) The spread of Bantu languages contributed to the linguistic and cultural diversity of West, Central, and Southern Africa.

60. How does the information on the map help scholars understand African American ancestry and heritage?
    (A) It proves that all African Americans descended from Northern African societies.
    (B) It demonstrates the role of European colonizers in shaping early African languages.
    (C) It reveals the West and Central African roots of many African Americans and highlights Bantu linguistic influence.
    (D) It supports the theory that African American ancestry originates mainly from North Africa and the Middle East.

PRACTICE TEST 2

Section II: Free-Response

TIME: 85 MINUTES—4 QUESTIONS

This section includes three short-answer questions (SAQs) and one document-based question (DBQ). You will have 85 minutes to complete all four questions.

Your responses should be written in complete sentences and paragraph form. Bullet points, outlines, or note fragments will not receive credit. Organize your ideas clearly, and support your responses with specific examples and historical reasoning.

Suggested time management:

- 40 minutes for the three short-answer questions (SAQ)
- 45 minutes for the document-based question (DBQ)

You may answer the questions in any order and revisit them as needed within the time limit.

NOTE: Although you may use scratch paper or planning space for outlines and notes, only your typed or written final responses will be scored. Make sure to review your work and submit your answers before time expires.

Short Answer Questions

1. Short-Answer Question, Text-Based Source

The Black Panther Party's Ten-Point Program, 1966

WHAT WE WANT

1. We want freedom. We want power to determine the destiny of our black community.
2. We Want Full Employment for Our People.
3. We Want An End to the Robbery By the Capitalists of Our Black Community.
4. We Want Decent Housing Fit For The Shelter of Human Beings.
5. We Want Education for Our People That Exposes The True Nature Of This Decadent American Society. We Want Education That Teaches Us Our True History And Our Role in the Present-Day Society.
6. We Want All Black Men To Be Exempt From Military Service.
7. We Want An Immediate End to Police Brutality and the Murder of Black People.
8. We Want Freedom For All Black Men Held in Federal, State, County and City Prisons and Jails.
9. We Want All Black People When Brought to Trial To Be Tried In Court By A Jury Of Their Peer Group Or People From Their Black Communities, As Defined By the Constitution of the United States.
10. We Want Land, Bread, Housing, Education, Clothing, Justice And Peace.

Source: The Black Panther Party, "Ten-Point Program" (October 15, 1966), *Helix* 3, no. 7 (May 9, 1968): 14 (The Seattle Public Library; Seattle Room Digital Collections).

DIRECTIONS: Respond to parts A, B, C, and D. Each response should be in complete sentences and paragraph form, demonstrating historical understanding, clarity, and critical thinking.

(A) Describe one demand made by the Black Panther Party in the Ten-Point Program, and explain its significance in the context of the 1960s Civil Rights Movement and Black Power movement.
(B) Identify one historical factor that influenced the creation of the Ten-Point Program.
(C) Explain how the Ten-Point Program reflects broader themes of systemic oppression and economic inequality.
(D) Apply your understanding by explaining how a modern social movement has drawn inspiration from the demands or strategies of the Black Panther Party.

2. Short-Answer Question, Visual Source

Photo of Elijah Muhammad Addressing Black Muslims at a Convention, 1966

DIRECTIONS: Respond to parts A, B, and C. Each response should be written in complete sentences and demonstrate deep understanding of historical and cultural developments.

(A) Describe one aspect of the Nation of Islam's ideology or objectives under Elijah Muhammad's leadership as reflected in the image.
(B) Identify one social or historical factor that contributed to the rise of the Nation of Islam in mid-twentieth-century America.
(C) Explain how Elijah Muhammad's leadership and message influenced broader discussions of Black empowerment and community control during the 1960s.

3. Short-Answer Question, No Source

DIRECTIONS: Respond to parts A, B, and C. Each response should be written in complete sentences and demonstrate deep understanding of historical and thematic concepts.

(A) Describe one example of African American cultural expression (such as music, art, or literature) that reflected resistance against systemic oppression.
(B) Explain how African American cultural expression changed from the Reconstruction era to the Civil Rights Movement.
(C) Compare the role of African American cultural expression during the Harlem Renaissance with its role during the Black Power era.

4. Document-Based Question

Explain how African American communities have pursued self-determination and economic independence in response to systemic racial barriers from the early twentieth century to the present.

In your response, you should do the following:

- Craft a defensible thesis or claim that directly responds to the prompt and establishes a clear line of reasoning.
- Describe a broader historical or disciplinary context that frames your argument and demonstrates understanding of the prompt's significance.
- Support your argument with evidence from at least three of the sources provided.
- Incorporate at least one additional piece of specific evidence beyond the provided sources to strengthen your argument.
- For at least two of the sources, explain how or why the source's perspective, purpose, context, and/or audience is relevant to your argument.
- Cite the sources you reference in your response by letter, title, or author to ensure clarity and attribution.

Source 1: *Photograph of a Convention of Madam C. J. Walker Agents at Villa Lewaro, 1924*

Source 2: The Map of the Great Migration

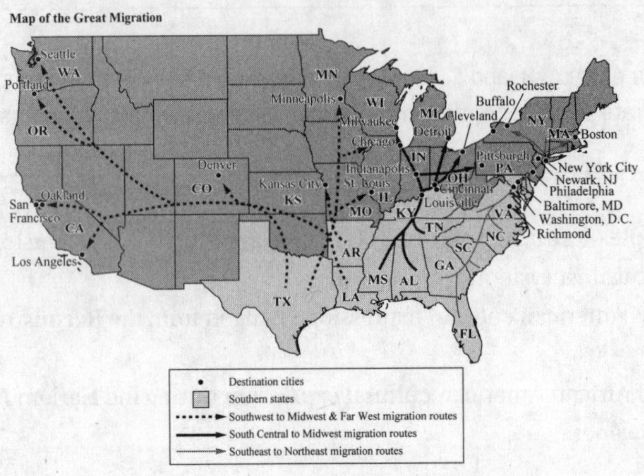

Source 3: *Marcus Garvey at His Desk, 1924*

Source 4: *Muhammad Speaks* Newspaper Salesmen, 1965

Source 5: Christine Tamir, "The Growing Diversity of Black America," Pew Research Center, March 25, 2021

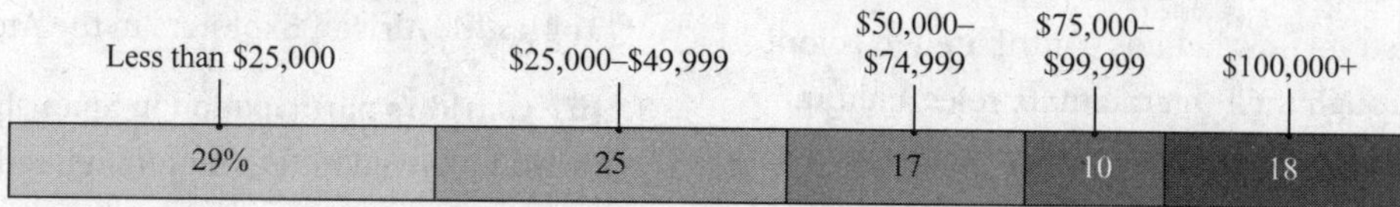

Note: Figures may not add to 100% due to rounding. The household population excludes people living in institutions, college dormitories and other group quarters. "Black households" are those headed by a household head who identifies as Black, inclusive of single-race Black, multiracial Black and Black Hispanic people.

Answer Explanations

Section I: Multiple-Choice

1. **(B)** Juan Garrido's petition and military involvement illustrate how ladinos contributed to colonization through their intermediary roles, cultural knowledge, and pursuit of freedom—characteristic of African conquistadores. (A) is incorrect. This response overlooks the importance of Juan Garrido's background as a ladino who was familiar with Iberian culture, which enabled his integration and service in the Spanish expeditions. (C) is incorrect. Although it references African presence in the Americas, it fails to connect their role specifically as skilled laborers or intermediaries, as seen with Garrido's unique status and experience. (D) is incorrect. This choice mistakenly emphasizes the transatlantic slave trade without recognizing the voluntary and strategic participation of ladinos like Garrido in early expeditions.

   Skill: 2B: Describe a source's perspective, purpose, context, and audience

   Learning Objective: LO 2.1.A: Explain the significance of the roles ladinos played as the first Africans to arrive in the territory that became the United States; LO 2.1.B: Describe the diverse roles Africans played during colonization of the Americas in the sixteenth century

   Topic: Topic 2.1: African Explorers in the Americas

2. **(B)** Garrido's experience reflects how Atlantic creoles operated as intermediaries with multilingual and multicultural skills that facilitated their roles in colonization. (A) is incorrect. This answer ignores Garrido's ability to communicate and navigate multiple cultural contexts, which was central to his identity as a ladino. (C) is incorrect. Although Africans did contribute to agriculture, this choice misses the broader influence and versatility of ladinos like Garrido. (D) is incorrect. The claim that they were unskilled and uninfluential is factually inaccurate and ignores the role of Atlantic creoles in conquest and diplomacy.

   Skill: 2B: Describe a source's perspective, purpose, context, and audience

   Learning Objective: LO 2.1.A: Explain the significance of the roles ladinos played as the first Africans to arrive in the territory that became the United States

   Topic: 2.1: African Explorers in the Americas

3. **(B)** Garrido's participation in Spanish expeditions in 1513 allowed him to maintain freedom and elevate his social status through military service. (A) is incorrect. Garrido was not enslaved during his time in the Americas, and his contributions extend beyond forced labor. (C) is incorrect. This choice inaccurately attributes Garrido's arrival to the Middle Passage, which does not apply to free Africans like him. (D) is incorrect. Garrido's role was not primarily religious; his historical significance lies in his military and exploratory service.

   Skill: 2B: Describe a source's perspective, purpose, context, and audience

   Learning Objective: LO 2.1.A: Explain the significance of the roles ladinos played as the first Africans to arrive in the territory that became the United States; LO 2.1.B: Describe the diverse roles Africans played during colonization of the Americas in the sixteenth century

   Topic: 2.1: African Explorers in the Americas

4. **(C)** Garrido and other ladinos actively contributed to early exploration and colonization through skilled labor and leadership roles. (A) is incorrect. This choice diminishes the leadership and contributions of ladinos like Garrido. (B) is incorrect. Although religion was part of colonization, Garrido's primary impact was through military and civic involvement. (D) is incorrect. Ladinos were not socially isolated; they often bridged African and European cultures in dynamic ways.

   Skill: 2B: Describe a source's perspective, purpose, context, and audience

   Learning Objective: LO 2.1.A: Explain the significance of the roles ladinos played as the first Africans to arrive in the territory that became the United States; LO 2.1.B: Describe the diverse roles Africans played during colonization of the Americas in the sixteenth century

   Topic: 2.1: African Explorers in the Americas

5. **(D)** The UNIA under Garvey promoted Black pride, global solidarity, and separatist economic and political institutions across the African diaspora. (A) is incorrect. This choice inaccurately presents the UNIA as primarily focused on integration with white society rather than on Black self-determination. (B) is incorrect. It overemphasizes the role of religion in the UNIA while underrepresenting Garvey's economic and political strategies. (C) is incorrect. Although the UNIA engaged internationally, this option ignores the central mission of economic empowerment and cultural pride.

Skill: 1B: Identify and explain the context of a specific event, development, or process

Learning Objective: LO 3.18.A: Describe the mission and methods of the Universal Negro Improvement Association (UNIA); LO 3.18.B: Describe the impact of Marcus Garvey and the Universal Negro Improvement Association (UNIA) on political thought throughout the African diaspora

Topic: 3.18: The Universal Negro Improvement Association

6. **(A)** Marcus Garvey's Back-to-Africa movement and the Black Star Line symbolized a bold effort to repatriate African Americans and unite the diaspora through pan-African nationalism. (B) is incorrect. This choice implies legal reform was the central aim, which misrepresents the core goals of the Back-to-Africa movement. (C) is incorrect. The UNIA was largely separate from mainstream civil rights organizations and operated with a more separatist nationalist agenda. (D) is incorrect. Garvey's goals focused on empowerment rather than on directly confronting European powers in Africa.

Skill: 1B: Identify and explain the context of a specific event, development, or process

Learning Objective: LO 3.18.A: Describe the mission and methods of the Universal Negro Improvement Association (UNIA); LO 3.18.B: Describe the impact of Marcus Garvey and the Universal Negro Improvement Association (UNIA) on political thought throughout the African diaspora

Topic: 3.18: The Universal Negro Improvement Association

7. **(D)** Garvey rejected integration, advocating instead for self-reliance and separate Black institutions globally. (A) is incorrect. Legal reform through te hcourts was not Garvey's focus. (B) is incorrect. Garvey rejected multiracial integration and instead promoted Black separatism. (C) is incorrect. Garvey emphasized Black-owned industry, not collaboration with white-owned corporations.

Skill: 1B: Identify and explain the context of a specific event, development, or process

Learning Objective: LO 3.18.A: Describe the mission and methods of the Universal Negro Improvement Association (UNIA); LO 3.18.B: Describe the impact of Marcus Garvey and the Universal Negro Improvement Association (UNIA) on political thought throughout the African diaspora

Topic: 3.18: The Universal Negro Improvement Association

8. **(C)** The UNIA established a model for later Black nationalist movements advocating global Black solidarity. (A) is incorrect. The NAACP pursued legal strategies, whereas the UNIA emphasized mass organizing and global Black empowerment. (B) is incorrect. The UNIA's primary legacy was not school desegregation but, instead, was the development of global Black political thought. (D) is incorrect. Garvey's focus was on political and economic independence, not primarily religious revivalism.

Skill: 1B: Identify and explain the context of a specific event, development, or process

Learning Objective: LO 3.18.A: Describe the mission and methods of the Universal Negro Improvement Association (UNIA); LO 3.18.B: Describe the impact of Marcus Garvey and the Universal Negro Improvement Association (UNIA) on political thought throughout the African diaspora

Topic: 3.18: The Universal Negro Improvement Association

9. **(D)** The Fifteenth Amendment granted voting rights to Black men, formally allowing them to engage in American politics. (A) is incorrect. The Fifteenth Amendment did not grant suffrage to women. (B) is incorrect. The Black Codes were challenged more directly by the Civil Rights Act and the Fourteenth Amendment. (C) is incorrect. Voting rights were expanded, but landownership was not guaranteed in every state.

   Skill: 1C: Identify and explain patterns, connections, or other relationships (causation, changes, continuities, comparison)

   Learning Objective: LO 3.1.B: Explain how the Fifteenth Amendment impacted African Americans' participation in American politics

   Topic: 3.1: The Reconstruction Amendments

10. **(C)** The image shows political achievement during Reconstruction that was later restricted under Jim Crow laws. (A) is incorrect. The federal government did allow Black representation in Congress during Reconstruction. (B) is incorrect. Black officeholders were not symbolic; many held legislative authority and helped draft state constitutions. (D) is incorrect. Black representation declined sharply after Reconstruction due to voter suppression, not steady growth.

    Skill: 1C: Identify and explain patterns, connections, or other relationships (causation, changes, continuities, comparison)

    Learning Objective: LO 3.1.B: Explain how the Fifteenth Amendment impacted African Americans' participation in American politics

    Topic: 3.1: The Reconstruction Amendments

11. **(A)** The Thirteenth, Fourteenth, and Fifteenth Amendments abolished slavery, ensured citizenship, and expanded suffrage. (B) is incorrect. Reparations and land grants were not widely implemented. (C) is incorrect. Many states continued to restrict civil rights in practice. (D) is incorrect. Political rights and citizenship—not economic reform—were central to the Reconstruction Amendments.

    Skill: 1C: Identify and explain patterns, connections, or other relationships (causation, changes, continuities, comparison)

    Learning Objective: LO 3.1.A: Explain how the Reconstruction Amendments impacted African Americans by defining standards of citizenship

    Topic: 3.1: The Reconstruction Amendments

12. **(B)** The Fourteenth Amendment established equal protection and citizenship, while the Fifteenth Amendment prohibited voter discrimination based on race. (A) is incorrect. Criminal justice reform was not the focus of either amendment. (C) is incorrect. Neither amendment repealed the other. (D) is incorrect. The amendments were not related to immigration.

    Skill: 1C: Identify and explain patterns, connections, or other relationships (causation, changes, continuities, comparison)

    Learning Objective: LO 3.1.A: Explain how the Reconstruction Amendments impacted African Americans by defining standards of citizenship

    Topic: 3.1: The Reconstruction Amendments

13. **(C)** These images reveal how convict leasing extended systems of forced labor and criminalized Black life as a means of social control. (A) is incorrect. Black landownership was severely limited during this period, especially through mechanisms like Black Codes. (B) is incorrect. The labor systems depicted do not reflect racial equality or industrial wage systems. (D) is incorrect. Southern labor remained exploitative, relying on unpaid or underpaid work through sharecropping and leasing systems.

    Skill: 2C: Explain the significance of a source's perspective, purpose, context, and audience

    Learning Objective: LO 3.3.B: Explain how new labor practices impeded the ability of African Americans to advance economically after the abolition of slavery

    Topic: 3.3: The Black Codes, Land, and Labor

14. **(C)** The presence of children in forced labor camps highlights how states used Black Codes to strip African American families of autonomy and labor rights. (A) is incorrect. There is no evidence of labor organizing by children in this era or context. (B) is incorrect. The image does not reflect voluntary apprenticeship but, rather, coerced labor. (D) is incorrect. The image captures

exploitative labor practices, not the expansion of educational access.

Skill: 2C: Explain the significance of a source's perspective, purpose, context, and audience

Learning Objective: LO 3.3.A: Explain how Black Codes undermined the ability of African Americans to advance

Topic: 3.3: The Black Codes, Land, and Labor

15. **(C)** Black Codes forced African Americans into exploitative labor arrangements and denied them access to wealth-building opportunities. (A) is incorrect. Black Codes actively denied property protection and did not guarantee voting rights. (B) is incorrect. Economic advancement was undermined, not supported, by labor restrictions. (D) is incorrect. Industrial integration was not a key feature of Southern labor practices postemancipation.

Skill: 1C: Identify and explain patterns, connections, or other relationships (causation, changes, continuities, comparison)

Learning Objective: LO 3.3.A: Explain how Black Codes undermined the ability of African Americans to advance

Topic: 3.3: The Black Codes, Land, and Labor

16. **(A)** Both images reflect how African Americans were systematically resubjugated through sharecropping and convict leasing—new forms of economic exploitation. (B) is incorrect. Northern migration was not depicted or referenced in these sources. (C) is incorrect. Slavery was abolished, but many practices replicated its conditions. (D) is incorrect. The Freedmen's Bureau did not succeed in establishing widespread Black landownership.

Skill: 1C: Identify and explain patterns, connections, or other relationships (causation, changes, continuities, comparison)

Learning Objective: LO 3.3.B: Explain how new labor practices impeded the ability of African Americans to advance economically after the abolition of slavery

Topic: 3.3: The Black Codes, Land, and Labor

17. **(D)** The majority opinion justified segregation by establishing the "separate but equal" doctrine. (A) is incorrect. The majority upheld segregation, claiming it was not unconstitutional. (B) is incorrect. Voting rights were not the subject of this case. (C) is incorrect. The majority did not acknowledge the inequality of separate facilities.

Skill: 3A: Formulate a defensible claim

Learning Objective: LO 3.4.A: Explain how Reconstruction era reforms were dismantled during the late nineteenth century

Topic: 3.4: The Defeat of Reconstruction

18. **(B)** Harlan famously argued that the Constitution is color-blind and all citizens are equal before the law. (A) is incorrect. Harlan did not support state autonomy in defining citizenship. (C) is incorrect. Harlan opposed precedent that reinforced segregation. (D) is incorrect. Harlan opposed separate facilities as unconstitutional.

Skill: 3A: Formulate a defensible claim

Learning Objective: LO 3.4.A: Explain how Reconstruction era reforms were dismantled during the late nineteenth century

Topic: 3.4: The Defeat of Reconstruction

19. **(B)** The decision legalized segregation through the "separate but equal" doctrine, allowing systemic inequality. (A) is incorrect. Desegregation occurred decades later through court rulings like *Brown v. Board of Education*. (C) is incorrect. The federal government did not enforce immediate equality. (D) is incorrect. African American rights were increasingly restricted after the decision.

Skill: 3C: Strategically select sources—evaluating the credibility of the evidence they present—to effectively support a claim

Learning Objective: LO 3.4.A: Explain how Reconstruction era reforms were dismantled during the late nineteenth century

Topic: 3.4: The Defeat of Reconstruction

20. **(C)** Legal analysis showing the reality of inequality under segregation provides strong support for Harlan's argument. (A) is incorrect. Literacy tests address voting, not public accommodations. (B) is incorrect. Equal appearance does not guarantee equal access or resources. (D) is incorrect. A cartoon offers limited evidentiary weight for a constitutional claim.

Skill: 3C: Strategically select sources—evaluating the credibility of the evidence they present—to effectively support a claim

Learning Objective: LO 3.4.A: Explain how Reconstruction era reforms were dismantled during the late nineteenth century

Topic: 3.4: The Defeat of Reconstruction

21. **(C)** The photographs depict separate and unequal conditions that were meant to degrade African Americans. (A) is incorrect. The photos clearly show inequality and humiliation in public accommodations. (B) is incorrect. Jim Crow laws spread beyond the South and were state and local policies. (D) is incorrect. There was no consistent guarantee of quality or equal access in segregated systems.

    Skill: 3B: Support a claim or argument using specific and relevant evidence

    Learning Objective: LO 3.5.A: Explain how the introduction of Jim Crow laws impacted African Americans after Reconstruction

    Topic: 3.5: Disenfranchisement and Jim Crow Laws

22. **(C)** The photographs show state-sanctioned segregation, upheld by *Plessy v. Ferguson* in 1896. (A) is incorrect. *Brown v. Board of Education* was decided in 1954, decades after these images were taken. (B) is incorrect. The Freedmen's Bureau was a Reconstruction-era agency and was not tied to the images. (D) is incorrect. New Deal programs often excluded or segregated African Americans. They did not eliminate discriminatory policies.

    Skill: 3B: Support a claim or argument using specific and relevant evidence

    Learning Objective: LO 3.5.A: Explain how the introduction of Jim Crow laws impacted African Americans after Reconstruction

    Topic: 3.5: Disenfranchisement and Jim Crow Laws

23. **(A)** Activists led organized protests like trolley boycotts and worked with the press to expose unjust conditions. (B) is incorrect. Emigration occurred but was not the primary response aligned with the visuals. (C) is incorrect. This misrepresents who led resistance to segregation. (D) is incorrect. Although white allies were involved, Black-led resistance was central.

    Skill: 3B: Support a claim or argument using specific and relevant evidence

    Learning Objective: LO 3.5.B: Describe the responses of African American writers and activists to racism and anti-Black violence during the nadir

    Topic: 3.5: Disenfranchisement and Jim Crow Laws

24. **(B)** Wells's writings documented lynchings and discrimination, offering direct evidence of how segregation was part of a wider racist system. (A) is incorrect. Design differences don't demonstrate systemic oppression. (C) is incorrect. A cartoon may offer commentary but not substantive evidence. (D) is incorrect. New England's integration laws would not represent the broader Southern reality.

    Skill: 3B: Support a claim or argument using specific and relevant evidence

    Learning Objective: LO 3.5.B: Describe the responses of African American writers and activists to racism and anti-Black violence during the nadir

    Topic: 3.5: Disenfranchisement and Jim Crow Laws

25. **(D)** Walker uplifted Black women by creating opportunities for entrepreneurship, beauty, and empowerment. (A) is incorrect. The sources highlight Walker's empowerment of Black women, not limitations due to beauty standards. (B) is incorrect. Although she was philanthropic, Walker's primary legacy was building economic independence. (C) is incorrect. Walker's business model focused on Black-owned networks, not integration.

    Skill: 3A: Formulate a defensible claim

    Learning Objective: LO 3.9.A: Explain how African Americans promoted the economic stability and well-being of their communities in the early twentieth century

    Topic: 3.9 Black Organizations and Institutions

26. **(A)** Walker's company created jobs and leadership roles for thousands of Black women and contributed to local community development. (B) is incorrect. Walker's focus was on Black-owned enterprises, not white-owned industrial jobs. (C) is incorrect. Walker did not receive federal loans during this era. (D) is incorrect. Walker's brand was specifically designed to affirm Black beauty standards.

    Skill: 3A: Formulate a defensible claim

    Learning Objective: LO 3.9.A: Explain how African Americans promoted the economic stability and well-being of their communities in the early twentieth century

    Topic: 3.9 Black Organizations and Institutions

27. **(D)** The images reflect the creation of Black-led economic systems in response to exclusion from white institutions. (A) is incorrect. The early twentieth century saw the growth of Black-owned businesses, not a decline. (B) is incorrect. The businesses celebrated African American culture, not European norms. (C) is incorrect. The focus was on urban business growth, not rural migration.

    Skill: 3A: Formulate a defensible claim

    Learning Objective: LO 3.9.A: Explain how African Americans promoted the economic stability and well-being of their communities in the early twentieth century

    Topic: 3.9 Black Organizations and Institutions

28. **(B)** Such an article would directly show how her agents advanced community leadership and business ownership. (A) is incorrect. This doesn't relate to Black business or Madam C. J. Walker's legacy. (C) is incorrect. Migration timelines do not address Walker's economic impact. (D) is incorrect. Church music is unrelated to Walker's business legacy.

    Skill: 3A: Formulate a defensible claim

    Learning Objective: LO 3.9.A: Explain how African Americans promoted the economic stability and well-being of their communities in the early twentieth century

    Topic: 3.9 Black Organizations and Institutions

29. **(D)** Bennett articulates a personal and emotional connection to Africa, underscoring her identity as part of the African diaspora. (A) is incorrect. Bennett embraces African ancestry rather than rejects it. (B) is incorrect. The poem celebrates connection rather than disconnection. (C) is incorrect. Slavery is not romanticized; Africa is reclaimed as a source of pride.

    Skill: 2C: Explain the significance of a source's perspective, purpose, context, and audience

    Learning Objective: LO 3.13.A: Explain how Harlem Renaissance poets express their relationships to Africa in their poetry

    Topic: 3.13 Envisioning Africa in Harlem Renaissance Poetry

30. **(B)** Bennett's poem paints Africa in rich, imaginative terms to reclaim its dignity and importance. (A) is incorrect. The poem contains no reference to Southern rural life. (C) is incorrect. The poem does not address legal systems or injustices directly. (D) is incorrect. Industrialization is not a theme of this poem.

    Skill: 2C: Explain the significance of a source's perspective, purpose, context, and audience

    Learning Objective: LO 3.13.A: Explain how Harlem Renaissance poets express their relationships to Africa in their poetry

    Topic: 3.13 Envisioning Africa in Harlem Renaissance Poetry

31. **(B)** The poem exemplifies how Harlem Renaissance writers explored African identity through personal and poetic reflection. (A) is incorrect. Legal desegregation efforts are not part of this artistic expression. (C) is incorrect. The poem does not address immigration or assimilation. (D) is incorrect. Jazz and blues were celebrated, not opposed, by Harlem Renaissance artists.

    Skill: 2C: Explain the significance of a source's perspective, purpose, context, and audience

    Learning Objective: LO 3.13.A: Explain how Harlem Renaissance poets express their relationships to Africa in their poetry

    Topic: 3.13 Envisioning Africa in Harlem Renaissance Poetry

32. **(C)** The letter serves as a persuasive call for African Americans to migrate North in search of safety, dignity, and opportunity. (A) is incorrect. The letter advocates for escape, not legal reform documentation. (B) is incorrect. It encourages leaving, not staging protests in the South. (D) is incorrect. The letter does not discourage industrial labor. It promotes industrial labor as an opportunity.

    Skill: 2C: Explain the significance of a source's perspective, purpose, context, and audience

    Learning Objective: LO 3.16.A: Describe the causes of the Great Migration

    Topic: 3.16: The Great Migration

33. **(B)** The letter speaks directly to African Americans suffering in the South under racial terror and economic hardship. (A) is incorrect. White laborers were not the intended audience. (C) is incorrect. The letter does not attempt to influence Southern legislators. (D) is incorrect. Although industrial employers benefited, this letter targets potential migrants.

    Skill: 2C: Explain the significance of a source's perspective, purpose, context, and audience

    Learning Objective: LO 3.16.A: Describe the causes of the Great Migration

    Topic: 3.16: The Great Migration

34. **(A)** The map shows massive movement from rural areas in the South to urban centers across the United States, illustrating a key pattern of the Great Migration. (B) is incorrect. White population shifts are not a central theme of the map. (C) is incorrect. Migration patterns show departure from the South, not departure from the North. (D) is incorrect. Economic, not educational, opportunity was the primary motivator.

    Skill: 2D: Describe and draw conclusions from patterns, trends, and limitations in data

    Learning Objective: LO 3.16.A: Describe the causes of the Great Migration

    Topic: 3.16: The Great Migration

35. **(B)** Both the map and letter reveal that racial violence and the lure of jobs were intertwined causes and that migration reshaped urban life and Black identity. (A) is incorrect. Racism persisted in cities in the North. (C) is incorrect. Agricultural opportunities were not the central draw. (D) is incorrect. Southern leaders generally opposed Black flight.

    Skill: 2D: Describe and draw conclusions from patterns, trends, and limitations in data

    Learning Objective: LO 3.16.B: Explain the impact of the Great Migration on Black communities and American culture

    Topic: 3.16: The Great Migration

36. **(B)** The Court ruled that segregated public schools violated the Equal Protection Clause of the Fourteenth Amendment because separate educational facilities are inherently unequal. (A) is incorrect because free speech rights were not the legal issue in this case. (C) is incorrect because self-incrimination protections were unrelated to segregation. (D) is incorrect because the Court determined that state laws permitting segregation conflicted with the U.S. Constitution.

    Skill: 1B: Identify and explain the context of a specific event, development, or process

    Learning Objective: LO 4.4.B: Explain the rationale for the *Brown v. Board of Education* decision to overturn "separate but equal"

    Topic: 4.4: Discrimination, Segregation, and the Origins of the Civil Rights Movement

37. **(C)** After ruling segregation unconstitutional, the Court restored the case to the docket to hear additional arguments on the appropriate remedies and timelines for desegregation. (A) is incorrect because the Court did not order immediate integration; implementation details were addressed later in *Brown II*. (B) is incorrect because there was no retrial in the lower courts. (D) is incorrect because the Court did not dismiss the case—it retained jurisdiction to oversee the remedy phase.

    Skill: 1B: Identify and explain the context of a specific event, development, or process

    Learning Objective: LO 4.4.A: Describe the enduring forms of segregation and discrimination in daily life that African Americans faced

    Topic: 4.4: Discrimination, Segregation, and the Origins of the Civil Rights Movement

38. **(A)** Despite earlier civil rights amendments, African Americans endured ongoing segregation in schools, housing, and public services. (B) is incorrect. Schools remained deeply segregated before 1954. (C) is incorrect. The Reconstruction Amendments remained active. (D) is incorrect. Voter suppression was one issue but was not the only reason *Brown v. Board of Education* was necessary.

Skill: 1B: Identify and explain the context of a specific event, development, or process
Learning Objective: LO 4.4.A: Describe the enduring forms of segregation and discrimination in daily life that African Americans faced
Topic: 4.4: Discrimination, Segregation, and the Origins of the Civil Rights Movement

39. **(C)** Many Southern states and school districts resisted by defunding or closing schools rather than integrate. (A) is incorrect. There was significant opposition across much of the South. (B) is incorrect. Integration often faced violent resistance. (D) is incorrect. Federal troops were deployed in support of integration in key cases, like Little Rock.

Skill: 1B: Identify and explain the context of a specific event, development, or process
Learning Objective: LO 4.4.C: Explain how different groups responded to school integration as a result of the *Brown v. Board of Education* decision
Topic: 4.4: Discrimination, Segregation, and the Origins of the Civil Rights Movement

40. **(B)** The map shows how "hazardous" zones—predominantly Black neighborhoods—were systematically denied access to home loans. (A) is incorrect. Access was unequal and based on race. (C) is incorrect. African Americans were often excluded from high-income zones. (D) is incorrect. Federal programs reinforced segregation rather than promote integration.

Skill: 2D: Describe and draw conclusions from patterns, trends, and limitations in data
Learning Objective: LO 4.5.A: Explain the long-term effects of housing discrimination on African Americans
Topic: 4.5: Redlining and Housing Discrimination

41. **(C)** Redlining was a racially coded policy used by government-backed lenders to deny loans in Black communities. (A) is incorrect. Redlining was the opposite of fair lending. (B) is incorrect. Redlining was not designed to desegregate housing. (D) is incorrect. Redlining discouraged investment, not reinvestment.

Skill: 2D: Describe and draw conclusions from patterns, trends, and limitations in data
Learning Objective: LO 4.5.A: Explain the long-term effects of housing discrimination on African Americans
Topic: 4.5: Redlining and Housing Discrimination

42. **(A)** Redlining restricted homeownership, denying Black families a key opportunity to accumulate and transfer generational wealth. (B) is incorrect. Wealth gaps were intensified, not eliminated. (C) is incorrect. Transportation disparities worsened, not improved. (D) is incorrect. Environmental conditions often declined in redlined zones.

Skill: 1C: Identify and explain patterns, connections, or other relationships
Learning Objective: LO 4.5.A: Explain the long-term effects of housing discrimination on African Americans
Topic: 4.5: Redlining and Housing Discrimination

43. **(C)** Patterns established by redlining contributed to long-standing disparities in wealth, housing, health, and urban infrastructure. (A) is incorrect. HOLC maps still reflect entrenched inequalities. (B) is incorrect. Racial inequality in housing remains pervasive. (D) is incorrect. Few redlined neighborhoods have received lasting reinvestment.

Skill: 1C: Identify and explain patterns, connections, or other relationships
Learning Objective: LO 4.5.A: Explain the long-term effects of housing discrimination on African Americans
Topic: 4.5: Redlining and Housing Discrimination

44. **(C)** Elijah Muhammad promoted Black self-reliance, faith in Allah, and cultural pride within a nationalist framework. (A) is incorrect. The Nation of Islam integrated Islamic beliefs, not Christian

theology. (B) is incorrect. Elijah Muhammad opposed racial integration. (D) is incorrect. The Nation of Islam discouraged direct engagement with the U.S. political system.

Skill: 1B: Identify and explain the context of a specific event, development, or process

Learning Objective: LO 4.9.A: Describe the origins and beliefs of the Nation of Islam

Topic: 4.9: Black Religious Nationalism and the Black Power Movement

45. **(C)** Elijah Muhammad encouraged followers to reject slave surnames by using the letter "X" until given a Muslim name. (A) is incorrect. Flag burning was not an encouraged practice. (B) is incorrect. Refusing to pay taxes was not promoted by the Nation of Islam. (D) is incorrect. The Nation of Islam embraced Islam, not Christianity.

Skill: 2A: Identify and explain a source's claim(s), evidence, and reasoning

Learning Objective: LO 4.9.A: Describe the origins and beliefs of the Nation of Islam

Topic: 4.9: Black Religious Nationalism and the Black Power Movement

46. **(C)** The image represents dialogue between civil rights leaders and Black Power advocates, reflecting evolving strategies within the movement. (A) is incorrect. The labor movement is not addressed here. (B) is incorrect. There was no agreement to form a political party. (D) is incorrect. The photo shows engagement, not avoidance.

Skill: 1C: Identify and explain patterns, connections, or other relationships

Learning Objective: LO 4.9.B: Explain how Black Freedom movement strategies transitioned from civil rights to Black Power

Topic: 4.9: Black Religious Nationalism and the Black Power Movement

47. **(C)** After leaving the Nation of Islam, Malcolm X pursued global human rights, connected with African and Islamic leaders, and redefined his activism internationally. (A) is incorrect. Malcolm X embraced Islam and Black identity. (B) is incorrect. Malcolm X did not serve in the military or hold political office. (D) is incorrect. Malcolm X remained politically engaged until his assassination.

Skill: 1C: Identify and explain patterns, connections, or other relationships

Learning Objective: LO 4.9.B: Explain how Black Freedom movement strategies transitioned from civil rights to Black Power

Topic: 4.9: Black Religious Nationalism and the Black Power Movement

48. **(C)** The interdisciplinary approach examined culture, history, and politics of African-descended peoples. (A) is incorrect. Early programs included modern as well as historical topics. (B) is incorrect. Courses were specific to Black identity and lived experience. (D) is incorrect. These courses were born from protest and self-determination, not from compliance with diversity requirements.

Skill: 1A: Identify and explain course concepts, developments, and processes

Learning Objective: LO 1.1.A: Describe the features that characterize African American Studies

Topic: 1.1: What Is African American Studies?

49. **(B)** The National Council for Black Studies reflected widespread interest and growing institutional legitimacy. (A) is incorrect. African American Studies was growing, not declining. (C) is incorrect. The movement included a wide range of institutions, not just HBCUs. (D) is incorrect. Political campaigning was not the primary aim of early conferences.

Skill: 2A: Identify and explain a source's claim(s), evidence, and reasoning

Learning Objective: LO 1.1.B: Describe the developments that led to the incorporation of African American Studies into United States colleges and universities

Topic: 1.1: What Is African American Studies?

50. **(C)** Programs like Hunter College's were established in response to Black student activism demanding inclusive education. (A) is incorrect. Interest in race-centered curriculum increased during this period. (B) is incorrect. Although the Voting Rights Act was significant, it was not the direct cause of curriculum development. (D) is incorrect. No federal mandates required this content.

Skill: 1A: Identify and explain course concepts, developments, and processes

Learning Objective: LO 1.1.B: Describe the developments that led to the incorporation of African American Studies into United States colleges and universities

Topic: 1.1: What Is African American Studies?

51. **(C)** The field of African American Studies emphasizes Africa's global connections and complex civilizations using evidence from multiple disciplines. (A) is incorrect. Although oral traditions are valued, they are part of a broader scholarly toolkit. (B) is incorrect. African American Studies includes what happened long before slavery. (D) is incorrect. Early Africa had international connections long before European colonization.

Skill: 2A: Identify and explain a source's claim(s), evidence, and reasoning

Learning Objective: LO 1.1.C: Explain how African American Studies enriches the study of early Africa and its relationship to communities of the African diaspora

Topic: 1.1: What Is African American Studies?

52. **(C)** The coin reflects Aksum's political independence, economic strength, and religious identity. (A) is incorrect. Aksum was politically centralized and urbanized. (B) is incorrect. Aksum was deeply connected to Mediterranean and Indian Ocean trade. (D) is incorrect. Aksum had its own script, Ge'ez, and an extensive written history.

Skill: 1A: Identify and explain course concepts, developments, and processes

Learning Objective: LO 1.4.A: Describe the features of, and goods produced by, complex societies in ancient East and West Africa

Topic: 1.4: Africa's Ancient Societies

53. **(D)** The sculpture shows Nok society's complexity and creative achievement. (A) is incorrect. Nok art predates European contact. (B) is incorrect. The designs are Indigenous, not European. (C) is incorrect. The artifacts reflect artistic sophistication.

Skill: 1A: Identify and explain course concepts, developments, and processes

Learning Objective: LO 1.4.A: Describe the features of, and goods produced by, complex societies in ancient East and West Africa

Topic: 1.4: Africa's Ancient Societies

54. **(C)** The legacy of Aksum and Nok enriches African American Studies by affirming historical complexity and identity. (A) is incorrect. Ancient African societies made major contributions to global history. (B) is incorrect. These societies were globally connected long before the transatlantic slave trade. (D) is incorrect. Their value to African American Studies goes far beyond just being compared with Europe.

Skill: 1D: Explain how course concepts relate to the discipline of African American Studies

Learning Objective: LO 1.4.B: Explain why Africa's ancient societies are culturally and historically significant to Black communities

Topic: 1.4: Africa's Ancient Societies

55. **(B)** Mali's economic power from trade enabled it to develop a strong cavalry that expanded its political dominance. (A) is incorrect. Horses were central to military strength, not just agriculture. (C) is incorrect. Horses were militarily significant, not just ceremonial. (D) is incorrect. The military use of cavalry was strategic, not symbolic.

Skill: 3A: Formulate a defensible claim

Learning Objective: LO 1.5.A: Explain how gold and trade shaped the development of the Sudanic empires

Topic: 1.5: The Sudanic Empires: Ghana, Mali, and Songhai

56. **(B)** The image reinforces Mali's use of cavalry to protect trade routes and extend influence. (A) is incorrect. Mali was internationally connected through trade and diplomacy. (C) is incorrect. Mali expanded through land-based trade routes, not maritime routes. (D) is incorrect. Mali rulers engaged with and promoted Islamic practices.

Skill: 3A: Formulate a defensible claim

Learning Objective: LO 1.5.B: Explain how Mali's wealth enabled expansion within and beyond Africa

Topic: 1.5: The Sudanic Empires: Ghana, Mali, and Songhai

57. **(B)** The image of the equestrian figure serves as credible evidence of Mali's military and cultural sophistication. (A) is incorrect. Mali's significance extends beyond architecture alone. (C) is incorrect. Islam was a prominent influence in Mali. (D) is incorrect. There's no historical basis for Mali collapsing due to overinvestment in cavalry.

Skill: 3C: Select credible sources to support a claim

Learning Objective: LO 1.5.C: Explain the connection between the Sudanic empires and early African American history

Topic: 1.5: The Sudanic Empires: Ghana, Mali, and Songhai

58. **(C)** Agricultural and technological innovation fueled population growth, prompting the Bantu expansion. (A) is incorrect. Agricultural productivity increased due to innovation. (B) is incorrect. Expansion occurred before sustained European contact. (D) is incorrect. Migration predated transatlantic slave trade influences.

Skill: 1C: Identify and explain patterns, connections, or other relationships

Learning Objective: LO 1.3.A: Describe the causes of Bantu expansion across the African continent

Topic: 1.3: Population Growth and Ethnolinguistic Diversity

59. **(D)** The expansion diversified linguistic and cultural landscapes across sub-Saharan Africa. (A) is incorrect. The spread of Bantu languages expanded diversity. (B) is incorrect. Bantu peoples migrated throughout Central and Southern Africa. (C) is incorrect. Bantu migrations predate European colonization.

Skill: 1C: Identify and explain patterns and connections

Learning Objective: LO 1.3.B: Explain how Bantu expansion affected linguistic diversity

Topic: 1.3: Population Growth and Ethnolinguistic Diversity

60. **(C)** The map reflects how the West and Central African origins of Bantu speakers contribute to African American ancestry. (A) is incorrect. Most African Americans trace their heritage to West and Central—not North—Africa. (B) is incorrect. The Bantu linguistic spread was internal to Africa. (D) is incorrect. African American heritage is not primarily from either North Africa or the Middle East.

Skill: 2D: Draw conclusions from data and make connections to course content

Learning Objective: LO 1.3.B: Explain how Bantu expansion shaped the genetic heritage of African Americans

Topic: 1.3: Population Growth and Ethnolinguistic Diversity

Section II: Free-Response

1. **Acceptable responses for Part A:**

- The demand to end police brutality reflects Black communities' response to systemic violence in the 1960s.
- The call for decent housing highlights economic inequality and segregation.
- Demands for education emphasize the need for curriculum that includes Black history and truth.
- These demands connect with broader Civil Rights and Black Power movements seeking systemic change.

Skill: 1A: Identify and explain course concepts, developments, and processes.

Learning Objective: LO 4.11.A: Explain how the Black Panther Party pursued political, economic, and social reforms in the twentieth century.

Topic: 4.11: The Black Panther Party for Self-Defense

Acceptable responses for Part B:

- The long history of racial discrimination and exclusion from economic and educational opportunities
- The rise of the Civil Rights Movement and Black Power ideology
- Urban poverty, police violence, and racial segregation in housing and schools
- The influence of global liberation movements and anti-colonial struggles

Skill: 1A: Identify and explain course concepts, developments, and processes.

Learning Objective: LO 4.11.A: Explain how the Black Panther Party pursued political, economic, and social reforms in the twentieth century.

Topic: 4.11: The Black Panther Party for Self-Defense

Acceptable responses for Part C:

- Reflects systemic oppression through police brutality and mass incarceration
- Highlights economic inequality with demands for employment, housing, and justice
- Emphasizes cultural empowerment through education that reflects true Black history
- Illustrates resistance to systemic racism in U.S. institutions and practices

Skill: 1A: Identify and explain course concepts, developments, and processes.

Learning Objective: LO 4.11.A: Explain how the Black Panther Party pursued political, economic, and social reforms in the twentieth century.

Topic: 4.11: The Black Panther Party for Self-Defense

Acceptable responses for Part D:

- The Black Lives Matter movement draws from the Black Panther Party's focus on police violence.
- Calls for community control and justice systems echo the Ten-Point Program.
- The use of direct action, community programs, and public statements mirrors tactics of the Black Panther Party.
- Modern movements emphasize economic justice, mirroring demands for housing and employment.
- Cultural pride and reclaiming history remain central to contemporary Black activism.

Skill: 1A: Identify and explain course concepts, developments, and processes.

Learning Objective: LO 4.11.A: Explain how the Black Panther Party pursued political, economic, and social reforms in the twentieth century.

Topic: 4.11: The Black Panther Party for Self-Defense

2. **Acceptable responses for Part A:**

- Emphasized Black self-determination and separation from white institutions
- Advocated for economic independence through Black-owned businesses
- Promoted cultural pride and religious identity within the Black Muslim community

Skill: 1B: Identify and explain the context of a specific event, development, or process.

Learning Objective: LO 4.9.B: Explain how Black Freedom movement strategies transitioned from civil rights to Black Power.

Topic: 4.9 Black Religious Nationalism and the Black Power Movement

Acceptable responses for Part B:

- Urban migration and racial segregation created economic and social challenges.
- Systemic racism and exclusion from mainstream institutions fostered alternative organizations.
- The Civil Rights Movement's focus on integration contrasted with the Nation of Islam's emphasis on independence.

Skill: 1B: Identify and explain the context of a specific event, development, or process.

Learning Objective: LO 4.9.B: Explain how Black Freedom movement strategies transitioned from civil rights to Black Power.

Topic: 4.9 Black Religious Nationalism and the Black Power Movement

Acceptable responses for Part C:

- Inspired broader discussions about Black nationalism and autonomy
- Influenced leaders like Malcolm X and later movements like Black Power
- Highlighted the importance of economic empowerment and cultural pride for community resilience

Skill: 1B: Identify and explain the context of a specific event, development, or process.

Learning Objective: LO 4.9.B: Explain how Black Freedom movement strategies transitioned from civil rights to Black Power.

Topic: 4.9 Black Religious Nationalism and the Black Power Movement

3. **Acceptable responses for Part A:**

- African American spirituals conveyed resistance through hidden messages of hope and escape.
- Blues music highlighted the struggles of Black life while asserting resilience.
- Harlem Renaissance literature celebrated Black identity and countered racist narratives.
- Gospel songs provided spiritual fortitude during the Civil Rights Movement.
- Hip-hop emerged as a tool to challenge systemic injustice and police brutality.

Skill: 1A: Identify and explain course concepts, developments, and processes.

Learning Objective: LO 4.8.A: Explain how artists, performers, poets, and musicians of African descent advocated for racial equality and brought international attention to the Black Freedom movement.

Topic: 4.8 The Arts, Music, and Politics of Freedom

Acceptable responses for Part B:

- Cultural expression expanded from oral traditions during Reconstruction to more public forms like jazz and literature in the Civil Rights era.
- Early cultural expression focused on survival and preservation, while later forms demanded social change.
- The shift from spirituals to protest music reflected changing political landscapes.
- Art evolved from hidden symbols of resistance to bold statements of pride and power.
- Black newspapers and media gained prominence as tools of advocacy and education.

Skill: 1C: Identify and explain patterns, connections, or other relationships (causation, changes, continuities, comparison).

Learning Objective: LO 3.14.A: Describe African Americans' contributions to American music in the 1930s and 1940s & LO 4.8.B: Explain how faith and music inspired African Americans to combat continued discrimination during the Civil Rights movement.

Topic: 3.14 Symphony in Black: Black Performance in Music, Theater, and Film & 4.8 The Arts, Music, and Politics of Freedom

Acceptable responses for Part C:

- The Harlem Renaissance emphasized artistic achievement and intellectual contributions.
- The Black Power era prioritized political activism and community control through cultural expression.

- Harlem Renaissance art aimed to prove Black excellence to the wider society, while Black Power art focused on internal pride and unity.
- The music of the Harlem Renaissance was jazz oriented, while Black Power embraced soul, funk, and protest lyrics.
- Literary works during the Black Power movement often included calls to action and highlighted systemic issues.

Skill: 1C: Identify and explain patterns, connections, or other relationships (causation, changes, continuities, comparison).

Learning Objective: LO 3.11.A: Describe ways the New Negro movement emphasized self-definition, racial pride, and cultural innovation & LO 4.10.A: Explain how the Black Arts movement (BAM) influenced Black culture in the 1960s and 1970s.

Topic: 3.11 The New Negro Movement and the Harlem Renaissance & 4.10 The Black Arts Movement

DBQ Scoring Guide: African American Self-Determination and Economic Independence

Reporting Category	Scoring Criteria	Decision Rules and Scoring Notes	Examples That Do Not Earn This Point	Examples That Earn This Point
Thesis/Claim (0–1 pts)	0 points: Does not state a thesis/claim that meets the criteria for one point. 1 point: Responds to the prompt with a defensible thesis/claim that establishes a line of reasoning. Additional Note: The thesis must appear as one or more sentences in a single location—either in the introduction or conclusion—and be clearly identifiable.	Responses that do not earn this point: ▪ Are not defensible. ▪ Only restate or rephrase the prompt. ▪ Do not respond to the prompt. ▪ Do not establish a line of reasoning. ▪ Are overgeneralized. Responses that earn this point: ▪ Provide a defensible thesis or claim about how African American communities pursued self-determination and economic independence in response to systemic racial barriers from the early 20th century to the present. ▪ The thesis or claim must either provide some indication of the reason for making that claim OR establish categories of the argument. ▪ The thesis must consist of one or more sentences located in one place, either in the introduction or the conclusion.	Provide a restatement of the prompt: ▪ "African Americans have pursued independence over the last century." Provide a defensible claim but no line of reasoning: ▪ "Black communities worked for economic self-reliance." Establish a line of reasoning but no defensible claim: ▪ "Economic growth happened because of community organizations."	Establish a line of reasoning that evaluates the topic of the prompt: ▪ "From the early 20th century to the present, African Americans pursued self-determination through Black entrepreneurship, migration to secure better opportunities, and creation of community institutions to resist systemic exclusion." Establish a line of reasoning with analytic categories: ▪ "African American self-determination emerged from three key strategies: building independent businesses, relocating through migration to access opportunity, and establishing social and religious institutions to foster economic and cultural independence." Establish a line of reasoning (minimally acceptable): ▪ "Economic self-reliance was a core goal for African American communities in the 20th century."

PRACTICE TEST 2

DBQ Scoring Guide: African American Self-Determination and Economic Independence (*Continued*)

Reporting Category	Scoring Criteria	Decision Rules and Scoring Notes	Examples That Do Not Earn This Point	Examples That Earn This Point
Contextualization (0–1 pts)	0 points: Does not meet the criteria for one point. 1 point: Describes a broader historical context relevant to the prompt.	Responses that do not earn this point: ▪ Mention a broader historical context without providing a description. ▪ Provide contextual information that is not clearly relevant to the topic of the prompt. ▪ Include contextualization that is too vague or general to support the argument. Responses that earn this point: ▪ Accurately describe a broader historical or disciplinary context relevant to African American economic self-determination and connect it to the prompt. ▪ This description can appear anywhere in the essay, but must be more than a phrase or reference—it must be a developed sentence or multiple sentences. ▪ Acceptable contexts include (but are not limited to): segregation under Jim Crow, exclusion from white-controlled economic institutions, the Great Migration, the rise of the Civil Rights Movement, the growth of Black Nationalism, or discriminatory housing and labor policies.	Mention a broader context but no description: ▪ "Jim Crow segregation existed during this time." Provide unrelated context: ▪ "The United States fought in World War I." Provide vague context: ▪ "Black people had it hard back then."	Connect African American self-determination to larger forces: ▪ "Following Reconstruction, Jim Crow laws and systemic racial exclusion limited African American access to banking, employment, and housing, forcing Black communities to create their own businesses, schools, and social institutions." Link to national movements: ▪ "The Great Migration, driven by the search for industrial jobs and escape from racial violence, shifted millions of African Americans to urban centers where they built strong community institutions that laid the foundation for modern Black economic activism." Include relevant cultural/intellectual context: ▪ "The Harlem Renaissance encouraged cultural pride and inspired parallel efforts to promote Black-owned businesses as a means of independence."

DBQ Scoring Guide: African American Self-Determination and Economic Independence (*Continued*)

Reporting Category	Scoring Criteria	Decision Rules and Scoring Notes	Examples That Do Not Earn This Point	Examples That Earn This Point
Evidence (0–3 pts)	0 points: Does not meet the criteria for one point. 1–2 points: Uses the content of at least two sources (1 pt) or three sources (2 pts) to address the topic of the prompt. 3 points: Uses the content of at least three sources to support an argument in response to the prompt AND provides at least one additional piece of specific evidence beyond the sources.	Responses that do not earn this point: ▪ Simply quote or paraphrase a source without connecting it to an argument. ▪ Describe fewer than two sources. ▪ Provide outside evidence that is vague, inaccurate, or irrelevant. Responses that earn this point: ▪ Describe the content of at least three sources AND use them to support an argument responding to the prompt. ▪ Provide at least one piece of accurate, relevant outside evidence—this must be specific and support the line of reasoning. ▪ **Outside evidence may include:** the Greenwood District ("Black Wall Street") in Tulsa, the 1921 Tulsa Race Massacre, Negro Business League, the rise of HBCUs, or the Civil Rights Movement's push for Black economic empowerment.	Quote sources without analysis: ▪ "The map shows the Great Migration." Mention vague outside evidence: ▪ "There were Black towns back then." Misidentify a source: ▪ "Marcus Garvey was a Civil Rights leader in the 1960s."	Use source content to support argument: ▪ "(S1) Madam C. J. Walker's national network of beauty agents empowered Black women economically and built community networks in the 1920s." ▪ "(S2) The Great Migration shifted millions of African Americans to industrial jobs in the North, increasing opportunities for business ownership." ▪ "(S3) Marcus Garvey's UNIA encouraged Black economic nationalism and independence from white-controlled markets." ▪ "(S4) The Nation of Islam's sale of Muhammad Speaks newspapers funded community programs and promoted self-reliance." ▪ **Outside evidence:** "Tulsa's Greenwood District, known as 'Black Wall Street,' demonstrated the potential of concentrated Black economic power before its destruction in the 1921 massacre."

PRACTICE TEST 2

DBQ Scoring Guide: African American Self-Determination and Economic Independence (*Continued*)

Reporting Category	Scoring Criteria	Decision Rules and Scoring Notes	Examples That Do Not Earn This Point	Examples That Earn This Point
Source Use (0–1 pt)	0 points: Does not meet the criteria for one point. 1 point: For at least two sources, explains how or why the perspective, purpose, historical situation, and/or audience is relevant to the argument.	Responses that do not earn this point: ▪ Identify the author, audience, or purpose without explaining how or why it matters. ▪ Give generic statements such as "This is biased" without further explanation. Responses that earn this point: ▪ For at least two sources, explicitly connect the sourcing element to the argument being made. ▪ Sourcing may address: perspective, purpose, historical situation, audience. ▪ Example: explaining that Garvey's context as a pan-Africanist leader influenced his advocacy for economic separation from white-dominated institutions.	Identify without analysis: ▪ "This source is from Marcus Garvey." ▪ "The audience was African Americans."	Explain perspective, purpose, and historical situation: ▪ "(S3) Marcus Garvey's perspective as a pan-African nationalist shaped his call to the African Diaspora for Black economic self-reliance, reflecting his belief that liberation required independence from white-controlled economies." ▪ "(S4) The Nation of Islam's purpose in selling Muhammad Speaks was both to spread religious and political messages of self-reliance and to financially sustain community programs, illustrating the link between ideology and economic practice."

DBQ Scoring Guide: African American Self-Determination and Economic Independence (*Continued*)

Reporting Category	Scoring Criteria	Decision Rules and Scoring Notes	Examples That Do Not Earn This Point	Examples That Earn This Point
Reasoning (0–1 pt)	0 points: Does not meet the criteria for one point. 1 point: Demonstrates a complex understanding of the topic by using historical reasoning (such as comparison, causation, or continuity and change) to frame or structure the argument.	Responses that do not earn this point: ▪ Present information as a disconnected list of facts. ▪ Use reasoning terms without actually showing a relationship. Responses that earn this point: ▪ Clearly use one or more reasoning skills to structure the argument. ▪ Causation: explain how systemic exclusion caused the rise of independent Black economic institutions. ▪ Continuity/change: show that strategies for economic self-determination evolved over time while the goal of independence remained constant. ▪ Comparison: compare strategies used in different eras, such as Garvey's economic nationalism vs. modern Black entrepreneurship.	Lists facts without connection: ▪ "Madam C. J. Walker started a business. Marcus Garvey made speeches." Misuse reasoning terms: ▪ "This caused change over time" without explaining what changed.	Apply reasoning to structure argument: ▪ "Systemic racial exclusion from mainstream banks and industries caused African Americans to develop alternative economic systems, from early-20th-century business networks to modern community investment strategies." ▪ "While methods evolved from Garvey's UNIA enterprises to Black-owned media and financial institutions, the emphasis on self-reliance remained constant across the 20th and 21st centuries."

PRACTICE TEST 2

DBQ Scoring Breakdown

This chart summarizes the document-based question (DBQ) scoring rubric for AP African American Studies. Use it to understand how your response will be evaluated and how you can earn all possible points.

Scoring Category	Points Available	Key Elements
Thesis/Claim	1	▪ Write a clear, defensible thesis or claim directly addressing the prompt.
Contextualization	1	▪ Provide a broader historical or disciplinary context. ▪ Go beyond prompt details.
Evidence from Documents	2	▪ 1 point Use the content of at least **two sources** to address the topic of the prompt. OR ▪ 2 points Support an argument in response to the prompt using at least **three sources.**
Additional Evidence	1	▪ Include at least 1 specific piece of evidence beyond the documents.
Source Use	1	For at least two sources, explain how or why the perspective, purpose, context, and/or audience of each source is relevant to an argument.
Reasoning	2	▪ Use reasoning (e.g., causation, comparison, change or continuity across time or geography) to set up an argument that addresses the prompt.
Total Points	7	**Maximum score available**

DBQ Success Checklist—Maximize Your Score

Checklist Item	Actionable Tips
Thesis/Claim	Craft a clear thesis that directly addresses the prompt and establishes a line of reasoning.
Contextualization	Describe a broader historical or disciplinary context to situate your argument.
Evidence from Documents	Use at least 3 pieces of evidence from documents and support your argument clearly.
Additional Evidence	Include 1 or more pieces of evidence beyond the provided documents.
Source Use	To earn this point, the response must explain—not just identify—how or why the perspective, purpose, context, or audience of at least two sources is relevant to the argument about the prompt.
Reasoning	To earn this point, the response must use reasoning to frame or organize an argument, even if the reasoning is uneven or the evidence is not highly specific.
Structure and Time Management	Structure your essay with clear paragraphs and manage your time effectively.
Source Citation	Cite sources by letter, author, or title to integrate evidence smoothly and clearly.

Index